October 24–26, 2016
Reno, Nevada, USA

I0047354

**Association for
Computing Machinery**

Advancing Computing as a Science & Profession

ASSETS'16

Proceedings of the 18th International ACM SIGACCESS Conference on
Computers and Accessibility

Sponsored by:
ACM SIGACCESS

Supported by:
**National Science Foundation, Microsoft Research, Facebook,
Google, and Towson University**

**Association for
Computing Machinery**

Advancing Computing as a Science & Profession

The Association for Computing Machinery
2 Penn Plaza, Suite 701
New York, New York 10121-0701

Notice to Past Authors of ACM-Published Articles
ACM intends to create a complete electronic archive of all articles and/or other material previously published by ACM. If you have written a work that has been previously published by ACM in any journal or conference proceedings prior to 1978, or any SIG Newsletter at any time, and you do NOT want this work to appear in the ACM Digital Library, please inform permissions@acm.org, stating the title of the work, the author(s), and where and when published.

ISBN: 978-1-4503-4124-0 (Digital)

ISBN: 978-1-4503-4709-9 (Print)

Additional copies may be ordered prepaid from:

ACM Order Department
PO Box 30777
New York, NY 10087-0777, USA

Phone: 1-800-342-6626 (USA and Canada)
+1-212-626-0500 (Global)
Fax: +1-212-944-1318
E-mail: acmhelp@acm.org
Hours of Operation: 8:30 am – 4:30 pm ET

Printed in the USA

ASSETS 2016 Foreword

We are happy to welcome you to the *18th International ACM SIGACCESS Conference on Computers and Accessibility (ASSETS 2016).* The ASSETS conference is the premier computing research conference exploring the design, evaluation, and use of computing and information technologies to benefit people with disabilities and older adults. In our 18th year, the ASSETS conference will continue its tradition of presenting innovative research on mainstream and specialized assistive technologies, accessible computing, and assistive applications of computer, network, and information technologies.

For the main (technical paper) track of the conference, the call for papers attracted submissions from across the world: Austria (1), Brazil (7), Canada (4), China (1), Denmark (1), Ecuador (1), Finland (1), France (1), Germany (3), India (1), Japan (3), Mexico (1), New Zealand (1), Pakistan (1), Portugal (2), Singapore (2), the United Kingdom (8), and the United States (56). Overall, we received 95 submissions from which we selected 24 for inclusion in the program, for an acceptance rate of 25%. Acceptance decisions were made by consensus of the program committee members, who discussed the papers online. The program committee consisted of 56 senior members of our research community who, along with 6 advanced doctoral students, produced a total of 288 reviews. We would like to thank them for their thorough reviews and thoughtful discussion and consideration of the submissions.

In addition to the main technical paper track of the conference, our program committee also reviewed 10 experience reports (4 accepted), 58 posters submissions (29 accepted), and 15 demo submissions (7 accepted). In addition, members of the program committee and other senior researchers helped to review submissions for the Student Research Competition and Doctoral Consortium events.

The ASSETS 2016 program is organized as follows:

On Monday (Day 1), the program starts with a keynote presentation by Dr. Richard Ladner who is a professor from the University of Washington, and his keynote is entitled "Accessibility is Becoming Mainstream." Professor Ladner is the recipient of the 2016 SIGACCESS Award for Outstanding Contribution, an award that recognizes individuals who have made significant and lasting contributions to the development of computing technologies that improve the accessibility of media and services to people with disabilities. Following the keynote, we will have a series of technical paper sessions organized around Deaf and Hard of Hearing Users, Users with Developmental Disabilities, and Tactile Information for Blind Users. The poster sessions during the day will feature poster and demo papers, along with Student Research Competition and SIGACCESS Travel Scholarship recipients. The day will end with a Reception at the conference hotel.

On Tuesday (Day 2), the program will continue with sessions on Big Data and Blind Users, Rehabilitation and Clinical Technologies, and Communication and Aging. During the morning, we will also have a special session for the Text Entry Challenge, featuring research in the area of text-entry technologies; this session is in memory of Torsten Felzer, a researcher in our community who passed away earlier this year.
We will also hear short talks from the finalists in the ACM Student Research Competition. The poster sessions on this day will include poster and demo papers, along with posters on the topic of text-entry and posters from our Doctoral Consortium participants. The day will conclude with a special reception at the National Automobile Museum.

On Wednesday (Day 3), the program will conclude with technical sessions on Users with Visual Impairments, Haptic and Audio Feedback for Blind Users, Social Issues and Assistive Technology, and Accessibility Education. After announcing the Best Paper and Best Student Paper Awards at the closing session, we will then introduce next year's chairs to tell you about ASSETS 2017.

Organizing ASSETS 2016 was a large collaborative effort. We would like to thank our authors for submitting high quality research to the conference, which has enabled us to assemble this exciting program. We are grateful to the program committee who worked together very hard in reviewing papers and providing feedback for authors. We also thank our Treasurer and Registration Chair Raja Kushalnagar, our Posters and Demos Chairs Stephanie Ludi and Kyle Montague, our Doctoral Consortium Chairs Amy Hurst and Karyn Moffatt, our Experience Reports chair Tiago Guerreiro, our Student Research Competition chairs David Flatla and Anke Brock, our Text Entry Challenge chair Adam Sporka, our Mentoring chair Leah Findlater, our Local Arrangements Chair Eelke Folmer, our Web chair Lourdes Morales-Villaverde, our Student Volunteers chair William Grussenmeyer, our Accessibility chair Erin Brady, and our Publicity chair Kyle Rector for all their contributions to the conference and these proceedings. Finally, we would like to thank our supporters: Microsoft Research, Facebook, Google, the Jess & Mildred Fisher College of Science & Mathematics at Towson University, and the National Science Foundation, and we thank our sponsors ACM and SIGACCESS for their support.

We hope that you will enjoy this exciting program of research in computing accessibility and that the conference will provide you with an opportunity to connect with other researchers and practitioners from institutions around the world. Welcome to ASSETS 2016!

Jinjuan Heidi Feng
ASSETS 2016 General Chair
Towson University, USA

Matt Huenerfauth
ASSETS 2016 Program Chair
Rochester Institute of Technology, USA

Table of Contents

Keynote Presentation
Session Chair: Matt Huenerfauth *(Rochester Institute of Technology)*

Session: Deaf and Hard of Hearing Users
Session Chair: Christian Vogler *(Gallaudet University)*

Session: Users with Developmental Disabilities
Session Chair: Kyle Rector *(University of Iowa)*

Session: Tactile Information for Blind Users
Session Chair: Shiri Azenkot *(Cornell Tech)*

Session: Communication and Aging
Session Chair: Karyn Moffatt *(McGill University)*

Session: Rehabilitation and Clinical Technologies
Session Chair: Shaun Kane *(University of Colorado Boulder)*

Session: Big Data and Blind Users
Session Chair: Kathleen McCoy *(University of Delaware)*

Session: Text Entry Challenge in Memory of Torsten Felzer
Session Chair: Adam Sporka *(Czech Technical University in Prague)*

Session: Users with Visual Impairments
Session Chair: Sergio Mascetti *(University of Milan)*

Session: Haptic and Audio Feedback for Blind Users

Session Chair: Hernisa Kacorri *(Carnegie Mellon University)*

Session: Social Issues and Assistive Technology

Session Chair: Erin Brady *(Indiana University-Purdue University Indianapolis)*

Session: Accessibility Education

Session Chair: Aqueasha Martin-Hammond *(Indiana University-Purdue University Indianapolis)*

Experience Reports

Poster and Demo Session I

Poster and Demo Session II

Student Research Competition (Undergraduate Students)

Student Research Competition (Graduate Students)

ASSETS 2016 Conference Organization

General Chair:	Jinjuan Heidi Feng *(Towson University, USA)*
Program Chair:	Matt Huenerfauth *(Rochester Institute of Technology, USA)*
Treasurer & Registration Chair:	Raja Kushalnagar *(Gallaudet University, USA)*
Posters and Demonstrations Chairs:	Stephanie Ludi *(University of North Texas, USA)* Kyle Montague *(Newcastle University, UK)*
Doctoral Consortium Chairs:	Amy Hurst *(University of Maryland Baltimore County, USA)* Karyn Moffatt *(McGill University, Canada)*
Experience Reports Chair:	Tiago Guerreiro *(University of Lisbon, Portugal)*
Text-Entry Challenge Chair:	Adam Sporka *(Czech Technical University in Prague, Czech Republic)*
Student Research Competition Chairs:	David Flatla *(Dundee University, UK)* Anke Brock *(Inria Bordeaux, France)*
Captioning Challenge Chair:	Raja Kushalnagar *(Gallaudet University, USA)*
Mentoring Chair:	Leah Findlater *(University of Maryland, USA)*
Local Arrangements Chair:	Eelke Folmer *(University of Nevada, Reno, USA)*
Accessibility Chair:	Erin Brady *(Indiana University-Purdue University Indianapolis, USA)*
Web Chair:	Lourdes M. Morales-Villaverde *(University of California Santa Cruz, USA)*
Student Volunteers Chair:	William Grussenmeyer *(University of Nevada, Reno, USA)*
Publicity Chair:	Kyle Rector *(University of Iowa, USA)*
Steering Committee Chair:	Shari Trewin *(IBM, USA)*
Steering Committee:	Yeliz Yesilada *(Middle East Technical University, Northern Cyprus)* Sri Kurniawan *(University of California Santa Cruz, USA)* Clayton Lewis *(University of Colorado Boulder, USA)* Matt Huenerfauth *(Rochester Institute of Technology, USA)*

Program Committee: Shiri Azenkot *(Cornell Tech, USA)*
Armando Barreto *(Florida International University, USA)*
Jeffrey Bigham *(Carnegie Mellon University, USA)*
Davide Bolchini *(Indiana University Purdue University Indianapolis, USA)*
Erin Brady *(Indiana University Purdue University Indianapolis, USA)*
Annelies Braffort *(LIMSI-CNRS, France)*
Giorgio Brajnik *(University of Udine, Italy)*
Anke Brock *(INRIA Bordeaux, France)*
Anna Cavender *(Google, USA)*
Elliot Cole *(Institute for Cognitve Prosthestics, USA)*
James Coughlan *(Smith-Kettlewell Eye Research Institute, USA)*
Lynn Coventry *(Northumbria University, UK)*
Michael Crabb *(Robert Gordon University, UK)*
Alistair Edwards *(University of York, UK)*
Leah Findlater *(University of Maryland, USA)*
David Flatla *(University of Dundee, UK)*
Eelke Folmer *(University of Nevada, Reno, USA)*
Jon Froehlich *(University of Maryland, USA)*
Nicholas Giudice *(University of Maine, USA)*
Tiago Guerreiro *(University of Lisbon, Portugal)*
Vicki Hanson *(Rochester Insititue of Technology, USA)*
Yun Huang *(University of Syracuse, USA)*
Matt Huenerfauth *(Rochester Institute of Technology, USA)*
Amy Hurst *(University of Maryland, Baltimore County, USA)*
Faustina Hwang *(Reading University, UK)*
Hernisa Kacorri *(Carnegie Mellon University, USA)*
Shaun Kane *(University of Colorado, USA)*
Ravi Kuber *(University of Maryland, Baltimore County, USA)*
Sri Kurniawan *(UC Santa Cruz, USA)*
Raja Kushalnagar *(Rochester Institute of Technology, USA)*
Richard Ladner *(University of Washington, USA)*
Walter Lasecki *(University of Michigan, USA)*
Jonathan Lazar *(Towson University, USA)*
Clayton Lewis *(University of Colorado, USA)*
Stephanie Ludi *(Rochester Institute of Technology, USA)*
Sergio Mascetti *(University of Milan, Italy)*
Kathy McCoy *(University of Delaware, USA)*
Scott McCrickard *(Virginia Tech, USA)*
Kyle Montague *(University of Dundee, UK)*
Hugo Nicolau *(University of Lisbon, Portugal)*
Christopher Power *(University of York, UK)*
Cynthia Putnam *(DePaul University, USA)*
Luz Rello *(Carnegie Mellon University, USA)*
John T. Richards *(IBM Watson Group, USA, University of Dundee, UK)*
Meredith Ringel Morris *(Microsoft Research, USA)*
Frank Rudzicz *(Toronto Rehabilitation Institute, Canada)*
Andreas Stefik *(University of Nevada, Las Vegas, USA)*
Hironobu Takagi *(IBM Research, Tokyo, Japan)*
Monica Tentori *(CICESE, Mexico)*
Shari Trewin *(IBM, USA)*

ASSETS 2016 Sponsors & Supporters

Sponsor:

Special Interest Group on Accessible Computing

Doctoral Consortium Supporter:

Student Research Competition Supporter:

Supporters: facebook   Google   

Accessibility Is Becoming Mainstream

Richard E. Ladner
Computer Science and Engineering
University of Washington
Seattle, WA 98195-2350
1-206-543-9347
ladner@cs.washington.edu

ABSTRACT

Since 1976, when California State University Northridge (CSUN) began its Annual International Technology and Persons with Disabilities Conference, there have been specialized conferences with an accessibility theme. The first ACM ASSETS Conference was held in 1994 when 22 papers were presented. The Rehabilitation Engineering and Assistive Technology Society of North America (RESNA) began its conference in 1979. The first biennial International Conference on Computers Helping People with Special Needs (under a different name) was held in 1988. Accessibility focused journals have existed since at least 1986. This history demonstrates that accessibility has grown into a separate field in research and practice. While this is true, more and more, accessibility has become mainstream.

The mainstreaming of accessibility can be seen in its integration into academic computing departments, HCI conferences, and conferences in supporting fields such as computer vision and natural language processing. Most importantly, accessibility can be seen in products and services provided by mainstream industry. One early example of this is the standardization of closed captioning for television. We now have built-in screen readers for iOS and Android devices and Augmentative and Alternative Communication (AAC) devices are being supplemented by lower cost AAC apps on mainstream touchscreen tablets. Technologies like video chat, personal texting, speech recognition, optical character recognition, and speech synthesis have their roots in solving accessibility problems. Slowly, accessibility is moving into the academic curriculum in computing departments [1]. Web design and development courses are starting to cover accessibility in the WCAG 2.0 and ARIA standards. There are capstone courses that focus on accessibility at several universities.

There will always be a need for specialized accessibility related devices and services, but moving forward accessibility will be provided by mainstream companies and accessibility solutions will become valuable to everyone, disabled or not. Mainstream technology companies are asking for more people with disabilities to join their diverse workforces.

Keywords

Accessibility; Disability.

SHORT BIOGRAPHY

Richard E. Ladner is a professor in Computer Science and Engineering at the University of Washington in Seattle, WA,

ASSETS '16, October 23-26, 2016, Reno, NV, USA
ACM 978-1-4503-4124-0/16/10.
http://dx.doi.org/10.1145/2982142.2982180

USA, where he has been on the faculty since 1971. He received in B.S. degree in Mathematics at St. Mary's College of California in 1965 and his Ph.D. in Mathematics from the University of California, Berkeley in 1971.

After many years of doing research in theoretical computer science, he turned his attention in 2004 to accessibility research, especially on technology for people who are blind, deaf, and deaf-blind. Some notable projects include the Tactile Graphics Project, MobileASL, ASL-STEM Forum, and MobileAccessibility. He has supervised or co-supervised 27 Ph.D. students, including ten in accessibility research. He has also supervised 60 undergraduates on various accessibility related projects. He wrote a short article for the SIGACCESS Newsletter about his transition from theoretical computer science research to accessibility research [2].

In addition to research, he has projects with the goal of increasing the participation and success of students with disabilities in computing fields. From 1994 to 2005 he held a one-week summer workshop for disabled high school students as part of the DO-IT Summer Scholars program. In 2006 he organized the Vertical Mentoring Workshop for the Blind in Science, Technology, Engineering, and Mathematics. From 2007-2013 he organized the Summer Academy for Advancing Deaf and Hard of Hearing in Computing. In 2014 he organized the Empowering Blind Students in Science and Engineering Workshop. He is the PI to two NSF-funded projects, AccessComputing and AccessCS10K that are working with students, teachers, computing departments, and organizations with the common goal getting more students with disabilities into computing fields.

He is on the editorial board of the ACM Transactions on Accessible Computing and served as program chair for the 2013 ASSETS conference. He has served on the Board of Trustees of Gallaudet University and on the Board of the Center for Minorities and People with Disabilities in Information Technology (CMD-IT). He is an ACM Fellow and IEEE Fellow. He is a recipient of the 2004 Presidential Award for Excellence in Science, Mathematics and Engineering Mentoring (PAESMEM). He is the 2014 recipient of the SIGCHI Social Impact Award.

ACKNOWLEDGMENT

This work was supported by NSF grant no. CNS-1539179.

REFERENCES

[1] Andrew Ko and Richard Ladner 2016. AccessComputing Promotes Teaching Accessibility. To appear in *Inroads*.

[2] Richard Ladner 2014. My Path to Becoming an Accessibility Researcher. SIGACCESS Newsletter. September 2014. http://www.sigaccess.org/wp-content/uploads/formidable/sigaccess_newsletter_1102.pdf

A Personalizable Mobile Sound Detector App Design for Deaf and Hard-of-Hearing Users

Danielle Bragg   Nicholas Huynh   Richard E. Ladner

Computer Science & Engineering
DUB Group, University of Washington
Seattle, WA 98195 USA
{dkbragg,huynick,ladner}@cs.washington.edu

ABSTRACT

Sounds provide informative signals about the world around us. In situations where non-auditory cues are inaccessible, it can be useful for deaf and hard-of-hearing people to be notified about sounds. Through a survey, we explored which sounds are of interest to deaf and hard-of-hearing people, and which means of notification are appropriate. Motivated by these findings, we designed a mobile phone app that alerts deaf and hard-of-hearing people to sounds they care about. The app uses training examples of personally relevant sounds recorded by the user to learn a model of those sounds. It then screens the incoming audio stream from the phone's microphone for those sounds. When it detects a sound, it alerts the user by vibrating and providing a pop-up notification. To evaluate the interface design independent of sound detection errors, we ran a Wizard-of-Oz user study, and found that the app design successfully facilitated deaf and hard-of-hearing users recording training examples. We also explored the viability of a basic machine learning algorithm for sound detection.

CCS Concepts

•Human-centered computing → Sound-based input / output; Accessibility systems and tools;

Keywords

Sound detection, accessibility, deaf, hard-of-hearing

1. INTRODUCTION

Knowing which sounds are happening in one's surroundings can be useful. Auditory cues can signify important events happening outside of the line of sight. For example, a person shouting or gun firing might be heard but not seen. Furthermore, society relies exclusively on sound for communicating certain information. For example, cars honk to alert other drivers; alarms ring to announce important times

and emergencies; loud speakers broadcast airport announcements; microwaves beep to tell us our food is cooked; and people ring doorbells and knock on doors to announce their arrival. These societal conventions make important information inaccessible to many deaf and hard-of-hearing people.

Non-technical sound awareness methods like visual inspection can be distracting and inconvenient, and technical solutions are often specific to individual sounds. For example, alarm clocks that ring loudly, flash bright lights, and vibrate are commercially available. Many deaf people also connect their doorbell to the home lights, so that the lights flash when the doorbell is rung. However, these solutions address individual sounds, and it can be expensive and inconvenient to purchase a different device for every sound. Even with many devices, some sounds cannot be covered because each person's life, and the sounds therein, is unique.

In this paper, we present the design of a personalizable mobile phone app to detect sounds that deaf and hard-of-hearing users find important. Guided by visual feedback, users train the app to identify the sounds they want to know about by providing recorded examples of those sounds. The user categorizes recordings into groups representing different sounds. Because the app learns models of sounds from training examples, it is flexible and gives the user control. Instead of buying a separate sound detector for each important sound, the user can download and train a single app. Furthermore, because it is a mobile app, the detector is portable. It accompanies the user throughout the day, detecting sounds in any location – at work, home, or in transit.

Our mobile app design provides sound detection for deaf and hard-of-hearing people through a ubiquitous device they likely already use. Most deaf and hard-of-hearing people we surveyed want a mobile sound detector (section 3.4). Because text messaging is so useful, mobile phone adoption is high in the deaf community, where vibration notifications are widely used. Deaf users typically choose phones that support vibration [28], one of the most useful mobile features for deaf users [29], and often carry their phone on the body to feel it vibrate [11]. Our app detects sounds with a familiar device (i.e., the mobile phone) and uses a popular notification medium (i.e., text and vibration).

We informed our app design through a survey on sounds that deaf and hard-of-hearing people want to know about, methods they currently use for sound awareness, and their design criteria for a sound detector app. We evaluated our app design through a Wizard-of-Oz in-lab user study where participants set up the app to listen for various sounds, and experienced the app detecting those sounds. We also ran an offline proof-of-concept for a GMM (Gaussian Mixture Model) based sound detection algorithm.

The key contributions of this paper include:

- A survey on the design preferences deaf and hard-of-hearing users have for a mobile sound detector app.

- The design of a mobile sound detector app independently trainable by deaf and hard-of-hearing users.

- A user study exploring the usability of our sound detector app design for deaf and hard-of-hearing users.

2. RELATED WORK

Sound awareness techniques include non-technical solutions, commercial products, and research ventures. This plethora of sound awareness methods highlights the importance of sound awareness. However, the usability of a trainable sound detector for deaf and hard-of-hearing users has not been explored, which we provide. The acoustic event detection required is an active research area spanning signal processing and machine learning.

2.1 Sound Awareness Techniques

There is a wide array of approaches that deaf and hard-of-hearing people use for sound awareness. Some deaf and hard-of-hearing people are not interested in sounds, but there are many approaches adopted by those who are. Many sounds are accompanied by visual cues that deaf and hard-of-hearing people pay attention to or check for. Some deaf and hard-of-hearing people use hearing aids or cochlear implants to improve sound sensing. It is possible to amplify only particular sound sources in hearing aids or cochlear implants, using wireless streaming with loop systems, FM, or infrared. Tactile hearing aids and tactile vocoders that vibrate to relay sonic information can also be used to identify sounds. Hearing dogs are also trained to alert their owners to important sounds.

There are many products that detect specific sounds, or replace them with other types of signals. In many deaf homes, the doorbell or phone feeds into the light system, so that the lights flash when somebody rings the doorbell or calls. Alarm clocks are available that emit loud sounds, vibrate, or flash bright lights. Several companies, including Harris Communications [12] and Sonic Alert [34], specialize in such products for deaf and hard-of-hearing consumers. Sound detectors for specific sounds are also marketed to consumers who are not deaf or hard-of-hearing. For example, baby monitors and breaking glass detectors can be useful for hearing, hard-of-hearing, and deaf consumers alike.

More comprehensive sound detection systems are emerging on the market, further signifying that sound detection is an important problem. For instance, the Leeo Smart Alert [16] plugs into an outlet and listens for smoke and carbon monoxide alarms. When it detects either alarm, it calls the subscribed phone and plays a recording of the sound so that the user can verify that the alarm is going off, and respond appropriately. Audio Analytic [3] sells a suite of sensors that are installed in the home to detect specific sounds like a baby cry, smoke alarm, or window breakage. Consumers must work with the company to develop custom sensors, and the system is designed specifically for the home. OtoSense [24] provides software for monitoring industrial machine sounds, with a recently released app for personal use. The app detects two types of smoke alarms and lets the user specify additional sounds they want it to detect. However, the usability of these designs for deaf and hard-of-hearing users has not been studied.

Several research projects have attempted to provide sound awareness for deaf people. Many of these systems focus on specific use cases, including detecting sounds in one specific deaf-blind person's home [8], and a chip for detecting sirens approaching from behind on the road [20]. Scribe4Me [18] is a mobile app that takes a more generalizeable approach to sound awareness. Users press a button to request detailed information about the last 30 seconds of audio, and the app uses a human-in-the-loop system for transcription. Peripheral displays depicting sounds for deaf people have also been explored (e.g. [13, 19]). Matthews et al. [19] provide a discussion of the sounds that deaf people care about. Because this research was conducted 10 years ago by interviewing a small set of people, we used it to inform our design of a large-scale web survey on deaf sounds of interest; we expect a higher quantity of responses, and those responses to be more up-to-date. Other applied sound detection research includes identifying stress in human voices (e.g., [17]), cough detection (e.g., [4, 15]), speech detection (e.g., [10, 33]), and voice recognition (e.g., [30, 21]).

2.2 Acoustic Event Detection

Acoustic Event Detection (AED) refers to the problem of identifying both when sounds occur within an audio stream and which sounds they are. Detection is more complex than sound classification because the temporal boundaries of the sounds must be determined. Creating a personalizeable sound detector app for deaf and hard-of-hearing users requires a particularly robust solution to AED. People care about a diverse set of sounds, ranging from babies crying to appliances buzzing, and the app must be able to model these different sounds. Training examples might be recorded with background noise or conflicting concurrent sounds; the phone's audio stream will include diverse environmental noise; and the microphone will be muffled when the phone is placed in a pocket. The AED algorithm must be robust to all these obstacles.

Model and feature choice greatly impacts AED accuracy. Spectral features like Mel-Frequency Cepstral Coefficients (MFCCs) represent the frequencies that make up a sound, and are commonly used to represent sounds. Because different features provide better signatures for different sounds, algorithms have been built to help determine the most effective features for particular classification tasks (e.g., [26]). The models for different sounds are built from these features. Researched models include Gaussian Mixture Models (e.g. [6, 31]), Support Vector Machines (e.g. [1, 9]), hierarchical models (e.g., [7, 1]), and random regression forests (e.g. [27]). Many of these solutions are tailored to specific sound types and environments, but a generalizable sound detection app must work well for any sound in any environment.

Once the sound model is built, different temporal methods are available for detecting sounds in the audio stream. Sliding window methods continuously determine whether a sound is present in a small window of recent sound. Hidden Markov Models represent the audio stream as a sequence of states (e.g. [6, 22, 23]). Each state represents the sound occurring at that time. Smoothing methods can help prevent the model from jumping from one sound to another.

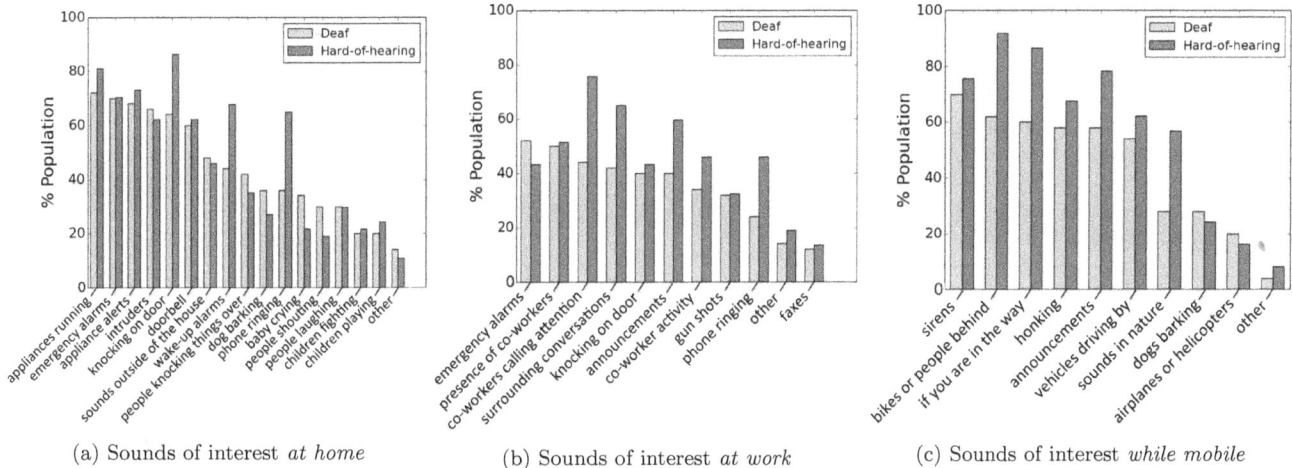

(a) Sounds of interest *at home*   (b) Sounds of interest *at work*   (c) Sounds of interest *while mobile*

Figure 1: Sounds of interest to deaf and hard-of-hearing participants (a) at home, (b) at work, and (c) while mobile.

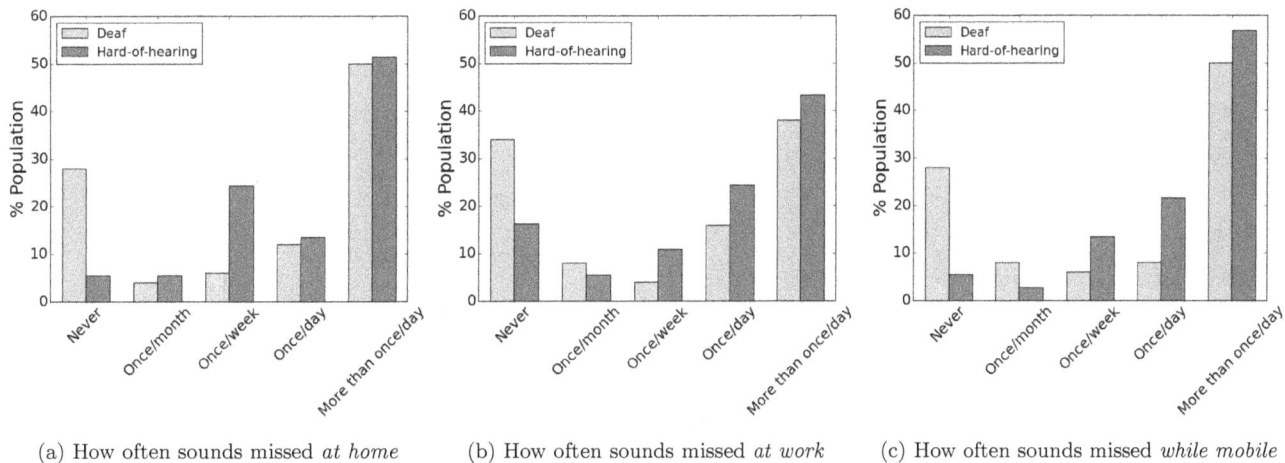

(a) How often sounds missed *at home*   (b) How often sounds missed *at work*   (c) How often sounds missed *while mobile*

Figure 2: Frequency of missed sounds (a) at home, (b) at work, and (c) while mobile.

Various onset detection methods have been developed and used to boost audio event detection accuracy (e.g., [5]). We explored the performance of a sliding window GMM sound detection algorithm using training data gathered in our user study. The state-of-the-art in sound detection is advancing, and we expect future work applying these algorithms to yield more accurate results.

3. SURVEY TO INFORM APP DESIGN

We conducted a survey to determine which sounds deaf and hard-of-hearing people care about, which methods they currently use for sound awareness, and what design criteria they would have for an app that detects sounds. The survey was approved by the University of Washington IRB and distributed online. It consisted of a combination of multiple-choice and free-response questions. Appendix A provides the exact questions. Participants were recruited by posting on Facebook and emailing relevant lists. We had 87 participants (51 female, 36 male). 50 were deaf, and 37 were hard-of-hearing. Ages ranged 18-99 (mean 42, std dev 17).

3.1 Sounds of Interest

The sounds that participants were interested in know-

ing about are presented in Figure 1. Participants selected sounds of interest from a list of options based on a previous sound awareness survey (i.e. [19]) and discussions with deaf colleagues. We also provided a write-in "other" option. They selected sounds for three scenarios: a) at home, b) at work, and c) while mobile.

The biggest differences between deaf and hard-of-hearing participants are likely explained by deaf participants having non-auditory ways of knowing when important sounds happen. For example, fewer deaf participants wanted to know about wake-up alarms and phones ringing than hard-of-hearing ones. Alarm clocks are available that ring loudly, vibrate, and have strong, flashing lights. Similarly, a phone can provide visual or tactile feedback when somebody calls, or can be connected to an external device that provides this feedback. It is likely that more deaf people know about and use these solutions. They are likely less concerned with knowing about a phone call or alarm clock going off because they already know when those events occur.

A small minority of participants wrote in additional sounds, which suggests our list was comprehensive. The home sounds participants added were: vehicles passing by, children having bad dreams, smoke and carbon monoxide detectors, appliances making unusual noises, water running, socializing, something dropping on the floor, gunshots, conversations, and distinguishing between multiple sources with similar frequency range. The sounds they wrote in for work were: dropping items, walking/running behind, moving carts, fire drill, printer, conversations, and baby sounds. The varied responses for work are likely due to varied work environments with different sounds. The sounds they added for mobile situations were: conversations, and sound location.

3.2 Missed Sound Frequency

To better understand where sound detection is needed, we asked participants how often they miss sounds of interest at home, at work, and while mobile. As shown in Figure 2, the majority of participants reported missing sounds in all three scenarios. About 50% of both deaf and hard-of-hearing participants thought they missed sounds more than once per day in each scenario. Most deaf participants either thought they never missed sounds, or that they missed sounds very frequently (more than once per day), as demonstrated by the U-shaped curve of the results in all three scenarios. Hard-of-hearing participants were more evenly distributed in how often they thought they missed sounds. It is possible that more deaf participants reported never missing sounds because they developed more reliable systems for knowing about the sounds they care about, or because they were less aware of missing sounds than hard-of-hearing participants.

3.3 Techniques for Sound Awareness

Participants reported using a wide range of techniques and devices for sound awareness, highlighting the importance of an all-purpose solution. The most widely used technique was to check to see if a sound happened (over 80% of both hard-of-hearing and deaf participants). The fewest participants relied on hearing dogs (under 30% of both hard-of-hearing and deaf participants). There was little variance in how much people relied on hearing dogs; each person either relied on a dog on a daily basis or not at all. Alarm clocks, and fire, smoke, or carbon monoxide alarms were the only alerting devices used by the majority of deaf participants. All other alert devices were used by a minority of both deaf and hard-of-hearing participants. The wide diversity of solutions with small user bases suggests that a general solution like a trainable sound detector app would be valuable. Instead of buying a separate device for many sounds they want to know about, users could download a single all-purpose app.

3.4 Need for a Mobile App

The vast majority of participants did not currently use any mobile apps for sound detection, but were interested in using a general sound detector app. Most participants did not use any mobile apps for sound detection (80% deaf, 89% hard-of-hearing). Those who did use sound detection apps reported using dictation software, software that connects to hearing aids or cochlear implants, and software that makes the phone flash or vibrate when receiving calls, alerts, or messages. None of the apps listed provide general sound detection (except OtoSense, which one participant used). Though most participants did not use mobile sound awareness apps, most wanted an app that would alert them to sounds of their choosing (88% deaf, 87% hard-of-hearing). The fact that the majority did not use any apps for sound awareness, yet wanted a sound detector app, demonstrates

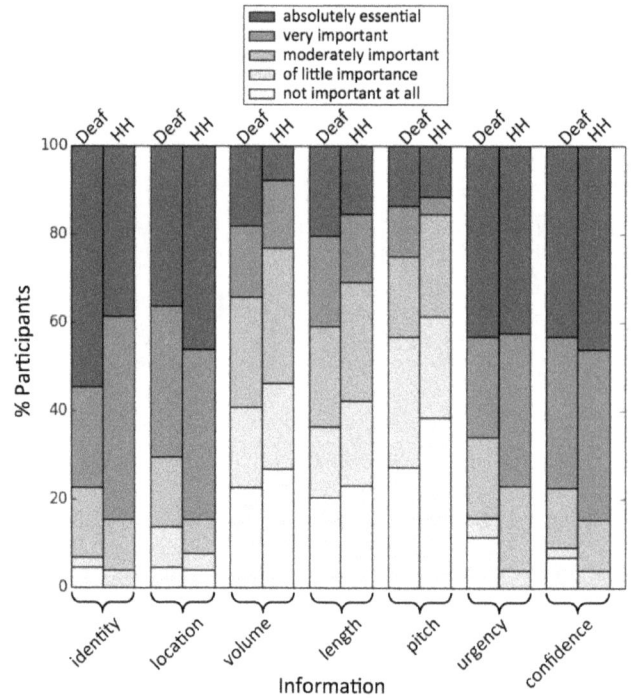

Figure 3: Desired information for app notifications. Pairs of bars represent deaf and hard-of-hearing (HH) participants.

an unfulfilled user need.

We explored participants' design criteria for such an app. Figure 3 summarizes desired information about detected sounds. Participants most wanted to know about sound identity, location, urgency, and confidence in detection. Volume, length (duration), and pitch are less important. Participants also reported a higher tolerance for extra notifications than for missed notifications. Deaf participants were more tolerant of both missed sounds and extra notifications. Twenty-six (59%) deaf and ten (38%) hard-of-hearing participants would tolerate at least one extra notification per day. Twenty (45%) deaf and eight (30%) hard-of-hearing participants would tolerate at least one missed sound per day. It is likely that deaf participants would tolerate more errors because a faulty app would still provide an appreciable benefit, whereas hard-of-hearing participants need a more accurate app to provide a comparable benefit.

Our survey results suggest that autonomy and privacy are important to users recording examples of sounds. Hard-of-hearing participants were generally willing to record more training samples. Fourteen (54%) hard-of-hearing participants were willing to provide at least five training examples for a sound, whereas thirteen (30%) deaf participants were willing to do the same. Three (7%) deaf participants did not want to record any examples, but all hard-of-hearing participants were willing to record some. It is possible that rich visual feedback during the recording process would increase deaf users' willingness to record examples of sounds they do not hear. About half of our participants were willing to ask a hearing person to help record sounds, but many (especially deaf users) preferred autonomy. All hard-of-hearing participants were willing to ask for help, compared to 84% of deaf participants. In terms of sharing, 73% hard-of-hearing and 59% of deaf participants were "very willing" to share recordings. Reluctance to share is likely due to privacy concerns.

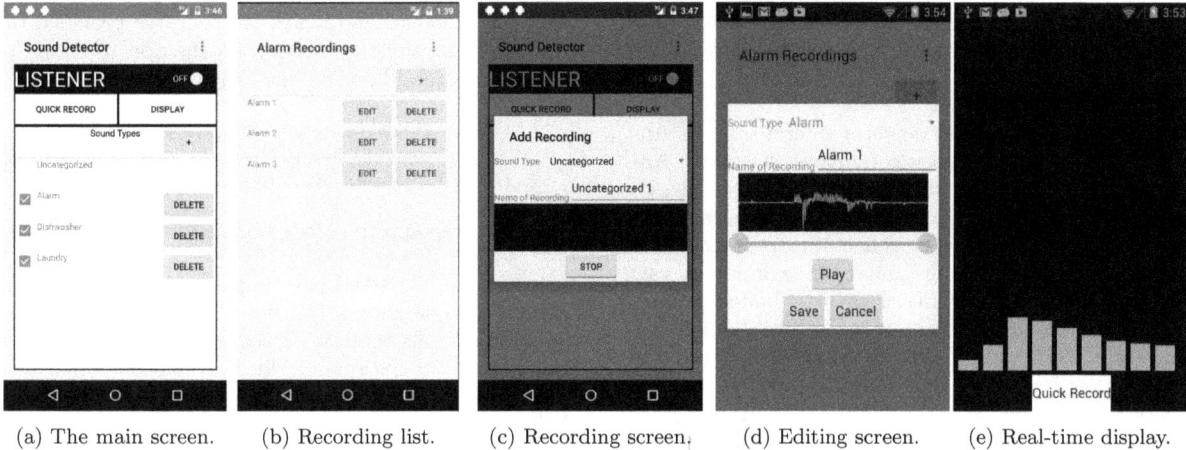

| (a) The main screen. | (b) Recording list. | (c) Recording screen. | (d) Editing screen. | (e) Real-time display. |

Figure 4: Screen shots of the app interface.

4. SOUND DETECTOR DESIGN

Informed by our survey and refined through iterative design, we designed a sound detector app to alert deaf and hard-of-hearing users to nearby sounds of interest. We implemented the design as an Android application using standard Android sound processing and data storage methods.

4.1 Interface Design

The app interface (Figure 4) allows users to train the app to identify sounds by recording examples of those sounds. The recording and editing screens provide visual feedback to support deaf and hard-of-hearing users independently recording sounds. Users create their own sound types (ex: "door knock" or "microwave beep"), and categorize their examples under the appropriate types. The app uses machine learning to model these sounds, and runs a sound detection algorithm on the incoming audio stream from the phone microphone to detect when these sound types occur. The user is then notified with a vibration and text notification letting them know which sound has occurred. The application also provides a display screen with a waveform of the current audio. The display can help users detect sounds that they want to record, gain an awareness of background noise, or find sound sources by seeing the waveform strengthen as they move closer to the source.

4.1.1 Main Screen

Because training the app to recognize different sound types is central to the app's functionality, the app's main menu provides a list of all sound types, as shown in Figure 4a. Users can check (or uncheck) the green box at the left of a sound type to make the app listen for (or ignore) that sound type. Sound types can be deleted by clicking DELETE or added by clicking the + at the top right. The "uncategorized" type appears at the top of the sound type list, and cannot be deleted. Clicking on a sound type brings the user to the recording list for that sound type. Through our iterative design process, we enlarged the listener switch to highlight the importance of turning it on and moved the sound display to a separate screen to avoid distraction.

4.1.2 Recording List

The recording list, displayed in Figure 4b, lists every recording that was given as an example of a particular sound

type. To keep the interface clean, the list only displays the user-given recording names. Additional details are available in the editing screen when the user clicks EDIT. Clicking DELETE deletes the corresponding recording. The + button allows the user to add a new recording. The recording interface that then appears automatically classifies the new recording under the current sound type.

4.1.3 Recording Interface

The recording interface, pictured in Figure 4c, provides a waveform visualization for visual feedback during the recording process. The "start" and "stop" buttons allow the user to start and stop recording. The recording interface can be accessed in two ways: 1) from the quick record button on the main menu or display screen, or 2) by navigating to a particular sound type and clicking the + button to add a sample. If the recording interface is accessed through a quick record button, the recording is put into the "uncategorized" type. Otherwise, it is saved under the currently selected type. To highlight the importance of categorizing the sample appropriately, the app verifies with the user before saving an "uncategorized" recording.

4.1.4 Editing Interface

The editing screen, pictured in Figure 4d, allows users to move a recording to a different sound type, change its name, or trim the recording. A static waveform visualization provides a visual representation of the recording. The visual feedback can help users evaluate the content of recordings. For example, a pulsing alarm will be visualized as a series of peaks. If the recording does not look as it should, the user is free to trim it or delete and try again. Recordings are trimmed by dragging two sliders along the waveform visualization to frame the desired portion of the recording. The user can also play back the recording if they want to listen to it themselves or ask a hearing friend to check the quality of the recording.

4.1.5 Real-time Display

The display screen, in Figure 4e, provides a visual representation of the current sound level. This feature can be used on its own to provide a sense of the current noise level, or can be used to help users identify when sounds they want to record happen. For example, if they want to record their dog barking, the visual display will jump every time their dog

7

barks. When a sound of interest occurs, it can be recorded directly from this screen using the quick record button.

4.2 Implementation

We implemented the sound detector interface as an Android application. Audio data was managed by native Android classes, AudioRecord and AudioTrack. The two classes are designed to be used in conjunction with one another and function in similar ways. When the user records a sound, AudioRecord stores the microphone input as raw Pulse Code Modulation (PCM) data in a buffer (<1 s), which is transferred to external storage. The AudioTrack class inversely reads data from the external file into the buffer and plays it from there. Metadata on the recordings is stored in the phone using Android's built-in SQLite database. The waveform displays are generated from the raw PCM data. Our implementation includes all functionality, except for algorithmic sound detection. For our user study, we pushed event detection notifications ourselves using Parse (i.e., [25]), an open source backend API.

5. INTERFACE USABILITY STUDY

We ran a formative in-lab study to evaluate the usability of the sound detector interface design for deaf and hard-of-hearing users. During the study, participants set up the app to listen for two sounds: door knocks and an alarm clock ringing. For each sound, participants recorded and edited examples of the sound, saved the sounds in the appropriate category, and set the app to listen for the desired sound. Participants answered questions and provided open-ended feedback about their experience. We obtained IRB approval through the University of Washington and recruited by posting on Facebook and emailing relevant lists.

We had 12 participants (9 female, 3 male). Age ranged from 19-60 (average 33). Five identified as deaf (all from birth); four as hard-of-hearing (1 from birth, 3 from childhood); one as both deaf and hard-of-hearing depending on the context (from infancy); one as "hearing impaired" (from childhood); and one as mostly hearing with difficulty in noisy environments (from young or mid-adulthood). Seven participants (58%) reported having their mobile phone with them over 80% of the time at home, eight (75%) reported the same at work, and ten (83%) reported the same when mobile. This smartphone-equipped majority would be able to detect sounds throughout the day using our app. One participant did not own a smartphone and expressed frustration with smartphones in general. No participants used apps to monitor sounds outside of the study.

5.1 Study Procedures

The study took place in a lab setting, and an American Sign Language interpreter was made available to each participant. The study consisted of several steps: 1) watching a short demo video, 2) setting the app up to detect door knocks, 3) setting the app up to detect an alarm, and 4) receiving a sound detection notification. Participants used a Samsung Android phone with the app installed. After each task, participants answered specific questions about their experience, and provided freeform feedback. Participants were encouraged to ask questions and talk about their experience.

We explained that the app will detect each sound more accurately if the user provides more recorded examples and trims them, and participants were free to decide how many

samples to record and which to trim. We provided the following instructions for setting up the app to listen for the door knock (and later for the alarm):

1. Create a sound category for door knocks (or the alarm).

2. Record examples of door knocks (or the alarm).

3. Tell the app to detect knocks (or the alarm).

In closing, we asked participants to configure the app to listen for door knocks but not the alarm, and triggered a door knock notification. Because we wanted to evaluate the usability of the app interface without detection accuracy confounding our results, we ran a Wizard-of-Oz experiment. Whenever a sound occurred that the app was configured to detect, we manually pushed a notification to the phone.

5.2 Study Results

We found the app design to be usable for deaf and hard-of-hearing users recording training examples of sounds. We evaluated usability through participants' ability to train and use the app, and their qualitative feedback. All participants successfully trained the app by recording, editing, and organizing samples appropriately, and noticed notifications. Participants' responses provide evidence that the training process was generally easy and notifications were appropriate. Areas for improvement include clearer instructions about sound categorization, larger buttons and checkboxes, and personalized notifications. We present participants' answers to questions about their experience in Figure 5, and provide a thematic analysis of their free-form feedback.

5.2.1 Recording and Organizing Recordings

All participants successfully recorded sound samples, and 91.7% agreed that "It was easy to record sounds." These participants understood that the user must categorize their recordings so that the app can "learn" those sounds, and felt that the app clearly supported this task. In the words of P9, it was "sleek and minimal which makes it easy to use." Others called it "intuitive," "simple," and "easy to use." Six participants specified the app's customizability as a strength. They liked that it could be trained to detect their personal sounds, and that it could handle a wide variety of sounds. They also enjoyed having control over their recordings.

The organization of sounds into categories confused some participants. Several asked us to clarify what a "sound category" was. Some expected the app to distinguish between individual recordings within a single category. Others thought a single example of a sound would be sufficient for the app to identify that sound. One person expected to provide more recordings for a variable sound (like knocking on different doors) than for a highly regular sound (like an electronic alarm). This expectation aligns with our vision of the app using the recordings in a single category to learn a model of that sound type. More training examples lead to more robust models, especially for highly variable sounds, and thus improved accuracy. Explanations satisfied our participants, and clearer instructions would likely reduce future confusion.

5.2.2 Editing Recordings

Participants generally enjoyed editing their training examples. The waveform visualization of the recordings was

8

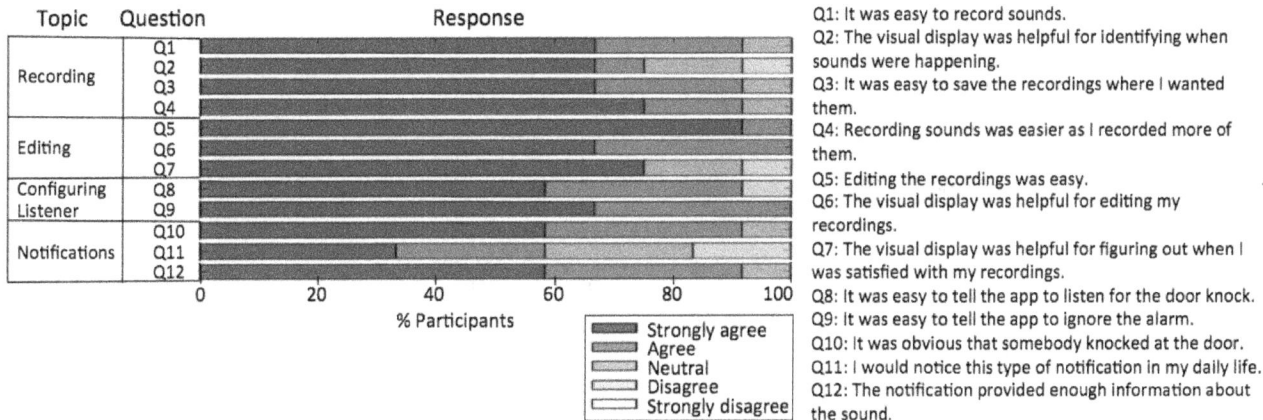

Topic	Question	Response

Q1: It was easy to record sounds.
Q2: The visual display was helpful for identifying when sounds were happening.
Q3: It was easy to save the recordings where I wanted them.
Q4: Recording sounds was easier as I recorded more of them.
Q5: Editing the recordings was easy.
Q6: The visual display was helpful for editing my recordings.
Q7: The visual display was helpful for figuring out when I was satisfied with my recordings.
Q8: It was easy to tell the app to listen for the door knock.
Q9: It was easy to tell the app to ignore the alarm.
Q10: It was obvious that somebody knocked at the door.
Q11: I would notice this type of notification in my daily life.
Q12: The notification provided enough information about the sound.

Figure 5: Participant responses to questions about their experience using the interface during the study.

a particular strength, with 91.7% of participants *strongly agreeing* that "The visual display was helpful for editing [their] recordings." The display provides a visual representation on recording content that allows deaf and hard-of-hearing users to evaluate them without hearing them. P4 explained how the display helps understand and trim recordings of repetitive sounds like an alarm: "if a deaf person could not hear it but wants to record whatever the sound is, they could possibly see the repetition and edit it down to a certain amount." Only half of our participants played back a sample, yet *all* participants successfully used the sliders to frame the part of their recordings they wished to keep. As P9 summarized, "VERY easy to use – just drag and stop." Once familiarized with the editing process, several participants described viewing and trimming recordings as "fun." Two participants expressed difficulty controlling the sliders. Enlarging the slider area would improve ease in the future.

5.2.3 Configuring the Listener

All participants successfully configured the app to listen for door knocks and ignore the alarm, though several asked questions along the way. Configuration involved selecting the door knock category, unselecting the alarm category, and sliding the listener on. All these actions take place on the main menu. All participants agreed that "It was easy to tell the app to ignore the alarm," and all but 8.3% agreed that "It was easy to tell the app to listen for the door knock." Of the participants who found configuration easy, one described the tasks as "easy peasy" and another elaborated, "it's easy to check on and off the options." Of the participants who had difficulty, four mentioned that the check boxes for selecting and unselecting sound categories were too small, and consequently had trouble checking the boxes with their fingers. One participant forgot to turn on the listener once they selected the sound categories, and suggested increasing the listener button's size to draw attention to the button.

5.2.4 Notification System

While most participants (58%) found the notification design sufficient to alert them to sounds in daily life, we received more feedback on the notification design than for any other part of the design. All participants received a door knock notification. If they did not test the door knock detection themselves, we knocked on the study door for them.

The combination of haptic and visual feedback caught each participant's attention. Many were impressed when the app notified them, and responded with "Cool!" or "Neat!" Those who criticized the text display wanted a larger notification, more information like a timestamp, and longer persistence on the screen. One participant was concerned about missing notifications if the phone was not physically on them, explaining, "it'd be hard to detect... if it only vibrates and the phone is not in my hand." Several participants wanted to customize the notifications for different sounds. For example, the phone could use a different sequence of vibrations to notify the user about each sound type. Others wanted alerts sent over another modality or to another device. They suggested email, SMS, flashing phone lights, sonic alerts, and amplifying the detected sound.

5.2.5 Use Cases

Participants envisioned many uses of our app in their lives. Picking out sounds while watching TV or in a noisy environment can be particularly difficult, and several participants hoped that the app would do so for them. Others noted that the app would be useful when they chose not to use their cochlear implants or hearing aids, or when they were using their cochlear implants to listen to music or other content besides their surroundings. Several participants stay near the door and periodically check for guests they are expecting, and using our app to detect door knocks would give them more freedom. They were also interested in using the app to detect distant sounds. For example, they might want to know when the tea pot boils in the kitchen downstairs. Several participants mentioned that they would like to take the app home and try it out on their personal use cases.

Participants also suggested design improvements for real-world usability. Some sounds are common but difficult to record (e.g. a fire-alarm or ambulance passing), and having these sounds built-in would be convenient. One participant was concerned about the presence of background noise or competing sounds while recording. While the app provides some feedback about background noise by visualizing sound level (i.e. volume), adding explicit feedback about conflicting sounds might improve usability. Three participants were concerned about the time it takes to set up the app, and streamlining the training process or allowing users to share training samples would likely lower barriers to use.

6. SOUND DETECTION EXPLORATION

To explore the viability of a sound detection app trained

9

by deaf and hard-of-hearing users, we implemented a basic sound detection algorithm and tested it on the training examples recorded in our user study. We model sounds as Gaussian Mixture Models (GMMs), a common technique in sound recognition and detection (e.x. [31]). The model's features are Mel-Frequency Cepstral Coefficients (MFCCs) which are commonly used for speech recognition [30]. We extract 14 MCFFs for each frame in the training samples.

We use a set of sliding windows to detect sounds in the incoming audio stream. Each sound (or class) has its own sliding window, spanning the average length of the class's training examples. The current window is classified as the sound whose GMM produces the highest normalized log-likelihood, the sliding windows are incremented, and the process repeats. The windows are incremented by 1/3 the size of the smallest window, a gap size found to perform well through experimentation. We smooth our classification by extending it to cover the expected duration of the sound, computed as the average duration of the training examples for that sound. We add a "white noise" class, trained on examples of office sounds and silence, to compete with the other sound types. An app notification is triggered when a window is classified as a sound other than "white noise" and the previous window does not share the same classification.

Table 1 shows our sound detection algorithm performance on recordings of door knocks and alarms from our user study. We ran 3-fold cross-validation on their examples. Test clips were formed by randomly inserting user recordings into longer streams of white noise collected in the study setting. We compared the events detected by our algorithm to the ground ground truth of audio events occurring where they were inserted in the longer streams. Each time the algorithm detected the inserted sound in the insertion range, we counted a true positive; each time the algorithm detected any other sound, we counted a false positive. Precision is the fraction of notifications sent that detected the right sound, and recall is the fraction of sounds that triggered a notification. F-score is a weighted average of precision and recall.

		Alarm	Knock
	Precision	1.00	0.41
Uncleaned	Recall	0.28	1.00
	F-Score	0.44	0.58
	Precision	0.71	0.77
Cleaned	Recall	0.98	0.41
	F-Score	0.82	0.54

Table 1: Accuracy of our sound detection algorithm using 3-fold cross-validation on recordings from our user study.

Our results demonstrate that background noise in training examples can impact detection accuracy. One researcher took notes with a portable keyboard during the study, and loud typing sounds were present in many training examples. Because loud typing sonically resembles knocking, keyboard sounds during alarm recordings were often mistaken for door knocks. We removed typing noises with Audacity's noise removal tool [2] to produce "Cleaned" training examples. This boosted performance, and in particular increased alarm recall. Because deaf and hard-of-hearing users might not be aware of or recognize the impact of background noise, providing additional visual feedback on training example quality would be a powerful addition to the app design. While

our algorithmic experiments are preliminary, the state-of-the-art in sound detection is advancing, and we expect that robust sound detection will be possible in the future.

7. CONCLUSION

In this work, we introduced the design of an app that detects sounds of interest to deaf and hard-of-hearing users. It is trainable by users who record examples of the sounds they want detected. Visual representations of both real-time audio and recorded sounds provide visual feedback on sonic content to allow deaf and hard-of-hearing users to independently train the app. Our design is informed by a widescale survey we ran on the design criteria that deaf and hard-of-hearing users have for such an app, including which sounds they want it to detect. We evaluated our interface design through a Wizard-of-Oz user study, and found the interface to be highly usable for deaf and hard-of-hearing users recording training examples of sounds. We also provided a preliminary exploration of a sound detection algorithm with training data from the user study.

A trainable sound detector app has many potential benefits: improved awareness in social situations where information is only communicated auditorily, freedom from visually checking if important events have occurred, the ability to turn off cochlear implants or hearing aids while still knowing about important sounds, and the consolidation of multiple detection methods into a single app. Allowing users to train the app gives users a great amount of control over the detector. They can customize it to personal sounds, and can expect high detection accuracy because it is trained on the exact sounds they want it to identify, recorded with the same device that will do the detection, and likely in the same environments where the detector will be expected to work.

There are several limitations to our current work. In particular, we did not implement a sound detection algorithm in the app because we did not achieve a high enough accuracy for diverse sounds in noisy environments with the methods we tried. Using Wizard-of-Oz sound detection for our user study allowed us to evaluate the app design without accuracy errors impacting the user experience. The algorithm we implemented is preliminary, and we expect to find appropriate algorithms in the future. Sensors are improving as industry pushes to gather data about users' environments, and virtual assistants already detect voice commands. The existence of virtual assistants like Apple's Siri (i.e. [32]) that run constantly but do not drain the battery suggests adequate efficiency is possible as well.

We plan to improve our interface design and release a complete working app. Because our study participants requested various notifications, we plan to support customization. For example, one participant could receive email alerts while another relays detected sounds to their cochlear implant. Sounds could even trigger complex responses, like turning on the porch lights when somebody knocks, by integrating into a smart environment or logic system like IFTTT (i.e. [14]). We will also explore active learning to help guide users about which categories of sounds need more examples. We plan to run a longitudinal study with the complete app to fully explore its usability. We hope that our work will result in a useful product, and encourage other sound detection researchers and developers to consider and evaluate the usability of their systems for deaf and hard-of-hearing users.

8. REFERENCES

[1] P. K. Atrey, N. C. Maddage, and M. S. Kankanhalli. Audio based event detection for multimedia surveillance. In *Proc. ICASSP*, volume 5, pages 813–816, 2006.

[2] Audacity. http://www.audacityteam.org, Accessed: 2015-09-28.

[3] Audio Analytic. http://www.audioanalytic.com, Accessed: 2016-05-06.

[4] S. Birring, T. Fleming, S. Matos, A. Raj, D. Evans, and I. Pavord. The leicester cough monitor: preliminary validation of an automated cough detection system in chronic cough. *European Respiratory Journal*, 31(5):1013–1018, 2008.

[5] S. Böck, F. Krebs, and M. Schedl. Evaluating the online capabilities of onset detection methods. In *Proc. ISMIR*, pages 49–54, 2012.

[6] M. Casey. General sound classification and similarity in mpeg-7. *Organised Sound*, 6(02):153–164, 2001.

[7] C. Clavel, T. Ehrette, and G. Richard. Events detection for an audio-based surveillance system. In *Proc. ICME*, pages 1306–1309. IEEE, 2005.

[8] R. I. Damper and M. D. Evans. A multifunction domestic alert system for the deaf-blind. *IEEE Transactions on Rehabilitation Engineering*, 3(4):354–359, 1995.

[9] G. Guo and S. Z. Li. Content-based audio classification and retrieval by support vector machines. *IEEE Transactions on Neural Networks*, 14(1):209–215, 2003.

[10] J. Haigh and J. Mason. Robust voice activity detection using cepstral features. In *Proc. TENCON*, volume 3, pages 321–324. IEEE, 1993.

[11] J. Harkins, P. E. Tucker, N. Williams, and J. Sauro. Vibration signaling in mobile devices for emergency alerting: A study with deaf evaluators. *Journal of deaf studies and deaf education*, 15(4):438–445, 2010.

[12] Harris Communications. http://www.harriscomm.com, Accessed: 2016-05-06.

[13] F. Ho-Ching, J. Mankoff, and J. A. Landay. Can you see what i hear?: the design and evaluation of a peripheral sound display for the deaf. In *Proc. CHI*, pages 161–168. ACM, 2003.

[14] If This Then That (IFTTT). https://www.ifttt.com, Accessed: 2016-05-06.

[15] E. C. Larson, T. Lee, S. Liu, M. Rosenfeld, and S. N. Patel. Accurate and privacy preserving cough sensing using a low-cost microphone. In *Proc. UbiComp*, pages 375–384. ACM, 2011.

[16] Leeo Smart Alert. http://shop.leeo.com/pages/about-leeo-smart-alert, Accessed: 2016-05-06.

[17] H. Lu, D. Frauendorfer, M. Rabbi, M. S. Mast, G. T. Chittaranjan, A. T. Campbell, D. Gatica-Perez, and T. Choudhury. Stresssense: Detecting stress in unconstrained acoustic environments using smartphones. In *Proc. UbiComp*, pages 351–360. ACM, 2012.

[18] T. Matthews, S. Carter, C. Pai, J. Fong, and J. Mankoff. Scribe4me: evaluating a mobile sound transcription tool for the deaf. In *UbiComp*, pages 159–176. 2006.

[19] T. Matthews, J. Fong, F. W.-L. Ho-Ching, and J. Mankoff. Evaluating non-speech sound visualizations for the deaf. *Behaviour and Information Technology*, 25(4):333–351, 2006.

[20] M. Mielke, A. Schäfer, and R. Brück. A mixed signal ASIC for detection of acoustic emergency signals in road traffic. *International Journal of Microelectronics and Computer Science*, 2:105–111, 2010.

[21] L. Muda, M. Begam, and I. Elamvazuthi. Voice recognition algorithms using mel frequency cepstral coefficient (MFCC) and dynamic time warping (DTW) techniques. *arXiv preprint arXiv:1003.4083*, 2010.

[22] P. Nordqvist and A. Leijon. An efficient robust sound classification algorithm for hearing aids. *The Journal of the Acoustical Society of America*, 115(6):3033–3041, 2004.

[23] S. Oberle and A. Kaelin. Recognition of acoustical alarm signals for the profoundly deaf using hidden markov models. In *Proc. ISCAS*, volume 3, pages 2285–2288. IEEE, 1995.

[24] OtoSense. http://www.otosense.com, Accessed: 2016-04-10.

[25] Parse. http://www.parse.com, Accessed: 2016-05-06.

[26] G. Peeters and X. Rodet. Automatically selecting signal descriptors for sound classification. In *ICMC*, pages 1–1, 2002.

[27] H. Phan, M. Maas, R. Mazur, and A. Mertins. Random regression forests for acoustic event detection and classification. *IEEE/ACM TASLP*, 23(1):20–31, 2015.

[28] M. R. Power and D. Power. Everyone here speaks txt: Deaf people using sms in australia and the rest of the world. *Journal of deaf studies and deaf education*, 9(3):333–343, 2004.

[29] M. R. Power, D. Power, and L. Horstmanshof. Deaf people communicating via SMS, TTY, relay service, fax, and computers in australia. *Journal of deaf studies and deaf education*, 12(1):80–92, 2007.

[30] L. Rabiner and B.-H. Juang. Fundamentals of speech recognition. 1993.

[31] D. A. Reynolds. Speaker identification and verification using gaussian mixture speaker models. *Speech communication*, 17(1):91–108, 1995.

[32] Siri. http://www.apple.com/ios/siri, Accessed: 2016-05-06.

[33] J. Sohn, N. S. Kim, and W. Sung. A statistical model-based voice activity detection. *Signal Processing Letters, IEEE*, 6(1):1–3, 1999.

[34] Sonic Alert. http://www.sonicalert.com, Accessed: 2016-05-06.

APPENDIX

A. SURVEY QUESTIONS

1. How often do you miss sounds that you want to know about? For example, a door knock, baby crying, or car honking.

	Never	Once per month	Once per week	Once per day	More than once per day
At home:	○	○	○	○	○
At work:	○	○	○	○	○
When mobile:	○	○	○	○	○

2. At home, what sounds do you care about? Check all that apply.

☐ Emergency alarms

☐ Wake-up alarms

☐ Doorbell

☐ Knocking on door

☐ Phone ringing

☐ People shouting

☐ People laughing

☐ Children fighting

☐ Children playing

☐ Baby crying

☐ People knocking things over
(ex: pots banging, vase breaking, plates breaking)

☐ Intruders

☐ Dog barking

☐ Appliance alerts (ex: dryer beeping, microwave beeping, tea pot boiling)

☐ Appliances running by accident
(ex: garbage disposal on, faucet on)

☐ Sounds outside of the house
(ex: people shouting outside the window)

☐ Emergency alarms

Other: [＿＿＿＿＿]

3. At work, what sounds do you care about? Check all that apply.

☐ Presence of co-workers

☐ What your co-workers are doing

☐ Co-workers trying to get your attention

☐ Surrounding conversations

☐ Knocking on door

☐ Emergency alarms

☐ Phone ringing

☐ Faxes

☐ Announcements

☐ Gun shots

Other: [＿＿＿＿＿]

4. When mobile, what sounds do you care about? Check all that apply.

☐ Vehicles driving by

☐ Honking

☐ Sirens

☐ Airplanes or helicopters

☐ Bikes or people coming up behind you

☐ Whether you are blocking another person
(ex: "excuse me", or "watch out")

☐ Dogs barking

☐ Sounds in nature
(ex: birds chirping, water in a stream, thunder)

☐ Announcements
(ex: airport or train station announcements)

Other: [＿＿＿＿＿]

5. How often do you use the following for sound awareness?

	Never	Once per month	Once per week	Once per day	More than once per day
Vibration sensing (ex: through the floor)	○	○	○	○	○
Checking to see if the sound happened (ex: checking to see if somebody knocked on the door)	○	○	○	○	○
Sound alerting devices (ex: flashing lights for the doorbell)	○	○	○	○	○
Hearing dog	○	○	○	○	○
Assistive hearing devices	○	○	○	○	○

6. What visual or tactile alerting devices do you use, if any?

☐ Baby monitor

☐ Sound monitor (for any type of sound)

☐ Doorbell or door knock signaler

☐ Fire, smoke, or carbon monoxide alarms

☐ Security alarms

☐ Motion detector

☐ Telephone signaler

☐ Alarm clock

☐ Weather alert

☐ Hearing dog

Other: [ ]

7. Do you use any apps on your mobile phone to provide sound awareness?
○ Yes
○ No

8. What mobile apps do you use for sound awareness?
[ ]

9. Suppose there is a new mobile phone app that can detect sounds. You tell it which wounds to listen for, and it sends you alerts when it hears those sounds. For example, you can tell it to listen for knocking on the door. Then every time it hears a knock on the door, it vibrates and a message appears on your phone screen. Would you be interested in using this app?
○ Yes
○ No

10. (If no:) Why would you not be interested in using such an app to detect sounds? [ ]

11. (If yes:) What sound would you most want the app to detect? [ ]

12. When the app detects your sound, how important is it that the app tells you the following information?

	Not important at all	Of little importance	Moderately important	Very important	Absolutely essential
What it is	○	○	○	○	○
Where it comes from	○	○	○	○	○
How loud it is	○	○	○	○	○
How long it lasts	○	○	○	○	○
How high or low the pitch is	○	○	○	○	○
How urgent it is	○	○	○	○	○
How sure the app is	○	○	○	○	○

13. Suppose the app tells you that your sound happened when it did not. How often can this happen, so that you would still use the app?

2-3 times per day	Once per day	Once per week	Once per month	Never
○	○	○	○	○

14. Suppose the app missed your sound and did not send you an alert. How often can this happen, so that you would still use the app?

2-3 times per day	Once per day	Once per week	Once per month	Never
○	○	○	○	○

15. In order to recognize a particular sound, the app needs samples of that sound. For example, before it can recognize your microwave beeping, the app needs recordings of the microwave beeping. How many samples would you be willing to record of your most important sound?

0	1-2	3-4	5-10	more than 10
○	○	○	○	○

16. How willing would you be to ask a hearing person for help to record sounds?

Not willing	Reluctant, but willing	Very willing
○	○	○

17. How willing would you be to share your recordings with other people using the app, so that they do not need to record the same sounds?

Not willing	Reluctant, but willing	Very willing
○	○	○

Improving Real-Time Captioning Experiences for Deaf and Hard of Hearing Students

Saba Kawas[1], George Karalis[1], Tzu Wen[1], Richard E. Ladner[2]
[1]Human Centered Design & Engineering, [2]Computer Science & Engineering
DUB Group | University of Washington
Seattle, WA 98195
{skawas, gkaralis, tzu}@uw.edu, {ladner}@cs.washington.edu

ABSTRACT

We take a qualitative approach to understanding deaf and hard of hearing (DHH) students' experiences with real-time captioning as an access technology in mainstream university classrooms. We consider both existing human-based captioning as well as new machine-based solutions that use automatic speech recognition (ASR). We employed a variety of qualitative research methods to gather data about students' captioning experiences including in-class observations, interviews, diary studies, and usability evaluations. We also conducted a co-design workshop with 8 stakeholders after our initial research findings. Our results show that accuracy and reliability of the technology are still the most important issues across captioning solutions. However, we additionally found that current captioning solutions tend to limit students' autonomy in the classroom and present a variety of user experience shortcomings, such as complex setups, poor feedback and limited control over caption presentation. Based on these findings, we propose design requirements and recommend features for real-time captioning in mainstream classrooms.

CCS Concepts

• **Human-centered computing~ User interface design** • **Human-centered computing~Participatory design** • **Human-centered computing~Empirical studies in accessibility** • **Human-centered computing~Accessibility technologies** • *Human-centered computing~ Accessibility design and evaluation methods*

Keywords

Deaf and Hard of Hearing; Co-Design; Real-Time Captions; Automatic Speech Recognition; Inclusive Classrooms.

1. INTRODUCTION

Many deaf and hard of hearing (DHH) students choose real-time captioning to access mainstream classes with hearing teachers and students. Today, real-time captioning solutions such as CART (communication access real-time translation) and C-Print have human captioners attend students' classes either in person or over a remote Internet call and transcribe course content as the instructor speaks. Captioners must be scheduled in advance, have limited availability and tend to be costly, making them difficult to offer by budget-conscious schools.

e

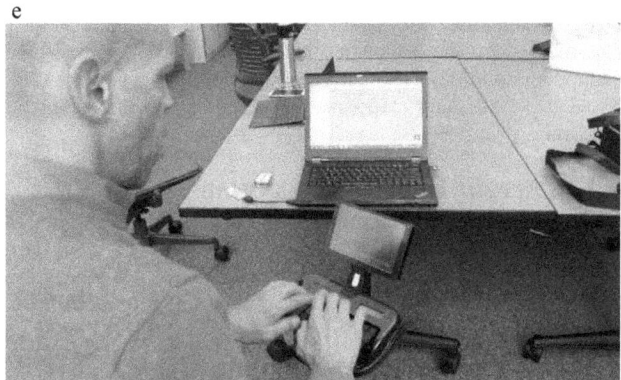

Figure 1. CART captioning setup.

Automatic speech recognition (ASR) is a machine technology that converts speech to text in real time, offering a low-cost alternative to human captioners. Poor accuracy and latency have been serious limitations of ASR as a real-time captioning tool, preventing it from catching on as a legitimate option for DHH students. However, as the technology improves ASR becomes increasingly viable as a classroom captioning tool.

Research taking a qualitative appraisal of real-time captioning experiences among DHH university students in mainstream classroom environments is scarce. Qualitative research into accessible technologies for DHH university students in the classroom do not dive into real-time captioning experiences specifically [14, 22]. Work addressing real-time captioning as a current solution for DHH students tends to focus on students' ability to retain course content [23, 24]. And while numerous studies have considered ASR as a tool for DHH students, these only assess the quality of the captions as measured by accuracy and/or performance of the technology itself [4, 9, 10, 13, 26].

While researchers have studied the technical and educational effectiveness of real-time captioning in the classroom, little work has been done to understand students' perspectives of real-time captioning from a user experience lens. We look holistically at students' experiences with real-time captioning solutions, considering existing human-based captioning solutions as well as potential ASR form factors. We consider usability and student sentiment along with technological factors.

To gather data about students' captioning experiences we employed a variety of qualitative research methods including in-class observations, interviews, diary studies, and usability evaluations. We also conducted a co-design workshop with 8 stakeholders after our initial research findings to tease out additional issues, brainstorm new solutions and evaluate concepts.

The contributions of this work are:
- This is the only work we know of that takes a holistic, qualitative approach to DHH students' experiences of real-time captioning.
- We involve DHH students and other stakeholders in the design process.
- Based on our studies, we propose design requirements and feature recommendations that can be implemented into new or existing real-time captioning systems.

2. RELATED WORK

DHH students may use a number of access technologies in their classrooms. In the following section we surveyed real-time captioning solutions commonly used today, potential new ASR-based solutions and experimental technologies attempted in academia.

2.1 Current Real-Time Captioning Tools

DHH students may use a variety of tools in the classroom to understand and communicate with hearing people [2, 5, 26]. Hard of hearing people often employ audio amplifiers such as hearing aids or personal FM systems that transmit sounds from a microphone to a person's hearing aids or cochlear implants. Students with more severe hearing loss may still use audio amplifiers, along with other methods like sign language interpretation or real-time captioning [5, 13]. Sign language interpreters who translate verbal speech into sign are a common choice for DHH students who are fluent in sign language [2, 26]. Some DHH students may prefer captioning because they are less fluent with sign language than with English. In this research we focus specifically on captioning, rather than other tools.

In human-based real-time captioning, a captioner listens to the speaker and types a transcript that the student can read along with as the speaker talks. Captioning solutions can either transcribe speech word-for-word (such as CART) or in a summarized fashion called meaning-for-meaning (such as C-Print) [6, 21]. ASR uses machine technology to generate word-for-word transcripts without a human captioner.

2.1.1 CART

The most reliable transcription service is CART (communication access real-time transcription), which provides word-for-word speech-to-text [13, 21]. Captioners use a shorthand typing keyboard enabling transcription at speeds of up to 225 WPM in real time, and sometimes faster in short bursts. The keyboard maps multiple key presses (chords) to phonemes of a word which expand into verbatim full text. [13] Abbreviations for frequent words and phrases immediately expand into the corresponding long form using a dictionary. A copy of the transcript is available on request. CART is the most expensive service, costing $100-200 per hour, due to the difficulty and length of training required to simultaneously listen and type on the specialized keyboard [13]. CART is available in person or remotely over an Internet call.

2.1.2 C-Print and TypeWell

C-Print and TypeWell are meaning-for-meaning real-time captioning services where a captioner produces a summarized transcription of the spoken information in the classroom. C-Print and TypeWell captioners are trained in text-condensing strategies [6, 21]. The cost of these services varies depending on need, demands, the captioner's skill and length of transcription [6]. C-Print is available as an in-person service as well as remotely, while TypeWell is available only remotely. Our research does not focus on these meaning-for-meaning solutions, as we did not encounter participants who use them at the location of our study.

2.2 ASR Systems

Automatic speech recognition (ASR) is a technology that recognizes and transcribes spoken language into readable text in real time. ASR has a wide range of applications such as supporting digital personal assistants like Siri and providing closed captions for online videos on websites like YouTube and Coursera [1, 12, 22]. However, ASR faces issues with accuracy, latency and context formalization due to the variability and complexity of human speech [1, 13, 19, 22]. Factors like background noise, speaker accent, speech rate, speaking style and spontaneous speech can degrade the quality of ASR transcriptions [3, 19].

2.2.1 ASR Applications

Many applications leverage ASR technology, though they tend to be for personal use or one-on-one communication. For example, Dragon NaturallySpeaking software is known for providing high quality speech-to-text for memo dictation. Skype Translator converts speech to text and provides machine translation in real time over a Skype video call, allowing speakers of different languages to communicate. These kinds of applications were not designed for real-time captioning in a classroom setting.

2.2.2 Real-Time Captioning with ASR

High quality real-time captioning with ASR becomes more realistic as the technology improves, implementing acoustic, pronunciation and context-aware language models [1, 3, 19]. For example, Papadopoulos and Pearson proposed an ASR model based on studies of human methods of recognition to increase the ASR performance and efficiency [18]. Additionally, with machine-learning technology, ASR systems can be trained to better recognize more specific vocabulary [19].

ASR is a desirable real-time captioning solution because of its low cost compared with human captioning services or sign language interpreters [13]. Researchers have thus begun to devise ASR-based solutions that can benefit DHH users. For example, Van Gelder et. al. leveraged ASR in a tabletop tool to help DHH users collaborate [25]. E-Scribe proposed the technology for a web-based ASR captioning solution for DHH users [4]. The APEINTA system provided automatic speech-to-text and text-to-speech on multiple platforms for DHH students inside and outside the classroom [8]. Gaur and Wald have both attempted to maintain high quality and low cost by using ASR as a starting point for human typists [7, 26].

However, ASR-based real-time captioning solutions for classrooms have only been used in experimental capacities.

2.3 Other Approaches to Classroom Captioning

Researchers have attempted to address issues of accuracy and cost of real-time captioning for DHH students with both human and machine-based solutions [7, 12, 16, 17]. Researchers have also considered other approaches to enhance captioning for DHH students. Legion:Scribe uses crowdsourcing where many non-expert captioners hear and type at the normal rate, collectively captioning speech in real time [16, 17]. This approach could be lower cost and more available than professional captioners, and it allows each typist to focus on a specific source while others focus on another source [13, 16].

Other researchers have focused on reducing DHH students' cognitive load in the classroom. Many things happen simultaneously during a university-level lecture: The instructor speaks and writes on the whiteboard, slides and other media are projected on a screen, classmates ask questions regarding the materials. DHH students often miss out or play catch up if they turned their attention away from the running captions or ASL interpreter.

Cavender et. al. developed ClassInFocus, which used the Adobe Connect service to bring lecture slides, a live video stream of an ASL interpreter, real-time captions and group chat together in one screen [5]. The tool provided visual cues to help students focus their attention. This approach could lower cost with remote interpreters and captioners and engage students with group chat and communal note taking. However, the researchers found that while students liked the interface, the various components made it difficult for students to notice changes outside of their current focus.

Another approach proposed by Kushalnagar et. al. projected real-time captions on the whiteboard, tracking the position of the speaker [11]. While DHH students found following the captions easier with this method, hearing students found the movement distracting. Additionally, this system required an involved set up, including a laptop, digital projector and Kinect 2 sensor to track the speaker location. Researchers didn't discuss the setup time nor who would be responsible for setting up the system before each class.

Lasecki et. al. developed a tool that allows users to control captioning speed and to highlight words [15]. This tool has the potential to help students attend to captions and other content, though it was only tested with pre-recorded online courses.

Currently, none of these experimental solutions has been used outside of controlled academic research environments. Likewise, practically all research focuses on comprehension or captioning accuracy rather than usability or students' experiences. We focused our research on tools available widely to students today.

3. QUALITATIVE STUDY DESIGN

We used a variety of qualitative research methods to triangulate insights from DHH students and other stakeholders including professors, captioners, technology providers and disability services coordinators.

3.1 Participants

To better understand the current solutions we recruited for several different research methods. We conducted 5 in-class observations with 2 DHH students. The same students also participated in a weeklong diary study. We conducted semi-structured interviews with 5 DHH university students, 2 professors, 2 disability services coordinators and 1 CART captioner. To begin to understand the opportunity of ASR as a classroom-captioning tool, we conducted usability tests with 3 DHH students in a classroom environment with Skype Translator, a tool that provides real-time transcripts over a Skype call. All DHH students in our study were female. Table 1 provides an overview of the research methods and participants.

Table 1. Participants in each research method.

Method	Participants
In-class observations	5 in-class observations with 2 DHH students
Diary studies	2 DHH students
Semi-structured interviews	5 DHH students 2 professors 2 disability services coordinators 1 CART captioner
Skype Translator usability evaluations	3 DHH students

3.2 Procedures

We recruited DHH students through the disability resources center email list and their social media web pages at the University of Washington. Interested DHH participants were asked to fill out a survey about their education history and the accessibility tools they've used before meeting with them in person. We recruited DHH students who use captioning services as their main accommodation. When we met with participants we explained the purpose and the research methods. We explained that they can participate in all or parts of our research. All DHH students received a gift card for their participation.

3.2.1 In-class Observations

We conducted a 30-minute interview with participants beforehand to understand their current in-class captioning accommodation experiences and preferences. We then sat with them in one of their regular class sessions, taking notes on setup, technological issues, behaviors and anything else of interest that we did not previously consider.

3.2.2 Diary Study

We had DHH participants keep a diary of at least 5 classes within one week. The students were asked to document their in-class experiences, frustrations and difficulties they may have faced with communication services and technologies using an online journal. Only the participants and researchers had access to the diary. We prompted participants with questions like "Did you encounter any difficulties or frustrations during this class period?" and "Describe any solutions or workarounds you found for these issues."

3.2.3 Interviews

We conducted semi-structured interviews with DHH students to ask about their current in-class captioning experiences including preferred accommodation, setup, quality of the captioning and in-class participation. For students who participated in the observations and diary studies, we followed up on specific things we observed or read. Likewise, we conducted interviews with other stakeholders including disability resources staff, professors, and a CART captioner to get a more holistic view of the students' experiences in the classroom.

3.2.4 Skype Translator Evaluation

We separately had several DHH university students pilot Skype Translator as an ASR-based captioning tool during lectures outside of their regular coursework. In these sessions we set up 2 computers running the Skype Translator app, which provides real-time speech-to-text for audio over a Skype call. We connected one computer to the lecturer's microphone and gave the other computer to the student to view the captions. Once a Skype call is initiated, a real-time transcription of the lecturer's speech appears in the Skype chat window, similar to real-time captions provided by CART or C-Print. We chose Skype Translator as opposed to other ASR tools because it is free, supports microphone connections, and displays word-for-word transcripts not unlike CART. During the sessions, we observed setup, technical and other issues that occurred and noted workarounds the participant tried. The students were then interviewed regarding their experiences with Skype Translator and completed a system usability survey.

3.3 Study Design Rationale

Using diary studies in addition to the interviews and the in-class observations not only allowed us to understand the biggest gaps in the existing solutions, it also helped us uncover subtleties that otherwise would not be clear through each method alone. Diary studies are one of the least intrusive methods for participants to express important, potentially sensitive personal experiences. Following up the diary studies and observations with semi-structured interviews allowed us to understand and make sense of what we had observed in the classrooms and read in participants' diary entries.

3.4 Analysis

We coded the data from the diaries, observations, interviews, and Skype Translator evaluations and conducted a qualitative analysis using affinity diagramming. We identified emerging insights through a thematic analysis. We then grouped our findings into various categories: benefits and limitations of solutions, user frustrations, system limitations, setup issues, system errors/crashes and troubleshooting. We also identified user interface issues such as font type, text size and background color that hindered the user experience. We distilled aggregated results from across the research methods.

4. RESULTS

We did not want to draw strong conclusions from individual research methods because the sample size for each method was small. We instead identified commonalities in the findings across the research methods to triangulate insights from multiple sources. Across the methods we uncovered benefits, limitations, and issues for both specific captioning solutions and classroom captioning more generally.

4.1 Captioning with CART

All participants use in-person CART in their classes. One participant uses CART for all classes except for Math, finding sign language interpretation more accessible for this subject. CART captioners arrive to the students' classes beforehand to set up the stenographic keyboard and a laptop that displays the captions. Students sit next to the captioner and refer to the laptop screen to read the captions. When the captioner is on vacation, sick or otherwise unavailable in person, the university provides students with equipment to connect to a captioner remotely. In this case, students are responsible for giving the instructor a microphone before each class and connecting to the remote captioner over an Internet call.

4.1.1 Benefits

DHH students strongly prefer CART with an in-person captioner to other captioning solutions because it provides the most accurate, high quality real-time captions. For example, a CART captioner can indicate multiple speakers, correct errors in near real time, and provide natural breaks in sentences for improved readability. When attending the class in person, the captioner also sets up the equipment, which is simpler on the student's part.

4.1.2 Limitations

Although CART caption accuracy is considered very high, participants in the diary study and interviews still complained about errors in the captions, especially when the speaker has an accent or speaks too fast, or with recognizing domain-specific words for specialized classes. As one participant said:

> "For certain subjects the captions can be kind of off. For example, one time we were learning about SQL, the programming language SQL. Instead the captions said 'sequel' as in a movie sequel" (Student P3, interview).

During an in-class session where the professor spoke quickly and used domain-specific terms, the captioner repeatedly made captioning errors. He was able to correct some errors quickly in near real time, but to keep up he had to make most corrections later during a break. While CART claims to have 90-100% accuracy, this figure accounts for corrections after the fact; in real-time the accuracy is somewhat lower. Students are usually provided with corrected transcripts later in the day, though only one of our participants said she has time to look at past transcripts.

Another observed CART limitation is the unreliability or unavailability of CART captioners. For example, during one in-class observation the captioner arrived late because he had to run across campus from his last session. By the time he set up the equipment, the student had missed more than 10 minute of the class. Another student mentioned her captioner is late every class because of scheduling:

> "My captioner usually has to be 5 minutes late because she is speed walking all the way...from South Campus to North Campus" (Student P1, diary entry).

Furthermore, the CART captioner's setup requires space and typically a connection to a power outlet, often dictating where the student can sit in the classroom.

> "You have to be near an outlet. I was once in an auditorium where there was only one outlet!" (Student P3, interview).

Because the captioner owns and operates the equipment, the student does not have direct control over the presentation of the captions. The student needs to ask the captioner to change font preferences or to scroll back to previous parts of the transcript if she or he missed something.

4.2 Captioning with ASR

We tested with Skype Translator in a medium-sized design seminar outside of participants' regular coursework and identified benefits and limitations.

4.2.1 Benefits

DHH students who evaluated the ASR-based Skype Translator tool found the interface intuitive: It was easy to follow along with the speaker and refer back to previous parts of the transcript. Every student mentioned the ability to scroll back as a benefit.

Figure 2. A hard of hearing student using Skype Translator during a lecture.

"It is easy to follow along, I can always look back at the captions if I'm not understanding something, I can scroll back up to see what the speaker said before, and it seems intuitive to use" (Student P1, Skype Translator post-evaluation survey).

Students also expressed that the Skype Translator solution made them feel more autonomous in the classroom than solutions that depend on human captioners.

4.2.2 Limitations
Students encountered a number of problems, especially compared with a CART captioner in person. The most common issue was low quality captions that included typos, incorrect grammar, extraneous words, and unnatural breaks in the caption blocks. Additionally, the Skype Translator setup involved 2 laptops with the software installed, which must be connected to the speaker's microphone. Students found this setup too complicated, similar to the set up of remote CART, and did not want to have to coordinate with the professor before every class. Students also found it problematic that Skype Translator was limited to a single microphone, so captions would not appear for other speakers or in groups.

"The translator was not accurate sometimes which made it difficult to follow along with… There was only one microphone, so I couldn't get the student questions translated" (Student P4, Skype Translator post-evaluation survey).

4.3 General Frustrations and User Experience Issues

4.3.1 In-class Structure and Activities
Participants expressed frustrations with having their attention divided between the speaker, lecture slides and captioning screen. This finding is consistent with the literature [5, 11, 14, 24]. As one participant in our research expresses:

"It would also help if the professor did not go through the slides very quickly, so that I could read both the slides and the transcript at once." (Student P1, diary entry).

Background noise was another issue affecting all captioning solutions, degrading transcription accuracy with both the human captioner and ASR technology. During one in-class observation,

the captioner had to ask other students to speak louder so he could hear well enough to transcribe their speech. This problem is especially common in situations where many people are talking at the same time, as one student notes:

"One area we struggle is when we have a breakout session. It becomes really noisy so it becomes really hard to transcribe. It can be hard to hear even for the CART transcriber" (Student P3, interview).

4.3.2 Speaker Behavior
All participants expressed frustration with the professor speaking too fast, as the captioner had a hard time keeping up. As one student writes:

"I talked to my captioner during the break, and he mentioned that the professor talks REALLY fast so it was harder for him to keep up. Which is understandable!" (Student P1, diary entry).

Professor's speech was a problem for both CART and ASR solutions. In addition to speaking too fast, participants noted that speakers' accents could pose issues with transcription accuracy.

4.3.3 Technology Errors
Likewise across solutions error reporting and troubleshooting posed problems. Technological issues were especially acute when a captioner was not there in person and the student was responsible for the setup, either with a human captioner remotely or with ASR. During our research, we encountered cases where CART (both in person and remote) and ASR crashed or otherwise failed without proper communication of the issue or how to resolve it. One student spoke with frustration about her experience trying to set up a remote CART session when her regular in-person captioner was on vacation:

"I had no clue how to set up the microphone [for a remote CART session], so weird to use it" (Student P1, interview).

When a professional captioner is present, she or he typically has the expertise to fix technical problems. When students are responsible, they found this to be a major burden. In either case, technical issues can disrupt students' access to the course content. For example, during one classroom session, we observed the captioner trying to fix a computer issue and had to restart the computer and the CART program. The student resorted to using her mobile phone to type and communicate with her classmates.

5. CO-DESIGN WORKSHOP
After analyzing the results of our research, we completed a stakeholder analysis, developed design requirements and ideated potential solutions for problems we uncovered. With our scoped set of ideas along with the design requirements, we created a list of features that captioning solutions might consider implementing to improve the experience for DHH students.

To validate our research findings, we came up with wireframes to help communicate and evaluate our ideas with stakeholders. We then conducted a co-design workshop to engage stakeholders in the design process, brainstorm new solutions and evaluate both our earlier research findings and the design ideas we created. We involved a variety of stakeholders to elicit feedback from different perspectives.

5.1 Participants

We conducted the 2.5-hour workshop in the evening at the University of Washington. In attendance were 5 university students (3 DHH, all ASL speakers), a Computer Science and Engineering professor and 2 technology providers, one of whom is deaf. A CART captioner and 2 ASL interpreters provided accommodations for the DHH participants.

5.2 Workshop Activities

We began with a quick icebreaker asking participants to imagine an idea for a new dessert and quickly sketch their idea. In doing so, we allowed the participants to get comfortable sketching and communicating their ideas to others in the group. We then asked participants to tell us the current limitations they face when using captioning services. For participants who are not deaf or hard of hearing and/or didn't use captioning, we asked them to draw parallels with metaphors like watching movies with captions or watching a lecture in a foreign language. Next, we asked our participants to imagine all possible solutions for the limitations and pain points brought up in the previous phase, forgoing all resource constraints.

For each activity we asked participants first to write down their thoughts individually on post-it notes, and then we asked each participant to share his or her ideas with the group. We gathered ideas on the board, grouped into ad-hoc categories to help prioritize and identify themes.

In our last activity, we evaluated the features our team had previously ideated by walking participants through mid-fidelity wireframes. For each feature participants judged the importance of the feature on a Likert scale and explained why they chose that rating. Last, we thanked our participants for joining us and handed out honoraria.

5.3 Analysis

We gathered all the feedback on the limitations of existing solutions from our participants and compared them with the results we gathered from our field research. We also looked at the new solutions that our participants had suggested and categorized the solutions based on their priority and feasibility.

5.4 Co-Design Results

5.4.1 Top Limitations

From the workshop critique phase, we found most of the limitations voiced by participants matched closely with our prior research. Caption accuracy, speaker behavior, setup and technical issues were among the top problem areas, in line with our past findings. One new finding was that all of the DHH students agreed that they were sometimes bothered by the brightness of the computer screen, especially if the classroom is dark while the professor is projecting slides. They wanted control over the brightness of the screen, if it could not automatically dim to be suitable for the environment.

5.4.2 Ideas for solutions

Participants came up with creative and forward-thinking solutions. Some of the solutions were futuristic, like contact lenses that beam captions into users' eyes or holographic captions that project off users' wrists. Other solutions were more grounded and practical for implementation. For example, the group agreed something as simple as a pre-class meeting with the teacher, student, disability services coordinator and captioner would go a long way.

Figure 3. Co-design workshop with stakeholders.

6. DISCUSSION

6.1 Technological Factors

The limitations we uncovered in our research generally reaffirm findings from the literature. Technological factors, especially accuracy, were among the top reported issues and have the largest impact on the user experience of ASR as a tool for classroom captioning. Across solutions including human-generated captions, situational factors like background noise or a speaker's accent exacerbate accuracy issues. ASR is considerably more susceptible to degradation as a result of such situational factors. ASR will face serious adoption difficulties in the classroom unless accuracy is on par with existing competitors across the same range of situations.

Reliability is another major technical factor for all captioning solutions. During our research, all solutions we observed including CART suffered from errors and crashes. The key difference between in-person CART and remote solutions including ASR, is that the human captioner is responsible for setting up and operating the CART technology. With CART when an error occurs or the system crashes, the captioner has the expertise to resolve the issue relatively quickly. Remote solutions including ASR count on the student to set up and operate the technology, and tend not to adequately communicate errors or provide troubleshooting steps to resolve issues.

6.2 Social and Behavioral Factors

While other research has noted that trained captioners are a limited resource [13, 26], the work does not discuss the scheduling issues that arise even when captioners are an option. Captioners arriving late to class or being unavailable while out on vacation or sick was an issue reported by all participants when talking about their CART experiences. Also, the quality of captioners varies based on their skill and the dictionaries they've built for school subjects. Given ASR can overcome its technical limitations, it provides an opportunity to resolve the issues of availability and inconsistency that students with human captioners face today.

Our findings validated that not enough thought is given to facilitating practices for professors and staff to better communicate in ways that accommodate DHH students using current real-time captioning services. A number of stakeholders suggested that instructors could receive resources with "best practices," such as speaking more slowly and repeating questions that were asked. Also, the student, professor, disability resource coordinator, and captioner could optionally have a meeting before the quarter to discuss how to best serve the student's needs. These ideas are consistent with the access technology literature, as Lartz and Stout observe:

"Previous literature has strongly recommended involving faculty and students in the AT [assistive technology] planning processes, whether for a single device or an entire AT program (Carey & Sale, 1994; Copley & Ziviani, 2004; Riemer- Reiss & Wacker, 2000; Todis & Walker, 1993). This recommendation is relevant to the current study in that AT planning for a classroom or entire program needs to involve all stakeholders: faculty, students who are Deaf, technology specialists, and interpreters" [15].

However, both of the professors we interviewed said they did not receive any specific instructions about how to best accommodate the DHH student(s) in their classes.

6.3 Student Autonomy

Interestingly, facilitating collaborative dialog between students, professors and others came somewhat at odds with another finding that students tend to desire autonomy in the classroom. This concept was reiterated by DHH students throughout our research in various forms. Students preferred solutions they could operate without coordinating with others and lacked interest in solutions that would require them to speak with the professor regularly. For example, students using remote CART need to give the professor a microphone before class. This can be problematic if students arrive late to class, for example, as one student describes:

> "The class had started, so I was waiting for a good time to give the professor the microphone so that he could wear it" (Student P1, interview).

Students wanted captioning to be less obtrusive and draw less attention. During interviews and in the diaries students expressed some discomfort with the CART setup, which involves considerable equipment and often dictates where they must sit in the classroom (in an aisle seat, near an electrical outlet, etc.).

Similarly, with CART the presentation of the captions is largely in the captioner's control. Students don't typically have the ability to scroll back to earlier parts of the transcript or change the font size or color unless they specifically request it of the captioner. Across our research methods, students expressed a desire to customize the presentation of the captions to better suit their preferences. Ideas from the co-design session also touched upon a desire for independence, from far-future concepts like captioning contact lenses to simpler ones like control over screen brightness so the caption screen is less distracting. Control over the caption display and presentation was a very desirable aspect of the ASR solution, which is entirely within the student's control.

7. IMPLICATIONS FOR DESIGN

Based on our research findings and our analysis of stakeholders' needs and goals, we came up with design requirements and a list of features. The design requirements, if realized in a design, would resolve the user experience issues and limitations we encountered in our findings. The features attempt to translate those requirements into a form consumable by technology providers.

7.1 Design Requirements

We developed these requirements after our initial research analysis and iterated as our research continued, especially based on the results of the co-design and evaluation workshop. We prioritized the list with all our stakeholders.

1. Captions have accurate spelling, grammar, punctuation, course content and context
2. Captions show in real-time with as little lag as possible
3. System is always available instantly and reliably
4. Students have control over captions display (font, size, scrolling, brightness, etc.)
5. Captioning can identify multiple speakers
6. Captions are segmented in a natural, conversational way
7. Captions are easy to read and comprehend
8. Students are able to quickly set up the system on their own
9. System clearly communicates errors and gives options to troubleshoot
10. System provides support for teachers of classes with both DHH and hearing students
11. Students don't need to interact with the professor to start using captions
12. Transcripts are available to the student after the class
13. System works in all classroom environments
14. System works on student's choice of device, e.g. laptop or tablet

7.2 Feature List

From the requirements, we designed features to address the top user needs. We evaluated initial ideas in the co-design workshop and iterated based on the results and as we reviewed them with stakeholders. We intend for the features to be general enough to be components of any real-time captioning tool for DHH students.

- **User interface for viewing captions**
  The interface displays accurate captions with natural language breaks and can identify multiple speakers.

- **Communicate errors and provide help**
  Resources help the student get set up with the captioning tool for the first time and resolve problems that occur. Resources are also provided to help the instructor to use the system and learn communication strategies to facilitate access for DHH students.

- **Microphone detection and connection**
  The system detects multiple nearby microphones so that the student can easily connect to one or more.

- **Dictionaries to increase captioning accuracy for different subjects**
  The student can select dictionaries specialized to specific subjects to increase caption accuracy, and students and teacher can upload content into the dictionaries to train them on domain-specific words.

- **Caption control**
  The student has control over the captions, with the ability to scroll back to previous parts of the transcript and change the size and style of the font.

- **Provide guidance to instructors**
  Professors get a guide with tips to help them speak to effectively accommodate students who need captions

8. LIMITATIONS

Our work had several limitations. Due to the small number of DHH students whose preferred access technology is real-time captioning at the university at which we recruited, the research sample size was relatively small and included only female participants. A larger sample size may have uncovered additional insights. Furthermore, all of the students who participated attended the same university, which provides a range of access technology options. We may have encountered different results at a more budget-conscious school or at a location where CART captioners are not available. While we were successful in testing with Skype Translator, it was not designed for the classroom setting nor for DHH students. An ASR-based captioning tool specific to DHH student needs, were such a tool available, may have provided a better comparison with CART.

9. FUTURE WORK AND CONCLUSION

We take a holistic, qualitative look at the experience of classroom captioning for deaf and hard of hearing students across new and existing solutions. Although accuracy and technical issues are still among the most problematic aspects of real-time captioning services and ASR tools, our qualitative research uncovered additional insights into user experience shortcomings in captioning solutions. Our design requirements and feature recommendations aim to provide technology providers with actionable guidance to improve real-time captioning for DHH students. The features aim to be implementation agnostic, such that they can be added to existing solutions like CART or Skype Translator, established classroom software like Microsoft PowerPoint, or new solutions we have yet to imagine.

10. ACKNOWLEDGMENTS

We would like to thank the follow people who assisted and guided us along the way: Liz Sanocki who served as our user research mentor for this project; Tanvi Surti, Will Lewis, and Ted Hart at Microsoft Research for supporting our research into ASR with Skype Translator; Jon McGough and Tobias Cullins at UW Disability Resources for Students who helped us in recruiting participants, and Erik Donnella an audio engineer at UW PCE. In particular, we thank all of the students and staff research participants at the University of Washington.

11. REFERENCES

[1] Araujo, G. F., & Macedo, H. T. (2014, April). Context formalization and its use on dynamic adaptation of language model in ASR systems. In Proceedings of the 7th Euro American Conference on Telematics and Information Systems(p.4).ACM.DOI:http://dx.doi.org/10.1145/2590651.2590655

[2] Bauman, H. D., & Murray, J. (2009). Reframing: From hearing loss to deaf gain. Deaf Studies Digital Journal, 1(1), 1-10.

[3] Benzeghiba, M., De Mori, R., Deroo, O., Dupont, S., Erbes, T., Jouvet, D., ... & Rose, R. (2007). Automatic speech recognition and speech variability: A review. Speech Communication, 49(10), 763-786.

[4] Bumbalek, Z., Zelenka, J., & Kencl, L. (2010). E-Scribe: ubiquitous real-time speech transcription for the hearing-impaired. In Computers Helping People with Special Needs (pp. 160-168). Springer Berlin Heidelberg.

[5] Cavender, A. C., Bigham, J. P., & Ladner, R. E. (2009, October). ClassInFocus: enabling improved visual attention strategies for deaf and hard of hearing students. In Proceedings of the 11th international ACM SIGACCESS conference on Computers and accessibility (pp. 67-74). ACM. DOI: http://dx.doi.org/10.1145/1639642.1639656

[6] Elliot, L. B., Stinson, M. S., McKee, B. G., Everhart, V. S., & Francis, P. J. (2001). College students' perceptions of the C-Print speech-to-text transcription system. Journal of deaf studies and deaf education, 6(4), 285-298.

[7] Gaur, Y. The Effects of Automatic Speech Recognition Quality on Human Transcription Latency. 2015. In Proceedings of the 17th International ACM SIGACCESS Conference on Computers & Accessibility (pp. 367-368). ACM. DOI: http://dx.doi.org/10.1145/2700648.2811331

[8] Iglesias, A., Ruiz-Mezcua, B., López, J. F., & Figueroa, D. C. (2013). New communication technologies for inclusive education in and outside the classroom.

[9] Keith Bain, Sara H. Basson, and Mike Wald. 2002. Speech recognition in university classrooms. In Proceedings of the 5th International ACM Conference on Assistive Technologies (Assets'02). ACM Press, New York, 192. DOI:http://dx.doi.org/10.1145/638249.638284.

[10] Kheir, R., & Way, T. (2007, June). Inclusion of deaf students in computer science classes using real-time speech transcription. In ACM SIGCSE Bulletin (Vol. 39, No. 3, pp. 261-265). ACM.DOI:http://dx.doi.org/10.1145/1269900.1268860

[11] Kushalnagar, R. S., Behm, G. W., Kelstone, A. W., & Ali, S. (2015, October). Tracked Speech-To-Text Display: Enhancing Accessibility and Readability of Real-Time Speech-To-Text. In Proceedings of the 17th International ACM SIGACCESS Conference on Computers & Accessibility (pp. 223-230). ACM. DOI: http://dx.doi.org/10.1145/2700648.2809843

[12] Kushalnagar, R. S., Lasecki, W. S., & Bigham, J. P. (2013, May). Captions versus transcripts for online video content. In *Proceedings of the 10th International Cross-Disciplinary Conference on Web Accessibility* (p. 32). ACM DOI: http://dx.doi.org/ 10.1145/2461121.2461142

[13] Kushalnagar, R. S., Lasecki, W. S., & Bigham, J. P. (2014). Accessibility evaluation of classroom captions. ACM Transactions on Accessible Computing (TACCESS), 5(3), 7. DOI: http://dx.doi.org/10.1145/2543578

[14] Lartz & Stout, "Perspectives of Assistive Technology from Deaf Students at a Hearing University," Assistive Technology Outcomes & Benefits, Fall 2008, Vol.5, Num. 1

[15] Lasecki, W. S., Kushalnagar, R., & Bigham, J. P. (2014, April). Helping students keep up with real-time captions by pausing and highlighting. InProceedings of the 11th Web for All Conference (p. 39). ACM. DOI: http://dx.doi.org/10.1145/2596695.2596701

[16] Lasecki, W. S., Kushalnagar, R., & Bigham, J. P. (2014, October). Legion scribe: real-time captioning by non-experts. In Proceedings of the 16th international ACM SIGACCESS conference on Computers & accessibility(pp. 303-304). ACM. DOI: http://dx.doi.org/10.1145/2661334.2661352

[17] Lasecki, Walter S.; Miller, Christopher D.; Sadilek, Adam; Abumoussa, Andrew; Borrello, Donato; Kushalnagar, Raja; Bigham, Jeffrey P. 2012b. Real-Time Captioning by Groups of Non-Experts. UIST'12, October 7–10, Cambridge, Massachusetts, USA. DOI: http://dx.doi.org/10.1145/2380116.2380122

[18] Miltiades Papadopoulos and Elaine Pearson. 2008. Accessible lectures: moving towards automatic speech recognition models based on human methods. In Proceedings of the 10th international ACM SIGACCESS conference on Computers and accessibility (Assets '08). ACM, New York, NY, USA, 273-274. DOI: http://dx.doi.org/10.1145/1414471.1414534.

[19] O'Shaughnessy, D. (2008). Invited paper: Automatic speech recognition: History, methods and challenges. Pattern Recognition, 41(10), 2965-2979.

[20] Richard Kheir and Thomas Way. 2007. Inclusion of deaf students in computer science classes using real- time speech transcription. In Proceedings of the 12th Annual SIGCSE Conference on Innovation and Technology in Computer Science Education (ITiCSE'07). ACM, New York, 261–265. DOI: http://dx.doi.org/10.1145/1268784.1268860.

[21] Seago, K. (Director), & Ladner, R., Burgstahler, S., & Roth, R. (Producers). (2014). Communication Access Realtime Translation: CART Services for Deaf and Hard-of-Hearing People [Video file]. Retrieved 2016, from http://www.washington.edu/doit/videos/index.php?vid=57

[22] Shiver, B. N., & Wolfe, R. J. (2015, October). Evaluating Alternatives for Better Deaf Accessibility to Selected Web-Based Multimedia. In Proceedings of the 17th International ACM SIGACCESS Conference on Computers & Accessibility (pp. 231-238). ACM. DOI: http://dx.doi.org/10.1145/2700648.2809857

[23] Steinfeld, A. (1998). The Benefit of Real-Time Captioning in a Mainstream Classroom as Measured by Working Memory. Volta Review, 100(1), 29-44.

[24] Stinson, M. S., Elliot, L. B., Kelly, R. R., & Liu, Y. (2009). Deaf and hard-of-hearing students' memory of lectures with speech-to-text and interpreting/note taking services. The Journal of Special Education, 43(1), 52-64.

[25] Van Gelder, Joris; Van Peer, Irene; Aliakseyeu, Dzmitry. 2005. Transcription Table: Text Support During Meetings. M.F. Costabile and F. Paternò (Eds.): INTERACT 2005, LNCS 3585, pp. 1002 – 1005.

[26] Wald, M. (2006). Captioning for deaf and hard of hearing people by editing automatic speech recognition in real time. In Computers Helping People with Special Needs (pp. 683-690). Springer Berlin Heidelberg.

SlidePacer: A Presentation Delivery Tool for Instructors of Deaf and Hard of Hearing Students

Alessandra Brandão[1], Hugo Nicolau[1,3], Shreya Tadas[1], Vicki L. Hanson[1,2]
[1]Rochester Institute of Technology, [2]University of Dundee
[3]INESC-ID, Instituto Superior Técnico, Universidade de Lisboa
ard6573@rit.edu, hman@inesc-id.pt, {sgt3895, vlhics}@rit.edu

ABSTRACT

Following multimedia lectures in mainstream classrooms is challenging for deaf and hard-of-hearing (DHH) students, even when provided with accessibility services. Due to multiple visual sources of information (e.g. teacher, slides, interpreter), these students struggle to divide their attention among several simultaneous sources, which may result in missing important parts of the lecture; as a result, access to information is limited in comparison to their hearing peers, having a negative effect in their academic achievements. In this paper we propose a novel approach to improve classroom accessibility, which focuses on improving the delivery of multimedia lectures. We introduce SlidePacer, a tool that promotes coordination between instructors and sign language interpreters, creating a single instructional unit and synchronizing verbal and visual information sources. We conducted a user study with 60 participants on the effects of SlidePacer in terms of learning performance and gaze behaviors. Results show that SlidePacer is effective in providing increased access to multimedia information; however, we did not find significant improvements in learning performance. We finish by discussing our results and limitations of our user study, and suggest future research avenues that build on these insights.

CSS Concepts

• **Human-centered computing---Accessibility---Accessibility systems and tools • Social and professional topics---User characteristics---People with disabilities**

Keywords

Deaf, Learning; Pace, Lecture; Interpreter, Multimedia; Visual Sources; Presentation.

1. INTRODUCTION

Over the past decades there has been a change in the face of deaf education. In the United States, the Education for All Handicapped Children Act (Public Law 94-142), passed in 1975, combined with the 1990 Individuals with Disabilities Education Act (Public Law 101-476) assured free and public education for children with disabilities. Since then, the number of deaf and hard of hearing (DHH) students in integrated or mainstream classrooms has increased considerably [28]. Still, DHH individuals struggle to achieve academic parity with their hearing peers [17].

ASSETS '16, October 23-26, 2016, Reno, NV, USA
© 2016 ACM. ISBN 978-1-4503-4124-0/16/10...$15.00
DOI: http://dx.doi.org/10.1145/2982142.2982177

A major assumption underlying mainstream education is that support services, such as sign language interpreters, provide access to classroom communication comparable to that of their hearing peers. Yet, the visual demands of learning through sign language interpreting are usually ignored. In addition to the interpreter, a typical university-level classroom includes the instructor and slides. In fact, educational researchers often cite the dependence of deaf students on the visual modality and encourage the use of visual materials and displays in the classroom [9, 11, 16]. Ironically, this practice forces students to divide their attention and rapidly change across simultaneous visual sources (interpreter, instructor, and slides), often resulting in missing critical information [10, 14, 18]. Thus, even though information is presented, students may not be able to simultaneously attend to all of it because their visual channel becomes overloaded. Moreover, because the interpretation and the instructor's spoken feedback are not synchronized, the likelihood of misunderstanding information on slides increases even more.

Previous work on classroom technologies has focused in assisting DHH students in managing multiple visual sources by integrating multiple views in a single screen and directing their attention to changes [2, 6, 7, 12]. However, students still have to integrate multiple (unsynchronized) sources of information, which takes working memory resources that could be used for learning [1].

Our work explores a different research avenue. Rather than focusing on the already overloaded student, we investigate how technology could facilitate and improve the delivery of instructions in mainstream classrooms to fit DHH students' learning needs. Instructors are often unaware of the specific challenges of DHH individuals and how to deal with them. To this end, we developed SlidePacer, a system that promotes better pacing behaviors for classroom multimedia presentations. The system opens a communication channel between interpreters and instructors, creating a single cohesive instructional unit, while synchronizing verbal and other visual resources (i.e. slides).

We base our design on cognitive load theory [29] and educational research. In fact, pace of instruction is widely mention as one of the main problems faced by DHH in mainstream classrooms, preventing them to access all classroom communication and engage in active learning (e.g. through participation) [3, 5, 8, 10]. Additionally, evidence from cognitive psychology research shows strong relationships between instructional pace and learning performance, particularly when using multiple sources of information [4, 20, 22]. Yet, there is a lack of empirical evidence on the effectiveness of adjusting the pace of instruction in mainstream classrooms. Therefore, our goal with this work is two-fold: 1) promote an adequate instructional pace by temporally integrate disparate sources of information, thus freeing cognitive resources for learning; and 2) assess the effectiveness of our approach by measuring learning performance.

We conducted a user study with 60 participants aimed at understanding whether SlidePacer enables more effective learning in multimedia classrooms. Results show higher access to visual materials. Learning performance was also higher than the control condition, although we did not find a significant effect.

The contributions of this paper include, first, SlidePacer, a novel system informed by multimedia learning and educational research that promotes a change in pacing behaviors. Second, we present results on the learning effect of our tool on both DHH and hearing participants. Third, we analyze the perceptions of students about presentations' pace. We close by discussing our results.

2. RELATED WORK

We discuss related work in three areas: first, we analyze previous work on multimedia learning and its implications for instructional design. Second, we discuss cognitive psychology research aimed at understanding how DHH individuals learn in mainstream classroom environments. Finally, we describe previous attempts to improve classroom accessibility using new technologies.

2.1 Multimedia Learning

Cognitive load represents the amount of mental effort in use in the working memory, which has a limited processing capacity. The cognitive theory of multimedia learning states that our working memory is capable of processing information received from visual and auditory channels simultaneously [19]; thus, separating content over both channels reduces the load on working memory.

For instance, aligning graphics (visual materials) to spoken text can be better processed in working memory rather than non-simultaneous information [19]. This is usually what happens in a classroom where hearing learners receive information through the auditory channel (speech) and visual channel (e.g. slides, notes). On the other hand, DHH students are at a disadvantage in comparison to their peers, since they do not have the opportunity to segregate verbal and visual information.

DHH learners need to be constantly shifting their attention between visual sources (lecturer, slides, accessibility services) in order to access information. As expected, this split-attention behavior impairs learning [1]. Although research in cognitive science has shown that aligning verbal information with graphics have clear benefits in retention and long-term recall [25, 30], most mainstream classrooms do not take into account these recommendations. The cognitive overload of learners prevents them to engage with information and organize the material in a rational structure, thus inhibiting the integration of the new content with the prior knowledge in the long-term memory [20].

Nevertheless, previous research has shown that presenting content sequentially and at a slower pace may have benefits, particularly when content is complex or words are unfamiliar [20, 22, 24]. Our work aims to leverage this knowledge as a new delivery tool.

2.2 Learning and Deafness

Previous studies [14] that investigate the differences between DHH (with interpreting services) and hearing students when accessing classroom content show that DHH students take away less from classroom lectures presented via sign language interpreting as compared to their hearing classmates. However, that difference does not appear to be related with either students' sign language skills nor interpreters' skills. Interestingly, Marschark et al. [14] do not provide a clear explanation on why removing the obvious communication barrier in mainstream classroom does not provide DHH learners with sufficient access to learning at a level comparable to their hearing peers.

Nevertheless, in a series of following experiments, the authors aimed to understand the extent to which interpreting provides deaf students with true access to education by comparing direct (instructor uses ASL) and mediated instructions (via ASL interpreter) [15]. Results showed that direct and mediated instructions can be equally effective; however, the quality of instruction for deaf students is more important than mode of communication per se; that is, when the class is well designed, there is no learning "gap". This highlights the importance of presentation delivery in classrooms.

Despite more than 40 years of research on the challenges that DHH students face in classrooms [13, 15, 26], there is little work done by cognitive scientists on potential solutions or guidelines to solve these issues, which include students not being able to attend to two different sources of visual information, classroom pacing, interpreters not being fully qualified, and interpreters being confronted by multiple conversations and interruptions,.

Previous studies have shown that instructors assume that the presence of support services is enough to guarantee an effective teaching [10]. In this paper, we offer a technological solution to be used by instructors and interpreters to delivery better presentations. Although it is still not clear what are the main characteristics of an effective class, lecture pace is perceived as one of the most important by DHH students and faculty [8].

2.3 Classroom Assistive Technologies

W3C offers a set of guidelines on making presentations accessible to all[1]. Still, these guidelines mostly focus on creating accessible presentation documents or general advice on content delivery, such as speak clearly, use simple language, and so forth.

ClassInFocus [2] attempts to assist DHH students in mainstream classrooms with the split-attention problem; that is, managing multiple visual sources. The system merges all visual sources in a single window and automatically notifies students of change in any visual source, such as slide changes. Results showed that students who gathered information from multiple visual sources performed better on content learning. Moreover, the tool enabled a reduction of visual dispersion.

More recently, Kushalnagar [7] addressed the same problem by leveraging hearing students' eye gaze to create reference cues in lecture videos. It was found that students who liked these cued notifications were more likely to demonstrate reduction in delay time associated with shifting visual attention. Lasecki et al. [12] investigated pausing and highlighting to help DHH students to keep up with classroom captioning. Results showed that the tool was effective and helped them to follow visual content that might otherwise have been missed.

Although some attention has been given to the split-attention challenges that DHH face in mainstream classrooms, all these new technologies put an extra cognitive (and sometimes physical) load on the students. On the other hand, much less attention has been paid on helping instructors and accessibility services in addressing DHH learners' needs. Moreover, it is crucial to assess the effect of technological interventions in terms of learning performance. Some studies solely rely on learning preference; however, there is little correspondence between students' perceptions of lesson effectiveness and actual instructional value [27].

3. SLIDEPACER

Previous research has shown that presentation delivery pace has an effect on learners' retention and understanding of information [20, 22, 24]. The effect is most noticeable when learners' working memory is overloaded with information. This is often the case for DHH students that receive all instructional content (verbal, images, text, etc.) via visual channel. Despite this knowledge there is a lack of delivery and practice tools for presenters that promote adequate pacing behaviors.

---

[1] https://www.w3.org/WAI/training/accessible

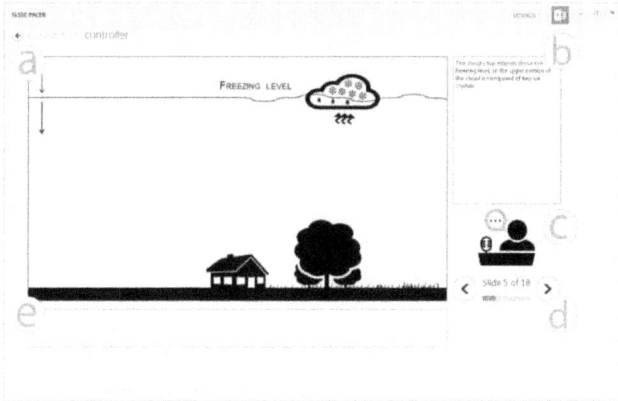

Figure 1. SlidePacer – presenter interface: a) current slide, b) presenter notes, c) illustration representing whether the instructor should wait to start speaking again; d) slideshow controls; and e) notification area.

3.1 Design

SlidePacer was designed to reduce information overload on learners by promoting a change in pacing behaviors during the delivery of multimedia presentations.

The main goal is to coordinate presenters and interpreters, turning them into a single unit of content delivery, and enabling DHH learners to read slide's content. We encourage presenters to wait for interpreters before advancing with the slideshow. Notice that interpreters can lag behind due to several reasons, such as: inherit overload related with interpreting (listen, understand, build interpretation, and verbalize), presenter's speech speed, complexity of content, etc. The lack of synchronization can dramatically hinder DHH learners' understanding of content, especially when there are references to visual materials.

SlidePacer reduces the lag between instructor and interpreter, and then waits for learners to shift attention and read visual materials. This gives DHH learners the opportunity to access slides, which are often missed in fast-paced presentations. The tool is intended to be used in mainstream classrooms and comprises two components: 1) a PowerPoint add-in to be used by instructors, and 2) an Android application to be used by interpreters. Both components are connected and communicate with each other in order to coordinate instructors and interpreters.

3.2 Instructor

The instructor component was implemented as a PowerPoint add-in. This means that SlidePacer works with any PowerPoint presentation file. We chose PowerPoint due to its popularity as a slideshow authoring tool. In order to use SlidePacer, which is a delivery tool, instructors need to enable the add-in. Once in presenter mode, SlidePacer consists of a familiar interface, similar to PowerPoint's built-in interface (Figure 1). SlidePacer was developed as a C# WPF application.

By default, SlidePacer behaves as a traditional presenter view with the same next/previous controls. However, if there is an interpreter available, instructors can connect to his/her app through Bluetooth. From then on, when they change slide, SlidePacer attempts to synchronize both interpreter and instructor by waiting for the interpretation to finish. Notice that the slide still has not changed at this point, since DHH students have not had the opportunity to see it. Pressing the forward/backwards key twice overrides the waiting time.

After the interpretation is finished there is a delay in order to give DHH students the chance to read the slide, before advancing to the next one. In the current implementation, the delay is a fixed but configurable value. Depending on the complexity or amount of content on each slide, the instructor can set the most appropriate delay in the settings menu. While waiting, instructors receive feedback through the presenter view, whether they are waiting on the interpreter or students (Figure 2).

3.3 Interpreter

The interpreter component has two main functions: 1) inform the interpreter that the instructor intents to advance the slideshow, and 2) inform the instructor that the interpretation is finished.

The component was implemented as an Android application. We first prototyped and informally tested a mobile app with professional interpreters. Feedback collected from 3 classroom interpreters showed that notifications needed to be subtle and inconspicuous, since they already deal with high cognitive load while performing their jobs. Moreover, all interactions should be eyes-free, short, and require minimal attention in order to keep users focused on their main task: interpreting.

Our final implementation consisted of a mobile and a companion smartwatch app. The app uses visual and vibrotactile feedback to inform interpreters that an action is required. When the instructor changes slide, the smartwatch gives a short (1 second) vibrotactile stimulus and changes the screen color to red (Figure 2). When the user finishes interpreting, s/he performs a single tap anywhere on the screen. This indicates that students are now free to look at the slides. After a delay (see previous section) the slide changes and the workflow restarts. Through this simple coordination mechanism in presentation delivery, we aim to provide DHH students with the opportunity to access multimedia content. Possible side effects of using SlidePacer are longer presentation times. Overall, we believe this to be a small limitation when considering we are providing both hearing and DHH students with equal access to information in classroom environments.

4. EVALUATION

This study focuses on assessing the effects of using SlidePacer during delivery of multimedia content. We conducted a laboratory study, replicating a validated experiment from the field of cognitive psychology to measure learning performance using multimedia presentations [19–21, 24].

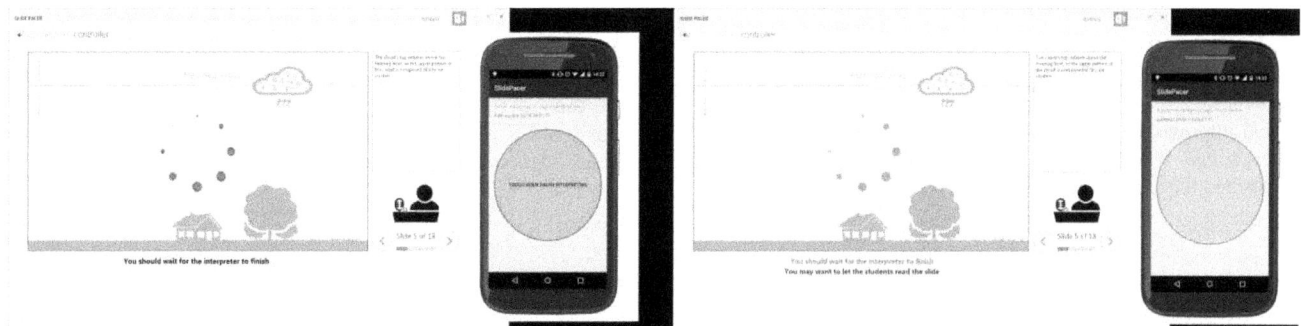

Figure 2. From left to right: presenter view waiting for interpreter to finish; mobile app is waiting for interpreter input to signal that interpretation is finished; presenter view waiting for students to read slide content; mobile app is inactive.

4.1 Research Questions

We aim to answer five main research questions: 1) Is SlidePacer effective in improving learning for DHH students? 2) Does SlidePacer improve DHH students' access to visual materials? 3) What is the learning effect on hearing students? 4) What is the relationship between DHH and hearing students performance? 5) What are students' perceptions about the lecture's pace?

4.2 Participants

Sixty participants took part in this study, 30 deaf and hard-of-hearing and 30 hearing. They were recruited at the Rochester Institute of Technology through flyers around the campus. Participants first filled an online screener questionnaire where they self-reported ASL skills. Participants were eligible for the user study if they 1) reported fluency with ASL (i.e. able to express yourself easily, articulated, and understand others), 2) used ASL on a daily basis, and 3) requested ASL services in mainstream classrooms. This criterion was only applied to DHH users. In addition, all participants needed to be college/university level students. Eligible participants were emailed to schedule their session and were assigned to one of two conditions: lecture without SlidePacer (control) or with SlidePacer. Participants were given a $20 compensation for their time.

4.3 Apparatus

To ensure internal validity and consistency, we used pre-recorded videos to simulate a classroom lecture. The lecture was about the process of lightning formation [19–21, 24] and featured an instructor, interpreter, and slides displayed in 3 similar computer monitors. We recorded two lectures; one with SlidePacer (5 minutes) and one without (control condition, 2 minutes and 20 seconds). An American graduate student acted as an instructor reading from a script, whereas a professional classroom ASL interpreter volunteered to record the lectures. He had access to the instructor's script in advanced in order to practice before the recording session. This was done to guarantee consistency in ASL instructions and to make sure all vocabulary was known beforehand. Slides illustrated verbal instructions and contained minimal text (Figure 1). We made sure both lectures were similar: same content, verbal instructions, and slides. The only difference was the pacing of the lecture and the interpreter's (subtle) interactions with the SlidePacer app. SlidePacer's delay between the interpretation and change of slide was set to 5 seconds.

During the experimental sessions, the computer displays were placed adjacent to each other in front of participants. The left monitor showed the slides, the middle monitor showed the ASL interpreter, and the monitor at the right showed the instructor. Participants had no control over the pre-recorded videos. Also DHH participants had no access to audio feedback in order to control for auditory abilities. They were asked to sit facing the middle screen, which had a built-in camera that was used to record the participant's face. These recordings were later used to analyze participants' eye gaze.

4.4 Procedure

At the beginning of each evaluation session, participants were told that the overall purpose of the study was to investigate how we could improve the delivery of multimedia lectures in mainstream classrooms. We then handed out the informed consent, which explained the experimental setup and procedure.

Before starting the lecture, participants were asked to fill a pre-questionnaire about demographic information, fluency in ASL, and previous knowledge of lightning formation [20]. They were asked to fill in a 5-point Likert scale ranging from very little to very much, to the questions: *1) I regularly read the weather maps in the newspaper / online; 2) I can distinguish cumulus and nimbus clouds; 3) I know what a low pressure system is; 4) I can explain what makes the wind blow; 5) I know what this symbol means* ▲▲▲ . *6) I know what this symbol means* ▲▲▲ .

After filling the pre-questionnaire, depending on their experimental condition, participants were informed that slideshow would advance after the interpretation was finished for the current slide (SlidePacer) or as the instructor spoke (control). After the lecture, participants were given a post-questionnaire with two questions: *1) how difficult was it for you to learn about lightning from the presentation you just saw? and 2) what do you think about the pace of the presentation?* Both questions had a 7-point Likert scale ranging from *very easy* to *very hard*, and *very slow* to *very fast*, respectively.

Afterwards, participants were given 20 minutes to complete two tests (10 minutes each) to assess their learning performance. The session took on average 45 minutes.

4.5 Dependent Measures

In this study we leverage the concept of *deep learning* [22], which is defined as "attention to important aspects of the presented material, mentally organizing it into a coherent cognitive structure, and integrating it with relevant existing knowledge". Learning is the ability to retain knowledge and apply it to new situations [23]. Therefore, we measured learning performance by using *retention* and problem-solving *transfer* tests. In addition to asking whether participants can recall what was presented in the lecture (*retention* test), we also ask them to solve novel problems (*transfer* test). Although learners may perform satisfactorily on retention tests, deep understanding may be limited.

The *retention* test consisted of the following instruction: *Please write down, to the best of your ability, a detailed explanation of how lightning works.* The *transfer* test contained the following 4 questions: *1) What could you do to decrease the intensity of lightning? 2) Suppose you see clouds in the sky but no lightning. Why not? 3) What does air temperature have to do with lightning? 4) What causes lightning?* In addition to learning performance measures, we also collected video recordings that were later analyzed to measure gazing behaviors. Finally, we collected participants' perceived difficulty and pace for the lecture.

4.6 Design and Analysis

We used a between subjects design to mitigate learning effects between conditions. Each participant tested one condition, either with or without SlidePacer. We had two groups of users (DHH and Hearing) with 30 participants per group and two conditions (with and without SlidePacer), resulting in a total of 15 participants per condition.

Both retention and transfer tests were scored individually by two of the authors. Scorers were not aware of the treatment condition of each participant. In order to achieve high agreement and cohesion, all scores were revised and differences were solved in a consolidation session with a third author.

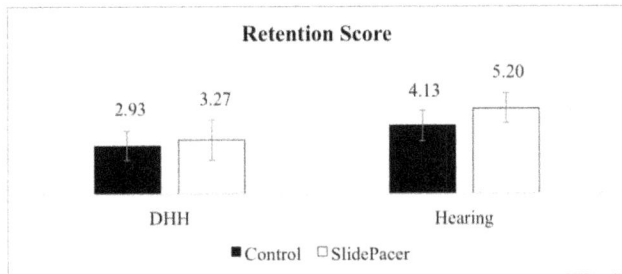

Figure 3. Mean retention score for both user groups and experimental conditions.

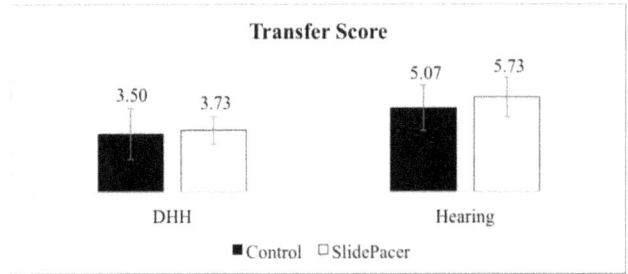

Figure 4. Mean transfer scores for both user groups and experimental conditions.

A *retention* score was computed for each participant by counting the number of major idea units (out of eight possible) that the participant produced [21]. One point was given for each of the following idea units: 1) air rises, 2) water condenses, 3) water and crystals fall, 4) wind is dragged downward, 5) negative charges fall to the bottom of cloud, 6) the leaders meet, 6) negative charges rush down, and 8) positive charges rush up. We also calculated *transfer* scores for each participant by counting the number of acceptable answers produced across the four transfer problems. Examples of acceptable answers for the first question could be removing negative charges from the clouds; acceptable answers for the second question include the top of clouds might not be above the freezing level; for the third question, an acceptable answer could be that the air must be cooler than the ground; for the fourth question, an appropriate answer included the transfer of charges between the clouds and the ground.

Regarding eye gaze, we annotated the recorded videos with the current monitor participants were looking at. Annotations were first done for a single participant by two of the authors. Differences between experimenters were within 1% for each monitor, which corresponded to a difference of four seconds. From then on, two of the authors annotated videos separately.

We performed Shapiro-Wilk test on all dependent measures. We applied parametric statistical tests, such as ANOVA and unpaired t-test, for normally-distributed values or non-parametric tests (Kruskal-Wallis and Mann-Whitney) otherwise. We applied Bonferroni corrections when performing pair-wise comparisons.

At the start of the study, participants were asked about their previous knowledge of lightning formation. We did not find any correlation between prior knowledge and retention performance [$r_{(7)}$=-0.034, p=0.802] or transfer performance [$r_{(7)}$=.223, p=.093], thus no participant data was excluded from the data analysis.

5. RESULTS

Our goal is to understand the effect of SlidePacer on mainstream classrooms. In this section, we describe participants' learning performance, gaze behaviors, and perceived pace.

5.1 Learning Performance

To assess learning performance we used retention and transfer scores. Figure 3 and Figure 4 illustrate the obtained results for both user groups and conditions.

DHH participants improved an average of 0.34 on retention score from the control (M=2.93, SD=.95) to SlidePacer (M=3.27, SD=.89) condition (Figure 3). Although there was an increase, we did not find a statistical significant effect [Z=.298, p=.766, r=.05]. Regarding transfer scores, DHH obtained an average of 3.5 (SD=1.39) in the control condition and 3.73 (SD=1.55) in the SlidePacer condition (Figure 4). Again, this difference was not statistically significant.

Considering hearing participants, we found a similar increasing tendency from the control to the SlidePacer condition. Participants improved, on average, 1.07 points on retention score from 4.13 (SD=0.93) to 5.20 (SD=1.23) (Figure 3). Nonetheless, we did not find a significant difference between conditions [Z=1.509, p=.131, r=.28]. Regarding transfer scores (Figure 4), hearing participants obtained similar results with both control (M=5.07, SD=1.22) and SlidePacer conditions (M=5.73, SD=0.84) [Z=.696, p=.486, r=.13]. Overall, although there was an increase in learning performance for both hearing and DHH participants, we did not find this difference to be statistically significant. Still, not finding a significant effect does not mean it does not exist. In Section 6, we will further discuss these findings and likely factors that might have influenced results.

Comparing user groups, hearing participants performed significantly better on the control condition in the retention test [Z=-1.939, p=.05, r=.35] but not in the transfer test [Z=1.55, p=.121, r=.28]. Regarding the SlidePacer condition, hearing participants seem to benefit more than DHH participants as the gap in learning performance increases, resulting in significant effect with larger effect sizes for both retention [Z=2.419, p<.05, r=.44] and transfer scores [Z=2.347, p<.05, r=.43].

5.2 Gaze Performance

Figure 5 shows the average time DHH participants spent looking at each monitor in the control and SlidePacer conditions. Most of the time was spent looking at the ASL interpreter in both conditions; however, participants significantly increased the time assessing visual materials from an average of 30 (SD=15) to 80 (SD=41) seconds in the control and SlidePacer conditions [$t_{(28)}$=-6.848, p<.001], respectively. These values correspond to an average of 2.7 seconds per slide in the control condition and 7.3 seconds per slide in the SlidePacer condition. Since the SlidePacer delay for students assess slides was only 5 seconds, it means that participants were still splitting their attention between visual sources, which in turn may have limited their learning gains.

Time looking at ASL interpreter also increased significantly

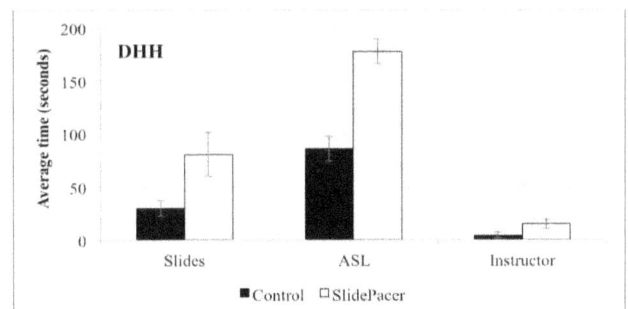

Figure 5. Average time DHH participants spent looking at each visual source.

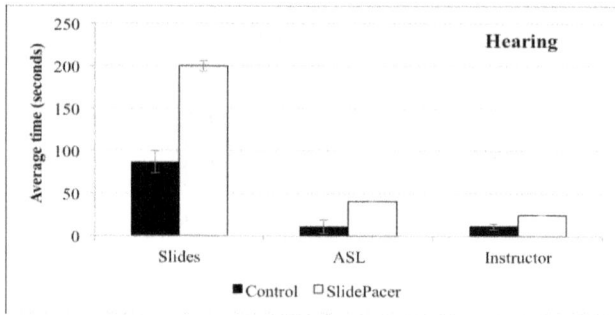

Figure 6. Average time hearing participants spent looking at each visual source.

$[t_{(28)}=-10.819, p<.001]$ from an average of 86 seconds (SD=23) in the control condition to 178 seconds (SD=23) in the SlidePacer condition. These results suggest that DHH participants choose to spend their additional time assessing visual materials and ASL, even though interpreting time was similar between experimental conditions. This result may be related with slides' complexity. Slides consisted of illustrations of verbal feedback and contained few text (1 or 2 words) and minimalistic images. Their content could be quickly assessed in less than 5 seconds. Additional time should be used to mentally organize information and integrate it with previous relevant knowledge [22]; however, it seems that DHH students spent it splitting their attention, monitoring when ASL interpretation would start again.

Analyzing the relative percentage of time DHH participants spent on each visual source, we found a significant decrease from 71% on control condition to 65% on SlidePacer condition for ASL $[Z=2.053, p<.05, r=0.37]$, and a small significant effect for Slides with an increase from 25% to 29% $[Z=1.597, p=.11, r=.29]$ on control and SlidePacer, respectively. There was also a significant increase for the time looking at the instructor ($M_{Control}=4\%$, $M_{SlidePacer}=6\%$) $[Z=2.012, p<.05, r=.37]$.

Regarding hearing participants, results show the opposite effect; that is, students spent relatively less time looking at slides ($M_{Control}=80\%$ $M_{SlidePacer}=75\%$) and instructor ($M_{Control}=11\%$ $M_{SlidePacer}=9\%$) and more time looking at the ASL interpreter ($M_{Control}=9\%$ $M_{SlidePacer}=15\%$) $[Z=1.929, p<0.05, r=.35]$. Nonetheless, in terms of average time, hearing participants assess all visual sources for longer periods of time (Figure 6).

As expected hearing and DHH participants had different gaze distributions across visual sources. While hearing students spent most of their time looking at the slideshow while receiving verbal auditory feedback, DHH students needed to focus on the ASL interpreter to received verbal feedback. Nonetheless it is noteworthy that SlidePacer enabled DHH participants to achieve the same degree of access to visual materials than hearing participants in the control condition (80 seconds vs. 86 seconds). The same rationale can be applied to learning performance;

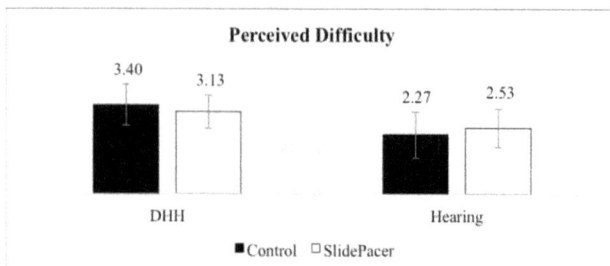

Figure 7. Perceived lecture difficulty for both user groups and conditions.

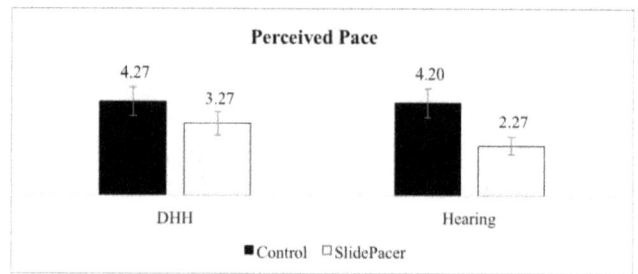

Figure 8. Perceived lecture pace for both user groups and conditions.

adjusting the lecture pace enables DHH students to achieve retention $[Z=1.452, p=.15, r=.27]$ and transfer $[Z=1.547, p=.122, r=.28]$ scores similar (no significant differences) to their hearing counterparts in current classroom settings. Although these results do not show that differences do not exist, they suggest that we are closing an accessibility gap between user groups.

5.3 Subjective Feedback

After watching the lecture, participants were asked about its difficulty using a Likert scale (1 - Very easy to 7 - Very hard). As shown in Figure 7, perceived difficulty was similar between experimental conditions. We did not find significant differences between control and SlidePacer conditions for DHH participants $[Z=.4, p=.689, r=.07]$ or hearing participants $[Z=.6, p=.519, r=.1]$.

Overall, hearing students perceived the lecture to be significantly easier than DHH students in control condition $[Z=1.909, p < .05, r=.35]$, but not in SlidePacer condition $[Z=1.085, p=.278, r=.2]$. This was due to a decrease of perceived difficulty from DHH. On the other hand, hearing participants perceived it as slightly harder with SlidePacer ($M_{Control}=2.27$ $M_{SlidePacer}=2.53$).

In addition to difficulty, we also asked participants about perceived pace using a 7-point Likert scale (1 - Very slow to 7 - Very fast), where 4 corresponded to appropriate pace. There was no difference of perception between DHH and hearing students in the control condition $[Z=.379, p=.705, r=.07]$. On average, both user groups rated the pace of the lecture as appropriate ($M_{DHH}=4.3$ $M_{Hearing}=4.2$). Although at a smaller extent to DHH students, SlidePacer had a significant negative effect on perceived pace. As shown in Figure 8 participants' scores were lower by 1 point (M=3.27 SD=1.28) $[Z=2.046, p<.05, r=.37]$, while hearing participants' scores dropped 1.93 points (M=2.27 SD=1.1) $[Z=3.916, p<.001, r=.71]$.

6. DISCUSSION

In this section, we answer our research questions and discuss the limitations of this work.

6.1 Answering the Research Questions

After analyzing the effect of SlidePacer for both user groups, we are now able to answer the proposed research questions.

1. *Is SlidePacer effective in improving learning for DHH students?*

The presented study assessed the effect of SlidePacer on DHH students' learning performance. Although there was an increase in both retention and transfer scores, we did not find a statistically significant effect. There are several plausible reasons for this result, which should be the aim of future research. First, our lecture content could have been too simple and easy to follow. Particularly, our slideshow content was mostly image-based, which is not always the case in college-level lectures. Programming classes are a good candidate for future research, since they place on DHH students a high demand to follow verbal instructions and slides full with textual information. Another reason might have been that the pace of our lecture was already slow. If we combine slow pace and minimalist slides, then students do not require additional time to access visual materials. Indeed, this is a known effect [20, 22, 24].

In this work, we were mainly interested in understanding the effect of SlidePacer on learning performance. However, DHH students face other challenges that might be alliviated by our proposed solution. For instance, reducing the pace of the lecture might enable students to engage in active learning by participating more in the classroom or take their own notes [10, 13, 15, 26].

2. Does SlidePacer improve DHH students' access to visual materials?

Overall, DHH students spend 2.7 more time looking at slides with SlidePacer, which corresponded to a significant increase in accessing visual materials. This results in a re-distribution of attention across visual sources in comparison with the control condition. Significantly less time (6%, 16.4 seconds) attending the ASL interpreter and more time (4%, 11 seconds) viewing slides.

Although participants had 5 seconds to attend to slides after verbal instructions, results suggest that DHH students still split their attention between verbal instructions and visual materials. This behavior may be natural to students, since it is their current strategy to cope with multiple visual sources in a classroom. However, it is not clear whether this behavior prevented them from receiving all verbal information from the ASL interpreter.

DHH students could spend an additional 4% of their lecture time looking at the slides, which corresponds to about 80 seconds. This value is similar to what hearing learners experienced in the control condition. Hence, results indicate that SlidePacer can support access to visual materials from DHH students.

3. What is the learning effect on hearing students?

Similarly to DHH students, we found a positive effect on learning performance for hearing students. Although there was a measurable increase for both retention and transfer scores, we did not find significant differences.

4. What is the relationship between DHH and hearing students performance?

Hearing participants performed better than DHH in both retention and transfer tests. This result goes in line with previous research on mediated learning research [14, 15]. Interestingly, hearing participants seemed to benefit the most from SlidePacer as their gains were higher than DHH participants. Moreover, results show that SlidePacer allows DHH students to achieve similar levels of learning performance as hearing students in the control condition. This is also true regarding access to visual materials. It is clear that mainstream classrooms are an unequal playfield regarding access to media materials used by instructors to support student's learning; that is, hearing students have constant access to verbal and visual information, while DHH students are restricted to one of these information sources. SlidePacer guaranteed a similar level of access to slides (~7 seconds per slide) to DHH as mainstream classrooms to hearing students.

5. What are students' perceptions about the lecture's pace?

SlidePacer had a significantly negative effect on perceived pace. Results from hearing and DHH questionnaires showed that the pace of the lecture was perceived as "slightly slow". Although it can be attributed to a novelty effect, since participants were not familiar to the change in pace from the *status quo*, it is still a significant result. Even more so for hearing students as the effect was higher. Interestingly, this user group benefited the most from the change in delivery pace.

6.2 Limitations

In this paper we propose a novel approach to improve classroom accessibility for DHH. Rather than building new tools for students, we focus on delivering better lectures that fit learners' needs. Changing the pace of multimedia presentations have previously shown to reduce students cognitive load, improving their learning performance [20, 24]. This effect is most noticeable when content is unfamiliar and complex. However, the slideshow used in this study featured almost no text, which does not represent a typical college class.

Also, in mainstream classrooms ASL interpreters usually refer (point) to content in the slides to illustrate a concept. However, due to the multi-camera setup of the experiment, such pointing reference was not possible to represent. Although it was consistent across experimental conditions, it might have had a negative impact on learning performance of DHH participants. Finally, SlidePacer inherently increases the duration of lectures. Still, we believe that its potential benefits outweigh this limitation. Moreover, instructors should have the flexibility (and obligation) to adjust covered content to better accommodate DHH students.

7. CONCLUSION

In this paper we introduce SlidePacer, a novel tool to be used by instructors and interpreters to collaboratively control the delivery of multimedia presentations. Our goal is to promote effective lectures by promoting better pacing behaviors that take into account the needs of DHH students. Coordinating verbal instructions and accessibility services can reduce the attention split effect and cognitive load that these students experience in mainstream classrooms, providing the opportunity to attend to visual materials and improve learning performance.

We have investigated the learning performance of 60 students using SlidePacer. Results show a positive effect, as DHH learners are able to give further attention to multimedia content. Although this did not result in significant learning improvements, participants achieved similar levels of access as hearing students in mainstream classrooms. We also found that DHH learners still split their attention during verbal instructions. Thus, additional research is needed to evaluate the effectiveness of SlidePacer in more demanding learning settings. Results are in line with previous research, showing that DHH students take away less from a lecture than their hearing counterparts. Interestingly, hearing students benefit the most from SlidePacer.

8. FUTURE WORK

One of the challenges instructors of students who are DHH face is managing the split attention implicit in multimedia learning; however, teachers are often unaware and assume that accessibility services deal with those issues [10]. In this paper we introduce a novel approach of creating the tools that can ease the process of delivering accessible and effective multimedia presentations. This is a design space fairly unexplored. As future work we propose three main research topics: First, improve SlidePacer prototype to better-fit students' behaviors and interpreters needs. This can include dynamically adapting slideshow delays based on slide content or smart classroom environments that are able to track students' head movements and infer when the current slide was read. Additionally, gesture recognition approaches can be added to the system in order to automatically identify when ASL interpretation is finished, removing the need (and cognitive load) for interpreter to actively advance slideshow.

Second, conduct further studies with new experimental designs to understand the effect of SlidePacer on different types of slideshows (text-intensive vs. image-intensive) and lectures (e.g. procedural vs. tutorials). It would also be interesting to measure the effect of SlidePacer beyond short-term learning and assess students' engagement (questions asked), note-taking behaviors or long-term retention. Finally, it is crucial to involve and understand the effect of presentation tools on all stakeholders, including accessibility services, presenters, DHH students, and their hearing peers. Does SlidePacer affect quality of interpretation? Does it reduce cognitive load of interpreters? Regarding instructors, can SlidePacer be included in real-world classroom activities? How would instructors cope with different pacing behaviors? How fast would they learn to adopt more adequate pacing behaviors? These questions should be thoroughly investigated in future work.

9. ACKNOWLEDGMENTS

We thank all participants for their time. We also thank Matt Huenerfauth, Raja Kushalnagar, and Daniel Ashbroock for their insights, and Mackenzie Willard and Brian Penly for their support. This work was partially supported by RCUK Digital Economy (EP/G066019/1), "Adaptive Technologies for Enhancing the Accessibility of Digital TV" from EPSRC and BBC, and INESC-ID (UID/CEC/50021/2013).

10. REFERENCES

[1] Ayres, P. and Sweller, J. 2005. The split-attention principle in multimedia learning. *The Cambridge handbook of multimedia learning*.

[2] Cavender, A.C. et al. 2009. ClassInFocus : Enabling Improved Visual Attention Strategies for Deaf and Hard of Hearing Students. (2009), 67–74.

[3] Foster, S. et al. 1999. Inclusive Instruction and Learning for Deaf Students in Postsecondary Education. (1999).

[4] Harskamp, E.G. et al. 2007. Does the modality principle for multimedia learning apply to science classrooms? *Learning and Instruction*. 17, 5 (Oct. 2007), 465–477.

[5] Knoors, H. and Hermans, D. Effective Instruction for Deaf and Hard-of-Hearing Students: Teaching Strategies, School Settings, and Student Characteristics.

[6] Kushalnagar, R.S. et al. 2010. Multiple View Perspectives: Improving Inclusiveness and Video Compression in Mainstream Classroom Recordings. *Proceedings of ASSETS*. (2010), 123–130.

[7] Kushalnagar, R.S. and Kushalnagar, P. 2014. Live and Collaborative Gaze Review for Deaf and Hard of Hearing Students. *International Conference on Computers Helping People*. (2014), 72–80.

[8] Lang, H. et al. 1992. Characteristics of Effective Teachers: A Descriptive Study of Perceptions of Faculty and Deaf College Students. (1992).

[9] Lang, H. and Pagliaro, C. 2007. Factors predicting recall of mathematics terms by deaf students: implications for teaching. *Journal of deaf studies and deaf education*. 12, 4 (Jan. 2007), 449–60.

[10] Lang, H.G. 2001. Higher Education for Deaf Students :

Research Priorities in the New Millennium. 1999 (2001).

[11] Lang, H.G. and Steely, D. 2003. Web-based science instruction for deaf students : What research says to the teacher. (2003), 277–298.

[12] Lasecki, W.S. et al. 2014. Helping Students Keep Up with Real-Time Captions by Pausing and Highlighting. (2014).

[13] Marschark, M. et al. 2005. Access to postsecondary education through sign language interpreting. *Journal of Deaf Studies and deaf education*. 10, 1 (2005), 38–50.

[14] Marschark, M. et al. 2006. Classroom Interpreting and Visual Information Processing in Mainstream Education for Deaf Students: Live or Memorex? 42, 4 (2006), 727–761.

[15] Marschark, M. et al. 2008. Learning via direct and mediated instruction by deaf students. *Journal of deaf studies and deaf education*. 13, 4 (Jan. 2008), 546–61.

[16] Marschark, M. et al. 2002. Teaching and the Curriculum. *Educating deaf students: From research to practice*.

[17] Marschark, M. and Hauser, P.C. 2008. *Deaf cognition: foundations and outcomes: foundations and outcomes*. Oxford University Press.

[18] Mather, S.M. and Clark, M.D. 2012. An Issue of Learning. (2012), 20–24.

[19] Mayer, R.E. Cognitive Theory of Multimedia Learning.

[20] Mayer, R.E. and Chandler, P. 2001. When learning is just a click away: Does simple user interaction foster deeper understanding of multimedia messages? *Journal of Educational Psychology*. 93, 2 (2001), 390–397.

[21] Mayer, R.E. and Moreno, R. 1998. A split-attention effect in multimedia learning: Evidence for dual processing systems in working memory. *Journal of Educational Psychology*. 90, 2 (1998), 312–320.

[22] Mayer, R.E. and Moreno, R. 2010. Nine Ways to Reduce Cognitive Load in Multimedia Learning Nine Ways to Reduce Cognitive Load in Multimedia Learning. December 2014 (2010), 37–41.

[23] Mayer, R.E. and Wittrock, M.C. Problem-solving transfer. *Handbook of educational psychology*. (1996), 47–62.

[24] Moreno, R. and Mayer, R.E. 2002. Verbal redundancy in multimedia learning: When reading helps listening. *Journal of Educational Psychology*. 94, 1 (2002), 156–163.

[25] Nelson, D.L. et al. 1976. Pictorial superiority effect. *Journal of Experimental Psychology: Human Learning and Memory*. 2, 5 (1976), 523.

[26] Schick, B. et al. 1999. Skill levels of educational interpreters working in public schools. *Journal of Deaf Studies and Deaf Education*. 4, 2 (1999), 144–155.

[27] Sitzmann, T. et al. 2008. A review and meta-analysis of the nomological network of trainee reactions. *Journal of Applied Psychology*. 93, 2 (2008), 280.

[28] Statistics, N.C. for E. 1999. *Integrated post-secondary education data system, Fall enrollment data file, Fall 1997*.

[29] Sweller, J. et al. 2011. *Cognitive load theory*.

[30] Weissman, J. 2008. *Presenting to win: the art of telling your story*. FT Press.

Would You Be Mine: Appropriating Minecraft as an Assistive Technology for Youth with Autism

Kathryn E. Ringland, Christine T. Wolf, LouAnne E. Boyd, Mark S. Baldwin, Gillian R. Hayes
Department of Informatics
University of California, Irvine
{kringlan, wolfct, boydl, baldwinm, hayesg}@uci.edu

ABSTRACT

Those with disabilities have long adopted, adapted, and appropriated collaborative systems to serve as assistive devices. In this paper, we present the results of a digital ethnography in a Minecraft virtual world for children with autism, specifically examining how this community has used do-it-yourself (DIY) making activities to transform the game into a variety of assistive technologies. Our results demonstrate how players and administrators "mod" the Minecraft system to support self-regulation and community engagement. This work highlights the ways in which we, as researchers concerned with accessible and equitable computing spaces, might reevaluate the scope of our inquiry, and how designers might encourage and support appropriation, enhancing users' experience and long-term adoption.

CCS Concepts

• **Human-centered computing** → **Accessibility** → **Accessibility technologies** • **Human-centered computing** → **Collaborative and social computing** → **Collaborative and social computing systems and tools.**

Author Keywords

Assistive technology; DIY; appropriation; modding; Minecraft; virtual worlds; autism; disability.

1. INTRODUCTION

Collaborative systems, like virtual worlds, have long been sites of adoption, adaptation, and appropriation. People with disabilities, in particular, have always found creative ways to pick up everyday objects—including information and communication technologies—to do the work of assistive devices. Indeed, many closed, proprietary, or heavily customized systems are often abandoned [13,40] in favor of lower cost, less stigmatized, and more prevalent "mainstream" technologies that can be easily adapted to suit specific needs [48].

Noting the challenges to adoption and widespread dissemination, many assistive technology researchers have called for new ways to augment existing systems, such as using lightweight browser plugins instead of expensive screen readers [3], alternative and augmentative communication software built into "off the shelf" tablets [34] in place of pricey (and typically more robust) assistive devices, or repurposing commercial products for unintended uses [19,20,46,51].

Going one step further, some have advocated for and tested the feasibility of those with disabilities developing their own assistive devices [24,26]. As Hurst *et al.* [24] have suggested, the ability to Do-It-Yourself (DIY) or appropriate "off the shelf" commercial products to create assistive technology may improve the quality of experiences with those devices and software. Users adopt, adapt, and augment technology in ways designers do not envision, to support needs that may not have been fully understood or anticipated [14]. Often, this kind of appropriation takes mainstream or "off the shelf" technology and changes it to suit the needs of those who have differing abilities [24,52].

With this in mind, we sought to understand the DIY culture surrounding and imbued in a virtual world that has been appropriated as a safe space [44], a social skills intervention [45], and, as we explore here, an assistive technology. Autcraft, a Minecraft virtual world for individuals with autism[1] and their allies, serves all of these functions at once.

Minecraft is an open-ended virtual world with no particular goals or play requirements [17,21,39]. Players can build and create new objects by manipulating blocks in the game. The base software of Minecraft can be modified with other programs, called "mods." According to the Minecraft End User License Agreement (EULA), *"If you've bought the Game, you may play around with it and modify it by adding modifications, tools, or plugins, which we will refer to collectively as 'Mods.'"* Although the makers of Minecraft explicitly discourage negative behaviors, they mostly leave the system open for any kind of modification users might envision [54]. Mods are popular across Minecraft instantiations [12] and have been explored for a variety of purposes in the research literature, including teaching children how to program [23]. The Autcraft community has taken advantage of the open and easily adaptable nature of Minecraft and this "modding culture" to tailor their server to multiple user needs, all while maintaining the creative and imaginative atmosphere characteristic of the virtual world.

In this paper, we present results from a virtual ethnography of Autcraft, specifically examining how this community has appropriated the platform, transforming features of the virtual world into a variety of assistive technologies. In particular, our results indicate that players use mods and other DIY techniques to support themselves in terms of self-regulation and to support the community in terms of their interaction with others and

ASSETS '16, October 23-26, 2016, Reno, NV, USA
© 2016 ACM. ISBN 978-1-4503-4124-0/16/10…$15.00
DOI: http://dx.doi.org/10.1145/2982142.2982172

---

[1] The term *autism* will be used throughout this paper to denote Autism Spectrum Disorder as well as Asperger's Syndrome as previously defined before the DSM-V changes [1].

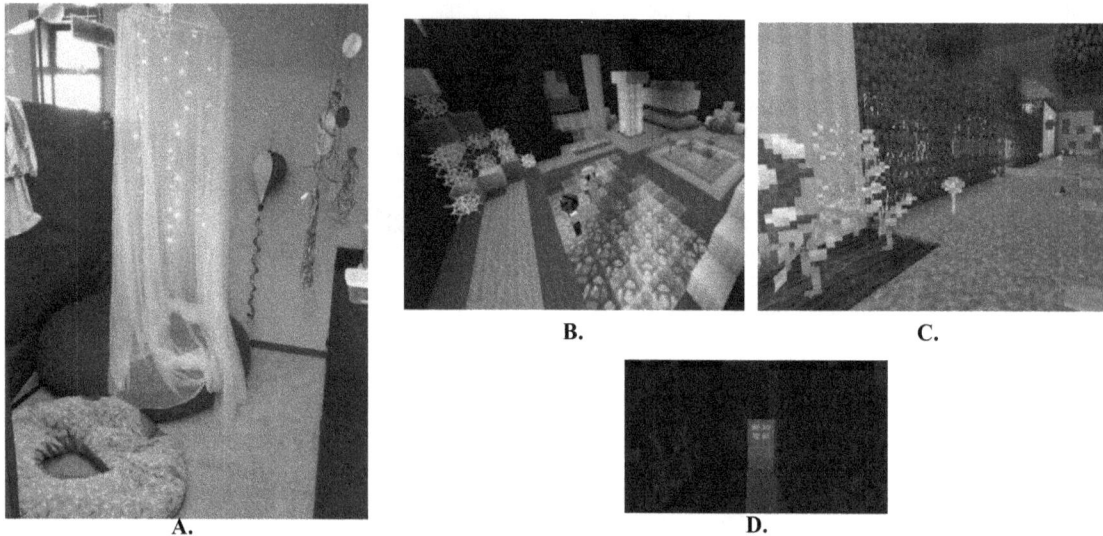

Figure 2. A. Multi-sensory environment in a physical classroom. B. Brightly rainbow colored Sensory Room in Autcraft. C. Calming garden in Autcraft. D. Dark room where the lights can be turned on and off in Autcraft.

monitor were turned off, but the avatar is also experiencing the black space, which is distinct from the experience of turning off the screen. Players enact virtual embodiment while controlling their avatars, highlighting the complex experiences of virtual and physical worlds [5].

Beyond simply supporting people with SPD, and other related challenges, when they need a break, therapeutic interventions also support teaching other coping processes. For example, multi-sensory environments (MSE) have been shown to help people support sensory integration. Typically, these physical environments, often called "sensory rooms," are saturated with visual, audible, and tactile stimuli and used therapeutically by trained professionals [47] (See Figure 2A).

Certainly, the complexities and nuance of a clinically designed MSE cannot be easily replicated in a virtual space. However, in noticing the player-driven self-regulation practices, the Autcraft community administrators built their own version of Sensory Rooms within the virtual world as a quiet space for members to go and relax. In these Sensory Rooms, chat is disabled and the environment is meant to be tranquil and with minimal sensory input. The administrators usefully "modded" and appropriated the Minecraft platform to create Autcraft, and the Autcraft platform to create carefully regulated spaces for sensory relief.

Members can choose three different styles of room, each tailored to meet different kinds of sensory needs (*i.e.,* a calm garden (See Figure 2C); a small, plain room with a light switch (See Figure 2D); and a brightly colored room (See Figure 2B)). In many ways, these rooms mimic the environments found in physical world Sensory Rooms. The community imbued the virtual spaces with assistive properties by mirroring physical therapeutic spaces.

In keeping with other Autcraft research [44], we see here that administrators manage the rules and norms of these spaces through multiple venues. They use the mods as the primary infrastructure, but build upon that visible set of instructions and policies for enforcing behavior. The instructions in reaching the Sensory Rooms say, *"Need a place to calm down? Quiet? Peaceful? Choose a Calm Room to visit here. In these rooms [t]here is no chat. It's a place to relax. Visit any time."* In an announcement

about the opening of these rooms, an administrator emphasized the importance of having the chat disabled in these rooms:

The best part is that in these rooms, chat is disabled! You can still private message back and forth with people but the public chat will be muted and you can't talk into public chat either. This means that you can experience the lights and the sounds and the calming nature of the rooms without a whole bunch of text flying across your screen. (forums, P29, age 30, m)[3]

Other members also used these Sensory Rooms to take a break from being in the public chat, which can be helpful when trying to self-regulate exposure to chat conversations:

This really helped me today there was a trigger for some bad memories in chat and it calmed me down wish i could visit this in real life[4]*. (forums, P31, age 15, f)*

Because these are virtual avatars, members are able to "transport" themselves to these Sensory Rooms at any time. Thus, in the virtual world players are able to regulate input in real time, nearly instantly. This player, however, points out that you cannot simply transport yourself to calming spaces in the physical world. This ability to instantly transport oneself into an environment that helps in self-regulation creates an assistive technology space—which is potentially better or used differently than in the physical world because it gives the player an ability and experience in the virtual world they might not otherwise have.

The actual interface of the game can also be overwhelming at times for some members, particularly if there are a lot of people logged in or a particularly chatty group are talking in chat. When the text scrolls too quickly in chat and visually becomes over-stimulating, players can seek relief simply by transporting to the Sensory Room:

i like going there when chat is going to fast and i need to take a break [really] calming and relaxing (forums, P4, f)

---

[3] Each quote includes: (source of quote, participant number, age of participant, and identified gender if available in member profile)
[4] Here participants use *"real life"* to indicate the physical, offline parts of their lives. Also, *"irl"* seen later means the same.

Not only do players use the community-created spaces for sensory self-regulation, they also contribute to these spaces. One member posted in the forums, informing others he had created an instruction manual of how to use the Sensory Rooms:

I think sensory rooms are a fantastic idea. And I added a book In calm room 1 its about what to do and about calm rooms (forums, P33, m)

Much like in the example above, the Autcraft virtual world is being shaped by each of the players as they participate in community life. This support can also be seen as administrators, noticing the players creating the sensory holes described at the beginning of this section, and then responding by building these sensory rooms. Each player, through their own acts of appropriation within the virtual space, shape what their virtual world looks like and how it functions to assist them as they engage with the world.

These spaces are also different from other virtual worlds in that they are specifically built for members with autism. Unlike other online communities, where adolescents socialize and "hang out," these platforms are being augmented for this specific population. Interestingly, despite sensitivity to sensory input, members interacting within the Autcraft community do not seem to have a problem with the overwhelming amount of choices given to them both within the Autcraft virtual world interface and throughout the various platforms the community uses. Community members are able to deal with a lot of the visual stimuli of the virtual world interface in spite of their SPD symptoms. In fact, members seem to be able to choose from the various options to create a social and sensory experience that feels right for them, giving them the opportunity to have the embodied experience they want—something that is more easily done in a virtual space than a physical one. This may be because Minecraft, although not a typical game with "levels" and other stated goals, follows a classic game-style genre, allowing the players familiarity as they navigate the world like they would in many other games with a typical, first person perspective.

Dealing with sensory overload can be a difficult experience for anyone with autism, particularly for children and adolescents who are still learning coping skills. Members of the Autcraft community have created spaces within the virtual world and the other platforms to help even the youngest members learn to deal with these sensory needs. As in the example of the sensory holes, one player appropriated materials at hand (in this case, virtual dirt) and inspired others to modify the actual software of Autcraft to create similar experiences for everyone. Individual players appropriate the Autcraft virtual world to suit their own needs, shaping their virtual environment, embodied experience, and, in time, influencing the overall experience for everyone in Autcraft.

4.1.2 Mood Regulation

Learning to manage one's moods is a fundamental part of human development. However, mood regulation is not straightforward for many with autism [27,32]. Not only are mood and anxiety disorders more prevalent in those diagnosed with autism [27], but there is some concern by clinicians that emotional regulation is simply a more difficult task for these individuals [32]. Youth with autism tend to ruminate over their negative moods and experiences [43]. This kind of behavior was evidenced in Minecraft among many other more positive emotional engagements. For example, one member described his strong emotions and some of the consequences:

I do notice that at least a few emotions are often stronger than others. Its mainly anger and fear that are the very strong emotions that I experience. I am generally not a super emotional person, but anger and fear are the hardest emotions for my mind to process. (forums, P35, age 17, m)

Members are able to put into words their emotional experiences, safely share and vent their feelings with others, on the forums and through in-game chat. They can do this in Autcraft without the fear of reprisal from bullies or trolls—which is something they fear in other online spaces [44]. While this type of behavior may not be unique to Autcraft, the ability to vent in this safe space is possibly unique for the community members personally. They may have communication challenges in their physical environments that limit their abilities to express their feelings fully [43].

Autcraft is a highly visual and active environment. Although much of this paper has so far focused on text chats, text from the forums, and so on, it is this visual and active orientation that may actually provide the most support for emotion and mood regulation. Just as members appropriated virtual "physical" tools like shovels to dig holes for sensory regulation, they appropriate other tools to manage their moods. For example, one early teenage boy described killing monsters in mini-games to release some anger to feel better:

"i also like to play the minigames on here It helps me take my anger out on [the monsters] :P… My parents say since ive joined i have been nicer irl If i am sad irl or angry on here i come and everyone brightens up my day I usally forget why i was sad/mad" (interview, P1, age 13, m)

Mini-games are group activities created by Autcraft administrators originally as a place for members to come together to play (*e.g.,* paintball tournaments, hide and seek). These games were created to support socialization and play, cornerstones of the Autcraft community [45]. While being able to let out some frustration and anger on digital monsters is helpful, it is also interacting with the community that elevates the interviewee's mood. When discussing mood moderation, he said that *"mostly the people"* help him feel better when he gets online and that *"sometimes i get so into talking i forget what i was doing :P"*. Because these interactions with others are an important part of being in the Autcraft community, members have also created many ways to help support interfacing and engaging with others.

Mini-games are an example of how community administrators in Autcraft have appropriated Minecraft to create a separate space within the virtual world. However, beyond this original appropriation, players in Autcraft have then appropriated these mini-games—originally as places to play and socialize—to help with other aspects of their life, including mood moderation.

4.2 Interacting with Others

Although Autcraft community members have creatively adapted and appropriated the platform to serve the needs of individuals, it is still fundamentally a collaborative platform. As such, it should come as no surprise that members of the Autcraft community have appropriated the entire ecosystem of technologies surrounding Autcraft to support interfacing and engaging with others. These efforts support engagement with both the internal community and across community boundaries by *supporting sociality* explicitly.

4.2.1 Supporting Sociality

Socialization and supporting the various ways members want to be and are social is an important aspect of the Autcraft community

Web accessibility (W4A), ACM, 73–82. Retrieved May 5, 2016 from http://dl.acm.org/citation.cfm?id=1368060

[4] Tom Boellstorff. 2010. *Coming of Age in Second Life: An Anthropologist Explores the Virtually Human*. Princeton University Press.

[5] Tom Boellstorff. 2011. Placing the virtual body: Avatar, chora, cypherg. In *A Companion to the Anthropology of the Body and Embodiment*. 504–20. Retrieved April 5, 2016 from http://www.socsci.uci.edu/~tboellst/bio/Body.pdf

[6] Tom Boellstorff, Bonnie Nardi, Celia Pearce, and T.L. Taylor. 2012. *Ethnography and Virtual Worlds: A Handbook of Method*. Princeton University Press.

[7] Moira Burke, Robert Kraut, and Diane Williams. 2010. Social use of computer-mediated communication by adults on the autism spectrum. *Proceedings of the 2010 ACM conference on Computer supported cooperative work*, ACM, 425–434. Retrieved February 29, 2016 from http://dl.acm.org/citation.cfm?id=1718991

[8] Jennie Carroll, Steve Howard, Frank Vetere, Jane Peck, and John Murphy. 2001. Identity, power and fragmentation in cyberspace: technology appropriation by young people. *ACIS 2001 Proceedings*: 6.

[9] Jennie Carroll, Steve Howard, Frank Vetere, Jane Peck, and John Murphy. 2002. Just what do the youth of today want? Technology appropriation by young people. *System Sciences, 2002. HICSS. Proceedings of the 35th Annual Hawaii International Conference on*, IEEE, 1777–1785. Retrieved April 28, 2014 from http://ieeexplore.ieee.org/xpls/abs_all.jsp?arnumber=994089

[10] Jane Case-Smith and Heather Miller. 1999. Occupational therapy with children with pervasive developmental disorders. *The American Journal of Occupational Therapy* 53, 5: 506–513.

[11] Kathy Charmaz. 2006. *Constructing Grounded Theory: A Practical Guide to Qualitative Analysis*. Sage Publications Ltd.

[12] Peter Christiansen. 2014. Players, Modders and Hackers. In *Understanding Minecraft: Essays on Play, Community, and Possibilities*, Nate Garrelts (ed.). McFarland & Company, Inc., Jefferson, NC, 23–37.

[13] Melissa Dawe. 2006. Desperately seeking simplicity: how young adults with cognitive disabilities and their families adopt assistive technologies. *Proceedings of the SIGCHI conference on Human Factors in computing systems*, 1143–1152. Retrieved November 9, 2013 from http://dl.acm.org/citation.cfm?id=1124943

[14] Alan Dix. 2007. Designing for appropriation. *Proceedings of the 21st British HCI Group Annual Conference on People and Computers: HCI... but not as we know it-Volume 2*, British Computer Society, 27–30. Retrieved May 12, 2014 from http://dl.acm.org/citation.cfm?id=1531415

[15] Paul Dourish. 2003. The appropriation of interactive technologies: Some lessons from placeless documents. *Computer Supported Cooperative Work (CSCW)* 12, 4: 465–490.

[16] Sebastian Draxler and Gunnar Stevens. 2011. Supporting the Collaborative Appropriation of an Open Software Ecosystem.

Computer Supported Cooperative Work (CSCW) 20, 4-5: 403–448. http://doi.org/10.1007/s10606-011-9148-9

[17] Sean C. Duncan. 2011. Minecraft, beyond construction and survival. *Well Played: a journal on video games, value and meaning* 1, 1: 1–22.

[18] Nirmala Erevelles and Andrea Minear. 2013. Unspeakable Offenses: Untangling Race and Disability in Discourses of Intersectionality. In *The Disability Studies Reader* (4th ed.), Lennard J. Davis (ed.). Taylor & Francis, 354–368.

[19] Alexander Fiannaca, Ilias Apostolopoulous, and Eelke Folmer. 2014. Headlock: a wearable navigation aid that helps blind cane users traverse large open spaces. ACM Press, 19–26. http://doi.org/10.1145/2661334.2661453

[20] Eelke Folmer and Tony Morelli. 2012. Spatial gestures using a tactile-proprioceptive display. *Proceedings of the Sixth International Conference on Tangible, Embedded and Embodied Interaction*, ACM, 139–142. Retrieved May 5, 2016 from http://dl.acm.org/citation.cfm?id=2148161

[21] Nate Garrelts (ed.). 2014. *Understanding Minecraft: Essays on Play, Community, and Possibilities*. McFarland & Company, Inc., Jefferson, NC.

[22] Goodley, Dan. 2011. Intersections: Diverse Disability Studies. In *Disability Studies: An Interdisciplinary Approach*. Sage Publications Ltd, Thousand Oaks, CA, 33–47.

[23] Sarah Guthals, Stephen Foster, and Lindsey Handley. 2015. *Minecraft Modding for Kids for Dummies*. John Wiley & Sons, Inc., Hoboken, NJ.

[24] Amy Hurst and Jasmine Tobias. 2011. Empowering individuals with do-it-yourself assistive technology. *The proceedings of the 13th international ACM SIGACCESS conference on Computers and accessibility*, 11–18. Retrieved November 9, 2013 from http://dl.acm.org/citation.cfm?id=2049541

[25] Lilly C. Irani, Gillian R. Hayes, and Paul Dourish. 2008. Situated practices of looking: visual practice in an online world. *Proceedings of the 2008 ACM conference on Computer supported cooperative work*, ACM, 187–196. Retrieved January 31, 2014 from http://dl.acm.org/citation.cfm?id=1460592

[26] Shaun K. Kane, Amy Hurst, Erin Buehler, Patrick A. Carrington, and Michele A. Williams. 2014. Collaboratively designing assistive technology. *interactions* 21, 2: 78–81.

[27] Joseph A. Kim, Peter Szatmari, Susan E. Bryson, David L. Streiner, and Freda J. Wilson. 2000. The prevalence of anxiety and mood problems among children with autism and Asperger syndrome. *Autism* 4, 2: 117–132.

[28] Yong Ming Kow and Bonnie Nardi. 2010. Culture and Creativity: World of Warcraft Modding in China and the US. In *Online Worlds: Convergence of the Real and the Virtual*, William Sims Bainbridge (ed.). Springer London, London, 21–41. Retrieved April 13, 2015 from http://link.springer.com/10.1007/978-1-84882-825-4_3

[29] Janet E. Lainhart and Susan E. Folstein. 1994. Affective disorders in people with autism: A review of published cases. *Journal of autism and developmental disorders* 24, 5: 587–601.

[30] Katherine A. Loveland. 2005. *Social-emotional impairment and self-regulation in autism spectrum disorders*. Oxford University Press.

[31] Sampada Marathe and S. Shyam Sundar. 2011. What drives customization?: Control or Identity? *Proceedings of the SIGCHI conference on human factors in computing systems*, ACM, 781–790. Retrieved May 5, 2016 from http://dl.acm.org/citation.cfm?id=1979056

[32] Carla A. Mazefsky, John Herrington, Matthew Siegel, et al. 2013. The Role of Emotion Regulation in Autism Spectrum Disorder. *Journal of the American Academy of Child & Adolescent Pschiatry* 52, 7: 679–688.

[33] Gabriele Meiselwitz. 2010. Universal Usability: Past, Present, and Future. *Foundations and Trends® in Human–Computer Interaction* 3, 4: 213–333. http://doi.org/10.1561/1100000029

[34] Maia Naftali and Leah Findlater. 2014. Accessibility in context: understanding the truly mobile experience of smartphone users with motor impairments. ACM Press, 209–216. http://doi.org/10.1145/2661334.2661372

[35] Bonnie Nardi. 2010. *My Life as a Night Elf Priest An Anthropological Account of World of Warcraft*. University of Michigan Press.

[36] Nigel Newbutt. 2013. *Exploring Communication and Representation of the Self in a Virtual World by Young People with Autism.*

[37] Elinor Ochs and Olga Solomon. 2010. Autistic Sociality. *Ethos* 38, 1: 69–92. http://doi.org/10.1111/j.1548-1352.2009.01082.x

[38] Celia Pearce and Artemesia. 2009. *Communities of Play: Emergent Cultures in Multiplayer Games and Virtual Worlds*. MIT Press.

[39] Markus "Notch" Persson. 2011. *Minecraft*. Mojang, Stockholm, Sweden.

[40] Betsy Phillips and Hongxin Zhao. 1993. Predictors of Assistive Technology Abandonment. *Assistive Technology* 5, 1: 36–45. http://doi.org/10.1080/10400435.1993.10132205

[41] Ravihansa Rajapakse, Margot Brereton, Paul Roe, and Laurianne Sitbon. 2014. Designing with people with disabilities: adapting best practices of DIY and organizational approaches. *Proceedings of the 26th Australian Computer-Human Interaction Conference on Designing Futures: the Future of Design*, ACM, 519–522. Retrieved May 4, 2016 from http://dl.acm.org/citation.cfm?id=2686694

[42] John T. Richards, Kyle Montague, and Vicki L. Hanson. 2012. Web accessibility as a side effect. *Proceedings of the 14th international ACM SIGACCESS conference on Computers and accessibility*, ACM, 79–86. Retrieved May 3, 2016 from http://dl.acm.org/citation.cfm?id=2384931

[43] C. Rieffe, P. Oosterveld, M. M. Terwogt, S. Mootz, E. van Leeuwen, and L. Stockmann. 2011. Emotion regulation and internalizing symptoms in children with autism spectrum disorders. *Autism* 15, 6: 655–670. http://doi.org/10.1177/1362361310366571

[44] Kathryn E. Ringland, Christine T. Wolf, Lynn Dombrowski, and Gillian R. Hayes. 2015. Making "Safe": Community-Centered Practices in a Virtual World Dedicated to Children with Autism. *CSCW 2015*, ACM.

[45] Kathryn E. Ringland, Christine T. Wolf, Heather Faucett, Lynn Dombrowski, and Gillian R. Hayes. 2016. "Will I always be not social?": Re-Conceptualizing Sociality in the Context of a Minecraft Community for Autism. *CHI 2016*.

[46] Kathryn E. Ringland, Rodrigo Zalapa, Megan Neal, Lizbeth Escobedo, Monica Tentori, and Gillian R. Hayes. 2014. SensoryPaint: A Multimodal Sensory Intervention for Children with Neurodevelopmental Disorders. *Proceedings of the 2014 ACM International Joint Conference on Pervasive and Ubiquitous Computing*, ACM, 873–884. http://doi.org/10.1145/2632048.2632065

[47] Roseann C. Schaaf and Lucy Jane Miller. 2005. Occupational therapy using a sensory integrative approach for children with developmental disabilities. *Mental Retardation and Developmental Disabilities Research Reviews* 11, 2: 143–148. http://doi.org/10.1002/mrdd.20067

[48] Kristen Shinohara and Jacob O. Wobbrock. 2011. In the shadow of misperception: assistive technology use and social interactions. *Proceedings of the SIGCHI Conference on Human Factors in Computing Systems*, ACM, 705–714. Retrieved April 28, 2014 from http://dl.acm.org/citation.cfm?id=1979044

[49] Karen Stendal. 2012. How do People with Disability Use and Experience Virtual Worlds and ICT: A Literature Review. *Journal of Virtual World Research* 5, 1.

[50] Karen Stendal, Susan Balandin, and Judith Molka-Danielsen. 2011. Virtual worlds: A new opportunity for people with lifelong disability? *Journal of Intellectual and Developmental Disability* 36, 1: 80–83. http://doi.org/10.3109/13668250.2011.526597

[51] Yu-Chi Tsai. 2012. Kinempt: a Kinect-based prompting system to transition autonomously through vocational tasks for individuals with cognitive impairments. *Proceedings of the 14th international ACM SIGACCESS conference on Computers and accessibility*, ACM, 299–300. Retrieved May 5, 2016 from http://dl.acm.org/citation.cfm?id=2385003

[52] Jacob O. Wobbrock, Shaun K. Kane, Krzysztof Z. Gajos, Susumu Harada, and Jon Froehlich. 2011. Ability-Based Design: Concept, Principles and Examples. *ACM Transactions on Accessible Computing* 3, 3: 1–27. http://doi.org/10.1145/1952383.1952384

[53] Pamela J. Wolfberg. 2009. *Play & Imagination in Children with Autism*. Teachers College Press, New York City, New York, USA.

[54] Minecraft End User License Agreement. *Mojang*. Retrieved April 30, 2016 from https://account.mojang.com/documents/minecraft_eula

Online Learning System to Help People with Developmental Disabilities Reinforce Basic Skills

Lourdes M. Morales-Villaverde[1], Karina Caro[2], Taylor Gotfrid[1], and Sri Kurniawan[1]

[1]Baskin School of Engineering
University of California, Santa Cruz
1156 High Street
Santa Cruz, CA 95064
{lommoral, tgotfrid, skurnia}@ucsc.edu

[2]Department of Computer Science
CICESE
Carretera Ensenada-Tijuana 3918
Ensenada, B.C. 22860, Mexico
karicaro@cicese.edu.mx

ABSTRACT

We present the development and evaluation of an online learning system for people with developmental disabilities (DD) of all ages in collaboration with Imagine! and Hope Services, two not-for-profit organizations that provide care services to people with DD. The system was implemented as an HTML5-based web application for iPad. It includes activities that aim to support and improve the process through which people with DD of all ages reinforce basic skills such as recognizing numbers, letters, money, shapes, and colors. User evaluations suggest that a system such as ours will be: 1) helpful in supporting people with DD reinforce basic skills, and 2) well-received by users.

CCS Concepts

• **Human-centered computing → Accessibility → Accessibility design and evaluation methods.**

Keywords

Developmental disability; basic skills; online learning; web application; iPad.

1. INTRODUCTION

People often take for granted the fact that they possess basic skills (e.g., recognizing numbers, colors, money) that they learned at a young age and now help them perform daily-living activities. For people with developmental disabilities (DD), performing daily-living activities can be a struggle, especially if they have not mastered the aforementioned basic skills. Consequently, people with DD often rely on other people, such as those in charge of their care, to carry out those activities. This limits these individuals' participation in valued and meaningful societal roles (e.g., adult, citizen, employee) and reduces their overall life satisfaction [2, 4, 9]. Also, this dependency on others increases their caretakers' workload.

ASSETS '16, October 23-26, 2016, Reno, NV, USA.
© 2016 ACM. ISBN 978-1-4503-4124-0/16/10...$15.00.
DOI: http://dx.doi.org/10.1145/2982142.2982174

Technology designed to support people with DD can provide them with new opportunities in terms of meaningful societal roles and positive outcomes (monetary and self-confidence) where they succeed in assuming one or more of those roles [1, 2, 3, 4, 6, 10].

Before the advent of touchscreen devices, such technologies included "*picture prompting*" [1, 3, 6], which involved giving individuals with DD pictures that depict how to complete each step required to complete a task, and video-based technologies that involved showing people with DD a video depicting how to complete a task in general (i.e., "*video modeling*") or step-by-step (i.e., "*video prompting*") [1, 2, 4, 8, 9]. The study by Lancioni et al. in [6] discussed two types of picture prompting systems designed to help people with DD perform "vocationally relevant" tasks: first, a physical card-based system with cards containing pictorial descriptions of instructions, and second, a computer-based system where pictorial instructions were shown on a portable device (i.e., a computerized card-based system). Their results suggest that most users had a higher percentage of correct steps with the computer-based system and that they preferred that system to the physical card-based one [6]. Similarly, Furniss et al. discussed their work on a computer-based picture prompting system, VICAID, designed to do two main things: first, enable individuals with DD to complete tasks (related to real work settings) by providing them access to pictorial instructions on how to complete the tasks; and second, alert and engage the job coach or supervisor of the individual with DD when his/her interaction with the system suggests that he/she is having difficulties [3]. Their results, like those of the work discussed in [6], suggest that computer-based systems were more effective than card-based systems in helping users with DD maintain accurate task-performance (in real-world work settings) and that most users preferred the computer-based systems [3].

Alberto et al. discussed the use of picture prompting and video modeling for teaching individuals with DD how to accomplish daily-living activities such as drawing money from an ATM and purchasing items using a debit card [1]. Ultimately, they found that both technologies were effective and efficient at teaching those skills. Similarly, in [2] Canella-Malone et al. researched the use of video modeling and video prompting technologies when teaching adults with DD daily-living skills such as setting up a table and putting away groceries. Their findings, unlike those of [1], suggest that video prompting was more effective than video modeling, and that certain video attributes (e.g. duration, number of clips, and perspective from which it is filmed) may influence the effectiveness of these technologies as teaching tools. Still, in [4] Goodson et al. found that not all individuals with DD learn from video prompting alone and that the addition of a video-based error correction procedure that plays the same clips as the video prompting when the user makes a mistake may help.

Although there are many works on the design of technology to support people with DD perform tasks, especially in employment and independent-living settings (e.g. setting up a table), there is not much work on developing technology that helps people with DD reinforce the basic skills they need to complete those tasks. For example, if an individual is given the instruction: "Place the number two screw on panel A." Then he/she must be able to recognize both numbers and letters to complete it.

The advent of touchscreen devices has spurred development of applications (apps) designed to teach and train users and to supplement rehabilitation therapy of users with all kinds of disabilities. Kagohara et al. conducted a review of works that involved the use of an iPad or iPod Touch as a learning tool for individuals with DD, which suggests that these devices are viable aids for people with DD [5].

The main problem is most of the apps that provide lessons on the basic skills are normally geared towards children. For example, the LetterSchool[1] iPad app (Figure 1, left) is an app that aims to teach letters to children aged 2-5. As Figure 1 shows, the app has very busy screens with lots of bright colors, images, and objects that move, which in addition to being childish, can be highly distracting to users with DD. Another example is the Learning Gems - Colors N Shapes[2] iPad app, which is designed to teach shapes and colors to children aged 2-6 (Figure 1, right). This app is more simplistic than the LetterSchool app, but it is also vibrantly colored and has a relatively busy design that may be inappropriate for adults with DD. Previous work also suggests that technology designed for children is generally not well-received by adults who acquired a cognitive disability (CD) (e.g., as a result of stroke) since they feel it is not appropriate for them as adults [7].

Figure 1. LetterSchool app (left) and Learning Gems - Colors N Shapes app (right).

The purpose of the work reported in this paper is to develop and evaluate an online learning system that provides individuals with DD of all ages activities that can reinforce basic skills. Working in collaboration with Imagine! and Hope Services, two not-for-profit organizations that provide support services to people with DD, we iteratively created and evaluated personas, storyboards, wireframes, and prototypes. The system includes seven activities that help users review numbers, colors, shapes, lowercase and uppercase letters, and U.S. currency; and practice gathering a set amount of money. The activities were designed to be simple, clear, rewarding, and appropriate for users with DD of all ages.

This paper is structured as follows: First, we give an overview of our methods for gathering system requirements and present a

subset of the requirements gathered, specifically those related to the features evaluated with primary users (individuals with DD). Secondly, we present the general design characteristics of the high-fidelity prototype of the system. Next, we give an overview of how we ran preliminary evaluations of our system and the main changes that resulted from those evaluations. Then, we discuss how we evaluated a high-fidelity prototype of the system through a comprehensive user study along with the results from that study. Finally, we present our conclusions along with future work.

2. METHODS
2.1 Gathering System Requirements
Working in collaboration with Imagine! employees and caregivers through focus group sessions, we gathered the system requirements (functional and non-functional) for the proposed system by iterating over the creation and evaluation of personas, usage scenarios, storyboards, wireframes, and prototypes.

Through the initial focus group sessions, we gathered information about our target users' desires in terms of what they would want out of the proposed system (e.g. the types of skills they want to work on), motivations for improving their skills (e.g. to be more independent), and activities of interest (e.g. activities where users interact with iPads or work on learning or improving basic skills that our proposed system is intended to help with), along with their surroundings during those activates (e.g. the people who are around them while they do those activities).

During this time, we noted that many of Imagine!'s clients had iPads (they were covered by their health insurance under the notion that they are needed for rehabilitation therapy). We also found previous work that supports that iPads are viable technological devices for teaching individuals with DD skills such as cooking and cleaning [5]. Hence, we decided to develop our proposed system as an iPad app and, as a first step, conducted a competitive analysis of existing iPad apps that could be used to help people with DD learn or improve the skills that our proposed system is intended to help with. We found that most of the apps that could help, like the LetterSchool and Learning Gems - Colors N Shapes apps, were geared towards children. As we explained before, using apps geared towards children to teach basic skills to individuals with DD can be problematic because: 1) their design normally includes elements that may be too distracting or overwhelming for adults with DD (e.g. too many bright colors, loud noises, animations), and 2) their strategy for motivating users to complete tasks may be appropriate for children but not necessarily appropriate for older individuals with DD (i.e., it may not be as motivating or as engaging for them).

Once we had established a preliminary set of system requirements for our proposed system, we created personas, usage scenarios, storyboards, wireframes, and low-fidelity prototypes; which guided the next round of focus group sessions with our collaborators. Those focus group sessions were centered on what the system should do, look and act like (i.e., its functionalities, interface, and complexity) in order for it to meet users' abilities and needs. Based on the feedback from the focus group sessions, we iteratively created low-fidelity prototypes (Figure 2, next page), which ranged from drawings on a white-board to slideshow presentations, and improved the system requirements until they were both accepted as a basis for a final prototype. As Figure 2 shows, the design evolved in many aspects, like the color choice for the background and highlight, and the size of the numbers.

[1] LetterSchool

[2] Learning Gems - Colors N Shapes

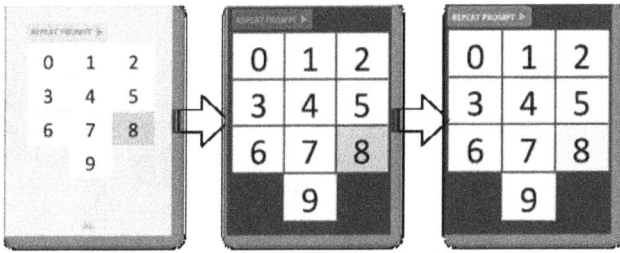

Figure 2. Iterations of activity on recognizing numbers.

2.2 System Requirements

Before presenting the system requirements, it is important to note:

1. Our primary users (users) are individuals with DD and their caregivers are the secondary users (administrators).
2. Typical usage scenarios depend on users' cognitive abilities:
   a. The two typical usage scenarios for users with limited cognitive abilities are: a) An administrator selects the activity that the user will attempt and helps the user attempt the activity, and b) An administrator checks the user's progress in previously attempted activities in order to assess the user's needs and decide which activity the user should attempt next.
   b. Otherwise, the typical usage scenario is: a user selects and attempts an activity independently.

The results of the above exercises are a list of functional and non-functional requirements, and their priorities and reasons as given by our stakeholders.

2.2.1 Functional Requirements
2.2.1.1 High Priority

1. Include activities that help people with DD review basic skills such as recognizing letters, money, colors, shapes, and numbers. *Reason*: Many daily-living activities require such basic skills.
2. Give users *positive reinforcers*[3] when they follow prompts (e.g., "touch number x") correctly during the activities. *Reason*: Positive reinforcers must serve as positive feedback and as an incentive to continue doing the activities.
3. When users do not follow a prompt correctly during an activity, give them various attempts (up to three) and hints on how to follow prompts correctly along with *learning reinforcers*[4] which also help users learn the correct response. On the last attempt, give users no other choice but to follow the prompt correctly and learn the correct response. *Reason*: In general, the system should not give users negative feedback. Also, the system should help users learn from their mistakes and not punish them.
4. Give users 90 seconds to respond to a prompt before issuing a timeout and proceeding as if an incorrect response was made or, if on the last attempt, ending the activity. *Reason*: The system should ensure that if users are distracted by other activities, they are informed that the system is still waiting for their interaction before terminating the session.

2.2.1.2 Low Priority

5. Display progress information to users during activities. *Reasons*: Users should know which round they are on out of the total number of rounds in an activity.

---

[3] *Positive reinforcer*: An image, video, or audio clip that users may enjoy seeing or hearing.
[4] *Learning reinforcer*: A visual cue (e.g. highlight) or audio clip that aims to help users learn.

2.2.2 Non-functional Requirements
2.2.2.1 High Priority

1. System should be computer-based and compatible with the ever-changing versions of iPad and iOS. *Reasons*: As mentioned before, previous work suggests that people with DD tend to prefer computer-based systems to paper-based ones [3, 6] and that iPads are aids for individuals with DD basic skills [5]. Plus, many of Imagine!'s clients had iPads and thus, some knowledge of their operation.
2. The system (specifically the activities) should: a) avoid distracting users (e.g., avoid using unnecessary sounds or buttons); b) be age-appropriate (i.e., not too childish for adults and not too complex for children to use); and c) use high-contrast and color-blind friendly colors, large fonts and buttons, and ample input space. *Reason*: The system (specifically the activities) should be usable, accessible and age-appropriate for people with DD of all ages who may have other disabilities (i.e., users may have limited cognitive, motor, and/or visual skills).

2.2.2.2 Medium Priority

3. System shall be easily maintainable and have an expected usage life of 2-3 years. *Reason*: The system should not increase caregivers' workload by requiring maintenance.

3. High-fidelity Prototype

Based on the system requirements that we gathered, we developed a high-fidelity prototype. Following the same process as with our low-fidelity prototype, we iterated over the prototype's design based on the feedback we got from focus group discussions with our collaborators. The main design characteristics of the final high-fidelity prototype of the proposed system are as follows:

- It was implemented as an HTML5 web-app for iPad so that it has a longer lifespan and is easier to maintain than a native iOS/iPad app. It also works on most desktop web browsers.
- It offers seven activities: Money Addition (MA), Money, Numbers, Lowercase Letters (LL), Uppercase Letters (UL), Shapes, and Colors. These consist of a set of prompts that aim to help users reinforce a basic skill while assessing their knowledge on that skill. In general, they help users practice gathering money (Figure 3, left) or recognize the following by name: U.S. currency (bills and coins most commonly used), numbers, letters in uppercase and lowercase, common shapes (Figure 3, right), and primary colors. The activities were designed to mimic how users normally perform such activities (i.e., activities where they reinforce the corresponding skills) at Imagine!.

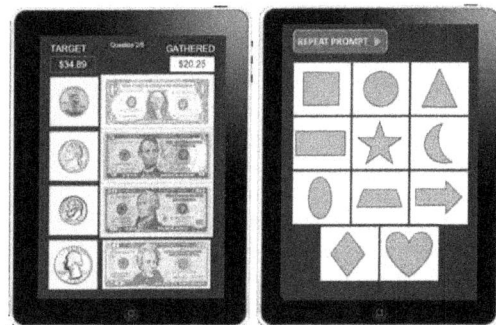

Figure 3. Money Addition (left) and Shapes (right) activities.

- Users respond to prompts by touching one of the options shown. For example, in the Numbers activity a grid is shown with all the numbers from 0 to 9 and users are prompted to touch a (randomly selected) number. The Money, Shapes, Colors, UL, and LL activities behave similarly.

- In the MA activity (Figure 3, left) a grid with the main bills and coins that make up the U.S. currency is shown (as in the Money activity) and users are asked to add those up (by touching them) to reach a target total (between $0.01 and $100) that is randomly generated in each of the five rounds that make up the MA activity. Note that, the currency that can be used to add up to the target total is highlighted in yellow. For example, if the user needs to reach $34.89 and has already gathered $20.25, then the twenty-dollar bill is not highlighted while the rest of the currency is (Figure 3, left). Although the goal of this activity is for users to reach the target total with the minimum amount of bills and coins (i.e., the minimum number of presses), reaching the target total will be noted as a success despite the total number of presses. That way the activity fulfills its purpose without giving users negative feedback. Likewise, when a user presses currency that is not highlighted, it is not marked as an error and the gathered amount is not changed.

- The Money and MA activities display images of real U.S. currency (Figure 3, left) instead of drawings to help users with recognition in real-life.

- The numbers and letters in the Numbers, UL, and LL activities are displayed in a random order.

- When users make a selection (right or wrong) after a prompt, they are given a learning reinforcer: an audio clip saying the name of the selection and, if the selection has another name, the other name too (e.g., "A penny, one cent.").

- When users do not follow a prompt correctly, all the activities (except the MA activity) give users three more attempts and hints on how to follow the prompt correctly (e.g., highlighting the correct choice and/or removing the 'incorrect' options). Hints get more direct with each attempt. Note that, while these techniques of prompting along with error-correction have proven to be effective at helping people with DD perform tasks [1, 2, 3, 4, 6], the main goal of the activities is to teach users the correct choice while helping them follow prompts correctly. That is why, besides the hints, the activity gives users the learning reinforcers. In general, the way the activities behave in this regard is:

  o When the user does not follow a prompt correctly on the first screen (i.e. on the first attempt), the second screen is shown with the correct choice highlighted in yellow (Figure 4(b)) or, as in the Colors activity, with black/white dashes. Then, the prompt is repeated.

  o When the user does not follow a prompt correctly on the second screen, the third screen is shown with the correct choice highlighted and the incorrect options are hidden (Figure 4(c)). Then, the prompt is repeated.

  o When the user does not follow a prompt correctly on the third screen, the last screen is shown with the correct choice (still highlighted) taking up most of the screen (Figure 4(d)) and the prompt is repeated.

- When users follow prompts correctly, they are given two positive reinforcers: an audio clip saying "Good Job!" or "That's right!" and a picture of something they might like. Since we were evaluating the prototype primarily with Imagine!'s clients, the pictures were of their favorite football team (the Denver Broncos). We used the same images when evaluating an improved prototype with Hope Services'

clients, and found that pictures of players from a popular sport work as positive reinforcers in general.

- Activities were designed to be simplistic, clear, and accessible by: 1) avoiding unnecessary buttons, sounds, and distracting objects; 2) making the activity the focus and the prompts and interface straightforward; 3) highlighting with colorblind-friendly colors (yellow), and using a high-contrast color-scheme (white on black), practical fonts (e.g., easily readable), and good quality images to make them accessible to users with visual impairments; 4) making choices (i.e., the numbers, shapes, colors, and images of objects) sufficiently large to make them accessible to users with visual and motor impairments; and 5) allowing users to provide input by just tapping the screen (no dragging or swiping) to make them accessible to users with motor disabilities.

Figure 4. Screens for the Numbers activity.

4. Evaluations and Results

In this paper, we focused primarily on evaluating the activities for primary users (individuals with DD) even though we have implemented other features for administrators (e.g., data collection of users' progress). We started by conducting heuristic evaluations of the activities at the beginning stages of development to test their usability and UI. Based on those evaluations, we improved the prototype and the list of requirements based on those evaluations. After getting IRB approval, we conducted preliminary user evaluations of the prototype, specifically the activities, in collaboration with Imagine!, with some of their clients with DD at their facilities. Based on the preliminary user evaluations, we further improved the prototype and the study. Then, in collaboration with Hope Services, we ran a more comprehensive user study with ten of their clients with DD at one of their facilitates.

4.1 Preliminary Evaluations and Results

We first ran preliminary evaluations of the prototype, specifically the activities, through heuristic evaluations. We chose to test the compliance of the system's UI design with Nielsen's 10 Usability Heuristics[5] since they are widely accepted and they cover all the usability properties that we want our UI design to comply with. Based on Nielsen's 10 Usability Heuristics and the usage scenarios we constructed when gathering system requirements, we developed a set of tasks for evaluators to perform in order for them to examine the UI design and usability of the system.

---

[5]http://www.nngroup.com/articles/ten-usability-heuristics/

Fifteen evaluators (not the authors) were asked to perform those tasks (with every activity) and judge the UI design's compliance with the chosen usability principles. Evaluators were between the ages of 21 to 28 (mean = 23) and they all had experience with iOS devices (e.g., iPad, iPhone), UI and heuristics evaluation. Based on these evaluations, we made the following improvements:

- Fixed timing for the transition between screens and the audio-based positive reinforcers so audio would not overlap.
- Progress information was added while the activity loads (i.e., the message "Loading" is shown while the activity loads the necessary graphics and audio) and while it is in progress (e.g., it specifies which round the user is on out of the total number of rounds that make up the activity). (Note: The latter helped us establish the 5th functional requirement.)
- The audio and images for the prompts and reinforcers were set to load before the activity begins in order to minimize the lagging that tends to occur while it is in progress (e.g., user's responses were either not detected or processed so slowly that they would not receive feedback regarding the correctness of their selections in a timely manner) if the strength and speed of the internet connection is weak or unstable. (Although we thought the issue had been resolved, we learned during user evaluations that the issue persisted.)

Next, in collaboration with Imagine!, we ran preliminary user evaluations of the prototype at their care providing facilities, including their smart group homes, with some of their clients with DD (primary users) and their caregivers or guardians (secondary users). Primary users were asked to try each activity (once) and to answer a set of follow-up questions after trying each one. Secondary users were asked to help researchers: 1) administer the activities to users, 2) make observations about users' interaction with the activities, and 3) answer questions about users' interaction with the activities. In order to avoid making the preliminary user evaluations too strenuous for primary users, the activities were divided into three groups and each group was evaluated on a different day: First, the Numbers, Colors, and Money activities were tested by seven individuals with DD aged 28-53 years old. Next, the Shapes and MA activities were tested by five individuals with DD aged 30- 58. Finally, the LL and UL activities were tested by three individuals with DD aged 39-45. Overall, the feedback sought and the follow-up questions was qualitative in nature and it consisted of how users interacted with and reacted to the activities and, from there, the improvements that needed to be made to the activities with regards to their UI, usability, and functionality in order for them to be more effective and provide a better user experience. The main findings were:

- The activities and the positive and learning reinforcers were well-received by participants.
- All the participants were able to complete the activities with little to no assistance.
- Participants found the touch-screen interface easier to use than paper when doing similar activities because of how easy it is to respond to prompts with the app (e.g., with paper they would have to write their answers).
- Improvements that needed to be made to the system:
  o Make the detection of user input (via touch or stylus) faster and/or more reliable.
  o Speed up loading times and response-time (i.e., make activities respond to users' input more quickly).
  o Add audio signals for when the activities start and end.
  o For the MA, make the audio of the target total more accessible (i.e., make button easier to see and press) and

make the hints about which currency cannot be used to make up the total more obvious (i.e. grey it out).
  o Ensure content displays properly in Portrait mode.

On another note, after stage 1, we found that to get a better idea of participants' interactions with the activities, we needed to ask caregivers more direct questions and some of the questions for the participants needed to be rephrased or omitted. So, we applied this to stages 2 and 3 of the preliminary user evaluations.

4.2 User Study and Results

Once the system was improved based on the results from the preliminary user evaluations, we ran a more comprehensive user study of the system, in collaboration with Hope Services, with ten of their clients with DD at one of their care providing facilities which offers day-programs. Participants, four males and six females, were between the ages of 23 and 36 (mean = 28.4). A summary of participants' demographics is shown in Table 1.

Table 1. Summary of participants' demographics

ID	Age	Gender	Disability
P1	23	M	Cerebral Palsy
P2	31	M	Autism
P3	25	F	Inverted X Syndrome
P4	36	F	Down Syndrome
P5	27	F	Cognitive/Intellectual Disability
P6	35	F	Mild Intellectual Disability
P7	27	F	Mild Intellectual Disability
P8	24	M	Autism
P9	26	M	Mild Intellectual Disability
P10	30	F	Down Syndrome

Participants were asked to try each activity on three different sessions over the course of a week and, after each session, to answer a set of follow-up questions that aimed to assess their experience with the activity and their feelings towards it. In order to avoid making the evaluations too strenuous, participants were asked to try three activities (picked and ordered randomly) one week and the remaining four activities the next week (ordered randomly again). Nine participants tried all the activities this way, except for P9 who completed the last session of the first three activities he/she was asked to try on the first week during the second week. The remaining participant (P10) only tried three activities: LL, Money, and Numbers.

Noting that our target users tend to be less critical and more positive when giving feedback, we also gathered user feedback through observations of the sessions. With consent from the participants and Hope Services, we recorded videos of all the session and audio of participants' responses to the follow-up questions. In addition, the activities recorded participants' (incorrect or correct) responses to prompts. Hence, the data gathered through the user study is both quantitative and qualitative in nature. Consequently, data analysis involved a mixed method approach. As a first step, in order to analyze the videos of the sessions through content analysis, four researchers went through the videos, noted the following themes, and defined a coding scheme based on them:

- Positive reaction: Physical (e.g., smile, laugh) or verbal indications that participant is enjoying the activity.
- Negative reaction: Physical or verbal indications that participant is not enjoying the activity (e.g., facial or physical signs of frustration or disinterest).
- Assistance: Participant needed assistance from researchers to perform specific actions without which they would not have been able to continue/complete the activity.
- Multiple presses to make a selection (MP): Participant had to press an option more than once to make a selection.

Three researchers then independently coded the same 8 videos (i.e., quantified the occurrences of the aforementioned themes) and obtained an acceptable interobserver agreement (90.5%). All the videos (198 in total) were then divided among the three researchers and coded independently. Video coding was done using the Behavioral Observation Research Interactive Software (BORIS[6]), an easy-to-use event logging software for video/audio coding of living observation. Data from the audio recordings was quantified when possible. Finally, all the quantitative data was analyzed using descriptive statistics, mainly summary statistics.

4.2.1 Results

Here we present our results from the analysis of the quantitative and qualitative data concerning participants' interactions with the activities. Due to space limitations, results will be presented in the following groups and order that follow: 1) Colors, Money, Numbers, and Shapes since they behave similarly. 2) LL and UL since they reinforce the general skill of recognizing letters and behave similarly. 3) MA will be discussed independently because it aims to reinforce a more advanced skill, plus it behaves a bit different from the other activities.

4.2.1.1 Colors, Money, Numbers, and Shapes

The Colors and Shapes activities were tested by nine participants, while the Money and Numbers activities were tested by all ten participants. Here we present all the data gathered while participants tried these activities.

1. **Positive and negative reactions**: A summary of the reactions displayed by participants (who displayed any reaction) while trying these activities is shown in Figure 5. Their reactions are further summarized below. On average:
   - Colors: 83.9% (SD = 0.34) of their reactions were positive and 16.1% (SD = 0.34) were negative.
   - Money: 95.8% (SD = 0.12) of their reactions were positive and 4.2% (SD = 0.12) were negative.
   - Numbers: 95.8% (SD = 0.06) of their reactions were positive and 4.2% (SD = 0.06) were negative.
   - Shapes: 97.1% (SD = 0.05) of their reactions were positive and 2.9% (SD = 0.05) were negative.

   While trying all four activities, P7 did not display any reactions. Likewise, P10 did not display any reactions while trying the Money and Numbers activities.

2. **Assistance needed from researchers**: P2 was the only participant who displayed this theme while trying all four activities: six times with Colors (during the third session) and Money (during S1), four times with Numbers (during S2), and one time with Shapes (during S1).

3. **Incorrect responses**: The total number of times each participant responded incorrectly to a prompt while trying

these activities is shown in Table 2 (Rows C, M, N, and S). P7 did not make incorrect responses during these activities.

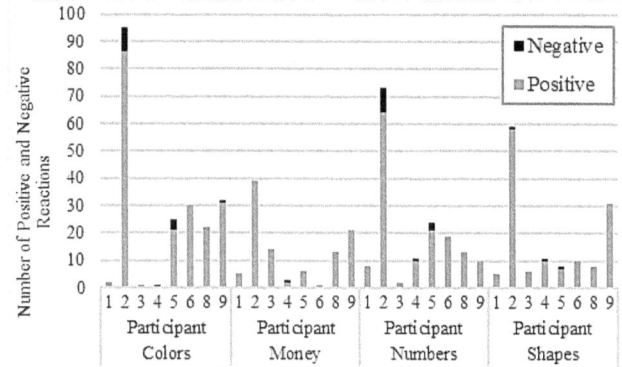

Figure 5. Positive and Negative Reactions with the Colors, Money, Numbers, and Shapes activities.

Table 2. Total number of incorrect responses

	P1	P2	P3	P4	P5	P6	P8	P9	P10
C	1	0	0	0	0	0	0	1	✕
M	3	3	2	3	1	0	1	3	3
N	0	0	0	0	1	0	0	0	0
S	7	1	0	8	0	0	0	7	✕
LL	4	0	2	2	0	1	0	5	2
UL	0	2	0	1	0	1	0	4	✕

Colors (C), Money (M), Numbers (N), and Shapes (S).

1. **MP**: The total and average number of instances of MP experienced by participants while trying these activities is shown in Table 3 (Rows C, M, N, and S). When researchers noted that many instances of MP occurred, they would ask participants if they were frustrated by that. Their responses are summarized in Table 4.

Table 3. Total number of instances of MP

	P1	P2	P3	P4	P5	P6	P7	P8	P9	P10	Avg
C	25	18	1	20	5	2	10	14	11	✕	11.78
M	7	11	2	10	3	1	3	10	10	3	6.00
N	14	16	0	6	10	3	10	4	13	1	7.70
S	20	8	2	7	3	2	12	9	10	✕	8.11
LL	9	15	3	10	1	12	7	12	14	6	8.90
UL	6	18	0	21	3	6	6	16	8	✕	9.33

Colors (C), Shapes (S), Money (M), Numbers (N), and average (Avg).

Table 4. Participants' responses to the question regarding MP being frustrating

Response	C	M	N	S	LL	UL	MA	T	%
Yes	1	1	1	1	0	0	3	7	35%
No	1	1	4	1	2	0	4	13	65%

Colors (C), Shapes (S), Money (M), Numbers (N), and Total (T).

2. **Responses to follow-up questions**: The main follow-up questions asked along with participants' responses regarding these activities are summarized in Table 5 (Columns C, M, N, and S, next page). The participant for whom the Money activity was not easy (P2) said it was hard because the iPad was not detecting his/her selections (input) properly.

[6] http://penelope.unito.it/boris/

Table 5. Summary of questions and participants' responses

Question	Response	C	M	N	S	LL	UL	MA
Easy?	Y	9	9.7	10	9	9	9	8.7
	N	0	0.3	0	0	1	0	0.3
Fun?	Y	9	10	10	9	10	9	8.7
	N	0	0	0	0	0	0	0
Helpful?	Y	9	10	10	9	10	9	9
	N	0	0	0	0	0	0	0
Liked it?	Y	9	10	10	9	10	9	9
	N	0	0	0	0	0	0	0
Use again?	Y	9	10	10	9	10	9	9
	N	0	0	0	0	0	0	0
Liked reinforcers?	Y	8	9	10	8	10	9	8.5*
	N	0	0	0	0	0	0	0.5*

* P3's answer was coded as "Y and N" since P3 expressed that she liked the positive reinforcers but not the learning reinforcers while trying the MA activity. Thus, 0.5 was assigned to both 'Y' and 'N'.

Note: Not all participants were asked or responded to these questions. If a question was asked during each session and participants' responses differed across sessions, the average was computed.

4.2.1.2 Lowercase Letters and Uppercase Letters

The LL activity was tested by all ten participants, while the UL activity was tested by nine participants. Here we present all the data gathered while participants tried these activities.

1. **Positive and negative reactions**: A summary of participants' reactions (if they displayed any reaction) while trying these activities is shown in Figure 6. Their reactions are further summarized below. On average:
   - LL: 89.5% (SD = 0.31) of their reactions were positive and 10.5% (SD = 0.31) were negative.
   - UL: 97.9% (SD = 0.04) of their reactions were positive and 2.1% (SD = 0.04) were negative.

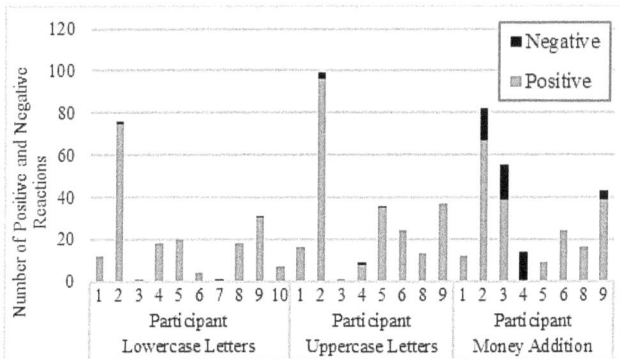

Figure 6. Positive and Negative Reactions with the LL, UL and MA activities.

2. **Assistance needed from researchers**: P1 was the only participant who displayed this theme while trying the LL activity: once during S1 and another time during S2.

3. **Incorrect responses**: The total number of times each participant responded incorrectly to a prompt while trying these activities is shown in Table 2 (Rows LL and UL). P7 did not make incorrect responses during both activities.

4. **MP**: The total and average number of instances of MP experienced by participants while trying these activities is

shown in Table 3 (Rows LL and UL). When researchers noted that many instances of MP occurred, they would ask participants if they were frustrated by that. Their responses are summarized in Table 4.

5. **Responses to follow-up questions**: The main follow-up questions asked along with participants' responses regarding these activities are summarized in Table 5 (Columns LL and UL). The participant who expressed that the LL activity was not easy (P1) explained that finding letters was hard because there were too many letters and they were unordered.

4.2.1.3 Money Addition

The MA activity was tested by nine participants. Here we present all the data gathered while participants tried these activities.

1. **Positive and negative reactions**: A summary of the reactions displayed by participants (who displayed any type of reaction) while trying this activity is shown in Figure 6 (right). Their reactions can be further summarized as follows. On average, 80.4% (SD = 0.34) of their reactions were positive and 19.6% (SD = 0.34) were negative.

2. **Assistance needed from researchers**: Four participants displayed this theme while trying the MA activity: P1 four times (two times during both S1 and S2), P2 twenty-three times (twelve times during S1, five times during S2, and six times during S3), and P4 and P6 one time (both during S1).

3. **MA responses**: Participants responses (i.e., the total number of bills and coins they pressed to get to the target total) were compared to the optimal responses (i.e., the minimum number of bills and coins needed to get to the target total) by dividing their responses by the optimal ones. The average of these comparisons are shown in Table 6. So, for example, on average, P1 would use 1.4 times the minimum number of bills and coins needed to get to the target total.

Table 6. Participants' responses versus the optimal responses

	P1	P2	P3	P4	P5	P6	P7	P8	P9
Average	1.4	2.2	2.4	2.4	1.9	2.2	1.1	1	1.1
SD	0.6	0.7	0.8	1	0.4	0.7	0.2	0	0.1

Standard deviation (SD).

6. **Strategies**: Based on the videos, we observed that four participants (P1-P4) seemed to normally choose bills and coins at random, three participants (P7, P8, P9) seemed to closely follow the optimal strategy, and the remaining two (P5, P6) seemed to normally touch bills and coins in order.

7. **Responses to follow-up questions**: The main follow-up questions asked along with participants' responses regarding the MA activity are summarized in Table 5 (Column MA). The participant who said that the MA activity was not easy during S1 (P1), expressed in later sessions that it got easier.

5. Discussion

From the user studies we gathered that all the activities were well-received since all the participants made positive remarks about each of the activities (e.g. they were fun, easy, helpful, and they liked them) and, on average, 80.4% of their reactions (or greater) were positive. This is in spite of the negative reactions displayed by participants while trying the activities, which researchers noted occurred generally when participants experienced instances of MP. On that note, all participants experienced instances of MP while trying almost all of the activities. When asked if those instances (of MP) were frustrating, 65% of the time participants expressed that those instances were not frustrating. Hence, despite its flaws (i.e., lagging and slow input detection that seems to occur when the internet connection is not good[7]) due to it being a web-app, our system has the potential to be well-received by target users and to help make the experience of reviewing basic skills easy and enjoyable for people with DD.

We also gathered that most participants were able to complete the activities on their own (with little to no assistance from researchers). Still, one participant in particular (P2) needed assistance from researchers while trying most of the activities (with five out of the seven activities). In addition, while trying the MA activity, many participants needed assistance from researchers (four out nine participants). Thus, the MA activity needs to be improved (by providing further guidance) so that users need little to no assistance from caregivers while doing this activity. With all the other activities, at most one participant needed assistance from researchers. Still, results suggest that the proposed system of activities has the potential to increase users' independence when doing these type of activities (while also decreasing the workload of their caregivers). That is, results suggest that our system has the potential to minimize how much help users need from their caregivers while completing these types of activities (i.e., caregivers will not need to be there all the time to say all the prompts that make up the activities and to tell them if their answers are correct or not).

Furthermore, we gathered from the user study that:

- The reinforcers seemed to serve their purpose since most participants expressed that they liked the reinforcers and that the learning reinforcers were helpful.
- Using pictures of things that are generally well-liked (e.g. sports, animals) will likely serve as good positive reinforcers.
- The following improvements can also be made:
  o Adding new activities: Activities that do not prompt users and allow them to review numbers, colors, letters, shapes, and money more freely. Also, activities that help users review more than one skill at a time (e.g. an activity that prompts the user to "Press the red three.") or more advanced skills like budgeting money.
  o Making MA activities more "real" by providing varying amounts of bills and coins and by allowing users to subtract from the gathered amount. It can also be made to allow users to turn on/off the learning reinforcers (i.e., allow users to decide whether they will hear audio-feedback regarding their selections within this activity).
  o For both activities related to money, make the pictures of the coins more truthful to their true size, especially in terms of the relative size between coins (e.g., the dime should be smaller than the nickel).
  o Increase difficulty as users progress through the activities; e.g., randomize the order of the letters and/or increase the number of letters, review bigger numbers, more shapes and colors, etc.
  o Add pictures of other things that are generally well-liked by most people (e.g., other sports, animals, race cars, superheroes, etc.).

6. Conclusions and Future Work

We present the development and evaluation of an online learning system for people with developmental disabilities (DD) of all

---

[7] *Note*: The wireless internet connection at the testing site was visibly slower than in our lab when loading some websites, so our best guess is that this caused the lagging.

ages. Overall, through the user study we gathered that, despite the improvements that need to be made and the system's inherent flaw as a web-app (i.e., its dependence on the strength and speed of the internet connection) and the issues that may arise because of that, our system has the potential to be a helpful learning tool for people with DD reviewing basic skills and for caregivers helping people with DD review basic skills.

From our preliminary (user) evaluations we learned how the system could be improved, but we were not able to implement some of the improvements since the system is a web-app that uses many media files (which means its use is limited to places with good internet connections). Then, through a comprehensive user study with individuals with DD we gathered that, despite the system's inherent flaws and issues due to it being a web-app and the improvements that need to be made, results suggest that the proposed system will likely be well-received by target users and that it has the potential to help: 1) make the experience of reviewing basic skills easy and enjoyable for people with DD, and 2) increase users' independence while doing the activities to review basic skills and, as a result, lessen their caregivers workload when they are trying to help them review basic skills. In summary, after making the necessary (and possible) improvements, we are confident that the proposed system will have the potential to be a practical and helpful learning tool for people with DD who need to reinforce basic skills.

One of the main contributions of our work lies in our methods for gathering feedback from people with DD. By combining debriefing interviews and an analysis of participants' behaviors during evaluations, we were able to gather a better assessment of participants' experiences and reactions to our system despite target users' tendency towards providing positive feedback.

The next steps for this project include: 1) improving the system based on the feedback we got from the user study (e.g., we will include a collection of stock photos and videos in various categories that will serve as positive reinforcers and we will allow users to choose the category of the positive reinforcers they see), 2) adding more activities that cover things like budgeting money, telling time, and recognizing street signs, common objects, and concepts with regards to object-relations (e.g., shorter, longer), and 3) evaluating the effectiveness of the activities by running a long-term user study (2 weeks) where participants will be asked to use the activities while we track their progress. In relationship to the latter, we conducted a preliminary assessment of the long-term effect of our system on the motivation of people with DD to reinforce basic skills by contacting our collaborating organizations (at least 4 weeks after the user study ended) and asking them whether users/caregivers were still using our system. The one collaborating organization who replied informed us that some of their clients were still using the system.

7. Acknowledgments.

This material is based upon work supported by the National Science Foundation through the Graduate Research Fellowship (grant No. DGE-1339067) and the UC MEXUS-CICESE scholarship. We would like to thank Imagine! Colorado and their clients as well as Hope Services and their clients for their help with the user evaluations. We would also like to thank Luke Buschmann for his crucial help with the development and evaluation of the Money, Colors, and Numbers activities; Mike Tan for his crucial help with the development of the Money Addition and Shapes activities, and Sonya Pita for her help with the preliminary evaluations, the analysis of the preliminary user evaluation results, and the development of the letters activities.

8. References

[1] Alberto, P. A., Cihak, D. F., & Gama, R. I. (2005). Use of static picture prompts versus video modeling during simulation instruction. Research in Developmental Disabilities, 26, 327–339.

[2] Canella-Malone, H., Sigafoos, J., O'Reilly, M., de la Cruz, B., Edrisinha, C., and Lancioni, G. E. (2006). Comparing video prompting to video modeling for teaching daily living skills to six adults with developmental disabilities (Doctoral dissertation).

[3] Furniss, F., Lancioni, G., Rocha, N., Cunha, B., Seedhouse, P., Morato, P., & O'Reilly, M. F. (2001). VICAID: Development and evaluation of a palmtop-based job aid for workers with severe developmental disabilities. British Journal of Educational Technology, 32(3), 277-287.

[4] Goodson, J., Sigafoos, J., O'Reilly, M., Cannella, H., and Lancioni, G. E. (2007). Evaluation of a video-based error correction procedure for teaching a domestic skill to individuals with developmental disabilities. Research in Developmental Disabilities, 28(5), 458-467.

[5] Kagohara, D. M., van der Meer, L., Ramdoss, S., O'Reilly, M. F., Lancioni, G. E., Davis, T. N., Rispolie, M., Langb, R., Marschikg, P. B., Sutherlandh, D., Green, V. A., and Sigafoos, J. (2013). Using iPods and iPads in teaching programs for individuals with developmental disabilities: A systematic review. Research in developmental disabilities, 34(1), 147-156.

[6] Lancioni, G. E., O'Reilly, M. F., Seedhouse, P., Furniss, F., and Cunha, B. (2000). Promoting independent task performance by persons with severe developmental disabilities through a new computer-aided system. Behavior Modification, 24(5), 700-718.

[7] Morales-Villaverde, L. M., Smith, S. R., and Kurniawan, S. (2013, October). Brain-training software for stroke survivors. In Proceedings of the 15th International ACM SIGACCESS Conference on Computers and Accessibility (p. 40). ACM.

[8] Sigafoos, J., O'Reilly, M., Cannella, H., Upadhyaya, M., Edrisinha, C., Lancioni, G. E., Hundley, A., Andrews, A., Garver, C. and Young, D. (2005). Computer-presented video prompting for teaching microwave oven use to three adults with developmental disabilities. Journal of Behavioral Education, 14, 189–201.

[9] Sturmey, P. (2003). Video technology and persons with autism and other developmental disabilities: An emerging technology for PBS. Journal of Positive Behavior Interventions, 5, 3–4.

[10] Wehmeyer, M. L., Palmer, S. B., Smith, S. J., Parent, W., Davies, D. K., and Stock, S. (2006). Technology use by people with intellectual and developmental disabilities to support employment activities: A single-subject design meta analysis. Journal of Vocational Rehabilitation, 24(2), 81-86.

[11] Wiemeyer, J. and Kliem, A. (2012). Serious games in prevention and rehabilitation—a new panacea for elderly people?. European Review of Aging and Physical Activity, 9(1), 41-5.

Comparing Tactile, Auditory, and Visual Assembly Error-Feedback for Workers with Cognitive Impairments

Thomas Kosch, Romina Kettner, Markus Funk, Albrecht Schmidt

University of Stuttgart (Pfaffenwaldring 5a, 70569 Stuttgart, Germany)
firstname.lastname@vis.uni-stuttgart.de

ABSTRACT

More and more industrial manufacturing companies are outsourcing assembly tasks to sheltered work organizations where cognitively impaired workers are employed. To facilitate these assembly tasks assistive systems have been introduced to provide cognitive assistance. While previous work found that these assistive systems have a great impact on the workers' performance in giving assembly instructions, these systems are further capable of detecting errors and notifying the worker of an assembly error. However, the topic of how assembly errors are presented to cognitively impaired workers has not been analyzed scientifically. In this paper, we close this gap by comparing tactile, auditory, and visual error feedback in a user study with 16 cognitively impaired workers. The results reveal that visual error feedback leads to a significantly faster assembly time compared to tactile error feedback. Further, we discuss design implications for providing error feedback for workers with cognitive impairments.

CCS Concepts

•**Human-centered computing** → **Human computer interaction (HCI); Empirical studies in accessibility;** *Haptic devices; Auditory feedback;* •**Computing methodologies** → **Mixed / augmented reality;**

Keywords

Multimodal Interfaces; Error Feedback; Assistive Systems; Cognitively Impaired Workers; Augmented Reality

1. INTRODUCTION

Sheltered work organizations are employing workers with cognitive disabilities for working on assembly tasks. Usually these assembly tasks can be broken down to very little complexity in order to fit the skill of cognitively impaired workers. Depending on the skill of the worker, this number of assembly steps is very little. To provide cognitive assistance

ASSETS '16, October 23-26, 2016, Reno, NV, USA

ⓒ 2016 ACM. ISBN 978-1-4503-4124-0/16/10. . . $15.00

DOI: http://dx.doi.org/10.1145/2982142.2982157

Figure 1: A participant is wearing an augmented glove providing tactile error feedback during assembly tasks.

for workers with cognitive disabilities during work tasks, assistive systems for the workplace have been proposed in the last years [15]. These systems usually use in-situ projection to provide information directly in the worker's field of view. Assistive systems can be used to continuously support workers and provide steady quality feedback, or they can be used to train workers to learn and adapt new assembly instructions very quickly.

The "United Nations Convention on the Rights of Persons with Disabilities" [1] describes how to ensure and protect fundamental rights of people with disabilities. This comprises of the inclusion in daily life tasks, such as work and public leisure activities. Cognitively impaired workers that are employed for conducting manual assembly tasks usually need a human instructor, who supports them during assembly tasks. The instructor is often responsible for multiple workers, which makes it difficult to check each assembly step of each worker for errors. Assistive systems providing assembly instructions can be used to reduce the number of assembly errors while decreasing assembly times [13]. However, errors can not be completely avoided. Therefore, assistive systems can be used to detect assembly errors and to provide appropriate error feedback if an assembly error occurs. Usually this error feedback shows the worker that the last assembly step has to be corrected in order to assemble the part correctly. Possible error feedback modalities delivered to the worker can be manifold but perceived diverse in terms of intrusiveness, comfortableness, and privacy aspects [11]. Related approaches conclude that a combination of haptic and visual feedback might be a suitable way of presenting error messages on assistive systems. As these results were collected with non-disabled participants, it is unclear if this error feedback is also suitable for cognitively impaired workers [11].

With this paper, we aim to close this gap by presenting a study with 16 cognitively impaired workers comparing the three most common modalities for providing error feedback: tactile, auditory, and visual. The contribution of this paper is twofold: (1) we present results of our user study favoring a visual presentation of errors and (2) we provide design implications for designing error feedback for cognitively impaired workers.

2. RELATED WORK

Over the last few years different approaches for providing context-aware information have been proposed. In the following, we provide an overview of different feedback approaches and introduce assistive systems for providing instructions at workplaces.

2.1 Feedback modalities

Different feedback modalities have been used for providing information in different scenarios. The most important categories are tactile, auditory, and visual feedback. Tactile feedback is for example used by Bial et al. [5] by using a glove that is equipped with vibrating motors. Results show that tactile feedback can be used for navigation tasks. They use the tactile feedback to provide information for motorcyclists during driving tasks. Considering auditory feedback, Rauterberg and Styger [20] proposed adding additional auditory feedback to traditional visual feedback for assembly tasks. Visual and auditory feedback has been provided at the same time while managing computer-numeric-controlled centres. Their study suggests that combining auditory and visual feedback leads to a more positive mood and improves the participants performance. However, the study was conducted with non-impaired participants. The multimodal representation of feedback could lead to a high mental demand for cognitive impaired participants. Plain visual feedback is for example used by Funk et al. [10] when comparing different visual approaches for providing feedback for workers with cognitive impairments at manual assembly workplaces. In their study, they compare video-based, pictorial and contour instructions. The results of the study suggest that visual contour instructions are perceived well among all Performance Index (PI) groups of cognitively impaired workers. Moreover, Cuvo et al. [9] use textual feedback while instructing persons with mild cognitive impairments. In their study, they found that performance feedback is crucial.

Other fields already experimented with combinations of haptic, auditory, and visual feedback. Akamatsu et al. [2] compared the three feedback types in a mouse pointing task. Their study revealed interesting design implications although no difference in Task Completion Time (TCT) was found. Further, Richard et al. [21] and Petzold et al. [18] compared the three feedback types when manipulating objects and assembling in virtual environments. Visual feedback was delivered on a screen, auditory feedback was provided by headphones and tactile feedback was triggered using pneumatic micro-cylinders, which applied pressure on the fingertips in a glove. Richard et al. found that both haptic and auditory feedback improve the workers' performance in manipulating virtual objects while Petzold et al. found that the performance is increased using additional haptic feedback.

2.2 Assistive systems for workplaces

In 1991, Pierre Wellner [25] suggested to use a camera-projector system to provide additional digital information for regular physical objects. In his prototype Wellner combined a digital and a physical workspace for enabling to use the best features of both spaces in one physical workspace. Later Pinhanez [19] was using a camera-projector system combined with a mirror for turning arbitrary surfaces into digital displays. Using Pinhanez's system, nearly every surface can become a display that shows information. Since then, systems using camera projector systems were deployed in different scenarios to provide cognitive assistance. E.g. Rüther et al. [22] provide assistance in sterile environments, Löchtefeld et al. [17] augment a shopping scenario, and Butz et al. [8] used it to support searching tasks. In 2008, Bannat et al. [3] used a similar setup for providing assembly instructions at manual assembly workplaces. Their system uses a camera to detect the position of picking bins and a projector, to provide pictorial instruction for the assembly process. Similarly, Büttner et al. [7] uses in-situ projection at manual assembly workplaces by providing pictorial instructions. They found that using in-situ projection is faster and leads to less errors compared to displaying instructions on smart glasses [6]. Further, Korn et al. [14, 16] used in-situ projection in combination with gamification approaches for motivating and instructing workers with cognitive impairments during assembly tasks. Their study with cognitively impaired workers revealed great potential for using gamification and in-situ instructions for instructing and motivating cognitively impaired workers at assembly workplaces. However, they did not find a statistically significant difference. Further, a comprehensive summary of assistive systems for supporting cognitively impaired workers at the workplace is provided by Korn et al. [15].

Recently, Funk et al. [13] used in-situ projection to provide instructions during assembly task at the workplace. Their results show that with increasing complexity, using in-situ instructions is leading to significantly less assembly errors and a significantly faster assembly time compared to pictorial instructions. In their system, they were providing red error feedback that illuminates the current picking bin when picking a wrong part. However, no scientific analysis of the error feedback was conducted. Therefore, Funk et al. [11] further investigated the effects of haptic error feedback, auditory error feedback, and visual error feedback by conducting a study with students. Their results reveal that a combination of haptic and visual feedback might be the best way to communicate errors while performing assembly tasks. However, this was only tested with students in a lab study.

As previous work suggests, adding haptic feedback for communicating errors during assembly tasks might be a privacy-presuming way of communicating errors at workplaces [11, 18]. Assistive systems will have a great impact on the inclusion of cognitively impaired workers in the work life [4, 23]. Thus, we are interested in whether the concepts of multimodal error feedback is also applicable to workers with cognitive impairments. This paper addresses this question.

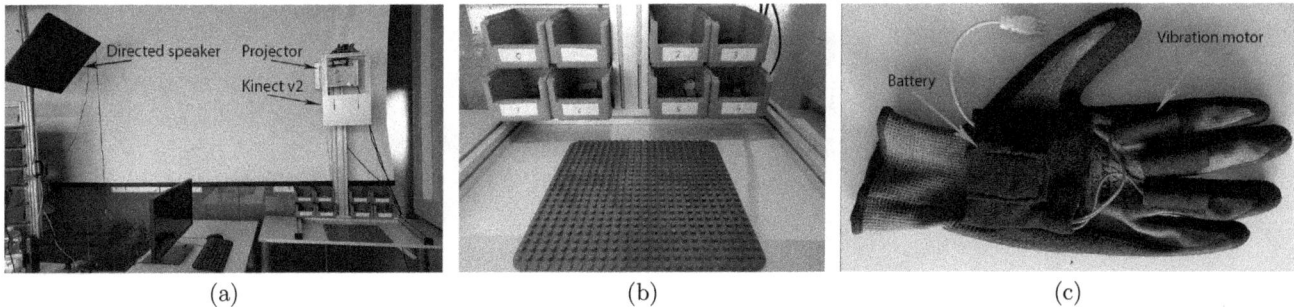

Figure 2: (a) The system uses a projector and a directed speaker for providing visual and auditory error feedback. Further, a Kinect_v2 observes the picking of items from bins. (b) Red light providing visual error feedback. In case of an error, the whole working area is highlighted. (c) A glove equipped with vibration motors is further used to provide tactile error feedback.

3. SYSTEM

To incorporate the use of tactile, auditory, and visual error feedback in an assistive system for workplaces, we extended the system presented by Funk et al. [13]. The system consists of modular components that are designed for providing different modalities of error feedback. The main system, which tracks assembly steps and provides feedback to the assembly area, is constructed out of multiple aluminum profiles. The profiles can be used to mount different hardware on top of the workplace. The system uses a top-mounted Kinect_v2 to detect picking steps. Therefore, the system can distinguish between correct and incorrect picks.

We placed the system on a table, and placed a height-adjustable chair in front of it. Therefore the workers can work while sitting at a comfortable height. The system is constructed in a way that the assembly area is $70\,cm$ wide and $49\,cm$ high. This is enough space for placing instructions and assembling Lego Duplo constructions. The system further features 2×4 picking bins which are filled with Lego Duplo bricks. Each picking bin is filled with one type of Lego Duplo bricks that is unique in either color or shape. In the middle of the system there is a Lego Duplo plate firmly taped to the work area (see Figure 2b). The system triggers an error when either a picking error was made, or an assembly error was made by the participants. Picking errors are detected automatically by the Kinect_v2 if the user places his or her hand in a wrong bin. For detecting assembly errors, the system uses a wizard of oz approach where a study assistant observes the assembly process and uses a wireless presenter for triggering an error. In a case of an assembly error or picking error, an error message is triggered. Depending on the condition, our system is capable of presenting error feedback using the following three modalities:

Visual error feedback is provided using a projector (see Figure 2a), which is mounted at the top of the assistive system. If an error occurs, a red light illuminates the whole work area (see Figure 2b). While previous approaches only highlight the incorrect picking bin or the incorrect assembly position if an error was made, we decided to illuminate the entire work area. Therefore, the error message is harder to miss.

Stimulus	Feedback Design	Duration in ms
Visual	Projecting red light	2500
Auditory	Playing deep error sound	2000
Haptic	Vibration in worker gloves	1200

Table 1: Feedback design and duration of each stimulus used in the study.

Auditory error feedback is provided using the Holosonics Audio Spotlight 24i[1] (AS24i) speaker. The speaker uses ultrasonic waves to prevent the sound from diffusing. Therefore, it is only noticeable by the person sitting at the workplace and therefore retains the user's privacy. As an error sound, we are using a deep error tone exactly as used by Funk et al. [11]. In case an error is made, the error sound is played by the speaker (see Figure 2a).

Tactile error feedback is provided using a glove equipped with two vibration motors (see Figure 2c). We decided to choose standard safety gloves, which are mostly used by workers while performing assembly tasks. The motors are placed on the index finger and the ring finger. Our glove uses an ESP8266 micro controller and a battery to receive the error trigger messages via WiFi. In comparison to Funk et al. [11], our glove can therefore be used without using a wire connection to a computer. This wireless feature makes the glove less obstructive while performing assembly tasks. In case an error is made, the glove uses an alternating vibration pattern that activates each motor twice directly after each other for 0.3 seconds each. This results in a vibration time of 1.2 seconds per error.

A summary of the design and duration of every error feedback modality can be found in Table 1.

4. EVALUATION

We conducted a user study with cognitively impaired workers to evaluate the usefulness and impact of different error feedback modalities. This section describes the used setup for the study, explains the procedure, and reports results of the quantitative measures. Ethical approval for this study

---

[1]www.holosonics.com/15-products - last access 08-08-2016

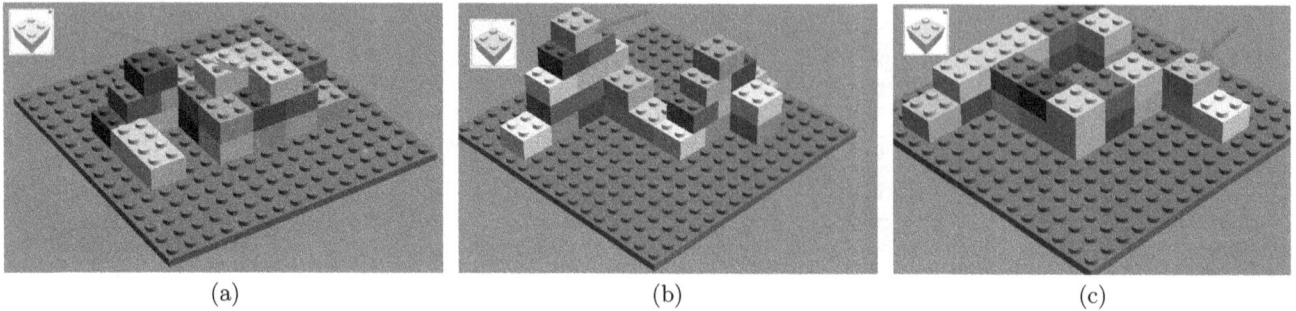

Figure 3: The assembly tasks used in the study. We used three different assembly tasks with equal complexity. The images depict the final step of the pictorial instructions.

was given by the employee organization of our partner sheltered work organization and by the German Federal Ministry for Economic Affairs and Energy.

4.1 Design

To find the most suitable error feedback modality for communicating errors to workers with cognitive impairments, we designed our experiment following a repeated measures design with the used error feedback modality as only independent variable. As dependent variables, we measure the TCT, the number of assembly errors, and the number of picking errors. We counterbalanced the order of the feedback modalities according to the Balanced Latin Square. Additionally, we collect qualitative feedback through semi-structured interviews and observations. We decided not to use a baseline condition that measures the time and errors without any error feedback as related approaches showed that error feedback is beneficial for workers with cognitive impairments. They usually ask their socio-educational instructors for feedback about the assembly [10, 13].

4.2 Apparatus

For our experiment, we use the system providing tactile, auditory, and visual error feedback described in the previous section. We configured it that only one feedback modality is active per condition. As previous work suggested, using Lego Duplo tasks provides a good abstraction of assembly tasks, which enables changing the complexity of tasks without changing the task itself [24, 13, 12]. Therefore we decided to use a Lego Duplo assembly task. As we designed the experiment to have three conditions, we created three unique Lego Duplo assembly tasks consisting of 24 bricks per task[2]. The tasks are mainly inspired by the tasks that were used by Funk et al. [13]. Therefore, we used their 24 bricks task, increased their 12 bricks task by 12 more bricks, and used their 48 brick task and stopped at 24 bricks. The instructions in their final assembly state are depicted in Figure 3. We printed the instructions on a single-sided A4 sheet of paper in a way that one assembly step is printed at one sheet of paper. The upper left corner of the instruction depicts the brick that has to be picked from one of the 8 picking bins. The assembly position is depicted in a way that the brick to assemble is shown in its final position. Further, a

red arrow highlights the assembly position that it can be found immediately. Further, the instructions were designed in a way that the same brick does not have to be picked twice directly after the first occurrence.

4.3 Procedure

In preparation of the study, we asked for a written consent from either the participants or their legal guardian before the study. As the study was conducted in our laboratory, which was a new environment for every participant, we initially made all participants familiar with our laboratory environment. Accompanied by their regular socio-educational instructors, we initially explained the assistive system and the three modalities that are used in the study. At first, we informed the participants that their participation in this study is voluntarily. We told them that they should inform us whenever they felt unwell or uncomfortable, as we would immediately abort the study in this case. Afterwards, we explained the intention of the study and why the tasks they perform are relevant. After explaining the course of the study, we made the participants familiar with the paper assembly instructions, i.e. which part to pick and where to assemble it. Once the participants felt confident using the paper assembly instructions, we introduced the error feedback modality for the current condition and explained what we count as an error and what the system will do if an error occurs. As the participants felt that they understood both error feedback and the paper assembly instructions, we began with the study and started measuring the TCT. During the study, 3 researchers were present at the scene. The first researcher triggered the assembly error feedback in case an assembly error was made as a wizard of oz. Picking errors were detected using a Kinect_v2, which triggered the error feedback automatically. The second researcher was measuring the TCT and counted the picking errors and assembly errors that were made for each condition. The third researcher was observing the worker reacting to the error feedback and taking subjective notes based on the observation. The error feedback was displayed immediately while performing the assembly, when an assembly or picking error was triggered. After the assembly was completed, we asked the participant for their opinion about the used error feedback. Then we repeated the procedure for the other two remaining conditions. At the end of the third condition, we asked each participant for a subjective rating which error feedback was perceived the best by her or him and we asked them why they preferred or disliked the feedback.

---

[2]We provide the created assembly instructions to other researchers for reproducing the study.
Link: www.hcilab.org/assets16instructions

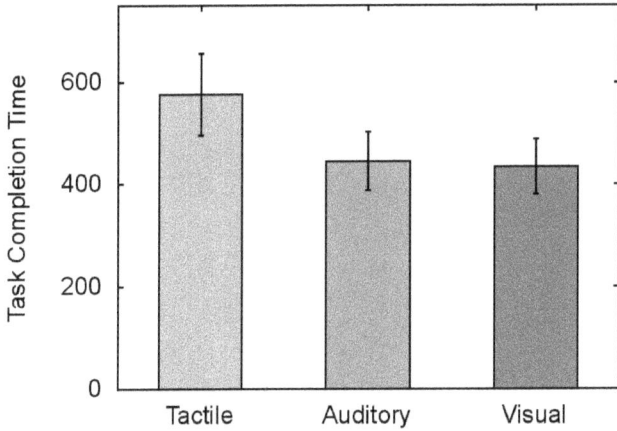

Figure 4: An overview of the average Task Completion Time to assemble the Lego Duplo construction using the different error feedback modalities. The error bars depict the standard error.

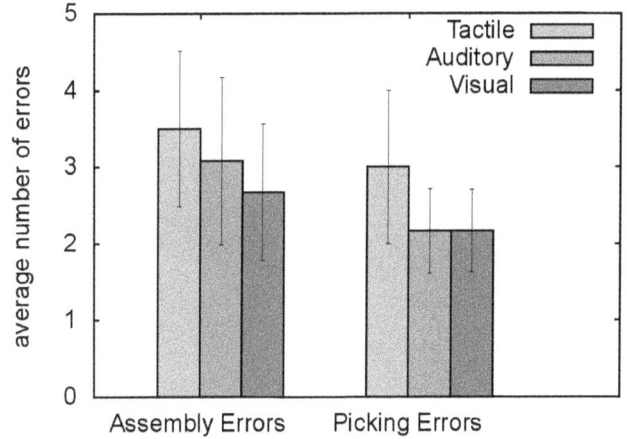

Figure 5: The average number of errors that were made using the different error feedback modalities for both assembly errors and picking errors. The error bars depict the standard error.

4.4 Participants

We invited 16 participants for our user study. The participants were aged from 34 to 53 years ($M = 40.33$, $SD = 6.36$) and were employees of a sheltered work organization working in manual manufacturing. All participants worked on manual assembly tasks on a daily basis. None of the participants were familiar with our system, the used task, or the error feedback modalities used in our study. We invited the participants according to their PI in a way that they represent the population of the sheltered work organization. Therefore, we used the PI of the sheltered work organization to categorize their capabilities. The PI is a percentage ranging from 0% to 100%, which indicates how capable a worker with cognitive impairments is of performing a work task. Inspired by previous work [10, 13], we divided the population to belong to one of three PI groups: 5-15%, 20-35% and above 40%. Accordingly, we invited 5 participants belonging to each of the three PI groups. The study took approximately 40 minutes per participant.

4.5 Results

During our study, 4 participants belonging to the 5-15% PI group aborted the study as they did not want to wear the glove anymore. Therefore, we excluded these 4 participants from the quantitative evaluation.

We statistically compared the TCT, the number of assembly errors, and the number of picking errors, between the error feedback modalities using a one-way repeated measures ANOVA. Mauchly's test showed that the sphericity assumption was violated for the number of assembly errors ($\chi^2(2)$=6.852, p=.033) and the number of picking errors ($\chi^2(2)$=9.201, p=.010). Therefore, we used the Greenhouse-Geisser correction to adjust the degrees of freedom (ϵ=.668 for the number of assembly errors and ϵ=.624 for the number of picking errors). Further, we used a Bonferroni correction for all the post-hoc tests.

Considering the TCT, the participants assembled the Lego Duplo construction fastest using the visual error feedback ($M = 434.42$ sec, $SD = 185.27$ sec), followed by the auditory error feedback ($M = 445.08$ sec, $SD = 197.40$ sec), and the tactile error feedback ($M = 575.42$ sec, $SD = $

276.71 sec). As the shapiro-wilk test did not show a non-normal distribution, we use a parametric one-way ANOVA. The one-way repeated measures ANOVA showed a statistically significant difference in the TCT between the feedback modalities $F(2,22) = 4.634$, $p = .021$. The post-hoc tests reveal a significant difference between the visual and tactile feedback. The effect size estimate shows a large effect ($\eta^2 = .296$). Figure 4 shows a graphical overview of the results.

Analyzing the number of assembly errors that were made by the participants using the different error feedback modalities, the visual error feedback resulted in the fewest assembly errors ($M = 2.67$, $SD = 3.09$), followed by the auditory error feedback ($M = 3.08$, $SD = 3.77$), and the tactile error feedback ($M = 3.5$, $SD = 3.5$). As a shapiro-wilk test showed a non-normal distribution for all three modalities (all $p < .05$), we use a non-parametric Friedman test. Accordingly the Friedman test did not reveal a significant difference between the error feedback modalities ($p > .05$). The results are depicted in Figure 5.

For the number of picking errors that were made using the different error feedback modalities, the visual error feedback ($M = 2.17$, $SD = 1.85$) and the auditory error feedback ($M = 2.17$, $SD = 1.89$) lead to the same number of picking errors. Using the tactile error feedback, the participants made the most picking errors ($M = 3.0$, $SD = 3.46$). As a shapiro-wilk test showed a non-normal distribution for all three modalities (all $p < .05$), we use a non-parametric Friedman test. However, the Friedman test could not reveal a significant difference ($p > .05$). The results are depicted in Figure 5.

5. QUALITATIVE OBSERVATION

Considering the qualitative observational feedback that was collected during the user study, two researchers continuously observed the participants during the study. The first researcher observed the interaction of the participants with different error feedback modalities and asked questions after the condition was finished in a semi-structured way. The second researcher was performing an observational study for subjectively analyzing the effect of the different error feedback modalities on the participants.

When asked about the Lego Duplo task itself, a participant stated that *"with increasing number of steps the task gets more complicated"* (P1). Another participant pointed out that the used task has several error sources as *"[he] had difficulties in distinguishing between the two different types of green bricks"* (P2). During the study, we subjectively observed that 10 of our 12 participants had difficulties to recognize bricks, whereas most of them stated that they did not have problems differentiating between the different colors.

We also asked the participants about how easy it was to perceive the different feedback modalities. One participant liked the visual feedback as it is *"directly in the field of view"* (P2), others said that the visual feedback is *"easy to see"* (P4). The participants were unsure about the tactile feedback as *"the vibration is rather unpleasant during the work task"* (P2) and *"[it] distracted me in my workflow"* (P4). Some participants (P3, P8) also did not feel or pay attention to the tactile stimulus. Further, four participants had to abort the study after the tactile feedback condition. Two of these participants stated that they did not feel well wearing a glove, the other two were uncomfortable or scared of the tactile vibration. Considering the auditory feedback a participant stated that the *"sound was very easy to perceive"* (P2). On the other hand, three participants (P3, P8, P14) stated that they was distracted by the auditory error feedback as it *"scared [them] when it triggered"*.

Considering the privacy implications of the different error feedback modalities, some participants stated that auditory feedback would be *"not that good because others can hear when [I] made an error"* (P2, P13). On the other hand considering the visual error feedback many participants told us that *"[they] don't care if others could see that they made an error"* (P2, P4, P5, P12, P14). When we asked why, the participants responded that *"usually the supervisors are watching the work steps as a quality control and are telling us when an error occurred"*. (P4) One participant was concerned that his supervisor would not be able to see anymore when an error was made as only he could perceive the tactile feedback (P16).

One participant (P7) stated after the study that he perceived working with the system using any error feedback as very easy as he could completely relax and rely on the system because it would tell him when he makes an error. Two other participants stated that they *"could imagine using the visual feedback on a daily basis"* (P4, P5).

At the end of the semi-structured interview, we asked the participants to rank the feedback modalities according to which modality they liked best and to also consider which error feedback they would use on a daily basis. One of our 12 participants who finished the study did not want to rank the error feedback modalities. The results reveal that participants' subjective impression of the visual error feedback was best (5× first, 4× second, and 2× third) followed by the auditory feedback (4× first, 4× second, and 3× third). The tactile feedback was perceived the worst (2× first, 3× second, and 6× third). The results are also depicted in Figure 6.

In addition to the interviews, 5 participants made comments on their performance or formulated their thoughts during the assembly task. In most cases these participants showed a higher TCT than other participants. Another 4

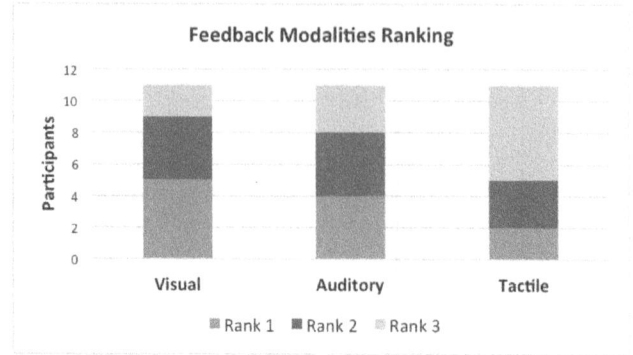

Figure 6: The subjective ranking of the feedback modalities ranked by the participants.

participants needed to be guided verbally during their tasks and reacted positively to the verbal help.

6. DISCUSSION AND IMPLICATIONS

The results of our study reveal that both the number of assembly errors and the number of picking errors are not significantly different between the error feedback modalities. We argue, that the number of errors is not different between the error feedback modalities as the error feedback occurs after the participant made the error. Thus, we could not measure that the used feedback modality is influencing the participant in the way they are working, e.g. paying more attention to a correct picking or to a correct assembly of the Lego Duplo construction or being insecure and making more errors due to an error feedback modality. However, the TCT is statistically different between tactile error feedback and visual error feedback. We assume that this difference in the TCT is caused by a faster error recovery after an error was made. The visual error feedback was perceived significantly faster than the error feedback provided by the tactile glove.

The qualitative observations and the answers we got from the participants through semi-structured interviews after using the different error feedback modalities tend towards using visual error feedback. Although some participants did not care about using error feedback that preserves their privacy at the workplace, an auditory error feedback was perceived as distracting. Considering the tactile feedback using the vibrating glove, some participants were able to perceive the tactile feedback while others did not react to the tactile feedback at all.

While using privacy presuming error feedback mechanisms might be a good decision in general [11], the implications for using these error feedback mechanisms for cognitively impaired workers are different. Through interviews we found that errors that are made at the assembly workplace are considered a non-private information, which is acceptable to communicate to supervisors. Compared to related work [11], which analyzed the error feedback for non-disabled workers the design implications are different as error privacy has a higher priority.

7. CONCLUSION

In this paper, we compared auditory, tactile, and visual error-feedback for cognitively impaired workers at manual assembly workplaces. In this user study, we obtained data from 12 participants to estimate the best feedback modality in terms of task completion time, measured errors, and qualitative feedback. We found a significant difference between visual and tactile error feedback regarding the task completion time, but could not find a significant effect between picking errors and assembly errors between each error feedback modality. We did not observe that altering the error feedback modality had an impact on the way the participants worked on assembly tasks. Therefore, the number of assembly errors throughout all error feedback modalities were not significantly different. However, we measured a significantly faster task completion time using visual error feedback compared to using tactile error feedback. Using visual error feedback, the participants were able to recover faster from errors than using tactile error feedback.

In future work, we want to perform a study, which addresses the limitations of working memory during assembly tasks. Assembly instructions will be provided as visual, auditory, and tactile representation to evaluate changes regarding performance and user acceptance of the error feedback modalities. Additionally we want to conduct a long term study in an industrial context to evaluate the user acceptance, performance, and learning effects of the proposed error feedback modalities, especially when used over a longer period of time. Furthermore, the presented vibration glove will be improved by reducing the size of electronic components within the glove for observing changes regarding the assembly and pick performance.

8. ACKNOWLEDGMENTS

This work is funded by the German Federal Ministry for Economic Affairs and Energy in the project motionEAP, grant no. 01MT12021E. We would like to thank Frank Raschhofer and Matthias Guth from the GWW - Gemeinnützige Werkstätten und Wohnstätten GmbH for their great help in organizing the study and making it possible. Further we thank Juana Heusler for her help in implementing the haptic glove.

9. REFERENCES

[1] United nations: United nations convention on the rights of persons with disabilities. http://www.un.org/disabilities/convention/conventionfull.shtml, 2008. [last accessed 02-May-2016].

[2] M. Akamatsu, I. S. MacKenzie, and T. Hasbroucq. A comparison of tactile, auditory, and visual feedback in a pointing task using a mouse-type device. *Ergonomics*, 38(4):816–827, 1995.

[3] A. Bannat, F. Wallhoff, G. Rigoll, F. Friesdorf, H. Bubb, S. Stork, H. Müller, A. Schubö, M. Wiesbeck, and M. F. Zäh. Towards optimal worker assistance: a framework for adaptive selection and presentation of assembly instructions. In *Proceedings of the 1st international workshop on cognition for technical systems, Cotesys*, 2008.

[4] H. Behrendt, M. Funk, and O. Korn. Ethical implications regarding assistive technology at workplaces. In *Collective Agency and Cooperation in Natural and Artificial Systems*, pages 109–130. Springer, 2015.

[5] D. Bial, D. Kern, F. Alt, and A. Schmidt. Enhancing outdoor navigation systems through vibrotactile feedback. In *CHI'11 Extended Abstracts on Human Factors in Computing Systems*, pages 1273–1278. ACM, 2011.

[6] S. Büttner, M. Funk, O. Sand, and C. Röcker. Using head-mounted displays and in-situ projection for assistive systems – a comparison. In *Proceedings of the 9th ACM International Conference on PErvasive Technologies Related to Assistive Environments*, New York, NY, USA, 2016. ACM.

[7] S. Büttner, O. Sand, and C. Röcker. Extending the design space in industrial manufacturing through mobile projection. In *Proceedings of the 17th International Conference on Human-Computer Interaction with Mobile Devices and Services Adjunct*, pages 1130–1133. ACM, 2015.

[8] A. Butz, M. Schneider, and M. Spassova. Searchlight–a lightweight search function for pervasive environments. In *Pervasive Computing*, pages 351–356. Springer, 2004.

[9] A. J. Cuvo, P. K. Davis, M. F. O'Reilly, B. M. Mooney, and R. Crowley. Promoting stimulus control with textual prompts and performance feedback for persons with mild disabilities. *Journal of applied behavior analysis*, 25(2):477–489, 1992.

[10] M. Funk, A. Bächler, L. Bächler, O. Korn, C. Krieger, T. Heidenreich, and A. Schmidt. Comparing projected in-situ feedback at the manual assembly workplace with impaired workers. In *Proceedings of the 8th ACM International Conference on PErvasive Technologies Related to Assistive Environments*, page 1. ACM, 2015.

[11] M. Funk, J. Heusler, E. Akcay, K. Weiland, and A. Schmidt. Haptic, auditory, or visual? towards optimal error feedback at manual assembly workplaces. In *Proceedings of the 9th ACM International Conference on PErvasive Technologies Related to Assistive Environments*, New York, NY, USA, 2016. ACM.

[12] M. Funk, T. Kosch, S. W. Greenwald, and A. Schmidt. A benchmark for interactive augmented reality instructions for assembly tasks. In *Proceedings of the 14th International Conference on Mobile and Ubiquitous Multimedia*, pages 253–257. ACM, 2015.

[13] M. Funk, S. Mayer, and A. Schmidt. Using in-situ projection to support cognitively impaired workers at the workplace. In *Proceedings of the 17th international ACM SIGACCESS conference on Computers & accessibility*, 2015.

[14] O. Korn, M. Funk, S. Abele, T. Hörz, and A. Schmidt. Context-aware assistive systems at the workplace: analyzing the effects of projection and gamification. In *Proceedings of the 7th International Conference on PErvasive Technologies Related to Assistive Environments*, page 38. ACM, 2014.

[15] O. Korn, M. Funk, and A. Schmidt. Assistive systems for the workplace: Towards context-aware assistance. *Assistive Technologies for Physical and Cognitive Disabilities*, pages 121–133, 2015.

[16] O. Korn, A. Schmidt, and T. Hörz. The potentials of in-situ-projection for augmented workplaces in

production: a study with impaired persons. In *CHI'13 Extended Abstracts on Human Factors in Computing Systems*, pages 979–984. ACM, 2013.

[17] M. Löchtefeld, S. Gehring, J. Schöning, and A. Krüger. Shelftorchlight: Augmenting a shelf using a camera projector unit. In *Conference on Pervasive Computing*, volume 10. Citeseer, 2010.

[18] B. Petzold, M. F. Zaeh, B. Faerber, B. Deml, H. Egermeier, J. Schilp, and S. Clarke. A study on visual, auditory, and haptic feedback for assembly tasks. *Presence: teleoperators and virtual environments*, 13(1):16–21, 2004.

[19] C. Pinhanez. The everywhere displays projector: A device to create ubiquitous graphical interfaces. In *Ubicomp 2001: Ubiquitous Computing*, pages 315–331. Springer, 2001.

[20] M. Rauterberg and E. Styger. Positive effects of sound feedback during the operation of a plant simulator. In *Human-Computer Interaction*, pages 35–44. Springer, 1994.

[21] P. Richard, G. Burdea, D. Gomez, and P. Coiffet. A comparison of haptic, visual and auditive force feedback for deformable virtual objects. In *Proceedings of the Internation Conference on Automation Technology (ICAT)*, pages 49–62, 1994.

[22] S. Rüther, T. Hermann, M. Mracek, S. Kopp, and J. Steil. An assistance system for guiding workers in central sterilization supply departments. In *Proceedings of the 6th International Conference on PErvasive Technologies Related to Assistive Environments*, page 3. ACM, 2013.

[23] A. L. Sauer, A. Parks, and P. C. Heyn. Assistive technology effects on the employment outcomes for people with cognitive disabilities: a systematic review. *Disability and Rehabilitation: Assistive Technology*, 5(6):377–391, 2010.

[24] A. Tang, C. Owen, F. Biocca, and W. Mou. Comparative effectiveness of augmented reality in object assembly. In *Proceedings of the SIGCHI conference on Human factors in computing systems*, pages 73–80. ACM, 2003.

[25] P. Wellner. The digitaldesk calculator: tangible manipulation on a desk top display. In *Proceedings of the 4th annual ACM symposium on User interface software and technology*, pages 27–33. ACM, 1991.

Gesture-based Interaction for Individuals with Developmental Disabilities in India

Sumita Sharma[1], Saurabh Srivastava[2], Krishnaveni Achary[3], Blessin Varkey[3],
Tomi Heimonen[4], Jaakko Hakulinen[1], Markku Turunen[1], and Nitendra Rajput[5]
[1]University of Tampere, Tampere, Finland
[2]Xerox Research Centre India, Bangalore, India
[3]Autism Research Center, Tamana School of Hope, New Delhi, India
[4]University of Wisconsin–Stevens Point, Stevens Point, WI, USA
[5]IBM Research, New Delhi, India
{firstname.lastname, sumita.s.sharma}@sis.uta.fi, saurabh.srivastava@xerox.com,
{krishnaveni.achary, blessinvarkey}@gmail.com, theimone@uwsp.edu, rnitendra@in.ibm.com

ABSTRACT

Gesture-based interaction provides a multitude of benefits to individuals with disabilities, for example, enhancing social, motor and cognitive skills. However, applications that encourage self-efficacy by promoting a life-skill through simulations of real world scenarios are largely missing. We explore the benefits of using a gesture-based application for individuals with developmental disabilities. The context is a special school in New Delhi, Nai Disha, where we designed and developed an application, *Kirana*, that integrates arithmetic and social interaction to teach purchasing of items from a local grocery store. In our study, 18 participants with developmental disabilities, previously unable to visit a grocery store, used *Kirana* for three weeks. Our results indicate that gesture-based applications can teach a life skill and enable self-efficacy for individuals with developmental disabilities by breaking down complex tasks that require social, mathematical and decision-making skills.

Keywords

Gesture-based interaction; Developing countries; Individuals with developmental disabilities

1. INTRODUCTION

Individuals with developmental disabilities require personalized care when using conventional educational methods. They face challenges in learning skills that promote self-efficacy – including the danger of being misunderstood and mistreated outside the classroom environment. In this work, we consider individuals with development disabilities as individuals with cognitive challenges, autism, or Down syndrome. Previous research has shown that interactive technology offers several desirable advantages for such individuals, including (a) controllable input stimuli ([5],[18],[32],[33]), (b) multisensory and safer learning environment ([1],[2],[3],[37]), (c) opportunities for customization for individualized learning ([1],[2],[7],[18],[19]), (d) structured, predicable and consistent learning environment ([1],[2],[18],[32]), (e) the possibility to introduce controlled modifications or difficulty levels ([1],[2],[7],[18],[19]), (f) assistance in

ASSETS '16, October 23 - 26, 2016, Reno, NV, USA
Copyright is held by the owner/author(s). Publication rights licensed to ACM.
ACM 978-1-4503-4124-0/16/10…$15.00
DOI: http://dx.doi.org/10.1145/2982142.2982166

generalizations between scenarios ([1],[2],[31],[32],[33]), and (g) possibility for self-paced repetition of learning activities ([18],[19],[32],[33],[37]).

However, research on gesture-based applications for individuals with developmental disabilities is mainly focused on therapeutic interventions and specific social, motor and cognitive skills. The potential benefits of designing and developing real world task-based interactive applications that promote essential life skills for self-efficacy are largely under-researched. For the purposes of interventions, complex social and cognitive tasks can be broken down. For example, buying something from a local store requires social interaction - talking or asking for something, and cognitive skills, like knowing what to ask for, knowing how much money there is to spend, and deciding if the item and cost are comparable.

There are several options for implementing interactive applications. Although virtual reality applications are known to assist individuals with developmental disabilities in understanding real world challenges [6] and [23], it can be argued that for children on the autism spectrum the fidelity of the representation is less important [32], and visual, auditory and motor experiences and feedback, when used together, result in more efficient learning and information retention [6]. This notion is also supported by the theory of embodied cognition [42]. Thus, simpler 2D interfaces employing immersive gesture-based interaction can potentially be sufficient to simulate real world environments.

However, novel technologies are often perceived to not be cost-effective, as catering to a limited group of people, and difficult to maintain and integrate into existing systems. This is particularly true in developing regions, including India, where access to such technologies is still limited, especially for individuals with developmental disabilities. Moreover, available resources are low, integration and inclusion of individuals with development disabilities into mainstream society is strained, and the digital divide – technical and economic barriers – is more pronounced. To overcome these challenges and perceptions, it is important to substantiate the potential of such technologies to build a stronger case for their mainstream adoption. These applications also need to consider the cultural implications of the real environment, as "what constitutes appropriate behavior is largely a social construct" [3]. Thus, it is important to collaborate with the different stakeholders, for example, teachers, therapists and caregivers, and follow a user-centered design approach.

This paper presents the potential benefits of using a gesture-based application that simulates a real world scenario to impart a life skill to individuals with developmental disabilities. We first conducted a user-centered design study to identify a suitable gesture vocabulary and life-skill. We designed and developed an application for mimicking the real world scenario of buying groceries from a local mom-and-pop store, *Kirana*, in New Delhi. We evaluated *Kirana* with 18 individuals with developmental disabilities, who were unable to shop independently. Our findings suggest that applications that employ gesture-based interaction to simulate real world scenarios in a safe and controlled environment can provide learning that is translatable from the virtual to real world. Our main contribution is demonstrating the potential of gesture-based applications to facilitate self-efficacy in individuals with developmental disabilities.

In the following, we first contextualize the research with the related work in this domain. This is followed by a detailed description of our user-centered design study and its results. We then present the application description, evaluation methodology and its results. We conclude by discussing our findings.

2. RELATED WORK
In the related research we (a) discuss gesture-based interactions for individuals with developmental disabilities and its potential benefits vis-à-vis the theory of embodied cognition, (b) present an overview of assistive technologies for Indian children, and (c) differentiate our work from previous work on virtual reality applications for learnings real world skills.

2.1 Gesture-based interaction
Employing gesture-based, *embodied* interaction for social, therapeutic and educational applications for individuals with developmental disabilities has gained momentum in recent years. There is strong evidence in support of embodied learning paradigms based on the theory of embodied cognition, whereby cognition is situated within the environment and learning occurs also through bodily interaction with the environment [22], [42]. The embodied learning paradigm has been extensively studied in neuroscience and cognitive sciences ([10],[15],[21],[40]), and has been adopted by research in educational technologies within the human-computer interaction (HCI) domain [11].

Studies by Bartoli et al. [1],[2] showcase the benefits of embodied learning via gesture-based interaction for children with autism. Our work expands Bartoli's work by extending it to individuals with developmental disabilities (including autism and Down syndrome), and to children from developing countries, by focusing on a life-skill. In line with Bartoli's findings, we also purport that learning from gesture-based interaction is applicable to real world scenarios where selection via pointing and moving of physical objects simulates interactions in everyday life.

Previous research in this space is largely focused on individuals with autism and in improving social, motor and cognitive skills. The focus of the research has been on attention and memory or the concept of self, and it has employed tangible interaction and/or sensory motor perception. For example, SensoryPaint is multimodal application that incorporates tangible interaction and whole–body interaction for therapeutic interventions to encourage social interaction [35]. Research by the Lakeside Center for Autism[1] and Kinems.com[2], taps into the potential of gesture-based

---
[1] http://lakesideautism.com/tag/kinect/

[2] www.kinems.com

---

interaction and its inherent affordances for kinesthetic learning experiences within the classroom environment. MEDIATE [13] is a multisensory interactive environment that utilizes real-time visual, aural and vibrotactile stimuli. There are also studies on gesture-based applications to match visual facial expressions [7], improve hand-eye coordination, attention and focus [1], detect repetitive behavior or tantrums [13], for promoting joint attention [38], and for cognitive rehabilitation and exercising [14]. However, there is limited research on using gesture-based applications to impart life skills, such as purchasing items. In this context, incorporating culturally sensitive gestures and interactions is particularly important [3].

2.2 Assistive technologies in India
There is a culturally misguided attitude towards children with disabilities in India. A study of teachers' attitude towards children with disabilities in schools in Mumbai showed that prior acquaintance with a person with a disability was a governing factor for teachers' to be more positive and welcoming towards inclusive education [29]. A World Bank survey in 14 developing countries, including India, indicated a "worrisome vicious cycle of low schooling attainment and subsequent poverty among people with disabilities in developing countries" [12]. While there are several schools for children with special needs across India, very few of them employ technology within their classrooms and there is limited research examining the role of assistive technologies. One study proposed developing assistive communication technologies for individuals with autism or dyslexia in India [37]. Another, called Jollymate, is a digital notepad for children with dyslexia that emulates a "phonetics system of teaching letter sounds and letter formation" [19].

There are challenges in introducing new technological interventions, especially for individuals with development disabilities in the developing world: (a) resource constrains within the environment, for example, infrastructure and access to electricity, (b) a huge digital divide, thus communities that can benefit the most from technology have the least access to it, (c) inclusivity and integration among children with disabilities and typically developed is low, (d) technologies are too costly, especially for individualized use, and (e) stronger cultural barriers for individuals with disabilities that lead to more pronounced digital exclusion even within the technology-capable communities. For example, economically stable and educated parents might provide a mobile phone to a typically developed child and but not to a child with autism. In fact, studies have shown that cultural, societal and socio-economic factors largely affect "the experience of autism" [3] [16]. However, we believe that several emerging technologies are now affordable and one device can cater to a larger number of children, so that a whole school can time-share the resource.

2.3 Simulating real world scenarios
Simulations of real world scenarios to provide learning tools for individuals with special needs have been studied from the late 90s. This work has primarily focused on virtual reality environments (VR) utilizing computer generated three dimensional (3D) worlds. Applications include therapeutic, social and skill-based learning, including solutions for individuals with developmental disabilities, most notably autism and ADHD [8]. Studies have examined the benefits for social interactions [20] [18], collaborations with peers [31], or avatars [27], understanding facial expressions [17], pediatric rehabilitation [33], physical rehabilitation [23] [34], sense of presence [26], [31], [41], and skill based learnings [39]. For example, Coles et al. [6] and [28]

taught road and fire safety skills to children affected by prenatal alcohol exposure using. However, much of this research is focused in the developed world, and so the applications are possibly socially and culturally unsuitable for developing countries [3]. Our work does not utilize 3D virtual reality, but a simplified 2D graphical representation with gesture-based interaction. The graphics and gestures for interaction are designed from a real world scenario.

3. USER-CENTERED DESIGN STUDY

We worked with one of India's oldest and most established special schools, called Nai Disha. Nai Disha is a part of Tamana.org, a nonprofit organization with four centers across Delhi. Nai Disha is dedicated towards providing young adults with developmental disabilities physical, emotional and functional independence by imparting vocational training and skill development. During the school's annual Diwali Mela (fair celebrating the Indian festival of lights), we conducted a user-centered design study by setting up two games in one of the school's classroom. The study had several purposes:

1. Capturing teachers', students' and their parents' initial reactions to such a system

2. Defining a gesture vocabulary for three main interaction goals, namely navigation, selection and object manipulation

3. Identifying application areas or topics where gesture-based interaction can assist the students.

Setting up the installation during the Diwali Mela provided an event to introduce the researchers to various stakeholders - school staff, teachers, children and their parents - in an informal public gathering. This helped create an open and relaxed atmosphere to experience and discuss gesture-based applications, and an opportunity to gain insights into the stakeholders' expectation and acceptance of such technology.

We designed two applications for the study to understand how the children interact with the screen space and select objects using free form gestures. The games provided an opportunity to identify gestures, which are fun, enjoyable and comfortable. The trials were recorded in short video clips, photos, questionnaires and observations. The data was analyzed by the researchers. The two applications and our findings from the user-centered design study are described next.

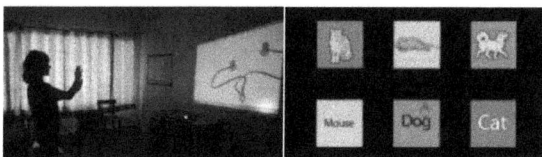

Figure 1: left) a researcher demoing the painting game, (right) interface of the flash card based animal matching game.

3.1 Free-form painting

The free-form painting application was used as an introduction to gesture-based interaction without pre-defined tasks. The objective was to observe natural, comfortable and intuitive hand gestures, a novelty in the educational setting, and to derive gestures for navigating the screen space. Participants could use their hands as paint brushes and draw on a white canvas. The right hand would draw in red while the left in blue. The width of the hand-brush was controlled by moving the hand away (thinner) or towards (thicker) the white canvas. The participants were free to draw any shape or image they liked, as shown in Figure 1(left).

3.2 Animal matching game

The animal matching game was based on flash cards used extensively in Autism interventions, and for example also in the TOBY Playpad [43]. The game used pointing, with a dwell time of one second for selection, and drag-and-drop for object manipulation. There were three cards on the top row and three placeholders on the bottom row (Figure 1, right). The top row of cards was initially stacked and opened up after a swipe gesture was made, similar to the gesture of spreading out a deck of cards.

Participants selected a card by pointing at it using their right hand for one second. A successful selection attached the card to the cursor following the right hand. The attached card had to be dragged close to the correct placeholder in the row below. Thus, when a card (animal picture) was near its correct placeholder (text), the card animatedly flew on top of the placeholder, resembling magnetism [25]. To make the game simpler for students who could not spell, the flash cards could also be matched based on the background colors.

3.3 System description

Both of the applications were based on an in-house framework, utilizing the Microsoft Kinect sensor for gesture recognition, and consisting of three main processes; a Kinect service, graphics engine and application core logic. The Kinect service is a thin client over the Microsoft Kinect SDK that connects to the core logic. The Kinect is used to track the user's body movements. For the two applications, we tracked only the upper body joints for the gestures. The graphical content is rendered using the Panda 3D[3] engine. The core logic is a Python[4] based application that takes the Kinect data as input, based on which the relevant content is displayed via the graphics engine.

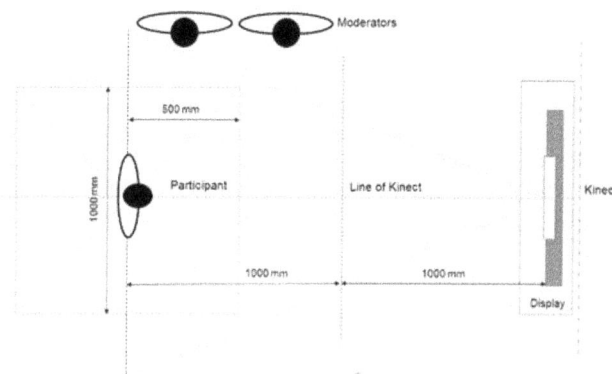

Figure 2: Game Setup showing the interaction space

The system responds to the user closest to the device in front of it in a 1 meter by 1 meter area, 1.5 meters away from the Kinect (see Figure 2). We call this the active area, that is, the area in which a user can interact with the application using gestures. An onscreen hand cursor was present in both the applications to help guide the gesture interaction. Each applications starts with a verbal welcome message when a user enters the active area, followed by a short music clip and the screen fades out from black to the game screen. While the user is in the active area, the system responds to her gestures as defined by the game. When there is no longer a user in the active area, the game screen goes back to black.

---

[3] https://www.panda3d.org/

[4] https://www.python.org/

3.4 Procedure

The students visited the Diwali Mela setup with their parents and were encouraged to try both applications. Students interacted one by one, first with the free form painting, and then the animal matching game. Students were asked to 'paint' something with the first application and their parents usually suggested an object, such as a tree, or to write their name. Instructions were kept brief to identify gestures that are intuitive and natural. Students interacted for as long as they liked, usually stopping once the white canvas was colored over 70%. For the second application, students were asked to 'match the animals'. The matching game was based on the already familiar flash cards, and students understood the task quite easily, and were able to finish the task.

Waiting students and parents, and other audience members were instructed to clap after every student interacted with an application. This was done as a reward for the students who tried out the unfamiliar environment and as a motivation for subsequent participants. Parents were interviewed after their child interacted with both of the applications and requested to fill in a feedback form. The feedback questionnaire aimed to understand the parents' experience of watching their child try the applications and their own expectations and initial reactions to the technology.

3.5 Findings

In total, 18 students with developmental disabilities, that is, individuals with mental retardation, autism, or Down syndrome, (IQ M=49.78, SD=10; SCQ M=51.6, SD=10) [36] participated in our user-centered design study out of which parents of 14 of them filled in the responses after their child had interacted with both the applications. For the remaining four parents' responses, either the parent was in a hurry or their child had interacted very briefly with only one of the applications.

3.5.1 Gestures for navigating the screen space

The onscreen cursor made it visually possible to imagine the hand-cursor as a brush to paint a red or blue line on the white canvas. From our observations of the gestures performed, the students formed circles using both hands with ease, as shown in Figure 3. Several participants, on the insistence of their parents, would try to write their name with large alphabetical gestures. Thus, we decided to design interaction-gestures using both hands with onscreen cursors for our main application.

3.5.2 Gesture for selection

There were two main gestures that were performed for selection: dwelling on an object or punching a fist towards the object. The punching gesture was popular and fun, but was not considered socially appropriate by the parents and teachers present. This is because the school experts shared concerns over the students' tendency towards repetitive behavior and the socially negative impact of a punching gesture outside of gameplay. This finding resonates with the role of culture and context in defining socially acceptable gestures [3].

For selection via pointing with a dwell-time, we observed that the dwell time of one second was too short for the participants and it triggered several unintentional selections, as the several participants verbally exclaimed 'oh' when a card was attached to their onscreen cursor. Thus, for our main application, we decided to use the dwell time of 1.5 seconds for selection. A participant making a selection by pointing is shown in Figure 4(left). Our applications also worked well for a participant using a wheelchair without using the Microsoft Kinect SDK's seated mode for gesture recognitions. Thus, with gestures requiring only upper body motion tracking, applications can be inclusive and comfortable for a larger group of participants.

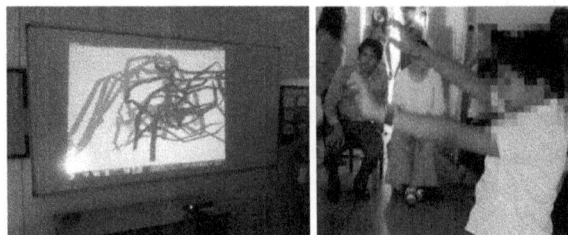

Figure 3: Participant creating midair circles

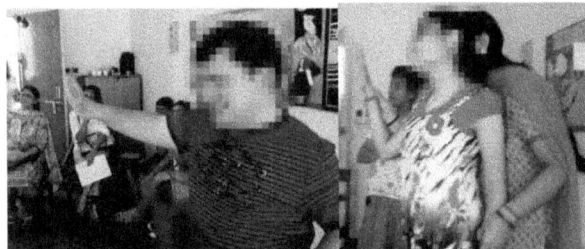

Figure 4: (left) Selection gesture with a one second dwell time and (right) parent helping a child with drag and drop gesture

3.5.3 Gesture for object manipulation

The animal matching game required moving a selected animal picture from the top row to a placeholder on the bottom row using the gesture inspired by the desktop drag and drop metaphor. Although all participants matched the three animal pictures to their placeholders, it was observed to be rather by chance than by choice, since the placeholders were *magnetic*. Thus, for object manipulation drag and drop was observed to be difficult. Figure 4 shows a participant being guided by her mother for the animal matching game. For our main application, we decided not to employ the drag and drop. Further research is required to identify a suitable gesture for this purpose.

3.5.4 Parent questionnaire

All of the parents agreed that their child enjoyed using the system and only 21% said it was tiring to use. Three out of the 14 children had used some form of gesture interaction before. Initial reaction of parents included excitement (50%) or being impressed (50%) by the games. 79% of the parents were enthusiastic about using gestures for educational interventions, while only one parent was skeptical and two did not comment. All but one parent had a positive overall impression of the system and that one parent had neither negative nor positive impression. 12 out of the 14 parents said they would consider using gestures for educational interventions in the future, while one parent wished the system worked better. Several parents, and also teachers, appreciated the inherent physical nature of the interaction, and commented that such games are good for body movement and encouraging physical activity. They hoped to see more rewards and motivation within the gameplay to encourage their child.

3.5.5 Potential application topics

Together with the teachers and parents at the Diwali Mela, we conducted a short focus group exercise to identify topics that are currently difficult to teach with traditional pedagogical methods and would greatly benefit from real world simulations with gesture-based interaction. These topics included monetary transactions, time management, planning or scheduling of events, working with constraints such as time or a budget, and the concept of currency (mainly because the size/shape/weight of Indian coins and notes does not relate to its value). Moreover, several teachers suggested designing an application that can simulate real world scenarios to assist in learning a life skill.

One of the life skills deemed important by the parents and teachers, was being able to purchase day to day items from a local *kirana* store, which are grocery stores in India (refer to Figure 5). The teachers explained that several students, who are able to communicate with strangers, are taken to the nearby market to practice buying an item, such as toothpaste, from the local store using a certain amount of money. However, sometimes a student is socially mistreated by strangers or the shopkeeper. Moreover, not all students are comfortable with all the processes involved in a visit to the local store, and the teachers are unable to extend the visit to these students. The school does not employ any other methods for teaching transactional calculations than traditional math classes and the occasional field trips to the local market.

Based on these discussions, it was decided that the real world scenario of buying an item from a *Kirana* store would be simulated in a gesture-based application and evaluated with the students who were not included in the monthly visits to the local store near the school. The details of the application, its interaction and design decisions are explained next.

Figure 5: A kirana store in India

4. KIRANA APPLICATION

In designing the *Kirana* application we broke down the life-skill into several smaller tasks: knowing the items to buy (decision making), asking for them from the shopkeeper (social interactions), looking up the price for each item, knowing if an item can be bought with the available cash (arithmetic), handing over the cash (social interaction), calculating the balance (arithmetic), and taking the balance and items (social interaction). In India, each item has an *M.R.P.* (maximum retail price), which is required by law to be printed on the item cover, and is usually the price charged by stores in New Delhi for the item. Therefore, students are also taught the concept of *M.R.P.*, which is contextually and culturally relevant for them.

These smaller tasks, which are independently achievable, bring out the bigger goal of 'buying groceries'. Furthermore, the application aimed to promote socially acceptable and expected behaviors within the Indian context of *Kirana* shops, making the learning from the application, when translated to the real world environment, culturally appropriate. We did not include a shopkeeper–avatar in the application, as simulating social interactions to the required degree is complex. The application was designed to allow a teacher or moderator to imitate the social interactions based on individual needs.

Our research goal was to *validate the potential of gesture-based interaction in translation of learning of a life skill from an application to real world scenarios for individuals with developmental disabilities,* with a focus on the Indian social and cultural context.

The *Kirana* interface simulates a typical store layout. Customers stand outside the counter of the store and point to items they want to purchase. The screen has two shelves behind a table counter-top containing food items that can be bought, as shown in Figure 6. The items are randomly arranged at the start of the sessions, removing learnability of item placements. The application was built on the same in-house framework as the games in the user-centered design study applications described in section 3.3. The setup was also similar, that is, participants could interact within the 1 m² active area 1.5 meters from the Kinect (see Figure 2).

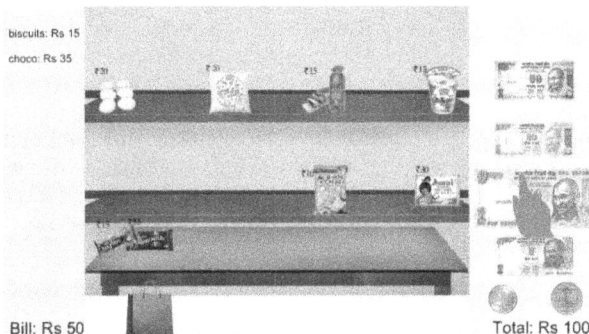

Figure 6: *Kirana*- buying items on the table by paying using a 10 rupees note

Based on the user-centered design study findings (section 3.4), gestures for interacting with the screen space and object selection used an onscreen cursor. Pointing with a dwell time of 1.5 second selects an object (item and money), which then animatedly slides to the table. This interaction eliminated the need of an explicit drag and drop gesture, which was found to be difficult (section 3.5.3). Moreover, since the application focus is primarily on three aspects of purchasing (decision making, social interaction and mathematics) the explicit gesture of handing over money was simplified in the application.

The session starts when a participant stands in front of the Kinect and is greeted by a female voice welcoming her to *Kirana*. The right side of the screen has the available money with the total amount displayed at the bottom. The left side shows the billing of items as they are bought allowing the participants to see the list of items they have bought and the total bill. The bill format is in line with *Kirana* shopkeepers who provide a written bill for all items purchased. The item's price is automatically added to the bill on the left. Once there is at least one item to pay for, the participant can select any denomination of money using her right hand. This two-handed selection mechanism was added to encourage increased bodily movement and isolate the item selection from the money selection. Each item and money is accompanied by its spoken name and each transaction process has audio feedback. For example, when the balance is returned, the female voice says *here is your balance*. The application caters to the various endings: running out of money, or not enough money left to buy an item. For these scenarios, the female voice informs, for example, *you have no money left*. This is followed by a textual *well done* and an audio feedback to indicate the end of the session.

The animations of items and money were slow and sequential: there was only one item or money movement, from the shelves or the wallet, to the table at a time. Once an animation was finished, the balance was returned back from the table to the wallet. Updating the bill and total amounts was also in sync with the series of animation. The application also supports customization; the type of item, its price and total available money in the wallet on the right hand side could be changed between sessions. However, this feature was not used in the evaluations.

5. EVALUATION AND RESULTS

The evaluation consisted of four phases. In the phases I and III, we conducted manual mathematical tests as a part of pre and post evaluation trials. These tests aimed to ascertain the mathematical ability (addition and subtraction) of the participant. The tests included single-digit subtractions, 2-4 digit additions, and single digit multiplications. The mathematical tests were evaluated by a teacher and a score was provided for each participant.

In phase II, *Kirana* was installed in a classrooms and sessions were conducted for three weeks - with every participant once per week. The setup is shown in Figure 2. A line was marked 1.5 meters away from the Kinect to help the students' positon themselves for good gesture recognition. The participant was given a grocery list by the teacher and a fixed amount of money which she had to use to purchase the items from *Kirana*. Each participant was asked to complete the following tasks per session:

(i) You need to select items for yourself for breakfast from *Kirana* using your grocery list. For example bread, chips, milk and biscuits.

(ii) You have a budget of 100 Rupees to pay for the items you selected. Also check the balance returned by shopkeeper.

Data from the sessions included automated system logs with task times, items bought and monetary transaction details, moderator observations and a behavioral analysis of the participant to record positive and negative emotional behaviors or signals.

In phase IV, participants visited an actual *kirana* store near the school and were asked to buy several items. A moderator observed participant behavior with respect to the three sub-tasks: decision making (choosing an item from the list to buy), social interaction (talking to the shopkeeper and asking for an item) and mathematical ability (knowing how much to pay and balance to expect). Pre-shopping evaluations were not carried out because all participants were previously unable to shop according to their parents and teachers, and we did not want to make them uncomfortable. In order to understand the learning offered by the application, participants were not taught mathematical concepts in other class sessions during the evaluation.

The evaluations were conducted by two school teachers. This reduced any anxiety and complex social dynamics the participant might experience due to an unfamiliar presence. Teachers are also better equipped to understood nuances and implications of the participants' behavior and reaction to the application or its tasks, responsible for and involved in all technical educational interventions within the school, and had participated in the design and development of the application. A workshop was conducted to discuss the evaluation goals and data collection requirements.

5.1 Participants

18 individuals (identified as P1-P18 in the following) with developmental disabilities participated in our evaluation (5 individuals with Down syndrome, 8 individuals with mental retardation, 3 individuals with autism and 2 individuals with cerebral palsy and mental retardation). There were 14 males and 4

females aged between 16 to 39 years ($M=26$, $SD=5.4$) with IQ ($M=46$, $SD=11$) and SCQ [36] ($M=58$, $SD=16$). The participants were recruited from the eighth grade of the school and they (a) understood the concept of left and right, (b) communicated verbally with the mediators, (c) understood instructions given to them, (d) had an awareness of self and body, (e) did not participate in the user-centered design study (mentioned in section 3), and (f) were previously unable to shop independently.

5.2 Results: Overview

While almost all the participants were excited and happy to play the game, two of them reported interaction fatigue. Four participants were observed to have limited left hand movement for two-hand interactions (items were selected using the left hand) although they did not explicitly mention any fatigue or pain. We also observed that the time taken to select items at the center of the screen was longer because five other participants first pointed to top-left corner of the screen and then moved towards the bottom right. Further research in required to identify optimum interaction gesture paths for individuals with varying motor capabilities.

The sessions were conducted during an Indian summer, and so surprisingly we observed that two participants expressed their desire to be able to buy cold beverages instead of food items from *Kirana*. One of the participants was upset at not being able to play more frequently because of her therapy schedules. We also observed that most of the participants felt bad if they were unable to complete a task or if they felt they were slow. At one instance, we noticed a participant slap her left hand to express her frustration.

With each progressive session, participants were more expressive and verbal than usual, and as expected, also showed improvements in the sub-tasks. For example, several participants navigated more carefully to items in the later trials. During the sessions, a line was drawn on the floor to enable participants to know the exact location from where to interact. In the later trials, we observed improvements in terms of understanding where to stand and reposition themselves.

5.3 Results: phase I and III

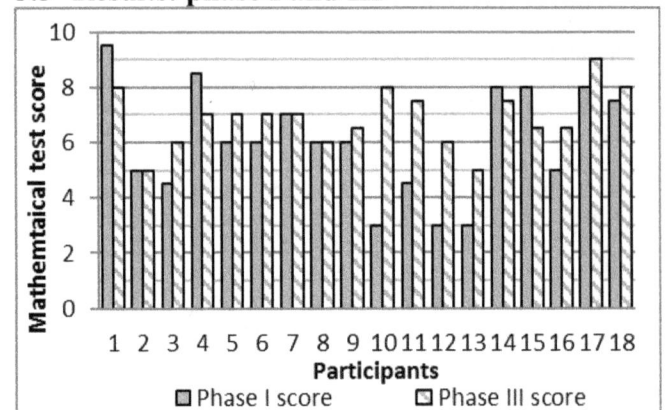

Figure 7: Phase I mathematical test scores with improvements seen in Phase III for participants P1 – P18

Figure 7 shows mathematical scores from phases I and III for each of the participants. In phase I (pre-trial) the highest score was 9.5 and lowest was 3 from a maximum 10 marks. In phase III, the lowest score was 5 and highest was 8. A score of 3 indicates knowledge of numbers from 1-10 and familiarity with money mainly notes, while a score of 6 indicates knowledge of numbers from 1-100, familiarity with notes and coins, and simple two-digit additions and single-digit subtractions. A score of 10 would ideally mean that the participant has knowledge of numbers from 1-100, is familiar with notes and coins, and is comfortable with mental arithmetic including single-digit multiplication.

We observed an average improvement of 8.3% between phases I and III. Four participants showed a decrease in performance. It can also be noted that participants with a lower score benefitted more from the application than those with a score of 6 or above in phase I. Further research is required to observe whether long term evaluations would be beneficial for participants with a score of 6 or above, or whether they require increased difficultly in tasks.

5.4 Results: phase II

A total of 218 items were purchased by the participants in the three-week pilot. During the first week, the participants spent an average of 9.3 minutes (*SD*=4.5) per session buying while during the second and third week they spent 6 minutes (*SD*=4.4) and 4.5 minutes (*SD*=2.2) respectively. Consequently, participants spent an average of 2 minutes 34 seconds per item (*SD*=1.39) during the first week, 1 minute 43 seconds (*SD*=1.94) during the second week and 1 minute 13 seconds (*SD*=0.57) during the third week. This reduction in buying time per item indicates that participants became comfortable with the transactions and interactions with the application, over the course of the evaluations. We note here the limitation in measuring task time; we cannot differentiate the time taken for decision making and that of the actual interaction.

The participants spent an average of 71 Rupees during the first week, 80 Rupees during the second week and 63 Rupees during the third week. The moderators gave each participant an option to either select the items to purchase from the list or to select on their own. Surprisingly, we observed a steady increase in the preference to buy the items from the list (16% in session 1, 50% in session 2 and 73% in session 3) over the three sessions.

5.5 Results: phase IV

Actual store visits in phase IV provided highly ecologically valid way of translating the learning from virtual to real world scenarios. 12 of the 18 participants were taken to a local *kirana* store near the school in one session. Four participants (P3, P5, P16 and P18) were not a part of this activity because the teachers assessed they needed more practice with the application and two participants (P2 and P11) had moved to another school after phase III. It should be noted this was the first time the participants had come to an actual store by themselves. A moderator observed the participants interact with the shopkeeper and buy items from a given list – similar to the task in phase II.

5.5.1 Decision-making

Participants were able to connect the tasks during the visit to the tasks in *Kirana,* and purchase items from the given shopping list. The moderator observed a high degree of cooperation among the participants and they helped each other out wherever possible. This included, for example, crossing the road. The most popular items during the visit were cold beverages due to the Indian summer.

5.5.2 Social interaction

Participants who were feeling shy would observe the others interact with the shopkeeper before approaching the store (P9, P12, P15, and P17). One participant (P17) made the valid observation that everyone should take a bill from the shopkeeper so that the purchasing amounts can be checked by an adult later. Surprisingly, three usually nonverbal participants (P12, P13 and P14) were very responsive and able to interact with the shopkeeper.

5.5.3 Mathematical ability

Participants who had a high mathematical score (greater than 6) were comfortable with the concept of money and transaction involving arithmetic (P1, P4, P6 and P9). However, two participants gave all money with them to the shopkeeper: one out of nervousness (P12) and the other (P7) had problems reading the decimal place in price because of the small font size on the packet.

Overall, all the participants were able to locate an item's M.R.P., understood that money is exchanged when *purchasing* the item, and expressed a positive attitude towards purchasing. However, as expected, the arithmetic aspect of calculating costs and balance was observed to be highly dependent on one's mathematical ability. Several participants understood the relation between items and costs such that they only selected items they knew they would be able to purchase with the amount of money they had.

6. DISCUSSION

The following summarizes the benefits of our work as uncovered during our user-centered design process and *Kirana* evaluations. With our promising findings, we wish to encourage others researchers to work on applications that simulate real world environments to promote self-efficacy for individuals with developmental disabilities.

6.1 Promoting self-efficacy

In our evaluations, we observed improvements in mathematical ability, based on the teacher's assessment, and translatable learning from the application to an actual local store. We believe that our application does the necessary groundwork in preparing individuals with developmental disabilities for purchasing items of need from local stores, thereby teaching them a valuable life skill that promotes self-efficacy.

However, when real life skills are being taught, particularly to individuals with developmental disabilities, cultural aspects must be considered. This is particularly relevant in the developing world where social awareness about individuals with disabilities varies greatly. The socio-cultural norms of a society dictate the degree of inclusivity and integration of individuals with developmental disabilities [3] and [16]. Additionally, individuals with developmental disabilities, such as autism, display a tendency towards repetitive behavior and teaching socially unacceptable gestures might increase their isolation, even if the gesture is fun during gameplay [1].

We developed an application that was culturally relevant and socially acceptable to the community by following a user-centered design approach and including the various stakeholders and decision makers – parents, caregivers, teachers, and therapists. Thus, applications that promote self-efficacy should employ gestures and interactions that are socially and culturally relevant and acceptable for the specific life-skill.

6.2 Simulating real world scenarios

Gesture-based applications can simulate real world scenarios in a safe and controlled environment through interactions that are appropriate and relevant to a life-skill. Using free form body gestures provides a mechanism for more inclusive social interaction and team work, especially when compared with touch screens that have limited form factor and surface area to support multiple users. The inherent nature of embodied interaction [42] makes for an immersive and engaging experience. In *Kirana*, even though it only supported a single active user, the interaction was visible to the moderators who could then prompt and encourage the participant, thus also involving them in the scenario.

6.3 Designing for technology acceptance

We note here the collaborative nature of our work, from the user-centered design study to the *Kirana* evaluations and analysis. Since the application was designed and developed with teachers, therapists and parents, who provided valuable insights and experience, there was no resistance towards technology acceptance or adoption. Thus, the technology was integrated within the classroom environment with ease.

Additionally, we identified ways to address the challenges in introducing new technological interventions for individuals with development disabilities in the developing world. First, economic barriers for technologies that are too costly can be overcome by designing applications that can be integrated within schools, and can be personalized and customized for use by a larger group of individuals. Second, resource constrains can be overcome through collaborations between schools, universities and industry partners. Third, the digital divide can be reduced by spreading awareness of the benefits of technology within schools and to parents.

Our main contribution is not the technology behind the *Kirana* application as such, but rather the focus on the currently overlooked potential of interactive technology for providing translatable learnings to real world scenarios, when using contextually appropriated gesture-based applications to teach life skills. In India, this technology is rare and novel, and thus its acceptance remains largely unexplored. Based on our findings, we can assume that following a user centered design approach helps reduce the challenges in technology integration.

6.4 Providing control to the teacher

Due to the wide range of abilities of an individual, the teacher or moderator should be able to customize the application based on individual capabilities and interest, as also stated in previous research by Bartoli et al. [1], [2], [38]. In *Kirana*, the teacher guided the social interaction and the task, for example, by giving a shopping list. This enabled the teacher to customize the learning, even on the fly. Moreover, number, type and price of items, and the total amount of money in the wallet could be changed easily between sessions. By providing control to the teachers, we believe we also increased the acceptance of technology within the classroom environment.

6.5 Providing multimodal feedback

Individuals with developmental difficulties find it easier to select items that have both visual (change in size) and auditory (name of the item is said aloud) feedback, instead of only one. This reinforced multimodal feedback helps overcome visual or auditory impairments, if any, and provides multiple stimuli for attention [1] [2]. In *Kirana*, each visual object, upon being selected, also had an auditory feedback.

6.6 Providing clear start and end of gameplay

To avoid ambiguity and confusion during interaction, it is extremely important to provide a clear start and end of gameplay. In *Kirana*, when the participant moves out of the Kinect's active area, the application screen turns black to indicate an end of interaction. The application also catered to various end-scenarios such as not enough money left to buy an item, or running out of money or items to buy. Each of these scenarios stated the reason for the end, followed by a visual and audio "well done" feedback to conclude the session.

6.7 Providing serial and structured content

Overall, our findings show that gesture-based applications that simulate real world scenarios can be used to teach a life skill to individuals with developmental disabilities. This is achieved by designing interaction that is socially and culturally appropriate and breaking down complex tasks that require social, mathematical and decision-making skills. We recommend such complex tasks to be broken down into a sequence of smaller achievable steps. If the animation and other visual media content also follow the same step by step order, individuals with developmental disabilities can follow the progress of the tasks with ease. As an example, in *Kirana*, the purchasing animations were slow and sequential.

7. CONCLUSION

This paper presented an application that employs gesture-based interaction for teaching a real world skill, of buying groceries, to individuals with developmental disabilities in India. By following a user-centered approach and including various stakeholders and decision makers – parents, caregivers, teachers, and therapists – we developed an application that was culturally relevant and socially acceptable by the community. *Kirana* simulated the real world scenario of pointing to an item to buy it, while interacting with a shopkeeper at a local grocery store in New Delhi. The results of our evaluations show promising translations of learnings from the application to a real world context. Our findings provide strong support in favor of gesture-based systems for enabling teachers and educationists across the globe to impart life skills to individuals with developmental disabilities.

8. ACKNOWLEDGMENTS

Our thanks to the school for their valuable time and guidance, and a special thanks to all the participants. We also like to thank Sanna Grönlund for developing the graphics for the game.

9. REFERENCES

[1] Bartoli, L., Corradi, C., Garzotto, F., & Valoriani, M. (2013, June). Exploring motion-based touchless games for autistic children's learning. Proc. Interaction Design and Children (IDC) (pp. 102-111). ACM.

[2] Bartoli, L., Garzotto, F., Gelsomini, M., Oliveto, L., & Valoriani, M. (2014). Designing and Evaluating Touchless Playful Interaction for ASD Children. Proc. Interaction Design and Children (IDC)

[3] Boujarwah, F. A., Hong, H., Abowd, G. D., & Arriaga, R. I. (2011). Towards a framework to situate assistive technology design in the context of culture. In The proceedings of the 13th international ACM SIGACCESS conference on Computers and accessibility (pp. 19-26). ACM.

[4] Bauminger-Zviely, N., Eden, S., Zancanaro, M., Weiss, P. L., & Gal, E. (2013). Increasing social engagement in children with high-functioning autism spectrum disorder using collaborative technologies in the school environment. Autism, 17(3), 317-339.

[5] Chang, Y. J., Chen, S. F., & Huang, J. D. (2011). A Kinect-based system for physical rehabilitation: A pilot study for young adults with motor disabilities. Research in developmental disabilities, 32(6), 2566-2570.

[6] Coles, C. D., Strickland, D. C., Padgett, L., & Bellmoff, L. (2007). Games that "work": Using computer games to teach alcohol-affected children about fire and street safety. Research in developmental disabilities, 28(5), 518-530.

[7] Christinaki, E., Triantafyllidis, G., & Vidakis, N. (2010). A gesture-controlled Serious Game for teaching emotion recognition skills to preschoolers with autism. In Proceedings of fdg. 2013, 417-418.

[8] Cromby, J. J., Standen, P. J., Newman, J., & Tasker, H. (1996). Successful transfer to the real world of skills practised in a virtual environment by students with severe learning difficulties. In Proc. 1st European Conference on Disability, Virtual Reality, and Associated Technologies (pp. 8-10).

[9] Dias, M. B., & Brewer, E. (2009). How computer science serves the developing world. Communications of the ACM, 52(6), 74-80.

[10] Damasio, A. R. (1999). The feeling of what happens: Body and emotion in the making of consciousness. Houghton Mifflin Harcourt.

[11] Dourish, P. (2004). Where the action is: the foundations of embodied interaction. MIT press.

[12] Filmer, D. (2008). Disability, poverty, and schooling in developing countries: results from 14 household surveys. The World Bank Economic Review, 22(1), 141-163.

[13] Firth, N. I. A. L. L. (2012). Kinect cameras watch for autism. New scientist, 214(2863), 17

[14] González-Ortega, D., Díaz-Pernas, F. J., Martínez-Zarzuela, M., & Antón-Rodríguez, M. (2014). A Kinect-based system for cognitive rehabilitation exercises monitoring. Computer methods and programs in biomedicine, 113(2), 620-631.

[15] Gover, M. R. (1996). The Embodied Mind: Cognitive Science and Human Experience (Book). Mind, Culture, and Activity, 3(4), 295-299.

[16] Grinker, R. R. (2008). Unstrange minds: Remapping the world of autism. Da Capo Press.

[17] Kandalaft, M. R., Didehbani, N., Krawczyk, D. C., Allen, T. T., & Chapman, S. B. (2013). Virtual reality social cognition training for young adults with high-functioning autism. Journal of autism and developmental disorders, 43(1), 34-44.

[18] Ke, F., & Im, T. (2013). Virtual-reality-based social interaction training for children with high-functioning autism. The Journal of Educational Research, 106(6), 441-461.

[19] Khakhar, J., & Madhvanath, S. (2010, November). Jollymate: Assistive technology for young children with dyslexia. In Frontiers in Handwriting Recognition (ICFHR), 2010 International Conference on (pp. 576-580). IEEE.

[20] Lahiri, U., Bekele, E., Dohrmann, E., Warren, Z., & Sarkar, N. (2013). Design of a virtual reality based adaptive response technology for children with autism. Neural Systems and Rehabilitation Engineering, IEEE Transactions on, 21(1), 55-64.

[21] Lakoff, G., & Johnson, M. (1999). Philosophy in the flesh: The embodied mind and its challenge to western thought. Basic books.

[22] Lindgren, R., & Johnson-Glenberg, M. (2013). Emboldened by embodiment six precepts for research on embodied learning and mixed reality. Educational Researcher, 42(8), 445-452.

[23] Lotan, M., Yalon-Chamovitz, S., & Weiss, P. L. T. (2009). Improving physical fitness of individuals with intellectual and developmental disability through a Virtual Reality Intervention Program. Research in developmental disabilities, 30(2), 229-239.

[24] Malinverni, L., MoraGuiard, J., Padillo, V., Mairena, M., Hervás, A., & Pares, N. (2014, June). Participatory design strategies to enhance the creative contribution of children with special needs. Proc. Interaction Design and Children (IDC) (pp. 85-94). ACM.

[25] Mäkelä, V., Heimonen, T., & Turunen, M. (2014). Magnetic Cursor: Improving Target Selection in Freehand Pointing Interfaces. In Proceedings of The International Symposium on Pervasive Displays (PerDis '14), 112, ACM,

[26] Mennecke, B. E., Triplett, J. L., Hassall, L. M., Conde, Z. J., & Heer, R. (2011). An examination of a theory of embodied social presence in virtual worlds*. Decision Sciences, 42(2), 413-450.

[27] Moore, D., Cheng, Y., McGrath, P., & Powell, N. J. (2005). Collaborative virtual environment technology for people with autism. Focus on Autism and Other Developmental Disabilities, 20(4), 231-243.

[28] Padgett, L. S., Strickland, D., and Coles, C. D. (2006). Case study: Using a virtual reality computer game to teach fire safety skills to children diagnosed with fetal alcohol syndrome. Journal of Pediatric Psychology, 31(1), 65–70.

[29] Parasuram, K. (2006). Variables that affect teachers' attitudes towards disability and inclusive education in Mumbai, India. Disability & Society, 21(3), 231-242.

[30] Parés, N., Carreras, A., Durany, J., Ferrer, J., Freixa, P., Gómez, D., & Sanjurjo, À. (2005, June). Promotion of creative activity in children with severe autism through visuals in an interactive multisensory environment. In Proceedings of the 2005 conference on Interaction design and children (pp. 110-116). ACM.

[31] Parsons, S., Mitchell, P., & Leonard, A. (2004). The use and understanding of virtual environments by adolescents with autistic spectrum disorders. Journal of Autism and Developmental disorders, 34(4), 449-466.

[32] Parsons, S., & Cobb, S. (2011). State-of-the-art of virtual reality technologies for children on the autism spectrum. European Journal of Special Needs Education, 26(3), 355-366.

[33] Parsons, T. D., Rizzo, A. A., Rogers, S., & York, P. (2009). Virtual reality in paediatric rehabilitation: A review. Developmental Neurorehabilitation, 12(4), 224-238.

[34] Reid, D. (2002). Virtual reality and the person-environment experience. CyberPsychology & Behavior, 5(6), 559-564.

[35] Ringland, K. E., Zalapa, R., Neal, M., Escobedo, L., Tentori, M., & Hayes, G. R. (2014, September). SensoryPaint: a multimodal sensory intervention for children with neurodevelopmental disorders. In Proceedings of the 2014 ACM International Joint Conference on Pervasive and Ubiquitous Computing (pp. 873-884). ACM.

[36] Michael Rutter, Anthony Bailey, and Cathrine Lord. 2003. The social communication questionnaire: Manual. Western Psychological Services.

[37] Sampath, H., Sivaswamy, J., & Indurkhya, B. (2010). Assistive systems for children with dyslexia and autism. ACM Sigaccess Accessibility and Computing, (96), 32-36.

[38] Sharma, S., Srivastava, S., Achary, K., Varkey, B., Heimonen, T., Hakulinen, J. S., ... & Rajput, N. (2016, February). Promoting Joint Attention with Computer Supported Collaboration in Children with Autism. In Proceedings of the 19th ACM Conference on Computer-Supported Cooperative Work & Social Computing (pp. 1560-1571). ACM.

[39] Standen, P. J., & Brown, D. J. (2005). Virtual reality in the rehabilitation of people with intellectual disabilities: review. Cyberpsychology & behavior, 8(3), 272-282.

[40] Thompson, E. (2007). Mind in life: Biology, phenomenology, and the sciences of mind. Harvard University Press.

[41] Wallace, S., Parsons, S., Westbury, A., White, K., White, K., & Bailey, A. (2010). Sense of presence and atypical social judgments in immersive virtual environments Responses of adolescents with Autism Spectrum Disorders. Autism, 14(3), 199-213.

[42] Wilson, M. (2002). Six views of embodied cognition. Psychonomic bulletin & review, 9(4)

[43] Venkatesh, S., Phung, D., Duong, T., Greenhill, S., & Adams, B. (2013, April). TOBY: early intervention in autism through technology. In Proceedings of the SIGCHI Conference on Human Factors in Computing Systems (pp. 3187-3196). ACM

Customizable 3D Printed Tactile Maps as Interactive Overlays

Brandon Taylor
Carnegie Mellon University
5000 Forbes Ave
Pittsburgh, PA 15213
+1 412 268 2000
bttaylor@cs.cmu.edu

Anind Dey
Carnegie Mellon University
5000 Forbes Ave
Pittsburgh, PA 15213
+1 412 268 2000
anind@cs.cmu.edu

Dan Siewiorek
Carnegie Mellon University
5000 Forbes Ave
Pittsburgh, PA 15213
+1 412 268 2000
dps@cs.cmu.edu

Asim Smailagic
Carnegie Mellon University
5000 Forbes Ave
Pittsburgh, PA 15213
+1 412 268 2000
asim@cs.cmu.edu

ABSTRACT

Though tactile maps have been shown to be useful tools for visually impaired individuals, their availability has been limited by manufacturing and design costs. In this paper, we present a system that uses 3D printing to (1) make tactile maps more affordable to produce, (2) allow visually impaired individuals to independently design and customize maps, and (3) provide interactivity using widely available mobile devices. Our system consists of three parts: a web interface, a modeling algorithm, and an interactive touchscreen application. Our web interface, hosted at www.tactilemaps.net, allows visually impaired individuals to create maps of any location on the globe while specifying (1) what features to map, (2) how the features should be represented by textures, and (3) where to place markers and labels. Our modeling algorithm accommodates user specifications to create map models with (1) multiple layers of continuously varying textures and (2) markers of various geometric shapes or braille characters. Our interactive application uses a novel approach to 3D printing tactile maps using conductive filament to provide touchscreen overlays that allow users to dynamically interact with the maps on a wide range of mobile devices. This paper details the implementation of our system. We also present findings from a user study validating the usability of our mapping interface and the utility of the maps produced. Finally, we discuss the limitations of our current implementation and the plans we have to improve our system based on feedback from our user study and additional interviews.

Categories and Subject Descriptors

• **Human-centered computing~Accessibility technologies** • *Human-centered computing~Haptic devices*

General Terms

Algorithms, Design, Experimentation, Human Factors.

Keywords

3D Printing; Tactile Maps

1. INTRODUCTION

Tactile maps are a well-established tool for providing visually impaired individuals with a spatial understanding of their

ASSETS '16, October 23-26, 2016, Reno, NV, USA
© 2016 ACM. ISBN 978-1-4503-4124-0/16/10...$15.00
DOI: http://dx.doi.org/10.1145/2982142.2982167

environment [10]. Unfortunately, the availability and utility of tactile maps are limited [27]. Whereas sighted individuals, thanks to online map repositories and modern graphical rendering techniques, can instantaneously produce virtually any map they may desire, visually impaired individuals are much more restricted in their access to customized maps. However, as the commercialization of 3D printers has driven down the cost of producing personalized physical artifacts [5], the opportunity to provide visually impaired individuals with tools for independently creating their own personal tactile maps, has arisen.

In this paper, we will introduce a set of tools and techniques that allow visually impaired individuals to create customized tactile map models. This work consists of three related parts. The first part is a website, designed with screen-reader compatibility in mind, which allows users to choose locations to map *and* specify a wide range of map features. The second part is a back end-algorithm which takes user-specified parameters from the website, downloads relevant data and generates 3D printable models of the specified region. Finally, we present an Android application that uses physical maps generated by our system and printed using a secondary conductive filament as a touchscreen overlay to provide dynamic touch interactivity to the maps.

This paper will provide an overview of previous literature related to creating customized tactile maps, highlighting the advantages that 3D printing can provide. It will then provide a detailed overview of each of the three parts of our system. Next, we will present the findings from our evaluation to verify that our system can be used independently and that our map models appropriately convey information. We will then discuss the limitations of our work, how it can be improved in the future and what the implications of such a system are.

2. BACKGROUND

There is a wide range of literature demonstrating the utility of tactile maps and specifying best-practice guidelines for the creation of tactile graphics [4,6,10,17,18]. Here we will focus on research most relevant to the various parts of our system.

2.1 3D Printed Maps

Tactile maps have a long history that predates 3D printing as a commercially available technology. Embossers and microcapsule paper can be used to automatically create maps from computer-generated images [23]. However, these techniques provide only two layers of depth and require expensive equipment. Braille embossers start at $1800 and can range up to $80,000 for high-speed machines [2]. Microcapsule, or swell paper, printers can be had for $1350 and also require specialized paper that costs more than a $1 per sheet [3]. Another production method, vacuum forming, offers a wider range of possible tactile features.

However, this comes with the cost of needing a master mold of the desired form, which does not readily lend itself to an automated process [25]. With the arrival of commercially available 3D printers, the possibility of obtaining the best of both approaches (automated modeling with a wider range of tactile surfaces) at a reduced cost has become a reality. 3D printers are already available for as little as a few hundred dollars [1] and unlike embossers or swell paper, the market for 3D printers is expected to continue expanding [5].

Unsurprisingly, a number of researchers began exploring the benefits 3D printing could provide to tactile map production. The HaptoRender project produced a 3D printed tactile map using OpenStreetMap data in 2009 [16]. Gotzelman and Pavkovic presented a more rigorous approach to automatically mapping OpenStreetMap data to flat, layered 2.1D models with braille annotations explicitly for use with 3D printers [14]. Ensuring that blind individuals could independently use their method was left to future work and their methodology is not publicly available at this time. Touch Mapper is a similarly motivated project, with a web interface that allows users to query addresses and download 3D map models of the surrounding area [20]. While Touch Mapper will generate maps that distinguish roads and rails, waterways, and buildings, it offers no labels (braille or otherwise) beyond a direction indicator and customization is restricted to a limited number of size and scale options.

In contrast to these efforts, we have explicitly focused on providing visually impaired individuals with the ability to create fully customizable maps. In doing so, we have developed a 3D modeling algorithm that moves beyond 2.1D layered maps to produce maps that can currently include: different textures for up to 5 different map features, topographical data, braille annotations, and the labeling of points designated by a set of geometric shapes or braille labels. Our system is designed to move beyond a one-size-fits all solution to automated map production and allow users to add, remove, and adjust how map features are represented tactilely.

2.2 Independently Customizable Tactile Maps
While designing algorithms that can produce 3D printable tactile maps from online repositories of geospatial data is certainly a necessary step in allowing visually impaired individuals to create customized maps, the algorithms themselves are not sufficient to solve the problem. An accessible interface that allows visually impaired individuals to independently produce the maps is also needed. Here we will examine the limits of projects that have explicitly focused on providing accessible interfaces.

The Smith-Kettlewell Eye Research Institute's Tactile Maps Automated Production (TMAP) project was an earlier effort with an explicit focus on allowing totally blind individuals to independently produce customized tactile street maps [23]. The TMAP project provided visually impaired users with an accessible web interface for specifying maps that would then generate digital files that could be printed using a braille embosser. The TMAP project was restricted to use within the United States as it relied on the US Census Bureau's Topologically Integrated Geographic Encoding and Referencing (TIGER) data. As of 2014, after an 11 year run, the TMAP project was decommissioned "due to aging digital infrastructure and is no longer available" [28]. A similar project was undertaken to provide independent tactile map creation within Japan [24]. The Japanese Tactile Maps Automated Creation System (TMACS) was later adapted to use OpenStreetMap [15] data allowing it to generate maps of locations across the globe [30]. To our knowledge, there are no other currently available services that have been demonstrated to allow visually impaired individuals to produce customized tactile maps.

Unlike these approaches, our system allows users to specify not only the locations they want to map, but also how and what geographic features should be represented on the tactile map. In this way, we have both a tool to help visually impaired individuals explore their environment and a platform by which we, as researchers, can examine user preferences and improve the design of 3D printed tactile maps.

2.3 Interactive Tactile Maps
One consistent difficulty in the generation of tactile maps lies in the problem of annotating features. While braille labeling, either directly on the map [14] or as a legend [23] is the most common solution, it is not without its own problems. Braille is understandable to only a small subset of the visually impaired population [11] and braille size requirements create real constraints on the density and size of maps that can be produced [6]. As a result of this and the constraints of the embossing machines commonly used, most tactile maps produced are printed on paper sizes A4 or larger [26]. It is perhaps unsurprising then, that most users indicate that they prefer to use tactile maps at home rather than while out and about [27].

Faced with these limitations, a number of researchers have explored methods for producing more interactive tactile maps. The TMAP project mentioned earlier, later incorporated Touch Graphics' Talking Tactile Tablet technology [22] to create the Talking TMAP [23]. The Talking TMAP used unique map numbers that users could manually enter into a tablet so that it could access a digital representation of the specified map. By aligning the embossed map with the tablet, touch interaction could then be registered with appropriate regions of the map. Unfortunately, this approach required both a specialized tablet and software that is no longer available.

By making use of commercially available multi-touch touchscreen devices along with raised line prints on paper, Brock et al. explored how various gestures could be used to enhance interactive tactile maps [7]. When evaluating their system, they reported a high level of user satisfaction; the fact that braille was not needed was the most frequently cited positive aspect [8]. Like the talking TMAP before it, this approach relies on a touchscreen that detects touches through a thin sheet of paper, precluding additional depth information that can be produced by 3D printing.

Efforts to provide interactivity to 3D printed tactile maps have been explored using computer vision. Linespace differs from other systems by using a much larger interactive surface (more than a square meter), which can allow for the persistence of more spatial information than other systems [29]. Users can also interact with the system by drawing or touching the surface with computer vision-based approaches detecting user actions. While Linespace is certainly a promising interface, the need for specialized hardware raises issues of availability while the scale clearly prohibits portability.

An explicitly portable approach that makes use of 3D printed maps has been explored by Gotzelmann [13]. By embedding visually detectable barcodes along the edges of 3D printable map models, a smartphone app can use the phone's camera to register uniquely produced maps. Additional computer vision can then be used to detect finger positions on top of the map and provide dynamic feedback. While the potential of such an approach is exciting, the need to hold the smartphone camera so that the map is in frame while pointing at features and tapping the phone leave an open question as to how usable such an approach may be for a visually impaired user.

Our approach to providing interactivity resembles the touchscreen overlay systems that relied on thin raised line maps. By using conductive filament for parts of our 3D prints, we are able to extend the touchscreen's sensitivity up to the surface of our maps. This allows for a wider range of depth information than earlier overlay approaches. It also eliminates the need to orient the maps to any camera, allowing for additional portability and ease of use. Also, by developing our maps so that they work with interactive applications that run on common touchscreen devices, our system does not face the barrier to entry that systems with custom hardware face.

3. SYSTEM DEVELOPMENT

Our system began as an exploration of how to make online mapping tools available to visually impaired individuals via 3D printing. While at the time, examples of 3D printed maps existed, the tools necessary for visually impaired individuals to independently create them were lacking. Thus began a development process of alternately adding features to our modeling algorithm and modifying the web interface to give users control of these features. Later, when we learned of conductive filaments, we began exploring the possibility of incorporating interactivity into our system as well. In this section, we will describe the system as it exists now, with an emphasis on reasons behind the design choices we made.

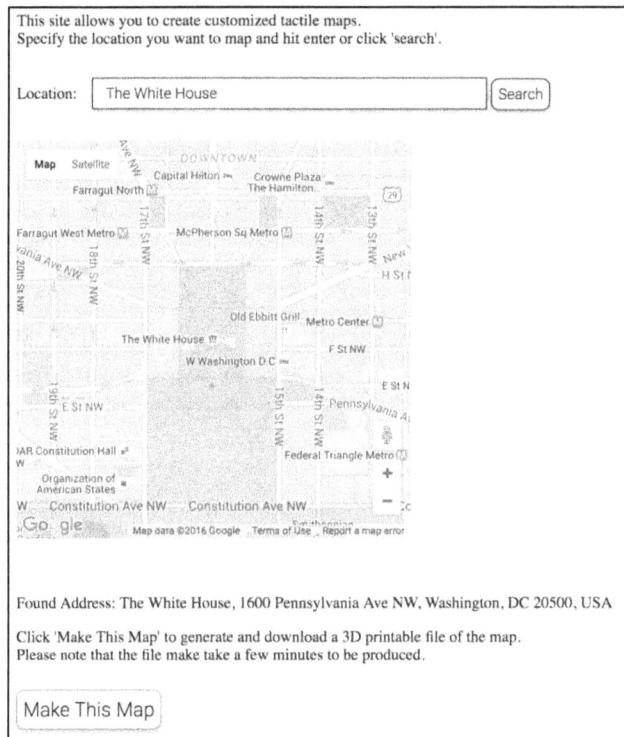

Figure 1. The simple web interface

3.1 Focus Groups

Throughout the development of this project, but prior to the evaluations described below, eight visually impaired individuals were interviewed either individually or as part of a focus group. The purpose of these interviews was to both explore potential use cases for customized maps and to receive feedback on models and web interfaces produced at various stages. While these discussions were informal, they did inform many aspects of our design.

3.2 Web Interface

Our web interface has evolved significantly throughout the development of our project. As we sought to balance intuitive interfaces and full customization, we created a series of interfaces exploring different levels of control.

3.2.1 Simple Interface

The simple interface is designed to generate a usable map with the absolute minimum amount of effort on the user's part. Users only have to search for an address and click 'Make a Map'. No customization options are available. The map is generated using a default set of parameters designed to provide an area of about .5 km^2. The web page, shown in Figure 1, does include a map image that displays the area centered on the location returned by the Google geocoding API. A text field labeled 'Found Address' conveys the resultant address or an appropriate error message in the case that no address can be found.

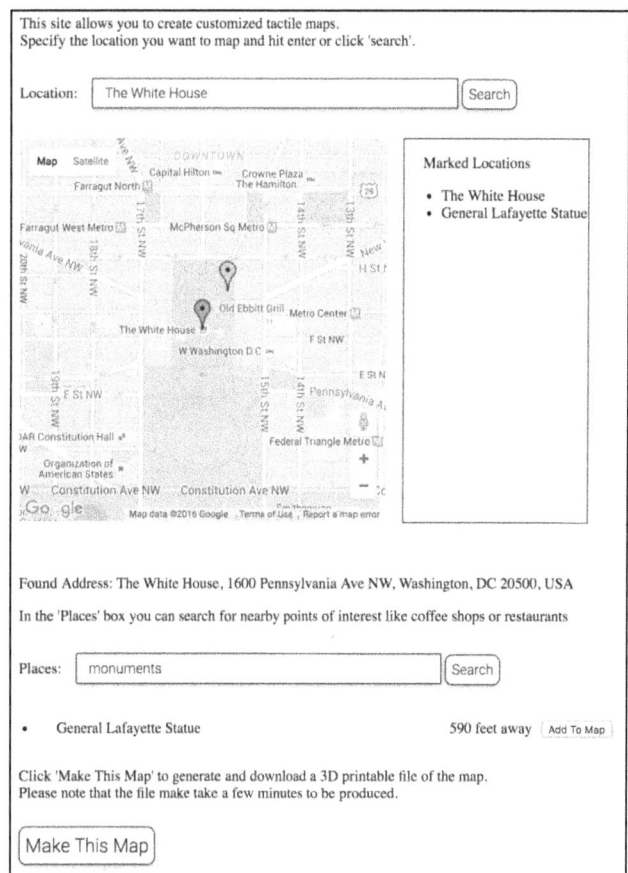

Figure 2. The places web interface

3.2.2 Places Interface

The places interface works much like the simple interface to create a map of a region using default parameters. However, users can then search for locations nearby using a second 'Places' text entry box (see Figure 2). The second box uses the Google Places API [12] to generate lists of relevant locations found within the map boundaries. Users can then select the locations they wish to tag and markers will be placed on the map models accordingly. Again, the 'Found Address' text field provides an indication of the map area and a separate 'Marked Locations' list provides a list of points that have been added to the map.

3.2.3 Advanced Interface

The advanced interface, shown in Figure 3, opens up a wide range of parameters to the user. Instead of merely specifying locations, users can adjust whether the locations are marked by geometric shapes or braille labels. Different map features can also be selected or removed from the maps and the textures and heights that will be used to represent the different features are also adjustable. Lastly, print sizes and coverage areas can be adjusted.

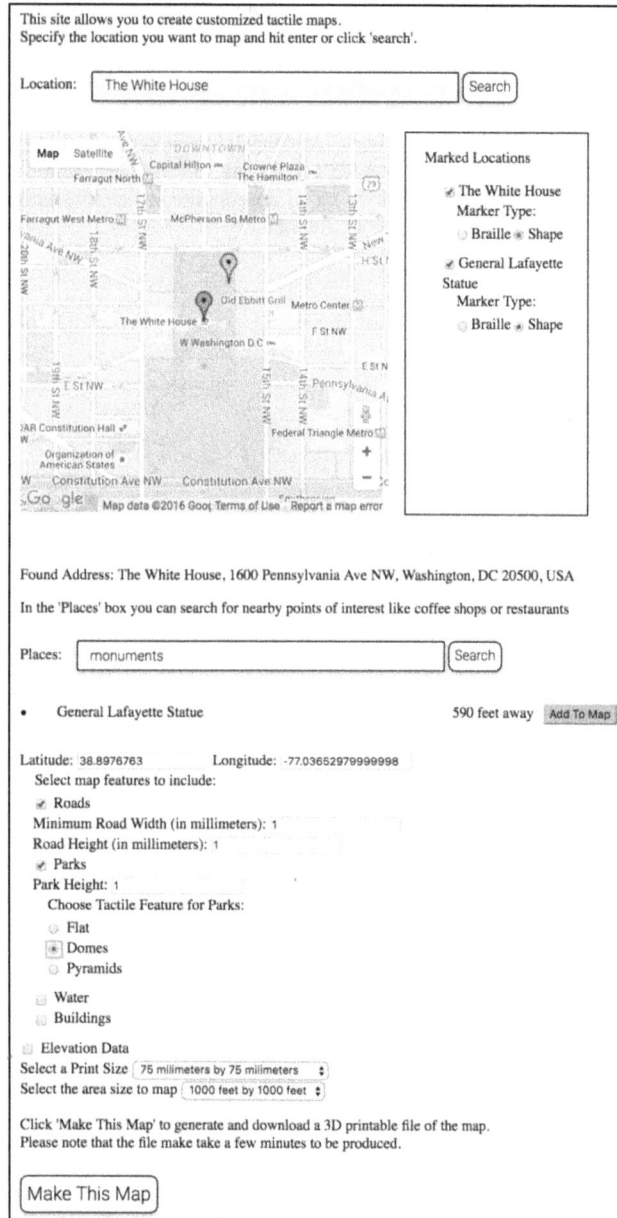

Figure 3. The advanced interface

3.3 Map Model Generation

Map models are generated by a set of Python modules that take various user-specified parameters. In this section we will describe the process by which our model-generating algorithm accesses data and generates 3D models to be printed.

3.3.1 Map Data

A majority of the data used to generate our map models is accessed via OpenStreetMap APIs [15]. Google APIs are also used to acquire elevation data and to geocode user-specified locations for both the maps and labels. Features designated in the OpenStreetMap corpus can then be represented as distinct tactile elements in our map models. Our current implementation can distinguish roads, walkways, buildings, waterways and parks. Additional features designated in the data corpus, such as pedestrian crossings or public transportation access, could be added to our models using a similar approach.

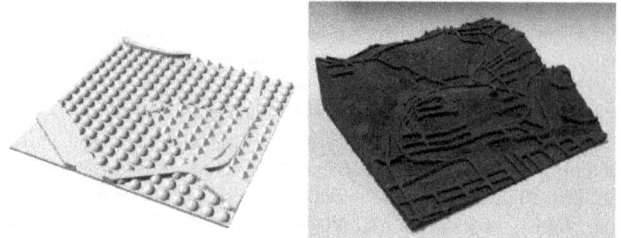

Figure 4. Tactile maps generated by our system. On the left, a rendering of a map model demonstrating different textures for different map regions. On the right, a printed example of a map including roadways overlaid on topographical elevation data.

3.3.2 Generating the Models

OpenStreetMap provides xml data containing the geographic coordinates of points, lines, and boundaries that define a number of map features (e.g., roads). Our code parses the xml data, grouping the relevant features into sets of polygons. Additional polygons are created for specified map labels and annotations. The polygons are trimmed to the specified boundaries and overlapping areas are hierarchically removed to leave a set of non-overlapping polygons that completely cover the specified region. Tactile features, specified by a layer height and a textured surface pattern, are then applied to each of the unique regions. Triangle meshes are then generated along all the surfaces, walls between adjacent features, and along the edges and bottoms of the mapped region. These meshes are then written out to an .stl file. Figure 4 (Left) shows an example of a generated model with four distinct tactile features. Water is represented by a pattern of domes, pyramids specify a park region, roads and non-defined regions both have flat surface textures, but roads are raised above the other features.

3.3.3 Feature Validation

Throughout the design process, we explored many variations in how different features could be represented. While we ultimately wanted to provide as much flexibility and customization to the end user as possible, we needed to establish usable default settings. To inform the default parameters, we created a set of example prints that demonstrated variations in how information could be represented. Some were designed to explore tactile perceptual preferences (e.g., what density of road patterns did users prefer) while others were more focused on the utility of potential representations of information. As an example, a print including direct representation of elevation data (Figure 4, Right) tended to draw more interest than flat maps, though most participants were skeptical of the utility of such a feature.

These example prints were shown to all focus group members as well as study participants to maximize feedback. The default settings for the maps generated with the simple interface (see

Section 3.2.1) are informed by this feedback. For the most part, user responses were consistent. Users preferred variations in width rather than height to distinguish different road types and, while they were often interested in additional map regions (e.g., waterways, parks), they expressed strong concerns over map complexity. However, one feature that received a decidedly mixed reaction was the approach to annotating roads by collocating braille labels on the back of the print. Figure 5 shows the two sides of such a map (the map was printed in two parts and later glued together). While some participants were intrigued by this approach, an equal number strongly disliked the idea of braille that was not horizontally aligned.

Figure 5. A neighborhood map (left) with the braille labels of major street names collocated on the back of the map (right). The image of the streets has been horizontally reversed to visually highlight the alignment between roads and labels.

3.4 Interactive App

Using tactile maps as overlays for touchscreen devices has been demonstrated as an effective way to provide interactivity and reduce the necessity of braille annotations [23]. Previous approaches, though, relied on the relatively low impedance of thin materials used to create raised line maps (typically either embossed or microcapsule papers). In contrast, our approach uses multi-material 3D printing that embeds isolated conductive regions in the passive plastic that forms the map. Through this process, we can extend our tactile maps into the 3rd dimension in ways that were not possible with other production methods without sacrificing interactivity.

3.4.1 Printed Components

In order to use custom printed maps with our interactive application, a customized case must be used. The case is designed to hold the maps in place against the touchscreen so that conductive touch points are properly aligned with the application's GUI interface. We designed a prototype phone case in which different maps can be slid in and out (see Figure 6). The phone case also has six static buttons that can be used to trigger specific application functions.

In addition to the custom cases, maps must be printed using a combination of passive plastic and conductive filaments. When placed on top of a touchscreen, the conductive filament will engage the touchscreen below when touched. In other areas, the plastic is thick enough to impede the user's touches so the touchscreen does not detect them. The maps are also given a Near Field Communication (NFC) tag to uniquely identify them.

3.4.2 Android Application

A custom application running on a phone or tablet identifies the particular map by its NFC tag and accesses the web interface's server to register the map. The conductive touchpoints, which can be user defined (see section 3.2.2) or automatically generated

according to map features (e.g., major intersections) prior to printing, will have corresponding touchscreen buttons to register responses. When users then touch a printed touchpoint, the application uses text to speech to inform the user of the location they pressed. For example, the map shown in Figure 6 has touch points that were automatically generated at the intersections of the region's primary roads. When users touch one of the points, the names of the two intersecting roads are spoken.

The fixed buttons on the case can also be used to trigger specific functions such as providing the user's current location via GPS or instructing the user to orient the map to their surroundings using the magnetometer. Since the touchpoints are 3D printed like the rest of the map, the regions can vary in size and shape to make specific points or whole regions interactive.

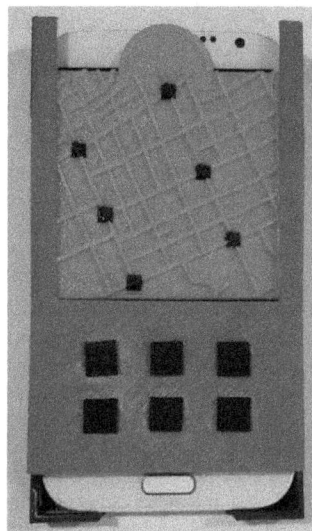

Figure 6. An interactive map with 6 black conductive touchpoints. The map is held in a case with 6 conductive buttons that houses a Samsung Note 2 with a 5.5-inch screen.

4. VALIDATION

While we are not the first to use OpenStreetMap data to 3D print tactile maps [14,16], our modeling algorithm does offer depth information and tactile features not previously explored. However, additional features are not necessarily better if the underlying models are incomprehensible or the interfaces to create them are unusable.

To verify our system's utility, we conducted three related studies. The first study focuses on the web-interface and demonstrates that visually impaired users are able to use our tool to generate map models without assistance. The second study verifies that maps printed from models generated by our tool are understandable and usable. Finally, a small qualitative study explores users' experiences using the interactive overlays.

4.1 Web Site Validation Approach

As described in the Section 3.2, we have developed a small set of interfaces for our web tool, each offering slightly different controls for map generation. We recruited seven severely visually impaired participants with prior experience with screen readers to test the various web interfaces. Participants were allowed to use their preferred screen reader, with six choosing to use JAWS and the seventh using NVDA.

Each participant was given an explanation about the www.tactilemaps.net web tool and then presented with a set of printed map examples that highlighted different map features and options. We explained that we were seeking to evaluate the interface for our tool and were interested in seeing if the web tool was designed appropriately so that an individual could independently use it. We explained that there were three different interfaces, and that we would provide specific tasks for each interface.

Each participant was first presented with the simple interface and then asked to generate a map of any location they wished. During the trial period, the investigators did not answer questions, though any issues or concerns were noted for later explanation. After each trial, users were asked to provide qualitative feedback about the interface.

After successfully completing the first trial, participants were then presented with the two more complex interfaces. For the places interface, users were asked to generate a map of a specific location, search for restaurants, and add one of their choosing to the map. For the advanced interface users were asked to adjust the area of the map to 2 km² and to include elevation data.

We do not have a consistent evaluation across participants as we made improvements to the interface in response to issues that arose in earlier trials. Even so, all but one participant was able to generate a map using the simple interface. That participant said they rarely used the internet and their difficulty came with navigating the browser more than the web interface itself. Success was decidedly more mixed for the more complex interfaces. Early on, there was a lack of feedback if a searched address returned no results. Some participants would continue, assuming the search had worked, but ultimately be unable to create a map. Another issue arose with an autocomplete menu that would pop-up when searching for places. Participants were given no warning about the menu, but it would change the effects of navigating in the text edit box. These issues and others were addressed following the trials in which they were observed. The result is a much improved interface which at least one participant has continued to use to generate maps for their own personal use.

4.2 Model Validation Approach

To demonstrate that maps generated by our modeling approach appropriately conveyed geographic information we conducted a study using two example maps generated by our web-tool. The maps, shown in Figure 7, represent actual regions in Nevada, MO and Austin, TX. The maps varied slightly in the information they contained and both were produced as 2.1D road maps to provide a more direct comparison with prior work. The Nevada, MO map was the simpler of the two with three levels (markers, raised roads, and undefined areas) and four marked locations designated by different geometric shapes (a square, a circle, a triangle, and a pentagon). The Austin, TX map has five layers (markers with braille above them, roads raised, waterways lowered, and undefined areas between) and included 4 locations designated by raised regions with braille labels reading 1, 2, 3, and 4.

Five participants with severe visual impairments or blindness were recruited to evaluate the maps. For each map, we first asked participants to explore as long as they wished and to describe their impressions as they did. We did not specify whether these should focus on descriptions of perceived tactile features or their symbolic representations, though most users did both. Users were instructed that the rounded or notched corner on the map represented the Northeast direction on the Nevada, MO map and the Southwest direction on the Austin Map. We asked users to orient the map so that the North edge was farthest away from them and recorded whether the orientation was correct.

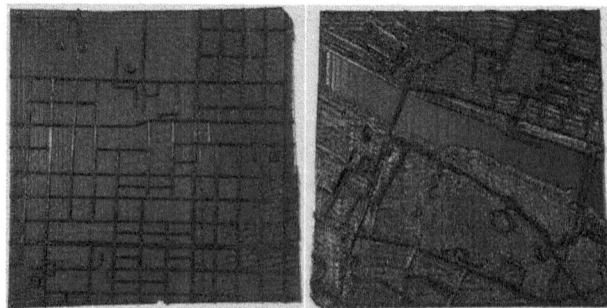

Figure 7. Test Maps. On the left, a map of Nevada, MO with 4 locations designated by geometric shapes. On the right, a map of Austin, TX, with 4 points designated by braille labels.

During their free exploration of the maps, every participant independently recognized the designated points on each map. For the Nevada, MO map, users were asked to (1) describe the shapes they felt, (2) specify which two marked points were closest to each other, and (3) provide directions from the triangle to the square, assuming the raised lines indicated roadways. On the Austin, TX map, users were additionally asked to identify the braille on the marked points. If they mentioned bodies of water in their description, participants were asked to indicate where the water was, if not, they were informed that the map did have a representation of water and asked to identify it. Due to a limited number of braille fluent participants and an issue with braille dots breaking off of the labels we did not collect proximity or direction information for the Austin, TX map. Table 1 lists the percentage of users able to accomplish the various tasks.

	Orientation	Labels Recognized	Nearest Points Identified	Water Feature Recognized
Nevada	5/5	5/5	5/5	N/A
Austin	5/5	5/5	N/A	3/5

Table 1. Map recognition tasks

As can be seen in Table 1, all users were able to orient the maps and located all marked points. Users easily identified the triangle, circle and square. The pentagon was easily distinguished as another, different marker, but slight warping during the printing process impacted users' ability to identify the shape. One participant described it as "a roundish shape with a point". Another participant thought that the triangle marker was an indicator of North rather than a marker like the others. Several participants did not notice the river in the Austin, TX map. However, all but one participant was able to correctly identify the lower region as a waterway when informed that one was present. That participant felt another area was water due to an unintended printing effect that created a surface texture that reminded them of how water was indicated on another map they had encountered prior to our study.

In additional to exploring and describing the features of the maps, we also asked the participants to provide directions from the triangle marker to the square marker on the Nevada, MO map while staying on roads marked on the map. The directions provided were unambiguous across four participants (e.g., "Go South on the road to the right of the triangle for 6 blocks then turn right..."). The fifth participant did not seem to understand the procedure and provided no directions. The paths described by the participants are marked in Figure 8 by the thicker lines with an

'X' indicating the final location after following the directions.

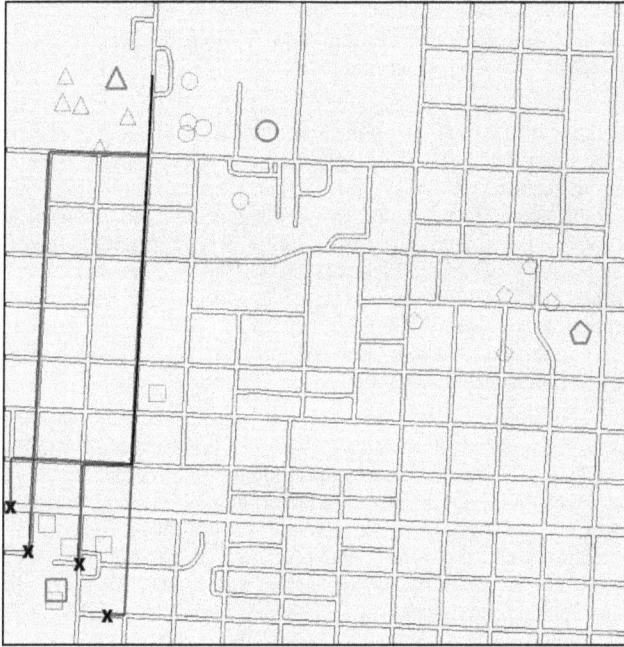

Figure 8. A map of Nevada, MO showing the same features represented on the tactile map presented to participants (see Figure 7). The larger red shapes show the actual locations of the marked points. The smaller corresponding shapes represent the locations marked when the participants recreated the maps. The shaded lines with X's at the end represented the path described by participants when asked to provide directions from the triangle to the square.

Finally, we employed a spatial cued response, as described by Kitchin, asking the participants to recreate the maps by drawing the locations of the marked points on a square piece of paper without tactile features [21]. The locations marked by each participant were then measured and transcribed (as the smaller geometric shapes) onto the map shown in Figure 8.

As we can see, users were able to provide generally correct, though often not exact, directions from the triangle to the square. Similarly, users were able to roughly recreate the maps. While we do not claim that our maps are better at conveying spatial information than previously tested approaches, we do feel that these results demonstrate a basic level of utility.

4.3 Interactive Overlay Exploration

Participants were provided with two prototype interactive maps. One was designed for an phone running our application (see Figure 6) the other was printed for use with a tablet (see Figure 9) . The participants were asked to freely explore the maps and describe their experiences. Feedback from their explorations will be discussed in the Future Work and Discussion sections.

5. DISCUSSION

In addition to the previously described tests, we also interviewed participants about their experiences with maps and navigation. Here we will focus on the most salient issues that will provide guidance to others interested in developing tactile maps.

Use Cases. From the beginning, we largely focused on developing maps for providing an understanding of an area covering a few blocks within an urban setting. While participants agreed that such a use case is reasonable, many other ideas were brought up that

we had not considered. P1 was interested in a small scale, shopping area map and had actually commissioned a custom made map of such an area near their home. P7 was interested in how city neighborhoods were arranged relative to each other. In the same way that visual maps use different zoom levels to let users see different types of information, tactile maps need to be able to provide different amounts of detail depending on the user's intent. Systems that optimize for a particular use case (such as our simple interface) inherently limit the utility of the maps they create. Flexible, customizable controls (such as our advanced interface) need to be explored to satisfy different user needs.

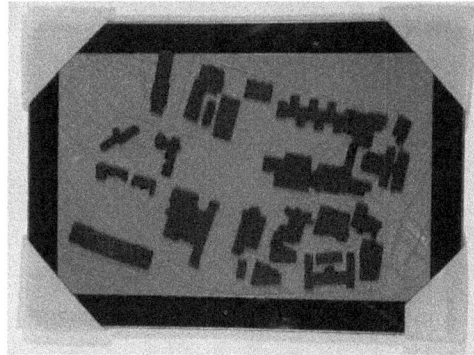

Figure 9. An interactive map of a college campus on a Samsung Galaxy Tab 10.1 tablet. The black buildings act as touchpoints and announce the building name when touched.

Holistic Explanations. Participants had a range of familiarity and interest with tactile maps, generally. However, none of them had particular experience with the 3D printed maps as we generated them. When introduced to the exemplar maps, many focus group members and study participants asked questions about features that were not present on a given map. For example, multiple users asked how big of a map we could create and others asked about labeling street names. For potential web users who have not been handed a physical map, the terse description, 'This site allows you to create customized tactile maps' almost certainly raises more questions than it answers. How to convey a sense of the tactile artifact that will result from learning to use our interface is a challenge that needs to be addressed.

Printing Limitations. An issue that we repeatedly encountered was that of the limitations of the 3D printer resolutions. When printing braille labels, the results, while usually legible, were suboptimal. P4 described it as "weird braille," saying, "It just doesn't feel good to me at all." Unintended print artifacts, such as a seam in a wider road or an area of the print that just happened to print more smoothly than others, also occurred. Participants noted several artifacts and often attributed meaning to the artifacts. As 3D printer quality continues to improve we expect many of these issues to be resolved, but in the meantime, care must be taken to use surface textures that exhibit clear, intentional differences.

Portability. In designing our interactive tactile overlays, we had imagined that users would find it advantageous to be able to interact with a map in the location. However, feedback about this idea was tepid, which is in line with surveys about tactile map preferences [27]. What remains unclear from our interviews though, is if this idea is biased by previous experiences with maps that are bulky and require considerable mental effort to decipher. Having interactive maps that could take advantage of location technology available in smartphones is not something they had experienced. Whether or not portability and customization would shift users' perception about tactile map technologies is something that we would be interested in exploring. Clearly, though, the first step is to make the underlying technology as available and usable as possible.

6. FUTURE WORK

While the system we have built is available online and is available for anyone to use, it would benefit from improvements. Each part of our system (the web interface, the modeling algorithm, and the interactive application) has a number of aspects that can be improved. Here we have highlighted the most pressing improvements we intend to work on.

6.1 Web Interface

Improve web interface usability. During the studies, there were some specific accessibility issues that were overlooked (e.g., buttons were not tagged in a way that brought them up on the JAWs screen reader's links list). However, most of these had straightforward solutions and have been addressed. A more systematic issue was a lack of properly detailed information about what the different website options would do and what the final result should be. Many users expected the generated map file to be immediately useful in some way. Simply providing a more detailed explanation of the process of generating the maps and providing links to 3D printing services would help.

Incorporate way-finding or path designations. One limitation of our current system is that there is no way to designate a specific path. While our modeling algorithm could easily raise specified road segments above others (or mark them with some tactile feature), users have no way to make such specifications. During our interview with an orientation and mobility specialist, it was brought to our attention that having an option to allow a sighted individual to designate a preferred pathway on a map could be a useful training tool. This idea was reinforced by P4, who mentioned that she often had her sighted husband check maps for audible crosswalks before planning routes. One can easily imagine a modified interface that allows a sighted individual to draw a designated path on a map. Alternatively, routing algorithms could be used to designate pathways.

6.2 Modeling Algorithm

Increasing the number of map features. OpenStreetMap currently recognizes 26 primary features, many of which contain a range of subfeatures. Due to time and resource limitations, we have not been able to incorporate all of these features. While too many different features on any given tactile map may leave it unusably complex, we believe providing the option to incorporate more features is better. In particular, features like public transit stops and audible crosswalks are high priorities for incorporation.

Increasing the number of surface textures. Currently our system only offers three different textures (flat surface or tessellations of domes or pyramids). The spacing and size of the tessellations, though, can be adjusted to create a wide range of textures. To expand upon this set, surface waves or randomized features could be implemented. Further exploration of how tactile perceptual limits and print resolutions interact to define readily distinguishable surfaces is needed.

6.3 Interactive Application

Explore additional touch interactions. Other interactive mapping approaches have explored accessing layers of information from a single region by distinguishing different tapping gestures (e.g., double or triple tapping) [23]. Thus far, we have only explored simple touch responses. In addition to tapping gestures, we intend to explore sequencing effects that could indicate sliding gestures

from one point to another or the designation of an intended pathway between multiple points. We also intend to explore adding interactivity to specific map features, such as roads, as suggested by two participants.

Increase interactive element density. Using a dual extruder 3D printer, it is possible to print both the interactive and the static map parts together into a single cohesive object [9]. We hope to soon acquire such a system so that we can more efficiently produce complex interactive maps. Our first exploration will be to produce a map with a grid of as many discrete interactive points as possible. In effect, the tactile surface will be the same as any other non-interactive map, but the touch sensitive regions will resemble a lower resolution touchscreen. We are interested in exploring how a denser array of interactive points can lead to more sophisticated interactions.

Directly incorporate into the web interface and modeling algorithm. As dual extruder printers or multi-material printing services become more readily available, integrating the interactive elements into both the web interface and the modeling algorithms will become a necessary step. While we have taken steps in this direction (e.g., the web interface for designating points creates a file that is accessed by the custom app to map UI elements on the touchscreen), many aspects are still not fully customizable (e.g., no option currently exists to specify the audio response to the designated points).

7. CONCLUSIONS

In this work we have shown a complete end-to-end system which allows visually impaired individuals to independently customize tactile maps, have the maps 3D printed, then interact with the maps as either passive objects or as an overlay for touchscreen phones or tablets. Our system allows visually impaired individuals to independently customize maps with a much greater degree of freedom than any previous mapping system. In addition to selecting particular locations to map, users can specify the scale, the tactile features, and the labels to present on the maps. The usability of the publicly available web interface (www.tactilemaps.net) has been tested by 7 visually impaired individuals and iterated upon to incorporate much of the feedback we received. The 3D printable map models generated by our system offer novel features such as elevation data and adjustable tactile patterns. The modeling algorithm is designed to incorporate users' specifications and a test using example maps confirmed that basic geographical information is conveyed by our models. Finally, we introduced a technique of producing 3D printed tactile maps with conductive regions that allow for dynamic interactions with a wide range of touchscreen devices. We produced an Android application and multiple example maps that demonstrated the proof of concept for how such interactive maps can be generated along with dynamic content to resolve many of the labeling issues that surround tactile maps. This system, taken together, represents a significant step towards making user-specified interactive, 3D printed tactile maps an affordable and accessible way for visually impaired individuals to explore the world around them.

8. ACKNOWLEDGMENTS

This work was supported by the National Science Foundation under grant IIS-1065336 and the NSF Quality of Life Technology Engineering Research Center unter grant EE-0540865. Special thanks to Carnegie Library for the Blind and Physically Handicap and the Blind and Vision Rehabilitation Services of Pittsburgh for their support with this work.

9. REFERENCES

[1] 3Ders.org. Price Compare 3D Printers. http://www.3ders.org/pricecompare/3dprinters/

[2] American Federation for the Blind. Braille Printers. https://www.afb.org/ProdBrowseCatResults.asp?CatID=45

[3] American Thermoform. www.americanthermoform.com

[4] Amick, N., Corcoran, J. 1997. Guidelines for Design of Tactile Graphics. American Printing House for the Blind. http://www.aph.org/research/guides/

[5] Berman, B. 2012. 3-D printing: The new industrial revolution. *Bus. Horiz.,* 55, 155-162.

[6] Braille Authority of North America. Size and Spacing of Braille Characters. http://www.brailleauthority.org/sizespacingofbraille/

[7] Brock, A. M. 2013. Touch the map!: designing interactive maps for visually impaired people. ACM SIGACCESS Accessibility and Computing, 105, 9-14.

[8] Brock, A. M., Truillet, P., Oriola, B., Picard, D., and Jouffrais, C. 2012. Design and User Satisfaction of Interactive Maps for Visually Impaired People. In *Computers helping people with special needs.* 544-551.

[9] Burstyn, J., Fellion, N., Strohmeier, P., and Vertegaal, R. 2015. PrintPut: Resistive and capacitive input widgets for interactive 3D prints. In *Human-Computer Interaction INTERACT 2015, 332-339.*

[10] Espinosa, M. A., Ungar, S. Ochaita, E., Blades, M. and Spencer, C. 1998. Comparing methods for introducing blind and visually impaired people to unfamiliar urban environments. *J. Env. Psych.* 18 (1998), 277-287.

[11] Giudice, N. A. and Legge, G. 2008. Blind navigation and the role of technology. In *Engineering handbook of smart technology for agin, disability, and independence.* A. Helal, M. Mokhtari and B. Abdulrazak, Eds. John Wiley & Sons, 479-500.

[12] Google. Google Places API. https://developers.google.com/places/

[13] Gotzelmann, T. 2014. Interactive tactile maps for blind people using smartphones' integrated cameras. In *Proceedings of the Ninth ACM International Conference on Interactive Tabletops and Surfaces.* ITS '14. ACM, New York, NY, 381-385.

[14] Gotzelmann, T. 2014. Towards automatically generated tactile detail maps by 3d printers for blind persons. In *Computers helping people with special needs.* Springer International Publishing, 1-7.

[15] Haklay, M. and Weber, P. 2008. OpenStreetMap: User-Generated Street Maps. *IEEE Pervasive Computing.* 7, 12-18.

[16] HaptoRender. 2009. http://wiki.openstreetmap.org/wiki/HaptoRender

[17] Hasty, L. Tactile Graphics: A How To Guide. http://www.tactilegraphics.org/index.html

[18] Jacobson, R. D. 1992. Spatial cognition through tactile mapping. *Swansea Geographer* 29, 79-88.

[19] Jacobson, W. H. *The Art and Science of Teaching Orientation and Mobility to Persons with Visual Impairments.*

[20] Karkkainen, S. Touch Mapper. https://touch-mapper.org/

[21] Kitchin, R.M. and Jacobson, R.D. 1997. Techniques to collect and analyze the cognitive map knowledge of persons with visual impairment or blindness: issues of validity. *J. Vis. Impair & Blindness.* (Jul-Aug 1997), 360-376.

[22] Landau, S. and Gourgey, K. 2001. Development of a Talking Tactile Tablet. *Information Technology and Disabilities E-Journal.* 7(2).

[23] Miele, J., Landau, S. and Gilden, D. 2006. Talking TMAP: automated generation of audio-tactile maps using Smith-Kettlewell's TMAP software. *The British J. of Vis. Impair.* 24, 2, 93-100.

[24] Minatani, K. Watanabe, T., Yamaguchi, T., Watanabe, K., Akiyama, J., Miyagi, M., and Oouchi, S. 2010. Tactile map automated creation system to enhance the mobility of blind persons- its design concept and evaluation through experiment. In *Computers helping people with special needs.* 534-540.

[25] Perkins, C. 2001. Tactile campus mapping: Evaluating designs and production technologies. *20th Int. Cartographic Conf.* 5, 2906-2913.

[26] Rowell, J. and Ungar, S. 2003. The world of touch: an international survey of tactile maps. Part 2: design. *The British J. of Vis. Impair.* 21, 3, 105-110.

[27] Rowell, J., Ungar, S. 2005 Feeling our way: tactile map user requirements- a survey. In *Proc. Of 22nd Int. Cartographic Conf.*

[28] Smith Kettlewell Eye Research Institute. Tactile Map Automated Production. http://www.ski.org/project/tactile-map-automated-production-tmap

[29] Swaminathan, S., Roumen, T., Kovacs, R., Stangl, D., Mueller, S., and Baudisch, P. Linespace: a sensemaking platform for the blind. In *Proceedings of the SIGCHI Conference on Human Factors in Computing Systems.* CHI '16. ACM, New York, NY,

[30] Watanabe, T., Yamaguchi, T., Koda, S., Minatani, K. 2014. Tactile map automated creation system using OpenStreetMap. *ICCHP 2015, Part II, 42-49.*

[31] Yatani, K., Banovic, N., and Truong, K. SpaceSense: representing geographical information to visually impaired people using spatial tactile feedback. In *Proceedings of the SIGCHI Conference on Human Factors in Computing Systems.* CHI '12. ACM, New York, NY, 415-424.

LucentMaps: 3D Printed Audiovisual Tactile Maps for Blind and Visually Impaired People

Timo Götzelmann
Nuremberg Institute of Technology
Keßlerplatz 12
D-90489 Nuremberg, Germany
+49 911 5880 1616
Timo.Goetzelmann@ohm-university.eu

ABSTRACT

Tactile maps support blind and visually impaired people in orientation and to familiarize with unfamiliar environments. Interactive approaches complement these maps with auditory feedback. However, commonly these approaches focus on blind people. We present an approach which incorporates visually impaired people by visually augmenting relevant parts of tactile maps. These audiovisual tactile maps can be used in conjunction with common tablet computers and smartphones. By integrating conductive elements into 3D printed tactile maps, they can be recognized by a single touch on the mobile device's display, which eases the handling for blind and visually impaired people. To allow multiple elevation levels in our transparent tactile maps, we conducted a study to reconcile technical and physiological requirements of off-the-shelf 3D printers, capacitive touch inputs and the human tactile sense. We propose an interaction concept for 3D printed audiovisual tactile maps, verify its feasibility and test it with a user study. Our discussion includes economic considerations crucial for a broad dissemination of tactile maps for both blind and visually impaired people.

CCS Concepts

• **Human-centered computing→Accessibility systems and tools**
• Human-centered computing→Auditory feedback • Human-centered computing→Ubiquitous and mobile devices
• **Hardware→Tactile and hand-based interfaces**
• Hardware→Touch screens.

Keywords

Tactile maps; audio-tactile; blind; orientation; global; accessibility; tangible user interfaces; functional; 3D printing; capacitive; touch screen; marker; capacitive sensing.

1. INTRODUCTION

Tactile maps are an essential means to support orientation and navigation of blind and visually impaired persons. These maps can be used to familiarize people with neighborhoods, for journey planning or can be used in situ to improve the spatial understanding of blind users in unfamiliar urban environments [6]. Many of these tactile maps are mainly designed for blind people. According to estimations of World Health Organization (WHO), globally there are about 39 million blind people, but nearly a quarter billion visually impaired persons [38]. A majority of these people live in low-income settings and in some countries, visually impaired persons do not get financial support from the government (such as blind persons do). Ideally, visually impaired people could also benefit from tactile maps, and these should be affordable to this target group.

Since several years electronic versions of the maps can be generated automatically. Their physical representations can be produced by multiple printing technologies (e.g., [33]). Braille *embossers* approximate line drawings of maps by punching series of dots into ordinary paper. *Microcapsule (swell) paper* can be printed with monochrome drawings of maps where the dark parts swell when they are treated with controlled heat from a *fuser*. More recently, tactile maps are being produced by 3D printers which print elevated 3D models generated from map material. This technology has several advantages that can be used for structuring map content as well as the simultaneous use of multiple materials which is leveraged in this paper.

However, printed tactile maps from all these technologies have one characteristic in common – they have to be kept simple. There are multiple reasons for excluding Braille annotations from tactile maps. First, only a smaller proportion of blind people are able to read Braille at all [2]. It can be assumed that an even smaller proportion of visually impaired people can read Braille labeled maps. Another argument to exclude Braille labels is to limit the tactile complexity of maps. As pointed out by Tatham [29], the extensive use of Braille annotations in tactile maps may worsen the overall legibility of the maps. Additionally, similar to visual maps, the alternative of using legends and keys may complicate the interpretation of tactile images due to reduced immediacy [11].

An alternative is the combination of tactile maps with an interactive component. Recent studies [3] have shown evidence that interactive audio support for tactile maps is advantageous in relation to the ISO 9241 usability design goals. There are numerous approaches for audio-tactile maps. In this paper, we present an approach that can be applied to existing approaches using different tactile map designs, but additionally addresses the visual modality of visually impaired persons. Because these tactile maps are interactively supported by both auditory and visual cues, we refer to them as *Audiovisual Tactile Maps*.

2. RELATED WORK

There are numerous approaches for audio-tactile maps which use various techniques to support blind people. We report some of the most relevant approaches from a technological perspective. These

ASSETS '16, October 23 - 26, 2016, Reno, NV, USA

Copyright is held by the owner/author(s). Publication rights licensed to ACM.
ACM 978-1-4503-4124-0/16/10…$15.00
DOI: http://dx.doi.org/10.1145/2982142.2982163

audio-tactile maps can be differentiated according to *Zeng&Weber's* classification [36]. In our paper we refer to these categorizations, nonetheless we structure the approaches in a more purpose oriented manner in relation to our solution.

2.1 Pure Software Approaches

There are approaches, which mainly rely on communicating cartographic map features and directions using software and standard hardware built in off-the-shelf computers or mobile devices. Some approaches, also called *Virtual Acoustic Maps*, rely on *sonification*, i.e., they encode tactile elements and directions as sound (e.g., *Timbremap* [27]). Other approaches use touch inputs to explore an electronic map by playing sound files when the user enters specific regions of the touch input (e.g., [13]). Experiments show that this strategy may contribute to the spatial understanding of blind and visually impaired people. *TouchOver map* [24] belongs to *Virtual Tactile Maps* and displays street networks on mobile devices and uses a vibration actuator and speech to guide blind users along displayed streets. Since it uses conventional paper maps, it is mainly designed for people with low vision. These approaches simulate tactile sensing, but without a physical representation, which induces the user to cognitively transfer his or her sensation.

2.2 Integrated Approaches

There are several approaches to so called *Braille Tactile Maps* which utilize *Hyperbraille*, a technology mainly for blind people that uses the combination of a tactile display (a matrix of piezo actuators) with a desktop computer. There are multiple approaches from *Zeng et al.* (e.g., [35–37]) for interactive tactile maps that adapt their tactile rendition due to a user's touch interaction. Another approach [25] addresses the tactile exploration of building plans and outdoor maps, which is supported by a text-to-speech (TTS) functionality.

Adaptability is a key strength of this technology. Displayed maps can adapt their tactile renditions dynamically and interactive augmentation techniques (such as blinking encoded by oscillating tactile elements) can be implemented. Another technology is *Linespace* [28], a combination of a camera and a modified 3D printer attached to a whiteboard. Map updates can be initiated by people who are visually impaired whilst preserving parts of the previous map contents. One main advantage compared to *Hyperbraille* is the significantly lower production costs, however its downside is the lack of immediacy. Both, Linespace and tactile displays address a major claim of *Jacobson* [21], that map updates, especially cause a high cognitive load to visually impaired users when no context information is preserved. However, the drawbacks of these technologies are their limited mobility and availability.

2.3 Approaches Augmenting Physical Maps

The following approaches partially belong to the category *Augmented Paper-based Tactile Maps* and use physical representations of tactile maps in conjunction with electronic devices. The aim of these technologies is to provide additional information stored as electronic content to map features the user is interested in. This helps to reduce the tactile complexity of maps and thus, addresses the issue of tactile cluttering particularly caused by textual map annotations. The use of these two independent components makes it possible to solve two main challenges of tangible user interfaces. First, the physical component has to be identified by the electronic system in order to couple both the electronic and physical entities. Second, to allow interaction with particular parts of the map, its position and orientation have to be determined or restricted to specific constraints.

A system of a touch-sensitive surface and a desktop computer linked by a USB interface in combination with tactile overlay sheets was presented by the *Talking Tactile Tablet* (TTT) [20]. When exchanging these sheets, they had a specified size and layout and had to be arranged exactly in the frame of the touch surface according to three calibration points. After justifying the sheets, the user had to touch multiple positions to register the map with the system. A graphical user interface was used to create graphics as source for the tactile sheets that are printable by local Braille embossers. A subsequent approach [22] allowed the automatic production of TTT sheets for US maps optionally by third party companies.

Wang et al. [32] described a system to analyze existing visual maps in order to transform them into a simplified image that can be printed by embossers or on microcapsule paper. These prints could be placed over the displayed image of the original map. During exploration of the tactile map, the automatically extracted metadata of street networks was used for auditory feedback to map features. Another approach, *Touchplates* [16] presented a system of a tabletop computer and acrylic plastic overlays combined with visual markers. It was able to recognize these overlays automatically by a technology called *infrared based diffused illumination*, which is integrated in tabletops such as Microsoft PixelSense. *Brock et al.* [3] used a system of a touch input space and raised-line drawings on microcapsule paper to examine multi-touch exploration of visually impaired people. The approach *Mappie* [5] extended this approach for a study focusing on visually impaired children, that incorporated 3D printed objects which could be placed on the tactile map.

These approaches allowed the exchangeability of tactile maps and, partially, to recognize tactile maps by performing a manual procedure of multiple steps. The necessity to place the map exactly in a certain way on the touch device and the restricted portability of these systems are the limitations of these approaches.

2.4 Mobile Approaches

There are also several approaches which allow the transportation of both the electronic component and the tactile map, which has been shown to be helpful in a study done by *Espinosa et al.* [6]. *McGookin et al.* [21] presented a combination of opaque, raised paper overlays for non-visual interaction with dedicated applications using touch screens. *Sennette et al.* [26] presented a portable approach which allowed the use of tactile microcapsule prints of the popular *OpenStreetMap* database as an overlay for tablets and smartphones. After electronic map contents were loaded manually, the tactile maps were constrained to be placed exactly in line with to the display's borders. Another portable approach [9] relied on a combination of smartphones and 3D printed tactile maps placed on a flat surface. Users were instructed by voice commands to hold the smartphone above the map to recognize it by inscribed barcodes. An optical finger detection allowed users to query information about map features. A user study with blind users verified its feasibility, but this approach was considerably dependent on lighting conditions and constrained users to a one-handed exploration of the tactile map.

Hence, some of these approaches are portable. But even when the system supports interchangeable tactile maps, users have to carry out a defined, multi-step procedure when changing a map. Additionally, there are hard constraints for the arrangement of the maps on the touch displays which could impede independent use for blind people. In the following, we introduce a novel approach to overcome these issues and additionally supports visually impaired persons by augmentation of individual map features.

3. APPROACH

As pointed out in Sec. 1, our aim was to develop a highly mobile solution for audio-tactile maps for both blind and visually impaired persons that uses auditory and visual augmentation. The development of our approach required several initial design considerations to solve general questions of technical LucentMap design to make them usable with capacitive touch displays. Next, the step of changing tactile maps, i.e., especially the effort required to mount the map on the touch display, had to be minimized. Finally, for the realization of user interaction, software related questions had to be addressed.

3.1 Technical Map Design Considerations

There are multiple web services which enable the production of tactile maps for different printing technologies, mostly for raised line drawings. An inherent limitation of creating detailed tactile maps using microcapsule paper is the support of only one elevation (height) level. Even worse, the elevation cannot be reliably controlled. Small features as well as thin lines may suffer from under-elevation whilst extensive elevated areas are prone to heating artifacts when the fuser's temperature is set too high.

In contrast, 3D printers are designed to fabricate spatial structures and thus do not have this limitation when printing tactile maps. This technical feature can be exploited to support the grouping and differentiation of individual map features, and thus the map's readability. Another advantage is that 3D prints can be produced in a single pass whilst integrating multiple printing materials. This fact is leveraged in this paper to permit automatic recognition of maps (see 3.2). However, currently available 3D printed tactile maps cannot be used without modification for the joint use with touch displays. Multiple technical and physiological constraints have to be harmonized to adapt existing 3D printed tactile maps.

Three main factors influence our design considerations: (i) the discriminability of the finger's skin, (ii) the effective resolution of consumer 3D printers, and (iii) the ability of capacitive inputs to recognize touches through multiple elevation levels of a map. The latter raises the requirement to minimize the height differences between elevation levels.

Resolution of Consumer 3D printers

There are 3D printers on the consumer market that work according to different printing techniques. The most common consumer 3D printers work according the *Fused Decomposition Modelling* (FDM) principle. Printers of this type use thermo-plastic polymers, usually in the form of filament wound up on coils. By using stepper-motors for the x- and y-axes, each point on the printing bed can be accessed. The printing head melts the filament and deposits it on points defined by the 3D model. This procedure is repeated layer per layer, whereas the printing bed (z-axis) moves away from the printing head(s) for a defined distance. By using printers with two or more printing heads, multiple printing materials can be used to fabricate (functional) multi-material 3D objects in a single turn.

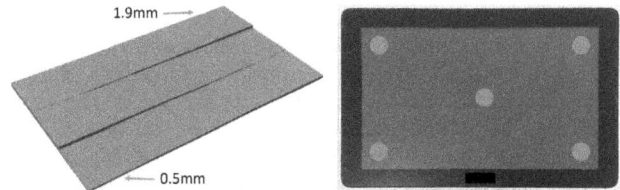

Fig. 1: Ramp of height differences to measure the range of distances for proximity touches of touch displays (at blue dots).

The resolution of these printers is dependent on numerous factors. The most important characteristic for realizing multiple elevation levels for tactile maps is the resolution on the z-axis (layer resolution). Current consumer FDM printers achieve up to 20 microns ($20\mu m$) layer resolution. However, printing with high resolutions may drastically increase printing time.

Discriminability of Elevation

Even fractions of a micron can be sensed due to deformations of the papillary ridges of the finger's skin [19]. However, this is only possible in specific settings which are not applicable to 3D printed map features. To ensure that the intended elevation of distinct map features is not confused with 3D printing artifacts, at least the nominal layer resolution should be used.

Smaller elevations require more time for reading [15]. The optimal elevation with regard to scanning time between two elevation levels has been determined to start at 160 microns [14]. According to *Way&Barner* [33], the exploration of tactile images follows two stages. First, the entire image is explored to gather a general overview and second, detailed information of specific parts is obtained. We adapt this strategy to the elevation levels of 3D printed tactile maps. On this basis, we propose that differences in elevation between categories of map features (area-, line-, point-features) should be elevated at least 160 microns. Only if needed, fractions of this value should be used to allow the discrimination of differences between individual map features within these categories.

Sensing Abilities of Capacitive Touch Inputs

Current mobile devices usually integrate capacitive touch displays which enable the registration of at least 10 concurrent touches by the device's software. The user interactions are tracked by frequent determination of the individual fingers' positions, which touch the display's surface. In order to locate the touch positions, a sensitive microcontroller (e.g., *Atmel maXTouch*) senses load changes in a uniform grid of sensor wires attached to the touch display. This grid may be located directly on the surface (surface capacitance) or be placed below an insulating surface, such as robust glass (projected capacitance). The latter type is used for modern mobile devices. An important factor is that load changes in the sensor grid can already be detected when a finger approaches the touch surface. Hardware manufacturers adjust their touch microcontrollers well to maintain an equalized touch sensitiveness over the whole display area. This controlled sensitiveness allows it to sense touches through thin non-conducting materials (e.g., paper, plastics, glass). In this paper, we make use of these technical characteristics and refer in the following discussion to such indirect touches as *proximity touches*.

To design tactile maps using multiple elevation levels, an initial study is necessary to find out the range of distances where proximity touches are detected by touch displays.

Methodology

We evaluated discriminable height differences in current mobile devices. We tested 20 devices to estimate the range of proximity to the display. We tested it through a 3D printed PLA ramp with ascending height differences by utilizing the open-source constructive solid modelling tool *OpenSCAD* [17]. It consisted of multiple adjacent platforms of $1.5cm^2$ and height differences of .1mm in the range of .5-1.9mm (see Fig. 1). For each device, five measuring points (center and the display's corners) were evaluated. Each measuring point was touched a total of five times in decreasing distances from 1.9mm. We recorded the maximum distance proximity touches when each of the touches could be correctly recognized.

Results

The range of medium distances between devices[1] was 0.58-1.90mm (Ø: 1.17mm, σ: .40mm). Hence, each of the devices was able to detect proximity touches on average up to 0.58mm distance. However, more than 75% of the tested devices were able to detect proximity touches of ≤ .99mm. According to the results of our preliminary study on touch proximity, 75% of the tested devices were not able to detect proximity touches from a distance above 1.43mm. This information is useful to define the minimum distance of conductive materials which should not cause a proximity touch (i.e., the bridging component of the capacitive codes descried in Sec. 3.2).

Discussion

Based on the results of this study we argue that the elevation levels used for encoding tactile map features should remain below 1.0mm to ensure that map interaction by proximity touches is possible. Combined with the physiological characteristics of tactile perception, this makes it possible to have 4-5 elevation levels. For this additional level of freedom in 3D printed tactile map design, a reasonable strategy has to be identified. Although an in-depth study of multi-elevation-level map design for 3D printed maps is not the focus of this paper: we propose the following strategy for this paper (see Table 1).

Elevation	Map features	Examples
Level 1	Superior areas	Building blocks, campuses
Level 2	Inferior areas	Buildings
Level 3	Walkable streets	Residential roads
Level 4	Footpaths	Pedestrian zones, walkways
Level 5	Points of Interest	Bus stops, shops, accessible crosswalks

Table 1: Elevation levels and their associated map features.

3.2 Map Recognition

Capacitive coupling of human fingers is sensed by touch surfaces. By using conductive materials, this coupling can be passed along

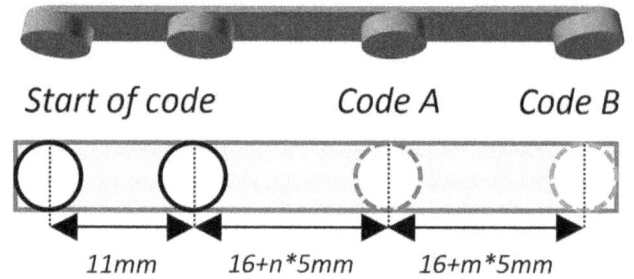

Fig. 2: The ID code which is embedded in the tactile map: varying distances by variables *n* and *m* encode a unique identifier which can be recognized through touch-displays.

the surface (e.g., *Sketch-a-TUI* [34]) or through objects (e.g., *CapWidgets* [18]).

When the capacitance of the user's finger is bifurcated to different locations on the touch surface, multiple concurrent touches are registered when the user touches this element [30]. The principle of bridging multiple points on the touch surface by conductive material can even be realized for untouched detection [31]. The concept of capacitive codes is based on the fact that distances between concurrent touch points can be measured. Because of this, these distances can be used to encode information.

We apply this principle to encode an identification of the tactile map[2]. Two touch points have at a minimum distance of more than 10mm to be detected as individual points. Larger distances between two points can be measured with an accuracy of at least 5mm. Our map ID code consists of four points in a row. The first two points are at the minimum distance of 11mm and mark the *start of code* (see Fig. 2). A third point (*Code A*) is placed at least at the minimum distance +5mm, to distinguish it from the beginning of the code. The fourth point (*Code B*) is placed in the same manner relatively to the third point. By varying the distances of Code A and B by multiples of 5mm, numerous combinations can be achieved. This code is integrated into the tactile map's 3D model and printed by conductive filament.

When the interactive application is started on the mobile device, it first requests that the tactile map with such an integrated capacitive code is placed on the touch display and for the user to touch or move it. This causes the registration of four concurrent touch points by the interactive application. The application detects the start of code (which is always two points at the distance of 11mm) and then measures the distances to both of the other touch points to extract the ID code. Besides the ID code, the exact position and orientation of the tactile map is extracted from the registered touch points.

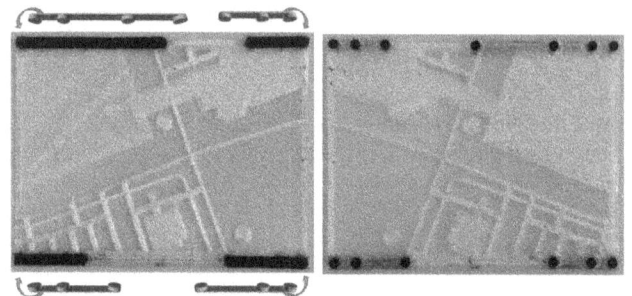

Fig. 3: Capacitive codes at tactile map's corners are printed with conductive filament. View from bottom side (right).

---

[1] Tested devices (Focus was on current lower cost tablets. Smartphones are marked italic): Acer Iconia One 10; Acer Predator 8; Apple iPad mini 4; Apple iPad Pro 12.9; Apple iPad Pro 9.7; Archos 101 Xenon Lite; Archos 7.0c Xenon; Asus Zenpad 10.1; Huawei MediaPad 10 Link+; Lenovo Yoga Tablet 3; *LG G Flex 2*; Odys Score Plug 3D 10.1; Samsung Galaxy Tab E 3G; Samsung Galaxy Tab E Wifi; Samsung Galaxy Tab 7; Samsung Tab S 10.5; Samsung Tab S2 9.7; Trekstor Surftab Breeze 7.0 Quad 3G; *Wiko Getaway*; Xoro Telepad 7 A3.

[2] Parts of this section have been previously published in Ref. [7].

For each map ID, there is a dataset which includes geographic coordinates of the map's corners, its real size and, optionally, a description of the map. This data as well as the information about the tactile map's position and orientation on the touch display serves to adapt the electronic rendition of the map and its touch interaction with the map to the overlaid physical tactile map. The visual representation on the map is aligned to the map's position on the touch display and its angle (when not parallel to the touch display).

The LucentMaps' cardinal direction north is always on the top side. Since the ID code is located to the upper left of the tactile map this serves as orientation for blind users who can feel the longish shape of the ID code. To make the maps also usable on small mobile devices, we integrated special codes for the remaining corners of the map (see Fig. 3). After the ID code of the map is recognized, these corner codes can be used to explore maps which are larger than the mobile device's display (see Fig. 4). These corner codes only contain the start code and a third point which encodes the corner by its distance to the start code analogous to Code A of the ID code (see Fig. 2).

3.3 Interaction

When a capacitive code is recognized, the actual user interaction starts. The user is able to explore the tactile map which is supported by touch interaction, speech input and output, and the visual augmentation of the map.

General

The integration of capacitive codes into the printed map minimizes the effort required to interchange tactile maps. The software offers a simple way to initiate an exchange of the tactile map.

LucentMaps are also designed to be used in situ to improve orientation. Due to their portability, both allocentric and egocentric exploration strategies [23] are possible. To support egocentric exploration, GPS and magnetic sensors, integrated in many mobile devices, can be used. If these modules can be activated by the software, the mobile application should be able to first communicate to the user whether she or he is currently located within the coordinates of the detected map. Secondly, the user should be able to know at which angle the map on the mobile corresponds to the real world's geographic directions.

Touch interaction

When exploring the map, users should have the opportunity to get immediate feedback about the map features they are interested in (such as its feature type and name). It is technically feasible to support many touch gestures through tactile maps. However, in order not disturb the tactile exploration, we decided to keep the touch interaction simple. For the immediate feedback on specific map features, double tapping on the desired map feature was used. We followed the suggestions of [3] to extend the time interval between the double tap to 700ms.

Since LucentMaps are designed to be used in an interactive context, we deliberately avoided integrating a scale into the tactile map. In contrast, the interactive application allows the determination of arbitrary distance measurements by a multi-touch gesture. One finger has to mark the starting point of the measurement (e.g., a crossing) and a second finger marks the end point of the measurement by simply touching the desired end position (e.g., a corner of a building). The exact real world distance is reported by the TTS. To not confuse blind or visually impaired users taking distance measurement with bimanual tactile

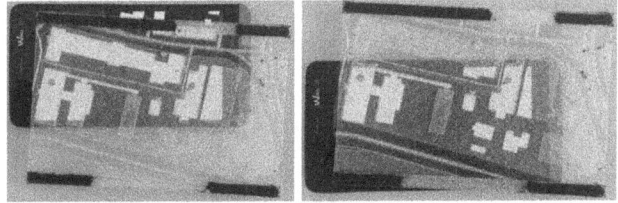

Fig. 4: User touches ID code at the map's top left corner and explores the map using a small device. By touching the code on the bottom left another part of the map can be explored.

exploration, this touch interaction has to be activated by an adequate voice command for each measurement.

Speech interaction

In order to facilitate the tactile exploration of the map, the touch interaction is kept simple. To access additional functionality, speech input is used. In order to ensure acceptable response times and to be independent of internet access during exploration (e.g., when maps are used in situ), the speech detection works offline on the mobile device. The functionality covers (i) showing all map features of a certain class (point-, line-, area features), (ii) showing map features of specific categories (Health, Eating&Drinking, Shops&Services, Culture&Entertainment, Nature&Leisure, Transport&Traveling, Accessibility) and should (iii) allow the user to obtain more detailed information about specific map features. Finally, the functionality mentioned before (measuring distances, locate and help user to be congruent to real world directions, changing maps) should be accessible by speech input. The results of these interactions are also communicated by speech output. In the case of multiple map features, the TTS speaks the number of the augmented map features.

Visual augmentation

The electronic map consists of area (e.g., buildings), line (e.g., streets) and point (e.g., traffic lights) map features. Visually impaired users should be able to augment each of these groups individually. Moreover, many of these map features are equipped with descriptive tags in order to characterize them (e.g., regarding their classification). Users should be able to augment each element of a specific class, (e.g., shops, pharmacies, public transport). Additionally, when selecting an area or line feature by double tap, the shape of this individual map feature should be augmented.

4. FEASIBILITY

To test the feasibility of the requirements defined in Sec. 3, we printed multiple maps and implemented a mobile application for detection of the maps and interactive components.

4.1 Creation of maps

There are several approaches for the automatic creation of 3D printable tactile graphics (e.g., [4]). For this paper we used a specialized web service (http://blindweb.org) to generate 3D models [8] usable for printing tactile maps. Its medium map detail level covers an area of 422x287 meters; the actual map's scale is depending on its printed size (1:1875 for a printed size of 22.5x15cm). By using its Python-API, we developed a plugin for the free open source 3D authoring tool *Blender 3D* [1] to automatically adapt these maps to the constraints of our approach and to substitute them with capacitive codes. The resulting multi-material 3D model was stored in two complementary 3D models (.STL) which share a joint coordinate system. This combination can be used by common 3D printing software for multi-material prints.

For the actual fabrication, we used an off-the-shelf dual-head 3D printer (*FelixPrinters FelixPro 1*), working according to the FDM principle. To print the map prototypes, we used a transparent filament, *FormFutura HDglass^TM*, for the tactile map itself and *Proto-pasta Conductive PLA* filament for the integrated capacitive codes. The fewer layers used, the less light scattering occurs. Hence, to both minimize printing time and to maximize translucency of printed maps we chose a layer resolution of 160 microns.

We intentionally omitted the integration of a wind rose or arrows for cardinal directions, because north on the maps is always represented by the upper bar containing the biggest capacitive code. On the one hand, this capacitive code can be used to find the cardinal directions relative to the map contents. On the other hand, the mobile device's compass could be used to obtain the orientation of the map contents relative to their real world entities. Likewise, a fixed scale was not printed in the map since the software allowed exact measurement of each distance the user is interested in by a two finger multi-touch gesture.

4.2 Mobile application

We implemented a mobile application for Android tablets and smartphones which run on at least API level 15 (Android 4.0.3), which is supported by the most current Android devices.

4.2.1 Implementation of functionality

For the recognition of the 3D printed tactile maps, we implemented an algorithm for detecting the capacitive codes embedded in the corners of the tactile map. When started, the application waits until it registers the four concurrent touch points in a line. Next, the detected touch points are classified. First, the start of code is extracted, followed by the classification of *Code A* and *B* based on their distance to the preceding point. When the map's ID is determined, its assigned geographic coordinates and real size are retrieved. Together with the computed coordinates and angle of the tactile map on the display, the electronic map is configured. The user is briefed about the recognized map.

For the map rendering and interaction, we relied on the *Mapsforge SDK*[3], which has also been used for numerous other research works. It uses compressed maps from the *OpenStreetMap* database. Our application determined the geographic coordinates from touch interaction with the map even when the map view was rotated by the angle determined by the capacitive codes. For example, a double-tap on one position in the map queried the map database for features at that position. Then the information about the map feature's type and name was communicated by the TTS. The results of queries (e.g., to highlight all buildings) were visually augmented by adapting the rendering styles of the map.

For the speech interaction, we utilized the *CMU PocketSphinx SDK* [12] developed for offline speech detection mobile devices. It supports multiple detection models, such as context-dependent phonetic search, which allows good recognition results. Because of likely performance issues on some mobile devices, we had to use context-independent search which had to be tailored to our application to achieve reasonable results. To limit the unintentional triggering of voice commands, we defined the keyword "Computer", which is needed to start the actual recognition. We implemented a state machine to navigate through our auditory menu. To increase the detection accuracy, in each level only a small dictionary of recognizable words was used. The auditory menu structure by its detected words is listed below (curly brackets for submenu):

- Overview {Buildings, Streets, Points}
  To show each representative of a feature class.
- Show {Eating, Health, Travel, Shop, …}
  To show representatives of a feature category.
- Which {Name, Type, Else}
  To obtain detailed information about a map feature the user points at.
- Map {Locate, Distance, Change}
  To get information about GPS and orientation to real world directions; to measure distances on the map; to change the tactile with another map (starting with recognition of capacitive code).

For text output, we used the standard Android TTS engine. For this study we only used the normal voice speed. However, the speed can be easily set to user's preferences for optimal use.

4.2.2 Usage scenarios

In the following, we define three intended usage scenarios in order to illustrate possible procedures of usage.

Blind person using tablet

Prior to a trip, the user wants to familiarize himself or herself with the target area. The user starts the application on a tablet computer and places an appropriate tactile map on its display. The user touches the capacitive code and waits for the acknowledgement that it has been recognized. Next, the user simply fixes the map by two strips of adhesive tape. Now, the user queries the map for public transport and street names to the destination, memorizes their shape and measures distances. The user is also interested in descriptions of buildings surrounding these streets. This scenario could also apply to a visually impaired person (e.g., when searching for the way from a bus stop to a building), who is additionally supported by visual augmentation (see Fig. 5).

Fig. 5: User queries map for public transport and traffic map features (left), followed by a double-tap on the street (center) and finally on the building (right). For each of these interactions the TTS tells name and type of the corresponding map features.

---

[3] https://github.com/mapsforge/

Visually impaired person using smartphone

A visually impaired user wants to consult a tactile map on a journey after arriving at the target area by bus. He or she retrieves the smartphone and a map out of their pocket, places the map on the smartphone and touches the capacitive code. Subsequently, the TTS reports the description of the map and the map is fixed by adhesive tape. She or he initiates the location feature in order to orient the map to real world directions and then explores a part of the map. Since the display is smaller than the map, another corner of the map is placed on the display and the corresponding corner code is touched. After the application recognizes the new corner of same map, it adapts and the map exploration continues.

Visually impaired person using tablet

The map is recognized just as in the previous scenarios. This time the user explores the map of a crowded area of a city center. By using voice commands, he or she gradually browses through the map feature categories and requests additional information about augmented map features of special interest.

5. EVALUATION

To assess whether blind and visually impaired people are able to use our approach and to obtain qualitative feedback, we conducted a brief application-driven user study. Because we think the target group for interactive tactile maps are mostly younger people, we cooperated with the regional school for visually impaired and blind persons.

We recruited nine participants (five females) with an average age of 15.67±5.57 years. Six of the participants were visually impaired (5-30% residual vision), one had residual vision of 2% and two were blind. Each of the participants had basic knowledge about tactile maps. For the study, we used an inexpensive off-the-shelf Android tablet (*Huawei MediaPad 10 Link+*) with our implementation of the detection of capacitive and the interaction with the tactile map as described in Section 3. The display was set to maximum brightness, augmented parts of the map' were represented by white color, whereas the remaining map features were indicated by a dark grey color.

Procedure

Initially the participants were given a brief description of the tactile maps and that mobile device touch displays are able to detect touches even through thin plastic. It was explained that capacitive markers are attached to the top and bottom sides of the map and that the tactile map can be automatically recognized by the tablet by touching or moving these markers on the tablet's display. Next, they had the chance to explore a trial map and were instructed to find the ID code which is the largest (black) structure located on the upper left side of the map. Subsequently, multiple use-oriented tests were carried out with each of the participants.

1. The participants were asked to grasp the tactile map from the table and to place it on the tablet computer's display. Next, they had to locate and touch or move the ID code until they heard the TTS message that the map had been recognized. Finally, they had to shift and tilt the map to another position at least three times, using the capacitive code each time to reorient the system. After each shifting or tilting action they had to rest for a short while until the TTS finished reporting the changes in coordinates and angle.
2. After that, participants had to explore a tactile map fixed by adhesive tape on the tablet. They had to find each of a point-, line- and area-feature and obtain verbal explanations by double tapping these map features. The visually impaired participants were asked to show the visually highlighted shapes of line- and area-features.

3. Next, voice commands were used to highlight
    a. all restaurants,
    b. all buildings and
    c. all point-features
    on the map. In each case, the visually impaired people were asked to determine the number of highlighted map features.
4. Finally, after activating the distance measuring feature by using the voice command, the participants were asked to measure the distance between two map features on the map by using a multi-touch gesture.

Results and Discussion

All of the participants were able to place the tactile map on the tablet's display and to use the capacitive code for detection of the map. When the users relocated the map, this was detected by the application and the correct angle was reported (1). All of the participants were successful, none of the users needed numerous trials, which resulted in registration timings considerably less than 10s. Multiple users tried to rotate the map more than ±90 degree which resulted in failure to recognize the code. However, this was a technical issue which could be solved by software in future versions.

All of the map users successfully managed the task to obtain additional information on point-, line- and area features (2). Visually impaired users recognized the rough shape of augmented map features and each of them recognized the correct number of augmented point features (3a+3c). Four visually impaired participants recognized the correct number of 11 augmented buildings on the tactile map, one counted only 6 buildings and another was not able to see adjacent buildings (see Fig. 6) as individual buildings. Each of the participants were successful to carry out the multi-touch gesture (4) in order to measure the distance between two map features.

Both groups of people, blind and visually impaired, were curious to use the interactive approach. They obviously liked the fact that the map is automatically recognized when its capacitive code is touched on the tablet's display. Multiple users mentioned that it should be combined with a popular navigation application called *BlindSquare*, in order to be able to "feel" individual map features. One participant proposed to invert the augmentation of the map features, i.e., to augment the whole map except selected map features. Another participant liked the mobility of the map and the fact that small maps usable with smartphones or tablets do not attract attention of sighted people in contrast to large maps. Finally, the users had multiple suggestions on improvements of the map design. Despite map design is not the focus of this paper this information can be used for our future work (see 6.3).

Voice commands had to be repeated in some cases. We expect that outdoor use could be problematic and suggest using a

Fig. 6: Augmented tactile map: adjacent buildings on the left weren t recognized as individual buildings by one participant.

Bluetooth headset for future applications. Despite the implemented keyword-search functionality, the voice recognition had to be disabled by the test supervisor between the individual tests, since sometimes unintentional commands were detected. For future versions, we suggest integration of a dedicated button in one of the display's corners which would allow speech-recognition when it is pressed instead of the keyword-search functionality.

6. DISCUSSION AND LESSONS LEARNED

This section discusses outcomes of our research and proposes improvements for future development of 3D printed *Audiovisual Tactile Maps*.

6.1 Costs and Availability

As discussed in the introduction, costs are an important factor for many in the target group. Exemplary 3D printed tactile maps of 10x15cm had an average weight of approximately 10g and consisted of ~90% transparent HDglass filament (750g: ~$40) and ~10% conductive PLA (500g: $48). On average, this means that the material costs of such a map usually is below $0.60. Even cheap 3D printers may be suitable for printing LucentMaps – we successfully tested prints with a dual-head 3D printer with a price point below $1000. Because there is a competitive market for 3D printers and filaments, it can be expected that this will continually drive quality and cost reduction of these mass products. Suitable tablet computers and smartphones can be purchased for less than $50.

6.2 Limitations

Besides the technical issues regarding the voice input, the magnetic sensor used for the compass functionality sometimes delivered skewed orientations. To prevent this behavior, users should always wave the device in an infinity-shaped manner before using the orientation feature. The offline map material used by the *Mapsforge* framework is freely available on the internet. However, it is pre-processed to be stored efficiently in a compressed format, which also incidentally excludes some special tags for accessibility. By using existing tools, specialized map material for blind and visually impaired people could be generated from the *OpenStreetMap* database and provided to the community through the internet.

Consumer 3D printers still lack standardization and their usability is still limited in terms of software and hardware. However, when these components are well adjusted, they can already produce 3D printed tactile maps in a consistently high quality. The main challenge to tackle in the future, however, is to identify how the tactile representation of automatically created maps should be and how this can be technically achieved in general (including multiple zoom levels). Since a similar task has been solved for electronic visual maps decades ago, the authors are confident that this can achieved for tactile maps as well. To realize this, the promising research results of user studies carried out to address these questions (e.g., [2,5,35]) have to be transferred to formal rules for computing functional and usable maps. Likewise, for volumetric tactile material there is an increasing number of publications (e.g., [10]) which could help to optimize the usage of multiple elevation levels (such as sketched in Sec. 3.1) for tactile map design. This has to be done with current and upcoming technologies in mind. Multiple tactile reproduction technologies should be addressed by an integrative approach to reach most of the blind persons.

6.3 Future Work

The visual augmentation of the transparent tactile maps is dependent on lighting conditions. In bright areas (e.g., outdoors) this could impede the recognition of augmented map features. Similar issues could occur for speech interaction. This is also true for standard use of mobile devices for sighted users. However, we plan to carry out a comprehensive user study to assess different augmentation techniques including varying light conditions, the effect of noise on speech interaction, and the benefits of using a Bluetooth headset for in situ orientation (such as Espinosa [6]).

Auditory and visual output should ideally be redundant to support blind and visually impaired people in equal measure. Currently, there is still a bias towards visual augmentation. Especially when the user prompts to highlight categories of map features (e.g., public transport), the application merely verbally reports *how many* of these map features are on the map, but not *where* they are located on the map. The individual map features are only visually highlighted. Hence, verbalization of the position of individual map features and, ideally, a verbal description of their shape as a complement to the tactile exploration of map features by blind people is in the focus of our future work.

Our approach can be applied to diverse tactile maps and thus, this paper did not focus on tactile map design. In our future work we plan to carry out a comprehensive user study about the discriminability of multiple elevation levels and on design considerations for 3D printed tactile maps.

7. CONCLUSION

We presented a novel approach designed for both blind and visually impaired persons. It extends the concept of audio-tactile maps by extending the visual modality. Particular map features are augmented by illumination and groups of map features sharing content-related characteristics are emphasized.

Our approach significantly simplifies the combination of mobile devices with physical tactile maps. By integrating conductive elements into the tactile map, the user is able to register maps by a single touch or movement of the tactile map placed on a touch screen. It does not require the placement of the map in a specific way or aligned to a specific axis. Even completely oblique arrangements of the map can be used immediately. A sufficient fixation of the map is possible by simply attaching two strips of adhesive tape on the borders to the map. No extra attachment system is needed; the strips can be reused and temporarily stored on the mobile device's backside. We carried out a study of capacitive displays in order to obtain characteristics of proximity detection. These results were used to propose usage of multiple elevation levels of tactile maps.

The maps used for our approach can be automatically generated by existing approaches. The conductive elements for the recognition of the maps can also be automatically integrated. This combination can be reproduced in a single turn by off-the-shelf 3D printers. Additionally, this approach does not necessarily need large displays, it also works with displays smaller than the tactile map. When at least one corner is placed on the display the parts overlaying the device's display can be explored by the user's fingers. This makes the maps pocket-portable and they can be used in situ with audio tactile maps on a normal smartphone. We implemented a mobile application to test feasibility and evaluated our approach by an application-driven user study. The authors think this could contribute to the broader dissemination of audio-tactile maps.

8. REFERENCES

[1] Blender Foundation. blender.org - Home of the Blender project - Free and Open 3D Creation Software.

[2] Anke M. Brock. 2013. Interactive Maps for Visually Impaired People: Design, Usability and Spatial Cognition.

[3] Anke M. Brock, Philippe Truillet, Bernard Oriola, Delphine Picard, and Christophe Jouffrais. 2015. Interactivity Improves Usability of Geographic Maps for Visually Impaired People. *Human–Computer Interaction* 30, 2: 156–194.

[4] Craig Brown and Amy Hurst. 2012. VizTouch: automatically generated tactile visualizations of coordinate spaces. *Proceedings of the Sixth International Conference on Tangible, Embedded and Embodied Interaction*, ACM, 131–138.

[5] Emeline Brulé, Gilles Bailly, Anke M. Brock, Frédéric Valentin, Grégoire Denis, and Christophe Jouffrais. 2016. MapSense: Multi-Sensory Interactive Maps for Children Living with Visual Impairments. *ACM CHI 2016-chi4good*, ACM.

[6] M. Espinosa, Simon Ungar, Esperanza Ochaíta, Mark Blades, and Christopher Spencer. 1998. Comparing Methods for Introducing Blind and Visually Impaired People to Unfamiliar Urban Environments. *Journal of Environmental Psychology* 18, 3: 277–287.

[7] Timo Götzelmann. 2016. CapMaps. In *15th International Conference on Computers Helping People with Special Needs (ICCHP'16)*. Springer, 146–152.

[8] Timo Götzelmann and Aleksander Pavkovic. 2014. Towards Automatically Generated Tactile Detail Maps by 3D Printers for Blind Persons. *14th International Conference on Computers Helping People with Special Needs (ICCHP'14)*, Springer, 1–7.

[9] Timo Götzelmann and Klaus Winkler. 2015. SmartTactMaps: A Smartphone-Based Approach to Support Blind Persons in Exploring Tactile Maps. *Proceedings of the 8th International Conference on PErvasive Technologies Related to Assistive Environments (PETRAE'15)*, ACM, 1–8.

[10] Jaume Gual, Marina Puyuelo, and Joaquim Lloveras. 2015. The effect of volumetric (3D) tactile symbols within inclusive tactile maps. *Applied Ergonomics* 48: 1–10.

[11] Ronald AL Hinton. 1993. Tactile and audio-tactile images as vehicles for learning. *Non-Visual Human-Computer-Interactions - Prospects for the Visually Handicapped*, John Libbey Eurotext Ltd., 169–180.

[12] David Huggins-Daines, Mohit Kumar, Arthur Chan, Alan W. Black, Mosur Ravishankar, and Alex I. Rudnicky. 2006. Pocketsphinx: A free, real-time continuous speech recognition system for hand-held devices. *Proc. of IEEE International Conference on Acoustics, Speech and Signal Processing*, IEEE, 185–188.

[13] R. Dan Jacobson. 1998. Navigating maps with little or no sight: An audio-tactile approach. *Proceedings of Content Visualization and Intermedia Representations*: 95–102.

[14] Sandra Jehoel, Snir Dinar, Don McCallum, Jonathan Rowell, and Simon Ungar. 2005. A scientific approach to tactile map design: minimum elevation of tactile map symbols. *Proceedings of XXII International Cartographic Conference A Coruña 2005 proceedings*, CD.

[15] Sandra Jehoel, Don McCallum, Jonathan Rowell, and Simon Ungar. 2006. An empirical approach on the design of tactile maps and diagrams: The cognitive tactualization approach. *British Journal of Visual Impairment* 24, 2: 67–75.

[16] Shaun K. Kane, Meredith Ringel Morris, and Jacob O. Wobbrock. 2013. Touchplates: low-cost tactile overlays for visually impaired touch screen users. *Proceedings of the 15th International ACM SIGACCESS Conference on Computers and Accessibility*, ACM, 22.

[17] Marius Kintel and Clifford Wolf. OpenSCAD - The Programmers Solid 3D CAD Modeller. Retrieved from http://www.openscad.org/. 2014-12-05.

[18] Sven Kratz, Tilo Westermann, Michael Rohs, and Georg Essl. 2011. CapWidgets: Tangible Widgets versus Multi-touch Controls on Mobile Devices. *CHI'11 EA Hum. Factors in Computing Systems*, ACM, 1351–1356.

[19] Robert H. LaMotte and Mandayam A. Srinivasan. 1991. Surface Microgeometry: Tactile Perception and Neural Encoding. In *Information Processing in the Somatosensory System*. Macmillan Education UK, 49–58.

[20] Steven Landau and Lesley Wells. 2003. Merging Tactile Sensory Input and Audio Data by Means of the Talking Tactile Tablet. *Proceedings of EuroHaptics' 03*, 414–418.

[21] David McGookin, Stephen Brewster, and WeiWei Jiang. 2008. Investigating touchscreen accessibility for people with visual impairments. *Proceedings of the 5th Nordic conference on Human-computer interaction: building bridges*, ACM, 298–307.

[22] Joshua. A. Miele, Steven Landau, and Deborah Gilden. 2006. Talking TMAP: Automated Generation of Audio-tactile Maps using Smith-Kettlewell's TMAP Software. *British Journal of Visual Impairment* 24, 2: 93–100. h

[23] Nazatul Naquiah Abd Hamid and Alistair D.N. Edwards. 2013. Facilitating route learning using interactive audio-tactile maps for blind and visually impaired people. *CHI'13 Extended Abstracts on Human Factors in Computing Systems*, ACM, 37–42.

[24] Benjamin Poppinga, Charlotte Magnusson, Martin Pielot, and Kirsten Rassmus-Gröhn. 2011. TouchOver map: audio-tactile exploration of interactive maps. *Proceedings of the 13th International Conference on Human Computer Interaction with Mobile Devices and Services*, ACM, 545–550.

[25] Bernhard Schmitz and Thomas Ertl. 2012. Interactively Displaying Maps on a Tactile Graphics Display. *SKALID 2012–Spatial Knowledge Acquisition with Limited Information Displays*: 13.

[26] Caterina Senette, Maria Claudia Buzzi, Marina Buzzi, Barbara Leporini, and Loredana Martusciello. 2013. Enriching Graphic Maps to Enable Multimodal Interaction by Blind People. In *Universal Access in Human-Computer Interaction. Design Methods, Tools, and Interaction Techniques for eInclusion*. Springer, 576–583.

[27] Jing Su, Alyssa Rosenzweig, Ashvin Goel, Eyal de Lara, and Khai N. Truong. 2010. Timbremap: enabling the visually-impaired to use maps on touch-enabled devices. *Proc. of the 12th International Conference on Human Computer Interaction with Mobile Devices and Services*, ACM, 17–26.

[28] Saiganesh Swaminathan, Thijs Roumen, Robert Kovacs, David Stangl, Stefanie Mueller, and Patrick Baudisch. 2016. Linespace: A Sensemaking Platform for the Blind. *Proc.*

SIGCHI Conf. Human Factors in Computing Systems, ACM (to appear).

[29] A. F. Tatham. 1991. The design of tactile maps: theoretical and practical considerations. *Proceedings of international cartographic association: mapping the nations*: 157–166.

[30] Timo Götzelmann and Daniel Schneider. 2016. CapCodes: Capacitive 3D Printable Identification and On-screen Tracking for Tangible Interaction. *Proceedings of 9th Nordic Conference on Human-Computer Interaction,* ACM (to appear).

[31] Simon Voelker, Kosuke Nakajima, Christian Thoresen, Yuichi Itoh, Kjell Ivar Øvergård, and Jan Borchers. 2013. PUCs: Detecting Transparent, Passive Untouched Capacitive Widgets on Unmodified Multi-touch Displays. *Proc. ACM Int. Conf. Interactive tabletops and surfaces*, ACM Press, 101–104.

[32] Zheshen Wang, Baoxin Li, Terri Hedgpeth, and Teresa Haven. 2009. Instant Tactile-audio Map: Enabling Access to Digital Maps for People with Visual Impairment. *Proceedings of the 11th International ACM SIGACCESS Conference on Computers & Accessibility*, ACM, 43–50.

[33] Thomas P. Way and Kenneth E. Barner. 1997. Automatic visual to tactile translation. i. human factors, access methods and image manipulation. *Rehabilitation Engineering, IEEE Transactions on* 5, 1: 81–94.

[34] Alexander Wiethoff, Hanna Schneider, Michael Rohs, Andreas Butz, and Saul Greenberg. 2012. Sketch-a-TUI: Low Cost Prototyping of Tangible Interactions Using Cardboard and Conductive Ink. *Proc. Conf. Tangible, Embedded and Embodied Interaction*, ACM, 309–312.

[35] Limin Zeng, Mei Miao, and Gerhard Weber. 2015. Interactive Audio-haptic Map Explorer on a Tactile Display. *Interacting with Computers* 27, 4: 413–429.

[36] Limin Zeng and Gerhard Weber. 2011. Accessible Maps for the Visually Impaired. *Proceedings of the IFIP INTERACT Workshop on Accessible Design in the Digital World*, 54–60.

[37] Limin Zeng and Gerhard Weber. 2012. ATMap: Annotated Tactile Maps for the Visually Impaired. In *Cognitive Behavioural Systems*. Springer, 290–298.

[38] WHO | Visual impairment and blindness. Retrieved from http://www.who.int/mediacentre/factsheets/fs282/en/. 2015-12-05.

Gesture-Based Interactive Audio Guide on Tactile Reliefs

Andreas Reichinger, Anton Fuhrmann, Stefan Maierhofer and Werner Purgathofer
VRVis Zentrum für Virtual Reality und Visualisierung Forschungs-GmbH
Donau-City-Str. 1, 1220 Wien, Austria
reichinger@vrvis.at

ABSTRACT

For blind and visually impaired people, tactile reliefs offer many benefits over the more classic raised line drawings or tactile diagrams, as depth, 3D shape and surface textures are directly perceivable. However, without proper guidance some reliefs are still difficult to explore autonomously.

In this work, we present a gesture-controlled interactive audio guide (IAG) based on recent low-cost depth cameras that operates directly on relief surfaces. The interactively explorable, location-dependent verbal descriptions promise rapid tactile accessibility to 2.5D spatial information in a home or education setting, to on-line resources, or as a kiosk installation at public places.

We present a working prototype, discuss design decisions and present the results of two evaluation sessions with a total of 20 visually impaired test users.

Keywords

Interactive Audio Guide; Tactile Reliefs; Finger Tracking; Gesture Detection; Evaluation; Blind Users;

1. INTRODUCTION

Tactile materials are widely used among blind and visually impaired (BVI) people that help to perceive and understand graphic content, that is otherwise difficult to convey. Such tools may be categorized according to the taxonomy in [26] into a) two-dimensional (*2D*) objects [1, 8] like tactile diagrams, line drawings or plans, e.g. on embossed paper, swell paper, and increasingly also with vibrotactile cues [17, 22], b) fully *3D* objects [23, 26, 30, 34] like anatomical models, 3D-printed reproductions or everyday objects, and c) the *2.5D* realm in-between, i.e., "height fields, surfaces that can be represented by a function $z = f(x, y)$, giving every point above a plane a single height value" [26]. The last group, tactile relief, is especially useful to ease access to the visual arts of images, photos and paintings, as it is important to keep the connection to the two-dimensional original, while

ASSETS '16, October 23 - 26, 2016, Reno, NV, USA

© 2016 Copyright held by the owner/author(s). Publication rights licensed to ACM.
ISBN 978-1-4503-4124-0/16/10. . . $15.00

DOI: http://dx.doi.org/10.1145/2982142.2982176

the plasticity of the added height makes it easier to recognize by touch. Depicted shapes can be geometrically formed in bas-relief, and painted textures can be made tactile as surface variations. The demand and importance is demonstrated by more and more art shows (e.g. [27]) all over the world incorporating tactile reliefs, as well as technical developments [10, 11, 25] in order to ease their creation.

While tactile material is good at conveying spatial cues, many aspects are difficult to mediate by touch alone. As stressed throughout the literature (e.g. [9]), verbal description is a very important part, especially for art. A painting is typically composed of several parts, all with their own appearance, colors and properties, and with relationships to each other. All of this is hard to encode into a single tactile image, but can easily be described verbally.

On the other side, a single monolithic text may not be satisfactory as well. While most appreciate a top-level introduction to orient themselves, detailed descriptions are better given on demand. Each person might be interested in different details and might rather request them when they find an interesting region, as opposed to getting the details in a pre-defined order and having to find the matching locations.

In museums and galleries, a BVI person is typically guided by a trained person, who is prepared to answer questions to different aspects, or who can guide the hand to desired locations. However, such a guide may not always be available, or a BVI person may want to be independent and explore the relief in a more autonomous way.

Therefore, we propose a gesture-based interactive audio guide, capable of giving a user exactly this freedom.

1.1 Requirements

The aim of this work is to create a system that enables BVI people to explore tactile materials in a more autonomous way. Motivated by project partners, our approach is mainly targeted at a museum setting with tactile reliefs of paintings, but the results may readily be used in a wider context. We therefore envision a largely self-contained system, in the form of a kiosk or installation that fits into a museum space. In order to keep the system maintainable, it should run on off-the-shelf, easily exchangeable, low-cost hardware. Custom software algorithms should not depend on specialized hardware to simplify adaption to different architectures. The same setup should be usable with several tactile objects, one at a time. The content for each object should be easily adaptable, flexible enough to add and change interaction locations, descriptions, and interaction modes. The interface should be simple, easy to use, self-explanatory, and robust to a wide variety of users. Although the first proto-

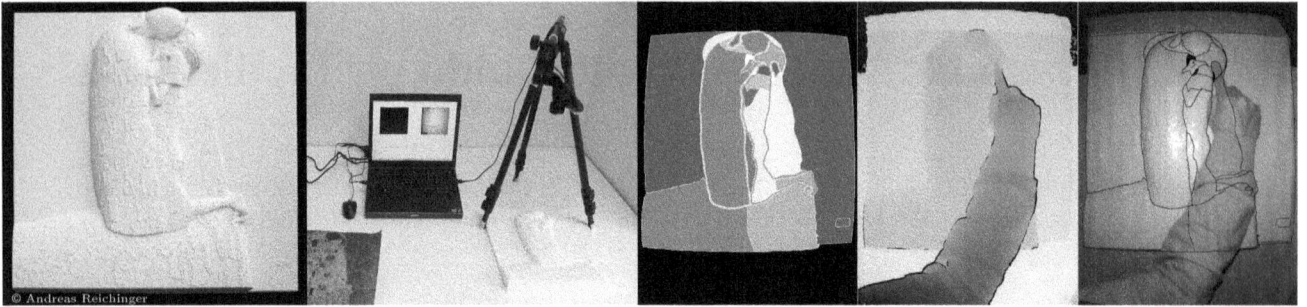

Figure 1: From left to right: a) Tactile relief interpretation of Gustav Klimt's "Der Kuss" (The Kiss, 1908/09); b) Test setup; c) Label image, warped to camera space. Outlines indicate merged base labels; d) Depth image; e) Infrared image with superimposed label borders and touched label (purple). © Andreas Reichinger

type is targeted at BVI people, according to a design-for-all philosophy, the system may be also interesting for children, elderly, people with cognitive impairments, and the general audience, possibly all with different interaction modes.

Based on discussions with BVI people, the main goal of our system is to allow users an *undisturbed* exploration, without unwanted explanations, and precise control over when and about what to get information. The user should be able to explore the relief with one or both hands without triggering unwanted audio and avoid Midas touch effects [14, p. 156]. This means, that only very distinct gestures should trigger audio comments, gestures that normally don't occur during tactile exploration and that can be reliably detected. This is in contrast to systems with embedded sensors (cf. Section 2), that are triggered by any kind of touch, whether intended or not.

2. RELATED WORK

A large body of work concentrates on augmentation of 2D graphics. The *Talking Tactile Tablet* [19] and *ViewPlus' IVEO* [13] detects touch-gestures on tactile diagrams put on a high-resolution touch pad. This technology clearly cannot be extended to relief surfaces of significant height.

Several projects utilize color cameras to track the user's fingertips: *Access Lens* [15] recognizes and reads texts on documents where the finger points at. The *Tactile Graphics Helper* [12] plays pre-recorded audio when the finger is over pre-defined labels, and is triggered by voice commands. *Tactile Graphics with a Voice* [2] is an app for cell phones and Google Glass, that reads labels indicated by QR codes. And, *Kin'touch* [3] studies the combination of optical finger tracking and touch events from a capacitive multi-touch screen. While these approaches focus on 2D documents, some could probably be extended to the third dimension. However, most require labels which we want to avoid, and tracking based on color alone is error prone, as it is dependent on skin color, background color and lighting conditions.

Talking Pen Devices[1] detect barely visible printed patterns, and take a somewhat special role: Although originally intended for printed documents, they are usable on 3D objects by applying stickers with the detectable pattern. However, stickers affect the tactile quality, and wear off.

---

[1]Multiple vendors offer talking pens, like the Talking-PEN (www.talkingpen.co.uk), Talking Tactile Pen (www.touchgraphics.com), Livescribe (www.edlivescribe.com) or Ravensburger tiptoi (www.tiptoi.com).

Several full 3D approaches are based on devices integrated *into* the tactile object. For instance, *Tooteko* [5] integrates NFC Tags in 3D models which are read by a wearable NFC reader. *Digital Touch replica* [32] have touch sensors integrated at interesting locations. Most recently, *3DPhotoWorks* (www.3dphotoworks.com) managed to print the color images directly on the relief surfaces [21] and integrated infrared sensors into their reliefs. While this is a robust solution for a museum setting, these approaches are less flexible. Once placed, trigger regions cannot be changed any more, and probably not reused on other objects. Only discrete trigger locations are possible, and interaction modes requiring fine-grained touch positions are not possible. Furthermore, the sensors react to any kind of touch, which conflicts with tactile examination by BVI people (cf. Midas touch).

Probably for the first time, Wilson [31] introduced the concept of using a depth camera as a touch sensor on non-flat surfaces. *CamIO* [29] extended the concept to touch-interaction on 3D objects targeted at blind users. A proof of concept implementation was given, with at least two different labels on an object, that could even be rotated. The probably most similar approach is a feasibility study [4], which uses a Microsoft Kinect with the CVRL FORTH Hand Tracker [20] to trigger audio by touch events of the right index fingertip on tactile reliefs. Little is reported about real-world experiences by the target group. Only the limited robustness of the tracking system is mentioned.

In contrast, our system is built around a custom hand detection algorithm that is very stable as it works independently on each frame. A carefully selected set of gestures already allows multiple actions, and was evaluated in a user study. The theoretical concept of our system was first presented in [24], and includes a review of current depth sensors.

3. INTERACTIVE AUDIO GUIDE (IAG)

The gesture-controlled IAG consists of a depth camera (currently an Intel RealSense F200) as the only sensor, connected to a computer and rigidly mounted above a tactile relief, which it observes (cf. Fig. 1b). In contrast to conventional color cameras that give an RGB color value for each pixel, a depth camera (or RGB-D camera) also returns a depth value, i.e., how far an object at this pixel is away from the camera. First, the system is initialized with only the relief present and the hands kept away. The system stores the acquired depth image, the so-called *background image*. Whatever is now put on top of the relief creates depth measurements that are nearer to the camera, and can therefore be easily detected. This process is called foreground segmentation (cf. Section 3.3.3), and creates a *foreground mask*, a set of pixels where new things are located. As any objects may be added, the foreground is carefully searched for hands, and whether these hands form certain input gestures (cf. Sections 3.3.5–3.3.8). Finally, depending on the gestures, real-time audio feedback is given to the user.

The use of a depth camera has multiple advantages over a conventional color camera: It is largely independent from the lighting situation, working even in complete darkness, as it has its own, for humans invisible lighting. In contrast to color images, depth allows a more reliable foreground segmentation, that is independent from relief and skin color, even gloves may be worn. Depth further allows to detect touch-events to trigger interaction, whereas systems using color cameras have to use, e.g., voice commands. It is more flexible than approaches with integrated sensors, works on arbitrary 3D surfaces, and allows gestures "beyond touch" [31]. Depth cameras are nowadays low-cost off-the-shelf technology that is estimated to be soon integrated into laptops (already available) and mobile devices. This makes the system also attractive for home use in the future.

In the remainder of this paper we will explain the development of our prototype, detail our design decisions and conclude with the results of the user evaluation.

3.1 Prototype

In order to test the proposed system, we developed a prototype for the interactive exploration of a tactile relief interpretation of Gustav Klimt's painting "The Kiss" (1908/09). This popular painting was chosen because many BVI people most certainly heard about it, but to date only descriptions, and a simple raised line diagram were available. The relief (cf. Fig. 1a) was created based on an approach by Reichinger et. al. [25], using custom software to segment and layer depicted objects and to extract surface textures. In addition, we integrated rigged 3D models for the figures, deformed to match their poses, and Beziér surfaces for the cloths.

In cooperation with experts on art history, regions of the painting have been labeled, named and short texts (20 seconds on average) have been recorded containing descriptions of the region, color composition, body poses, and relations between parts. The image was divided into 6 basic regions (like background, meadow, male and female figure), and the two figures were further subdivided for a total of 20 different labels of varying size (cf. Fig. 1c). In addition five short general texts (50–60 seconds each) about the painting, its history, interpretations and the artist have been recorded.

3.2 Interaction Design

Despite ongoing research on gestures for BVI people (e.g. [16]) and user-elicited gestures (e.g. [33]) these are only valid for dynamic interaction on flat screens, and are not directly applicable. For our specific case with static reliefs and depth sensors, careful interaction design was important.

We distinguish between two kinds of information: location specific information that describes a specific part on the explored object, and general information that is unrelated to any specific location on the object. Correspondingly we require two groups of gestures: Location specific information should be triggered with gestures *on* the object, directly touching the part of interest. Gestures *off* the

object can be used for all other interactions, e.g., to trigger the above-mentioned general information, but also for application commands, like audio controls.

Our design choices are based on typically used exploration strategies we derived from informal discussions with BVI people and from observations in previous projects: Most BVI people touch the relief with both hands, often keeping one hand as a reference. Both hands are almost always on or close to the relief. The exploration is usually divided into two phases, although not strictly separated: In a first "overview" phase users try to familiarize themselves with the overall composition of the painting, typically observing it with their whole hands, and in larger motions. In a second "detail" phase, they are exploring selected parts in more detail, typically with the tips of individual fingers.

3.2.1 On-Object Interaction

For on-relief interaction it feels natural to use gestures directly touching the region of interest. Using a single finger avoids ambiguous situations, and also matches motions occurring naturally in the detail exploration phase. We allow any finger to be used for interaction, so BVI people can choose whichever they feel most comfortable with. This is in contrast to Buonamici et al. [4] who require using the right index finger. We decided for the typical pointing gesture, having all fingers but one contracted into a fist. This gesture feels very natural, while at the same time it is only rarely used during normal exploration, which mostly avoids triggering unwanted audio.

In order to account for the two exploration phases, we at first play back the region name of the selected part, and only after a longer touch gesture (until the name was played), the detail description follows. Every playback can be interrupted by triggering another region. This enables the user to quickly scan the object during exploration and to easily locate parts of interest for more detailed information. Each new trigger is accompanied by a short click sound, as an important feedback to the user and also to avoid confusion when a text was unintentionally interrupted.

3.2.2 Hierarchical Exploration

As mentioned before, two basic regions (male and female figure, cf. Fig. 1c) were further subdivided into smaller parts, mainly the parts of the bodies and cloths. The idea is, that in the beginning only the six basic regions are used to gain a quick overview. Once the user has heard the full detail description of a figure (which includes important information about the posture and relation to other regions) the subdivided parts of the respective figure will become available instead of the basic region.

3.2.3 Off-Object Interaction

As most users keep their hands on or close to the relief, we use the space above the relief to trigger off-object interactions. A *closed fist* gesture at least 10 cm above the relief will stop the current playback. The other hand may still remain on the relief to stay oriented. According to our main goal of an undisturbed exploration, this command is the most important, as it allows to cancel unwanted or unintentional audio. Background information can be triggered by *number-gestures*. As our number of general texts (cf. Section 3.1) is exactly 5, we chose to simply count the number of extended fingers of the lifted hand, which also generalizes to different number gestures in different cultures. More chapters are unlikely for paintings in a museum context, but different gestures may be implemented in a future work. Once the gesture is detected, a click sound followed by the number of fingers and the title of the chapter is played. Again, a newly detected gesture interrupts the playback of the former. This allows the user to correct the hand pose until the desired number of fingers is detected, and to browse through the headings of the available texts until the desired one is found. Once the user is satisfied with the choice, the text starts directly after its title, and the users can lower their hand and continue the tactile exploration while listening.

3.2.4 Making it Self-Explanatory

The current prototype was designed as an installation in a museum, for people who are not familiar with the system. Therefore, the first interaction is to simply put the hands on the relief, which triggers a short introduction explaining the interface. After the system is not used for a given amount of time, the system is reset and waits for the next user.

3.3 Implementation

Based on the selected set of gestures, the requirements for the gesture detection system are as follows: 1) a reliable detection of hands and individual fingers, 2) measurement of the palm height for off-relief gestures, 3) detection of touch events of a pointing finger and the position of the touch.

3.3.1 Sensor Selection

In [24] the concept for our setup is described, requirements for a tracking camera are analyzed, and several state-of-the-art cameras are reviewed. We follow the suggestion to use the *Intel RealSense F200* as the currently most suitable sensor for our application. It has a sufficient resolution of the depth sensor (true 640×480 pixels) with up to 60 fps and a low noise level. Combined with its near operating range and suitable field-of-view we achieve an effective resolution of more than 10 pixels per cm (25 dpi) on the relief. In our setup the sensor is centered approximately 40–45 cm above our 42×42 cm relief, overlooking the whole relief including a few centimeters of its surrounding (cf. Fig. 1). We chose portrait orientation, as it is more important to detect the hands beyond the relief towards the user. At the depth in our setup, the sensor does not give measurements at an up to 40 pixels wide region on one side, which we rotated beyond the top of the relief, away from the user (cf. Fig. 1d).

The RealSense F200 is a time-sequential structured light scanner. For each depth measurement frame, several Gray-coded stripe patterns are projected with an infrared (IR) laser projector and filmed with a high-frame-rate infrared camera. The projector consists of an on-off modulated laser, a cylindrical lens to create a laser line, and a swinging micro-mirror to scan over the whole area [6]. A set of IR camera images with different Gray-code patterns are combined to compute the final depth image. In addition to the depth image (D, cf. Fig. 1d), two other images are transmitted via USB 3.0: an IR image of the scene is generated, that appears fully lit by the laser projector (cf. Fig. 1e), and an RGB image is generated using a separate RGB camera mounted approximately 2.5 cm away from the IR camera.

This technology has only recently become available for low-cost depth cameras. It has a low noise level in the depth values, with a standard deviation below 1 mm on smooth surfaces. However, noise levels vary in a moiré-like pattern (cf. Fig. 2b), possibly caused by interferences between the projector and camera. On steep edges, where a multitude of depth measurements are equally correct, depth measurements get less reliable. Despite low noise and high resolution, the scanner has 3 caveats that need to be dealt with:

1) Like most structured light scanners, objects near the scanner cast a projection shadow on more distant objects. Therefore, foreground objects are surrounded by pixels with no, or erroneous measurements.

2) Since the scanner requires multiple frames per measurement, fast moving objects, or more specific, depth-changes at a pixel during the measurement, result in unreliable measurements. This results in blurred and unusable measurements around the edges of hands and arms, when in motion.

3) We measure significant drifts in the depth measurements of a static scene over time, possibly caused by timing issues during pattern projection with the swinging mirror. These are noticeable as a tilt of the depth values, slowly changing over time, and some abrupt changes. The tilt exists mainly in x-direction, and was measured in our setup to be up to 15 mm between the left and right end of the sensor after a cold start, and still varying over 5 mm after warm-up.

3.3.2 Software Implementation

As pointed out by Reichinger et al. [24], the optimum for the proposed system would be "an out-of-the-box solution for articulated finger tracking, [that works] on relief surfaces". The only publicly available implementation we found is the CVRL FORTH Hand Tracker [20] already tested by [4] for a similar application. However, we could not use the software, because a) it currently only supports sensors of the Kinect family, b) the demonstrator only tracks a single hand and requires an initialization pose,[2] and c) according to [4] it loses tracking for fast movements. Similar approaches have been published (e.g. [28]) or created by www.NimbleVR.com but implementations are not or no longer available.

As such approaches are very hardware demanding, and an implementation from scratch was beyond the scope of our work, we decided to implement a simpler, silhouette-based approach, which is basically a 2D problem, for which a lot of well-studied algorithms are available. These basically work, when the hand is more or less parallel to the camera plane, and the relevant fingers can be detected in the silhouette (cf. Fig. 2a), i.e., do not touch. With the selected set of gestures, and the camera setup with an almost parallel view of the hands, these requirements are satisfied.

Because of the demonstrated robustness and the detailed documentation we based our implementation on [35]. We will shortly outline the original approach, and detail the parts that had to be modified in order to make it work on our specific setup, directly on a relief surface.

3.3.3 Silhouette Detection

The original paper addresses both color-based foreground segmentation using RGB cameras, and depth segmentation using a depth camera. In our prototype we use the depth measurement as main segmentation key, complemented by the infrared image, which proved adequate for our requirements. We do not currently use color information in our prototype, although it could be interesting as an extension

---

[2]Extensions where published (e.g. [18]) but their implementations are not publicly available.

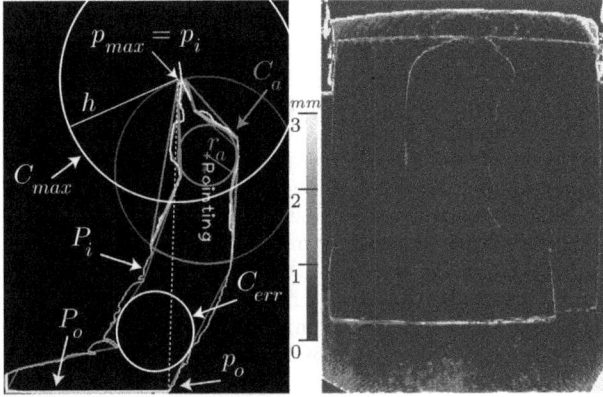

Figure 2: From left to right: a) Hand detection output and palm detection diagram; b) Standard deviation of background measurements over 100 frames.

in the future. Due to the sensor's low noise in depth measurements (with a variance below 1 mm) we are able to reliably segment the hands, even at a fingertip pressed against the surface, with a height difference as low as 5 mm.

In contrast to hand-tracking approaches that operate in free space, we cannot use a constant depth threshold, as the hand is supposed to operate directly on the surface. However, we can exploit the fact that in our static setup, the background does not change and can be calibrated once. This is in contrast to other setups [4, 29], where the object and/or camera are allowed to move relative to each other, and more complex tracking solutions have to be used.

During background calibration, the mean μ and standard deviation σ of each pixel in the depth and IR images are computed from 100 consecutive frames, yielding a Gaussian distribution. A foreground probability based on depth p_D is computed as the one-sided p-value at the current depth, offset by a safety margin of 5 mm. p_{IR} is computed as the two-sided p-value. The combined foreground probability p is the weighted average $p = (w_D p_D + w_{IR} p_{IR})/(w_D + w_{IR})$, where the weights are computed as $w_D = \alpha/\sigma_D$ and $w_{IR} = 1/\sigma_{IR}$, and $\alpha = 100$ trades off depth for IR.[3]

As outlined in Section 3.3.1, rapid depth-changes at a pixel caused by fast moving objects, results in unusable measurements around the edges of hands and arms when they are in motion. In order to still extract a meaningful silhouette, we track the standard deviation of the depth measurements σ_M of the last 5 frames, compute a depth-motion-penalty $\beta = 0.3 \, \text{mm}/\sigma_M$ clamped to $[0.2, 1]$ and replace $\alpha = 100/\beta$. If an object moves fast, the variance of an edge-pixel is high, β gets low, and less weight is given to the depth probability p_D, effectively falling back to a foreground detection based on the infrared channel values. Detection based on a single intensity value is of course rather error prone. Nevertheless, skin and worn cloths often have a significantly different infrared reflection than the tactile relief (cf. Fig. 1e), giving an additional clue as to where the correct silhouette is located.

The resulting probability image is smoothed (Gaussian blur σ=3 pixels), thresholded to 0.5 and eroded with a 3×3 kernel to yield the foreground segmentation mask.

---

[3]If background (I_B) or current (I_C) or both (I_{BC}) measurements are invalid, special (p, w) pairs are used: $I_B = (0.5, 0)$, $I_C = (0.7, 1)$ and $I_{BC} = (0.2, 1)$.

3.3.4 Continuous Sensor Calibration

As outlined in Section 3.3.1, the depth measurements show significant drift over time, which compromises the tight tolerances of the depth-based segmentation and therefore requires continuous detection and calibration with respect to the stored background image. We model the drift d at a pixel (x, y) as an additive tilt to the raw metric depth measurements d_{raw} in the form of $d(x, y) = d_{raw}(x, y) + \delta_0 + x\delta_x + y\delta_y$. This approximation proves to be sufficient for our application, but is presumably not very accurate.

The tilt-parameters δ_0, δ_x and δ_y are estimated as a 2D linear regression on the difference between the stored mean background $\bar{b}$ and a running average of the latest 5 depth values $\bar{c}$. Currently detected foreground regions (enlarged by a safety margin of 12 px) are excluded, as well as unreliable measurements of b and c, which yielded invalid measurements during the average computation. The differences are clamped to ±3 mm to avoid excessive outliers, and weighted by the inverse of the computed standard deviations of b and c, to lower the impact of noisy regions. The changes are applied gradually to avoid abrupt changes, using an IIR filter mixing in only 10% of the new solution. Due to performance, the adjustments are only performed once every 4 frames.

3.3.5 Palm Detection

Following [35], the hands are detected solely based on their silhouettes. From the foreground mask of Section 3.3.3, all connected components larger than 5000 pixels are chosen as potential hand regions, and their contours are extracted. Of course, this approach only works if the hands and arms do not touch or overlap. This is satisfied for the selected gestures, since the user can be instructed to move the other hand away from the interacting hand. In a future implementation this can be improved, using multiple sensors, and/or a fully articulated hand tracker that allows overlap (e.g. [18]).

Assuming the region contains a single hand, the position of the palm has to be found. The original approach [35] finds the largest circle C_a inscribed in the silhouette. However, this often fails, e.g., when the user is wearing loose cloths (cf. Fig. 2a, C_{err}). Our solution is as follows:

We first intersect the contour with a rectangle, 5 pixels from the image border, and find the largest consecutive contour-part P_i that does not touch the border. If no part touches the border, we assume that the hand was segmented without the arm, and continue with the largest circle search. Otherwise, we close the polygon P_i along the rectangle with one or more line segments P_o. We then find the point p_{max} on P_i that is most distant to all the points on P_o as

$$p_{max} = \arg\max_{p_i \in P_i} \min_{p_o \in P_o} \|p_i - p_o\|. \tag{1}$$

We create a bounding circle (50 pixel radius) around p_{max} and compute the average depth measurement $\bar{d}$ of all valid points inside this circle and the contour. We estimate the expected maximum hand size h at such a distance as $h = 200px \times 390mm/\bar{d}$. The maximum inscribed circle C_a with radius r_a is then only searched inside a bounding circle C_{max} around p_{max} with radius h. We compute the depth of the palm as the average depth of all valid points inside C_a.

3.3.6 Fingertip Detection

Fingertip detection is similar to [35]. The hand silhouette is clipped to a bounding circle 3.5 times the radius of the palm, the resulting polygon is simplified, convexity defects are computed and filtered whether they could represent the empty space between fingers.[4] Between neighboring pairs of all accepted convexity defects we test for potential fingertips. We modified the criteria as follows: a) The arc-distance along P_i between two consecutive convexity defects and their angle must be below certain thresholds. b) Similar to [35], we require the k-curvature to be below 60°. But instead of using a constant $k = 30$, we take the curvature as the minimum k-curvature computed using a number of different k varying from 30 to 60 px, to allow for locally flat but still elongated fingertips to be detected. c) We limit the width of such a potential fingertip, to eliminate cases like two fingers pressed together that still may pass the k-curvature test.

We also modified the fingertip localization. While in [35] the fingertip location is determined from the k-curvature points, we found this too unreliable, due to the often rather jagged contours occurring in our setup. Instead we take the part of the finger contour between the two k-convexity end points, and compute the oriented bounding box to get more reliable estimates for the finger's direction and width. In order to extract the tip region, we take the valid pixels inside the top square region of the bounding box. We estimate the center of the fingertip as the centroid of these pixels, and compute the z-location of the finger as the average depth values of these pixels. Finally, we classify the fingertip's quality into three categories: If the tip-region has too few pixels (<50) it is not classified as finger. If the finger is too wide for the given depth (width $\times$ depth > 25 px $\times$ 400 mm) it is labeled as *blob*, being probably a union of two fingers, and only if it satisfies both, it is labeled as a single finger.

3.3.7 Gesture Recognition

We do not perform frame to frame tracking, as this is not necessary for the current gestures, and would introduce recovery problems once a hand was lost. Nevertheless, we need to make the gesture recognition robust, as the detected hands and fingers may vary each frame. Our solution is to require a gesture to be detected in the majority of the latest frames. For instance, off-object gestures are triggered if the palm-to-sensor distance is below a certain value in 75% of the last 20 frames, *with* the same amount of fingers detected.

3.3.8 On-Object Touch Event

In order to relate the detected touch events to regions on the relief, and therefore to different audio files, the regions have to be labeled by the content author (cf. Fig. 1c). Since our setup is static, we simply sketch the labels on a once acquired IR image of the relief (cf. Fig. 1e). While this of course does not adapt to a different camera placement as in [29] and [4], it proved accurate enough for our rigid setup. For added flexibility, a future implementation might incorporate an automatic and dynamic calibration. Manual initialization [4] and fiducial markers [29] might be eliminated by detecting the base plane and corners of rectangular reliefs, or by using novel 3D feature based algorithms [7].

Finally, the fingertip location has to be mapped to the regions. While Buonamici et al. [4] use a complex 3D search for the nearest point of a point cloud of the relief to the

fingertip, we again use a simpler 2D approach. Since the camera observes the relief almost straight on and the labels are defined in camera space, the xy-location of the finger is already given with maximum precision in the foreground mask. We simply take all pixels of the detected fingertip that are within some depth tolerance to the depth background, and collect the labels of these pixels. If at least 90% of these pixels are on the same label, the detection is considered unique. Otherwise, the finger might be on a border between labels and it is not decidable, which label the user meant. A touch event is generated, when at least 70% of the last 10 frames detected the same unique label (cf. purple area in Fig. 1e). With a sufficient depth tolerance to robustly detect touch, actual touch is not distinguishable from a slightly hovering finger. However, no participant seemed to have noticed that, as they mostly kept the finger on the relief.

4. EVALUATION

The implemented system was evaluated in two sessions in two different European countries. The first session was an informal 2.5 hours long evaluation with 7 mostly elderly BVI people, with the majority having some rest of sight. Based on this first feedback we implemented a structured evaluation which took place in the course of 2 full days with 13 people (5 female, aged 11–72, avg. 50).

Of the 13 volunteers, 6 were fully blind with no sense of sight, 4 had a minimum rest of sight below 1% that did not help them perceive images and 3 had some rest of sight. Nine participants have been visually impaired for the majority of their lives, three at least 20 years and one for 9 years. Seven are able to read Braille, and all are very interested in museums, going at least twice a year, four at least 4–5 times, two even over 20 times. Most participants reported, that touch tools are important for them (on a Likert-scale from 1 to 10, six reported 9–10, four between 6–8, three <3).

The presented prototype was part of a larger evaluation with four different devices. However, we concentrate here on the questions regarding the present system. The results of the full evaluation will be presented elsewhere. Only one relief was tested to keep the load of the evaluation tractable, but during development a number of reliefs were used. Each participant spent at least 30 minutes evaluating this device, and could test it as long as they wanted. Afterwards, the examiner asked 24 questions in a structured interview. Most questions asked for a ranking on a 10 point Likert-scale, 1 being the most negative, 10 the most positive ranking, giving no answers allowed. These are summarized in Figure 3.

The testers where seated in front of the relief, so they could comfortably reach it. The introduction was kept minimal, stating the general idea of the IAG, and showed them where the relief and camera were located, so that nobody accidentally crashed into it. No interface was initially described as we wanted to test whether the introductory text was sufficient. However, one examiner was always present, prepared to answer questions or help with the interface.

4.1 General Impression

We got very good feedback for the system in general. On the question, whether the IAG helped gaining a better understanding of the painting, all gave a rating above 8 (average 9.5). Several people spontaneously praised the system, calling it "super", "perfect", "cool", "I am in love with it", "It has to go into the museum, for eternity" and "finally I have

---

[4] We use slightly different criteria than [35]. Following their notation, instead of $r_a < l_d < r_b$ we require for both $l \in \{l_a, l_b\}$ that $l > 0.1\,r_a$ and at least for one l that $l > 0.4\,r_a$. The criterion $\theta_a < 90°$ was removed.

1	2	3	4	5	6	7	8	9	10	avg.
How important are touch tools for you?										
1	1	1				1	2	1	2	4 |→ 7.2
How did you get along with the system?										
			1		4	1		2	5	8.4
Did IAG help to better understand painting?										
							1	5	7	9.5
How understandable is the introduction?										
		1				2	1	6	3	8.5
How easy is it to perform the gestures?										
			1		1		2	3	5	8.8
How easy is it to trigger a desired comment?										
			1		1	6	2		3	8.3
How satisfied with number of described parts?										
							3	5	3	9.1
How satisfied with description texts?										
						1	2	3	7	9.3
How import that audio only played when wanted?										
							1	2	10	9.5
Is this technology meaningful in museums?										
							3	1	9	9.5
Would you rather go to a museum offering IAG?										
1	1					1		1	1	8 → 8.2
Would you use this technology at home?										
1		1	3			1		3	4	7.2
Would you buy such system (approx. 200 EUR)?										
	1			1			1	3	6	8.6
Your general impression of the relief?										
			1				1	2	7	9.2
How good did you get the overall composition?										
			1	1				4	7	9.0
How good did you get the details of painting?										
		1			1		2	4	4	8.4

Figure 3: Results of ranking questions on a Likert scale from 1 to 10, 10 being the "best". Translated abbreviated questions, histograms and averages.

a mental picture of 'The Kiss'". They liked the direct interaction with the finger, the intuitive interface, its simplicity and the combination of 3D touch and simultaneous audio, the in-depth descriptions, and that the texts are "pleasantly short". Some felt that the independence of a human guide gives them the freedom to explore it without pressure, as long and as detailed as they wanted. One person expressed that they "felt guided", probably caused by descriptions that cross-reference nearby regions, guiding from one region to the next. Another put a thought into the future, and liked the fact, that the object to be observed could be exchanged below the camera, and began to sketch scenarios, where he could choose between different reliefs and put them under the camera in a kiosk in the museum or at home.

Negative feedback was rare. One person with rest of sight questioned the necessity of such a system, concluding that it probably depends on the complexity of the relief. In general, it seemed that completely blind people appreciated the system most, as people with rest of sight are not that dependent on touch and audio. One person wished to have a description about the painting first, but did not follow the suggestion in the introduction to first listen to the general text about the painting. When asked, how good they were getting along with the system, all but one ranked it above 7, two gave it a 9, and five a full 10. One person ranking 7 noted: "the functions are clear but it did not always work".

4.2 Interface

Since the system is designed as a kiosk in a museum, an introductory text should be sufficient to use the interface. Indeed, nine people rated the understandability of the introduction above 9. Participants giving lower ranks stated that they did not pay full attention, that the text was too fast or too long, or that they simply did not memorize everything. Some wished for a possibility to repeat the introduction, or to include an interactive tutorial session.

Four participants immediately mastered the interface, and could reproduce all gestures without any intervention from the examiner. Others needed tips or slight manual corrections of their hands. After a short training phase, nearly all could perform the gestures on their own. When asking for how easy it was to perform the gestures, eight participants rated 9 or higher. Comments included, that it is "as simple as possible", "as good as it gets", and "even funny to silence it with the fist". Especially significant was the confirmation of our design goal, to only have the system play audio when it is explicitly requested by the user. Ten participants gave a ranking of 10, stating that it is very important to concentrate on the tactile exploration every now and then, without being disturbed by constant audio information.

4.2.1 Off-Object Gestures

Off-object gestures worked for most people as they got audio feedback about the number of detected fingers when reaching the desired height, allowing instant corrections. Problems were mostly caused by the hand not positioned at the required minimum height, or the camera not detecting all fingers for the chapter selection. Either the hand was partly outside the camera, or was not held fully frontal to the camera. Some people frequently lifted their hands up from the relief, and accidentally triggered off-object commands. This mainly occurred with people with a rest of sight, and while talking to the examiner. Participants encountering such problems suggested to use hardware buttons, voice-commands or knocking-signals instead of the gestures. Some also expressed the desire for additional playback-commands, like pause, back/repeat, or the change of reading speed. Others disliked the idea of browsing the text headlines with the finger gestures, and requested a table of content.

4.2.2 On-Object Gestures

The pointing gesture worked for most people, at least after some training. A common problem was, that sometimes more than one finger was detected when the fist was not fully closed. Mostly, the thumb was still extended as the testers did not think of it as part of the fist. Some participants mentioned, that the gesture is uncomfortable or feels unnatural, and expressed their wish to relax the gesture and to allow more fingers being extended, at least the thumb. It is yet unclear, how to best select the interacting fingers in such alternative gestures. Maybe by performing a kind of double-tap with the specific finger?

Another source of error and probably also the main course of the discomfort, is the current requirement to perform it in a very flat way, required by the the silhouette-based hand detector. Especially elderly people from the first evaluation session had problems performing the required flat pointing gesture, as their hands were already less flexible, or had medical conditions like arthritis. Some participants thought, the pointing gesture was more like pressing a button, and held the finger steep down, making it difficult to detect. This gets more severe at the top of the relief: As the camera is mounted over the center of the relief, the observation angle gets steeper to the top edge, and even with a flat hand position, the fingertip detection gets less reliable. A possible solution would be a different camera placement, observing the hands from a lower perspective. However, this might have negative implications on the localization. Maybe a combination of multiple cameras can solve this in the future.

Another limitation of the current setup occurs near the left, right and lower edges. We placed the scanner as low as possible to maximize the effective resolution, with only a few centimeters around the relief still captured by the scanner. When the finger touches a feature near an edge, the hand typically protrudes beyond the relief and outside the scanning region, hindering proper hand detection. A future setup with possible higher resolution scanners should keep ample space around the relief.

The hierarchical exploration was not specifically tested, but seemed to work for most users. People going into detail listened to the top-level description and explored further without noticing the transition. Others were either satisfied with the general description or did not even fully listen to it. In the future, an explicit level control may be investigated.

Lastly, localization accuracy has some room for improvement. The majority of testers rated the question "How easy is it to trigger a desired comment?" with 8. There were no problems selecting larger areas. However, most participants had problems selecting the smallest regions like the hands of the figures, which are not much larger than the fingertip itself. This is probably caused by the current algorithm, that requires 90% of the fingertip pixels to be over a single area. Although, it is possible to select all regions, especially for sighted users with visual feedback from the tracking system, it is currently unknown how to make it easier at small regions as well as at borders between two regions. Maybe the single point interaction of [4] is of advantage here.

4.3 Content

Nearly all participants were satisfied with the presented content. High rankings confirm a good readability of the created relief: The average rating for the general impression was 9.2, 9.0 for getting the overall composition, and 8.4 for getting the details of the painting. All but one stated, that the amount of detail was chosen right, one said it was too much. They liked the high elevation, the three-dimensional plastic appearance, the size, the detailed textures, the smooth, rounded parts, the recognizable body parts and the faithfulness to the original painting. Some wanted it slightly larger and higher, or suggested detachable parts for easier recognition. The material (Corian) was comfortable for most, only two people did not like it at all. Four people mentioned, that it would be nice to have a colored relief for people with rest of sight, while others found it irrelevant as long as the original can be seen next to it.

People were highly satisfied by the texts (average 9.3), and by the number of described parts (9.1). One very eager participant would have liked to know the number of descriptions in advance, in order to check to have not missed anything. On the question whether they were missing descriptions, four mentioned a better description of color and texture, possibly not only for the area, but more specifically at the location of the fingertip. This was especially apparent at the comparatively large area of the male figure's coat, where several people expected more descriptions than just a single text covering the whole area.

4.4 Acceptance and Field of Application

All test users found the presented technology to be meaningful in a museum setting with an average ranking of 9.5. However, not all would *rather* go to a museum if it was offering an IAG (average 8.2), as they would go to the museums in any case. Even less would consider it for home use (7.2) as they would not have space and time to use it. However, after telling them, that the technology is very low-cost, possibly included in many future devices and that it could be extended to any objects, not just reliefs, six would buy it without hesitation, and another four ranked it 8–9. They would like to use it for the annotation of plans, for object detection ("which bottle was the good wine?"), for photo exploration, geography, education, and would like to see it also in schools or other educative institutions (e.g. at the zoo).

5. CONCLUSION AND FUTURE WORK

We presented a gesture-controlled interactive audio guide that allows access to location-specific content, triggered directly with the fingertips on relief surfaces, and demonstrated its real-world usability. The prototype is targeted at a museum setting, but the low-cost sensor hardware and the perspective that these sensors will soon be integrated in laptop and mobile devices, makes it very attractive also for home use, or in educational institutions. The algorithms are lightweight and may run on embedded systems, like the ORBBEC Persee, the first depth camera with integrated computer. Although this work focused on 2.5D tactile reliefs of paintings, the techniques should generalize to any 2D, 2.5D and 3D object.

The majority of the 20 test users found it useful and worth further developments. It seemed to be especially interesting for fully blind people, who like to go into detail, and to do this autonomously. Based on the feedback, we will critically review the selected gestures and the interface design with the target group. We will investigate fully articulated finger trackers, alternative sensor placement, or multiple sensor setups, to better observe the fingertip, especially near the top edge, and to relax the need for flat finger gestures.

Although the system remained stable during several consecutive days without restart, accumulated sensor drift made it less reliable. A future implementation might overcome this limitation by performing a background calibration right before a new user is detected. Finally, we would like to investigate new interaction possibilities. Planned features include multiple knowledge layers, multi-finger gestures, educative games, sonification of color, and an extension to exchangeable 3D objects with arbitrary and dynamic placement.

6. ACKNOWLEDGMENTS

This work was performed within the framework of the project Deep Pictures, supported by the Austrian Science Fund (FWF): P24352-N23, and within the Erasmus+ project AMBAVis (http://www.ambavis.eu) and has been funded with support from the European Commission. This publication reflects the views only of the authors, and the Commission cannot be held responsible for any use which may be made of the information contained therein.

7. REFERENCES

[1] E. S. Axel and N. S. Levent, editors. *Art Beyond Sight: A Resource Guide to Art, Creativity, and Visual Impairment*. AFB Press, 2003.

[2] C. M. Baker, L. R. Milne, J. Scofield, C. L. Bennett, and R. E. Ladner. Tactile Graphics with a Voice: Using QR Codes to Access Text in Tactile Graphics. In *Proceedings of the 16th International ACM SIGACCESS Conference on Computers & Accessibility*, ASSETS '14, pages 75–82, New York, NY, USA, 2014. ACM.

[3] A. Brock, S. Lebaz, B. Oriola, D. Picard, C. Jouffrais, and P. Truillet. Kin'touch: understanding how visually impaired people explore tactile maps. In *CHI'12 Extended Abstracts on Human Factors in Computing Systems*, pages 2471–2476. ACM, 2012.

[4] F. Buonamici, R. Furferi, L. Governi, and Y. Volpe. *Universal Access in Human-Computer Interaction. Access to Interaction: 9th International Conference, UAHCI 2015, Held as Part of HCI International 2015, Los Angeles, CA, USA, August 2-7, 2015, Proceedings, Part II*, chapter Making Blind People Autonomous in the Exploration of Tactile Models: A Feasibility Study, pages 82–93. Springer International Publishing, Cham, 2015.

[5] F. D'Agnano, C. Balletti, F. Guerra, and P. Vernier. Tooteko: a case study of augmented reality for an accessible cultural heritage. Digitization, 3D printing and sensors for an audio-tactile experience. In *Int. Arch. Photogramm. Remote Sens. Spatial Inf. Sci.*, volume XL-5/W4, pages 207–213, 2015.

[6] S. Dixon-Warren. Inside the Intel RealSense Gesture Camera. http://www.chipworks.com/about-chipworks/overview/blog/inside-the-intel-realsense-gesture-camera, accessed May 2016.

[7] B. Drost and S. Ilic. 3d object detection and localization using multimodal point pair features. In *3D Imaging, Modeling, Processing, Visualization and Transmission (3DIMPVT), 2012 Second International Conference on*, pages 9–16. IEEE, 2012.

[8] P. K. Edman. *Tactile Graphics*. American Foundation for the Blind, New York, 1992.

[9] Y. Eriksson. How to make tactile pictures understandable to the blind reader. In *65th IFLA Council and General Conference*, Bangkok, Thailand, August 1999.

[10] R. Furferi, L. Governi, Y. Volpe, et al. Tactile 3D Bas-relief from Single-point Perspective Paintings: A Computer Based Method. *Journal of Information & Computational Science*, 11(16):5667–5680.

[11] R. Furferi, L. Governi, Y. Volpe, L. Puggelli, N. Vanni, and M. Carfagni. From 2D to 2.5D i.e. from painting to tactile model. *Graph. Models*, 76(6):706–723, 2014.

[12] G. Fusco and V. S. Morash. The Tactile Graphics Helper: Providing Audio Clarification for Tactile Graphics Using Machine Vision. In *Proceedings of the 17th International ACM SIGACCESS Conference on Computers & Accessibility*, pages 97–106. ACM, 2015.

[13] J. A. Gardner and V. Bulatov. Scientific diagrams made easy with IVEO™. In K. Miesenberger, J. Klaus, W. L. Zagler, and A. I. Karshmer, editors, *ICCHP 2006*, volume 4061 of *LNCS*, pages 1243–1250, Heidelberg, 2006. Springer.

[14] R. J. K. Jacob. The Use of Eye Movements in Human-computer Interaction Techniques: What You Look at is What You Get. *ACM Trans. Inf. Syst.*, 9(2):152–169, Apr. 1991.

[15] S. K. Kane, B. Frey, and J. O. Wobbrock. Access lens: a gesture-based screen reader for real-world documents. In *Proceedings of the SIGCHI Conference on Human Factors in Computing Systems*, pages 347–350. ACM, 2013.

[16] S. K. Kane, J. O. Wobbrock, and R. E. Ladner. Usable Gestures for Blind People: Understanding Preference and Performance. In *Proceedings of the SIGCHI Conference on Human Factors in Computing Systems*, CHI '11, pages 413–422, New York, NY, USA, 2011. ACM.

[17] R. L. Klatzky, N. A. Giudice, C. R. Bennett, and J. M. Loomis. Touch-screen technology for the dynamic display of 2D spatial information without vision: Promise and progress. *Multisensory Research*, 27(5–6):359–378, 2014.

[18] N. Kyriazis and A. A. Argyros. Scalable 3D Tracking of Multiple Interacting Objects. In *IEEE Computer Vision and Pattern Recognition (CVPR 2014)*, pages 3430–3437, Columbus, Ohio, USA, June 2014. IEEE.

[19] S. Landau and K. Gourgey. Development of a Talking Tactile Tablet. *Inf. Technol. Disabil.*, 7(2), 2001.

[20] I. Oikonomidis, N. Kyriazis, and A. Argyros. Efficient model-based 3D tracking of hand articulations using Kinect. In *BMVC 2011*. BMVA, 2011.

[21] J. S. Olson and A. R. Quattrociocchi. Method and apparatus for three-dimensional digital printing, June 23 2015. US Patent 9,061,521.

[22] S. OÂŠModhrain, N. A. Giudice, J. A. Gardner, and G. E. Legge. Designing Media for Visually-Impaired Users of Refreshable Touch Displays: Possibilities and Pitfalls. *IEEE Transactions on Haptics*, 8(3):248–257, July 2015.

[23] S. Oouchi, K. Yamazawa, and L. Secchi. Reproduction of Tactile Paintings for Visual Impairments Utilized Three-Dimensional Modeling System and the Effect of Difference in the Painting Size on Tactile Perception. In K. Miesenberger, J. Klaus, W. Zagler, and A. Karshmer, editors, *ICCHP 2010, Part II*, volume 6180 of *LNCS*, pages 527–533, Heidelberg, 2010. Springer.

[24] A. Reichinger, A. Fuhrmann, S. Maierhofer, and W. Purgathofer. A Concept for Re-Usable Interactive Tactile Reliefs. In K. Miesenberger, C. BÃijhler, and P. Penaz, editors, *ICCHP 2016, Part II*, volume 9759 of *LNCS*, pages 108–115, Heidelberg, 2016. Springer.

[25] A. Reichinger, S. Maierhofer, and W. Purgathofer. High-Quality Tactile Paintings. *J. Comput. Cult. Herit.*, 4(2):5:1–5:13, 2011.

[26] A. Reichinger, M. Neumüller, F. Rist, S. Maierhofer, and W. Purgathofer. Computer-Aided Design of Tactile Models. In K. Miesenberger, A. Karshmer, P. Penaz, and W. Zagler, editors, *ICCHP 2012, Part II*, volume 7383 of *LNCS*, pages 497–504, Heidelberg, 2012. Springer.

[27] L. Secchi. Seeing with the Hands - Touching with the Eyes, Work of Art Reading as a Hermeneutical Act.

[28] T. Sharp, C. Keskin, D. Robertson, J. Taylor, J. Shotton, D. Kim, C. Rhemann, I. Leichter, A. Vinnikov, Y. Wei, et al. Accurate, robust, and flexible real-time hand tracking. In *Proceedings of the 33rd Annual ACM Conference on Human Factors in Computing Systems*, pages 3633–3642. ACM, 2015.

[29] H. Shen, O. Edwards, J. Miele, and J. M. Coughlan. Camio: A 3D computer vision system enabling audio/haptic interaction with physical objects by blind users. In *Proceedings of the 15th International ACM SIGACCESS Conference on Computers and Accessibility*, page 41. ACM, 2013.

[30] Y. Teshima, A. Matsuoka, M. Fujiyoshi, Y. Ikegami, T. Kaneko, S. Oouchi, Y. Watanabe, and K. Yamazawa. Enlarged Skeleton Models of Plankton for Tactile Teaching. In K. Miesenberger, J. Klaus, W. Zagler, and A. Karshmer, editors, *ICCHP 2010, Part II*, volume 6180 of *LNCS*, pages 523–526, Heidelberg, 2010. Springer.

[31] A. D. Wilson. Using a Depth Camera As a Touch Sensor. In *ACM International Conference on Interactive Tabletops and Surfaces*, ITS '10, pages 69–72, New York, NY, USA, 2010. ACM.

[32] J. Wing. Ancient hieroglyphics meet cutting-edge technology at Loughborough University. http://www.lboro.ac.uk/service/publicity/news-releases/2012/197_Manchester-Museum.html, accessed March 2015, November 2012.

[33] J. O. Wobbrock, M. R. Morris, and A. D. Wilson. User-defined Gestures for Surface Computing. In *Proceedings of the SIGCHI Conference on Human Factors in Computing Systems*, CHI '09, pages 1083–1092, New York, NY, USA, 2009. ACM.

[34] K. Yamazawa, Y. Teshima, Y. Watanabe, Y. Ikegami, M. Fujiyoshi, S. Oouchi, and T. Kaneko. Three-Dimensional Model Fabricated by Layered Manufacturing for Visually Handicapped Persons to Trace Heart Shape. In K. Miesenberger, A. Karshmer, P. Penaz, and W. Zagler, editors, *ICCHP 2012, Part II*, volume 7383 of *LNCS*, pages 505–508, Heidelberg, 2012. Springer.

[35] H.-S. Yeo, B.-G. Lee, and H. Lim. Hand Tracking and Gesture Recognition System for Human-computer Interaction Using Low-cost Hardware. *Multimedia Tools Appl.*, 74(8):2687–2715, Apr. 2015.

Tactile Accessibility:
Does Anyone Need a Haptic Glove?

Andrii Soviak[1], Anatoliy Borodin[2], Vikas Ashok[1], Yevgen Borodin[1], Yury Puzis[1], I.V. Ramakrishnan[1]

[1]Department of Computer Science   [2]Department of Physics and Astronomy

[asoviak,vganjiguntea,borodin,ypuzis,ram]@cs.stonybrook.edu   anatoliy.borodin@stonybrook.edu

Stony Brook University, NY, USA

ABSTRACT

Graphical user interfaces (GUIs) are widely used on smartphones, tablets, and laptops. While GUIs are convenient for sighted users, their accessibility for blind people, who use screen readers to interact with GUIs, remains to be problematic. Even the most screen-reader accessible GUIs are far less usable for blind people compared to sighted people, because the former group cannot benefit from the geometric layout of GUIs. As a result, blind people often have to listen through a lot of irrelevant content before they find what they are looking for. *Haptic interfaces* (those providing tactile feedback) have the potential to make GUI interfaces more accessible and usable for blind people. Alas, mainstream computer devices do not have haptic screens that would enable high-resolution tactile feedback, and specialized haptic devices are very limited and/or are exuberantly expensive and bulky.

In this paper, we describe a low-cost haptic-glove system, FeelX, which can potentially enable usable tactile interaction with GUIs. The vision of FeelX is to enable blind users to connect it to any computer or smartphone, and then interact with it by moving their hands on any flat surface such as the desk or table. To establish the practicality and the desirability of using haptic gloves, we evaluated the initial prototype of the glove in a user study with 20 blind participants. Throughout the study, we performed a comparative evaluation of several design options for the tactile interface. The participants were asked to identify simple geometric figures such as lines, rectangles, circles, and triangles that are the basic building blocks of any GUI interface. Although the FeelX prototype is far from being a usable product, the results of the study indicate that blind users want to use haptic gloves.

CCS Concepts

• **Human-centered computing~Haptic devices**
• **Human-centered computing~Accessibility technologies**

Keywords

Haptic glove; tactile interaction; haptic display; blindness; GUI accessibility; screen reader; tactile exploration.

ASSETS '16, October 23-26, 2016, Reno, NV, USA

© 2016 ACM. ISBN 978-1-4503-4124-0/16/10…$15.00

DOI: http://dx.doi.org/10.1145/2982142.2982175

1. INTRODUCTION

Computers and mobiles have become ubiquitous in our daily lives, and many of us are interacting with multiple graphical user interfaces (GUIs) on our smartphones, tablets, and laptops throughout the day. While the accessibility of GUIs for blind screen-reader users has improved in recent years, a large gap remains in the efficiency of access for people with and without vision impairments; the latter group spends significantly more time interacting with content in web pages, documents, and apps.

To give a sense of the size of the affected population, according to the World Health Organization, there are 39 Million blind worldwide [35]. In the U.S. alone, according to the American Foundation for the Blind [3], there are over 21M Americans who have significant vision loss. These numbers are growing as baby boomers, already relying on computers, continue to develop vision impairments associated with age-related diseases.

Since the introduction of computers, researchers and practitioners have been striving to make computer interfaces accessible to blind people. The best-known results of their work are assistive technology tools such as magnifiers for people with low vision and screen readers for those who are blind. Magnifiers (e.g., Zoomtext [40] and MAGic [19]), which are primarily controlled either with the touch or mouse input, allow their users to zoom in and even narrate the content of the screen. Screen readers (e.g., JAWS [17], Window-Eyes [37], VoiceOver [33], NVDA[22]) enable blind people to interact with and narrate the content of the screen relying either on the touch or keyboard input.

Due to the limitations of assistive technology interfaces, neither magnifier nor screen-reader users can use GUI interfaces as effectively as sighted people. In our experience, the majority of time ends up being spent on searching the screen for relevant content and controls such as links, buttons, and form fields. Magnifiers require a lot of panning, since only a small portion of the magnified screen can be displayed at a time; so, the efficiency depends on the size of the screen, the type and extent of the vision loss, zoom level, and familiarity with the GUI. In contrast, screen readers require an extensive use of touch gestures and, more frequently, keyboard shortcuts to navigate even the most screen-reader accessible interfaces. The efficiency of screen-reader users can vary drastically based on their screen-reader proficiency, speech rate they use, and the familiarity with a particular GUI.

Over the years, screen readers have come a long way from simple and limited tools [11, 12, 25] to sophisticated productivity applications [17, 22, 31, 33, 37]. Nevertheless, the majority of screen readers continue to operate the same way, allowing users to navigate sequentially by pressing arrow keys on the keyboard, and now also with gestures on touch-screens. If a GUI has accessible tags for headings, buttons etc., then, with additional shortcut keys or gestures, users can "jump" to the next/previous heading, paragraph, button, etc. Alas, due to the limitation of audio modality, using screen readers boils down to navigating a one-dimensional list of GUI elements, thereby losing any semantic information and utility of the two-dimensional GUI layout.

The introduction of touch-screen devices such as iPhones allowed blind users to listen to the content they touch, i.e. the screen reader narrates the text under the finger. Touch screens allowed blind users to benefit from the 2-D layout, i.e. if the user knows where the content is on the screen, s/he can slide the finger right to it, in contrast to navigating through items one by one.

Regrettably, screen reading on touch screens has numerous limitations: (1) just as with keyboard browsing, one can determine if some content is relevant *only* after listening to it; (2) one can go directly to the particular content *only* if one is very familiar with the content layout; however, it is difficult to orient oneself on a flat surface just with the audio feedback; and (3) touch screens are often small, which makes it easy to miss content due to the "fat finger" problem [18, 30]. It should be noted that blind users do not normally use zoom to avoid horizontal scrolling. Our user studies [4] revealed, for example, that non-visual web browsing on touch-screens is not any faster than browsing with keyboards. In the end, any text-to-speech interface is ultimately limited by the inherent throughput of the audio channel and by the speech rate.

Haptic interfaces (with tactile feedback) have the potential to overcome some of the above limitations. Haptics engages the sense of *touch*, providing multiple simultaneous channels of information (e.g., one for each finger). If touch screens could render any GUI in tactile form, the user would be able to feel the sections of the interface, or the lines of text, or individual controls such as buttons. Prior studies [21] revealed that understanding webpage layout would be easier if users could feel section borders, enabling them to explore webpages faster than with audio alone. Regrettably, mainstream devices do not have haptic screens that would enable that kind of interaction, and specialized devices have very limited haptic capability (Section 2). Thus, accessible haptic interfaces remain to be the technology of the future.

To enable low-cost tactile interaction with GUIs, we developed *FeelX* – a haptic glove system. The vision of FeelX is to enable blind users to connect it to any computer, tablet, or smartphone, and then interact with the device by moving their hands on any flat surface such as the desk or the table. The architecture of FeelX is briefly reviewed in Section 3.1. The working area (i.e. the surface on which one can use the FeelX glove) can be several feet wide and deep. Therefore, while using the FeelX glove, one can easily avoid the "fat finger" problem, since a larger working area allows for bigger objects and wider space between them. The FeelX glove system is envisioned to be used in conjunction with regular screen readers and audio feedback. The gloves, however, will provide users with more ways of exploring GUIs and will enable users to interact with GUIs more efficiently, in this way, transforming the computer interaction experience for blind users.

In this paper, we evaluated the first prototype of a single FeelX glove with 20 blind participants for the purpose of establishing the practicality and the desirability of using haptic gloves. In our experiments, we have questioned the need to use more than one finger, the orientation of the hand relative to the interface, and we tested the ability of the glove users to tell apart basic geometric figures that are the basic building blocks of any GUI.

2. RELATED WORK

The research and development detailed in this paper uses haptic feedback devices for computer accessibility. Our research is based on the prior work on haptic interfaces and requires finger tracking to enable the FeelX system. Prior work has been done in all these areas; so, we provide a representative literature review to demonstrate our knowledge of the state of the art and, at the same time, contrast it with the innovations of the proposed approach.

There are a number of **haptic display** prototypes in existence: displays with electro-vibration (electrostatic) feedback [7, 28] that can give a feeling of varying friction; surfaces with temperature-sensitive hydrogel [26], which are slow and have no touch input or real screen; soft flexible displays with magnet or heological fluid actuated by an array of electromagnets to create different tactile sensations, though with low resolution [16]; etc. Some of these technologies are already making their way to the mainstream market, e.g., Phorm iPad case [32] with fluid-filled dynamically appearing buttons from Tactus Technologies and screens from Senseg [28] with electrostatic feedback. While these solutions are innovative, they are still very limited. Tactus case has large round buttons that can *slowly* appear only in the *predefined* locations and are *too large* to be useful for rendering webpage structure. Electrostatic screens have very small latency, and they could theoretically be used to render a webpage structure; however, 1) the feedback will be limited to the screen size, while the haptic gloves could enable interaction over a much larger area, e.g., the table; 2) existing devices provide the *identical* sense of friction over the *entire screen*, so blind users will be limited to using a single finger, while they naturally explore objects with all of their fingers; 3) the finger has to be moving to feel the friction, while, with the glove, the finger can feel the feedback (including the sense of pulsation) with or without finger movement; and 4) the electrostatic feedback is very subtle and depends on the moisture of the skin, while the proposed glove uses mechanical feedback.

Another type of haptic feedback is based on the tactile belts [13] with embossed dots on them. This sort of feedback is designed to reproduce the sensation of both lateral and rotational slip on the user's fingertip. Unfortunately, such displays are limited to representing only simple graphics and textures and are not suitable for interaction with web pages.

Thus, a number of haptic devices have been prototyped, but none of them can render a computer screen with high resolution and low latency. Perhaps the most relevant haptic technology is the pin-matrix device. For example, BrailleDis [34] can raise mechanical pins to form a tactile picture, but it is not portable, has small resolution (e.g., 120x60 in BrailleDis9000), and is exuberantly expensive, e.g., if an OEM Braille cell with 8 pins can cost around $100, a Braille display with 20 Braille cells costs $3K-$5K, then a pin-matrix device with just 120x60 pins will cost tens of thousands of dollars. In the FeelX glove prototype, we use small matrices of pins attached to each finger of the glove and, in this way, simulate a pin-matrix display that is portable, relatively inexpensive ($500 for a single glove), and is as wide as practically feasible, limited by the span of hands and the area covered by the hand-tracking camera. The FeelX prototype already supports the resolution of 320x240 pins, with the desk space of only 80x60cm.

Extensive research has been done on **haptic interaction**, both with static objects and dynamic computer screens. The use of tactile textures has been explored in [15]. The effectiveness of vibro-tactile feedback for typing on mobile phones has been investigated in [14]. The use of tactons, which stands for tactile icons, has been explored in [9], where authors investigate the use of varying frequency, duration, and amplitude of tactile pulse, to help the user distinguish icons from one another. In [21], the authors combined a 120x60 pin-matrix display with vibration feedback to enable blind and low-vision people to access complex STEM (Science Technology Engineering and Mathematics) educational materials.

Some early prior work exists even on tactile web browsing. In [27], haptic rendering of web-based images and Support Vector Graphics is proposed on a 120x60 pin-matrix display. In [6], auditory and vibration feedback were used to represent visual effects in web pages, such as the appearance of dynamic content. Unfortunately, all haptic research has been limited by the lack of inexpensive haptic technology that could provide high resolution of dynamic tactile feedback.

A wide variety of haptic glove designs have been proposed in research literature. For example, one of the early gloves, proposed in [39], had plastic tubes, light sources and detectors to record joint angles. The major drawbacks of this type of glove are: the fabric from which they are made is limiting the user movements, and the glove by itself requires complex user specific calibration, but does not provide haptic feedback. The majority of haptic gloves [8, 24] focus on virtual reality scenarios trying to give users the feeling of resistance, when they grab objects, and the feeling of touch.

Simple gloves have even been proposed for accessibility, e.g., [20] describes an inexpensive haptic glove which could be used in combination with a touch screen to interact with basic algebra graphs to enable navigation along the plot. A pager motor is placed on the tip of each finger and the motors are used to indicate the direction in which the hand should move. This setup only allows for guiding the user in the interface. This type of tactile feedback could be added to FeelX, but it would essentially provide only a single tactile dot per finger. Another glove that uses vibration feedback was proposed for way finding [38]. The FeelX glove technology is innovative in that it provides high resolution (2x4 pins for each finger) and haptic feedback to enable blind users to interact with GUIs. However, the existing research gave us useful insights that will help us improve the FeelX gloves and avoid common pitfalls.

The component that is needed for the success of the FeelX sytem is **finger tracking**, which is a well-studied field, offering numerous approaches to identifying finger positions. Finger tracking could be performed in a way it is done on capacitive displays (iPads); however, a large capacitive display would not be cheap or portable. Capacitive displays also suffer from their inability to detect fingers that share (X,Y) coordinates; therefore, where possible, finger tracking is done with cameras. In [10], a single finger was tracked using a bounding box-match method applied to camera video; although this approach assumed a contrast background and had limitations in finger orientations. Multiple fingertips were detected in [23] with the help of a thermal camera and fingertip geometry analysis; the use of the thermal camera made this approach rather expensive. A cheaper approach is described in [29], where two cameras are used to track finger positions, and the multiple graphics filters are applied to detect the edges; unfortunately, this approach is rather intensive computationally and sensitive to the surrounding environment. In [5], the authors use a mobile device camera to detect fingers based on the skin detection approach, which has similar limitations. A simpler approach is described in [36], where a custom-made glove with two infrared light-emitting diodes (LEDs) is used to track finger position. One LED is placed on the tip of the pointing finger, and the other – on top of the hand, which enables the support of simple gestures. Since the hand will be

wearing the FeelX glove, we simplify finger detection by placing LEDs on the tips of the fingers, making the fingers easier to track. The FeelX system uses off-the-shelf computer vision libraries [2] to identify finger positions captured by an infrared camera (Section 3.4).

3. THE DESIGN OF FEELX

3.1 General Architecture

FeelX, our Haptic Glove system (Figure 1), is composed of the Camera, Finger Tracker, Controller, Haptic Glove, and Interface Manager. The Camera, set up over the table on a portable foldable crane, sends a live video feed of the glove to the Finger Tracker, which uses a standard computer vision algorithm to resolve the $(X,Y)_i$ coordinates for each finger i, and sends the coordinates to the Interface Manager.

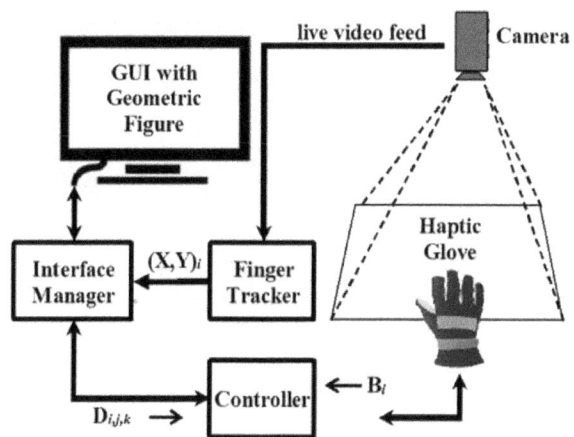

Figure 1 - The Architecture of FeelX

The Interface Manager processes geometric figures in the GUI, and maps the $(X,Y)_i$ finger coordinates to the GUI coordinates. Then, the Interface Manager outputs haptic instructions that are sent via the Controller to the haptic gloves in the form of $D_{i,j,k}$, where (j, k) are the row and column of a tactile "dot" rendered on finger i. Each finger in the glove is equipped with a hardware unit capable of rendering a tactile matrix of size j by k on the finger.

3.2 Haptic Glove

The FeelX glove is designed in the shape of a human hand (See Figure 2). The first working prototype of the glove, manufactured from laser-cut acrylic parts glued together, is made for the right hand. . Each finger is attached to the palm-platform in a way that allows the user to spread the fingers, as well as extend and collect them by a quarter of an inch. The device can further be adjusted to hands of various sizes by configuring the length of the finger appendages. In addition, the glove has a vertical hand position stabilizer on the left side for the thumb to hold on to. The stabilizer enables a more comfortable placement of the hand on the glove, which results in greater control over the hand movements. Although the glove, to a certain degree, resembles a mouse, each finger can be lifted from the table and moved around individually.

Figure 2 – The FeelX glove prototype

The glove integrates four Braille cells (Figure 2), one on each of the four fingertips. We aligned the cells with the *distal phalanx*, which is the most sensitive part of the finger. In our current design, we chose to limit tactile feedback to four fingers because: 1) the thumb wraps around the stabilizer; and 2) when the hand is placed naturally on the surface of the table, the thumb lies on its side, which does not work well with the Braille cell. With the miniaturization of tactile hardware, a future design that engages the thumb as well may be possible.

Figure 3 – Metec Braille cell and specifications

Each Braille cell is a 2x4 pin matrix with two columns of 4 pins. Each pin is approximately 1.2mm in diameter, and the distance between pin is around 1.3mm. Braille cells are typically operated by piezoelectric actuators that push the pins up or release them to go down. A Braille cell is typically used to render 2x6 Braille characters, with the bottom 2 pins used for other purposes, e.g., the letter case. We use all 8 pins to translate visual information into tactile form. For instance, by activating any two horizontal pins, we can depict a horizontal line; by activating another 4 vertical pins, we can depict two lines intersecting at 90 degrees. Activation and deactivation of horizontal pairs of pins one by one, going from top to bottom, give an impression of a horizontal line moving down. A

2x4 layout can even enable the user to feel lines placed at an angle, and even curves, as illustrated in Figure 4.

We placed two infrared LED lights on each finger to keep track of the finger orientation. We placed one more infrared LED near the thumb on the top of the stabilizer for easier identification of the hand orientation. We believe that, in future designs, this last LED may be eliminated.

3.3 Controller

The glove operates via a Controller that is connected to a computer via a USB port. The controller [1] was produced by Metec, a German company specializing in manufacturing Braille devices. We used a Metec's driver to communicate with the cells programmatically via a TCP socket. The payload of one socket transaction is a matrix data structure encoding the information about the pins that should be raised on a particular Braille cell.

3.4 Finger Tracker

To enable finger tracking, we removed the infrared filter from a Logitech C210 webcam and converted it into a pseudo-infrared camera. This enabled us to decrease the noise of the picture as well as the camera's sensitivity to the surrounding environment. Then, we made a few standard computer-vision preprocessing steps. Firstly, we converted the camera frame to a gray-white picture and inverted the image. As a result, we received a white image with a black blob representing the positions of the infrared LEDs. The size of the blob depends on the voltage applied to the LED. In our set up, the diameter of each blob was approximately 3 pixels. Then, we smoothed the image using Gaussian smoothing and increased the contrast of the picture to make the borders of the blobs more prominent. After the frame preprocessing, we applied Simple Blob Detection algorithm to detect center (X,Y) coordinates of the blobs on the frame; all image processing steps were made using OpenCV [2], an open source Computer Vision library. If the system lost track of the LEDs, which usually happened when the user moved the hand out of the camera sight range, we raised all pins to notify the user of the fact.

3.5 Field Representation

In this paper, we will use the term *field* to describe the GUI that contains a single geometrical figure. We will later refer to the pixel representation of the field as the *field grid*. The resolution of the field is 640 by 480 pixels, limited by the resolution of the camera used in our setup. By using a higher resolution infrared camera, the resolution of the field can be dramatically increased. However, even with the 640 x 480 resolution, blind users were able to recognize geometric shapes successfully, as we will discuss later.

We will refer to the part of the table viewable with the camera as a *working area*. The size of the working area on the table depends on the distance of the camera from the table. The higher above the table the camera is, the larger the working area is. In our setup, the camera was positioned 80cm above the table; the resulting width of the working area was 80cm, and the depth was 60cm.

A Braille cell is represented by a 2 by 4 table of cells in the field grid. Each table cell is a square of 5 by 5 pixels. In addition to Braille cell representation, the field grid contains a geometric figure, represented by one or more line segments or curves.

3.6 Interface Manager

The Interface Manager is the mediator of all the modules of the FeelX system. It receives an array of nine point coordinates from the Finger Tracking module: locations of infrared bulbs on the glove. Then the Interface Manager classifies the point coordinates into five categories: the pointing finger, the middle finger, the ring finger, the pinky finger, and the stabilizer bar. The process of classification of points consists of two steps. First, we are looking for the *pivot point*, i.e. a point with the highest cumulative distance from the other points. This point corresponds to the LED located on the hand stabilizer. Then, we sort the remaining eight points based on the distance to the pivot point. Since the position of all the points is dictated by the shape of the hand (i.e. fingers cannot change order), we assign each consecutive pair of points from the sorted array to each of the fingers, in the clockwise order, starting with the index finger.

Using the coordinates of two points on each finger, the Interface Manager builds a representation of the Braille cell in the field. For this purpose, we draw the line connecting these two points and calculate the position of a 2 by 4 grid with that line serving as the main axis of the grid. The resulting grid is the representation of the Braille cell in the field discussed in Section 3.5.

The final responsibility of the Interface Manager is to prepare and send the state of the Braille cells to the Controller to update the state of the pins on the Braille cells. In order to calculate the state of the Braille cells, the Interface Manager is looking for intersections of the grid that represents the Braille cell with the geometrical shape located in the field. If the geometrical shape intersects the (i,j) cell of the Braille cell grid, the corresponding pin on the cell should be raised. Then, the Interface Manager converts this information to the binary matrix and sends it to the Controller.

4. STUDY DESIGN

4.1 Overview

We evaluated the effectiveness of the Haptic Glove in a user study with 20 blind participants who had to recognize simple geometric figures presented in tactile form.

In preparation for the user study, we singled out 3 possible types of alignment of the haptic feedback grid:

1. Finger-aligned: the haptic feedback grid is always aligned with the user's finger and the field grid is fixed.
2. Field-aligned: the haptic feedback grid is always aligned with the field grid and the field grid is fixed.
3. Field-rotated: the haptic feedback and the field grids are aligned with the finger and the fields are fixed relative to one another.

If the finger is positioned as shown in (Figure 4a), the user gets the exact same haptic feedback in all three types of alignment. However, the feedback changes if the user rotates a finger. The finger-aligned Figure 4b) set up is the most intuitive and represents the way we typically interact with the physical world. The field-aligned set up (Figure 4c) keeps the Braille cell table representation borders aligned with the filed grid boarders. We thought this could decrease the noise of the user feedback at a given point, because, irrespective of the finger position in terms of rotation, the user would get the same feedback from the Braille cell. The field-rotated set up (Figure 4d) attempted to keep the glove and each finger always aligned with the field; so, rotating the hand also rotated the field. This last condition was eliminated during the pilot studies because, when the participants were trying to trace a straight line, their hand invariably rotated and they perceived the line as curved.

To verify if blind users cared about using more than one finger, we evaluated the Haptic Glove by providing tactile feedback to 1 finger (index) and 4 fingers (no thumb). Using the index finger is natural for pointing and touching as it is the most sensitive finger; also, it is the finger that blind people use for reading Braille. The 4-finger condition was chosen to maximize the number of input channels. As already mentioned, when the hand is placed naturally on a surface, the thumb lies on its side and, hence, it cannot be used effectively with the current design of the glove.

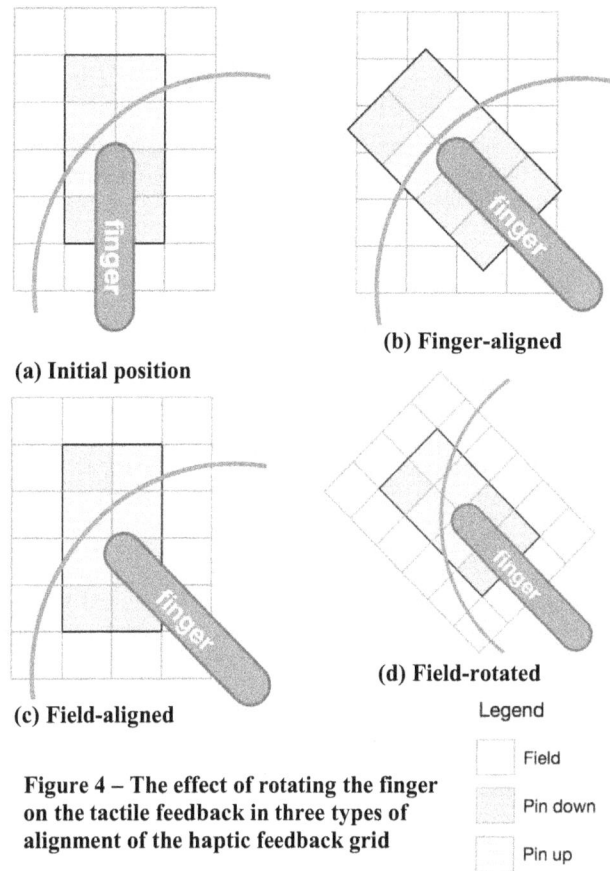

(a) Initial position

(b) Finger-aligned

(c) Field-aligned

(d) Field-rotated

Legend

	Field
	Pin down
	Pin up

Figure 4 – The effect of rotating the finger on the tactile feedback in three types of alignment of the haptic feedback grid

4.2 Hypotheses

In the user study, we focused on the following main hypotheses:

H1: "Blind users can recognize simple geometric shapes using the Haptic Glove Interface with at least 80% accuracy, in at least one test condition." – This hypothesis tested the overall suitability of the FeelX prototype for interacting with the basic geometric figures – the basic building blocks of any GUI.

H2a: "Irrespective of alignment, blind users can recognize simple geometric shapes significantly faster with the 4-finger Haptic Glove Interface compared to the 1-finger Interface."

H2b: "Regardless of the number of fingers used in the glove, blind users can recognize simple geometric figures significantly faster with the finger-aligned haptic feedback grid than with the field-aligned one." – H2a and H2b compared the two viable interface design options identified in the preliminary pilot studies.

H3: "The haptic-glove interface has an overall good usability rating (an SUS score of at least 75)" – This hypothesis tested the overall user satisfaction with the glove interface.

4.3 Subjects

The user study involved 20 blind participants; however, we had to exclude 4 of them; the first one did not have an understanding of what geometric figures are (the participant was elderly and was unaware of the terms "triangle", "rectangle" and "circle"), the second one had an unusually small hand that did not work with our haptic glove prototype, the third one kept falling asleep and was unable to concentrate, and with the fourth participant, we experienced hardware failure. The results of the study are based only on the data collected from the 16 remaining participants.

The participants were pre-screened to be: a) blind screen-reader users, as our user study was concerned only with the participants who had severe vision impairments; b) right-handed, as our Haptic Glove prototype was designed for right-handed users; c) Braille users, as we wanted the participants to have a well-developed sensitivity to subtle Braille feedback, and we wanted to eliminate the advantage that Braille users would have had over the participants who had no previous experience with Braille; however, in the experiment, the participants did not use their knowledge of Braille.

The participants included 43% females and 57% males and were on average 41 years old (median: 36.5). The participants were Hispanic (5), Black (5), White (2), Other (2), Asian (1), Native American (1). Education levels were Graduate (6), Undergraduate (6), High-school (3), and Post-Graduate (1). The participants were, on average, experienced computer and screen-reader users; both average and median experience using computers was 15.5 years. With regard to computer experience, 4 participants considered themselves "experts", 7 – "very confident", 3 – "confident", 2 – "mildly confident". Finally, 4 participants were self-identified "experts" with Braille, 5 were "very confident", 2 – "confident", 3 – "mildly confident", and 2 – "not confident".

4.4 Methodology

The evaluation was designed as a within-subjects experiment with counterbalancing. Each task involved using the Haptic Glove to identify a horizontal line, a vertical line, a triangle, a rectangle or a circle; we chose to show one geometric figure per task to keep the experiment focused. Each task was to be performed using either 1 finger or 4 fingers, with either finger-aligned or field-aligned feedback delivery (a total of 2x2=4 conditions). Overall, each participant had to identify each of the 5 figures 4 times, once per each condition, resulting in 20 tasks per participant.

Each time the figure was placed in a different place in the field. The dimensions of the working field were 640x480px. We randomized the positions of the figures to be in central part of the screen from 1/3 to 2/3 along the X-axis and from 50px to 250px along the Y-axis. We did this to have comparable results for different conditions and still have variability of placements. The geometric figures had a consistent orientation. The dimensions of the rectangle were 100x250px, the radius of circle: 100px, the dimensions of the triangle: 250x150x150px. The lines crossed the entire field. Larger figures would be difficult to identify because the user would be sliding the hand out of the field. Smaller figures would be more difficult to identify because of the limited resolution of the field, which could jeopardize the study. We did not attempt to use smaller figures because the goal of the study was not to identify the limitations of the early prototype, but to determine its general feasibility and test several interface design options. In addition, in an envisioned tactile interface, users would be able to zoom in and make the figures the desired size.

Prior to the study, the participants were explained how to use the Haptic Glove, given an opportunity to practice, ask questions, and express concerns. The participants were explained the difference between the finger-aligned and field-aligned glove interfaces. The participants were explained the difference between all evaluation conditions and were asked to practice with all 5 geometric figures listed above. During the practice session, the participants were given the time to find the workflows that were comfortable to them, rather than were forced to follow specific instructions. The practice session lasted between 15 and 60 minutes depending on the participant's ability to adapt to the new technology. The practice session ended when the participants explicitly indicated that they were comfortable with the settings.

The learning effect in somewhat repetitive tasks was mitigated by: (a) having intensive practice sessions that lasted for as long as necessary for the participant to get comfortable with the glove, and (b) randomizing the order of the tasks and conditions.

5. RESULTS AND DISCUSSION

In this section, we present our findings, as well as discuss the subjective feedback from the participants. We also present the results of the statistical significance tests we conducted to compare the participants' performances under various conditions.

5.1 Analysis of Objective Measure

As explained in the previous section, the participants were asked to identify various geometric figures such as circles, rectangles, etc., under different conditions. Table 1 presents a detailed report on the participants' recognition accuracies for various combinations of figures and conditions. These accuracy measurements were computed based on *successful* task completions, i.e. the tasks where the participants correctly recognized the figure under a given condition. As seen in Table 1, in the 4-finger conditions, the recognition accuracy is over 80% for each figure, which validates hypothesis H1.

Table 1 Figure recognition accuracy (Avg. w/ Std. Dev.)

	Finger aligned 1-finger	Finger aligned 4-fingers	Field aligned 1-finger	Field aligned 4-fingers	*Overall*
Horizontal Line	81% (40%)	88% (34%)	94% (25%)	81% (40%)	**86% (35%)**
Vertical Line	100% (0%)	81% (40%)	81% (40%)	100% (0%)	**91% (29%)**
Rectangle	56% (51%)	88% (34%)	81% (40%)	88% (34%)	**78% (42%)**
Triangle	69% (48%)	81% (40%)	81% (40%)	88% (34%)	**80% (41%)**
Circle	75% (45%)	81% (40%)	63% (50%)	94% (25%)	**78% (42%)**
Overall	**76% (43%)**	**84% (37%)**	**80% (40%)**	**90% (30%)**	**83% (38%)**

It is notable that, with 4 fingers, the recognition accuracy of each shape was above 80%, regardless of alignment. Except when working with vertical and horizontal lines, the participants mostly struggled to recognize the remaining figures under the Finger-aligned 1-finger condition; this is evident from the low accuracy statistics in Table 1. When inquired about the difficulties, most participants mentioned that, under this condition, it was hard and confusing for them to detect the intersection points. The participants struggled to trace the curve of the circle in all 1-finger conditions, especially, in the field-aligned condition. The overall accuracy was the highest in the field-aligned condition.

Table 2 shows the average task-completion times based on the following groupings: (i) the type of alignment (finger-aligned vs. field-aligned); and (ii) the number of fingers used (1 finger vs. 4 fingers). We generated these statistics by merging the data from 4 conditions according to 2 factors: the number of fingers and the alignment paradigm. The statistical t-tests for comparison between groups were performed on the merged data in order to safeguard against Type I errors. We also checked the normality of data in these groups using statistical plots.

Table 2 Average task completion times

Group	Time in ms
Finger-aligned	μ: 1:06 σ: 0:46
Field-aligned	μ: 0:59 σ: 0:43
1 finger use	μ: 1:11 σ: 0:48
4 finger use	μ: 0:54 σ: 0:38

As can be seen in Table 2, users could identify figures faster when exploring the geometric figures with 4 fingers, compared to using only 1 finger. Between these 2 conditions, the difference in task-completion times was found to be statistically significant (p < 0.0001, paired t-test), thereby validating hypothesis H2a. The difference can be attributed to the fact that it may be easier to find a figure with 4 fingers because 4 fingers can cover a larger surface area in less time. Feeling the shape of the figure with multiple fingers also leaves less chance for a mistake (the difference in accuracies for 1 finger vs. 4 fingers was found to be statistically significant, p = 0.026 – paired t-test). In addition, the participants reported that the extra tactile stimulus available with 4 fingers made it easier for them to identify figures.

Table 3 Participants' task-completion times (avg. w/ std.dev) by shapes and conditions. The winning values are in bold.

Shape	Finger aligned 1-finger	Finger aligned 4-fingers	Field aligned 1-finger	Field aligned 4-fingers	Overall
Horizontal Line	1:06 (0:44)	0:52 (0:43)	0:58 (0:42)	0:44 (0:41)	**0:56 (0:42)**
Vertical Line	0:46 (0:42)	0:55 (0:43)	0:55 (0:44)	0:41 (0:20)	**0:51 (0:38)**
Rectangle	1:14 (0:43)	1:09 (0:46)	1:13 (0:49)	0:43 (0:20)	**1:05 (0:42)**
Triangle	1:25 (0:47)	1:05 (0:45)	1:18 (0:48)	0:58 (0:45)	**1:11 (0:47)**
Circle	1:25 (0:56)	0:55 (0:41)	1:29 (0:57)	0:47 (0:28)	**1:09 (0:49)**
Overall	**1:11 (0:48)**	**0:59 (0:43)**	**1:11 (0:49)**	**0:46 (0:32)**	**1:02 (0:44)**

The statistics in Table 2 show that the participants, on average, took slightly less time to recognize the figures in the field-aligned

condition compared to the finger-aligned feedback. However, this difference was not found to be statistically significant – we conducted a paired t-test, p=0.102; therefore, we cannot validate H2b. Although the finger-aligned design may seem to be more intuitive, blind participants had no problem using the field-aligned design. The results demonstrate the viability of both designs, at least, for the types of tasks performed in the user study.

Table 3 presents a more detailed breakdown of the task-completion times, by considering different combinations of figures and conditions. We conducted a 2x2 2-way Anova test, and the results showed that there was indeed a statically significant difference (p=0.0002) among the 4 conditions with respect to the Fingers (1 vs. 4) and Alignment (Field vs. Finger) independent variables. Furthermore, there was no significant interaction effect (p=0.16) between these two independent variables.

5.2 Usability Analysis

At the end of the experiment, we administered several questionnaires to elicit feedback and opinions regarding the Haptic Glove. These included a standard System Usability Scale questions (SUS). The SUS questionnaire is a Likert scale with positive and negative questions, with responses expected to be on the scale from 1-strongly disagree to 5-stongly agree, and 3 being neutral. The average SUS score for the haptic glove, in general, was 62.2 (std. 22.6); therefore, we could not validate hypothesis H3.

The main concerns of the participants were related to the comfort and ergonomics of the glove. Given that it was an early prototype, there were various issues such as the inability to fit the glove on/OR: to small/large hands, insufficient flexibility to bend the fingers, lack of ergonomics, etc. However, the fact that the participants could still achieve a high accuracy (Table 1) indicates the glove's potential to become a viable assistive technology tool.

Since the overall SUS score was influenced by user experience in 4 different conditions, we also administered separate SUS questionnaires for the two types of alignment as well as the number of fingers. However, many participants were getting confused due to multiple SUS questionnaires, and also getting mixed up between the two types of alignment, thereby making the obtained data unreliable. In future, we plan to evaluate different conditions in a between-subjects study to minimize the cognitive load on the participants and obtain more reliable feedback.

5.3 User Preferences

Table 4 presents the participant's preferences about the finger conditions. The main takeaway of those results is that the majority of the participants preferred to use 4 fingers; this indicates that the haptic glove is desirable compared to other devices that can only provide tactile feedback for a single finger.

Table 4 Post-evaluation questionnaire comparing haptic feedback with different numbers of fingers.

Question	4 fingers	1 finger	Both	None
Which number of fingers would you prefer to use?	50%	37.5%	12.5%	0%
Which number of fingers did you find the most complex?	37.5%	43.75%	0%	6.25%
Which number of fingers did you find the easiest to use?	43.75%	43.75%	12.5%	0%

Which number of fingers would need the most support from a technical person?	18.75%	31.25%	12.5%	25%
Which number of fingers was the most well integrated?	50%	18.75%	31.25%	0%
Which number of fingers was the least consistent?	6.25%	37.5%	6.25%	37.5%
Which number of fingers do you imagine most people would learn to use most quickly?	43.75%	37.5%	12.5%	6.25%
Which number of fingers did you find the most cumbersome to use?	37.5%	25%	0%	18.75%
Which number of fingers did you feel most confident using?	50%	37.5%	12.5%	0%
Which number of fingers did you feel required you to learn the most before using it?	37.5%	25%	6.25%	18.75%

5.4 Feature Requests and Opinions

Finally, we conducted a brief questionnaire to get the participants' opinions on the future development of the haptic glove (Table 5). We asked each participant to rate the importance of a prospective feature on the scale from 1 to 5, where 1 was "unimportant" and 5 was "very important". As can be seen in Table 5, the most desirable feature (Avg. 4.31 with the smallest Std. Dev. of 1.13) was the ability to click on the tactile screen to have a more interactive experience with the glove. The participants also favored the ability to spread fingers to help them cover a bigger portion of the working area during the exploration process, the ability to zoom in/out the interaction field for busier GUIs, and the ability to read Braille. The participants were undecided about being able to use two gloves or about using the gloves for typing, but we believe further experimentation is needed to determine the utility and usability of these features, as the participants based their ratings on the experience with the current glove design.

Table 5 Post-evaluation questionnaire for glove development

Question	Avg.	Std. Dev.
How important is it to be able to spread the fingers	3.56	1.67
How important is it to be able to change the zoom level?	3.68	1.62
How important is it to be able to use two gloves?	2.75	1.77
How important is it to be able to click on the tactile screen while wearing the glove?	4.31	1.13
How important is it to be to able to read Braille with haptic gloves?	3.68	1.74
How important is it to be able to type using a virtual keyboard enabled by the glove?	2.81	1.51

TESTIMONIALS

In this section, we present a selection of the testimonials made by the participants during the debriefing session:

"It is a great generalization tool which can be applied for reading the graphs, images, etc."

"The system has a lot of potentials in different areas such as Maps representation, graphics, charts even games such as Maze."

"Receiving the information from a hard copy diagram is too slow. Haptic glove is a faster and more efficient solution."

"I was never able to follow a straight line [in a computer interface] before using the Haptic Glove"

The Haptic Glove system has also received a fair amount of criticism from the participants. The major area of concern was the ergonomics of the glove. While we were trying to make the glove configurable to fit any hand size, we still had problems with the participants who had unusually small or large hands.

6. CONCLUSION AND FUTURE WORK

In this paper, we presented the FeelX haptic glove prototype. The results of the preliminary user study indicate that haptic gloves could be a viable solution for interacting with GUI interfaces. The experiments showed that, at least with the current design of the glove and the resolution of the Braille cells, the participants could identify geometric figures more accurately and faster when using 4 fingers compared to using a single finger. The observations showed that most of the participants were exploring the figures with multiple fingers at the same time. We hypothesize that, even if tactile resolution increases, blind users would still want to use more than one finger for tactile interactions. Despite being crude, the FeelX prototype received good System Usability Scale scores from the more experienced participants. The majority of the participants wanted to utilize the haptic glove for their everyday computer use despite the limitations of the early FeelX prototype.

Now that we have identified the desirability and the utility of the haptic glove, in our future work, we will improve the design of the glove to be more ergonomic and start 3D printing the prototypes to accelerate the design cycles. We will experiment with using gloves on both hands and explore alternative camera-less approaches to finger tracking. We will enable the glove users to hear the touched content narrated by text to speech. We will test the usability of the gloves with real GUI interfaces such as spreadsheets, web pages, and graphs. We will also experiment with using the gloves as input devices, e.g., clicking and dragging objects in GUIs. Finally, we expect that the tactile technology will eventually undergo miniaturization, which will enable the gloves to become smaller and increase the resolution of tactile feedback.

7. ACKNOWLEDGMENTS

This material is based upon work supported by the National Science Foundation under Grants: No. IIS-1447549, CNS-1405641, and IIS-1218570. We would also like to thank Lighthouse Guild for helping us recruit participants for the user study and conduct the experiments. We will like to thank our accessibility consultant, Glenn Dausch, for helping us develop a more accessible technology and formulate the goals for the study.

REFERENCES

[1] *Metec Controller.* 2016; Available from: http://web.metec-ag.de/P20.pdf.

[2] *OpenCV.* 2016 [cited 2016]; Available from: opencv.org.

[3] AFB. *Facts and Figures on American Adults with Vision Loss.* http://www.afb.org/Section.asp?SectionID=15&TopicID=413&DocumentID=4900.

[4] Ahmed, F., M.A. Islam, Y. Borodin, and I.V. Ramakrishnan, *Assistive web browsing with touch interfaces*, in *Proceedings of the 12th international ACM SIGACCESS conference on Computers and accessibility.* 2010, ACM: Orlando, Florida, USA. p. 235-236.

[5] An, J.-h. and K.-S. Hong. *Finger gesture-based mobile user interface using a rear-facing camera.* in *Consumer Electronics (ICCE), 2011 IEEE International Conference on.* 2011: IEEE.

[6] Asakawa, C., H. Takagi, S. Ino, and T. Ifukube, *Auditory and tactile interfaces for representing the visual effects on the web*, in *Proceedings of the fifth international ACM conference on Assistive technologies.* 2002, ACM: Edinburgh, Scotland. p. 65-72.

[7] Bau, O., I. Poupyrev, A. Israr, and C. Harrison, *TeslaTouch: electrovibration for touch surfaces*, in *Proceedings of the 23nd annual ACM symposium on User interface software and technology.* 2010, ACM: New York, New York, USA. p. 283-292.

[8] Blake, J. and H.B. Gurocak, *Haptic glove with MR brakes for virtual reality.* Mechatronics, IEEE/ASME Transactions on, 2009. 14(5): p. 606-615.

[9] Brewster, S. and L.M. Brown, *Tactons: structured tactile messages for non-visual information display*, in *Proceedings of the fifth conference on Australasian user interface - Volume 28.* 2004, Australian Computer Society, Inc.: Dunedin, New Zealand. p. 15-23.

[10] Brown, T. and R.C. Thomas. *Finger tracking for the digital desk.* in *User Interface Conference, 2000. AUIC 2000. First Australasian.* 2000: IEEE.

[11] Chieko, A. and C. Lewis, *Home page reader: IBM's talking web browser*, in *Closing the Gap Conf. Proceedings.* 1998.

[12] Edwards, A.D.N., *Outspoken software for blind users*, in *Extra-ordinary human-computer interaction.* 1995, Cambridge University Press. p. 59-82.

[13] Ho, C., J. Kim, S. Patil, and K. Goldberg. *The Slip-Pad: A haptic display using interleaved belts to simulate lateral and rotational slip.* in *World Haptics Conference, IEEE.* 2015.

[14] Hoggan, E., S.A. Brewster, and J. Johnston, *Investigating the effectiveness of tactile feedback for mobile touchscreens*, in *the SIGCHI Conference on Human Factors in Computing Systems.* 2008, ACM: Florence, Italy. p. 1573-1582.

[15] Hollins, M., S. Bensmaïa, K. Karlof, and F. Young, *Individual differences in perceptual space for tactile textures: Evidence from multidimensional scaling.* Attention, Perception, & Psychophysics, 2000. 62(8): p. 1534-1544.

[16] Jansen, Y., T. Karrer, and J. Borchers, *MudPad: tactile feedback and haptic texture overlay for touch surfaces*, in *ACM International Conference on Interactive Tabletops and Surfaces.* 2010, ACM: Saarbrücken, Germany. p. 11-14.

[17] JAWS. *Screen reader from Freedom Scientific.* 2013 [cited 2015]; http://www.freedomscientific.com/products/fs/jaws-product-page.asp.

[18] Kane, S.K., J.P. Bigham, and J.O. Wobbrock, *Slide rule: making mobile touch screens accessible to blind people using multi-touch interaction techniques*, in *Proceedings of the 10th international ACM SIGACCESS conference on Computers and accessibility.* 2008, ACM: Halifax, Nova Scotia, Canada. p. 73-80.

[19] MAGic. *Magnification software from Freedom Scientific.* 2013: http://www.freedomscientific.com/products/lv/magic-bl-product-page.asp.

[20] Manshad, M.S. and A.S. Manshad, *Multimodal vision glove for touchscreens*, in *Proceedings of the 10th international ACM SIGACCESS conf. on Computers and accessibility.* 2008, ACM: Halifax, Nova Scotia, Canada. p. 251-252.

[21] Namdev, R.K. and P. Maes, *An interactive and intuitive stem accessibility system for the blind and visually impaired*, in *Proceedings of the 8th ACM International Conference on PErvasive Technologies Related to Assistive Environments.* 2015, ACM: Corfu, Greece. p. 1-7.

[22] NVDA, *Non-Visual Desktop Access.* 2011.

[23] Oka, K., Y. Sato, and H. Koike, *Real-time fingertip tracking and gesture recognition.* Computer Graphics and Applications, IEEE, 2002. 22(6): p. 64-71.

[24] Popescu, V., G. Burdea, and M. Bouzit. *Virtual reality simulation modeling for a haptic glove.* in *Computer Animation, 1999. Proceedings.* 1999: IEEE.

[25] Raman, T.V., *Emacspeak - direct speech access*, in *Proceedings of the second annual ACM conference on Assistive technologies.* 1996, ACM: Vancouver, British Columbia, Canada.

[26] Richter, A. and G. Paschew, *Optoelectrothermic Control of Highly Integrated Polymer-Based MEMS Applied in an Artificial Skin.* Advanced Materials, 2009. 21(9): p. 979-983.

[27] Rotard, M., S. Knödler, and T. Ertl, *A tactile web browser for the visually disabled*, in *Proceedings of the sixteenth ACM conference on Hypertext and hypermedia.* 2005, ACM: Salzburg, Austria. p. 15-22.

[28] Senseg. *Senseg's Tixel Technology.* 2011; Available from: http://senseg.com/technology/senseg-technology.

[29] Shaker, N. and M. Abou Zliekha. *Real-time finger tracking for interaction.* in *Image and Signal Processing and Analysis, 2007. ISPA 2007*: IEEE.

[30] Siek, K., Y. Rogers, and K. Connelly, *Fat Finger Worries: How Older and Younger Users Physically Interact with PDAs Human-Computer Interaction - INTERACT 2005*, M. Costabile and F. Paternò, Editors. 2005, Springer Berlin / Heidelberg. p. 267-280.

[31] SuperNova. *Screen Reader from Dolphin.* 2013 [cited 2015]; http://www.yourdolphin.com/productdetail.asp?id=1.

[32] TactusTechnology. *Phorm Case for iPad.* 2015; Available from: http://www.getphorm.com/.

[33] VoiceOver, *Screen reader from Apple.* 2015.

[34] Völkel, T., G. Weber, and U. Baumann, *Tactile Graphics Revised: The Novel BrailleDis 9000 Pin-Matrix Device with Multitouch Input Computers Helping People with Special Needs*, K. Miesenberger, et al., Editors. 2008, Springer Berlin / Heidelberg. p. 835-842.

[35] WHO. *Visual impairment and blindness.* 2012 [cited 2015]; http://www.who.int/mediacentre/factsheets/fs282/en/.

[36] Williams, R.C. *Finger tracking and gesture interfacing using the Nintendo® wiimote.* in *Proceedings of the 48th Annual Southeast Regional Conference.* 2010: ACM.

[37] Window-Eyes, *Screen Reader GW Micro.* 2010.

[38] Zelek, J.S., S. Bromley, D. Asmar, and D. Thompson, *A haptic glove as a tactile-vision sensory substitution for wayfinding.* Journal of Visual Impairment and Blindness, 2003. 97(10): p. 621-632.

[39] Zimmerman, T.G., *Optical flex sensor.* 1985, Google Patents.

[40] ZoomText, *Magnification tool from aisquared.* 2010.

The Cost of Turning Heads: A Comparison of a Head-Worn Display to a Smartphone for Supporting Persons with Aphasia in Conversation

Kristin Williams[1,3], Karyn Moffatt[2], Jonggi Hong[3], Yasmeen Faroqi-Shah[4], Leah Findlater[3]

[1]Human Computer Interaction Institute Carnegie Mellon University Pittsburgh, PA

[2]School of Information Studies McGill University Montreal, QC

[3]Human Computer Interaction Lab University of Maryland College Park, MD

[4]Aphasia Research Center University of Maryland College Park, MD

{krismawil@cs.cmu.edu, karyn.moffatt@mcgill.ca, jhong12@umd.edu, yfshah@umd.edu, leahkf@umd.edu}

ABSTRACT

Current symbol-based dictionaries providing vocabulary support for persons with the language disorder, aphasia, are housed on smartphones or other portable devices. To employ the support on these external devices requires the user to divert their attention away from their conversation partner, to the neglect of conversation dynamics like eye contact or verbal inflection. A prior study investigated head-worn displays (HWDs) as an alternative form factor for supporting glanceable, unobtrusive, and always-available conversation support, but it did not directly compare the HWD to a control condition. To address this limitation, we compared vocabulary support on a HWD to equivalent support on a smartphone in terms of overall experience, perceived focus, and conversational success. Lastly, we elicited critical discussion of how each device might be better designed for conversation support. Our work contributes (1) evidence that a HWD can support more efficient communication, (2) preliminary results that a HWD can provide a better overall experience using assistive vocabulary, and (3) a characterization of the design features persons with aphasia value in portable conversation support technologies. Our findings should motivate further work on head-worn conversation support for persons with aphasia.

CCS Concepts

• **Human-centered computing** →**Accessibility** → **Empirical Studies in Accessibility**

Keywords

Aphasia; head-worn display; conversational support; AAC; wearable computing; accessibility.

1. INTRODUCTION

Aphasia is a language disorder acquired from damage to the brain through, for example, a stroke or car accident. Symbol-based dictionaries to support persons with aphasia in speaking provide groupings of text, images, and sound for dialogue or vocabulary. However, these tools are often treated as a last resort by persons with aphasia [7]. One issue is that, unlike commonly worn sensory

ASSETS '16, October 23-26, 2016, Reno, NV, USA
© 2016 ACM. ISBN 978-1-4503-4124-0/16/10...$15.00
DOI: http://dx.doi.org/10.1145/2982142.2982165

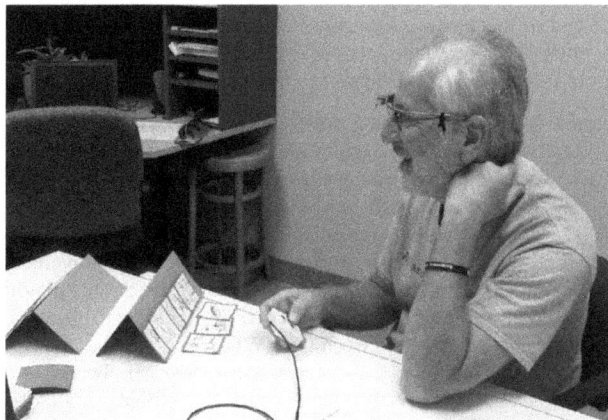

Figure 1. A participant is shown using vocabulary prompts from the head-worn display to support conversation during the study task (playing the card game Go Fish). The head-worn display sits over the participant's prescriptive lenses: positioning a small screen in front of his right eye.

aids such as eyeglasses or hearing aids, the dictionary support is typically provided through an external augmentative and alternative communication (AAC) device (e.g., Dynavox[1]) or a smartphone application (e.g., ProLoquo2Go[2]). The external form factor makes it difficult to employ the supported vocabulary unobtrusively as attention is explicitly diverted away from the conversation partner to operate the device. This diversion interferes with important aspects of communication such as managing speaking role, verbal inflection, error monitoring, or continuing the dialogue's pace [15, 34, 35]. Further, these solutions often generate text-to-speech from the words or phrases in the dictionary, which can replace the user's own natural voice and disrupt their speaking turn [35].

As an alternative, a recent study explored head-worn displays (HWD) for vocabulary support [47]. In that work, 14 participants with aphasia were able to successfully use vocabulary prompts from a HWD in conversations in both private and public settings. Participant feedback suggested that, compared to existing communication tools, the HWD may allow the wearer to access support less obtrusively and better maintain focus on their conversational partner. However, that study did not directly compare the HWD to equivalent support on more traditional devices such as smartphones, nor did it include a detailed

---

[1] http://www.tobiidynavox.com/t-series/
[2] http://www.assistiveware.com/product/proloquo2go

examination of how the vocabulary prompts were used within conversation.

To address these limitations, we conducted a study with 20 persons with aphasia. Participants used vocabulary support both on a HWD (Figure 1) and on a smartphone to support conversation during a simple card game (an adaption of Go Fish using picture cards) that requires primarily verbal interaction between two partners. Following Faroqi-Shah and Virion [37], we employed this game to simulate a natural, yet controlled conversation. We compared the two devices in terms of subjective experience, via measures of overall experience and perceived ability to focus on the conversation, and in terms of conversational success, via measures of how often participants employed the vocabulary prompts and how efficiently they were able to complete the conversation tasks in the game.[3] Finally, at the end of the session, we conducted a semi-structured interview to elicit feedback about the devices and the design of future unobtrusive, vocabulary support solutions.

Despite participants having little to no prior experience with HWDs, the quantitative results are promising and confirm the predicted benefit from previous work that the near-eye display of the HWD allows for efficient access to information [47]: the HWD was at least comparable to the smartphone on all quantitative measures, and resulted in a significant improvement in communication efficiency (i.e., how quickly participants played each game turn). Surprisingly, however, no significant subjective differences were found between the HWD and the phone in terms of supporting focus on the conversation or partner. During our semi-structured interview participants identified trade-offs between the HWD and the smartphone in terms of aesthetic choices, fit within current communication support strategies (both other tools and other people), compatibility with prescriptive lenses, and the ability to blend the use of the device with their current practices. Our work contributes (1) evidence that a HWD can support more efficient communication, (2) preliminary results that a HWD can provide a better overall experience using assistive vocabulary, and (3) a characterization of the design features persons with aphasia value in portable conversation support technologies. Our findings should motivate further work on head-worn conversation support for persons with aphasia.

2. RELATED WORK

2.1 Aphasia and Conversation

Aphasia is an acquired language disorder that occurs from damage to the central nervous system [7, 36]. It ranges in severity from mild complications in the selection of an appropriate word to complete loss of the ability to comprehend or formulate language. A typology has emerged which classifies aphasia according to different combinations of deficits in naming, fluency, repetition, auditory comprehension, grammatical processing, reading, and writing [7, 36]. Aphasia affects people of all ages. However, the most common cause of aphasia is stroke, and so, the prevalence of aphasia increases with age [7].

Persons with aphasia encounter a sudden loss of language skills after a lifetime of proficiency, which can severely limit daily interaction. The challenges are particularly evident in public settings where conversation partners may not know anything about aphasia. Aphasia is often mistaken for incompetence and, as a result, persons with aphasia are often excluded from

conversation and decision-making [3, 16]. Conversational success often depends on the facilitation skills and cooperation of the conversational partner [4, 16]. Yet, unfamiliar partners are not likely to assume the role of a language resource by anticipating and providing vocabulary just-in-time [16] as may be required to jointly establish meaning during conversation [8, 15, 16]. Assistive technology for conversation support may be able to address this need by providing these vocabulary prompts.

Picture-based support may help with initiating conversation, but can be difficult to access when needed to sustain conversation. Conversation partners put pressure on persons with aphasia to respond quickly, and long delays responding can lead to losing a conversation turn and can highlight the person's problems with speaking [46]. As a result, speakers with aphasia may adapt their speaking style to vocabulary content using more nouns and dropping function words and verbs in order to be perceived as competent [14, 46]. One study showed that picture-based assistive technologies facilitate this adaptive strategy by quickly communicating complex information such as progress on a gardening project or purchasing an item in a store through direct reference to the displayed image [2]. Similarly, one case study showed how directly referencing picture-based support contributed to rehabilitative goals: the participant independently named objects in a personal, living room photo using audio-recorded prompts on an interactive pen [32]. However, the technique did not extend to naming objects in her actual living room. By providing private access to audio prompts and picture-based support in the wearer's line of sight, HWDs may support both social and rehabilitative speaking goals by making prompts readily available in the desired context.

2.2 Computerized AAC for Aphasia

Research on assistive technology to support aphasia can be strongly influenced by the conception of the language disorder and what is being targeted for assistance. For example, AAC might draw "on a theory of the underlying language deficit; and, importantly, the efficacy of [the] device may provide a test of [the] theory" [23]. This has led some researchers to categorize assistive technologies as "disorder oriented" or "communication oriented" [35]. To this end, some research has focused on supporting persons with aphasia in activities of daily living to achieve functional goals that may be impacted by language (e.g., daily planning [5, 29] and cooking [40]) instead of providing general linguistic support.

As mentioned in the Introduction, symbol-based dictionaries of images, text, and sound (e.g., Lingraphica[4] or Proloquo2Go) are a common linguistic support tool. Navigating through their hierarchies, however, can be time consuming, so manual customization is often supported though requires effort to set up. Navigation time may also be reduced by organizing vocabulary based on semantic associations [30], or dynamically adapting the vocabulary based on the user's location or conversation partner [18], possibly using automated means of generating these contextual predictions [10]. While these approaches provide promising directions for content organization, issues remain with employing support mid-conversation. For many individuals, the audio and visual stimuli are sufficient for prompting speech, but most devices make the support audible and visible to others, effectively replacing rather than augmenting the user's own voice [21]. By providing private perceptual access to the device's content in a wearable form, HWDs may better support the wearer

---

[3] In comparisons of quantitative data, we considered only the first device each participant used, due to a software bug, as described in Section 3.6.

[4] https://www.aphasia.com/

in using the assistive vocabulary in conversation [47], a question we directly examine in our study.

Another class of computer-based tools for persons with aphasia support storytelling. These approaches attempt to address problems with diverting attention to external devices by supporting language composition prior to speaking. Storytelling scaffolds speaking by leveraging narrative structure [36], and emphasizing independent speaking while still realizing social goals such as indirect communication, self-expression, and establishing social proximity [9, 45]. Further, narrative provides for reusable language like prerecording material to later introduce conversation topics (e.g., TalksBac [44]). Yet, storytelling applications use a linear, temporal order through pre-recording [45] or creation of a timeline for the story [9], and are challenging to break with when there is a need to revise plots to make them relevant to the current telling [28]. Revision is important for engaging the conversation partner in co-constructing the narrative [8, 9, 28], and highlight issues with design approaches that align personal narrative with a specific temporal order. While our study focuses on dictionary-based support, investigating how our findings translate to storytelling tools could be a useful line of future work.

2.3 Head-Worn Communication Support

The design of an appropriate form factor for AAC must balance perceptual access to device content with sociolinguistic facets of communication. A clear view of the conversation partner's face can impact both the comprehension and formulation of language. Facial expressions, eye contact, and lip reading provide feedback on whether conversation partners have a shared understanding [12, 32], and further, can play an important therapeutic role [11].

As previously discussed, persons with aphasia have responded positively to the idea of using a HWD for vocabulary support in an exploratory study that, unlike our work, did not include a direct comparison to a control condition [47]. Other work with persons with aphasia used a head-mounted camera (without a visual display) to capture content for later use in storytelling, but not as a means of supporting communication in situ [25].

Beyond aphasia, a few studies have looked at HWDs to provide assistive support to older adults [20], persons with Parkinson's disease [27], and persons with cognitive decline [13]. These studies identified potential application areas such as short-term memory aids, experience capture, and instructions (e.g., for cooking), but did not look at how HWDs are incorporated into an active dialogue. Two studies developed algorithms for AAC on a HWD, but evaluation minimally involved only two individuals with cerebral palsy [42, 43].

Outside the realm of assistive technology, researchers have studied the use of HWDs during face-to-face communication and their impact on conversation quality and efficiency. When displaying information that is not directly related to what is being said, researchers have found that it can negatively impact eye contact and attention [26] and should be delivered visually, in batches, when the wearer is not speaking [31]. Similar issues with information timing while speaking were revealed in a study of a contextually appropriate speech command interface: the wearer had the most difficulty negotiating communication with their partner while also manipulating the HWD [24]. It is unclear whether these prior findings extend to AAC, where information shown on the display is directly relevant to the wearer's conversation. Others, in studying the role of a prompting tool for public speaking, found that when the information has a direct role it can have a positive impact [39]: one to two words delivered in

short intervals can support the wearer in actively changing speaking speed and volume, and wearers preferred textual feedback to information visualizations for interpretability while speaking. These studies leave open the potential for symbol-based dictionaries on a HWD to provide support while speaking, but highlight the need for careful design in conversation contexts where AAC is most likely to be used.

3. STUDY METHOD

This study employs a controlled conversation task (playing the game Go Fish) to subjectively and objectively explore potential differences between vocabulary support on a HWD versus a smartphone. Our HWD prototype includes a custom-built remote control for Google Glass to address motor accessibility issues that arose in earlier work [47]. Further, we elicit discussion of device design for conversation support and the device's fit within a conversation ecology.

3.1 Participants

We recruited 20 persons with aphasia (5 females, 15 males) through local aphasia community centers, support groups, speech-language pathologists, listservs, and rehabilitation service providers. They ranged in age from 31 to 78 ($M = 56.6$; $SD = 14.5$). Fifteen participants owned a phone, 10 of which were smartphones. Six participants had used a HWD (Google Glass) for at least a few hours 6–12 months beforehand in a previous study we ran; these participants were evenly split in terms of device presentation order (HWD or phone first; Section 3.6). Based on discussion with caregivers and on participants' self-report, we screened participants for right-sided neglect (loss of visual awareness in the right-sided field of view which would interfere with our evaluating of the right-sided monocular display of Google Glass) and moderate to severe apraxia (problems with the articulation of sounds dependent on the motor system). We compensated participants $25 for the 90-minute study.

3.2 Apparatus

We wrote identical custom dictionary applications for Google Glass and a Samsung Galaxy Nexus 4G LTE smartphone, and built a remote control for the HWD to address motor accessibility with Google Glass [47]. Similar to the proof-of-concept prototype evaluated in [47], these applications consisted of a two-level hierarchy of words, where each item in the hierarchy included an image, text, and audio. Only one item was shown on the screen at a time (Figure 2 shows examples). The top level always consisted of two categories: *actions* and *objects*. The second level of the hierarchy included 10 action (e.g., 'balance', 'celebrate', 'wash') and 10 object (e.g., 'bird', 'pirate', 'telescope') words, which were configured to match the specific set of cards used for different versions of Go Fish card decks used in the study procedure (Section 3.4). Category images were black and white icons taken from the Noun Project [1], while the vocabulary in the second level of the hierarchy used black and white line drawings from the University of California of San Diego (UCSD) International Picture Naming Project [38]. To provide context in the second level of the hierarchy, a small version of the category icon appeared in the top-right corner of the screen.

For both the HWD and the phone, we designed similar controls to navigate the word hierarchy (Figure 2). While Google Glass offers manual control (swipes, taps) via a touchpad on the right-hand side of the device, persons with aphasia can have right-sided hemiparesis (weakness or paralysis) caused by a stroke, which makes it difficult to access these controls. To address this issue, previous work controlled Google Glass using gestures on a wrist-

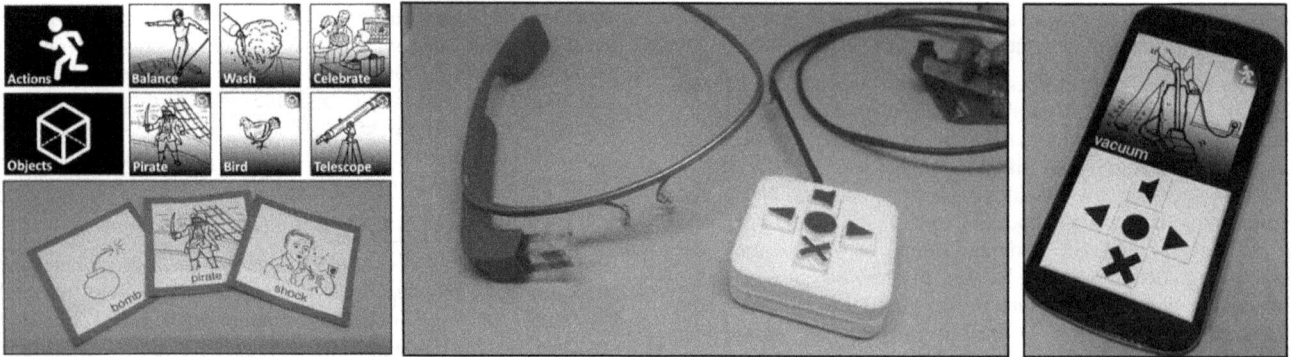

Figure 2. Top-left: Words from the vocabulary-prompting software, showing both the top level of the hierarchy ('actions' and 'objects') and examples of words from the second level. Bottom-left: Examples of Go Fish cards used for introducing the game; card sets used for the training and testing tasks were identical except they did NOT include text. Middle: HWD with remote control for navigation: cycle through words in the current level of the hierarchy (left/right arrows), select a top-level category and view its contents (circle), cancel out of the second level and return to the top level ('X'), and play audio for the current word (speaker icon). Right: Smartphone version, showing an action word above the navigational controls.

worn smartphone (similar to a smartwatch setup), but participants felt this solution was distracting [47]; an alternative recommendation was to use a button-based control. Thus, we created an Arduino Uno-based remote control (Figure 2, center) that linked to Google Glass via Bluetooth through a Galaxy Nexus mobile phone using the Amarino library [19].

We consider eyes-free input to be an integral aspect of an overall HWD user experience, so we created a 3D-printed case to minimize the need for visual attention to the remote control. It housed five buttons (each 12mm across); each with a raised icon (2mm in height) to allow for tactile identification. The buttons, shown in Figure 2, were: *forward* and *back* (right/left arrows) to cycle through words in the current level of the hierarchy; *select* (circle) and *cancel* ('X') to switch between the top-level and the second-level of the hierarchy; and *audio* (speaker icon) to activate text-to-speech for the current vocabulary word. For the smartphone, we created a comparable touchscreen button layout.

3.3 Conversation Task: Playing Go Fish

The conversation tasks consisted of playing the game *Go Fish* with different sets of cards. Go Fish requires structured requests and responses between two players. Each player is dealt the same number of cards (in our case, five cards) and the remaining ones are placed face down on the table. Players take turns requesting a card from the other person to match a card in their own hand. The object of the game is to make as many matches as possible. On each game turn, if the opponent holds a matching card, they hand it over and the player can make a new request; otherwise, the player draws a card from the deck and the game turn passes to the opponent. Following Faroqi-Shah and Virion [37, 41], we selected this language game as the basis for conversation tasks so as to strike a balance between constraining dialogue in a targeted manner and simulating natural conversation that can offer some generalization to everyday life [33].

We created five different decks with 10 pairs of action cards and 10 pairs of object cards each (40 total cards per deck). One deck was used for *learning* to play the game itself, two were used for *training* with the devices (HWD and smartphone), and two were used for *testing* with the devices. Each card consisted of the same black and white line drawings used in the HWD and smartphone software (Figure 2, bottom-left). The deck used for initially learning to play Go Fish also included text, but the four other decks did not. Each deck was created using a process that took into account frequency of words in the English language based on

the picture naming study of Szekely et. al [38], that is: (1) one object and one action word were randomly selected from each tenth percentile (1st–10th percentile, 11th–20th, etc.) so that each deck included 20 pairs of cards that represented a variety of more common and less common words; (2) no word was selected twice across the decks; and (3) finally, cards were swapped across decks or replaced so that each deck contained the same number of one, two, and three syllable words at an equivalent frequency percentile.

3.4 Procedure

The study procedure lasted up to 90 minutes and was video recorded. At the beginning of the session, participants completed a baseline naming evaluation to roughly gauge their ability to name the cards that would be later used for testing. Here, participants described a series of 40 picture cards using a single word for each; the 40 pictures corresponded to those used across the two test decks. Then, to ensure that participants were familiar with the rules of Go Fish, they played the game once without the smartphone or HWD, using the card deck that contained both pictures and words.

Each participant then completed a training task and a test task with each device. The order of presentation of the devices was counterbalanced, as was the pairing of training and testing card decks with a given device. The tasks were as follows:

Training task. The researcher loaded the appropriate vocabulary set (to match the assigned Go Fish card deck) on the device, then introduced the device and controls to the participant—forward, back, audio, select, and cancel. The participant briefly tried out each function and explored the software. Each participant was free to hold and position the mobile phone and remote control however worked best for him/her. For the HWD, the researcher helped the participant to put on the device and to adjust the display arm to ensure full view of the display. The researcher then presented the 20 pictures from the card deck in series and asked the participant to locate each one in the software and say the associated word when they had found it. Participants were cut off at the 10-minute mark whether or not they had proceeded through all 20 pictures.

Test task. After loading the appropriate vocabulary on the device, the researcher and the participant played Go Fish with the assigned card deck. The two players sat across a table from each other, and stands were constructed to hold the cards and prevent the opponent from seeing a player's hand (Figure 1). Before beginning play, we instructed participants to use the device to support communication as needed during the game. The game proceeded until all cards in the deck had been matched or 10 minutes had passed, whichever was sooner. Following the game, participants rated the device in terms of overall experience and ability to maintain focus on the conversation as a whole and on the game partner.

Finally, following use of both devices, we conducted a semi-structured interview (about 15 minutes), with questions about each device's design, potential communication and social impacts of using vocabulary support with the two devices, and ideals for communication support tool design.

3.5 Research Questions

This study compares how well vocabulary support provided on a HWD versus a smartphone supports conversation for individuals with aphasia. Our goals were both to assess the projected benefits of HWDs identified in previous non-comparative work [47], particularly the ability to maintain focus on the conversation partner due to the glanceable nature of the display, and to explore additional dimensions of conversation quality, such as how efficiently the user can communicate with a partner. Specifically, our research questions included: How do the two devices compare in terms of overall user experience and perceived ability to maintain focus on the conversation and partner? How do the devices compare in terms of supporting efficient and accurate communication, measured indirectly through speed and success at playing the card game? Do participants employ vocabulary from the device more with the HWD versus the smartphone? Finally, we were interested in the more general question of how participants envisioned an ideal technology-based vocabulary support solution, as discussed in the end-of-session semi-structured interview.

3.6 Design and Analysis

We used a single-factor within-subjects design to allow for subjective comparison between the two devices. The independent variable was the device (HWD or smartphone), and the order of presentation for the two conditions was fully counterbalanced. However, after running 15 participants, we discovered that due to a software bug, the HWD test task cutoff was 15 minutes rather than the intended 10 minutes, while the smartphone test task was cut off at 10 minutes as intended. Although we fixed the problem for the remaining five participants, we chose a conservative approach for analyzing our quantitative data, by only examining data that is comparable across participants: objective measures from the first 10 minutes of gameplay for the first device used and subjective measures from only the first device used. Note that for completeness, we also conducted a within-subjects analysis on all data, which provided results consistent with the between-subjects analysis presented here. To compare measures between the two conditions, we employed unpaired t-tests or, when appropriate (e.g., with the rating data), non-parametric Mann-Whitney U tests.

For each device, we collected subjective ratings using 7-point Likert scales (1-poor, 7-excellent) for *overall experience*, *ability to maintain focus on the conversation*, and *ability to maintain focus on the conversational partner*. We included separate measures for focus on the conversation and conversational partner, distinguishing the former as the ability to concentrate on one's own speaking ability, word finding, and conversation planning and the latter as the ability to concentrate on the partner's behaviors, including eye contact, facial expressions, and intonations. However, as suggested by the results, it is unclear whether or not participants made a distinction between the two.

For objective measures, we divided the video from the test tasks into game turns using transcription software supported by the aphasia research community, CHAT/CLAN[5], and transcribed the conversation for each turn. From the video and log data, we then extracted three main measures to address our research questions: the *number of card pairs matched* out of the 20 possible matches (i.e., how far players made it through the game); the *number of vocabulary words* the participant retrieved from the device and employed; and the *average time per game turn*, only for turns where the participant used the device—that is, a direct indication of how device interaction impacted the speed of the turn.

Responses to the design questions were transcribed, subdivided by speaking turns [4, 47], and coded for themes of interest (*e.g.* aesthetics or discrete use) by a person trained in supported conversation techniques and who had prior experience interviewing persons with aphasia [16]. We applied a coding method that allowed for inductive codes tied closely to the data to also emerge [6]. A person independent of the research group with a background designing technology for persons with cognitive disabilities (though not language disorders) independently coded two randomly selected transcripts. Coding differences were reconciled through discussion. The independent coder was later asked to assess the resulting summarization, and its match with the groupings identified in the data; no questions or problems were identified.

We excluded four participants from the final analysis. Two were excluded because their log data revealed that they did not use the device at all during the task, so their subjective ratings and performance data did not reflect device experience. Further, they did not appear to need its support: one completed 20 turns (higher than average), while the other completed the full game. Two more were excluded due to much lower language ability than the rest of the group: they scored only 1 and 0, respectively, on the baseline language evaluation test, compared to an average score of 19.1 (SD=6.7) for the 20 participants overall. Our final participant set included eight participants who used the HWD first and eight who used the phone first.

4. Findings

We present subjective and objective quantitative findings before going into more depth on the qualitative findings that arose from the semi-structured interview portion of the study.

4.1 Task Performance and Experience

As noted in Section 3.6, we analyzed quantitative data only for the first device that participants used, effectively employing a between-subjects analysis. Over the 10-minute test task period, participants using the HWD completed 14.8 game turns on average (SD=4.8), while smartphone participants completed 13.4 (SD=4.1). Of course, the device's vocabulary support was not employed for all of those turns. With the HWD, the vocabulary support was used on average in 8.3 turns (SD=2.9), while the smartphone was used in 5.0 (SD=3.4) turns. Participants were closely matched in naming ability across the two devices as evaluated in the baseline naming task: for the HWD, M=18.6 (SD=7.5, range=6-28), and the phone, M=19.6 (SD=5.8, range=8-29). With this context, we present our primary quantitative measures.

4.1.1 Comparing Form Factors

We begin with our main analysis, comparing the HWD to the smartphone over our dependent measures.

---

[5] More detail at Aphasia Bank, http://talkbank.org/AphasiaBank/

Communication efficiency. The HWD supported more efficient communication than the smartphone, as evidenced primarily by the elapsed time for turns where participants used the vocabulary support. On average, time per turn in the HWD condition was 36.3s (SD=12.9s), compared to 71.0s for the smartphone condition (SD=47.9s). An unpaired t-test showed that this difference was significant (t_{14}=-1.85, p=.043, d=1.00).

Providing additional support that the HWD improved communication efficiency, participants matched on average 11.3 (SD=5.4) pairs of cards in the HWD condition, compared to only 7.6 pairs (SD=4.0) in the phone condition; again, the total number of possible matches is 20. Although this difference is not significant at p < .05, the effect size is large (t_{14}=1.45, p=.087, d=0.82).

Vocabulary words used from the device. Participants using the HWD, retrieved and employed on average 6.8 (SD=3.5) vocabulary words from the device, compared to an average of only 4.6 (SD=2.9) for the phone. This result did not reach significance (t_{14}=1.37, p=.119, d=0.66), but the effect size is large and suggests that the HWD may have made it easier to access vocabulary, in turn spurring greater use of the words. This possibility should be revisited in a future study with greater statistical power.

Overall experience. Participants rated the overall experience of using the HWD higher, at 6.1 (SD=0.8) on average, compared to using the smartphone, at 4.6 (SD=1.9). However, a Mann-Whitney U test revealed this difference was not significant (U=17, p=.064, r=0.38).

Focus. Although a predicted advantage of the HWD over a phone is that it should allow for greater focus on the conversation [47], measures of focus were similar across the two devices, with no statistically significant differences for perceived focus on the conversation (p=.480) or on the partner (p=.374). This result is evident in the raw ratings. Participants did not rate the HWD substantially higher than the smartphone for focus on conversation (HWD: M=5.6, SD=0.9; phone: M=5.1 SD=1.9), nor, for focus on the partner (HWD: M=5.4, SD=1.3; phone: M=5.6, SD=1.3).

4.1.2 Comparing Fast vs. Slow Performers
As we observed a high degree of variability among participants (e.g., large standard deviations observed for time for turns reported in Section 4.1.1), we further analyzed the data to better understand this diversity. When the 16 participants were divided into two evenly split groups based on time per turn—a fast group (<45s time per turn, M=28.7s, SD=9.2s, range=18.5–43.7s) and a slow group (>45s time per turn, M=78.6s, SD=41.6s, range=48.6–149.4s)—some trends emerged that could inform the design of conversation support technologies. The two subgroups were almost evenly exposed to either device first (5 used the HWD first in the fast group vs. 3 in the slow group) and had similar baseline naming abilities (on average 18.6 vs. 19.6 words named in the fast and slow groups, respectively). Since this is a secondary analysis, we report only descriptive statistics, and did not perform any inferential analyses that would imply generalizations beyond our sample.

The fast group matched a greater number of card pairs than the slow group (11.4 vs. 7.5 matches), and retrieved and used more vocabulary from the device (7.6 vs. 3.8 words used). While it is perhaps not surprising that the fast group accomplished more during their study sessions, the fast group also used the device—whether HWD or phone—almost twice as often as the slow group (in 8.6 vs. 4.6 turns), emphasizing the adeptness with which the

faster participants appeared to use the device. The fast group also reported a higher perceived ability to focus on the conversation (average rating of 6.1 vs. 4.6 for the slow group) and on the partner (5.75 v. 5.25).

When asked to expand on their ratings for the ability to focus on the conversation, fast participants said they felt mentally sharp, had helpful prior experience multitasking, had a fluid rapport with the conversation partner, were able to establish eye contact, and found the device (regardless of form factor) supplied supportive vocabulary. In contrast, participants from the slow group may have had to attend more to operating the device and struggled more with multitasking. Two participants from the slow group reported being confused trying to simultaneously navigate the software and conduct the conversation, and two others thought they could learn to use the device over time to overcome the difficulties experienced during the study's time frame. Overall, this analysis suggests that the fast group was both objectively and subjectively more effective at interacting with the device (HWD or phone) than participants in the slow group and that this difference may explain their greater efficiency.

4.2 Semi-Structured Interview
We summarize participant responses to open-ended questions organized around themes such as previously predicted advantages of HWDs [47], aesthetics, and fit within current communication practice.

4.2.1 Privacy, Discreet Use, and Glanceability
While previous work highlighted privacy, discreet use, and glanceability as important potential advantages of vocabulary support on HWDs over smartphones [47], our participants identified further nuance to these characteristics.

The ability to access the displayed contents and text-to-speech on the HWD without exposing that content to others was generally seen as advantageous by eight of our participants (despite the concern mentioned above), because it supported control over who could see the device's contents and when. Five participants mentioned they disliked having audio prompts loud enough to be overheard by others, with C21 pointed out that such noise is inappropriate in some contexts like a library. The privacy of the near-eye display was also not always seen as a positive, however; C20 and C21 highlighted how the phone screen, unlike the HWD, could be easily displayed to others, which in some cases could aid in efficiently sharing information. An ideal form factor would be one that provides control over what gets shared and when.

Moreover, although the HWD provided privacy and the ability to be discreet about what support was being accessed, it was also described as more noticeable than a mobile phone because it is worn on the face. Three participants criticized the remote control for the HWD for being too visible and required managing an additional object. Participants suggested: severing its cord, integrating its functionality with their existing phone, or hiding the tactile control in their pocket.

In terms of glanceability, one participant (C6) felt that the near-eye display disrupted visual perception of the conversation partner, forcing attention to the display or to the partner, but not both. In essence, glanceability was not effective for this participant. While putting the HWD back on to demonstrate a point, an unexpected change in the visual content curtailed C6's speaking, further emphasizing the forced choice of how to allocate attention.

4.2.2 Aesthetics and Practicality

Seven participants discussed how the device fit within their current aesthetic or fashion choices, and especially with how it fit with current eyewear. C15 remarked, "I mean it was cool having 'em over my glasses and not everybody needs glasses." While C3 and C17 wanted the HWD to be integrated with their glasses, C19 only needed reading glasses so did not want to fully commit to having glasses on all the time. C8 desired the ability to selectively attach or remove the HWD from eyeglasses much like clip-on sunglasses. The need to accommodate glasses was not simply one of preference, but also due to vision requirements. For example, C17 used bifocals and wanted to make glanceable switches between optic support as supported by bifocals, and C7 complained that the current HWD display caused her to develop a headache during the time worn.

Three participants described how they wanted to miniaturize the HWD so that it was as thin as their current frames and receded into their glasses. For example, C8 wanted the nose pads of the HWD incorporated into a smooth bridge like his current glasses. Notably, C19 and C21 thought the current visibility of the HWD design would distinguish them as being trendsetters or signal that they, as wearers, were technology insiders. C19 describe the HWD as "Funky, glass is funky." While C19 and C21 regarded this as a positive feature of the HWD design, they thought that it would lead them to only use the HWD in exceptional circumstances when they wanted to standout as "future[istic]" or "geeking". Overall, C15, C19, and C21 desired a design that blended the HWD support with eyeglass fashion and could likewise be adopted by persons without aphasia.

In terms of other practical issues, six participants expressed a desire to separate features of the HWD so that they could be selectively employed. C21 wanted to be able to fold the HWD and reduce its size to easily stow away: "Close it up, close it up, fold it up." C7 and C8 wanted the ability to simply push the glasses up on top of their head as is currently done with other sorts of glasses. C6, C8, and C13 voiced concerns of having to switch between multiple pairs of glasses and thought the HWD would not be suitable for outdoor use because of the need to wear sunglasses. To provide more flexibility in interaction, C21 recommended separating the visual display from the audio prompts, by moving the display to a wristwatch and the audio speaker to a discreet earpiece. C19 thought that decoupling access to the audio prompt from access to the visual display would facilitate selective use similar to how headphones can be used (or not used) with a phone.

4.2.3 Fit Within a Communication Ecology

Nine participants described how the smartphone or HWD may fit within their current communication ecology. C3 and C7 described how the device needed to work in a larger language support system of artifacts and conversation partners. The points from C6, C7, C20, and C21 to do with glanceability and privacy (above) touch on how the technology could positively or negatively impact the connection with a conversation partner. C8, C15, and C19 wanted a form factor design that could facilitate selective engagement of the device since they frequently shifted between familiar and unfamiliar conversation partners. C19 depicted a situation in which the closeness of the communication partner would impact when they used the device: he would not need a vocabulary prompting device when talking with family and friends, but would for strangers. Finally, C15 envisioned the glasses as providing robust vocabulary support in conversations that could be easily scripted like pushing a restaurant's menu to

the HWD: "I still struggle to get the words out, but if those words are in there, I'm looking around and I like, 'Oh, I want chicken with French fries'."

4.2.4 Role of Mainstream Devices

Eleven participants described features of a smartphone that they would want incorporated in future HWD designs or that highlighted limitations of the HWD. Responses reflected a desire for support using mainstream devices, a common sentiment with mobile accessible technology [17]. Participants wanted HWDs to enjoy the current ubiquity of smartphones because it ensured that the device had robust community support and allowed them to blend in. C7 liked that she could simply ask a stranger for help with a smartphone because they would be likely to know how to help. Unlike HWDs, smartphones supported blending in because they could be stowed away in a pocket or could be used as a general-purpose device (e.g., a smartphone allows for vocabulary assistance, but also a range of other tools). C6 thought that he could obviate any need for the HWD simply by augmenting his phone with an earpiece; such a design would no longer offer the glanceable and private visual display. In contrast, C4 was more optimistic about how HWDs would evolve, predicting that over time they would become more common, support a range of activities like shopping, and develop informal community support.

4.2.5 Summary

Participants identified trade-offs between the HWD and the smartphone for supporting aesthetic choices, fitting within their current communicative and technological practices, and support for vision prescriptions. While the smartphone excelled at blending with popular usage and concealing aphasia-specific support, participants identified many features of the HWD that could be customized to signal fashion consciousness, facilitate speaking, and conceal or reveal use of supportive vocabulary prompts.

5. DISCUSSION

Our study explored the potential benefits of vocabulary support provided on a HWD by directly comparing its use to a more traditional smartphone approach. Our findings confirm predicted benefits of HWDs made in previous work [47], including the ease of accessing information on the near-eye display compared to the phone—seen in quantitative measures of conversation efficiency such as time per game turn—and the importance of the HWD's private visual and audio output. At the same time, the varying adeptness with which participants used the devices (HWD or phone) and themes from the semi-structured interview highlight additional complexities of providing effective vocabulary support on either a HWD or phone.

Value of direct comparison. By asking participants to employ two prototypes representing two different form factors during a controlled conversation task, we were able to elicit detailed feedback and trade-offs on design dimensions that impact conversation dynamics. In contrast to prior research on HWD conversation prompts [47], where the authors articulated concern that "positive feedback was not clearly attributable to the head-worn form factor" (pg. 239, Limitations), we were able to elicit more nuanced feedback, including differences specifically arising from the form factors. For example, participants identified trade-offs in whether the visibility of the conversation assistance facilitated information sharing and help from others, versus empowering the wearer to speak for themselves and manage others' perceptions.

Design trade-offs. One motivation for using a HWD was the potential to provide private and unobtrusive support, but our results revealed a tradeoff, indicating that this unobtrusiveness may come at a cost. While participants described the HWD as empowering wearers to speak for themselves and providing a way to manage external perceptions of language ability, in some cases, that very privacy may inadvertently limit social assistance. Persons with aphasia can sometimes have difficulty translating a prompt into speech; for example, some individuals commonly replace the first phoneme with that of a different word (*i.e.,* they might say "present" in place of "pheasant"). Within our data, we saw a small number of instances where such transformations happened, and while these were easily mitigated in the phone condition (as the listener could hear and see the original prompt), such problems were less readily resolved with the HWD. A shared display or audible text-to-speech would have helped ground the conversation, allowing the partner to infer what the participant intended to communicate. This observation highlights the importance of accommodating each user's needs and preferences, suggesting the best form factor may depend on the individual characteristics of the user, including their specific communication profile, and the degree to which unobtrusive support is valued.

Balancing conversation and device use. Findings from our study provide preliminary support for using HWDs to balance the challenging task of conversing while accessing assistive vocabulary. In particular, our results suggest the HWD enabled more efficient, and possibly more effective, communication. Participants took significantly less time per turn with the HWD. As well, despite lack of statistical significance, large effect sizes suggest participants may have gotten further in the game (as measured by the proportion of correct matches), and had a better overall experience with the HWD. The underlying mechanism for these gains, however, is less clear. Contrary to our initial expectations, there were negligible differences between the HWD and the phone for perceived impacts on focus. This lack of difference may be related to individual adeptness with using the device, whether the HWD or phone, as seen in our secondary analysis comparing fast versus slow participants. Those who were more adept with the technology (i.e., fast) also reported a higher ability to focus on the conversation and partner, which suggests that technology training could be important for participants who experienced more struggle with the device interaction, or that other cognitive factors (e.g., fluid intelligence) influence success.

Lessons learned. Constructing the study task as a language game supported comparison of speaking turns and time frames of device interaction while still enabling participants to proceed through the trials and advance toward a larger objective: winning the game [22]. This allowed the study to model how assistive devices may be employed during the dynamic shifts of naturally occurring conversation, and to examine how participants used the device when challenged by the required vocabulary (a language game has also been used for aphasia emulation [14]). This shifts focus from the device as a support tool for speaking to its fit within broader aspects of conversation such as listening, clarifying, and comprehending. Overall, we found the language game task successful in simulating a conversational ecology to examine device use in a lab setting. Surprisingly, we saw in the video-taped sessions a few participants using the device as a reflexive tool to verify guessed words against the supplied picture, to coach their own pronunciation, and to resolve ambiguity on whether they understood what the researcher was requesting. These kinds of uses are so minute as to be difficult to catch in a field study, and suggest future work on how a language game task could help

investigate when participants might appropriate a vocabulary support tool to help with their personal language challenges.

Limitations. One limitation of our study is that, discarding half of our data for the quantitative measures and switching to a between-subjects analysis substantially reduced statistical power. Nonetheless, absolute differences were generally in the direction favoring the HWD, and even comparable findings between the HWD and smartphone are encouraging given that participants had limited to no experience with HWDs but many had at least some experience with smartphones. A related limitation is that our study only included a single session, which allowed for only a short training period with both of the devices. Future work should revisit our research questions after longer-term exposure to the technology. Finally, the particular HWD design we used may have impacted results. We used Google Glass—a HWD that offers a visual display that is offset to the right and above the user's center of vision—which may have negatively impacted participants' ability to maintain visual focus on their conversation partner while accessing support. Further, we did not examine to what extent the use of a remote control to address accessibility issues with Glass's right-sided touchpad supported eyes-free input and diverted visual attention. Other HWD designs, particularly those with a display in the viewer's line of sight and supporting eyes-free input accessible to individuals with aphasia, may provide different results.

6. CONCLUSION

In order to employ assistive technology in conversation, individuals with aphasia must balance interaction with the device and maintaining the conversation. Our comparative study confirms a previously predicted advantage of HWDs over smartphones: providing vocabulary support on the HWD allowed for more efficient communication than doing so on the phone. Subjective ability to focus on the conversation partner, however, was found to be no different between the two conditions, possibly due to the offset display of the particular HWD device we used (Google Glass). These findings should motivate future work on using HWDs for language support, including investigating the effectiveness of the support after longer-term use and with greater experience, and examining issues of social acceptance and obtrusiveness in field settings.

7. ACKNOWLEDGMENTS

We thank Melissa Richman, the Snyder Center for Aphasia Life Enhancement, the Stroke Comeback Center, and the Montgomery County Stroke Association and their members for all of their help and support for this research. Software icons are from the Noun Project and created by Jessica Lock and Ilsur Aptukov. This research was funded by NSF grant IIS-1350438, a Google Faculty Research Award, and a Career Development Grant from AAUW.

8. REFERENCES

[1]   About | NounProject: *https://thenounproject.com/about/*. Accessed: 2015-07-08.

[2]   Allen, M., McGrenere, J. and Purves, B. 2007. The design and field evaluation of PhotoTalk: A digital image communication application for people. *Proc. of the ACM SIGACCESS Conf. on Computers and Accessibility* (Tempe, Arizona, USA, October 15-17, 2007). ASSETS '07. ACM, New York, NY, 187–194. DOI=http://doi.acm.org/10.1145/1296843.1296876.

[3]   Arnott, J.L., Newell, A.F. and Alm, N. 1992. Prediction and conversational momentum in an augmentative

communication system. *Communications of the ACM.* 35, 5 (May 1992), 46–57.

[4] Ball, M.J., Muller, N. and Nelson, R.L. eds. 2014. *Handbook of Qualitative Research in Communication Disorders.* Psychology Press.

[5] Boyd-graber, J., Nikolova, S., Moffatt, K., Kin, K., Lee, J., Mackey, L., Tremaine, M., Klawe, M. and Vt, B.C. 2006. Participatory Design with Proxies: Developing a Desktop-PDA System to Support People with Aphasia. *Proc. of the SIGCHI Conf. on Human Factors in Computing* (Montreal, Quebec, Canada, April 22-27 2006). CHI'06. ACM, New York, NY, 151–160. DOI=http://doi.acm.org/10.1145/1124772.1124797.

[6] Braun, V. and Clarke, V. 2006. Using thematic analysis in psychology. *Qualitative Research in Psychology.* 3, 2 (Jan. 2006), 77–101.

[7] Chapey, R. 2001. *Language intervention strategies in aphasia and related neurogenic communication disorders.* Lippincott Williams & Wilkins.

[8] Clark, H. 1996. *Using Language.* Cambridge University Press.

[9] Daemen, E., Dadlani, P., Du, J., Li, Y., Erik-Paker, P., Martens, J.-B. and De Ruyter, B. 2007. Designing a Free Style, Indirect, and Interactive Storytelling Application for People with Aphasia. *Proc. of the IFIP TC 13 International Conf. on Human-computer Interaction* (Rio de Janeiro, Brazil, September 10-14, 2007). INTERACT '07. Springer, Berlin, Germany. 221–234. DOI=http://dx.doi.org/10.1007/978-3-540-74796-3_21.

[10] Demmans Epp, C., Djordjevic, J., Wu, S., Moffatt, K. and Baecker, R.M. 2012. Towards providing just-in-time vocabulary support for assistive and augmentative communication. *Proc. of the ACM Conf. on Intelligent User Interfaces* (Lisbon, Portugal, February 14-17, 2012). *IUI '12.* ACM, New York, NY. 33-36. DOI=http://dx.doi.org/10.1145/2166966.2166973.

[11] Fridriksson, J., Hubbard, H.I., Hudspeth, S.G., Holland, A.L., Bonilha, L., Fromm, D. and Rorden, C. 2012. Speech entrainment enables patients with Broca's aphasia to produce fluent speech. *Brain: a journal of neurology.* 135, (Dec. 2012), 3815–29.

[12] Galliers, J., Wilson, S., Muscroft, S., Marshall, J., Roper, A., Cocks, N. and Pring, T. 2011. Accessibility of 3D Game Environments for People with Aphasia: An Exploratory Study. *Proc. of the ACM SIGACCESS Conf. on Computers and Accessibility* (Dundee, Scotland, October 24-26, 2011). ASSETS'11. ACM, New York, NY. 139–146. DOI=http://doi.acm.org/10.1145/2049536.2049562.

[13] Ha, K., Chen, Z., Hu, W., Richter, W., Pillai, P. and Satyanarayanan, M. 2014. Towards wearable cognitive assistance. *Proc. of the International Conference on Mobile Systems, Applications, and Services - MobiSys '14* (New York, New York, USA, Jun. 2014), 68–81.

[14] Hailpern, J., Danilevsky, M. and Harris, A. 2013. ACES: a cross-discipline platform and method for communication and language research. *Proc. of the ACM Conf. on Computer Supported Cooperative Work and Social Computing* (San Antonio, Texas, USA, February 23-27, 2013). CSCW'13. ACM, New York, NY, 515–525. DOI=https://doi.acm.org/10.1145/2441776.2441835.

[15] Higginbotham, D.J., Shane, H., Russell, S. and Caves, K. 2007. Access to AAC: present, past, and future. *Augmentative and alternative communication.* 23, 3 (2007), 243–257.

[16] Kagan, A. 1998. Supported conversation for adults with aphasia: methods and resources for training conversation partners. *Aphasiology.* 12, 9 (Sep. 1998), 816–830.

[17] Kane, S.K., Jayant, C., Wobbrock, J.O. and Ladner, R.E. 2009. Freedom to roam. *Proc. of the ACM SIGACCESS Conference on Computers and Accessibility* (Pittsburgh, Pennsylvania, USA, October 25-28, 2009). ASSETS'09. ACM, New York, NY, 115-122. DOI=http://doi.acm.org/10.1145/1639642.1639663.

[18] Kane, S.K., Linam-Church, B., Althoff, K. and McCall, D. 2012. What We Talk About: Designing a Context-aware Communication Tool for People with Aphasia. *Proc. of the ACM SIGACCESS Conf. on Computers and Accessibility* (Boulder, CO, USA, October 22-24, 2012). ASSETS'12. ACM, New York, NY, 49–56. DOI=http://doi.acm.org /10.1145/2384916.2384926.

[19] Kaufmann, B. and Buechley, L. 2010. Amarino: a toolkit for the rapid prototyping of mobile ubiquitous computing. *Proc. of the International Conference on Human Computer Interaction with Mobile Devices and Services.* (Lisbon, Portugal, September 7-10, 2010). MobileHCI'10. ACM, New York, NY, 291–298. DOI=http://doi.acm.org/ 10.1145/1851600.1851652.

[20] Kunze, K., Henze, N. and Kise, K. 2014. Wearable Computing for Older Adults – Initial Insights into Head-Mounted Display Usage. *Proc. of the ACM International Joint Conference on Pervasive and Ubiquitous Computing* (Seattle, WA, USA, September 13-17, 2014). UbiComp'14. ACM, New York, NY, 1–4. DOI=http://doi.acm.org/10.1145/2638728.2638747

[21] Lasker, J. and Bedrosian, J. 2001. Promoting acceptance of augmentative and alternative communication by adults with acquired communication disorders. *Augmentative and Alternative Communication.* 17, 3 (2001), 141–153.

[22] Lewis, D. 1979. Scorekeeping in a Language Game. *Journal of Philosophical Logic.* 8, 1 (1979), 339–359.

[23] Linebarger, M. and Schwartz, M. 2005. AAC for hypothesis testing and treatment of aphasic language production: Lessons from a "processing prosthesis." *Aphasiology.* 19, 10-11 (Nov. 2005), 930–942.

[24] Lyons, K., Skeels, C., Starner, T., Snoeck, C.M., Wong, B.A. and Ashbrook, D. 2004. Augmenting Conversations Using Dual–Purpose Speech. *Proc. of the ACM Symposium on User Interface Software and Technology* (Santa Fe, NM, USA, October 24-27, 2004). UIST'04. ACM, New York, NY, 237-246. DOI=http://doi.acm.org/10.1145/1029632.1029674.

[25] Al Mahmud, A. and Gerits, R. 2010. XTag: Designing an Experience Capturing and Sharing Tool for Persons with Aphasia. *Proceedings of the 6th Nordic Conference on Human-Computer Interaction* (Reykjavik, Iceland, October 16-20, 2010). NordiCHI'10. ACM, New York, NY, 325–334. DOI=http://doi.acm.org/10.1145/1868914.1868953

[26] McAtamney, G. and Parker, C. 2006. An examination of the effects of a wearable display on informal face-to-face communication. *Proc. of the ACM SIGCHI Conf. on Human Factors in Computing Systems* (Montreal, Quebec, Canada, April 22-27, 2006). CHI'06. ACM, New York, NY, 45–54. DOI=http://doi.acm.org/10.1145/1029632.1029674

[27] McNaney, R., Vines, J., Roggen, D., Balaam, M., Zhang, P., Poliakov, I. and Olivier, P. 2014. Exploring the acceptability of google glass as an everyday assistive device for people with parkinson's. *Proc. of the ACM SIGCHI Conf. on Human Factors in Computing Systems* (Toronto, Canada, April 26-May 1st, 2014). CHI'14. ACM, New York, NY, 2551–2554. DOI=http://doi.acm.org /10.1145/2556288.2557092

[28] Mishler, E.G. 2006. Narrative and identity: the double arrow of time. *Discourse and Identity*. A. De Fina, D. Schiffrin, and M. Bamberg, eds. Cambridge University Press.

[29] Moffatt, K., McGrenere, J., Purves, B. and Klawe, M. 2004. The participatory design of a sound and image enhanced daily planner for people with aphasia. *Proc. of the SIGCHI Conf. on Human Factors in Computing Systems* (Vienna, Austria, April 26-May 1st, 2004). CHI'04. ACM, New York, NY, 407–414. DOI= http://doi.acm.org/10.1145/985692.985744.

[30] Nikolova, S., Tremaine, M. and Cook, P.R. 2010. Click on Bake to Get Cookies: Guiding Word-finding with Semantic Associations. *Proc. of the ACM SIGACCESS Conf. on Computers and Accessibility* (Orlando, FL, USA, October 25-27, 2010). ASSETS'10. ACM, New York, NY, 155–162. DOI=http://doi.acm.org/10.1145/1878803.1878832

[31] Ofek, E., Iqbal, S.T. and Strauss, K. 2013. Reducing disruption from subtle information delivery during a conversation: mode and bandwidth investigation. *Proc. of the SIGCHI Conf. on Human Factors in Computing Systems* (Paris, France, April 27-May 2, 2013). CHI'13. ACM, New York, NY, 3111–3120. DOI=http://doi.acm.org /10.1145/2470654.2466425

[32] Piper, A.M., Weibel, N. and Hollan, J.D. 2011. Write-N-Speak. *ACM Transactions on Accessible Computing*. 4, 1 (Nov. 2011), 1–20.

[33] Pulvermüller, F., Neininger, B. and Elbert, T. 2001. Constraint-induced therapy of chronic aphasia after stroke. *Stroke*. 32, (2001), 1621–1626.

[34] Roelofs, A. 2004. Error biases in spoken word planning and monitoring by aphasic and nonaphasic speakers: comment on Rapp and Goldrick (2000). *Psychological review*. 111, 2 (Apr. 2004), 561–80.

[35] van de Sandt-Koenderman, M. 2004. High-tech AAC and aphasia: Widening horizons? *Aphasiology*. 18, 3 (2004), 245–263.

[36] Sarno, M. ed. 1998. *Acquired Aphasia*. Academic Press, Inc.

[37] Shah, Y. and Virion, C. 2009. Constraint-Induced language therapy for agrammatism: Role of grammaticality constraint. *Aphasiology*. (2009), 977–988.

[38] Szekely, A., Jacobsen, T., D'Amico, S., Devescovi, A., Andonova, E., Herron, D., Lu, C. C., Pechmann, T., Pleh, C., Wicha, N., Federmeier, K., Gerdjikova, I., Gutierrez, G., Hung, D., Hsu, J., Iyer, G., Kohnert, K., Mehotcheva, T., Orozco-Figueroa, A., Tzeng, A., Tzeng, O., Arevalo, A., Vargha, A., Butler, A. C., Buffington, R., & Bates, E. A new on-line resource for psycholinguistic studies. *Jour. of Memory and Language*. 51, 2 (2004), 247–250.

[39] Tanveer, M.I., Lin, E. and Hoque, M.E. 2015. Rhema : A Real-Time In-Situ Intelligent Interface to Help People with Public Speaking. *Proc. of the Int. Conf. on Intelligent User Interfaces* (Atlanta, GA, USA, March 28-April 1, 2015). IUI'15. ACM, New York, NY, 286–295. DOI= http://doi.acm.org/10.1145/2678025.2701386

[40] Tee, K., Moffatt, K., Findlater, L., MacGregor, E., McGrenere, J., Purves, B. and Fels, S.S. 2005. A Visual Recipe Book for Persons with Language Impairments. *Proc. of the SIGCHI Conf. for Human Factors in Computing Systems* (Portland, OR, USA, 2005). CHI'05. ACM, New York, NY, 501–510. DOI=http://doi.acm.org/10.1145/1054972.1055042.

[41] Virion, C.R. 2008. *"Go Aphasia!": Examining the Efficacy of Constraint-induced Language Therapy for Individuals with Agrammatic Aphasia*. Master's Thesis. URI=http://hdl.handle.net/1903/8611. University of Maryland.

[42] Vörös, G., Rabi, P., Pinter, B. and Sarkany, A. 2014. Recommending Missing Symbols of Augmentative and Alternative Communication by Means of Explicit Semantic Analysis. *Natural Language Access to Big Data: Papers from the AAAI Fall Symposium* (2014).

[43] Vörös, G., Verő, A., Pintér, B., Miksztai-Réthey, B., Toyama, T., Lőrincz, A. and Sonntag, D. 2014. Towards a Smart Wearable Tool to Enable People with SSPI to Communicate by Sentence Fragments. *Proc. of the Int. Symposium on Pervasive Computing Paradigms for Mental Health* (Tokyo, Japan, May 8-9th, 2014). MindCare'14. Springer International, 1–10. DOI=http://dx.doi.org/10.1007/978-3-319-11564-1_10

[44] Waller, A., Denis, F., Brodie, J. and Cairns, A.Y. 1998. Evaluating the use of TalksBac, a predictive communciation device for nonfluent adults with aphasia. *International Journal of Language and Communication Disorders*. 33, 1 (1998), 45–70.

[45] Waller, A. and Newell, A. 1997. Towards a Narrative Based Augmentative Communication System. *European Journal of Disorders of Communication*. 32, (1997), 289–306.

[46] Wilkinson, R., Gower, M., Beeke, S. and Maxim, J. 2007. Adapting to conversation as a language-impaired speaker: changes in aphasic turn construction over time. *Communication & medicine*. 4, 1 (Jan. 2007), 79–97.

[47] Williams, K., Moffatt, K., McCall, D. and Findlater, L. 2015. Designing Conversation Cues on a Head-Worn Display to Support Persons with Aphasia. *Proc. of the ACM SIGCHI Conf. on Human Factors in Computing Systems* (Seoul, South Korea, 2015). CHI'15. ACM, New York, NY, 231–240. DOI=http://doi.acm.org/10.1145/2702123.2702484

A Computer Vision-Based System for Stride Length Estimation using a Mobile Phone Camera

Wei Zhu[1], Boyd Anderson[1,2], Shenggao Zhu[1,2], Ye Wang[1,2]
[1]School of Computing, National University of Singapore, Singapore
[2]NUS Graduate School for Integrative Sciences and Engineering, National University of Singapore,
Singapore
juilangchu@icloud.com,{boyd,shenggaozhu}@u.nus.edu, wangye@comp.nus.edu.sg

ABSTRACT

Conditions such as Parkinson's disease (PD), a chronic neurodegenerative disorder which severely affects the motor system, will be an increasingly common problem for our growing and aging population. Gait analysis is widely used as a noninvasive method for PD diagnosis and assessment. However, current clinical systems for gait analysis usually require highly specialized cameras and lab settings, which are expensive and not scalable. This paper presents a computer vision-based gait analysis system using a camera on a common mobile phone. A simple PVC mat was designed with markers printed on it, on which a subject can walk whilst being recorded by a mobile phone camera. A set of video analysis methods were developed to segment the walking video, detect the mat and feet locations, and calculate gait parameters such as stride length. Experiments showed that stride length measurement has a mean absolute error of 0.62 cm, which is comparable with the "gold standard" walking mat system GAITRite. We also tested our system on Parkinson's disease patients in a real clinical environment. Our system is affordable, portable, and scalable, indicating a potential clinical gait measurement tool for use in both hospitals and the homes of patients.

Keywords

Gait Analysis; Computer Vision; Mobile Camera; Video Analysis; Parkinson's Disease; Movement Disorder

1. INTRODUCTION

The world population has been growing rapidly in recent decades, with more than seven billion people living worldwide[1]. Along with this growing trend, the world population is aging at an unprecedented rate, and this brings profound implications for many facets of human life[2]. One of the most serious implications is age-associated chronic diseases that deteriorate the quality of life of elderly people, such as neurodegenerative disorders including Parkinson's disease, Huntington's disease, and Amyotrophic Lateral Sclerosis.

Parkinson's disease (PD) affects an estimated seven to ten million people worldwide, and its incidence increases with age[3]. PD is characterized by decreased motor control abilities, causing symptoms which typically include bradykinesia (slowness of movement), rest tremors, rigidity, and postural and gait impairment. Currently there is no cure for PD, and PD patients rely on medicine such as Levodopa to control the symptoms.

As a chronic disease, PD progresses slowly and its onset is usually difficult to detect. It has a long progression time, which can be divided into different stages. Diagnosis of the PD stage of a patient is an important clinical task that also affects the treatment of the patient. In rural or community hospitals where neurologists and specialized medical equipment are not available, doctors have to diagnose a patient's PD stage based on experience and some simple tests. Therefore, there is a great need for inexpensive, accessible, and objective tools that can be used for PD diagnosis in rural hospitals or hospitals in developing countries.

Mobility assessment is a standard non-invasive PD test, which aims to assess the degree of mobility impairment via the quantification of limb movement. Specifically, gait analysis is widely used to evaluate lower motor performance. Some of the fundamental gait measures include stride time and stride length, as well as the variability of these measures. Experiments have shown that PD patients usually have reduced cadence and increased variation during walking. For example, a study showed that PD patients had a much larger step time variability (7%) than healthy controls (4%) [6].

Clinical gait measurement normally uses pressure sensitive walking mats [17] or motion-capture cameras or camera arrays [19]. These devices are costly and often require technical expertise to use, and thus are difficult to scale up. For those motion-capture systems, usually highly specialized cameras are used, such as Vicon cameras[4]. However, cheap, general-purpose cameras on mobile phones are now ubiquitous. Many smartphone (e.g., iPhone 6S, Samsung Galaxy S5 and newer) cameras are capable of recording videos at 4K resolution at 30 frames per second (FPS) or higher. These modern smartphones have become a potential platform for camera-based gait analysis.

---

[1]https://ourworldindata.org/world-population-growth/
[2]http://www.un.org/esa/population/publications/worldageing19502050/

ASSETS '16, October 23-26, 2016, Reno, NV, USA

© 2016 ACM. ISBN 978-1-4503-4124-0/16/10. . . $15.00

DOI: http://dx.doi.org/10.1145/2982142.2982156

---

[3]http://www.pdf.org/en/parkinson_statistics
[4]http://www.vicon.com/

2. RELATED WORK

There are many studies that focus on analyzing PD patient's activities using different methods and tools. Inertial sensors such as accelerometers and gyroscopes have been used to record patient motion [23, 12, 33, 5]. A mobile phone application [18] was introduced to quantify the Timed-up-and-go test which is common for PD assessment. It also uses the inertial sensors of the mobile device to capture the signals of the patient's gait. One study [23] designed a biometric suit with inertial sensors to simultaneously measure the gait oscillation from eight major joints (knees, hips, elbows and shoulders) of a human body. Another inertial measurement system was developed with several IMUs attached to the subject's feet [12]. These studies use multiple wearable inertial sensors to collect motion data, and then calculate gait parameters based on the collected data, which is not very convenient, especially for severe PD patients. Moreover, the data collected from inertial sensors is not straightforward to analyze, requiring complicated algorithms to extract even simple gait parameters.

Many studies also use specialized cameras for motion analysis. Microsoft Kinect cameras are commonly used in markerless tracking systems which provide both a color and depth image. There are some studies which use these images to extract motion parameters. For example, a Kinect camera was used in a study [8] to track the center of mass of a person. Another study [22] focuses on the effects of playing Kinect Adventures on the postural control of patients with Parkinson's disease. These studies use relatively expensive and specialized cameras to track human motion, which require simple environments to avoid noise caused by background objects and lighting. A disadvantage of marker-less tracking systems is that their accuracy is affected by complicated movements. This is not ideal for tracking PD patients with abnormal gait patterns.

There are some other commercial gait measurement tools based on pressure sensors, such as GAITRite[5] [17] (a mat embedded with pressure sensors) which records foot steps when the subject walks on the mat. It does not require the subject to wear any special sensors on the body. However, it is unable to detect foot movement above the mat and thus can not obtain the full picture of the gait cycle. Moreover, GAITRite is too expensive to be widely adopted in the homes of patients or even some hospitals.

Based on the above analysis, this paper presents a computer vision (CV) based gait analysis system using a smartphone camera. It records a video of a subject walking on a mat, and calculates the subjects stride times and lengths. The stride length measurement accuracy is comparable with the "gold standard" walking mat GAITRite. A set of video analysis algorithms are developed to segment the videos, locate the mat and shoes, and estimate stride lengths. The detailed system description and algorithms will be presented in the following sections.

3. SYSTEM OVERVIEW

Due to clinical constraints, the proposed system needs to meet certain usability requirements. We placed a strong emphasis on portability, ease of use, cost reduction, and accuracy. As our target users are rural hospitals, hospitals in developing countries, and home users, we require the sys-

[5]http://www.gaitrite.com

Figure 1: System test environment. Note the smartphone on a tripod and the mat on the ground.

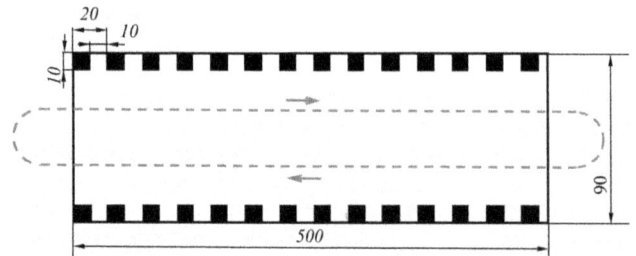

Figure 2: Walking mat. All sizes in the figure are in cm. The red dashed line denotes the walking path in our experiment.

tem to cause minimal interference to the patient and work in a wide range of environments with differing lighting conditions, backgrounds, and walking styles. The basic idea of the system is to use video footage of patients walking on a specially designed mat (see Figure 1 & 2) to automatically locate the foot position on the mat and then estimate the stride lengths of the patient. The system should be a complete solution for gait analysis, providing important gait information and statistical analysis. To this end, the system accepts a recorded video of a patient walking on a mat and outputs estimations of stride lengths.

The pipeline of the system is presented in three main components: Mat Extraction, Shoe Detection and Stride Length Estimation. Figure 3 illustrates how the components are connected, with a detailed work-flow for each component. The first component (Mat Extraction) analyses the recorded video to find sections where the patient is not in the frame. It uses these sections to extract the relative orientation of a specially designed mat to the camera and acts as a ruler for later stride length estimation. The second component (Shoe Detection) uses the same video and selects the sections where the patient is walking on the mat. This component finds the closed contour of the shoe using a selection of computer vision and Computer Aided Geometric Design (CAGD) algorithms. The third component (Stride Length Estimation) uses this closed shoe contour in combination with the previously extracted mat information to map the shoe contour position to real world units and thus estimate stride length. This component uses a mapping function which relates pixels to meters, and uses dif-

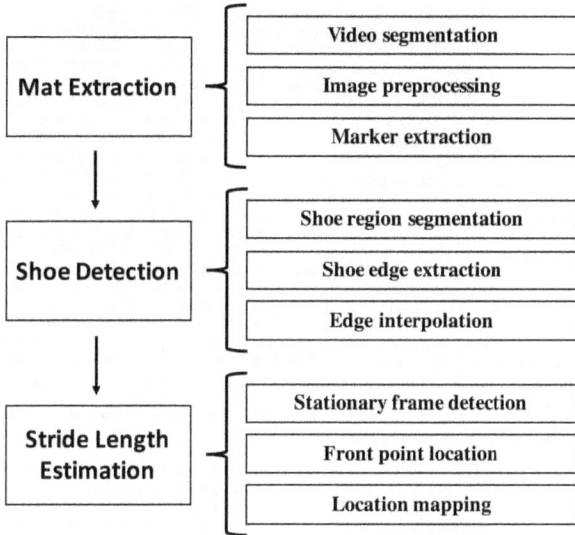

Figure 3: System Pipeline

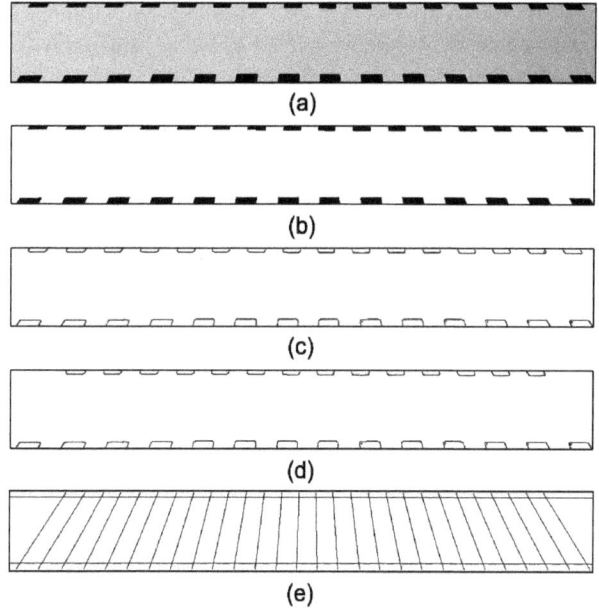

Figure 4: Mat extraction stages. (a) Original cropped mat image from video. (b) Binary mat image. (c) Marker contours. (d) Paired markers. (e) Perspective lines.

ferent strategies to determine where the front of the shoe is (even under perspective change).

To keep within a modest budget, our system consists of a Samsung S5 phone, a printed PVC walking mat, and a pair of shoes which have distinct and uniform colors. The camera is placed on a tripod and pointed at the mat (See Figure 1). We record 1080p video at 30fps and then transfer the video to a computer running our gait analysis software. In the next three sections we will detail the three components of the system.

4. MAT EXTRACTION

In order to extract stride lengths from a video we will need some point of reference to figure out the scale and orientation of the recorded environment. Therefore we design a simple mat which acts as this reference point, giving us both scale, and relative orientation of the mat to the camera. It also serves as a ruler for stride length estimation. In this section, we will describe the mat used in our system, and then discuss the method for automatically extracting perspective information from it.

4.1 Mat Design

We designed our mat to be durable, low cost, simple, and to not cause undue dizziness or vertigo in those walking across it. The mat consists of alternating black and white markers printed on the long edges of a 0.9 m × 5.0 m sheet of PVC material. The markers, each 10 × 10 cm in size, are used to calculate the orientation of the mat and provide a ruler in the final system component (Section 6) for stride length estimation. The middle of the mat is clear in order to both simplify shoe detection in Section 5 and to stop the subject getting vertigo from the high contrast edges. The completed mat design is shown in Figure 2.

We selected PVC material as it is easy to find in printing shops around the world and can be printed to any length or width. It is also durable, easy to clean, and heavy enough that it will sit flat on the ground. Furthermore, this material is non-reflective and therefore it will not interfere with video recording.

4.2 Perspective Information

In our system a smartphone camera is placed on a tripod and pointed towards the mat, but this position may not always be exactly the same. Therefore the goal of this component is to find the relative size, location, and orientation of the mat automatically so that the camera position does not have to be re-calibrated every time it is set up or bumped.

Before we do any processing on the recorded video it must be segmented into multiple sections, those with walking (walking videos) and those without (mat videos). This is performed using a simple background subtraction approach to detect motion [31, 4]. In this section we will process the mat videos, and in the next section we will use the walking videos. We define the perspective information as the extracted set of paired markers which make up the mat. From this set of paired markers we can ascertain the relative orientation of the mat to the camera and estimate distances in our real world co-ordinate system.

A procedure overview is detailed in Algorithm 1. The procedure for extracting perspective information from a video is automatic with the exception of the following step. First, we manually crop the frames of the mat video to include only the mat itself using a simple UI. Figure 4a shows the cropped image. We have not automated this step because it needs to be able to handle different conditions and environments and it is possible that the mat could blend into the background. Therefore we ask the user to specify the location of the mat. This step reduces both overall processing time and the impact of other objects in the frame. From this step onward, the system is completely automatic.

Next, we use a few basic image processing algorithms [21] to prepare the image for analysis. First we use the histogram equalization method to compensate for differing lighting.

Then we use use a basic Gaussian filter to remove the noise in the middle of the empty mat. Lastly, we transform the color image to a binary one using a threshold method. Figure 4b shows the processed image from the video.

With this binary image we now locate, count, and pair off the mat markers. For simplicity sake, we will define the bottom of the mat as the edge of the mat that is closest to the camera, and conversely the top of the mat is the edge furthest away from the camera. The idea is straightforward: we count the number of markers in the bottom of the original mat and then align these markers to the markers in the top of the mat. We use the Canny operator [2] to find the contours of all of the markers (see Figure 4c).

Due to the perspective of the camera, we find that there are a few markers at the top of the mat that have no corresponding markers on the bottom of the mat and therefore these need to be excluded. Here, we choose the line that passes through the left edge of the bottom first marker and shift the line 5 to 10 pixels to left. All top markers to the left of this line are removed from the binary image of the mat. Likewise, we do this on the right using the bottom rightmost marker, and therefore only the markers which can be paired remain. Figure 4d shows the mat after all of the markers have been paired, with the redundant markers removed.

Finally we choose critical points from each marker's left and right edges to draw the line between the bottom and top markers. We take the top and bottom marker edges, and then we calculate the line of best fit that connects them. This is repeated for all pairs of markers. To improve the success of this method we only use the edge points between 5% and 95% of the total height of the marker, thus removing any influence of the corner of the marker. Figure 4e shows the final perspective information as displayed on the mat.

Algorithm 1 Mat Extraction Algorithm

1: **procedure** MAT-EXTRACTION
2:     Crop frame of mat video
3:     Perform histogram equalization operation
4:     Remove noise using Gaussian Filter
5:     Convert frame to binary image
6:     Use Canny operator to extract edges of markers
7:     Count the number of markers
8:     Exclude unpaired markers
9:     Connect paired markers with a line of best fit
10: **end procedure**

To get high accuracy perspective information we recommend the following steps. Ensure the camera is stable and record in as close to a uniform lighting environment as possible. It is also important to fine tune the parameters for the techniques used to get a clear contour of the edge of the markers. Even with this calibration we may not always get a continuous contour of the edge, in this event we can use the technique described in Section 5.2 to find a continuous contour. Next, we describe the process to detect the shoe and find its contour.

5. SHOE DETECTION

This component analyses the sections in a video where the patient is walking on the mat whilst wearing uniformly colored shoes. The goal here is to find the contour of both shoes to be used in the final component to estimate stride

Figure 5: Shoe region segmentation. (a) Original frame. (b) Left shoe region. (c) Right shoe region.

length. In this section, we describe the procedure for shoe detection. The procedure involves detecting the regions of the shoes based on the color of the shoes, and then extracting the closed contour of the shoes. To make the computation easily parallelizable, the video is first decomposed into a sequence of images, and shoe detection is performed on each image independently.

5.1 Shoe Region Segmentation

First, each source image is cropped to the same size and location as the empty central region of the mat. This step removes both the background and the mat markers from the frame. Next, we need to reduce the noise from the cropped image. There are many sources of noise such as those caused by shadows under the feet, lighting differences, and objects that have fallen on the mat during walking (such as dust and hair). Here we choose the median filter, because our goal is to extract the contour of the shoe, and the median filter performs better at preserving edges compared to simple average filters. After applying the median filter to the image, most of this noise is removed.

In order to track both feet, our system needs the colors of the left and right shoe. In our experiments, we use red for the right shoe and black for the left, as shown in Figure 5a. While it is not necessary for the feet to use these exact colors, we recommend that the feet colors have high contrast with each other and the mat. This is because the lighting conditions may vary over a recording or even vary within the same walk. This causes the shoe color in the image to change significantly. Thus using shoe colors which are sufficiently different from the mat color will produce the best results.

Given the color of each shoe, we can segment the shoe region from the image based on the similarity between the shoe color and the color of each pixel. The shoe region is formed by the pixels which have a high color similarity (using a predefined threshold) to the shoe color. Figure 5b and 5c show the segmented left and right shoe regions, respectively. In our system, we adopt the commonly used CIE94 algorithm to compare two colors [16].

5.2 Contour Detection

After finding the shoe regions, we need to find the closed contour of each shoe, which is used to determine the exact location of the shoe. To obtain an accurate contour of each shoe, we first detect the edges of the shoe, which can be achieved using the Canny operator [32, 1, 20, 27]. For our system we choose to modify the normal operator to achieve a better edge detection result. In a normal Canny operator, an image is first filtered using a Gaussian filter before finding the intensity gradient of the image. However, the Gaussian filter is not very good at preserving the edges. There-

Algorithm 2 Shoe Detection Algorithm

1: **procedure** SHOE DETECTION
2:     Crop frame of walking video
3:     Detect edges using modified Canny operator
4:     Use edge traversing to find edges belonging to shoe
5:     **while** largest gap between edges $> \epsilon$ **do**
6:         Lower edge detecting threshold for operator
7:         Detect edges using modified Canny operator
8:         Use edge traversing to find edges
9:     **end while**
10:    Interpolate edges to get the closed contour
11: **end procedure**

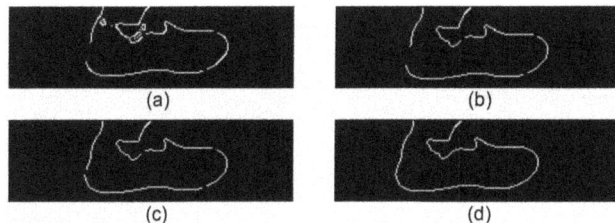

Figure 6: Modification on Canny operator result. (a) Original detected result. (b) Edge traversing result. (c) Reducing gap size. (d) Interpolation result.

fore, to achieve better edge detection results, we modify the Canny operator by instead using the bilateral filter [26, 29] to remove noise, as it performs better at edge-preservation. Although computationally expensive, it is possible to use general purpose GPU computing techniques to speed up the Canny operator [11, 25] even on mobile hardware.

Next we use our modified Canny operator to detect the edges of the shoe (see Figure 6a). We find that the initial edges obtained by the Canny operator cannot guarantee a closed contour of the shoe region. Instead, there are often many gaps in the front of the shoe. This makes it difficult to find the front point of shoe and will cause large errors in the estimation of shoe location. One of the solutions for this problem is to adjust the parameters of Canny operator, but this method usually causes other side effects (e.g., too many unwanted edges) and is not suitable for the automation of the whole processing procedure. Another solution is to use Computer Aided Geometric Design (CAGD) algorithms [9, 24] to modify the initial edges.

Since we cannot always obtain a closed contour using the edges extracted by the Canny operator, we need to use fitting methods to fill in the gaps between edges to make it closed. For this task we use B-spline curves, which have the advantages of being continuous and allowing fine local control. For the B-spline interpolation curve, the main question is how to calculate the so called control points on the shoe edges [15, 13, 30, 14]. Since there are many different types of shapes on the contour, we cannot simply use a uniform function to choose the feature points [28]. In this paper, we propose a new algorithm to find the feature points from all of the discrete points located on the shoe edges. Then we use non-uniform cubic B-spline interpolation method to obtain a closed shoe contour.

Edge traversing methods normally come from two main strategies. One is based on Run-length [7], and the other is based on Chain Code methods [3]. Regardless, both of them have the disadvantage of repeatedly outputting some edges or missing some interior edges. Our method is based on 3D reconstruction techniques used in medical imaging [28] which can quickly extract a complex contour in one scan. After the edge traversing process, we get a single pixel-width contour as shown in Figure 6b. If we find large gaps between adjacent edges, we can dynamically adjust the parameters of the Canny operator to decrease the gaps to be smaller than a predefined threshold ϵ. The trade off is we will also extract more redundant edges in the process. The improved edges extracted are shown in Figure 6c.

To fill the gaps among the edges to form a closed contour, we used an interpolation algorithm based on the non-

uniform cubic B-spline curve. First, we need to find the feature points from an edge line. As illustrated in Figure 9c, for the j−th point (i.e., a pixel) P_j in an edge line, two of its neighbor points P_{j-s} and P_{j+s} are selected, where s is a predefined neighbor range (e.g. $s = 4$). We proposed a new method for easy estimation of the vertex curvature at P_j, which is calculated as the perpendicular distance (H_j) from P_j to the line formed by P_{j-s} and P_{j+s}. If H_j is less than a preset threshold, P_j is selected as a candidate of the feature points. Then, a non-minimum suppression method [28] is adopted to choose the final feature points from the candidates. After obtaining the feature points, we apply the bi-directional accumulated arc length method [24] for parameterization in B-spline interpolation. Finally, control points are computed and non-uniform cubic B-spline interpolation curves are generated to connect the edges to form a closed contour [24]. The final closed contour is shown in Figure 6d. An overview of the procedure can be seen in Algorithm 2.

6. STRIDE LENGTH ESTIMATION

This component finds the front point of the closed shoe contour and maps it to real world units using the previously extracted mat information. It also separates each stride from continuous walking and thus estimates stride length. An overview of the procedure can be seen in Algorithm 3.

Algorithm 3 Stride Length Estimation Algorithm

1: **procedure** STRIDE LENGTH ESTIMATION
2:     Find stationary frames
3:     Find front point on shoe contour
4:     Convert from pixels to cm using mapping function
5:     Estimate stride length
6: **end procedure**

6.1 Stride Detection

Stride length is the displacement between two successive foot strikes on the ground of the same foot. We denote the video frame that separates two adjacent strides as a "stationary frame" (i.e., the frame in the middle of the stationary stance phase). Therefore, the stride length can be calculated as the distance traveled by the same foot at two adjacent stationary frames.

We propose two methods to find the stationary frames. In the first method, we take advantage of the nature of walking as there are alternating periods when the foot is stationary on the ground and periods when the foot is moving above the

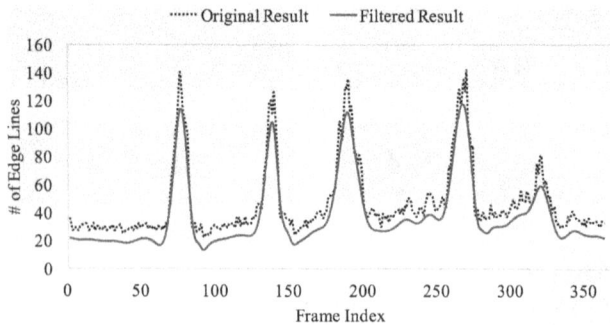

Figure 7: Stationary frame detection based on the number of edge lines in each frame.

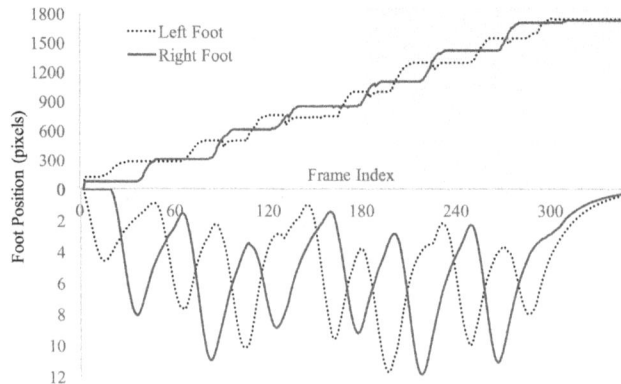

Figure 8: Front point position on foot contour

ground. This leads to our key observation that the frames are less blurred when the foot is stationary and more blurred when the foot is in motion. As noted earlier, the Canny operator will output more edge lines if the image is blurred. So we can use this feature to find the number of edges in each frame of the whole image sequence. The dashed line in Figure 7 illustrates the detected number of edges in every frame. We can easily find, for one foot, that there are a few peak points. The middle point between two adjacent peaks is therefore the frame in which the foot is on the ground (i.e., the stationary frame). To facilitate peak detection, we apply a low-pass filter on the original signal to smooth out the waveform (the solid line in Figure 7).

This stationary frame detection method is simple and effective. However, it may be affected by other noise in the frame. For example, if the clothing of the subject is still moving after the foot is stationary, the captured frame can still be blurred. If the subject is walking at a very slow speed, the frame will not be blurred much, which leads to less dominant peaks in the waveform of the edge lines. Nevertheless, with well-tuned parameters in filtering and peak detection, this method worked successfully in stride detection in our experiments.

The second method we propose for stationary frame detection is based on the position of the foot in the frames. We can take the rightmost point in the shoe contour as the position of the foot. The upper panel of Figure 8 shows the foot position (in pixels) in each frame. We can observe that the foot position remains level when the foot is stationary on the ground, and it increases along a rising edge when the foot moves forward. The foot furthest away from the camera has small fluctuations in its foot position waveform which are caused by the foot closest to the camera occluding it as it moves by. These small fluctuations can be smoothed out using a low-pass filter.

To separate the strides, we take the first order difference of the foot position signal, resulting in an approximately periodic waveform with clear peaks and troughs. This difference waveform is then low-pass filtered, as shown in the lower panel of Figure 8. As before, a peak detection algorithm is used to find the local minimum points in the difference waveform, which correspond to the stationary frames. Unlike the first method, this method is more robust to slow walking.

6.2 Mapping Function

For each stationary frame, we find the front point in the shoe contour, which is used to represent the foot position at pixel-level. First, we obtain the x−coordinate (along the mat direction) of each point in the shoe contour. We also use the edge traversing method to find the front point in the shoe contour, which is the rightmost point for left-to-right walking, or the leftmost point for right-to-left walking.

Once we obtain the front points, we use a mapping function to transform the front point position (x) at pixel-level into real world position (d) in cm. There are several choices for the mapping function. A basic algorithm uses the average distance of a pixel (d_p), which is calculated as the total mat length (in cm) divided by the total pixels of the mat. The real position of the front point is obtained as $d = xd_p$. However, the above algorithm ignores the perspective differences for the pixels.

To mitigate these problems, we designed a new mapping function (referred to as Method-1 in Section 7), which is illustrated in Figure 9a. This method first finds two marker edge lines (L_1 and L_2) that are closest to the front point. The real position of these two lines (d_1 and d_2 respectively) are known from the markers. Then the perpendicular distances (λ_1 and λ_2) from the front point to the two lines are calculated at pixel level. The real position is derived proportionally as

$$d = \frac{\lambda_2 d_1 + \lambda_1 d_2}{\lambda_1 + \lambda_2}. \tag{1}$$

Since the two marker lines L_1 and L_2 are generally not parallel due to the perspective of the camera, we designed a second mapping function (referred to as Method-2 in Section 7), as illustrated in Figure 9b. If L_1 and L_2 are parallel, it reduces to the first mapping function. Otherwise, we assume L_1 and L_2 intersect at point Q. Similarly, we estimate the real position based on the proportion of the arc length α_1 (formed by line PQ and L_1) and arc length α_2 (formed by line PQ and L_2), where the arc lengths are proportional to the $\sin$ of the angle θ_1 (between line PQ and L_1) and θ_2 (between line PQ and L_2), respectively.

$$d = \frac{\alpha_2 d_1 + \alpha_1 d_2}{\alpha_1 + \alpha_2} = \frac{d_1 \sin \theta_2 + d_2 \sin \theta_1}{\sin \theta_1 + \sin \theta_2}. \tag{2}$$

Another strategy which provided an improvement in accuracy was to compensate for the small errors in the man-

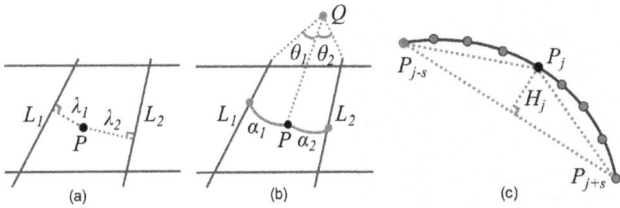

Figure 9: (a) Mapping function using perpendicular distance. (b) Mapping function using arc length. (c) Estimation of vertex curvature.

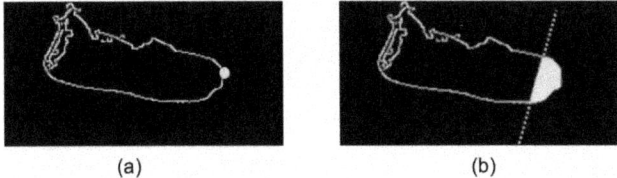

Figure 10: Finding the front point. (a) Original method. (b) Finding a small region in the front of the contour.

ufacture of the mat. Instead of using the assumed width of each marker we measure them individually, and directly use the real distance rather than our print specifications and then apply the Method-2 approach. This method is denoted as Method-3 in Section 7.

6.3 Front Point Selection

The previous analysis used a naive approach to find the front of the shoe, taking the maximum point on the shoe contour (see Figure 10a). Certainly, this maximum point on the contour may not always be the front most point on the shoe as the contour can change under rotation. To compensate for this issue we propose a new iterative testing method to find a better estimate for the location of the front of the shoe.

This method is based on the assumption that the true front of the shoe exists in the small region enclosed in the front of the foot contour. We first use a threshold to define a small region near the maximum point on the contour. Next, we use the mapping function to calculate the position in real units of all the points inside this region. Finally, we pick the rightmost point in this region as the front point on the foot. Figure 10b shows the area that we use in this method. This refined front point selection method in combination with Method-3 is labelled as Method-3+R in Section 7.

7. SYSTEM ACCURACY

Now that we have a system for estimating stride length we must quantify the accuracy of its output. To test our system we designed some imitation experiments in different environments. To do this we must compare our CV stride length estimates against ground truth measurements. We aligned a ruler to the edge of the mat and took a high quality photo for every step taken using a secondary camera and then directly measured the stride length. Whilst this ground truth measurement is simple and inexpensive, it is also cumbersome and requires a lot of busywork.

We invited five subjects to mimic PD patients with differ-

ent walking requirements. The accuracy of the system was tested in one room, over multiple days, at numerous times during the day. This caused a large variation of lighting and coloring on the mat. The non-PD subjects were shown videos of PD patients and were asked to imitate their movements: failing to initiate walking (in PD fields known as "start hesitation"), walking with asymmetric gait patterns, and simulating the common "freezing of gait" symptoms. In this experiment, we collected 128 video sessions with 382 strides. Table 1 shows the accuracy of all three methods. It can be seen that Method-2 outperforms Method-1, and Method-3 outperforms both. Additionally, using the improved front point selection approach in combination with Method-3 further decreases the error (Method-3+R in Table 1). We found the mean absolute error of the stride length of both feet to be 0.62 cm for Method-3+R, which is comparable with "gold standard" tools such as GAITRite.

8. CLINICAL TEST

Now that we have an estimate of the accuracy of our system, we try to investigate its practicality and usefulness in practice. Therefore we tested our system in a real world clinical environment using real patients with severe gait issues.

8.1 Procedure

We recruited 55 elderly subjects, 44 PD patients and 11 healthy controls with help from Huashan Hospital located in Shanghai, China. The PD patients came from four severity groups according to the Hoehn and Yahr Scale (HY) [10]. The subjects recruited in our experiment were classified into HY1 (10), HY2 (14), HY3 (10), HY4 (10) and healthy controls (11) by neurologists. Our inclusion criteria only allowed subjects who (1) were 50 to 75 years old, (2) were able to walk by themselves without help, (3) had no other serious diseases, (4) were able to understand and sign the consent forms. This test had IRB approval and was performed in accordance with hospital ethics board requirements.

The procedure in this test involved a subject walking from left to right, turning around at the end and walking back as shown in the Figure 2. We did not limit the duration for walking, and encouraged subjects to walk for as long as they were able such that we could get a minimum of thirty strides on each foot. One "session" was defined as walking from one side to the other side (Left to Right or Right to Left). Subjects would repeat this process numerous times.

8.2 Results

We obtained 98 videos consisting of 1947 walking sessions from the 55 subjects over a period of two weeks. In our test, we processed all videos and our system was able to correctly identify every shoe contour in comparison with human annotated data. It also correctly counted every stride even in severe patients with abnormal cadence or gait patterns. Finally, it correctly extracted the walking mat in all videos. While we were unable to test the stride length accuracy on these patients due to the cumbersome nature of our ground truth measures, we were able to test the practicality of using the system in a real world scenario. Importantly, we could detect all subject's shoe contours even under very different lighting conditions, gait styles, gait abnormalities, and with subjects who wore a wide array of different clothing.

Table 1: Absolute stride length error between ground truth and estimations from different methods

	Left Foot				Right Foot			
	Method-1	Method-2	Method-3	Method-3+R	Method-1	Method-2	Method-3	Method-3+R
Max (cm)	11.36	4.10	2.77	1.75	12.14	4.50	4.07	1.87
Min (cm)	1.45	0.65	0.01	0.04	0.06	0.04	0.15	0.06
Mean (cm)	5.97	2.52	1.31	0.59	5.83	2.54	1.62	0.65
SD (cm)	2.79	0.84	0.67	0.40	2.96	1.12	0.97	0.48

Table 2: Example of a basic statistical report

Parameters	Left Foot	Right Foot
Basic Statistical Analysis		
Mean Stride Length (cm)	73.69	73.66
Mean Stride Time (s)	0.96	0.96
# of Strides	75	74
Stride Length		
Standard Deviation (cm)	11.14	9.5
Coefficient of Variation	0.15	0.13
Stride Time		
Standard Deviation (s)	0.06	0.05
Coefficient of Variation	0.15	0.05

To provide information to doctors or clinicians, the system is able output the subject's basic statistical information, including mean, coefficient of variation, and standard deviation of left and right stride lengths and times (an example is shown in Table 2). These results can be used to generate many gait measures of interest to clinicians. The system can be used in combination with other systems as it imposes minimal interference to the subject. Some patients preferred to have someone walk beside them as they performed the walking task. Our system could handle this scenario, meaning that aided walking (for severe PD patients) could also be analyzed.

9. CONCLUSIONS

This paper presented a novel system for accurate estimation of stride lengths of Parkinson's disease patients based on computer vision techniques. It serves the needs of neurologists who want to ascertain PD progress by way of gait analysis, even in rural hospitals or hospitals in developing countries. Our clinical test demonstrated that our system supports various testing environments and is suitable for use in a clinical setting.

Our system has a few limitations, mostly due to the use of the contour of the shoe which is not invariant under rotation. This requires clever techniques to compensate for this perspective shift which does not occur in other motion based systems. We also have a limited recording width as we are constrained by the field of view of the camera, however with the use of higher resolution cameras in modern smartphones and external optics such as fish eye lenses it is possible to overcome this limitation without losing accuracy. Stride times are also limited by the refresh rate of the camera, however modern smartphones can support 60 fps or higher.

The accuracy of the system is dependent on many factors, such as lighting, filming distance, lens type, frame rate, and video quality. In our experiments and trials, we fixed the video quality, frame rate, and filming distance. However, lighting changed throughout recording and despite this we were able to identify the contour of the shoe correctly, in part due to the high contrast colors used between the shoes and mat. Two major errors were identified, those associated with the parallax effect between the shoe and the markers, and the fact that the front part of the shoe contour does not always coincide with the front part of the shoe. In the paper we proposed methods to get around these constraints and limitations.

Despite these limitations our system has many advantages over other commercial systems such as high accuracy, low price, portability, and scalability. The cost of our system is less than $800 USD: $200-$700 USD for a smartphone (which many users already have), $50-$80 USD for the printed mat, and $20 USD for the camera tripod. In contrast, commercial gait measurement systems are orders of magnitude more expensive. GAITRite (a pressure sensitive mat-based system) costs $36,000 USD, Vidcon motion capture systems can retail for $45,000 USD, and APDM (an inertial measurement sensor-based system) costs approximately $10,000-$18,000 USD. As the system only has two main components (the smartphone and the mat), it can be easily transported and set up. The system does not require a lab setting, or clinicians and is therefore suitable for the home.

For future work, we believe the system could be scaled to run entirely on a smartphone as the algorithms have low time complexity and could be computed on mobile GPU hardware. The use of improved mapping functions, perspective modeling, and better front point selection will definitely reduce estimation errors. A study of the stride and step length accuracy on a group of elderly subjects (including PD patients) is also an important step for the validation of the system. Additionally, these same algorithms proposed in this paper could be used to detect the hand movements of PD patients to quantify tremor, another important symptom for PD progression. Finally, testing the system concurrently with commercial systems such as GAITRite is the next step to validating the system.

In conclusion, we have presented a pipeline for a low cost system for gait analysis which is easy to use, portable, and accurate. The use of CV algorithms and smartphone cameras has the potential to make gait analysis cheap, accessible, and ubiquitous even in hospitals in rural areas or in developing countries.

10. ACKNOWLEDGEMENTS

The authors would like to thank Prof. Jian Wang, Miss. Ke Yang, and the entire Huashan team for their assistance in the data collection. This project was partially funded by a NUS Cross-faculty research grant R-252-000-567-133 and a FOE-SOC Joint Collaboration grant R-252-000-588-112.

11. REFERENCES

[1] S. Agaian, A. Almuntashri, and A. Papagiannakis. An improved canny edge detection application for asphalt concrete. In *Systems, Man and Cybernetics, 2009. SMC 2009. IEEE International Conference on*, pages 3683–3687. IEEE, 2009.

[2] J. Canny. A computational approach to edge detection. *Pattern Analysis and Machine Intelligence, IEEE Transactions on*, PAMI-8(6):679–698, 1986.

[3] V. Chalana, W. S. Costa, and Y. Kim. Integrating region growing and edge detection using regularization. In *Medical Imaging 1995*, pages 262–271. International Society for Optics and Photonics, 1995.

[4] D. Chinchkhede and N. Uke. Image segmentation in video sequences using modified background subtraction. *International Journal of Computer Science & Information Technology*, 4(1):93–104, 2012.

[5] B. T. Cole, S. H. Roy, C. J. De Luca, and S. H. Nawab. Dynamic neural network detection of tremor and dyskinesia from wearable sensor data. In *Engineering in Medicine and Biology Society (EMBC), 2010 Annual International Conference of the IEEE*, pages 6062–6065. IEEE, 2010.

[6] M. F. del Olmo and J. Cudeiro. Temporal variability of gait in parkinson disease: Effectsof a rehabilitation programme based on rhythmic sound cues. *Parkinsonism & related disorders*, 11(1):25–33, 2005.

[7] S. Di Zenzo, L. Cinque, and S. Levialdi. Run-based algorithms for binary image analysis and processing. *IEEE Transactions on Pattern Analysis & Machine Intelligence*, 18(1):83–89, 1996.

[8] A. Dubois and F. Charpillet. A gait analysis method based on a depth camera for fall prevention. In *Engineering in Medicine and Biology Society (EMBC), 2014 36th Annual International Conference of the IEEE*, pages 4515–4518. IEEE, 2014.

[9] G. E. Farin. *Curves and surfaces for CAGD: a practical guide*. Morgan Kaufmann, 2002.

[10] C. G. Goetz, W. Poewe, O. Rascol, C. Sampaio, G. T. Stebbins, C. Counsell, N. Giladi, R. G. Holloway, C. G. Moore, G. K. Wenning, M. D. Yahr, and L. Seidl. Movement disorder society task force report on the hoehn and yahr staging scale: Status and recommendations the movement disorder society task force on rating scales for parkinson's disease. *Movement Disorders*, 19(9):1020–1028, 2004.

[11] H. Gupta and D. S. Antony. Implementation of gaussian and box kernel based approximation of bilateral filter using opencl. In *Digital Image Computing: Techniques and Applications (DICTA), 2015 International Conference on*, pages 1–5. IEEE, 2015.

[12] D. Korotkin and K. Artem. Inertial measurement system for human gait analysis. In *Proceedings of the 8th International Conference on Body Area Networks*, pages 414–419. ICST (Institute for Computer Sciences, Social-Informatics and Telecommunications Engineering), 2013.

[13] H. Lin, G. Wang, and C. Dong. Constructing iterative non-uniform b-spline curve and surface to fit data points. *Science in China Series: Information Sciences*, 47(3):315–331, 2004.

[14] Y. Lu, K. Shi, J. Yong, H. Gu, and H. Song. A b-spline curve extension algorithm. *Science China Information Sciences*, pages 1–9, 2015.

[15] E. Margolis and Y. C. Eldar. Interpolation with nonuniform b-splines. In *Acoustics, Speech, and Signal Processing, 2004. Proceedings.(ICASSP'04). IEEE International Conference on*, volume 2, pages ii–577. IEEE, 2004.

[16] R. McDonald and K. J. Smith. Cie94-a new colour-difference formula*. *Journal of the Society of Dyers and Colourists*, 111(12):376–379, 1995.

[17] H. B. Menz, M. D. Latt, A. Tiedemann, M. M. San Kwan, and S. R. Lord. Reliability of the gaitrite® walkway system for the quantification of temporo-spatial parameters of gait in young and older people. *Gait & posture*, 20(1):20–25, 2004.

[18] M. Milosevic, E. Jovanov, and A. Milenkovic. Quantifying timed-up-and-go test: A smartphone implementation. In *Body Sensor Networks (BSN), 2013 IEEE International Conference on*, pages 1–6. IEEE, 2013.

[19] T. B. Moeslund, A. Hilton, and V. Krüger. A survey of advances in vision-based human motion capture and analysis. *Computer vision and image understanding*, 104(2):90–126, 2006.

[20] H. S. Neoh and A. Hazanchuk. Adaptive edge detection for real-time video processing using fpgas. *Global Signal Processing*, 7(3):2–3, 2004.

[21] M. Petrou and C. Petrou. *Image Processing: The Fundamentals*. John Wiley & Sons, Ltd, 2011.

[22] J. E. Pompeu, C. Torriani-Pasin, F. Doná, F. F. Gananв̧a, K. G. da Silva, and H. B. Ferraz. Effect of kinect games on postural control of patients with parkinson's disease. In *Proceedings of the 3rd 2015 Workshop on ICTs for improving Patients Rehabilitation Research Techniques*, pages 54–57. ACM, 2015.

[23] S. Shahid, A. Nandy, S. Mondal, M. Ahamad, P. Chakraborty, and G. C. Nandi. A study on human gait analysis. In *Proceedings of the Second International Conference on Computational Science, Engineering and Information Technology*, pages 358–364. ACM, 2012.

[24] F.-Z. Shi. Cagd & nurbs. *China Higher Education Press*, 2001.

[25] S. Srisuk, W. Kesjindatanawaj, and S. Ongkittikul. Real-time bilateral filtering using gpgpu. In *Applied Mechanics and Materials*, volume 781, pages 568–571. Trans Tech Publ, 2015.

[26] C. Tomasi and R. Manduchi. Bilateral filtering for gray and color images. In *Computer Vision, 1998. Sixth International Conference on*, pages 839–846. IEEE, 1998.

[27] S. Vasilic, V. Hocenski, et al. Improved canny edge detector in ceramic tiles defect detection. In *IEEE Industrial Electronics, IECON 2006-32nd Annual Conference on*, pages 3328–3331. IEEE, 2006.

[28] Y. Wang, J. Zheng, H. Zhou, and L. Shen. Medical image processing by denoising and contour extraction. In *Information and Automation, 2008. ICIA 2008.*

International Conference on, pages 618–623. IEEE, 2008.

[29] Q. Yang, N. Ahuja, and K.-H. Tan. Constant time median and bilateral filtering. *International Journal of Computer Vision*, 112(3):307–318, 2015.

[30] L. Zhang, X. Ge, and J. Tan. Least square geometric iterative fitting method for generalized b-spline curves with two different kinds of weights. *The Visual Computer*, pages 1–12, 2015.

[31] S. Zhang, P. Li, L. Wang, and Y. Zhang. Gait image segmentation based background subtraction. In

Intelligent Computing Theories and Methodologies, pages 563–569. Springer, 2015.

[32] P. Zhou, W. Ye, Y. Xia, and Q. Wang. An improved canny algorithm for edge detection. *Journal of Computational Information Systems*, 7(5):1516–1523, 2011.

[33] S. Zhu, R. J. Ellis, G. Schlaug, Y. S. Ng, and Y. Wang. Validating an iOS-based Rhythmic Auditory Cueing Evaluation (iRACE) for Parkinson's disease. In *Proceedings of the ACM International Conference on Multimedia*, pages 487–496. ACM, 2014.

Uncovering Challenges and Opportunities for 3D Printing Assistive Technology with Physical Therapists

Samantha McDonald[1], Niara Comrie[1], Erin Buehler[1], Nicholas Carter[1], Braxton Dubin[1],
Karen Gordes[2], Sandy McCombe-Waller[2], Amy Hurst[1]

[1]Information Systems Department
University of Maryland, Baltimore County
Baltimore, MD 21250 USA
{sam30, cniara1, eri4, ni6, bdubin1,
amyhurst}@umbc.edu

[2]Department of Physical Therapy
University of Maryland, School of Medicine
Baltimore, MD 21201 USA
{KGordes,
SMcCombeWaller}@som.umaryland.edu

ABSTRACT

Physical therapists have a history of modifying and making assistive technology (AT) to fit the unique needs of their patients. However, lack of materials, time, and access to training can restrict what they can create. While 3D printing has the opportunity to empower physical therapists to develop highly customized, economical, and timely assistive technology; little is known about the feasibility of using 3D printing in a clinical setting, and how to teach and engage physical therapists in physical prototyping. We collaborated with physical therapy professors and students at a medical university to integrate 3D printing and AT design into a graduate-level physical therapy class. Our investigation showed 3D printing is a viable tool for clinical production of AT. We found opportunities and barriers to 3D printing in the physical therapy field, and we present four considerations relevant to integrating 3D printing into clinical practice: 1) exploring augmentations versus novel AT designs, 2) improvements to novice 3D modeling software, 3) adjusting for prototype fidelity, and 4) selecting 3D printing materials. This paper contributes knowledge toward the understanding of practical applications of 3D printing in a clinical setting and teaching 3D modeling to non-engineers.

CCS Concepts

• **Human Centered Computing ~ Accessibility**

Keywords

3D Modeling; 3D Printing; Assistive Technology; Digital Fabrication; Education; Physical Fabrication; Physical Therapy.

1. INTRODUCTION

Clinicians, such as physical therapists (PTs), have a history of modifying and augmenting standardized assistive technology (AT) or creating new AT to better fit the needs of their patients [3]. Customization can be crucial to the success of an AT device. When a piece of AT is ill-fitted or otherwise falls short of a user's needs, the user may abandon their device all together [16]. Tasks such as making casts for broken bones, adding padding to crutches for patient comfort, and creating ad hoc assistive

ASSETS '16, October 23-26, 2016, Reno, NV, USA
© 2016 ACM. ISBN 978-1-4503-4124-0/16/10…$15.00
DOI: http://dx.doi.org/10.1145/2982142.2982162

augmentations from materials such as tennis balls or tape can all be considered experiences in the modification and creation of assistive technology.

By augmenting standardized devices instead of purchasing professionally customized devices, PTs are typically providing more affordable and timely improvements to AT which could be difficult for users to obtain otherwise. For example, adding softer materials such as foam to a crutch handle can provide increased comfort and support to a patient. This augmentation is typically faster and less expensive than purchasing a professionally customized crutch handle through insurance. Although these augmentations improve the AT, PTs are restricted in their ability to produce customized AT for certain patient needs. Materials such as Velcro, tape, string, paper, and cardboard are typical products PTs use as augmentations to AT [3]. These materials are suitable for quick fixes but may not withstand long term use. The motivations for PTs to build customizations with these temporary materials are availability and time constraints. PTs are limited in the amount of time they can invest in sourcing alternate materials and in learning new tools and techniques. Learning new technology takes time, and PTs may feel they do not have the time to explore an emergent technology like 3D printing [3]. Even if PTs had the time to invest in more modern fabrication tools such as 3D printing, there is limited access to training for these tools in a clinical environment. If the limitations of material, time, and training are removed, and 3D printing is integrated into their practice, we believe 3D printing can empower PTs to create better fitted AT for their patients out of more robust materials.

We present our work understanding needs and perceptions regarding 3D printing as a means to customize AT in clinical settings by working with practicing PTs, PT professors, and PT students at a local medical university. Results from our analysis provide insight into how 3D printing can be integrated into their practice. Through surveys and collaborative design sessions with practicing PTs and PT professors, we demonstrated 3D printing as a viable tool for PT production of AT, and gathered information on the current perceptions of 3D printing in PT. We collaborated with PT professors to integrate three 3D printing class sessions into the curriculum of a course with 65 graduate physical therapy students. During these classroom sessions, researchers taught students introductory lessons on the use of 3D printing in medicine, and gave students the opportunity to design and evaluate 3D printed assistive technologies. As a result, our

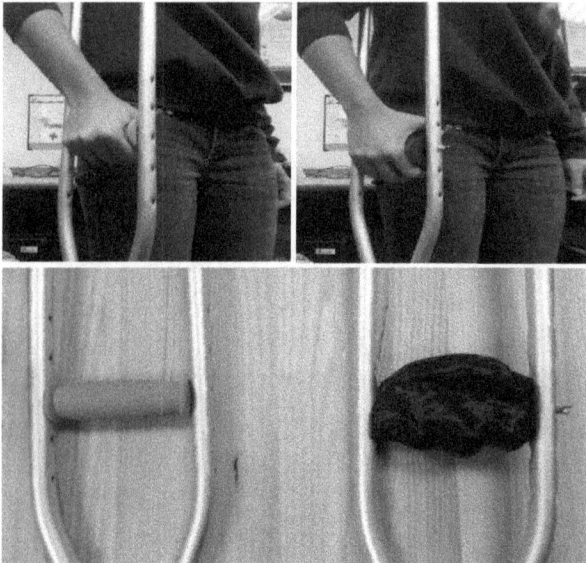

Figure 1. Standard crutch grip (left) and custom, ergonomic 3D-printed crutch grip co-designed with PT professors (right). Each is shown in use (above) and on its own (below).

investigation showed that 3D printing can be a viable tool for clinical production of AT.

In this paper, we contribute to the knowledge of 3D printing as a form of assistive technology production and the use of 3D printing technologies in the physical therapy field. We describe our collaboration with practicing PTs, PT professors, and PT students; present our observations on the opportunities for 3D printing in physical therapy education; and suggest future technology designs to promote this new group of assistive technology designers.

2. RELATED WORK

Our research builds on existing explorations of 3D printing as a tool for AT development, the use of 3D printing in do-it-yourself (DIY) and clinical settings, and 3D printing education for novices. We describe relevant work from each area to frame our research.

2.1 Applications of 3D Printing and Assistive Technology Development

2.1.1 Assistive Technology Abandonment
AT is defined as "any item, piece of equipment, or system, whether acquired commercially, modified, or customized, that is commonly used to increase, maintain, or improve functional capabilities of individuals with disabilities" [1]. AT can facilitate greater independence for users and allow the completion of a task, which may not originally be accomplished independently. Unfortunately, 35% of all ATs purchased are unused or abandoned [16, 19]. This can result from lack of user consideration in the design process, ease of device procurement, poor device performance, and change in user needs [16]. 3D printers can potentially mitigate these issues of abandonment and provide highly customized, economical, and timely AT. One of our goals in this research is to provide a method for local AT fabrication and augmentation which could reduce AT abandonment, ultimately improving the adoption rate of AT.

2.1.2 3D Printing Assistive Technology
The applications of 3D printing in medicine have skyrocketed over the past decade. Objects such as prosthetics, medical equipment, drugs, medical models, and biological cells have been

produced using 3D printing [18, 20, 13]. 3D printing is particularly useful for AT production because of its ability to localize production and customize 3D models to user's exact specifications. Consumer 3D printer materials are inexpensive in comparison to other AT material and can reduce economic burdens usually associated with customized AT.

3D printers allow for rapid development and prototyping, enabling patients to test different devices and change devices over time as their needs change. For example, pediatric prosthetic hands are inevitably abandoned because children outgrow their prosthetic. As a result, children are actively obtaining new customized prosthetics until they stop growing. This active need for new AT can be costly to the user and their family, especially if a prosthetic must be customized to a child's individual needs. 3D printing has the potential to resolve these issues by providing an iterative production of low cost and rapidly fabricated prosthetics fitted to the child's needs as they grow [21].

2.2 Do-It-Yourself and Clinical Production of Assistive Technology
Past work has begun to explore the empowerment end-users experience when creating their own assistive technology [8, 10, 11, 21]. Hurst et al. conducted studies on DIY and 3D printing with a focus on empowering individuals with disabilities to build their own assistive technology [10, 11]. Their studies suggested empowering users to make their own customized AT can improve the adoption process and decrease the likelihood of user abandonment [11]. This enables users to address their specific needs and avoid limitations of standardized AT on the market [10]. 3D printing's ability to increase customization supports the goal of empowerment and decreased user abandonment.

Buehler et al. studied the backgrounds and motivations of AT designers in an online 3D model-sharing repository and found very few medical professionals designing AT [2]. A handful of studies describe the collaborations between clinicians, users, and researchers to develop and choose AT [6, 14, 21]. Hofmann et al. conducted a case study into the design of prosthetics and the need for modularity when creating custom, task-specific devices co-designed by end-users [8]. However, there is a lack of exploration into specifically educating and empowering clinicians to develop ATs and AT modifications in collaboration with their patients. We believe 3D printing can be incorporated into the physical therapy practice, and the combination of PTs' pre-existing making skills and medical expertise, and their patients' AT user expertise, is advantageous to AT development.

2.3 Teaching 3D Printing to Novices
Although 3D printing can be advantageous to AT development, novice users of 3D modeling and 3D printing technology encounter common obstacles. Previous studies (described below) have found similar disconnects in regards to the obstacles faced with teaching 3D printing and 3D modeling to novices.

Buehler et al. conducted studies on populations with disabilities learning 3D modeling tools [3]. They found that novice tools for 3D modeling were not intuitive, that students struggled with scaling objects, making holes, and accidental selections resulting in undesired changes to models. They also described users' difficulty understanding the physical capabilities and limits of 3D printers. Stangl et al. reported highly disparate levels of 3D modeling ability across a diverse set of stakeholders using 3D printing to create accessible tactile graphics for children's picture books, and suggested amateur 3D designers might benefit from working in teams to complement design, accessibility knowledge, and modeling skills [22].

In studies of youth without disabilities, Follmer et al. found challenges related to children's ability to conceptualize models, "getting young children to grasp 3D modeling concepts, and striking a balance between ease of use and complexity can be a challenge." [7] As with students with disabilities, Leduc-Mills et al.'s, study working with children confirmed that novice interfaces are not always intuitive and that youth had issues designing simple tangible shapes due to issues of "virtual camera angles, extrusion, [and] polygonal meshes." [12]. While children as users have their own unique needs, we anticipate some of their struggles in learning 3D modeling tools will translate to other populations such as adults with little or no experience designing or manipulating objects in three-dimensional space.

We have taken into consideration the challenges faced by novice designers and, through our classroom exercises with PT students, are contributing to previous literature by exploring ways to reduce barriers to this technology. For 3D printing software to be usable for all novice populations, the challenges must be identified and addressed. Comparing the novice experience of our PT students to those populations in previous literature can help identify key challenges to be addressed in future 3D printing software.

3. EXPLORING 3D-PRINTED AT WITH PT PROFESSORS AND PRACTICING PTS

We worked with PT professors and practicing PTs to understand how 3D printing could be integrated into their practice. These activities provided an in-depth analysis of PT perceptions of 3D printing and validated 3D printing as a means to customize or otherwise augment AT.

3.1 Online Survey with Experienced PTs

We conducted an online survey to learn the perceptions of 3D printing AT and liability in the practice and education of PTs. We were interested in their thoughts regarding liability since DIY can produce non-standardized 3D objects and AT augmentations. Our primary PT collaborator distributed this survey to four colleagues, two practicing PTs and two PT professors (Table 1). We collected information about current liability practices, coverage, and PTs' perceived concerns for increased liability though 3D printing. We also asked about their previous experience augmenting and creating AT and how different methods of prototyping could affect their ability to design AT effectively.

Table 1. Demographic information for the experienced PTs who participated in our online survey.

	Demographic Information
PT1	Practicing Physical Therapist (Female)
PT2	Practicing Physical Therapist (Male)
PT3	Assistant Professor of Physical Therapy (Female)
PT4	Director of Faculty & Student Affairs, Assistant Professor of Physical Therapy (Male)

3.1.1 Survey Results

Even though we only worked with four participants, each provided significant insight. All four practicing PTs and PT professors had clear optimism for 3D printing in their practice. Participants' concerns over liability and specific AT developments were mixed.

Figure 2. (Left) Black 3D printed crutch grip designed by scanning the smaller red play-dough prototype (Right) made by a PT professor.

The prescription of AT is straightforward for PTs. According to PTs 1 and 3, when patients are given standardized AT devices, PTs must demonstrate that the AT chosen fits properly and is appropriate for the patient. This prescription is true for all AT regardless of the production process. PT 1 and PT 4 stated PTs are constantly concerned about liability when prescribing AT. When asked if PTs would be worried about increased liability from creating new AT, the responses were split. Both practicing PTs believed there may be increased liability, while the PT professors did not. PT 2 explained this potential increase in liability, *"If a product fails, the manufacturer is liable. If I were to print a piece of equipment for my patient to use, I am now the designer and the manufacturer. I hadn't thought about this before, but it makes sense that this would be a concern with 3D printing." – PT2*

We also asked participants to describe preferred prototyping methods for the construction of AT. Sometimes prototypes of products are miniaturized or produced with different materials for easier prototyping. We wanted to know if 3D printed miniature prototypes or prototypes printed out of materials other than the intended final product would change or impede the PTs' ability to test the usability of that device. Three of the four PTs (PT1, PT2, and PT4) thought the change in scale in material would impede their ability to test a device. A change in size would make it difficult to determine the proper fit for a patient, and differing material would make it difficult to assess the effectiveness and maximum load/resistive forces of the product. As such, 3D printed prototypes must be to-scale and printed in the final material, else risk impeding testing and development of AT.

3.2 Collaborative Design Sessions with Physical Therapy Instructors

We conducted a series of collaborative design sessions with P3 and P4 to produce multiple 3D printed AT augmentations (Figures 1, 2, and 3). These augmentations were initially used to demonstrate the capabilities of 3D printing to the PTs. These artifacts were later used as design probes to solicit feedback from PT students (See Section 4).

We asked both PT professors to identify any specific issues related to patient AT that could potentially be addressed by 3D printing. PT professors were interested in developing 3D printed augmentations to standardized axillary crutches in order to customize grips to mitigate discomfort and replace missing crutch tips. We worked with these participants over six months to collaboratively design these augmentations. This section will describe the interest and motivations for these applications and the design process of those augmentations.

3.2.1 Designing a Crutch Grip (Figure 1)

Standardized axillary crutch grips are where a crutch user rests their hand. These are designed to alleviate pressure, promote proper postural alignment, and improve biomechanics of the upper extremity (Figure 1). However, long-term use of crutches can lead to overuse injuries of the upper extremity. Specifically, long-term users are at risk for development of wrist pain, carpal tunnel syndrome, and calloused/blistered hands. Patients of the PTs using crutches for a prolonged period of time complained of wrist pain and discomfort. Our PTs believed an augmented assistive grip could mitigate their discomfort, and were interested in using 3D scanning and printing technology to customize grips to the exact shape, size, and position of a user's hand to minimize strain. These grips could be 3D printed quickly at home or the clinic and be made out of comfortable material for long-term use.

We first conducted two prototyping sessions with two former long-term crutch users in order to prototype potential augmentations to mitigate grip discomfort. From these sessions, we developed a set of crutch grip prototypes. During collaborative design sessions with the PT professors, we provided play-dough as a form of 3D modeling for customized hand size and grip specifications The play-dough mold created by the PT professors was taken back to our university and 3D scanned to create a digital 3D model for printing (Figure 2). We conducted an iterative process of design and feedback from clinicians to evaluate and modify the grip design.

3.2.2 Designing a Crutch Tip (Figure 3)

Crutch tips are located at the bottom ends of the crutches and support the user's weight and maintain balance while the user is mobile. Due to a high volume of student users, the PT professors' crutch tips frequently go missing and a third of their crutch tips are lost every year. PT professors believed 3D printed crutch tips could replace missing crutch tips on their pre-existing crutches.

We 3D printed a standard crutch tip model found in an online repository for usability testing [5]. Because most crutch tips are made of a rubbery material, we had to test multiple flexible 3D printing materials to identify materials with similar flexibility and structural integrity as a standardized crutch tip (Figure 3). The crutch tips were printed in several types of filament: Polylactic acid (PLA), Acrylonitrile Butadiene Styrene (ABS), NinjaFlex™, and SemiFlex™. Through iterative prototyping, we aimed to develop an example crutch tip that had both the compression and traction of standardized crutch tip rubber. We printed a variety of crutch tips for the PT professors to review. Although the tips were not developed for the long term testing, these tips provided examples of varying materials for PTs to potentially use in their practice.

3.3 Outcome of Collaborative Sessions

The purpose of these sessions was not to design novel objects, but demonstrate the capabilities of 3D printing in the field of PT. The augmentations provided examples of 3D printing familiar and standardized products (crutch tips) and new designs customized to a patient's needs (crutch grips). Through these collaborative sessions, we learned a lot about PT expectations of 3D printing, and how to teach these skills. We built on this knowledge when working with the PT professors to create materials to teach these skills in a graduate-level PT class. Specifically, we developed realistic design scenarios where customized AT would be needed.

Figure 3. (Left) A 3D printed crutch tip installed onto a crutch. (Top Right) Different iterations of 3D printed material to test crutch tips. (Bottom Right) A 3D printed crutch tip in comparison to original crutch tip.

4. INTEGRATING 3D PRINTING INTO PHYSICAL THERAPY EDUCATION

Our surveys and collaboration activities with practicing PTs and PT professors confirmed our belief that 3D-printed AT has a home in PT practice. To take this concept further, we co-designed an educational unit incorporating 3D printing into a graduate-level physical therapy course over three class sessions. Introducing this concept into the classroom may be a starting point to address PT concerns over time constraints and required technical skills. By incorporating 3D modeling into the PT classroom, students gain expertise and knowledge about this technology they can use in their future practice.

We conducted three class sessions where students received an introduction to 3D modeling software and printing technology, and completed a hands-on design activity. PT students took pre- and post-class surveys to evaluate their educational progress and their perceptions of 3D printing. In this section, we will discuss these three class sessions and present our findings specific to the classroom experiences.

4.1 Student Demographics

Class sessions on 3D printing were provided to a total of 65 first-year, physical therapy students. All 65 students were expected to attend all three sessions, and fill out the surveys. An average of 53 students (82%) completed each survey.

Table 2. Demographic information and experience with AT, 3D printing, and 3D modeling for all 65 PT students.

Age		Gender	
Average Age: 25		Male: 21 (35%)	
Age Range: 22-41		Female: 39 (65%)	
3D Printing Experience		**Yes**	**No**
Experience creating Assistive technology		1 (1.7%)	59 (98.3%)
Experience using a 3D printer		0 (0%)	60 (100%)
Experience using 3D modeling software		3 (5%)	57 (95%)

4.2 Classroom Sessions

Our 3D printing educational series consisted of three classroom sessions that were one to two hours long. Class One served as an introduction to 3D printing. Class Two focused on assistive device design and the basics of 3D modeling tools. Class Three consisted of collecting class feedback and an evaluation of AT design.

All classes were taught at the medical university during regularly scheduled class time in the students' usual classroom. Students were asked to attend all three classes on 3D printing.

Pre-class surveys and post-class surveys were distributed to students to gather information on class expectations and experiences. Our goals for the educational series were for PT students to gain insight into how 3D printing can be utilized in physical therapy, experience with 3D modeling, and experience with designing AT or AT augmentations.

4.2.1 Class One: 3D Printing Introduction

Class One included an introductory presentation on 3D printing, overviews of the use of 3D printing in the medical field, 3D modeling software, and locations for 3D printing and 3D printing resources. Two members of our research team presented the information to a class of 65 first-year physical therapy students. The classroom session was approximately one hour long, including a 20-minute presentation and 40-minute Q&A session. During the presentation, Thingiverse[1], a repository website with a collection of 3D models, was specifically highlighted to the students for its variety of 3D models for printing. The researchers encouraged the PT students to gain familiarity with Tinkercad[2], an introductory 3D modeling software that would be used to create 3D models in Class Two.

4.2.2 Class Two: AT Design and 3D Modeling

In Class Two we gave a lesson on 3D modeling software and design and 3D printed AT. The class was approximately two hours long with an hour-long tutorial on 3D modeling and an hour-long AT design session. During the 3D modeling tutorial, we provided a video demonstrating a step-by-step process to create a simple 3D snowman in Tinkercad. The snowman was chosen because of its simple shapes and coverage of all basic modeling tools (rotating, scaling, stretching, subtracting, and combining shapes). Students followed along with the instructional video and worked together to make the snowmen. There were five 3D printing experts from our research group in addition to the instructor offering 3D modeling assistance.

After the video tutorial, we split students into five groups to create individualized assistive devices for simulated patient case scenarios (Table 3). The simulated patient case scenarios were created by the PT instructor and focused on designing augmentations to pre-existing assistive devices. These scenarios reflected current PT student learning objectives centered around walking aids such as canes, crutches, and walkers.

Table 3. Scenarios presented to PT students during Class Two. Each scenario includes patient age, patient gender, a clinical description of the scenario, and a laymen translation.

	Patient	Description
Scenario 1	Age: 62	Clinical: Status post left hemorrhagic stroke, requires use of hemiwalker, limited ability to grasp with his left hand.
	Gender: Male	Laymen: Patient had a hemorrhage in the brain that reduced his ability to control movement. Patient has trouble grasping his one-handed walker with his left hand
Scenario 2	Age: 45	Clinical: Status post TBI, requires use of right quad cane, limited by right wrist flexor synergy
	Gender: Female	Laymen: Traumatic brain injury caused patient to have limited balance and reduced control of movement of her wrist. Patient uses a cane with four legs.
Scenario 3	Age: 32	Clinical: Status post right humeroradial fracture, requires axillary crutches for recent ankle sprain, limited by right elbow flexion range (AROM/PROM 0-10 degrees)
	Gender: Male	Laymen: Patient has limited range in the right elbow from a prior fracture and is using crutches for a recent ankle sprain.
Scenario 4	Age: 60	Clinical: Right adhesive capsulitis, requires use of straight cane for balance issues, limited by shoulder flexion range (AROM/PROM 0-10 degrees).
	Gender: Female	Laymen: Patient has limited motion in the right shoulder making it difficult to advance her cane forward during walking.
Scenario 5	Age: 8	Clinical: Scoliotic curve, requires walker for CP related balance issues, limited by fixed trunk flexion to 20 degrees, fixed trunk right side bend / rotation to 10 degrees.
	Gender: Male	Laymen: Patient has cerebral palsy and uses a walker for balance. Patient has limited ability to lean forward and leans to the right when standing.

After a 30-minute brainstorming and sketching period, groups were given two hours to 3D model their design. Because students were introduced to 3D modeling software during the beginning of class, we provided play-dough as an additional form of 3D modeling (Figure 4). Play-dough models were 3D scanned into digital 3D models for printing. After Class Two, we 3D printed the student groups AT designs and brought the 3D models back for the third classroom session for evaluation (Figure 4).

---

[1] Thingiverse.com
[2] Tinkercad.com

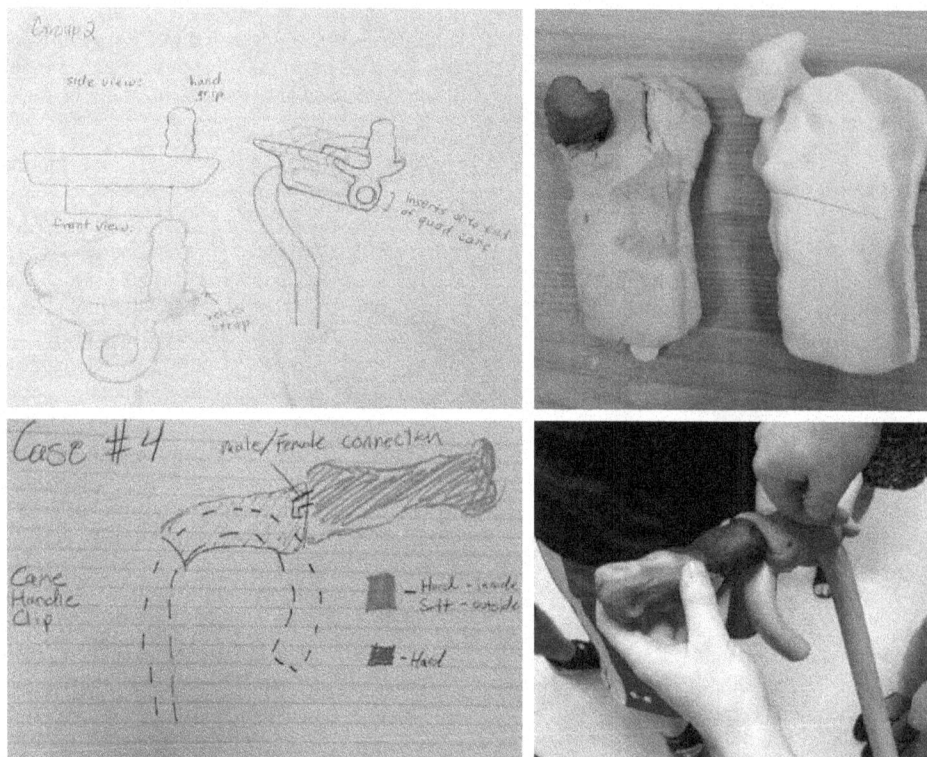

Figure 4. Student designs for Scenario 2 (Top) and Scenario 4 (Bottom). Students working on Scenario 2 created an arm-rest grip augmentation to assist a patient with limited wrist mobility. Students working on Scenario 4 augmented a cane with a grip extension to alleviate stress to the scenario patient's elbow. 3D printed version of the Scenario 2 model is provided (Top-Right).

4.2.3 Class Three: AT Presentations and Discussion

During the third class, each PT student group was provided a 3D printed version of their designed AT and tasked with assessing the usability of their designed product. After group discussions, each PT student group selected two to three group members to present their design process, final product review, and suggestions for future improvement of their design. Each presentation included the group's impression with designing and 3D modeling AT and their thoughts on 3D printing as construction for generating individualized modifications for their patient case scenario. After the five groups presented, we requested feedback from the full class on their participation in the 3D printing educational series along with their recommendations for future 3D printing class experiences.

4.3 Classroom Outcomes

4.3.1 Student Designs

All design groups successfully created an AT model for their simulated patient. Each group provided one paper sketch of their design and one play-dough model to be 3D scanned into a digital 3D model (Figure 4). The group for patient Scenario 3 was the only group to modify their 3D model on 3D modeling software after it had been 3D scanned.

Students were knowledgeable in the medical needs of their simulated patients and knew what modifications were needed to assist them. Four of the five groups (patient Scenarios 1-4) focused their designs on grips augmented to the simulated patient's original standardized AT. The group for patient Scenario 5 created crutch tips similar to our own standardized tip 3D printed for PT professors' evaluation, but modified for the simulated patient's specific need.

4.3.2 Student Reactions to 3D Printing and Modeling

We conducted surveys before and after classes to better understand student reactions and knowledge. In the first pre-class survey, we found students had minimal to no background experience in 3D modeling, printing, or design of AT. 59 of the 60 students who participated in this survey (98.3%) stated they did not have experience creating assistive technology, 60 students (100%) stated they had never used a 3D printer, and 56 students (93.4%) had never used 3D modeling software. We saw a clear increase in personal 3D printing knowledge in the Class Two post-survey (Figure 4). For Class Three, personal knowledge of 3D printing wasn't compared because students did not receive additional lectures on the topic.

On a scale of 1-5, 5 being an expert, how much do you know about 3D printing?

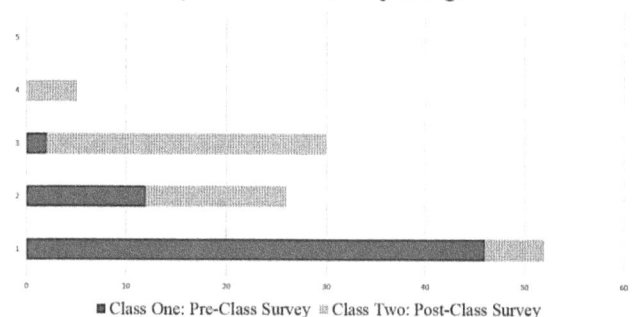

Figure 5. Bar graph of students' change in personal knowledge of 3D printing between Class One and Class Two.

For the pre- and post-survey of Class One, we asked students if they saw 3D printing technology rapidly growing in the physical

136

therapy field. Before Class One, 53.3% believed 3D printing was a rapidly growing topic in the PT field. After Class One, students' responses increased to 92%. This may be attributed to PT students learning the capabilities of 3D printing in their field during Class One. In the post-class survey of Class One, multiple students mentioned an initial lack of knowledge in the capabilities of 3D printing in their field. *"I didn't realize 3D printing could be used for less complicated things than prosthetics (i.e., cane and walker nubs, grips). I'm looking forward to learning how I can utilize it creatively in my field,"*. 94% of PT students enjoyed working on the case studies in Class Two. During the post survey of Class Two, students explained they enjoyed the simulated patient scenarios because it made 3D printing more applicable to their practice.

Due to time constraints, two of the five 3D printed AT designs were printed in a smaller scale than the original model. All models were printed using PLA filament because of its printing reliance and efficiency in comparison to more flexible material. During Class Three, student satisfaction with prints was 49%, most likely a result of low fidelity prototypes. In the third class post-class survey, PT students said 3D printed models were non-functional, not scanned properly, made from the wrong material, and/or were not the size they expected

Based on our discussions with students and an informal in-class poll, most students felt the 3D modeling software was challenging and they would prefer having more time to learn 3D modeling in future classes. In the Class Three post-survey, 74% of students stated they would rather use a 3D scanner than a 3D modeling software to create their AT.

5. OPPORTUNITIES AND BARRIERS TO 3D PRINTING IN THE FIELD OF PT

Through our surveys, design collaborations, and classroom sessions with PT professors, practicing PTs, and PT students, we identified opportunities for 3D printing in this clinical setting and barriers to its successful integration into existing practice.

5.1 DIY-AT Opportunities for PTs

We have identified the following attributes that make PTs good candidates for 3D printing technology adoption.

5.1.1 Low-Tech DIY-AT Experience

Augmenting and adjusting off-the-shelf assistive technologies and creating new devices is a common part of many PTs clinical work [3]. This experience and training is useful in low-tech DIY activities, but their ability to brainstorm solutions, determine design requirements, and work around constraints will transfer when working on 3D modeling design tasks.

5.1.2 Medical Expertise

PTs provide important medical expertise to evaluate the functionality of AT as well as generate and implement ideas for improvements in AT design. Physical therapy students at our interviewing university are taught the underlying biomechanical and anatomical implications of designing basic technologies in order to effectively treat variable patient disabilities. An AT user without this training developing their own personal AT may not have the medical knowledge to develop optimal devices. However, when designing usable AT, medical knowledge isn't enough and it is crucial to acknowledge the expertise, insight, and preferences of end-users. Strategic collaborations between clinicians and end-users can yield functional and usable AT.

5.1.3 User Access

PT clinicians treat patients with a broad spectrum of medical diagnoses and have the capacity to reach a large number of users with varying abilities. 3D printing technology and existing shared design repositories can address this diverse set of AT users and expand PT knowledge and expertise in developing AT and AT augmentations.

5.2 Clinical Barriers to 3D Printing Adoption

We found PTs to be interested in producing 3D printed assistive devices, but we observe that they may face a series of problems that can prevent them from adopting these tools.

5.2.1 Limited Experience and Time

PTs lack experience in 3D printing and modeling. This is due to many clinicians believing they do not have the time available to fully learn and use 3D printing and modeling services [3, 13]. With increasing productivity demands, clinicians are likely to lean towards the treatment techniques they are most familiar with. Also, 3D printing is a new technology growing in use over the past decade. Clinicians are just starting to realize the potential of 3D printing in their practice. Therefore, knowledge and expertise about 3D printing may be difficult for clinicians to obtain.

5.2.2 Ease of Purchase

Fully customized AT can be costly and can have lengthy insurance and billing processes [6]. Standardized AT is easily acquired through medical catalogs and is typically covered by medical insurance. The ease of acquiring standardized AT could deter PTs and their users from taking the time to produce their own AT when standardized devices are available.

5.2.3 Standardized Reliability

Standardized AT provides reliable and rigorously tested devices. Because novel AT designs and DIY technologies are not rigorously tested, therapists may be hesitant to prescribe novel products to their patients. Clinician concerns over loss of product warranty and professional liability risk may also limit consideration for modifying a standardized assistive device.

5.2.4 Liability of DIY-AT

The liability of DIY-AT is a concern for PTs. Generally, when AT fails, liability falls to the manufacturer of that device. By becoming the manufacturers of their patients' devices, the PTs are accepting a potential increased liability for that new device. Also, materials for 3D Printed AT are unregulated and not tested for medical use. This could be concerning for patients who are constantly in contact with their devices, as unregulated materials may cause unforeseen reactions or irritation. However, if 3D printing continues to grow in the medical field, we could see a natural progression towards more regulated development of AT augmentations and materials to alleviate this barrier.

6. DISCUSSION

In this section we will discuss key topics extrapolated from our findings. These topics include: 1) exploring augmentations versus novel AT designs, 2) improvements to novice 3D modeling software, 3) adjusting for prototype fidelity, and 4) selecting 3D printing materials.

6.1 Augmentation vs. Novel Designs

Our PTs were more interested in customizing off-the-shelf AT through various augmentations rather than creating novel AT customized to the patient's needs. During our investigation, we noticed every simulated patient scenario in class and every 3D printed assistive device requested by the PTs were augmentations to pre-existing standardized assistive technologies, and not standalone pieces of assistive technology. We asked both the practicing PTs and PT students about this observation in the surveys. Approximately 75% of both PT students and practicing PTs preferred augmenting pre-existing technology in comparison to creating a novel device. There were several reasons for this preference that were different for each clinician and student. Many students discussed the benefits of potentially lower cost, reduced liability risk to PTs, faster construction, and reliance on universal standards. Our practicing PTs mentioned concerns over liability, a discomfort in creating their own designs, and a lack of need for innovation. This finding is expected considering the large portion of highly regulated and universally approved devices available for clinicians to prescribe.

We suggest future 3D modeling software should take augmentation of standardized technology into account by implementing software features that can integrate standard AT items and measurements into their design systems.

6.2 3D Modeling Software

Despite their technical backgrounds, students experienced difficulty using the Tinkercad software. This is similar to previous research that found novice 3D modeling tools to be less usable than expected [3]. Basic shape combinations such as the snowman example were often skewed as a result of inexperience working in 3D workspaces. Multiple students expressed their frustration and mentioned their appreciation for being able to work in groups to 3D model. *"...that fact that we were working in groups...I know that if I did it by myself I probably would have just thrown my computer...so it was nice to have a collaborative effort."* – Student, Class Three.

During class, students had the option of using 3D scanning and play-dough modeling, 3D modeling software, or both in the development of an AT device for the patient scenario. By the end of the second class, 73.6% of students preferred 3D scanning and play-dough modeling over 3D modeling software to produce their AT designs. This could potentially be a result of familiarity with physical modeling in comparison to 3D modeling, but is useful in determining the level of usability in 3D modeling software.

Although there are many personal 3D printing technologies made for novice users, it is clear there is still a steep learning curve that needs to be addressed in the design of 3D modeling software. There is also room for potential specialization of 3D modeling software. PTs would greatly benefit from automated software that caters to their 3D modeling needs. We hope software can be improved upon in the future for PT AT development.

6.3 Prototype Fidelity

When designers create prototypes, they must choose the level of fidelity they are working at and what compromises come with that level. For designers such as architects, fidelity requirements are inherently low as a result of smaller scale prototypes being necessary for testing and analysis. This is because an architect is typically unable to make a full-scale prototype building before making the final building. For clinicians, we found high fidelity AT prototypes to be very important when testing their design. During our third class session, two of the five groups were given small-scale versions of their original design. This was a result of time constraints to 3D print the full product. As a result, the models did not represent the proper sizing needed to be usable for their patient scenarios. Students expressed concern with the downscaled prototypes because they did not allow for realistic analysis. A grip customized to a person's hand cannot be tested unless the prototype is scaled for the intended hand. As a result, prototyping for clinicians requires models with high levels of fidelity to provide for the most realistic analysis of usability.

Although high fidelity models are preferred, we found PT students also preferred 3D scanning, a lower fidelity tool, instead of 3D modeling. This could possibly be tied to the PT students' level of experience with 3D modeling software. In the third class post-class survey, we asked student what 3D printing topics they would like to continue learning in future classes. 19 of the 27 students (70%) who responded to this open-ended question mentioned if given the opportunity to continue 3D printing, they would like to learn more about 3D modeling. Student preference to scanning may be tied to current skill level and change with increased use of 3D modeling software.

6.4 3D Printing Materials

In PT, the type of material used is often important for the overall function of the device. Because the majority of AT designs made by students were made for direct hand contact, many of our students were not satisfied with the comfort level of the solid plastic AT. Multiple groups of students wanted to modify their 3D print by adding softer material to improve the level of comfort for their patient. If these materials are used, there may still be the need to modify 3D prints for comfort and usability.

More flexible 3D printing materials such as NinjaFlex™ could be great alternatives to solid plastics, but like most personal 3D printer filaments is unregulated for medical devices. Further research into 3D printing material options in comparison to standard assistive device material should be explored in order to ensure proper usability and safety for the patient.

7. LIMITATIONS

Unfortunately, the realities of conducting research in a graduate-level classroom limited some aspects of our investigation. The investigation was limited to students in one section of an introductory physical therapy class that we worked with over one semester. Although we encouraged students to look at Tinkercad between the first and second class, most students were unable to do so. Increasing the time dedicated to 3D modeling education and exposure may increase students' levels of familiarity and comfort with 3D modeling systems.

8. CONCLUSION

Through our collaborations with PTs and the education of PT students, we have demonstrated a clear potential for 3D printing in the PT production and augmentation of AT. We identified benefits of 3D printing in the PT practice, barriers to 3D printing and the PT practice, and opportunities for integration of 3D printing in the PT practice. In the future, we hope to continue teaching more 3D printing classes to PT students. PTs would also like to see this expanded to include development of AT for other patient populations as well as incorporating events that involve actual patients so that the patient may participate in the development and feedback of the adapted device.

9. ACKNOWLEDGMENTS

We would like to thank the students, instructors, and clinicians who participated in our study. This material is based on work supported by the National Science Foundation under Grant No. IIS-1451661. Any opinions, findings, and conclusions or recommendations expressed in this material are those of the authors and do not necessarily reflect the views of the National Science Foundation. Additional funding provided by the CRA-W's Collaborative Research Experiences for Undergraduates.

10. REFERENCES

[1] Assistive Tech Act of 1998, Section 3, https://www.access-board.gov/guidelines-and-standards/communications-and-it/about-the-section-508-standards/section-508-standards, accessed: 4/30/2016

[2] Buehler, E., Branham, S., Ali, A., Chang, J. J., Hofmann, M. K., Hurst, A., & Kane, S. K. (2015, April). Sharing is caring: Assistive technology designs on thingiverse. In Proceedings of the 33rd Annual ACM Conference on Human Factors in Computing Systems (pp. 525-534). ACM. DOI=http://dx.doi.org/10.1145/2702123.2702525

[3] Buehler, E., Comrie, N., Hofmann, M., McDonald, S., & Hurst, A. (2016). Investigating the Implications of 3D Printing in Special Education. ACM Transactions on Accessible Computing (TACCESS), 8(3), 11. DOI=http://dx.doi.org/10.1145/2870640

[4] Buehler, E., Kane, S. K., & Hurst, A. (2014, October). ABC and 3D: opportunities and obstacles to 3D printing in special education environments. In Proceedings of the 16th international ACM SIGACCESS conference on Computers & accessibility (pp. 107-114). ACM. DOI=http://dx.doi.org/10.1145/2661334.2661365

[5] "Crutch Tip",© 2011 darthcarter, http://www.thingiverse.com/thing:13591

[6] Dawe, M. (2006, April). Desperately seeking simplicity: how young adults with cognitive disabilities and their families adopt assistive technologies. In Proceedings of the SIGCHI conference on Human Factors in computing systems (pp. 1143-1152). ACM. DOI=http://dx.doi.org/10.1145/1124772.1124943

[7] Follmer, S., & Ishii, H. (2012, May). KidCAD: digitally remixing toys through tangible tools. In Proceedings of the SIGCHI Conference on Human Factors in Computing Systems (pp. 2401-2410). ACM. DOI=http://dx.doi.org/10.1145/2207676.2208403

[8] Hofmann, M., Harris, J., Hudson, S., and Mankoff, J. (2016, May). Helping Hands: Requirements for a Prototyping Methodology for Upper-limb Prosthetics Users. In Proceedings of the 2016 CHI Conference on Human Factors in Computing Systems (CHI '16). (pp 1769-1780). ACM. DOI=http://dx.doi.org/10.1145/2858036.2858340

[9] Hook, J., Verbaan, S., Durrant, A., Olivier, P., & Wright, P. (2014, June). A study of the challenges related to DIY assistive technology in the context of children with disabilities. In Proceedings of the 2014 conference on Designing interactive systems (pp. 597-606). ACM. DOI=http://dx.doi.org/10.1145/2598510.2598530

[10] Hurst, A., & Kane, S. (2013, June). Making making accessible. In Proceedings of the 12th International Conference on Interaction Design and Children (pp. 635-638). ACM. DOI=http://dx.doi.org/10.1145/2485760.2485883

[11] Hurst, A., & Tobias, J. (2011, October). Empowering individuals with do-it-yourself assistive technology. In The proceedings of the 13th international ACM SIGACCESS conference on Computers and accessibility (pp. 11-18). ACM. DOI=http://dx.doi.org/10.1145/2049536.2049541

[12] Leduc-Mills, B., & Eisenberg, M. (2011, June). The UCube: a child-friendly device for introductory three-dimensional design. In Proceedings of the 10th International Conference on Interaction Design and Children (pp. 72-80). ACM. DOI=http://dx.doi.org/10.1145/1999030.1999039

[13] Leukers, B., Gülkan, H., Irsen, S. H., Milz, S., Tille, C., Schieker, M., & Seitz, H. (2005). Hydroxyapatite scaffolds for bone tissue engineering made by 3D printing. Journal of Materials Science: Materials in Medicine, 16(12), 1121-1124.

[14] Lin, H. W., Aflatoony, L., & Wakkary, R. (2014, April). Design for one: a game controller for a quadriplegic gamer. In CHI'14 Extended Abstracts on Human Factors in Computing Systems (pp. 1243-1248). ACM. DOI=http://dx.doi.org/10.1145/2559206.2581334

[15] Lutz, R. (2013, October). Enhancing information technology education (ITE) with the use of 3D printer technology. In Proceedings of the 14th annual ACM SIGITE conference on Information technology education (pp. 157-158). ACM. DOI=http://dx.doi.org/10.1145/2512276.2512327

[16] Phillips, B. and Zhao, H. 1993. Predictors of assistive technology abandonment. In Assistive Technology. Taylor & Francis. 5(1): 36--45.

[17] Ribas-Xirgo, L., & López-Varquiel, F. (2015, September). DIY computer mouse for special needs people. In Proceedings of the XVI International Conference on Human Computer Interaction (p. 27). ACM. DOI=http://dx.doi.org/10.1145/2829875.2829895

[18] Rengier, F., Mehndiratta, A., von Tengg-Kobligk, H., Zechmann, C. M., Unterhinninghofen, R., Kauczor, H. U., & Giesel, F. L. (2010). 3D printing based on imaging data: review of medical applications. International journal of computer assisted radiology and surgery, 5(4), 335-341.

[19] Scherer, M. J. 1996. Outcomes of assistive technology use on quality of life. In Disability & Rehabilitation. Informal Healthcare. 18(9): 439--448.

[20] Schubert, C., van Langeveld, M. C., & Donoso, L. A. (2013). Innovations in 3D printing: a 3D overview from optics to organs. British Journal of Ophthalmology, bjophthalmol-2013.

[21] Schull, J. (2015, October). Enabling the Future: Crowdsourced 3D-printed Prosthetics as a Model for Open Source Assistive Technology Innovation and Mutual Aid. In Proceedings of the 17th International ACM SIGACCESS Conference on Computers & Accessibility (pp. 1-1). ACM. DOI=http://dx.doi.org/10.1145/2700648.2809870

[22] Stangl, A., Hsu, C., and Yeh, T. (2015, October). Transcribing Across the Senses: Community Efforts to Create 3D Printable Accessible Tactile Pictures for Young Children with Visual Impairments. In *Proceedings of the 17th International ACM SIGACCESS Conference on Computers & Accessibility* (ASSETS '15). (pp 127-137). ACM. DOI=http://dx.doi.org/10.1145/2700648.2809854

WeAllWalk: An Annotated Data Set of Inertial Sensor Time Series from Blind Walkers

German H. Flores
Dept. of Computer Engineering
Baskin School of Engineering
University of California
Santa Cruz, CA 95064
ghflores@ucsc.edu

Roberto Manduchi
Dept. of Computer Engineering
Baskin School of Engineering
University of California
Santa Cruz, CA 95064
manduchi@soe.ucsc.edu

ABSTRACT

We introduce WeAllWalk, a data set of inertial sensor time series collected from blind walkers using a long cane or a guide dog. Blind participants walked through fairly long and complex indoor routes that included obstacles to be avoided and doors to be opened. Inertial data was recorded by two iPhone 6s carried by our participants in their pockets and carefully annotated. Ground truth heel strike times were measured by two small inertial sensor units clipped to the participants' shoes. We also show comparative examples of application of step counting and turn detection algorithms to selected data from WeAllWalk.

CCS Concepts

• **Human-centered computing→Ubiquitous and mobile computing→Ubiquitous and mobile devices** • **Human-centered computing→Accessibility→Accessibility technologies**

Keywords

Inertial sensing; Wayfinding; Step counting.

1. INTRODUCTION

For someone who cannot see, tasks such as finding one's own location or figuring out how to reach a certain location in a building can be daunting, especially if this person is not familiar with the building layout or if he or she has poor orientation skills. Lacking access to visual landmarks, a blind traveler can quickly become disoriented; and if he or she at some point finds himself or herself being lost, tracing back their own steps can be equally challenging. For this reason, many blind individuals do not visit new places (office buildings, hospitals, schools) without a sighted guide who can show them around and lead them to the desired destination. Without the ability to travel independently, people in this community may miss opportunities for education, employment, leisure, socialization, and participation.

Personal navigation systems are designed to provide their users with spatial information and directions when traveling to new places. While outdoor navigation is to some extent already solved by the use of GPS, this is not an option for indoor navigation, and various technologies are being explored. Of course, systems for indoor navigation are useful not only for blind travelers; anyone may need directional information at times. Indeed, there is increasing commercial interest in technology that may help one locate a shop in a mall, a room in a building, or one's own car in a parking lot. Several research groups have started building assistive applications on top of this technology, adapting it to the particular needs of specific communities of users.

This contribution focuses on systems that support indoor wayfinding using dead reckoning from inertial sensors. This approach has the advantage that it requires no external infrastructure (as with iBeacons or similar technologies) or use of a camera (as with image-based technologies). Note that, until wearable cameras are socially accepted and widely used, users of a camera-based localization system would need to take pictures of the environment with their cell phone, something that for a blind person may be difficult and possibly awkward in social settings. In contrast, inertial sensing can be conducted with a smartphone conveniently tucked in one's pocket.

Dead reckoning uses data from the inertial sensors (and from magnetic sensors, when the data they produce is reliable) to estimate the trajectory taken by the user. In theory, data from a tri-axial accelerometer could be doubly integrated to obtain its location. In practice, this is only possible with sensors attached to the walker's feet; by detecting when one's foot is resting on the ground, it is possible to perform a zero velocity update, thus largely limiting errors due to drift. When the sensors are worn elsewhere on one's body or garments, a safer strategy is to use them for step counting[1], and to indirectly recover one's position using an estimated stride length, as well as orientation information from the gyroscope. Various versions of this approach have been used to track a person walking in a place with known geometry (obtained, for example, from a floor plan). Even when the geometry of the environment is not known, it is possible to use dead reckoning (e.g., by means of step counting and robust turn detection) to help a person re-trace a path taken in a building.

Step counting and turn detection with a smartphone placed in one's clothing can be computed reliably if one walks with a steady gait and in mostly rectilinear paths. Blind individuals, however, often exhibit body motion patterns during gait that are

ASSETS '16, October 23 - 26, 2016, Reno, NV, USA
Copyright is held by the owner/author(s). Publication rights licensed to ACM.
ACM 978-1-4503-4124-0/16/10...$15.00
DOI: http://dx.doi.org/10.1145/2982142.2982179

---

[1] Note that many blind individuals prefer receiving information about distances in steps, rather than in feet or in time [21].

markedly different than those of sighted people [15] (e.g., due to "scuttling" [9]). In addition, cane users, who are trained to execute the 2-point touch or constant sliding technique [4], swing their cane-holding arm left and right, resulting in additional upper body rotation. As already observed by other authors [9], step counting may be difficult (or require specific parameter tuning) to work robustly with these individuals and for any smartphone placement. Likewise, blind individuals, especially when walking in large spaces, and unless they use a guide dog, do not always walk on straight paths with sharp and clearly detectable turns. Rather, they often veer involuntarily, and need to correct their path when they realize that they are getting close to a wall or an obstacle.

This paper introduces a new, openly accessible and annotated data set of inertial sensor time series collected from blind individuals walking through relatively long and complex paths in realistic conditions, and carrying two smartphones in different locations on their clothing. The primary purpose for creating this data set was to allow other researchers to benchmark their algorithms (step counting, turn detectors, or other) on a common ground. This follows the example of other similar data sets (described in Sec. 2.3), with the critical difference that our WeAllWalk data was obtained from blind walkers, using either a long cane or a guide dog. More important, this data set does not just contain measurements from people walking on a straight line, as in previous collections [5][29]. Instead, our participants walked on multiple paths with different levels of complexity, including turns at 45, 90, and 180 degrees, as well as through doors that needed to be opened. While walking, our participants occasionally veered off the straight path, got caught in wall openings, and collided with obstacles. These events (which are faithfully recorded in the WeAllWalk data set) are to be expected when walking without sight. We carefully annotated our measurement time series, indicating the start and end time of each such event. In addition, we provide ground truth data in the form of heel strike times, measured by accessory inertial sensors clipped to the participants' shoes. We believe that this annotated data is representative of typical situations encountered by blind walkers, and that it should be very useful for anyone who wants to test their dead reckoning algorithms in realistic scenarios.

This article is organized as follows: After the related work, presented in the next section, we introduce the WeAllWalk data set in Sec. 3. We describe the sensor platform, the paths and their characteristics; we introduce the participants to this study, the procedures that were followed, and our criteria to annotate the data collected. In Sec. 4, we present some simple results of automatic step counting and turn detection on this data. Sec. 5 has the conclusions. The WeAllWalk inertial sensor time series data set is available at **http://n2t.net/ark:/b7291/d1cc7g**. It is released under the terms of the Creative Commons Attribution license (CC-BY-4.0).

2. RELATED WORK
2.1 Indoor Navigation via Inertial Sensing
There has been increasing interest over the past decade in personal navigation systems that support users in determining their location and in finding a path to a desired destination. While outdoor localization can be obtained, at least with an accuracy of a few meters via GPS, this is not possible indoors, where the GPS signal becomes too weak for detection. Indoor navigation represents the "last frontier," with whole conferences devoted to this subject [16][18]. A variety of techniques have been proposed [10] for indoor localization, including radio-frequency triangulation [37],

image-based recognition [22], Bluetooth beacons [27], visual markers placed in specific locations [7], and dead-reckoning using inertial sensors (see survey by Yang et al. [35]). The use of inertial sensors for blind indoor wayfinding has also been considered by several authors [6][8][9][23][28][30][31][35].

2.2 Step Counting
Automatic step counting (e.g., for physical activity tracking) has received considerable attention by the research and industry world alike. Commercial pedometers use sensors that can be embedded in shoes (e.g., the Adidas Micropacers), in a smartwatch, in a smartphone, and attached to ankles or a belt. We refer the reader to [36] for a review of different sensing modalities for step counting and other physical activity monitoring. A variety of algorithms have been proposed for stride event detection from inertial sensor time series; an excellent review of some of the main algorithms is presented in [5]. Sensor placement certainly has a role in the characteristics of the data collected. For example, ankle or foot worn sensors usually provide more accurate step counting [13] than waist worn sensors. However, step counting accuracy does not seem to be greatly affected by the specific location of the sensor on other parts of the body [14][5] (including on head-mounted displays [3]).

Whereas the vast majority of step counting algorithms have been developed for able-bodied ambulators, some authors have addressed the performances of these algorithms with sensors carried by people with some level of mobility impairment. For example, [25] evaluated different algorithms with ten mobility-

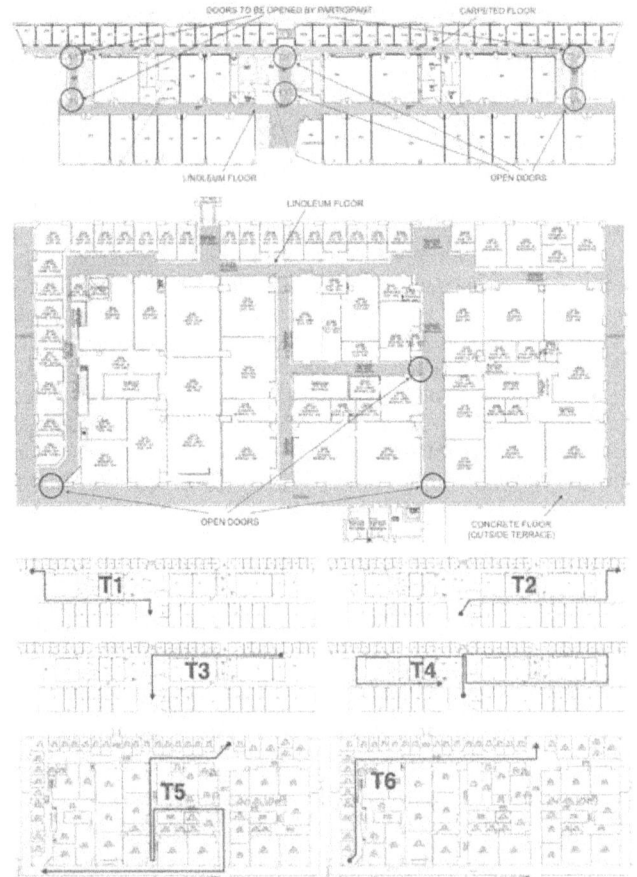

Figure 1. Top two rows: the floor plans of E2 and BE, respectively. Lower rows: the trajectories taken by our participants. T1–T4 were located in E2, T5-T6 in BE.

impaired geriatric patients, while [38] designed and tested robust stride event detectors for users with Parkinson's disease. In both cases, participants carried an accelerometer on a belt around their waist. While none of the blind individuals who contributed to the WeAllWalk data set could be considered to have mobility impairment, use of a long cane or a guide dog may result in a gait pattern that is quite different than for sighted walkers.

2.3 Similar Data Sets

We are aware of two existing openly accessible data sets with inertial time series collected from walkers carrying a smartphone; these data sets are briefly described below. Other similar data sets exist, but with different sensors and body placement (e.g., foot-mounted sensors [2]) which are not directly relevant to our intended use case.

The Walk Detection and Step Counting on Unconstrained Smartphones dataset [5] consists of time annotated sensor traces (accelerometer, gyroscope, and magnetometer) obtained from 27 participants walking a route at three different walking paces, and carrying one or two smartphones placed in various positions while walking.

The OU-ISIR Gait Database [29] consists of walking data from 744 participants wearing four sensors (three units with accelerometer and gyroscope, and one smartphone containing an accelerometer) located in a belt around the participants' waist. Participants walked on straight paths at varying inclinations.

WeAllWalk differs from these prior data sets in two main aspects. First, it contains data from blind walkers, both using a long cane and a guide dog. Second, the path traversed by our participants are much more complex and realistic than the straight routes considered in the previous data sets. The routes in WeAllWalk include turns at corridor junctions, active door openings, as well as sporadic stops or short re-routings due to involuntary collisions with objects or walls, as should be expected during regular blind ambulation. We carefully annotated the time series to identify intervals corresponding to walking in a straight line, taking a turn, or opening a door, as well as specific "features," such as when the walker stopped for a short moment, bumped into an obstacle or a wall, or deviated momentarily from the path, because for example, he or she missed a door or got stuck in an opening in the wall.

3. THE WEALLWALK DATA SET

3.1 Sensor Platform

3.1.1 Sensors

Our participants carried two smartphones (Apple iPhone 6s), placed in different locations on their garments. Each smartphone recorded data from its tri-axial accelerometers, gyroscopes, and magnetometers. Data was sampled at a rate of 25 Hz. In addition, we recorded derived data produced by the iOS' Core Motion

Figure 2. Examples of placement of the CPRO shoe-mounted sensor for ground truth step detection. The sensor is contained in the white small case, attached to a plastic padded clip.

framework via proprietary sensor fusion algorithms. This derived data includes the estimated direction of the gravity force, the device's actual acceleration (obtained by subtracting the estimated gravity acceleration from the data measured by the accelerometer), the corrected magnetic field, and the device's attitude (the 3-D rotation of the device with respect to a static reference frame). Each data sample was time-stamped with the clock of the phone that originated it.

In addition to the smartphones, our participants carried two small inertial sensor units clipped to their shoes (see Fig. 2). We would like to emphasize that we do not assume or expect that blind walkers would wear these shoe-mounted sensors in their daily life. These sensors were added for the sole purpose of enabling ground truth step counting (since placement at the foot level enables robust step detection [13]). Algorithms for step counting from inertial sensors in the smartphone can then be benchmarked against this ground truth data. We used MetaWear-CPRO[2] units (shown in Fig. 2), which contain a 16-bit tri-axial accelerometer and gyroscope IMU from Bosch (BMI160). The accelerometers can work at a programmable range of ±2g, ±4g, ±8g, or ±16g, whereas the gyroscope can work between ranges of ±125°/s, ±250°/s, ±500°/s, ±1000°/s, or ±2000°/s. For the experiments, we set the accelerometer range to ±2g, and the gyroscope range to ±500°/s. The inertial sensor time series measured by the shoe-mounted sensors (sampled at 25 Hz) are recorded together with data from the smartphones, and later processed to detect the ground truth heel strike times. Foot strike events for each foot are detected from these sensors using data from the Y-axis gyroscope (as in [32]) using a modified version of the UPTIME algorithm [1] (see Fig. 3).

All of the devices carried by our participants (two iPhone 6s and two foot-mounted sensors) are controlled via Bluetooth by a single iPhone 5 (called "control phone") carried by one of the experimenters. The system makes use of the Multipeer connectivity Framework to communicate between multiple iOS devices, and the MetaWear iOS Objective-C API to communicate with the MetaWear-CPRO sensors. The "control phone" is paired with each of the smartphones carried by the participant in order to broadcast commands to them, as well as receive status updates (e.g., acknowledgement that a command was received, or battery life status from the MetaWear-CPRO sensors). The smartphones carried by the participant are then paired with each of the MetaWear-CPRO sensors, one per smartphone. This pairing is done remotely from the "control phone." Once the "control phone" is paired with the two smartphones carried by the participant, and each one of these is paired with a MetaWear CPRO sensor, the "control phone" broadcasts a series of commands. Some of these commands include starting and stopping the inertial sensors, synchronizing the smartphones and the MetaWear-CPRO sensors so that all sensor readings reference the same starting time, saving all the sensor data from the smartphones and the MetaWear-CPRO sensors, restarting the system for the next experiment, and more. All of this is done remotely and without having to physically interact with the smartphones carried by the participants during the experiment (e.g., having to take the smartphones out at the end of each trial in order to restart the system or save the data). All the sensor data from the MetaWear-CPRO sensors is streamed to the smartphone paired with and recorded along with all the sensor data produced by the iOS Core Motion framework.

---

[2] https://store.mbientlab.com/product/metawear-cpro/

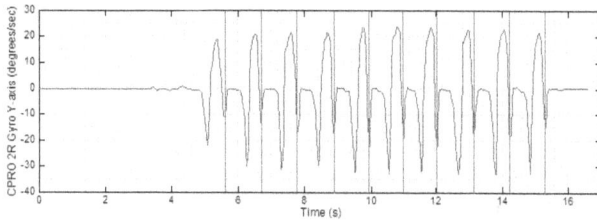

Figure 3. Time series of measurements from the Y-axis gyroscope in the CPRO sensor clipped to one of our participants' right shoe during the calibration pre-trial. The green vertical lines represent heel strike times.

3.1.2 Calibration Pre-Trial

Before starting to walk on the prescribed paths, each participant went through a "calibration" pre-trial, which consisted of walking along a straight corridor for twenty steps. The approximate time of each heel strike for each foot was recorded manually by an experimenter (by tapping on the screen of the control phone each time the participant placed a foot on the ground). This pre-trial phase is used to calibrate the parameters of the ground truth step detector from the shoe-mounted sensors described earlier (this calibration is performed off-line after data collection.) The ground-truth step detector is assumed to be well calibrated when the steps events it identifies correlate well with the steps that have been manually input by the experimenter. Note that the manual step input is performed only during pre-trial.

3.2 Paths

Our participants walked on 6 different paths in two different buildings in our campus (called the E2 and the BE building in this paper). The first paths (T1 to T4) are located in the E2 building, while the last two (T5 and T6) are located in the BE building. Floor maps of the buildings and the routes are shown in Fig. 1. Paths were all indoors and on level terrain (one path contained a stretch on an outdoor terrace). We decided against including staircases in the paths, due to safety concerns. Routes where chosen to have a variety of lengths and complexities. The shortest path was about 75 meters long and only included one 90 degrees turn; the longest path was about 300 meters long along an 8-

Table 1. BLIND PARTICIPANTS LIST

ID	Mobility tool	Phone 1 placement	Phone 2 placement
P1	Cane Dog	Left breast pocket	Jacket right side pocket
P2	Cane	Jacket left side pocket	Tucked under shirt on right shoulder
P3	Cane	Pants left front pocket	Pants right back pocket
P4	Dog	Jacket left side pocket	Pants right back pocket
P5	Cane	Pants left front pocket	Pants right back pocket
P6	Cane	Holster clipped to front right belt	Pants left front pocket
P7	Cane	Jacket right side pocket	Pants left front pocket
P8	Cane Dog	Pants right front pocket	Pants left front pocket

shaped route, included seven turns and required the participant to open three doors. One path included a 180 degrees turn, while three paths included a 45 degree turn. The path order was designed in such a way that the end point of a path in the sequence corresponded to the start point of the next path.

For most of the time, participants walked in a corridor (with the width of the corridor varying from 120 cm to 210 cm), but some paths included traversal of an open space (an elevator hall or an entrance hall) as well as a passage next to a stairwell. In some cases, a turn was preceded or followed by a door that needed to be opened. In these cases, we informed the participant in advance of the presence of a door, and of whether the door had to be opened by pushing on a crowd bar, or be pulled open by a handle. In two places, the path went through a door that required substantial force for opening; in these cases, one experimenter opened the door for the participant.

Floor surface varied from industrial carpet to linoleum to rugged concrete (in the outside terrace). In addition, two industrial flat mats were placed in an elevator hall, and a metal plate was placed across a corridor. Some of our participants got their cane tip or their shoe briefly stuck at the edge of these floor coverings. Most environments were devoid of obstacles, although a few corridors contained large pillars, couches, chairs, tables, garbage bins, and obstacles in the form of appliances, which were kept on one side of the corridor. In these situations, we advised the participant to keep close to the opposite side of the corridor. Some corridors contained openings to rooms or to other corridors, and a few participants occasionally moved close to these openings and got caught in the wall corner; this typically caused a short stop before the participant was able to get back to the intended route. At times, the participant also had to stop and move to the side to avoid walking into people who were standing in the corridor or were walking towards the participant. On the day participant P6 visited, some corridors were encumbered by one or more ladders due to ongoing work. In this case, we directed the participant by voice to avoid the ladder.

3.3 Participants and Procedure

Eight blind volunteers and five sighted volunteers participated in the study. The blind participants were recruited through the network of acquaintances of the second author, while the sighted participants were graduate students or faculty members in our school. Note that the focus of this data set is on blind walkers; we added data from sighted participants only as a "control," for comparison in identical settings.

3.3.1 Blind Participants

Participant P1 is a 66-year-old woman who has been blind since she was very young. She has a guide dog, a Labrador Retriever, who is functioning, but close to retirement. P1 feels that her dog is becoming distracted and is not as good as he used to be at staying away from obstacles, and for this reason she recently took some classes to refresh her long cane skills. She walked paths T1 to T4 with the dog first, then again with the cane. She then walked paths T5 and T6, with the dog first, and then again with the cane. She felt that using the dog allowed her to walk on a straight line, while she tended to veer while walking with the cane; this was confirmed by our observations. Her dog, which she held on a harness with her left hand tended to keep very close to the right side of the wall. When walking with the cane, P1 sometimes got stuck in a wall opening and had to walk away from it to resume her path. She slides her pencil-tipped cane left and right, synchronized with her gait.

Participant P2 (aged 46) lost her sight over the past five years due to diabetic retinopathy (the diabetes also caused some neuropathy at her feet). She uses a long cane for mobility, although she is looking forward to receiving a guide dog in the near future. She is still perfecting her mobility skills, and feels that she is not moving as gracefully as other people in her condition. Her cane has a ball tip; she slides it left and right, synchronized with her gait. She often hit a sidewall with her cane, and sometimes bumped into obstacles along the way (e.g., a garbage bin or a chair).

At 26 years of age, P3 was the youngest participant in our study and she has been blind since birth. An expert cane user, she had a guide dog in the past. She, however, admits that her orientation skills are poor, so she was glad to hear that this study required no route memorization. P3 was able to walk on straight paths without much veering; however, she did get caught in a wall opening a few times. She uses a cane with a ball tip, sliding it on the floor in a swinging motion that, however, is generally not synchronized with her gait.

Participant P4 is a 65-year-old woman who lost her sight soon after birth. She didn't bring her cane, and thus was tested only with her dog, an energetic German Shepherd, who walked very fast as she held the harness with her left hand. The guide dog followed P4's commands faithfully, although at one point, while in the stairwell that joins two corridors, the dog almost started leading P4 downstairs instead of walking straight past the staircase. P4 explained that the dog might have been wanting to walk to P4's husband, who was waiting downstairs in the parking lot.

Participant P5, aged 59, is a man who lost his sight at 18 months of age. He never had a guide dog, and is not interested in one. He is an expert traveler, with excellent orientation skills. He often travels independently by public transit. He had a peculiar way of using his pencil-tipped cane. Instead of swinging his cane left and right, he holds it at an angle in front of him, and taps it on the ground at regular intervals. He explained that, by listening to the sound and its echo, he could tell the presence of nearby surfaces. He walked, for the most part, with very little veering.

Participant P6 is a 68-year-old man. He lost his sight due to a traumatic brain injury as a teenager. P6 used a telescopic cane with a round metallic glide tip, which he maneuvers in a swinging motion synchronized with his gait. He slid the cane on the floor except for the outside terrace with rugged concrete surface, where he instead tapped it (2-point touch). P6 explained to us that he normally uses a different, heavier cane when walking outdoors. He was able to walk in straight lines and avoided almost all obstacles, without hitting any wall or being caught in wall openings.

Participant P7 is a man, aged 46, who has been blind since birth. He has excellent orientation skills and regularly travels even long distances using public transportation. He uses a single piece long cane with round metallic glide tip, which he slides on the floor in a swinging movement synchronized with his gait. In our trials, he walked with little veering. In a couple of occasions, he bumped his shoulder into large obstacles along the path.

Participant P8 is a 69-year-old woman who lost her sight progressively during her young age. Similar to P1, she walked all paths twice, one time with her guide dog and the other time using a long cane (pencil tip). She is a proficient traveler, yet she often times veered off the straight direction when walking in a corridor and had to correct her path.

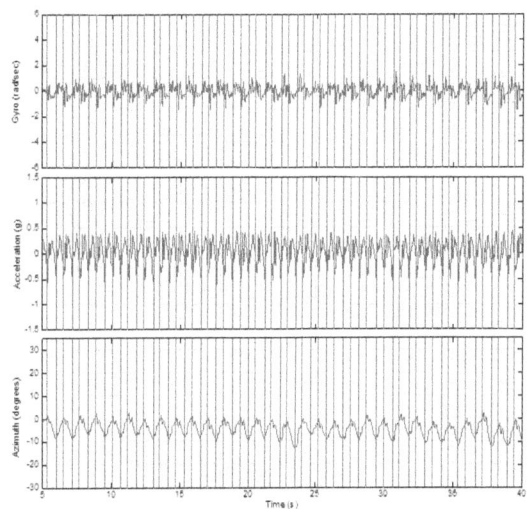

(a) A sighted participant

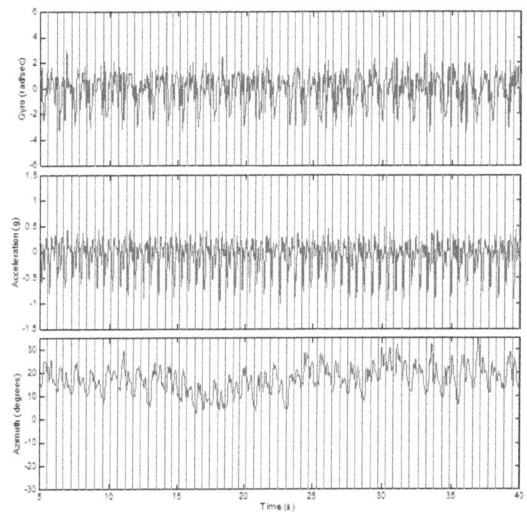

(b) Participant P3 using a long cane

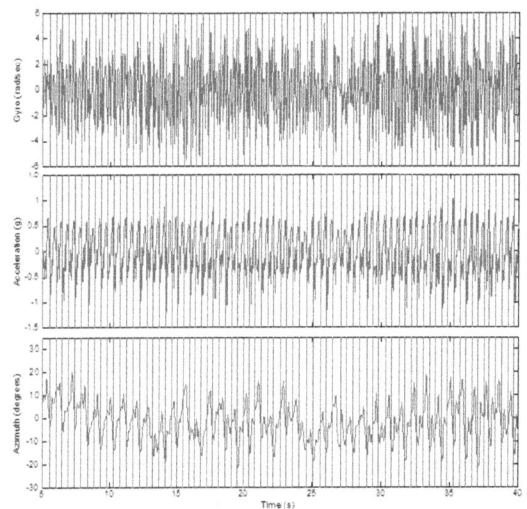

(c) Participant P6 using a guide dog

Figure 4. Time series of measurements from accelerometer, gyroscope, and azimuth. The magenta and green vertical lines mark the left and right foot strikes.

3.3.2 Smartphone Placements

Each participant was asked to choose a comfortable location for the two smartphones used in order to take inertial measurements during the trials. Preferences varied: sometimes a smartphone was placed in the front or back pants pocket, while in other cases it was placed in a holster clipped to the participant's belt, in a jacket pocket at waist or breast height, or tucked under the participant's shirt at shoulder level. Tab. 1 shows the different placements for our blind participants. Informal surveys (e.g., [19]) have shown that the majority of people keep their phone in their pocket, and for this reason we didn't consider placement of the smartphones in the participants' handbag or backpack. In addition, step counting with smartphone in a handbag was shown to be inaccurate [5] due to extra swinging of the bag. We also didn't consider the case of a smartphone held in one's hand while walking, as this may be inconvenient for blind people who already have one hand occupied holding a cane or a guide dog.

3.3.3 Procedure

After signing the IRB-approved consent form, each participant was shown the CPRO sensors in their clip cases, and asked to clip each sensor case to the back, if possible, or to the side of their shoe (see Fig. 2). (Note that participants were advised in advance of their visit to wear comfortable shoes, and to wear clothing with pockets.) Then, the participant was asked to position the two smartphones, as discussed in Sec. 3.3.2. Participants were advised not to pay attention to any speech produced by the smartphones (which were programmed to utter short synthetic speech verification sentences upon successful pairing with the control phone). Participants were also advised to begin walking when prompted by an experimenter, and to walk straight until asked by the experimenter to turn left or right (or, in the case of path T5, to turn around), to push or pull open a door, or to stop at the end of the path. These were the only verbal directions provided to the participants, except for occasional safety warnings (e.g., as mentioned earlier, participants were advised to walk closer to one side of a corridor if there were obstacles on the other side).

Figure 5. Four of our blind participants dealing with specific situations. Top two images: being caught in a wall opening. Bottom left: pushing open a door. Bottom right: avoiding an obstacle (a ladder) in the way.

No training on the use of the system was necessary, since the task was for the participants to simply walk naturally. Each participant first went through the pre-trial described in Sec. 3.1.2 for ground truth calibration. Then, he or she was accompanied to the start position of the first path, and asked to start walking in the designated direction. Before the start of each path, participants were oriented to face the correct direction; this was particularly important for paths T2, T5 and T6, which started with diagonal traversal of an entrance or elevator hall. All trials with blind participants were supervised by two experimenters. One of the experimenters managed the start and end of data collection from all sensor platforms via the control phone, and recorded videos of all sessions by means of a GoPro HERO Session camera attached to a head strap. The other experimenter walked at a close distance behind or sometimes in front of the participant, and was in charge of ensuring the participant's safety.

Fig. 4 shows an example of time series collected during a straight path in route T3 for three individuals: a sighted participant, a blind participant using the long cane, and a blind participant using a guide dog. For the accelerometer and the gyroscope sensors, the first and second subfigures plot a linear combination of the time series from the three axes, corresponding to the principal component. The azimuth data (angle around the vertical) was obtained from the iOS CoreMotion Framework, and is defined with respect to an arbitrary horizontal axis. (Note that the magnetometer is not used for this purpose, as we found that it decreases the quality of the azimuth in indoor environments.) The plots also display the heel strikes times (shown by vertical lines) for each foot. Observation of the azimuth time series provides some insight into the gait characteristics of each individual. In particular, the sighted walker maintained a steady heading direction (with oscillation due to natural body swinging). The azimuth time series of the blind walker with a cane shows a more variable pattern, with variation in heading direction as large as 20 degrees. The blind participant using a guide dog maintained a more stable heading direction, but with a wider swinging action.

3.4 Data Annotation

After completion of all trials for a participant, the data from all sensors was offloaded to a desktop computer for post-processing. In particular, all data streams were synchronized as discussed in Sec. 3.1.1. The video streams collected from the GoPro camera were also synchronized to the same time base used for the sensors. The heel strikes times for each foot (computed by the CPRO sensors, Sec. 3.1.1) were recorded.

The time lapse during traversal of a route was divided (by visual inspection of the video) into contiguous intervals, where each interval corresponds to either a straight segment in the path, or to a "turn" event. For example, traversal of route T1 (shown in Fig.1) was divided into seven contiguous time intervals, corresponding to four straight patches interleaved with three 90 degrees turns. The cardinal direction of each straight path, or of the paths joined by a turn, was recorded in the annotation file, together with the start and end time of each interval, and with the number of steps taken during the interval. In addition to the segmentation into straight paths and turns, we created annotations of particular events such as opening a door, bumping into an obstacle, being caught in a door opening, or stopping momentarily (see Fig. 5). These events are normally associated with anomalous characteristics in otherwise regular inertial data time series (see Figs. 6–8). Also note from these figures that when participants are engaged in tasks such as opening a door, the shoe-mounted

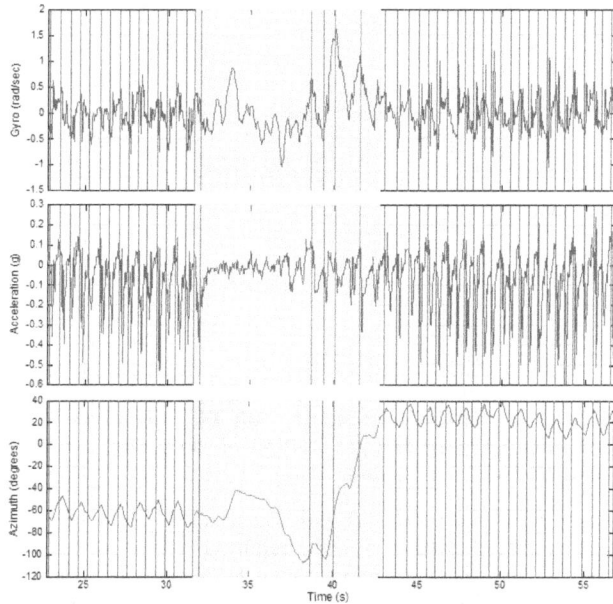

Figure 6. Sensor data from a participant pulling a door open then making a left turn.

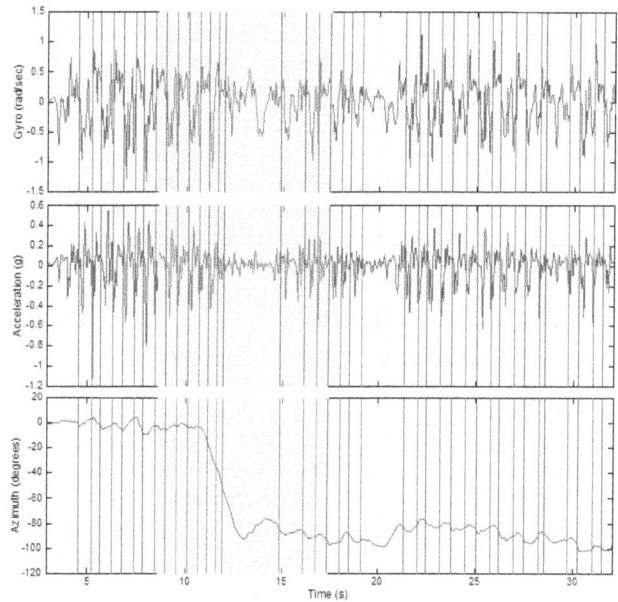

Figure 7. Sensor data from a participant making a right turn then pushing a door open.

sensors sometimes detected "phantom steps" when in fact the participants were simply balancing themselves on their feet. We did not manually remove these phantom steps, as they occurred only sporadically in our study. All of the data was annotated by one experimenter and independently checked and verified by another experimenter. The annotation file, which is stored using the Extensible Markup Language (XML) format, also includes other relevant information such as the type of mobility tool used, as well as some general gait pattern observations.

4. DERIVED DATA EXAMPLES

In this section, we show some simple examples of the different types of analysis that can be carried out on the inertial data in WeAllWalk. These examples are not meant to test specific hypotheses, but simply to highlight the richness of the data in our data set, and to suggest directions for future research.

4.1 Step Counting

After experimenting with several of the algorithms mentioned in Sec. 2.2, we found that the best step detection results for our data were produced by the AMPD technique of Scholkmann et al. [34]. This algorithm was used to process the magnitude of the acceleration, and finds the peaks associated with heel strikes by detecting local maxima. We used a Savitzky-Golay filter [33] to smooth the accelerometer magnitude before computing the local maxima. We then compared the step detections (computed on the data from the iPhones) with the ground truth data from the foot-mounted sensors. Rather than simply counting the total number of steps in a certain path, we used a more conservative metric, defined as following. Given the interval T between two consecutive ground truth heel strike times, and the number n of steps detected within this interval, we declare an *undercount event* if $n = 0$ (no steps detected within interval T) and number $n - 1$ of *overcount events* if $n > 1$ (more than one step detected within T). We then report errors in terms of rates of undercount and overcount events. Fig. 9 shows step counting errors computed over the whole set of trajectories for sighted participants, blind participants using a cane, and blind participants using a guide dog.

Note that the same algorithm (with the same parameters) was used for all participants. This data seems to suggest that larger errors are obtained with this algorithm for blind walkers; a thorough statistical analysis to evaluate this hypothesis is planned as future work.

4.2 Turn Detection

An indoor route can often be expressed in terms of a sequence of turns, along with the number of steps taken in the path between two consecutive turns. For example, one may specify a route as: "Walk straight through this corridor for about 50 steps, then make a left at the junction, walk for 20 more steps and take a right at the first corridor." Note that for most buildings, corridors intersect at angles of 90 or, in some cases, 45 degrees. Robust detection of turns from inertial data from a smartphone, combined with step

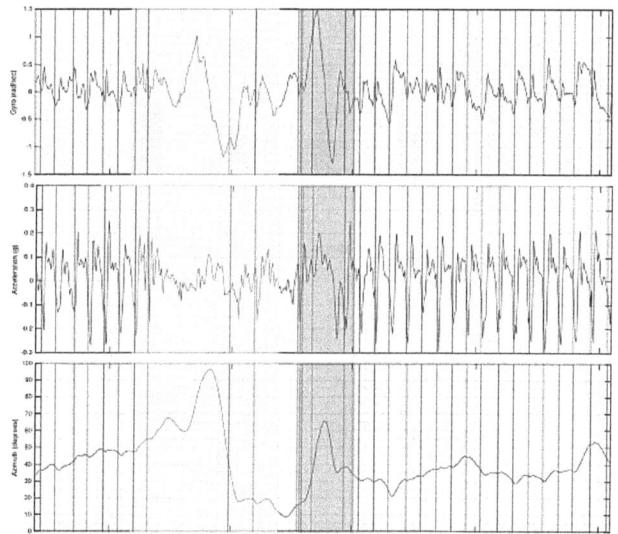

Figure 8. Sensor data from a participant being caught in a door opening (yellow area) then hitting her arm against the wall (magenta area).

147

counts between turns, may help blind travelers keep track of their progress in an indoor route. If a walker at some point feels lost, he or she may be able to return to the starting point (e.g., an entrance door) by simply following the sequence of recorded turns in reverse order.

Turn detection can be achieved by analyzing azimuth data, which represents the walker's heading direction. However, care must be taken in the case of wide swinging or veering during walking, which may trigger false turn detection. In addition, drift in the measured azimuth may accumulate during a long path, which may complicate the job of algorithms that detect turns by simply thresholding the heading direction.

An algorithm for robust turn detection based on a hidden Markov model (HMM) was introduced by Flores et al. [11]. This algorithm was shown to be resilient to drift. It can be designed to detect turns of 45 or of 90 degrees; in the case of 45 degrees turn detection, consecutive detected turns within a short time interval are "clustered" together to form a 90 degree turn.

We show results of turn detection based on azimuth data using this algorithm in Figs. 10 and 11 for two different routes (T4 and T5) and for two different individuals: a sighted participant, and a blind participant using a long cane. The system was set to detect turns of 90 degrees in the first case, and turns of multiples of 45 degrees in the second case (note that T5 begins with a 45 degree turns). As noted earlier, the heading direction for the blind participants tend to be less steady than for sighted walkers, which may complicate the job of the turn detector and, as in the case of these examples, result in occasional false positives.

5. CONCLUSIONS

We have introduced a new data set with inertial sensor time series collected from blind walkers. Our participants walked through fairly long and complex routes; on their way, they sometimes had

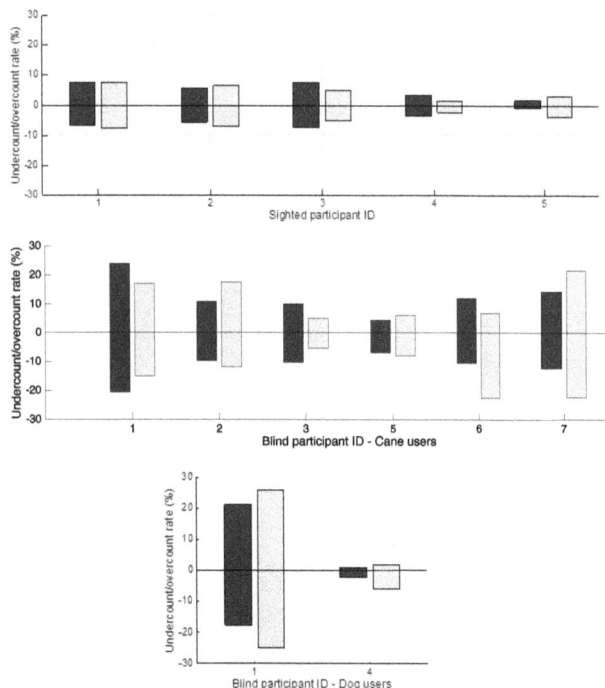

Figure 9. Step over count rate (positive bars) and undercount rate (negative bars) for sighted participants, blind participants using a long cane, and blind participants using a guide dog.

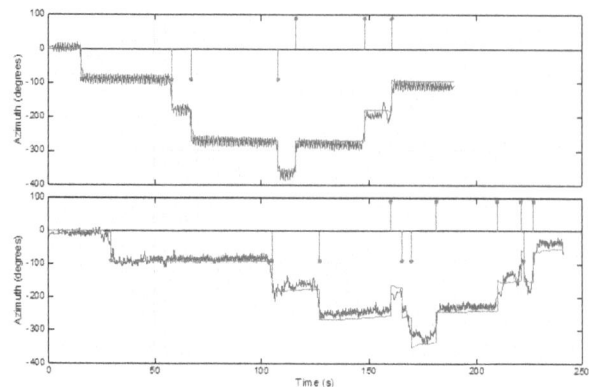

Figure 10. Azimuth time series for a sighted (top) and a blind participant (bottom) walking on Path T4. Pink stems: turn angles (left or right) that are multiple of 90 degrees. Red line: estimated heading direction.

to open doors and avoid obstacles. The data has been subdivided into straight paths and turns, and carefully annotated, with special events (such as bumping into an obstacle) individually identified and marked. Simple examples of applications such as step counting and turn detection have been presented, which highlight some of the peculiar characteristics of blind ambulation as measured by these sensors.

While we believe that this data can be useful to several researchers who are interested in personal mobility, we are also aware of some of its shortcomings. For example, although our participants were asked to walk naturally, they didn't have to find their way independently (as they were instructed when to turn). Participants may also have felt self-aware, as they were being followed and observed, and thus may not have been fully natural (for example, they may have put extra effort to avoid obstacles). All of our routes were indoors, and thus our data is not representative of outdoor ambulation. As one of our participants explained, some blind travelers pay attention to different things when walking indoors and outdoors. For example, when walking indoors, they may be careful to avoid obstacles such as a door left ajar; while walking outdoors, typical concerns include the condition of the pavement, and the possibility of a hole or a curb.

6. ACKNOWLEDGMENTS

Research supported by a Seed Grant from CITRIS, the Center for Information Technology Research in the Interest of Society.

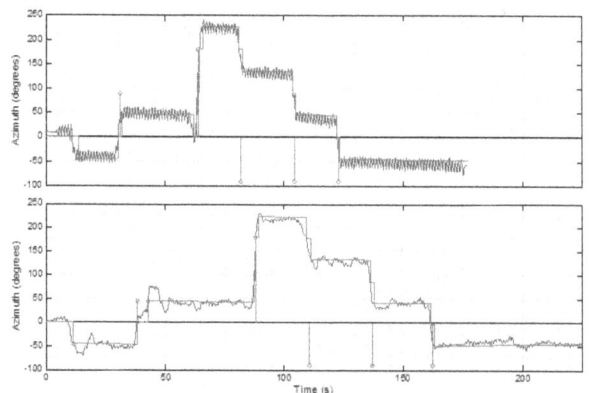

Figure 11. Azimuth time series for a sighted (top) and a blind participant (bottom) walking on Path T5. Red stems: turn angles (left or right) that are multiple of 45 degrees. Pink line: estimated heading direction.

7. REFERENCES

[1] Alzantot, M., & Youssef, M. (2012, April). UPTIME: Ubiquitous pedestrian tracking using mobile phones. In Wireless Communications and Networking Conference (WCNC), 2012 IEEE (pp. 3204-3209). IEEE.

[2] Angermann, M., Robertson, P., Kemptner, T., & Khide, M. (2010, September). A high precision reference data set for pedestrian navigation using foot-mounted inertial sensors. In Indoor Positioning and Indoor Navigation (IPIN), 2010 International Conference on (pp. 1-6). IEEE.

[3] Apostolopoulos, I., Coming, D. S., & Folmer, E. (2015, April). Accuracy of pedometry on a head-mounted display. In Proceedings of the 33rd Annual ACM Conference on Human Factors in Computing Systems (pp. 2153-2156). ACM.

[4] Blasch, B. B., LaGrow, S. J., & De l'Aune, W. R. (1996). Three aspects of coverage provided by the long cane: Object, surface, and foot-placement preview. Journal of Visual Impairment and Blindness, 90, 295-301.

[5] Brajdic, A., & Harle, R. (2013, September). Walk detection and step counting on unconstrained smartphones. In Proceedings of the 2013 ACM international joint conference on Pervasive and ubiquitous computing (pp. 225-234). ACM. Data set available at www.cl.cam.ac.uk/~ab818/ubicomp2013.html

[6] Chen, D., Feng, W., Zhao, Q., Hu, M., & Wang, T. (2012). An infrastructure-free indoor navigation system for blind people. Intelligent Robotics and Applications, 552-561.

[7] Coughlan, J., Manduchi, R., & Shen, H. (2006, May). Cell phone-based wayfinding for the visually impaired. In 1st International Workshop on Mobile Vision.

[8] Dias, M. B., Steinfeld, A., & Dias, M. B. (2015). Future directions in indoor navigation technology for blind travelers. In Hassan A. Karimi (Ed.), Indoor Wayfinding and Navigation, CRC Press.

[9] Fallah, N., Apostolopoulos, I., Bekris, K., & Folmer, E. (2012, May). The user as a sensor: navigating users with visual impairments in indoor spaces using tactile landmarks. In Proceedings of the SIGCHI Conference on Human Factors in Computing Systems (pp. 425-432). ACM.

[10] Fallah, N., Apostolopoulos, I., Bekris, K., & Folmer, E. (2013). Indoor human navigation systems: A survey. Interacting with Computers.

[11] Flores, G. H., Manduchi, R., & Zenteno, E. D. (2014, November). Ariadne's thread: Robust turn detection for path back-tracing using the iPhone. In Ubiquitous Positioning Indoor Navigation and Location Based Service (UPINLBS), 2014 (pp. 133-140). IEEE.

[12] Flores, J. Z., & Farcy, R. (2014). Indoor navigation system for the visually impaired using one inertial measurement unit (IMU) and barometer to guide in the subway stations and commercial centers. In Computers Helping People with Special Needs (pp. 411-418). Springer International Publishing.

[13] Foster, R. C., Lanningham-Foster, L. M., Manohar, C., McCrady, S. K., Nysse, L. J., Kaufman, K. R., ... & Levine, J. A. (2005). Precision and accuracy of an ankle-worn accelerometer-based pedometer in step counting and energy expenditure. Preventive medicine, 41(3), 778-783.

[14] Graser, S. V., Vincent, W. J., & Pangrazi, R. P. (2007). Effects of placement, attachment, and weight classification on pedometer accuracy. J Phys Act Health 4, 359–69.

[15] Horvat, M., Ray, C., Ramsey, V. K., Miszko, T., Keeney, R., & Blasch, B. B. (2003). Compensatory analysis and strategies for balance in individuals with visual impairments. Journal of Visual Impairment and Blindness, 97(11), 695-703.

[16] Hub, A. (2008, July). Precise indoor and outdoor navigation for the blind and visually impaired using augmented maps and the TANIA system. In Proceedings of the 9th International Conference on Low Vision (pp. 2-5).

[17] International Conference on Indoor Positioning and Indoor Navigation (IPIN). ipin-conference.org

[18] International Conference on Ubiquitous Positioning, Indoor Navigation and Location-Based Services (UPINLBS). upinlbs.sjtu.edu.cn

[19] Jackson, R. (2013). In what pocket do you keep your phone? http://phandroid.com/2013/03/25/in-what-pocket-do-you-keep-your-phone-poll/

[20] Jayalath, S., Abhayasinghe, N., & Murray, I. (2013, October). A gyroscope based accurate pedometer algorithm. In International Conference on Indoor Positioning and Indoor Navigation (Vol. 28, p. 31st).

[21] Kalia, A. A., Legge, G. E., Roy, R., & Ogale, A. (2010). Assessment of indoor route-finding technology for people with visual impairment. Journal of visual impairment & blindness, 104(3), 135.

[22] Košecká, J., Zhou, L., Barber, P., & Duric, Z. (2003, June). Qualitative image based localization in indoors environments. In Computer Vision and Pattern Recognition, 2003. Proceedings. 2003 IEEE Computer Society Conference on (Vol. 2, pp. II-3). IEEE.

[23] Ladetto, Q., & Merminod, B. (2002). In step with INS: Navigation for the blind, tracking emergency crews. Gps World, 13(10).

[24] Mannini, A., & Sabatini, A. M. (2011, August). A hidden Markov model-based technique for gait segmentation using a foot-mounted gyroscope. In Engineering in Medicine and Biology Society, EMBC, 2011 Annual International Conference of the IEEE (pp. 4369-4373). IEEE.

[25] Marschollek, M., Goevercin, M., Wolf, K. H., Song, B., Gietzelt, M., Haux, R., & Steinhagen-Thiessen, E. (2008, August). A performance comparison of accelerometry-based step detection algorithms on a large, non-laboratory sample of healthy and mobility-impaired persons. In Engineering in Medicine and Biology Society, 2008. EMBS 2008. 30th Annual International Conference of the IEEE (pp. 1319-1322). IEEE.

[26] Mason, S. J., Legge, G. E., & Kallie, C. S. (2005). Variability in the length and frequency of steps of sighted and visually impaired walkers. Journal of visual impairment & blindness, 99(12), 741.

[27] Murphy Kelly, S. (2014). San Francisco Airport Tests Beacon Sensors to Guide Blind Travelers. http://mashable.com/2014/07/31/san-francisco-airport-beacons/

[28] Nakamura, K., Aono, Y., & Tadokoro, Y. (1997). A walking navigation system for the blind. Systems and computers in Japan, 28(13), 36-45.

[29] Ngo, T. T., Makihara, Y., Nagahara, H., Mukaigawa, Y., & Yagi, Y. (2014). The largest inertial sensor-based gait database and performance evaluation of gait-based personal authentication. Pattern Recognition, 47(1), 228-237. Data set available at www.am.sanken.osaka-u.ac.jp/BiometricDB/

[30] Pressl, B., & Wieser, M. (2006). A computer-based navigation system tailored to the needs of blind people. In Computers Helping People with Special Needs (pp. 1280-1286). Springer Berlin Heidelberg.

[31] Riehle, T. H., Anderson, S. M., Lichter, P. A., Whalen, W. E., & Giudice, N. A. (2013, July). Indoor inertial waypoint navigation for the blind. In Engineering in Medicine and Biology Society (EMBC), 2013 35th Annual International Conference of the IEEE (pp. 5187-5190). IEEE.

[32] Sabatini, A. M., Martelloni, C., Scapellato, S., & Cavallo, F. (2005). Assessment of walking features from foot inertial sensing. Biomedical Engineering, IEEE Transactions on, 52(3), 486-494.

[33] Schafer, R. W. (2011). What is a Savitzky-Golay filter?[lecture notes]. Signal Processing Magazine, IEEE, 28(4), 111-117.

[34] Scholkmann, F., Boss, J., & Wolf, M. (2012). An efficient algorithm for automatic peak detection in noisy periodic and quasi-periodic signals. Algorithms, 5(4), 588-603.

[35] Yang, Z., Wu, C., Zhou, Z., Zhang, X., Wang, X., & Liu, Y. (2015). Mobility increases localizability: A survey on wireless indoor localization using inertial sensors. ACM Computing Surveys (CSUR), 47(3), 54.

[36] Yang, C. C., & Hsu, Y. L. (2010). A review of accelerometry-based wearable motion detectors for physical activity monitoring. Sensors, 10(8), 7772-7788.

[37] Yang, Z., Wu, C., & Liu, Y. (2012, August). Locating in fingerprint space: wireless indoor localization with little human intervention. In Proceedings of the 18th annual international conference on Mobile computing and networking (pp. 269-280). ACM.

[38] Yoneyama, M., Kurihara, Y., Watanabe, K., & Mitoma, H. (2014). Accelerometry-based gait analysis and its application to Parkinson's disease assessment—Part 1: Detection of stride event. Neural Systems and Rehabilitation Engineering, IEEE Transactions on, 22(3), 613-622.

Supporting Orientation of People with Visual Impairment: Analysis of Large Scale Usage Data

Hernisa Kacorri
Carnegie Mellon University
hkacorri@cmu.edu

Sergio Mascetti
Università degli Studi di Milano
and EveryWare Technologies
sergio.mascetti@unimi.it

Andrea Gerino
Università degli Studi di Milano
and EveryWare Technologies
andrea.gerino@unimi.it

Dragan Ahmetovic
Carnegie Mellon University
dragan1@cmu.edu

Hironobu Takagi
IBM
takagih@jp.ibm.com

Chieko Asakawa
Carnegie Mellon University
chiekoa@cs.cmu.edu

ABSTRACT

In the field of assistive technology, large scale user studies are hindered by the fact that potential participants are geographically sparse and longitudinal studies are often time consuming. In this contribution, we rely on remote usage data to perform large scale and long duration behavior analysis on users of iMove, a mobile app that supports the orientation of people with visual impairments.

Exploratory analysis highlights popular functions, common configuration settings, and usage patterns among iMove users. The study shows stark differences between users accessing the app through VoiceOver and other users, who tend to use the app more scarcely and sporadically. Analysis through clustering of VoiceOver iMove user interactions discovers four distinct user groups: 1) users interested in surrounding points of interest, 2) users keeping the app active for long sessions while in movement, 3) users interacting in short bursts to inquire about current location, and 4) users querying in bursts about surrounding points of interest and addresses.

Our analysis provides insights into iMove's user base and can inform decisions for tailoring the app to diverse user groups, developing future improvements of the software, or guiding the design process of similar assistive tools.

CCS Concepts

•Human-centered computing → Accessibility design and evaluation methods; •Computing methodologies → Cluster analysis; •Social and professional topics → People with disabilities;

1. INTRODUCTION

Nonvisual understanding of the environment is far more ineffective and inefficient as well as potentially dangerous than scanning the surroundings by sight [3]. In fact, orientation, a person's awareness of position and heading in the environment [10, 23], is a challenge for people with severe visual impairment and the main difficulties derive from the inability to efficiently obtain a mental map of the surrounding area while moving. To address this problem, many researchers and developers of assistive technology, surveyed in [10, 11], have explored technological approaches such as laser canes, sonar devices, and GPS navigation tools.

The design of these technological solutions is typically guided by supervised experiments with few participants, such as formative studies (e.g. [26]), Wizard-of-Oz experiments (e.g. [8]), and evaluation studies (e.g. [17]). These approaches may be attractive for the advantages they offer. Researchers can conduct experiments with prototype applications, or in some cases, even prototypes without working software. They can also conduct such experiments in controlled situations and with users whose characteristics (e.g., form of disability, age) are known in advance. However, these approaches are also limited in many ways. First, it is not possible to explore many real world scenarios. Second, these studies generally involve participants that live in close proximity to the physical location where the experiment is conducted, leading to the possibility of cultural bias. Third, these experiments are susceptible to the Hawthorne effect [1], where users may act differently when they know they are being watched. Finally, and most important, these approaches are not scalable both in terms of number of involved subjects and length of the study as stressed in [10].

We are interested in advancing state-of-the-art technologies for supporting orientation and mobility of people with visual impairment. For these applications, we want to study the following questions. Which are the most frequently used functionalities? What are the most common user interaction patterns? Can users be grouped based on their interaction patterns? How do users benefit from these applications? Being able to answer these questions makes it possible not only to improve existing applications but also to guide the design of similar applications supporting outdoor mobility (e.g., [15, 14]) as well as indoor navigation (e.g. [2] among others).

To answer these questions, we analyze large scale usage data remotely collected from iMove[1], a GPS-based mobile application that supports outdoor orientation of people with

ASSETS '16, October 23-26, 2016, Reno, NV, USA

© 2016 ACM. ISBN 978-1-4503-4124-0/16/10...$15.00

DOI: http://dx.doi.org/10.1145/2982142.2982178

---

[1]https://itunes.apple.com/us/app/imove/id593874954

visual impairments. The app provides information about nearby "landmarks" that help the user construct a mental map of their environment.

Our analysis is conducted both with inferential and exploratory methods using statistical tools. We also employ machine learning tools for unsupervised discovery of user clusters based on common interaction patterns. To the best of our knowledge, this is the first study adopting this methodology in the field of mobility of people with visual impairments.

Specifically this paper presents three main contributions:

- First, the analysis highlights a number of usage properties of *i*Move, including commonly used functions and preferences for applications settings. We examine the differences both in application use and preferred settings across screen-reader users and other users. We also discover clusters of users based on common interaction patterns and identify features that are primarily responsible for cluster formation. The proposed feature space is intuitive enough to interpret the meaning of the clusters.

- Second, we describe our collected dataset and release it for use by other researchers.

- Third, the analysis methodology proposed in this contribution may be adapted to the study of other applications in the field of assistive technologies.

2. RELATED WORK

Understanding user behavior during interactions with a software application is of paramount importance for evaluating the application's effectiveness, for guiding the iterative design process, and for informing the design of similar applications. However, there are inherent challenges in conducting behavioral studies both over long periods and with large samples of participants with disability. Thus, fewer contributions in the field of assistive technologies adopt methodologies involving analysis of collected real-world usage data and often, their participants' demographics are known a priori or collected through questionnaires. To name a few, [4] automatically collected user actions during web browsing to assess the accessibility of web pages by visually impaired users. Usage log analysis is also performed in [18] to evaluate the localization error of a navigation assistance tool using Video Light Communication (VLC) for guiding people with visual impairments. In [12], log data from real-world tasks over a long period were used to build predictive models in distinguishing users by pointing performance. Last, in [22], behavior anomalies perceived during user interaction with a sensor-enabled smart home environment act as a diagnostic tool for detecting mild cognitive impairments in senior patients.

In the broader field of human computer interaction, where the pool of participants tend to be much larger, it is more feasible for the researchers to perform behavior analysis on large scale datasets available to the research community (e.g. [7, 9, 13, 20]). These analyses often combine data-driven approaches from many fields such as classification, clustering, and time-series analysis from machine learning, sentiment analysis from natural language processing, and community detection from network analysis. The work of Wang et al.,

2016 [25] is the closest to our analysis. The authors applied natural language processing techniques to detect similarity among Facebook social network users. Specifically, they analyzed "clickstreams", timed sequences of interactions with website, and performed hierarchical clustering on users' clickstream to identify common user profiles (e.g., those who like others' pages and those who update their status often).

Prior work in cognitive science related to spacial representation and navigation in people with visual impairments [24, 23] discuss limitations in user studies which compare orientation and mobility performance among sighted, early blind, and late blind participants. Their discussion on adopted and preferred navigation strategies among these users made us wonder whether similarities in these strategies also lead to similarities across user interaction with supportive orientation and navigation technologies. Motivated by this question, we investigate approaches, similar to Wang et al. [25], that automatically discover user clusters based on streams of interactions with *i*Move. However, the link between these clusters and underlying user-adopted navigation strategies is beyond the scope of this paper.

3. *i*Move APP AND DATASET

*i*Move is an iOS application that is accessible through VoiceOver screen reader and magnifier. The app informs users about outdoor geo-referenced information such as current address, nearby Points Of Interest (POIs), and *geonotes* i.e., user-defined notes associated to a geographical location. Users can access this information either explicitly, e.g., ask for current address in the root screen (Fig. 1(a)) and list of nearby POIs (Fig. 1(b)), or periodically while in motion by turning on the "Notify me" toggle button in the root screen. The frequency of such periodic updates can be tuned both in terms of time and proximity (i.e., a minimum temporal/spatial distance between two readings). Geo-notes can be created and edited as audio recordings or text entries (Fig. 1(c)) and they are organized into "routes" (Fig. 1(d)).

*i*Move is designed to be highly customizable: users can specify the categories of POIs they are interested in, activate automatic readings of surrounding information, and modify settings related to system verbosity. Therefore, beyond user visited screens, actions, and received notification, we also collect data related to their settings modifications.

3.1 Remote Logging System

Since *i*Move version 2.0, released on December 8, 2015, the application implements a remote logging system that makes it possible to collect anonymous app usage information. Logging is supported by a client library within *i*Move communicating with a REST server and a non-relational database back-end.

A detailed description of the released dataset is available online[2]. Data was collected in compliance with European regulations[3] and user logs were recorded in anonymized form. Thus, the dataset does not include location-related information, e.g. POI, or user-generated content, e.g. geo-

---

[2] http://webmind.di.unimi.it/assetsim16/

[3] Directive 95/46/EC of the European Parliament and of the Council of 24 October 1995 on the protection of individuals with regard to the processing of personal data and on the free movement of such data, OJ L 281, 23.11.1995, 31-50.

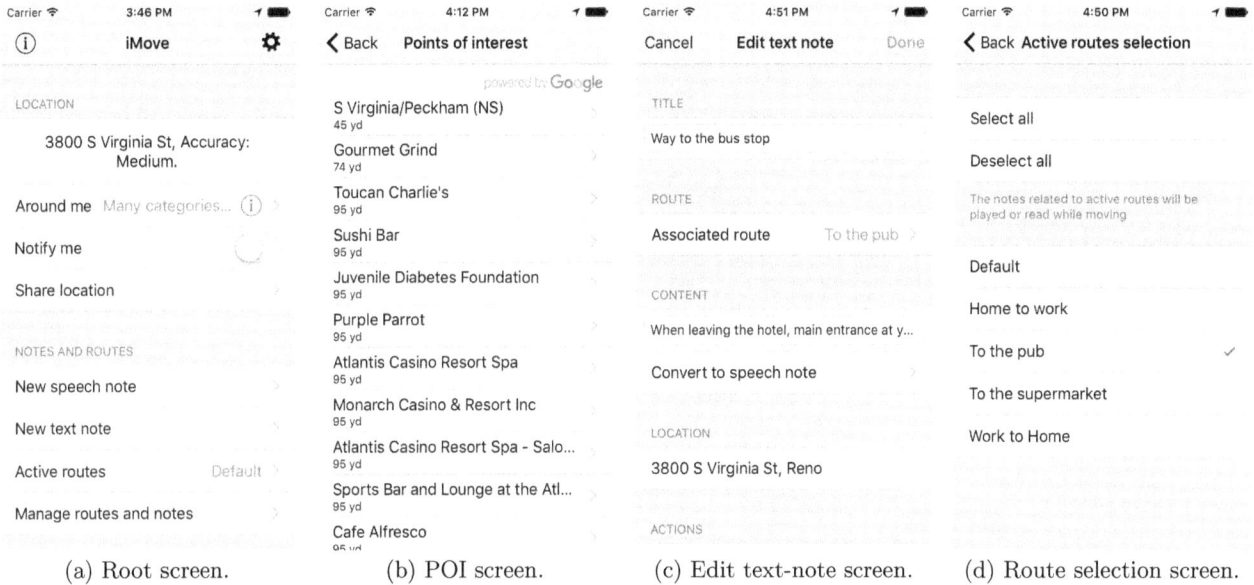

| (a) Root screen. | (b) POI screen. | (c) Edit text-note screen. | (d) Route selection screen. |

Figure 1: Main screens of the iMove application.

notes. To reconstruct user-interaction history, each log includes a unique pseudo-identifier associated with an anonymized user.

Each log record has two main components. The first component contains data about the user and the device on which iMove is running: the user's pseudo-identifier, the device model, the system language, whether VoiceOver is enabled or not, the application version (we collected data for build versions 31 and 32) and log creation timestamps in the user's time zone, UTC, and the server time.

The second component contains the application usage data. In iMove, we partition log entries into four different categories of usage data:

Screen logs capture user navigation between iMove screens. Each screen log records the screen name and an "enter" or "exit" label when a user enters or exits a screen.

Action logs record iMove function activation by a user such as recording a new speech note.

Notification logs are generated when the application automatically provides information to the user (e.g. when the user gets close to a POI).

Preference logs are generated every time a user changes iMove settings. A preference log lists the name of the modified parameter, its old value, and its new value.

3.2 iMove Dataset Overview

The iMove dataset was collected during the December 2015 - April 2016 period and contains a total of 771,975 log records across 17,624 unique user pseudo-identifiers ($\mu = 43.8, \sigma = 105.15$) log records per user with range 1 - 7,299. From the feedback we received by email and on the app-store, we realized that a number of users, who we call "incidental" users, installed the application without realizing its functionality and its intended use for people with visual impairments. For example, some users confused iMove with iMovie, a popular application for video editing.

To filter out these users, we introduce the concept of "interaction session" (or simply, session): a period of time during which a user frequently interacts with the application (e.g., navigates in the screens, performs actions or receives system notifications). A session is extracted from app usage data as a sequence of consecutive log entries such that: i) the sequence begins with a "screenRootEnter" record, which signals that the user opened the main screen of the application, and ii) there is at least a 5 minutes gap between the session starting log and the previous log. This constraint captures the intuition that the user might temporarily exit the app for a short time within an interaction session.

Based on the intuition that users who are uninterested in iMove would not use it for more than one session, we consider only users having two or more sessions. There are a total of 4,055 such users generating a total of 255,004 logs ($\mu = 62.89, \sigma = 211.51$ logs/user with range 2-7,296).

4. ANALYSIS

4.1 iMove Use Properties Across All Users

We analyze log records from all 4,055 users with the goal of highlighting iMove use properties such as commonly used functions and user preferred values for interaction parameters. Using both inferential and exploratory methods we examine four categories of log records: preferences, screen activity, actions, and notifications.

One interesting aspect of iMove is the support of user-defined geo-notes, where users can either record a speech note associated with a location or type it as text. While both options are available, we expect that the former will be the one adopted by the users since the purpose of the app is to support mobility and it is has been observed that typing in mobility is particularly challenging for people with visual impairments [16]. Specifically, we formulate and examine the following hypothesis:

H1: iMove users will favor speech over text for input modality when creating geo-notes.

Results and Interpretation

Preference logs account for 3.41% of the total log records. Figure 2 reports, for each preference setting, its default value and how many times it has been set to a given value. We observe that the parameter "keepUserInformed", which toggles all notifications, was changed far more frequently. This interaction was expected by our intuition that users will frequently toggle off when they do not want to be disturbed by notifications. Anticipating such an interaction during the design of *i*Move, we position the toggle button in the root screen (see Figure 1(a)). Indeed, 22.2% of the users changed this value twice or more, while 20.9% of the users changed it more than once for at least one session.

We also explore log records for other parameters, whose semantics are detailed online[4], to assess the default values provided by *i*Move. This analysis cannot take into account only the values changed by the users. Since all logged changes necessarily involve modification of default values, the logged data does not inform us of how many users intentionally choose to stick with the default value for a given parameter. To estimate this, we compute, for each parameter, the percentage of users that changed the parameter value at least once, among the users that actually visited that parameter's settings screen (values are reported in Figure 2).

For example, only 4% of the users who entered the "Settings_location" screen actually changed the value of the "locationSpatialThreshold" parameter. On the other hand, 22% of the users who entered the System settings page changed the "prevent screen lock" option that by default is set to false. Similarly, 23% of the users changed the preference "sayCity" and more than 16% of the users changed the "saySpeed", "sayHeading" and "sayCourse". These are parameters whose default values are candidates for change in future versions of the app. More generally, we observe the four parameters above are all related to the type of information provided to the user when a location notification occurs. To avoid verbosity in the application, we limited location notifications to the name and number of the street by default. Apparently, many users prefer to have more detailed information.

Screen, Notification, and Action logs account for 66.23%, 29.55%, and 0.76% of the total 255,004 log records, respectively. Figure 3 illustrates the distribution of these records across the subsequent categories. We observe that "Location" is the most common notification followed by "POI" and the two geo-notes. Interestingly, the "NavigateToPOI" function, suggested by many users and introduced with app build 31, is the most frequent user action. Geo-notes notifications ("SpeechNote" and "TextNote") are less frequent than "Location" and "POI" notifications, accounting for 3% of the total notifications. This is due to the fact that 83% of the users never created a geo-note. Among users creating a geo-note, the percentage of geo-note notifications is 10% of the total notifications.

Figure 4 shows the distributions of per-user screen, action, and notification logs related to speech and text geo-notes (box indicates quartiles, center-line indicates median, square symbol indicates mean, whiskers indicate 1.5 inter-quartile ranges, and crosses indicate outliers). In *support of hypothesis H1*, there is a significant difference between the pairs of

---

[4]*i*Move parameter semantics is detailed in http://webmind.di.unimi.it/assetsim16/#param_semantics.

these graphs determined by Mann-Whitney U test. Specifically, users visit the "NewSpeechNote" screen significantly more times than the "NewTextNote" screen ($p < 0.001$) and perform significantly more "SavedNewSpeechNote" actions than "SavedNewTextNote" actions ($p < 0.05$). Not surprisingly, users receive significanlty more "SpeechNote" notifications than "TextNote" notifications ($p < 0.05$).

4.2 Voiceover-Based User Comparison

As mentioned in Section 3.1 for each log record we collect the VoiceOver field, which reports whether VoiceOver was active when the record was generated. This field is particularly relevant for our analysis as it allows us to distinguish users that are likely to have severe visual impairments. Therefore, we partitioned the *i*Move users into two groups: VO-group users (VO-users) have at least one VoiceOver-active record and NVO-group users (NVO-users), have no VoiceOver-active records.

We formulate and examine the following hypotheses:

H2: VO-users will have different settings preferences than NVO-users.

H3: VO-users will make more intense use of *i*Move as measured by the number of actions and notifications as well as the span of days using the app.

Results and Interpretation

VO-group consists of $1,025$ users whereas NVO-group includes the rest $3,030$ users. We observe that while VO-group includes a smaller percentage of the overall *i*Move users (25.28%), the number of records generated by this group accounts for more than half of the logs (56.34%) along with a higher mean records per user ($\mu = 140.16, \sigma = 403.91$) than the NVO-group ($\mu = 36.74, \sigma = 45.05$). We also observe a small positive correlation in our dataset between the number of records for a user and the percentage of records with activated VoiceOver for the same user.

Users in VO-group generated logs with a high mean percentage of active-VoiceOver records ($1\%-100\%, \mu = 95.26\%, \sigma = 16.6\%$). This suggests that, while by definition a user in VO-group can only have one record with VoiceOver-active, in practice users in VO-group have VoiceOver activated almost all the time during use of *i*Move. We suspect that users in VO-group are mostly people with severe visual impairments and a few users with low vision that sporadically activate VoiceOver while users in NVO-group either use magnifier in their interaction with the app or are non visually impaired ("incidental" users, see Section 3.2).

Figure 5 illustrates side-by-side the distribution of threshold preference from both groups. In *support of hypothesis H2*, we find that users in VO-group set smaller temporal and spatial threshold values determined by Mann-Whitney U test (p<0.05). Even though different threshold parameters have different semantics, smaller temporal values result in more frequent notifications, while smaller spatial values for "PoiProximity" and "GeoNoteProximity" indicate preference for notification only in close proximity to the target place (POI or geo-note). These findings suggest that users in VO-group prefer to receive information more frequently than users in NVO-group and only in close proximity to the target.

To examine hypothesis H3, we consider the number of notifications and actions, as well as the period of *i*Move use

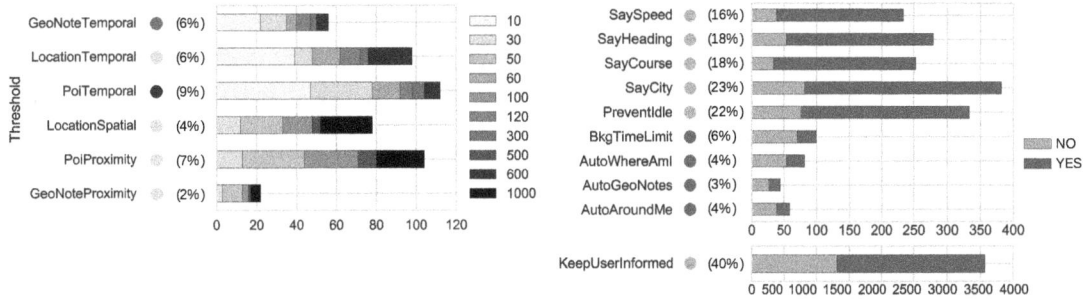

Figure 2: Number of preference records generated from the subset of users that modified the default values. Colored circles indicate preferences' default values, while the percentages represent how many users changed the value at least once, among those who visited the corresponding settings screen.

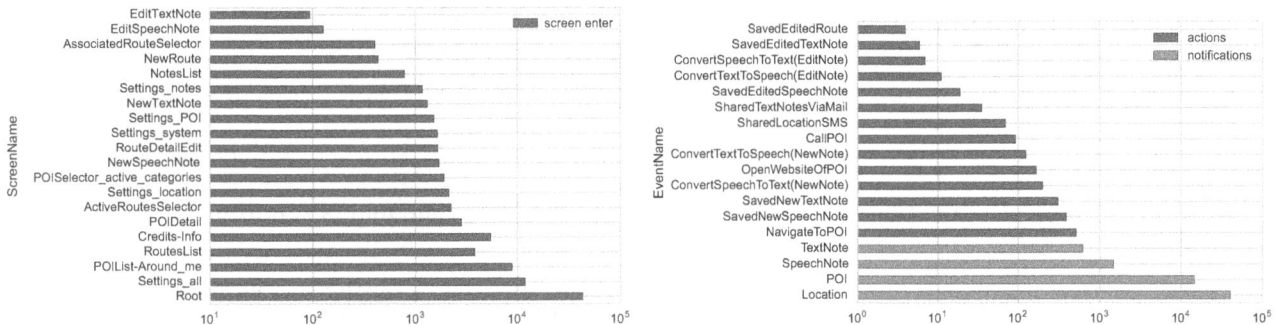

Figure 3: User log records distributed across the screens, actions, and notifications logs.

per user in each group and compare their mean ranks with Mann-Whitney U test. In *support of hypothesis H3*, we find that users in VO-group receive significantly more notifications ($p < 0.001$) such as the "Location" notifications shown in Figure 6(a). Similarly, users in VO-group perform significantly more actions ($p < 0.001$), for example Figure 6(b) shows how the number of times a VO-user asks for directions to navigate to a POI is significantly higher than for a NVO-user. Users in VO-group use the application for a significantly longer period than the NVO-users ($p < 0.0001$), where the period of use is measured as the span of days between the first and last time a user enters the *i*Move root screen. On average, this duration is of 53.95 days for users in VO-group and of 20.45 days for users in NVO-group (as shown in Figure 6(c)).

4.3 User Clustering Based on *i*streams

While the exploratory and inferential analyses in the previous sections reveal interesting patterns, they do not take into account the sequential relationship between the log entries. In order to learn richer patterns of interaction, we use unsupervised learning techniques on record streams, which preserve the temporal structure of the data. We anticipate that users naturally fall into clusters based on common interaction patterns with *i*Move. The automatic discovery of these clusters can help us identify: what are the major interaction categories; which is the most prevalent interaction; and what is the relationship between different types of interactions. This clustering is performed on the $1,025$ users residing in VO-group, who are likely to have severe visual impairments and, as shown above, make intensive use of the application.

Clustering Methodology

As discussed in related work, HCI researchers have adopted prior work in machine learning, natural language processing and network analysis, to better understand user behavior, with the social network analysis in [25] being the closest to our work. Our methodology builds upon previous methods to understand and support assistive orientation of people with visual impairment. One of the inherent challenges in analyzing our data is that users can interact with the app either by actively navigating the screens and using their functions, captured by screen and action logs, or by physically changing their location thus generating notifications logs. We introduce the notion of sessions (defined in Section 3.2) into our feature engineering (described below) to yield more intuitive and high level descriptions for the discovered clusters.

Specifically, we represent each user by the stream of interactions (*i*stream) with the app. We map users to a feature space extracted from these streams, construct a similarity graph by comparing users in this feature space, and identify clusters of similar users by graph partitioning. Finally, we interpret the meaning of the clusters by isolating primary features that are responsible for forming the clusters. To assist future researchers in adopting this methodology for analysis of their data, we describe the above steps, implementation, assumptions, and the hyper-parameters used in our clustering.

Obtaining user *i*stream. We define an *i*stream as a sequence of interactions between the user and *i*Move, extracted from user's log records ordered by timestamp. It captures both the type of the log entry (i.e. screen, action,

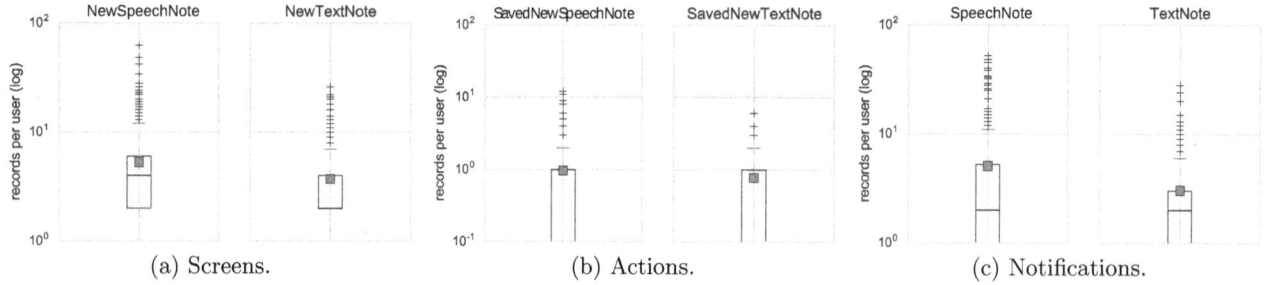

Figure 4: Distribution of log records highlighting differences between speech and text geo-notes logs.

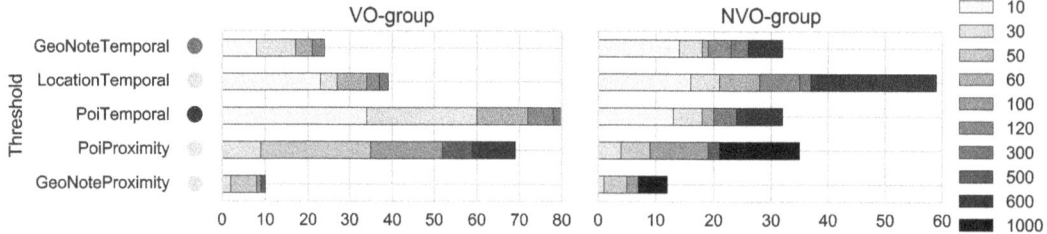

Figure 5: Preference log records across users in VO-group and NVO-group.

or notification) and the magnitude of time gaps between two consecutive log entries. Precise time gap values are omitted if the log entries belong to the same session (defined in Section 3.2) and are represented by the symbol "|" if they denote session boundaries. Figure 7 illustrates an example of this approach for obtaining a discrete user *istream*.

Mapping users to an intuitive feature space. We treat *istreams* as text sentences and adopt n-gram-based text representation, a common practice in natural language processing. We consider three classes of records: screen enters, actions and notifications. Each of these three classes is defined as a set of atomic strings, which are dented by A_s (screen enters), A_a (actions), and A_n (notifications). For example, the string "s-Root" $\in A_s$ represents an entrance in the root screen; "a-navigateToPOI" $\in A_a$ represents the action of getting the navigation instructions to a POI; and "n-Location" $\in A_n$ represents the location notification. We define an *istream* as a sequence $S = (s_1 s_2 ... s_m)$, where $s \in A_s \cup A_a \cup A_n \cup \{|\}$ and m is the total length of the *istream*. We define F_n as the set of all possible n-grams (n consecutive elements) from all the users' *istream* sequences: $F_n = n\text{-gram}(S_1) \cup n\text{-gram}(S_2) \cup ... \cup n\text{-gram}(S_{\#users})$. For each user *istream* we calculate the normalized frequencies of the n-grams in F_n. We experimented with different values of n in the n-gram and chose 5-grams for our analysis, though 4-grams and 3-grams reveal similar clusters. As discussed in [25], intuitively, a larger value of n for the n-gram captures longer subsequences that are unlikely to repeat as a pattern in the *istream*. For the above calculations we use the NLTK platform [5].

Constructing a similarity graph. We create a fully connected graph where each node represents a user and each edge between a pair of users represents the weight based on their pairwise similarity score. To calculate the similarity score between two users, we compute the cosine similarity of their n-gram feature vectors using scikit-learn [21].

Clustering and identifying primary features. We partition the graph into clusters of similar users with com-

munity detection using the Louvain method[5] described in [6]. To interpret cluster meaning, we isolate the primary features responsible for a cluster by performing feature selection based on Chi-square statistics (χ^2) [27]. For each cluster, we build a classifier that distinguishes users belonging to that cluster from the remaining users. Then we select the top k features with the highest discriminating power in separating the two classes using the "SelectKBest" method from scikit-learn [21].

Results and Interpretation

The clustering procedure generates 9 clusters with a modularity of 0.47, where modularity [19] is a widely-used metric to assess the quality of a graph's partition into communities. Loosely speaking, it measures the density of edges inside clusters to edges outside clusters with values in the $[-1, 1]$ range, where a higher value indicates better clustering. Five of the detected clusters contain a total of 6 outlier users which we omit from the following discussion, hence focusing on four clusters with many users. Figure 8 visualizes the resulting clusters and the top 3 features with the highest discriminating power per cluster.

The first cluster (C1) contains 370 users. From the 5 primary features: two indicate that short sessions, in which the user simply opens the application without further interaction, appear with lower normalized frequency for users in C1 than those outside C1; one indicates that long sessions with many consecutive location notifications appear with low frequency as well; last, the remaining two primary features indicate that sessions in which the user navigates *iMove* screens with the list of POIs and their details have higher frequency for users in C1 than the rest. We can infer that users in this cluster often open the application to check the list of nearby POIs and their details.

The second clusters (C2) contains 247 users. From the 5 top features characterizing this cluster, three indicate high

---

[5]Library: http://perso.crans.org/aynaud/communities

156

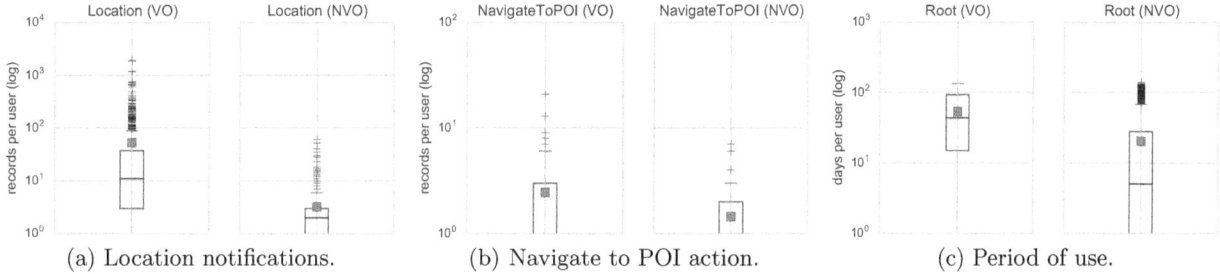

(a) Location notifications. (b) Navigate to POI action. (c) Period of use.

Figure 6: Differences between users in VO-group and NVO-group.

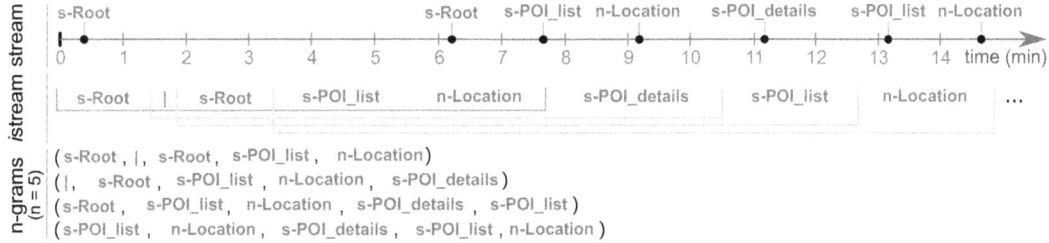

Figure 7: Mapping interaction streams to n-grams.

frequency of location and POI notification sequences in a single session for users in C2; and the remaining two primary features indicate low frequency of "empty" sessions, e.g., "| screenRootEnter | screenRootEnter |". These features suggest that C2 is a set of users running the application for long sessions during which they frequently receive many location and POI notifications.

The third cluster (C3) contains 198 users. In this case four of the 5 primary feature denote high frequencies of short "empty" sessions; and feature points to lower frequency of consecutive location notifications within the same sessions for users in C3 than outside C3. These features suggest that C3 contains users that starts the application, do not wait for any notifications, and then close the application. We speculate C3 users often open iMove simply to read (though VoiceOver) the current address.

The fourth cluster (C4) contains 154 users. All 5 primary features have high frequencies of short sessions with some location and POI notifications. Our interpretation is that these users start iMove and listen to one or two notifications without any further interactions.

To get a confirmation of the semantics we associate to each cluster, and to further study these clusters, we analyze user characteristics across clusters. We consider the average session length per user, computed as the distance between timestamps of the last and first records in each session. As shown in Figure 9(a), users in C2 have longer sessions that the other users. This supports our earlier interpretation based on the primary features. Figure 9(b) shows that users in C2 also have a higher number of sessions, followed by users in C3 and C4. We can interpret this observation in two ways. First, given the particular use of the app (keeping iMove active while moving), users in C2 tend to use it more frequently (e.g., every day, commuting to work). A second interpretation is that more experienced users of iMove tend to use it for longer sessions and hence belong to C2. Distinguishing these two cases requires additional analysis that we leave as future work. Last, Figure 9(c) shows that C1 users

have a higher rate of records corresponding to POI details screen enters. This is in support of the primary features extracted for this cluster, identifying C1 as a user group with higher frequency of sessions that explore POI-related screens.

5. CONCLUSIONS AND FUTURE WORK

This paper presents an analysis of users interactions with iMove, a mobile app that supports the orientation of people with visual impairment. The initial dataset contains more than $17,000$ users, many of which are "incidental" users, not really interested in the functions of the app. To filter these users out, we adopted a session-based heuristic that eliminates 77% of the users and 67% of the log records.

The data analysis performed on about $4,000$ remaining users, highlights a number of iMove use properties, including commonly used functions and users' preferred values for settings parameters. In summary:

- While initial iMove settings favored sporadic and brief notifications, we observed that users, in particular those with severe visual impairments, prefer to have frequent and detailed information about the current location, which should include city, speed, heading and course.

- Applications similar to iMove are recommended to activate the "prevent screen lock" option by default.

- iMove users favored speech over text for input when creating notes associated to geographical locations.

- We observed that points of interest (POIs) were important in iMove functionality. Many users checked the list of nearby POIs (the third most visited screen) and the most popular action was navigating to a POI.

- VoiceOver users (VO-users) received more notifications, made intensive use of core iMove functions, and used the app for longer periods than other users. While

157

c1(370 👤): Check list and details of nearby POIs

feature space	normalized frequency	
	in cluster	not in cluster
(s-POI_list, n-Location, s-POI_details, s-POI_list, n-Location)	0.013078	0.001167
(s-Root, |, s-Root, |, s-Root)	0.002553	0.073674
(n-Location, n-Location, n-Location, n-Location, n-Location)	0.000192	0.046369

c2(247 👤): Long sessions of location and POI notifications

feature space	normalized frequency	
	in cluster	not in cluster
(n-Location, n-POI, n-Location, n-Location, n-Location)	0.021846	0.000411
(n-POI, n-Location, n-Location, n-Location, n-Location)	0.016155	0.000411
(n-Location, n-Location, n-Location, n-Location, n-Location)	0.175919	0.000615

c4(154 👤): Short sessions with few notifications

feature space	normalized frequency	
	in cluster	not in cluster
(|, s-Root, n-Location, |, s-Root)	0.024224	0.001708
(n-Location, |, s-Root, n-Location, |)	0.036877	0.001331
(|, s-Root, n-POI, n-Location, |)	0.023818	0.001058

c3(215 👤): Very short sessions of only Root screen entrances

feature space	normalized frequency	
	in cluster	not in cluster
(s-Root, |, s-Root, |, s-Root)	0.222907	0.001778
(|, s-Root, |, s-Root, |)	0.186638	0.000567
(n-Location, n-Location, n-Location, n-Location, n-Location)	0.000361	0.056407

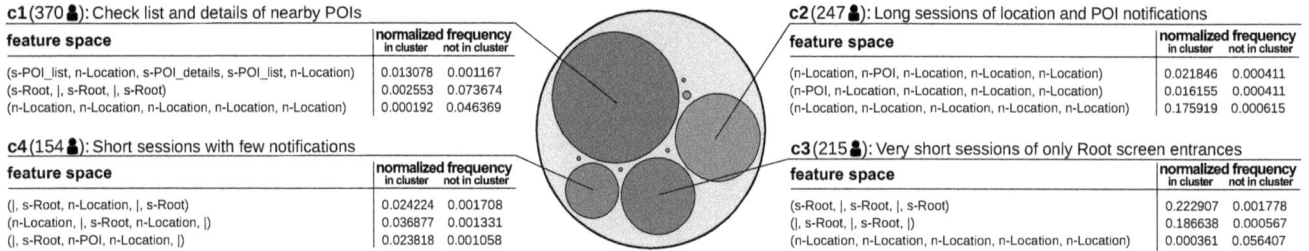

Figure 8: Clustering results.

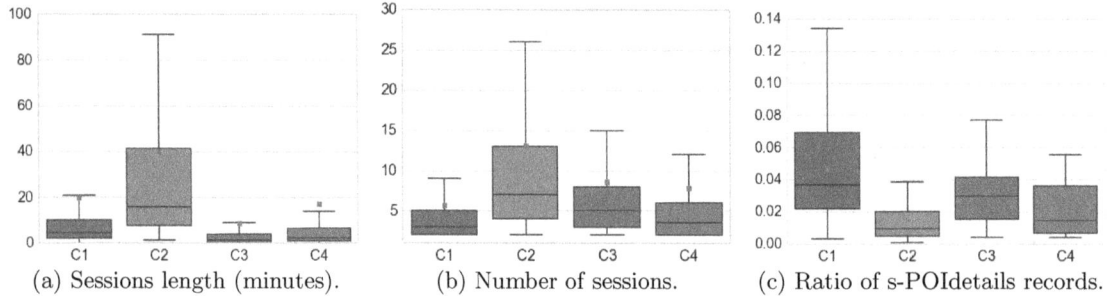

(a) Sessions length (minutes).   (b) Number of sessions.   (c) Ratio of s-POIdetails records.

Figure 9: Analysis of the four clusters.

*i*Move was designed with blind users in mind, the observed differences with non-VoiceOver users, possibly including people with low vision, raises concerns about the app design in support of this population.

*i*Move was designed with a main user target in mind: people with visual impairment that would keep the app active along a route to get notifications. By clustering about 1,000 *i*Move VO-users based on common interaction patterns, our user target base was successfully identified from one of the major clusters (C2), which contained 25% of the VO-users. In addition, our clustering method was able to capture and provide semantics for the remaining 75% of the VO-users with three more clusters; indicating those users who interact with the app in short sessions. We speculate that users in those clusters avoid interacting with the app while moving, because they do not want to be distracted or do not feel comfortable walking while holding their smartphone. Hence, they use the app in short bursts when they feel comfortable.

The identification of additional user clusters, other than C2, can help improve *i*Move by designing new interaction patterns and functions that support these usage patterns. For example, since many users (those in C1) often open the app to check nearby POIs, it may be possible to optionally show the list of POIs in the first app screen. Similarly, we speculate that users in C1 often open the app to check current address and close it. To support these operations, researchers could investigate different interaction modalities like an accelerometer-based interface to determine when the user wants to read the current address while the device is in the user's pocket.

This contribution highlights a number of possible future works. First, the analysis was conducted from data collected in a period of four months during which *i*Move has been downloaded on average more than 4,000 times each month. We expect the number of users to grow linearly with time so that in few months it will be possible to conduct the same analysis on a larger set of users and adopt hierarchical clustering that can potentially refine our higher-level clusters into more descriptive sub-clusters. On the other hand, collecting data for a longer period will enable better analysis of a user's learning curve and evolution of interactions over time, possibly characterizing the behavior of novice users with respect to experienced ones.

In the future it will also be possible to collect additional types of log data. For example, while it is not possible to collect users' location or user-defined geo-notes due to privacy concerns, it may be possible to collect additional context-related information, like users' speed and whether users are walking or traveling on a bus/car.

From the point of view of users' clustering, there are three directions along which we intend to extend this contribution. First, we want to explore hierarchical clusters and dimensionality reduction approaches that can further improve our clustering quality and preserve an interpretable feature space. Second, we intend to investigate the link between preferences for user settings and the automatically detected user clusters. Third, we intend to experiment with clustering techniques for effectively identifying "incidental users" so that it is possible to remove them more reliably.

We see the results, methods, and data provided in this paper to improve existing applications, provide guidance, and advance the state of art in the field of assistive orientation and navigation – ultimately leading to a better experience of independent mobility for people with visual impairment.

6. ACKNOWLEDGMENTS

Chieko Asakawa acknowledges support from Shimizu Corporation. Sergio Mascetti was partially supported by grant "Fondo Supporto alla Ricerca 2015" under the project "Assistive Technologies on Mobile Devices". Authors are grateful to Valeria Alampi who assisted in the *i*Move development.

7. REFERENCES

[1] J. G. Adair. The hawthorne effect: A reconsideration of the methodological artifact. *Journal of applied psychology*, 69(2):334, 1984.

[2] D. Ahmetovic, C. Gleason, K. M. Kitani, H. Takagi, and C. Asakawa. Navcog: turn-by-turn smartphone navigation assistant for people with visual impairments or blindness. In *Proceedings of the 13th Web for All Conference*. ACM, 2016.

[3] A. Arditi, J. D. Holtzman, and S. M. Kosslyn. Mental imagery and sensory experience in congenital blindness. *Neuropsychologia*, 26(1):1–12, 1988.

[4] J. P. Bigham, A. C. Cavender, J. T. Brudvik, J. O. Wobbrock, and R. E. Ladner. Webinsitu: a comparative analysis of blind and sighted browsing behavior. In *Proceedings of the 9th international ACM SIGACCESS conference on Computers and accessibility*, pages 51–58. ACM, 2007.

[5] S. Bird, E. Klein, and E. Loper. *Natural language processing with Python*. " O'Reilly Media, Inc.", 2009.

[6] V. D. Blondel, J.-L. Guillaume, R. Lambiotte, and E. Lefebvre. Fast unfolding of communities in large networks. *Journal of statistical mechanics: theory and experiment*, 2008(10):P10008, 2008.

[7] M. Böhmer, B. Hecht, J. Schöning, A. Krüger, and G. Bauer. Falling asleep with angry birds, facebook and kindle: a large scale study on mobile application usage. In *Proceedings of the 13th international conference on Human computer interaction with mobile devices and services*, pages 47–56. ACM, 2011.

[8] E. L. Brady, D. Sato, C. Ruan, H. Takagi, and C. Asakawa. Exploring interface design for independent navigation by people with visual impairments. In *Proceedings of the 17th International ACM SIGACCESS Conference on Computers & Accessibility*, ASSETS '15, pages 387–388, New York, NY, USA, 2015. ACM.

[9] S. Chennuru, P.-W. Chen, J. Zhu, and J. Y. Zhang. Mobile lifelogger–recording, indexing, and understanding a mobile userâĂŹs life. In *Mobile Computing, Applications, and Services*, pages 263–281. Springer, 2010.

[10] N. A. Giudice and G. E. Legge. Blind navigation and the role of technology. *Engineering handbook of smart technology for aging, disability, and independence*, pages 479–500, 2008.

[11] M. Goldberg. *Assisting Visually Impaired People with Mobility through Technology in the Age of Context*. PhD thesis, City University of New York, 2015.

[12] A. Hurst, S. E. Hudson, J. Mankoff, and S. Trewin. Distinguishing users by pointing performance in laboratory and real-world tasks. *ACM Transactions on Accessible Computing (TACCESS)*, 5(2):5, 2013.

[13] Q. Li, Y. Zheng, X. Xie, Y. Chen, W. Liu, and W.-Y. Ma. Mining user similarity based on location history. In *Proceedings of the 16th ACM SIGSPATIAL international conference on Advances in geographic information systems*, page 34. ACM, 2008.

[14] S. Mascetti, D. Ahmetovic, A. Gerino, and C. Bernareggi. Zebrarecognizer: Pedestrian crossing recognition for people with visual impairment or blindness. *Pattern Recognition*, 2016.

[15] S. Mascetti, D. Ahmetovic, A. Gerino, C. Bernareggi, M. Busso, and A. Rizzi. Robust traffic lights detection on mobile devices for pedestrians with visual impairment. *Computer Vision and Image Understanding*, 148:123–135, 2016.

[16] S. Mascetti, C. Bernareggi, and M. Belotti. *TypeInBraille: quick eyes-free typing on smartphones*. Springer, 2012.

[17] S. Mascetti, L. Picinali, A. Gerino, D. Ahmetovic, and C. Bernareggi. Sonification of guidance data during road crossing for people with visual impairments or blindness. *International Journal of Human-Computer Studies*, 85:16–26, 2016.

[18] M. Nakajima and S. Haruyama. New indoor navigation system for visually impaired people using visible light communication. *EURASIP Journal on Wireless Communications and Networking*, 2013(1):1–10, 2013.

[19] M. E. Newman and M. Girvan. Finding and evaluating community structure in networks. *Physical review E*, 69(2):026113, 2004.

[20] B. Pang and L. Lee. Opinion mining and sentiment analysis. *Foundations and trends in information retrieval*, 2(1-2):1–135, 2008.

[21] F. Pedregosa, G. Varoquaux, A. Gramfort, V. Michel, B. Thirion, O. Grisel, M. Blondel, P. Prettenhofer, R. Weiss, V. Dubourg, J. Vanderplas, A. Passos, D. Cournapeau, M. Brucher, M. Perrot, and E. Duchesnay. Scikit-learn: Machine learning in Python. *Journal of Machine Learning Research*, 12:2825–2830, 2011.

[22] D. Riboni, C. Bettini, G. Civitarese, Z. H. Janjua, and R. Helaoui. Smartfaber: Recognizing fine-grained abnormal behaviors for early detection of mild cognitive impairment. *Artificial Intelligence in Medicine*, 2016.

[23] V. R. Schinazi, T. Thrash, and D.-R. Chebat. Spatial navigation by congenitally blind individuals. *Wiley Interdisciplinary Reviews: Cognitive Science*, 7(1):37–58, 2016.

[24] C. Thinus-Blanc and F. Gaunet. Representation of space in blind persons: vision as a spatial sense? *Psychological bulletin*, 121(1):20, 1997.

[25] G. Wang, X. Zhang, S. Tang, H. Zheng, and B. Y. Zhao. Unsupervised clickstream clustering for user behavior analysis. In *SIGCHI Conference on Human Factors in Computing Systems*, 2016.

[26] M. A. Williams, A. Hurst, and S. K. Kane. Pray before you step out: describing personal and situational blind navigation behaviors. In *Proceedings of the 15th International ACM SIGACCESS Conference on Computers and Accessibility*, page 28. ACM, 2013.

[27] Y. Yang and J. O. Pedersen. A comparative study on feature selection in text categorization. In *ICML*, volume 97, pages 412–420, 1997.

An Evaluation of SingleTapBraille keyboard:
A Text Entry Method that Utilizes Braille Patterns on Touchscreen Devices

Maraim Alnfiai
Faculty of Computer Science
Dalhousie University
Halifax, Canada
mrim@dal.ca

Srinivas Sampalli
Faculty of Computer Science
Dalhousie University
Halifax, Canada
srini@cs.dal.ca

ABSTRACT

This paper provides an evaluation of the SingleTapBraille keyboard, designed to assist people with no or low vision in using touchscreen smartphones. This application allows blind users to input characters based on braille patterns. To assess SingleTapBraille, this study compares its performance with that of the commonly used QWERTY keyboard. We conducted an evaluation study with 7 blind participants to examine the performance of both keyboards on Android platforms. Overall, participants were able to quickly adjust to SingleTapBraille and type on touchscreen devices using their knowledge of Braille patterns within fifteen to twenty minutes of introduction to the system. The SingleTapBraille keyboard was better than the QWERTY keyboard in terms of both speed and accuracy, indicating that SingleTapBraille represents an improvement over existing alternatives in making touchscreen keyboards more accessible for blind users. Based on the evaluation results and the feedback of our participants, we discuss the strengths and weaknesses of previous keyboards that have been used by participants, as well as those of SingleTapBraille. In doing so, we consider possible design improvements for the future development of accessible keyboards for blind users.

Keywords

Accessibility; text entry; blindness; touchscreens; smartphone devices; single-touch interaction; braille patterns; tapping, gestures.

1. INTRODUCTION

Smartphone accessibility for people with visual impairments has improved dramatically in recent years. One of the areas of greatest improvement is the screen reader function of smartphones, which has improved quality of life among the visually impaired by enabling them to more easily may access all kinds of information from the Internet and from their devices.

Compared to other interventions, integration of screen readers into smartphone devices has brought numerous benefits to people with no or low vision. Notably, smartphone devices are cheaper and smaller than screen reader machines [1].

The VoiceOver service in the Apple platform and the TalkBack service in the Android platform are the fundamental accessibility features that enable blind users to interact with the system. While these are beneficial, blind users still experience difficulties associated with typing on touchscreen devices, primarily because touchscreen devices do not have physical buttons that would allow them to easily identify their functions; the elimination of such physical landmarks on touchscreen devices represents the loss of a key element of how blind users interact with their mobile devices. As a result, typing on a touchscreen device using the QWERTY keyboard requires a user to slide his/her finger on a screen searching for an intended character, without the benefit of any tactile input. According to Nicolau et al. (2010), text entry on the QWERTY keyboard is time consuming and prone to errors for blind users [3]. This sort of text entry also requires the use of both hands in order to interact with the keyboard, which is inconvenient for blind users that typically must use one of their hands to employ a cane or a guide dog. Thus, such users often have only one hand available for interaction with their smartphone devices.

Recently, we addressed these difficulties by developing SingleTapBraille, a new braille-based text entry method for touchscreen devices [4]. For blind people, braille is an essential tool for reading and writing. The main purpose of our keyboard is to employ principles of braille in order to allow users to hold the smartphone device using one hand and type using only a thumb. Developing accessible text entry tools for blind people has been a challenge for a long time.

2. RELATED WORK

Historically, there have been many interventions designed to assist blind users in communication. In 1892, Frank Hall invented the braille typewriter, which has six knobs representing in the six possible dot positions in the braille code. In 1951, Abraham designed the Perkins Brailler, which remains the standard mechanical keyboard for blind people. He improved on the Hall typewriter by adding such features as a space key, a backspace key, and a line space key. Similar to the braille typewriter, the Perkins Brailler has six dots, which are arranged in two columns: the first column has 1st, 2nd, and 3rd dots and the second column has the 4th, 5th, and 6th dots [2].

Figure 1: Perkins Brailler device

Currently, the standard input method on touchscreens on smartphone devices is the QWERTY keyboard. Using smartphone touchscreens has been made more accessible for blind and visually impaired users through the integration of audio feedback on android devices. The QWERTY keyboard is based on particular location of keys including letters, number and symbols, with letter and number keys presented on the first layer and symbols presented on the second layer.

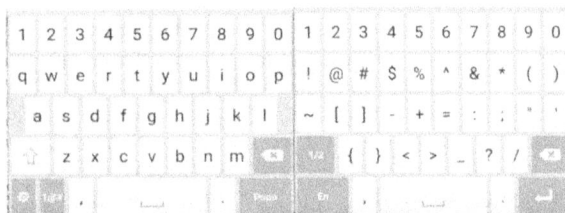

(a) Layer 1- QWERTY   (b) Layer 2- numbers and symbols

Figure 2: The two layers of the on-screen keyboard

Blind users on Android devices use the QWERTY keyboard in conjunction with the TalkBack service, which reads out the name of any object under the user's finger on a screen, thus making interaction with the touchscreen devices accessible. The QWERTY keyboard with TalkBack service provides a double tap typing mode for blind users to enter text: the user can slide their finger on a screen to hear the description of soft keys until they find the desired key, at which time they can perform a double tap in order to activate that key.

The most promising approach to assisting blind users in entering text on a touchscreen is to use an interface based on braille patterns. There are several keyboards that have been designed to combine braille coding and with audio feedback. The differences among these keyboards relate to how many hands are required to enter text and exactly how blind users can interact with the screen. The vast majority require two hands to enter braille dots to represent a letter, while others require only one hand.

With TypeInBraille [5][6], users can insert a braille letter using one hand to activate dots in each braille row at a time; three steps, each requiring sequential gestures, are required to type a character. The other hand is used to stabilize the mobile device while the user is typing. The average speed of this keyboard was 10 wpm with an error rate of 10 % after practicing it for 2 months.

Similarly, Jalaliniya et al. (2015). developed the Eyedroid keyboard, which requires users to swipe on a touchscreen to activate braille dots using their index finger while the other hand holds and stabilizes the mobile device [7]. It also requires three steps for each character. Its speed and error rate are unknown.

In BrailleType, developed by Oliveira et al. [8], each braille dot occupies a specific position on the screen. The user must use one

hand to hold the mobile device and the index finger of the other hand to tap on the braille dots that appear on the screen. BrailleType's speed was measured at 1.45 words per minute (WPM), with an error rate of 9.7% [8].

Frey, Southern, and Romero (2012) developed BrailleTouch [9][10]. As with the previous programs, it requires two hands: one to hold the device and one to operate the keyboard. Users need to find the exact locations of fixed soft keys representing the six dots in braille coding. It also requires that the screen is held in an orientation facing away from the user, which is awkward and inconvenient. Its speed was 23.2 WPM and the error rate was 14.8%.

Mattheiss et al. (2014) developed the EdgeBraille keyboard, wherein the user swipes one finger along the edges of the touchscreen to activate one braille dot or combinations of dots in order to enter a letter. Similar to other alternatives, one hand is required to hold the device while the other swipes on the screen. Its speed was 3.97 WPM and its error rate was 8.43% [11].

Another braille touchscreen keyboard is Perkinput, developed by Azenkot, Wobbrock, and Prasain [12]. Perkinput enables users to enter a character in two steps, and users can activate three dots at a time using three fingers. As with other keyboards, it requires the use of one hand to stabilize the keyboard. Its speed was 6.1 WPM and the error rate was 3.5%.

Two hands are also required for BrailleEasy, developed by Sepic, Ghanem and Vogel (2015) [13]. Each character requires two gestures. The user can activate the first braille column by tapping using one, two or three fingers to produce braille dots. This keyboard is challenging to use because it requires the user to locate particular reference points for his/her finger positions in order for the keyboard to identify the location of the user's fingers. Its speed was 7 WPM and its error rate was not indicated.

There is also an assortment of text entry solutions for blind users that do not rely on Braille patterns. For example, Guerreiro, Nicolau, Jorge, and Gonçalves (2008) developed the NavTouch keyboard, which divides the alphabet into five rows, each of which starts with a different vowel. Users can navigate through these rows, performing swiping gestures in four different directions (vertically up and down, and horizontally left and right) with audio feedback in order to locate the desired letter [14]. Like the braille-based options mentioned above, this keyboard requires two hands.

No-Look Notes, developed by Bonner, Brudvik, Abowd, and Edwards (2010), employs pie-menus, with each part including 3 or 4 letters. The user slides a finger on the pie-menus in order to find a specific group and then finds the desired letter within that group using voice feedback [15]. Here, the user has to use one hand to hold the device and the other to slide on a screen.

The main motivation for designing SingleTapBraille was to provide a more accessible input method for touchscreen devices – one that overcomes the limitations of existing keyboards for people with low or no vision. We designed SingleTapBraille to allow blind users to tap anywhere on a screen without looking for specific objects on a touchscreen. It also allows users to hold the mobile device with one hand and enter text using the thumb of the same hand to tap on the screen, similar to the concept of the slate and stylus braille device. Thus, while mobile and using one hand to hold a cane or guide dog, the user can use the dominant hand both to hold the phone and to operate the touchscreen. We allow users to tap one or a combination of dots to enter a braille letter.

As mentioned after, the keyboard is based on the braille system with which blind users are already familiar. Users can enter dots from left to right, matching the way blind users read braille. Each braille dot is activated individually using a single tap on the touchscreen. Once the user stops touching the screen for a short interval, the braille pattern is translated and the corresponding letter is typed and the software speaks out the letter using text-to-speech. For example, if the user taps the screen once and then pauses, the letter "A" is typed and spoken by the text-to-speech software. When the character has more than one active dot, users can tap that series of dots anywhere on the screen and the algorithm will analyze the relationship between dots based on the number of dots in each character, the distance between taps and the coordinates of series of dots, as described in [4].

In addition of character entry, we implemented a number of other typing tasks using gestures. For example, flicking from right to left adds a space, flicking from left to right to performs a backspace, and flicking up and down switches between the letter, number, and symbols keyboards.

We integrated our keyboard into an SMS application that can be used to type and edit text, and to send written text to any receiver using our proposed approach. Integration of the SMS application also allows for evaluation of the SingleTapBraille keyboard. We implemented the SMS application in the Android platform.

To send SMS messages, users can perform a long press to accomplish each of the involved tasks, entering the user's number and sending the message. After typing a message, the user can do a long press on the touchscreen, at which time the app will speak out, "please enter the number". Then the user can tap on the touch screen to enter a receiver's number and then perform another long press to send the message. We chose to use the same gesture to perform each of the required tasks in order to simplify the users' interaction with the touchscreen and to increase learnability.

In the SMS application, we used the TalkBack service to provide users with verbal feedback from the application. This also allows the users to listen to what has been typed by them and what has been edited. Along with allowing users to operate the touchscreen with a single hand, integration with an SMS application represents one of SingleTapBraille's key advantages over existing alternatives. A detailed comparison of existing braille keyboards, including SingleTapBraille, is shown in Table 1.

The objective of this research is to evaluate a new text entry method for blind users, SingleTapBraille, and test its accessibility, learnability and usability. Eventually, we hope that this technology will eliminate many of the difficulties that blind people face when they enter text or send messages. One of the major limitations for people with visual impairments is their inability to locate an exact object on a touchscreen. Therefore, the essential motivation of our project is to develop a smartphone application that, by overcoming that obstacle, will help visually impaired people to enter text and send messages easily. Ultimately, our input method will improve the accessibility of touchscreen devices for people with no vision.

To assess our keyboard, we compared it to the QWERTY keyboard on a smartphone device with respect to speed, accuracy, and how users interact with the keyboards. We chose to compare our keyboard with the QWERTY keyboard because the interfaces for most applications on smartphone devices force users to use the QWERTY keyboard to enter text (e.g., PIN). As a result, it is the existing keyboard that users, including blind users, are most familiar with. This study assessed SingleTapBraille by testing it with blind users at the Canadian National Institute for the Blind (CNIB) in Halifax, Nova Scotia, not only measuring speed and accuracy but also collecting user feedback and suggestions. In doing so, this study evaluates the accessibility, learnability, and usability of the keyboard. Thus, this study aims not only to assess the performance of the SingleTapBraille keyboard but also to

Table 1: Summary of existing braille keyboards' features

	Is easy to learn	Is easy to use	Requires one hand	Requires one finger to interact with a screen	Uses VoiceOver service	Uses tactile feedback	Eliminates switching between layers	Eliminate looking for a specific location	Supports number, alphabets, punctuation	Allows editing	Integrates the keyboard with an application
BrailleTouch	✓	×	×	×	✓	×	✓	×	✓	✓	×
BrailleType	✓	✓	×	✓	✓	×	✓	×	✓	×	×
Perkinput	✓	✓	×	×	✓	×	✓	×	✓	✓	×
BrailleEazy	✓	✓	×	×	✓	×	✓	×	✓	✓	×
No-Look Notes	✓	✓	×	×	✓	×	×	×	×	×	×
NavTouch	✓	✓	✓	✓	✓	×	×	✓	×	×	×
EdgeBraille	✓	✓	×	✓	✓	✓	✓	×	×	×	×
Eyedroid	×	×	×	×	✓	×	×	✓	✓	✓	×
TypeInBraille	×	×	×	×	✓	×	✓	✓	✓	✓	×
SingleTapBraille	✓	✓	✓	✓	✓	×	✓	✓	✓	✓	✓

enhance its overall effectiveness of our user interface, ultimately bringing it closer to becoming a widely available alternative for visually impaired smartphone users.

3. METHODS

3.1 Study Design

In this study, evaluation of SingleTapBraille relied on having blind and visually impaired participants use our proposed keyboard and the QWERTY keyboard to perform the same tasks that involve composing and sending SMS text messages. Afterwards, we were able to evaluate and compare the performance of both keyboards based on performance data and the feedback of the participants.

We also examined the accessibility, learnability and usability of the SingleTapBraille keyboard.

3.2 Participants

Evaluation was conducted with blind users. We had seven blind users (2 males and 5 females) ranging in age from 28-52 years old (mean age: 40). Recruitment of participants was undertaken with the assistance of the director of the Canadian National institute for Blind.

All participants had prior experience with touchscreens, the QWERTY keyboard, and TalkBack service. All of them use braille regularly and were familiar with the six dots braille system. The participants' demographic data is detailed in Table 2.

3.3 Methodology

The following sections describe the evaluation process for the SingleTapBraille application with respect to interface usability, learnability, accuracy and speed. The main task for the participants was to listen to phrases and enter those phrases as messages using each of the keyboards, QWERTY and SingleTapBraille.

3.3.1 Phrase set

We obtained a set of short message phrases from an English for Students website [16]. In selecting phrases, we were aware of two factors, unrelated to the particular keyboard being used, that might cause errors in text entry. To address one of these, the possibility

Table 2: Participants' demographic data

P	Age	G	Sigh	PIB	BD	ESP	MTT
P1	48	M	blind	expert		6 years	A QWERTY keyboard
P2	34	F	blind	expert		7 years	AQWERTY keyboard, MBraille
P3	40	F	blind	expert	Perkins Braille, slate and stylus	5 years	A QWERTY keyboard
P4	50	M	blind	expert		5 years	A QWERTY keyboard
P5	46	F	blind	expert		3 years	A QWERTY keyboard
P6	36	F	blind	expert		3 years	A QWERTY keyboard
P7	29	F	blind	expert		5 years	A QWERTY keyboard

P = Participant number, G = Gender, PIB = Proficiency in Braille, BD = Braille device they use, ESP = Experience with smartphones and touchscreens, MTT= method used to enter text on a touchscreen.

that the user may not know the spelling of a word, we provided simple short sentences containing common words. To overcome the second problem, the possibility that users may not grasp the phrases, we implemented a dictation application to allow users to listen to a sentence and repeat it in order to enhance comprehension.

3.3.2 Dictation of phrases

While sighted people can both type and see phrases with ease, people with no vision need support in order to read text, either from sighted people or from an app that can accomplish the same function. In the dictation app, we employed a text-to-speech function to speak out phrases, allowing blind users to type out what they hear. In the context of this study, we implemented the dictation application in order to enable blind users to listen to the set of phrases that they would have to enter using the SingleTapBraille keyboard. Users were able to listen to a given phrase repeatedly while typing, and could also move quickly to the next phrase using the developed dictation application. Users were able perform the following gestures to accomplish these tasks:

- Swipe from bottom to top to listen to a new phrase
- Swipe from top to bottom to repeat the previous phrase

3.4 Study Procedure

The study was conducted at the Canadian National Institute for the Blind (CNIB). For each participant, the study consisted of a pre-test questionnaire, a training session with SingleTapBraille, test sessions using SingleTapBraille and QWERTY, another questionnaire, and an interview. The initial -questionnaire was used to collect basic demographic data and other details related to the input methods typically used for text entry on a touchscreen.

In the beginning of the study, an overview of the objective of the study discussed. In the training session, we explained SingleTapBraille's operation and functions, described how to do the finger tap on a touchscreen, and demonstrated how the finger taps relate to the braille code and to the letters of the alphabet. To familiarize the participants with the input method, we provided a 20-minute training period during which they could practice using the application to type letters and numbers and to send a set of phrases as SMS messages using the SingleTapBraille application. In order to avoid potentially confounding effects related to participants memorizing particular phrases and learning how to type them, the set of phrases provided for training differed from those used for the test session. Data associated with the training session were not analyzed as part of this study.

In the first part of the test session, which lasted 20-30 minutes, participants listened to dictated phrases, typing each of them using the SingleTapBraille keyboard before moving on to the next phrase. Fourteen short phrases were chosen in order to maintain a reasonable session length that would not discourage people from participating; the number of phrases used here was similar to other studies [8]. Participants were asked to type as quickly and accurately as possible. These phrases were sent as texts to the researcher's phone number. The text typed and the time required to type it were recorded in order to assess typing accuracy and typing speed, respectively. We used a video recorder in order to help us understand exactly how the participants interacted with a touchscreen.

After the participants had texted all the phrases, they answered a post-study questionnaire regarding the usability and learnability of the SingleTapBraille approach and the SMS application.

Following that, we asked participants to type the same phrases using the QWERTY keyboard, providing another 20-30 minute session. After that, the participants were further interviewed with respect to the strengths and weaknesses of the two keyboards assessed in the study; as part of this interview, participants were invited to suggest improvements with respect to the SingleTapBraille method.

4. RESULTS

During the study, each participant typed 14 short messages for each keyboard, totaling 1596 characters including space and symbols. The results of the study include quantitative measures of typing speed and accuracy, as well as qualitative findings related to the participants' experiences using the keyboards.

4.1 Quantitative results

4.1.1 Speed

The measure used to assess text entry speed was Words-Per-Minute (WPM), calculated as (transcribed text length/ entry time in seconds * 60 seconds in a minute) / (5 characters per word). The designation of five characters, including letters, numbers, spaces and symbols, as the accepted word length was based on previous studies [17]. Typing speed was significantly higher using the SingleTapBraille keyboard (average = 4.71 WPM) compared to the QWERTY keyboard (average = 3.72 WPM) (paired t-test; p = 0.03).

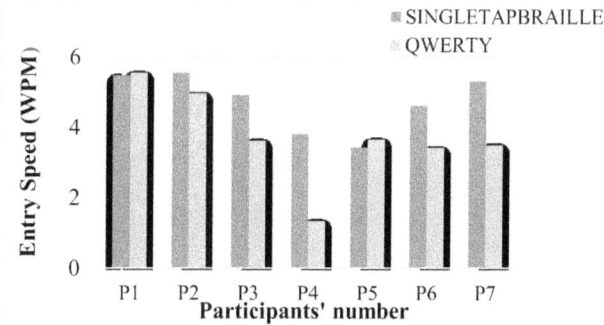

Figure 3: Text entry speeds (WPM) for each participant for SingleTapBraille and QWERTY keyboard.

4.1.2 Accuracy

Participants were permitted to insert text without restrictions during the study, such that they may or may not correct any typing errors. Therefore, to measure accuracy we chose to use Minimum String Distance (MSD) and keystrokes per character (KSPC) [19] [20]. The MSD method analyzes three types of primitives, insertion, deletion, and substitution. Keystrokes are classified into four categories within the input stream: correct keystrokes (C), the number of erroneous keystrokes that are not corrected in the transcribed text (INF), the number of erroneous keystrokes and they are corrected in the transcribed text (IF), and the number of keystrokes used to correct errors, such as delete or backspace (F). This classification enables us to measure several statistics, including the total error rate:

$$\text{Total Error Rate} = \frac{(INF+IF)}{(C+INF+IF)} * 100\% \qquad (1)$$

Total error rate (TER) represents the number of errors made while typing the phrases. The total error rate was trend lower for the SingleTapBraille keyboard (average = 11.23) than it was for the QWERTY keyboard (average = 20.54) (paired t-test; p = 0.193), indicating higher accuracy using the SingleTapBraille method (Figure 5).

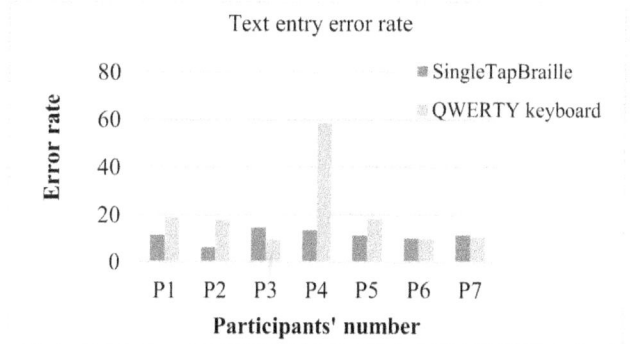

Figure 4: Average total error rate for each participant for SingleTapBraille and QWERTY keyboard.

The amount of time required to type the messages differed greatly, both between input methods and across participants. Besides input method, the time required may be influenced by the effort made and time needed to correct errors. To address this, we chose to use Corrected Error Rate (CER), which represents the number of errors made and then corrected, and Not Corrected Error Rate (NCER), which represents errors made but not corrected, in order to better understand the processes that participants undertake while typing messages [19]. We also used KSPC (keystrokes per character) in order to measure the cost of making typing errors and correcting them, as well as the effort that participants chose to invest in error correction [19].

$$\text{Corrected Error Rate (CER)} = \frac{IF}{(C+INF+IF)} * 100 \qquad (2)$$

$$\text{Not Corrected Error Rate (NCER)} = \frac{INF}{(C+INF+IF)} * 100 \qquad (3)$$

$$\text{KSCP} = \frac{C+INF+IF+F}{C+INF} \qquad (4)$$

Not corrected error rate was trend lower for the SingleTapBraille keyboard (average = 1.3) than it was for the QWERTY keyboard (average = 4.9) (paired t-test; p = 0.065) (Figure 6).

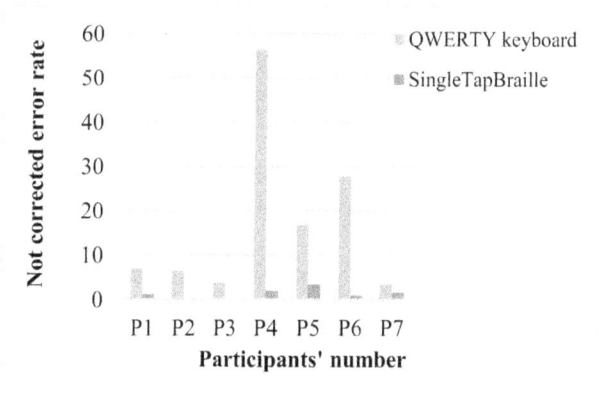

Figure 5: Average not corrected error rate for each participant for SingleTapBraille and QWERTY keyboard.

Corrected error rate was higher for the SingleTapBraille keyboard (average = 9.9) than it was for the QWERTY keyboard (average = 4.9) (paired t-test; p = 0.034), indicating that participants were more willing to fix their mistakes using SingleTapBraille, perhaps because it is easier (Figure 7). Despite that difference, it is interesting to note that the corrected error rate was actually lower using the SingleTapBraille for one of the seven participants.

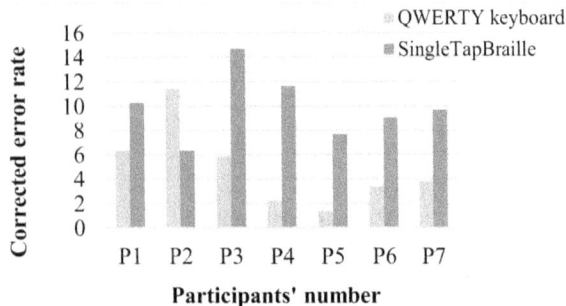

Figure 6: Average corrected error rate for each participant for SingleTapBraille and QWERTY keyboard.

Keystrokes per character, which is a measure of how much typing participants had to do in order to successfully enter each message (and, therefore, the occurrence of errors and the effort made to fix them), did not differ between the two keyboards (Figure 8).

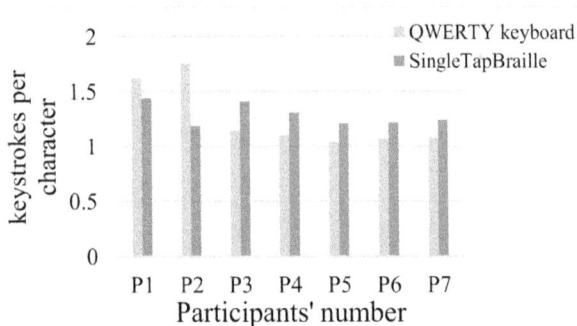

Figure 7: Average keystrokes per character rate for each participant for SingleTapBraille and QWERTY keyboard.

4.2 Qualitative Feedback

4.2.1 Pre-questionnaire

The participants were asked for their opinions regarding the possibility of a new input method, as well as the strengths and limitations of the keyboards they had used. Most of participants were most familiar with the QWERTY keyboard with audio feedback. All participants agreed that audio feedback is the best solution confirming that they have located the intended letter.

The users were asked about the main difficulties associated with using touchscreen keyboards. The most common complaint was related to the slowness of the QWERTY keyboard; for example, Participant 5 stated that "because I have to swipe my finger and listen to all letter I have passed. Finding a specific location of symbol takes time". Similarly, QWERTY keyboard in your phone it is much slower than a keyboard that you can have your finger tips to type with on a Bluetooth keyboard".

Another obstacle reported was interference by alternative keyboards that pop up when a user pressed for a long on a letter (as shown in figure 9). For example, Participant 3 stated that "I found something frustrating on a touch screen, which is if you swipe your finger across the screen to locate a certain letter, another keyboard or something else pops up and it says "Alternative keyboards", and then it types something else not the one I am looking for".

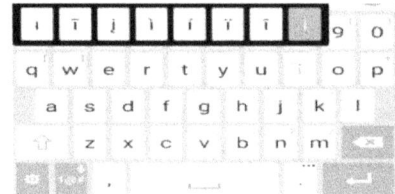

Figure 8: Alternative keyboard

Five participants made reference to the difficulty of locating the keys for specific letters, numbers and symbols. Participant 7 said, "I found difficulty to find the symbols and numbers more than letters. Because sometimes it layout differently and also because again it is a touchscreen. I always guessing where I put my finger". Reflecting this difficulty, Participant 4, the only participant with limited experience using the QWERTY keyboard and sending short messages, only reached 1.10 wpm with audio feedback, indicating considerable difficulty in locating the requires characters.

One participant that uses MBraille keyboard, which is similar to BrailleTouch, said "I use six fingers to type based on Braille patterns and my thumbs hold the device from the back, which is awkward". She also did not like some other features of MBraille, including the need to copy text from MBraille to other applications (e.g., Facebook) and its tendency to shut down unexpectedly.

We also asked participants about how they hold their smartphones and interact with touchscreens while typing. Most participants use one hand to stabilize the smartphone device while using the index finger of the other hand to tap on the screen. Unlike the other participants, participant 3 reported a preference for using her thumb to type on a screen because she lost her sight when she was 20 years old; this method contrasts with the tendencies of most people who are born blind, who typically use their index finger to read Braille and type on a touch screen. We also asked the participants about sending messages while walking; only two participants do this, with the others reporting it was too difficult because they do not have two free hands while walking.

4.2.2 Usability questionnaire

After the participants completed typing messages using the SingleTapBraille keyboard during the test session, they answered questions about the usability, learnability and accessibility of the new keyboard. The usability questionnaire contained 19 statements regarding the keyboard, with participants required to indicate their level of agreement with each statement on a 5-point Likert scale (1 = disagree strongly, 5 = agree strongly). As Table 3 demonstrates, the participants rated the keyboard highly with respect to usefulness, ease of use, and learnability. Nonetheless, they were less satisfied with some aspects of speed and usability. Overall, however, the results of the questionnaire parallel the quantitative improvements in speed and accuracy, and reflect improvements related to usability, learnability and accessibility.

Table 3: Usability questionnaire results, the average of participants' responses given on a Likert scale

PERCEIVED USEFULNESS	Avg
Accomplish typing tasks more quickly.	3.8
Enter text more independently.	5.0
Improve my typing performance.	4.4
Increase my productivity.	4.2
Enhance my effectiveness on entering text.	4.0
make it easier to enter texts and send messages.	4.6
useful in general	4.8
PERCEIVED EASE OF USE	
It was easy to use the keyboard to enter what I wanted to text.	4.0
My interaction with the keyboard was clear and understandable.	4.8
It would be easy for me to become skillful at using the keyboard.	4.6
The letters, numbers, and punctuation was easy to type.	4.8
The interaction techniques was easy to understand	5.0

PERCEIVED EASE OF LEARNING	
Learning to operate the SingleTapBraille keyboard would be easy for me.	5.0
Editing text was clear.	5.0
Switching between keyboard was clear	5.0
Remembering the gestures and touch commands was easy.	5.0
Performing tasks like entering text, making capital and small letters were straightforward	5.0
Voice feedback were helpful to define the gesture function	5.0
I found my skills at using the app improved with practice	5.0

4.2.3 Interview

All participants successfully used the interface to enter text using SingleTapBraille with the help of the text-to-speech feature built into the keyboard itself. All participants found the audio to be clear and easy to follow. After the participants completed their test session, we asked them about various elements of their experiences using the keyboard.

All participants liked that interaction with the touchscreen did not involve a button or looking for a specific location. For example, Participant 3 said "I like it because I did not have to look all over the screen looking for something, it's just a matter of tapping in or swiping, it is simple to use."

Participants also liked the use of swiping gestures, reporting that swiping from bottom to top and vice versa are easy gestures that

blind users can perform quickly. Interviews also revealed that the swiping gesture to switch between layers and to capitalize letters is easier for blind users than finding the switch or shift button on the QWERTY keyboard. As Participant 1 said, "It is simple, it is straightforward, it is intuitive, that particular function, I like better than buttons in the normal keyboard because it is quicker to flick up anywhere and switch between number, letters, and symbols than finding the little button." Likewise, Participant 7 said "switching up and down is quite efficient and easier than trying to navigate with a QWERTY keyboard." This finding is supported by previous research; for example, Shaun et al. (2011) found that the easiest gestures for blind users involve swiping rather than typing [21]. Participants also reported that using a long press gesture anywhere on a touchscreen to perform a specific task is easier than finding a specific button. Participant 5 stated, "it was great: on my Ipad, If I want to send message, I have to swipe over to locate send button. I mean, it is much easier, pressing for long anywhere on a screen." Participant 2 also said "that's cool because you do not need to look for send button."

Four of the participants were not satisfied with the keyboard speed, and they provided different possible reasons for its inadequate speed. Participant 7 stated that "I was not fast, because I have to think about because I have never obviously typed with Braille on a touch screens. When ever, I typed Braille, I used six keys right in front of me, so it kind of the same I was typing on computers versus being on a regular keyboard with a voiceOver, I can type faster and it gets easier as I go." In contrast, Participant 5 found the keyboard speed is normal, stating, "normal, a little of delay because I think that's good because it gives you time to correct mistakes if you made one." Most participants also suggested the implementation of Braille grade 2 in order to minimize the number of letters required to type a word.

The users were also asked about the features that they liked the most, as well as what they saw as the primary limitations of the SingleTapBraille keyboard. All seven participants liked the way of using Braille to enter text on a screen. Participant 2 said "the advantage is using something I grow up with it, I use Braille for 30 years."Participant 3 agreed with that and added, "I am very keener for Braille, you will not forget Braille, if you keep using it, you will not not forget the Braille combination of dots to type a letter. It is so straight forward and it is very simple to use."

The use of the swiping gesture and the long press gesture to perform different tasks were both strengths according to the participants. Participant 2 also appreciated the ability to hold the smartphone using one hand, saying "I am walking it is difficult to feel the screen where is my d, a, s etc; Here user can use one hand to enter text based on the shape of Braille letter, which is for somebody who knows Braille and use it well is more natural than slid your finger on the keyboard to find a specific letter."

Nonetheless, participants agreed on some limitations for the keyboard. One criticism, brought up by three of the participants, was that the keyboard does not repeat the word that has been typed out, an action that helps blind users confirm that they entered the correct word. Another limitation is the delay associated with users having to enter the Braille dots individually. Three participants had difficulty typing some letters, like n, p and r, due to the similarity of Braille code for these letters.

5. DISCUSSION

In this study, we compared the newly developed SingleTapBraille keyboard with the standard QWERTY keyboard, with respect to speed and accuracy. Below, we summarize that comparison. We then discuss the suggestions from the participants regarding how to improve this keyboard. We also discuss the key factors that should be considered in developing an input method or application for the visually impaired.

5.1 Speed and accuracy

The SingleTapBraille keyboard demonstrated improvements in terms of speed and accuracy compared to the QWERTY keyboard. The main advantage of the SingleTapBraille, underlying the differences in performance, is that it allows blind users to enter letters based on Braille coding. The reliance on Braille coding reflects one of SingleTapBraille's limitations, as the need to enter letters in several dot-based steps potentially slows the text entry process. Along with this, this keyboard requires care and accuracy because the tapping of the first dot directly influences how the following dots are interpreted. Nonetheless, it is still faster than the standard keyboard, as well as other options available for this population.

The average error rate was less in the SingleTapBraille keyboard compared to the QWERTY keyboard. Further analysis of error rate revealed that participants in the SingleTapBraille correct their typing mistakes more often than they do using the QWERTY keyboard. The results indicated that the SingleTapBraille keyboard is less prone to errors than the QWERTY keyboard prone errors, perhaps because users, when using QWERTY, got confused while hearing all the letters that have passed along with the letter that they have typed. In our keyboard, users only get audio feedback once they have typed the letter. Just as sighted people have to spend a lot of effort to understand a lot of presented visual information at once, blind users need to obtain audio feedback when necessary; thus, eliminating unnecessary sounds can increase accessibility and minimize cognitive load.

Based on our examination, there are two main reasons for the occurrence of typing errors using SingleTapBraille. One possibility is that users do not follow the correct order of braille dots while tapping It also may be that users make large gaps between taps, possibly because users have a big space on the screen and they intend to make it spaced. Typically, the gap between Braille dots is only 10 mm (what is braille, 2008).

One possible limitation of the study is that we did not consider the effect of phrase order on speed and accuracy. However, previous studies have found no such effect of phrase order [12] [15].

5.2 Keyboard Features

Using a single tap to enter text based on Braille patterns significantly improves the accessibility for blind and visually impaired people while using touchscreens. The blind participants expressed that the SingleTapBraille keyboard makes typing text easier than it is with the QWERTY keyboard. It is much easier for blind users to tap anywhere on a screen rather than trying to locate a specific key on a screen and worry about hitting a wrong key. Swiping on a touch screen to perform a specific task was also considered an easy and fast way to accomplish tasks. Most participants found flicking up and down to switch between keyboards and flicking left to right to add or backspace character to be much easier than finding a shift key on a QWERTY keyboard or finding a switch sign in order to switch to other layers, or finding specific buttons for those functions. Overall, it is also much faster to flick than it is find a specific button on a touch screen.

Some user interfaces on smartphones force blind users to use the QWERTY keyboard and do not support the various alternative keyboards that have been designed to serve this population. For example, in the PIN (passcode) interface for a smartphone device, blind users must enter a password using the QWERTY keyboard. Based on information provided by the participants, blind users, because they find it easier to located buttons near the corner and screen edges, often create simple passwords that rely on these landmarks. Thus, blind users are at a disadvantage with respect to security, underlining the need to provide them with the ability to easily create and formulate any password combination.

Based on my observation, none of the participants were able to use predictive words on the QWERTY keyboards, indicating that this feature is essentially inaccessible for blind users. This feature therefore needs improvement in order to increase accessibility.

All participants liked the keyboard because it allows them to use Braille, the language they use in daily life. Participant 4 stated that "the main benefits of this keyboard is learning Braille, let's people who know Braille keep Braille skills," adding that "it brings to me that I can use Braille continually."

6. CONCLUSION AND FUTURE WORK

Because keyboards based on Braille provide an accessible input method on touch screen devices, we tried to develop a text entry method for blind people in order to make smartphones more accessible for all populations. We have described a non-visual text entry method, SingleTapBraille, that does not require users to locate a particular object on a touch screen; instead, text can be inserted by tapping on a touch screen based on Braille shapes. The SingleTapBraille keyboard was evaluated with blind participants, enabling us not just to quantify how such users interact with touch screens but also to understand more subtle aspects of phone use, like how they hold devices in order to use them while walking. Our evaluation also enabled us to identify the advantages and limitations of the SingleTapBraille prototype and to obtain feedback for improvements.

The main contribution of our research is that we have used Android mobile devices to build an accessible keyboard to help blind people overcome some of the difficulties they face while typing on a touch screen using the standard keyboard (QWERTY keyboard). The evaluation provided promising feedback and also suggested possible improvements for further development. It also showed that using the thumb to interact with a touch screen and holding the smartphone using only one hand is not a method that has been commonly used by blind users. Indeed, the ability to use this system with only one hand while walking is a critical advantage over other keyboards, especially for a population that often has to use one hand for a cane or guide dog. Our results indicate that entering characters based on Braille significantly enhances accessibility and usability, and has the potential to be a valuable text entry tool for blind users.

In the future, there are definitely opportunities for improvement to the SingleTapBraille keyboard. Firstly, because seven is a relatively small sample size, future work will test the keyboard with larger groups of people in order to better understands its strengths and weaknesses. We will also run another study to train users how to hold the mobile phone using one hand and type using only the thumb of that same hand. To better measure the improvement of our keyboard, we will quantitatively compare it with other available Braille keyboards on both Android and Apple platforms.

We will also address existing suggestions. For example, we will attempt to increase typing speed by using grade 2 Braille, which employs shortened word forms such that a complete word can be represented using only six dots (what is braille, 2008). We will also improve the SMS application and other aspects of the keyboard. Future work will increase the keyboard's usefulness by integrating it with existing communicating apps and implementing it with wearable technology such as the Apple Watch in order to make it even more convenient for blind people to text short messages while walking. Further, we will try to find a way by which blind users can use the predictive text feature with SingleTapBraille. Lastly, we will try to increase security and privacy through a keyboard based entirely on Braille. Other possible future directions include implementation of efficient error correction interfaces. With regard to the SMS application, we are going to allow users to select the receiver from their contacts using voice commands. Lastly, we will try to increase security and privacy through a keyboard based entirely on Braille.

7. ACKNOWLEDGMENTS

We thank the Canadian National Institute for Blind, and especially the study volunteers. We also gratefully acknowledge support from Taif university and the Saudi Arabian Cultural Bureau in Canada.

REFERENCES

[1] Accessibility. 2016. Accessibility features. Retrieved from http://www.lenovo.com/lenovo/us/en /accessibility/

[2] Tobe, C. B., Callahan, E., and Callahan, M. 2000. Embossed Printing in the United States, in *Braille: Into the Next Millennium*, J. M. Dixon, Editor. National Library Service for the Blind and Physically Handicapped of the Library of Congress: Washington, D.C., 41-71.

[3] Nicolau, H., Guerreiro, T., Jorge, J., and Gon, D. 2010. Proficient blind users and mobile text-entry. In Proc. of the 28th Annual European Conference on Cognitive Ergonomics, ECCE '10, New York, NY, USA,. ACM,19–22.

[4] Alnfiai, M., Sampalli, S. (2016). SingleTapBraille: Developing a text entry method based on braille patterns using a single tap. The 11th International Conference on Future Networks and Communications (FNC 2016).

[5] Mascetti, S., Bernareggi, C., & Belotti, M. (2012). TypeInBraille: quick eyes-free typing on smartphones (pp. 615-622). Springer Berlin Heidelberg.

[6] Mascetti,S., Bernareggi,C.,Belotti, M.(2011).TypeInBraille: A braille-based typing application for touchscreen devices. *Proc. ASSETS '11*. ACM, New York, NY, USA

[7] Jalaliniya, S., Mardanbegi, D., Sintos, I., and Garcia, D. 2015. EyeDroid: an open source mobile gaze tracker on Android for eyewear computers. In *Adjunct Proceedings of the 2015 ACM International Joint Conference on Pervasive and Ubiquitous Computing and Proceedings of the 2015 ACM International Symposium on Wearable Computers* (UbiComp/ISWC'15 Adjunct). ACM, New York, NY, USA, 873-879. DOI=http://dx.doi.org/10.1145/2800835.2804336

[8] Oliveira, J., Guerreiro, T., Nicolau., H, Jorge, J., and Gonçalves, D. 2011. BrailleType: Unleashing Braille over

[9] Frey, B., Southern, C., and Romero. M. 2011. BrailleTouch: mobile texting for the visually impaired. In *Universal Access in Human-Computer Interaction. Context Diversity.* Springer,19-25.

[10] Southern, C., Clawson, J., Frey, B., Abowd, G., and Romero. M. 2012. An evaluation of BrailleTouch: mo- bile touchscreen text entry for the visually impaired. In *International Conference on Human-computer interaction with mobile devices and services*. ACM.

[11] Mattheiss, E, Georg, R, Johann, S, Markus, G., Schrammel, J, Garschall, M., & Tscheligi, M. 2015. EdgeBraille: Braille-based text input for touch devicesnull. *Journal of Assistive Technologies*, 9(3), 147–158.

[12] Azenkot, S., J., Wobbrock, O., Prasain, S., and Ladner., R. E. 2012. Input finger detection for nonvisual touch screen text entry in Perkinput. In *Graphics Interface*.

[13] SEPIC, B., GHANEM, A., and VOGEL, S. 2015. BrailleEasy: One-handed Braille Keyboard for Smartphones. *Qatar Computing Research Institute, Qatar Foundation*

[14] Guerreiro, T., P. Lagoa , P., Santana, P., Goncalves, D., and Jorge., J. 2008. NavTap and BrailleTap: non-visual texting interfaces. In *Resna*.

[15] Bonner, M. N., Brudvik, J. T., Abowd, G. D. and Edwards. W. K. 2010. No-look notes: accessible eyes-free multi-touch text entry. In *Pervasive Computing*. Springer.

[16] English for Students. 2015. SMS Message Sentences. Retrieved from http://www.english-for-students.com/SMS-Message-Sentences.html

[17] Yamada, H. (1980). A Historical Study of Typewriters and Typing Methods: from the Position of Planning Japanese Parallels. Journal of Information Processing, 2, 175-202.

[18] Barbara Pierce. Braille--what is it? What does it mean to the blind? *The World Under My Fingers: Personal Reflections on Braille*. [serial online] 1995 [cited 2016 Mar 14]; 15(1), Available from: URL: Retrieved from https://nfb.org/images/nfb/publications/fr/fr15/issue1

[19] R.W. Soukoreff, & I.S. MacKenzie, Recent developments in text entry error rate measurements. Extended Abstracts, *Proc. ACM Conference on Human Factors in Computing Systems*, New Y ork, NY , 2004, 1425-1428.

[20] R.W. Soukoreff, & I.S. MacKenzie, Metrics for text entry research: An evaluation of MSD and KSPC, and a new unified error metric. *Proc. ACM Conference on Human Factors in Computing Systems – CHI 2003*, New Y ork, NY , 2003, 113 -120.

[21] Shaun, K. Kane, Jacob O. Wobbrock, Richard E. Ladner. 2011. Usable gestures for blind people: understanding preference and performance, Proceedings of the SIGCHI Conference on Human Factors in Computing Systems, May 07-12, 2011, Vancouver, BC, Canada, doi:10.1145/1978942.1979001

How People with Low Vision Access Computing Devices: Understanding Challenges and Opportunities

Sarit Szpiro
Jacobs Technion-Cornell
Institute, Cornell Tech
New York, USA
sarit.szpiro@cornell.edu

Shafeka Hashash
Jacobs Technion-Cornell
Institute, Cornell Tech
New York, USA
snh57@cornell.com

Yuhang Zhao
Jacobs Technion-Cornell
Institute, Cornell Tech
New York, USA
Information Science,
Cornell University, NY, USA
yz769@cornell.edu

Shiri Azenkot
Jacobs Technion-Cornell
Institute, Cornell Tech
New York, USA
shiri.azenkot@cornell.edu

ABSTRACT

Low vision is a pervasive condition in which people have difficulty seeing even with corrective lenses. People with low vision frequently use mainstream computing devices, however how they use their devices to access information and whether digital low vision accessibility tools provide adequate support remains understudied. We addressed these questions with a contextual inquiry study. We observed 11 low vision participants using their smartphones, tablets, and computers when performing simple tasks such as reading email. We found that participants preferred accessing information visually than aurally (e.g., screen readers), and juggled a variety of accessibility tools. However, accessibility tools did not provide them with appropriate support. Moreover, participants had to constantly perform multiple gestures in order to see content comfortably. These challenges made participants inefficient—they were slow and often made mistakes; even tech savvy participants felt frustrated and not in control. Our findings reveal the unique needs of low vision people, which differ from those of people with no vision and design opportunities for improving low vision accessibility tools.

ACM Classification Keywords

• **Social and professional topics~Assistive technologies** • Human-centered computing~User studies • Human-centered computing~Empirical studies in accessibility

1. INTRODUCTION

Visual impairments have different manifestations and can affect seeing in a variety of ways, from a simple need for glasses, through low vision to no vision at all. Low vision is used to describe a variety of visual conditions that cannot be corrected with glasses or contact lenses and affect daily functions (e.g., Stargardt's Disease or Retinitis Pigmentosa). Low vision is pervasive, at least 3.3 million Americans over the age of 40 have low vision [34], and this estimate is expected to increase dramatically in the coming decades due to age related eye disease [7, 22]. People with low vision may have limited peripheral or central vision, blurred vision, extreme light sensitivity, or tunnel vision [6], thus their visual experiences are very different from people who have no vision.

ASSETS '16, October 23-26, 2016, Reno, NV, USA
© 2016 ACM. ISBN 978-1-4503-4124-0/16/10...$15.00
DOI: http://dx.doi.org/10.1145/2982142.2982168

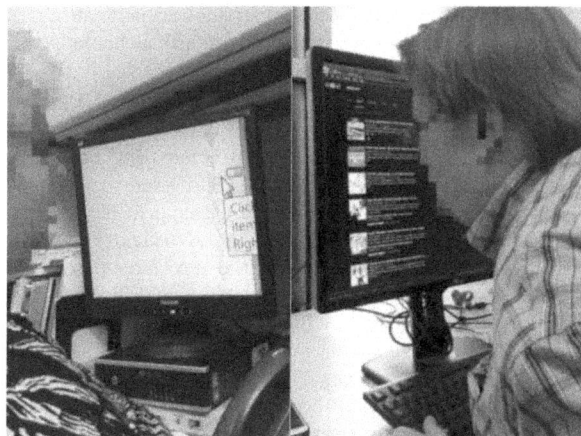

Figure 1: On the left, a participant uses Microsoft Outlook with a screen magnifier leading to two problems. First, the flag symbol appears on her screen but the corresponding email cannot be viewed simultaneously. Second, her mouse initiated a context menu that is out of view. On the right, a participant sits close to the screen because he doesn't want to use a screen magnifier; the display colors are inverted, which distorts the images.

Today, technology assumes an increasingly important role in many aspects of our lives, and accessing digital information is required for education, employment and leisure. It is thus important to minimize the digital gap in our society, especially for people with disabilities and the first step to that end is to understand what factors lead to the divide. Thus, we conducted a study that examined how people with low vision interact with their personal computing devices (smartphones, tablets, and laptop and desktop computers) when performing common daily activities such as reading an online article. Specifically, we asked how do people use their devices: *what* accessibility tools do they use, *how* do they use these tools, and *what challenges* do they face when using them.

Low vision people use a variety of mainstream computing devices such as smartphones, tablets, and e-books [9], but there has been little research on how software low vision accessibility tools are used to interact with these devices. Previous research on accessibility tools has focused on accessing print materials with low vision aids (e.g., optical lens magnifiers). Low vision aids (LVAs) are somewhat useful for low vision people [21], but many LVAs are abandoned [10]. It is unclear whether and how LVAs help access digital interfaces. There has been little research on software low vision accessibility tools. One study examined browsing with a screen magnifier and found that participants struggled to get an overview of a webpage due to the limited view of the screen magnifier [30]. Some studies examined performance on computer tasks (e.g., icon identification tasks and mouse movements) and found that low vision people did not perform well on them [18, 27, 28]. Still, it remains understudied how people with low vision access interfaces on mainstream devices (such as smartphones) and whether and how they use low vision accessibility tools.

For our study, we recruited 11 low vision participants where we observed them as they completed several common tasks on their personal computing devices (i.e., smartphones, tablets and computers) such as reading online news and writing an email. We used contextual inquiry [34] to interview and observe them in-situ. This method, in which researchers observe participants' behavior in a daily activity in real-time, allowed us to discover how people with low vision access interfaces with technology and whether and how they use accessibility tools.

Our study revealed three key findings:

1. Low vision software accessibility tools did not meet participants' needs. Participants struggled trying to constantly adjust to changes in visual content (e.g., when switching between applications or websites), but still preferred visual information to text-to-speech options.
2. Low vision software accessibility tools were difficult to use. Even though software accessibility tools required many gestures to manipulate, they did not provide enough control for participants to see content comfortably. Even proficient technology users had difficulties performing simple tasks like reading an online news article. This prevented some participants from using accessibility tools such as screen magnifiers. Moreover, the inefficiency of interacting with technology made participants feel loss of control and disorientation.
3. Participants often felt uncomfortable disclosing their disability, which also prevented them from using certain tools.

In summary, our findings illuminate the gaps between existing accessibility tools and the needs of low vision people. Our study highlights opportunities to improve the design of accessibility tools for the large and understudied low vision population.

2. RELATED WORK
2.1 Use of Low Vision Aids

Several studies found that using low vision aids (LVAs) like lens magnifiers and video magnifiers can be effective. In many cases, researchers measured the effectiveness of LVAs by asking people to read newsprint. For example, a study conducted in Britain found that LVAs significantly improved newsprint reading for low vision people [21] and a study in Finland found that 91.4% of low vision participants were able to read newsprint with low vision aids [31]. Yet, these studies only examined reading printed material with magnification in controlled lab experiments.

Although LVAs can be helpful, several studies found that they are often not used. A survey study in the U.S. found that 19% of prescribed devices were abandoned (defined as not used in the last three months) [10]. Surveys in Europe have found even larger abandonment rates. In Scotland, a third of low vision participants reported that they never used their LVAs [23] and in Britain this number was as high as 77% [16]. It remains unclear why people abandon their LVAs: while in one study abandonment of LVAs was associated with non-central vision loss, but not with age, time

from prescription, or visual acuity [10], in another study decreased visual acuity and increased age were significant factors that decreased the use of LVAs [23].

One method that increases the use of LVAs is training and vision rehabilitation services. In the U.S., training and vision rehabilitation are often provided by private optometry practices and state agencies [25]. These training services can teach people how to effectively use their residual vision and how to use prescribed LVAs [24]. Training enables people to use their LVAs more effectively and was even associated with lowering depression rates [15]. However, despite the fact that rehabilitation services are helpful and available, they are not fully taken advantage of. Only 44% of ophthalmologists and 27% of optometrists referred low vision patients to rehabilitation [35], and one survey of low vision adults showed that the percent of participants receiving rehabilitation services was as low as 6% [4]. Importantly, people who receive training are more likely to use their devices. For example, in a survey of American veterans with low vision most reported receiving more than 20 hours of training and continued to use their devices frequently [32].

These studies illustrate the gaps between the availability, effectiveness, and use of LVAs, and the availability of vision rehabilitation services. Critically, these studies examined the usability of LVAs for reading print. It is unclear whether and how these aids are used for accessing computer interfaces.

2.2 Use of Technology by Low Vision People

People with low vision use technology frequently, but the patterns and challenges of their use of technology remain understudied. Electronic books have been shown to improve access to books for people with low vision [8, 9, 12]. For example, one study found that reading on digital readers, such as the iPad, was faster than reading print (with the same text size), for age-related macular degeneration patients [13]. A recent survey examined the use of electronic consumer devices by people with visual impairments, and found that most people with low vision used a smartphone and nearly half used a tablet [9]. Smartphones were used for phone calls (94% of users), text messaging (90%), email and internet (80%), and other applications (77%); tablets were used for internet browsing (100%), reading books (60%), and for using applications (54%). Most participants reported that changing the text size was the most useful function on their smartphones; unfortunately, the authors did not discriminate between methods that modify the text size, so it remains unclear how they changed fonts (by changing the font size, using pinch-to-zoom, or using screen magnifiers). Other useful functions were text-to-speech (36%), followed by using a large screen (34%), and the ability to modify contrast (30%) and font type (26%). On tablets, similar functions were indicated as useful, though to a lesser degree. Interestingly, nearly half of the participants indicated that they used the device's camera to see objects more easily, most likely as a digital magnifier. It is important to note however that in the study participants were recruited via social media and thus the sample is not representative. The authors recommend, "that device and content manufacturers consider the needs of people with vision impairment when designing and upgrading their systems," but they do not describe any specific challenges low vision people may have or make any specific recommendations about how to modify devices and applications to make them more suitable for low vision people.

Pseudo-nym	Age/Gender	Employment	Diagnosis And Visual Acuity	Diagnosis Onset	Computing Devices
Richard	56/M	Retired programmer	Bilateral Optic Atrophy; 20/220	Birth	Samsung Galaxy 4, Windows Computer
Lora	55/F	Part time dance instructor	Steven Johnson Syndrome; left: 20/150, right: 120/200	4	Feature phone, Windows Computer
Gordon	23/M	Student; Programmer	Stargardt's Disease; Unknown	21	iPhone, MacBook Pro, Apple Watch
Joanna	55/F	Unemployed	Pathological myopia (right eye), detached retina (left eye); 20/200	25	iPhone, Sony Xperia tablet, MacBook Pro
Yasmin	68/F	Part time teacher at a senior center	No vision in the right eye; tunnel vision in the left eye; left: 20/80	55	iPhone, Windows Computer
Adam	36/M	Math Tutor	Reverse Retinitis Pigmentosa; 20/300	6	iPhone, iPad, Windows Computer
Marie	58/F	Teacher for the visually impaired	Retinopathy of Prematurity; left: 20/400; right: 20/300	Birth	iPhone, Windows Computer
Ethan	31/M	Private contractor	Albinism; 20/200	Birth	iPhone, iPad, Windows Computer
Megan	30/F	Student	Nystagmus; Unknown	Birth	LG smartphone, Windows Computer
Oprah	20/F	Student	Stargardt's Disease; Unknown	19	iPhone, MacBook Pro
Kate	59/F	Technology sales	Retinitis Pigmentosa (Usher syndrome); 20/50	50	iPhone, iPad, MacBook Pro, Apple Watch

Table 1: Participant information and devices they used.

Some studies examined the challenges of performing tasks on the computer by people with low vision. Theofanos and Redish observed how low vision participants use ZoomText [33] when browsing a U.S. government site and described several challenges participants experienced [30]. For example, participants struggled to get an overview of a webpage due to the limited view of a screen magnifier. Another challenge was that participants missed items on the screen. Menus on the right of the webpage were rarely viewed, and white space in a webpage layout caused confusion when magnified because it became huge. Some developed strategies to overcome their challenges like copying text material to a word document. The authors made several recommendations for web-design, such as not relying on color to convey information (because some users modify the color view) and checking that style sheets and fonts enlarge properly when enlarging the text size using the browser.

Several studies examined how age-related macular degeneration patients use computers. In one study the majority of participants (70.6%) used a computer at least a few times a month, mainly for using email clients, web browsing, and word processing [3]. However, using the computer was difficult for participants with age-related macular degeneration: two studies found that performance on icon identification tasks (accuracy and speed) decreased as visual function decreased [28], and that smaller and more icons on the screen made it harder to identify icons [27]. Another study examined cursor movements by people with age-related-macular degeneration and found that movement speed and velocity were lower for people with lower visual acuities, and that performance improved when targets were larger [18].

Although prior work examined some aspects of computer use by people with low vision, the challenges they experience when accessing interfaces during daily tasks remain understudied. For example, it is unclear what tools low vision people use on smartphones to access information, how they use them, and whether these tools provide appropriate support. Several publications emphasized the need for more studies that explore the needs of low vision people when using technology [5, 17]. Our goal is to address this need with the study we present here.

2.3 Stigma and Technology Use
Beyond the difficulties of using low vision aids and performing tasks on the computers, studies found that people with low vision were concerned about social stigma. Shinohara and Wobbrock

studied the social factors of interaction with assistive technology faced by people of different types of disabilities (motor, hearing, and visual impairments) [29]. They interviewed three participants with low vision and found that these participants felt self-conscious about using specialized devices, because it made their disability apparent. Kane et al. studied the accessibility of mobile devices in everyday life [20]. They found that situational impairments affected the use of mobile devices on-the-go for low vision people (e.g., lighting), and also observed low vision participants modify settings on their phones to see content. A low vision participant in their study described feeling socially awkward when using an optical magnifying glass to read text on her phone. At the time of the study only two of the nine low vision participants owned a smartphone (while today this number is likely to be higher [9]). Thus, the accessibility of touch devices was not explored in depth. Moreover, while previous studies examined the social aspects of using devices, we were also interested in examining the interactions in non-social setting, what motivated or frustrated participants when using accessibility tools.

3. METHODS
3.1 Participants
We recruited 11 participants (see Table 1) from local mailing lists of low vision people and word of mouth. We conducted a brief screening interview over the phone to determine whether the volunteers were indeed low vision by asking whether they used aids that enhanced their vision. Although all participants were low vision, they had different visual conditions. It was beyond the scope of this work to study specific types of low vision in depth. Participants varied in age from 20 to 68 (mean=44.6, SD=16.8), gender (four males, seven females), employment status (four full time, five part-time or students, and two were unemployed), and technology experience (from a computer programmer to participants who used a computer only occasionally).

3.2 Procedure
Our study consisted of a two-hour session, which started with a brief semi-structured interview about participants' demographics, employment status, visual condition, and use of computing devices.

Our goal in the study was to observe how participants used their devices to access information across applications. To that end, we brainstormed common tasks people perform on their devices and used the following: find an online news article related to finance and read it aloud, find an email and write a short response, write a grocery list, send a text message, and pick an item from a take-out menu. We asked participants to perform all of these tasks on all of their devices. We did not expect participants to use specific applications because participants owned different devices and had their own preferences. If participants did not perform a task frequently or were not able to do so, we did not insist that they complete the task, because we were interested in observing tasks that participants completed routinely. For example, Richard did not read news online, and Yasmin forgot her password and could not login to her email. We also asked participants to demonstrate how they used any other frequently used applications.

While participants performed the tasks, we observed them and occasionally interrupted with questions. We encouraged participants to explain what they did and why, to understand their motivations and thought processes, following a master-apprentice relationship model of contextual inquiry [1]. We sought to identify the challenges they encountered accessing information when performing tasks: when they chose to use assistive tools, what tools they used and why (e.g., screen magnifier versus screen reader), how they used these tools (e.g., panning or modifying magnification level), how the completed the task (e.g., whether it was efficient) and how they felt performing it (e.g., frustrated).

For nine participants, the study was conducted in the lab, and for two it was conducted at their homes. We asked participants who came to the lab to bring their computing devices and if not possible (e.g., Lora did not own a computer but regularly used one at her local library) we made sure to have in the lab the assistive software they used (e.g., ZoomText).

3.3 Analysis

We audio-recorded all interviews and had them transcribed by a professional service. During the interviews, we took pictures of scenarios that illustrated participants' challenges.

We initially developed codes using open coding during data collection. After data collection was finished, two researchers independently read the transcripts and categorized the data. The researchers met periodically and discussed the coding categories (the challenges, strategies, and tools participants used). In the rare cases when coders disagreed, they discussed the issue until they reached agreement. We continued recruiting participants until we reached saturation: no new challenges or strategies were revealed.

Subsequently, the researchers developed themes using axial coding [26] and affinity diagrams [1].

4. RESULTS

Participants struggled to use technology for a variety of reasons. Except for one case, none of the participants used LVAs to access their devices; instead they used software accessibility tools. We describe specific challenges with the most frequently used accessibility tools like screen magnifiers. We also describe challenges that were evident across tools and tasks, such as knowing what tools are available or the difficulty using gestures.

4.1 Specific Challenges With Low Vision Accessibility Software

The first thing we noticed when participants used their devices is that they used many accessibility tools. We summarize the tools participants used in **Tables 2-3**, however we note that this list of tools only represents tools that were frequently used by participants and many more are available in the market. Participants also appropriated existing tools for accessibility (e.g., the phone's camera or display settings). Moreover, participants often used several tools simultaneously or switched between them depending on the task or their ability to see content. Overall, the experience of using such tools was challenging. Ethan explained the difficulty using low vision accessibility tools:

You're either stuck with reading a bunch of stuff that you just don't want to read [with VoiceOver] or you're stuck with just using all these gestures and fighting to find your position of where you want to be [with Zoom]. (Ethan)

4.1.1 Screen Magnification

Five participants used screen magnifiers on their personal computers (ZoomText, Magic, or Zoom) and three used it regularly on their touch devices (e.g., Zoom). However, participants encountered different challenges with screen magnifiers. These challenges with screen magnification led participants to struggle using them and even avoid screen magnifiers altogether. Instead, some enlarged text if possible, and all participants positioned the screen of the device very close to their eyes at some point during the study.

On computers, the main challenge with screen magnifiers was that participants had difficulty panning. Several screen magnification applications are available on computers (see **Table 3**). Users move the cursor to pan them. Participants did not like panning. For example, Adam did not use screen magnifiers at all on his computer, because of the difficulty panning; instead, he moved his head very close to the part of the screen he wanted to see (see **Figure 1**). Kate summarized why she didn't like to use Zoom on her MacBook because it was "tedious and time-consuming."

Another challenge with screen magnifiers was that the field of view was small, making it difficult to see the context and leading participants to miss items. For example, Marie tried to understand whether an email was important in Outlook. In Outlook there are flag symbols to indicate importance of emails, and they appear inline with the title of the email. However, because Marie used a screen magnifier the space between the email and the corresponding symbol became huge, which made it hard to understand which email matches which symbol (See **Figure 1**).

Yet another challenge with screen magnifiers was that magnification was uniform across the screen regardless of content, making it difficult to navigate and understand content. For example, pictures became huge and thus hard to see. When Marie read an online news article she explained she couldn't see pictures and read the text simultaneously because the level of magnification she required for reading, makes the pictures "overwhelming," which made her feel "lost". She ended up switching back and forth between magnification levels to read the article comfortably.

Technique	Tools	Platform	Description	Designed For LV?
Magnification	Zoom	OSX	Screen Magnifier. Activated by the keyboard, panning performed with the cursor.	Yes
	Windows Magnifier, ZoomText, Magic	Windows	Screen Magnifiers. Activated by the keyboard, panning performed with the cursor.	Yes
Inverted Colors	Dark Mode	OSX	Inverts the colors of menus.	No
	Negative Colors	OSX, Windows	Inverts colors of content.	Yes
Text-to-Speech	Speak Selection	OSX	A text-to-speech option that allows users to select text to be read aloud.	No
	VoiceOver, ZoomText, Magic	OSX, Windows	A screen reader that allows the user to access content on their device with synthesized speech.	Yes

Table 3: Tools used by participants on laptop or desktop computers.

In some cases using the screen magnifier made it impossible to perform certain actions. For example, when Marie was using Outlook, she moved her cursor on an item leading a context menu to appear, but because of magnification, the menu was outside the field of view, when she panned to see the menu, she moved the cursor causing the menu to disappear (see **Figure 1**).

On touch devices (smartphones and tablets), participants either did not know about the screen magnification option, were confused about it (see section **4.2**), or struggled with panning which led them not to use it. On touch devices, panning required multiple fingers to move the view (see **Table 2**) and participants complained that that was especially cumbersome. Participants explained panning meant too much "back and forth" (Yasmin) and "was not easy to manipulate" (Oprah). Adam said he sometimes used his smartphone in landscape orientation to reduce the need for panning. Another strategy, both Adam and Ethan used on their touch devices, was to avoid using screen magnifiers when browsing by switching from mobile versions of websites to desktop versions because desktop versions allow users to pinch-to-zoom to magnify content. Many participants simply held their devices very close to their eyes instead of using a screen magnifier, though this strategy could make their disability apparent to their surrounding (see section **4.3**).

4.1.2 Inverted Colors

Inverting colors was a popular method to access text among participants. Six participants inverted colors to allow them to read text comfortably on their touch devices and one used it on the computer. However, this method inverts *all* colors on the screen regardless of content, which was not always helpful and in many cases confusing. For example, pictures were also inverted, and all participants mentioned they did not like viewing distorted pictures (see **Figure 1**). Oprah explained she even avoided using this method for that reason, "When I do the inverse thing it affects the pictures, and that bothers me. If it would just reverse the text and leave the pictures alone that would be great. I don't use it, because it freaks me out."

Another problem was that in some cases the content's style was already "inverted." Some websites were designed with light text over a dark background, causing a need to un-invert, as Kate explained:

Another trouble with inverting colors is let's say you're in one part of an app and the background is white and you've got it inverted, now I have that nice dark color but another page in the app or an app like the weather apps, uses the dark backgrounds already and you go to those, you're, "Oops! Okay I've got to hurry up and turn my inverted colors off because that one's already inverted now I have to un-invert it in order to read it". (Kate)

Switching between the "normal" and the "inverted" mode was tiring for participants. Adam explained he sometimes simply avoided switching between modes. For example, when shopping on Amazon, he only viewed the shapes of products and read the product descriptions for color information, because products pictures were inverted.

Kate, who worked in technology sales, found it difficult to communicate at work because she inverted colors on her devices, "People use color to reference things all the time. At work, it's a real problem when people go and click on the blue button while I have inverted colors, so it happens to be, orange or something." She was also disturbed that the esthetic design of a webpage changes so dramatically when colors are inverted. All the participants who used this feature expressed a desire for a "smart" invert option, which will invert text, but intelligently, making sure that only text is inverted and that the color schemes will be chosen to accommodate the needs of low vision people.

4.1.3 Text-to-Speech

Participants had mixed feelings about text-to-speech options. Although many used text-to-speech (six participants), they tended to prefer accessing materials visually. Participants explained that even though their vision is not like a sighted person, they preferred using it than converting information to audio because visual text was easier to comprehend. Lora explained that when she was taking a college course, she was only offered auditory learning materials because of her visual impairment, but she was not able to process auditory information as well as she could visually, "I need to see it to retain it. When listening to something, I couldn't absorb learning the material as quickly as I could when I was able to see it." Adam said that reading visually helps him comprehend the text and described himself, "I'm kind of a weird blind person, I'm very visual. Not that I couldn't understand it if I was listening, but it's just easier [to read visually]." Myra as a teacher for the visually impaired, said she recommends low vision students screen readers when their visual reading was so slow that they lost the meaning of the text. It is worth noting that Kate, who was hard of hearing, found it difficult to use text-to-speech options.

Although most participants preferred reading visually, six participants still used text-to-speech options, mostly on touch

Main Function	Tools	Platform	Description	Designed For Low Vision?
Magnification	Zoom, Magnifying Gestures	iOS, Android	Screen Magnifier. Activated by triple tap, panning performed with three (iOS) or two (Android) fingers.	Yes
	Pinch-to-Zoom	iOS, Android	Allows enlarging content by pinching two fingers. Works only on some applications and websites.	No
	Camera	iOS, Android	The camera can be appropriated as a magnifier to enlarge objects in the user's surroundings.	No
	Magnification Applications, KNFB Reader	iOS, Android	Applications that magnify objects in the environment using the camera. KNFB Reader converts printed text to digital text using the camera and OCR technology.	Yes
Inverted Colors	Invert Colors, Negative Colors	iOS, Android	Inverts all colors on the screen.	Yes
Text-To-Speech	VoiceOver, TalkBack	iOS, Android	A screen reader that allows the user to access content on their device based on spoken descriptions.	Yes
	Speak Selection	iOS	A text-to-speech option that allows users to select text to be read aloud.	Yes
Speech Input	Dictation	iOS, Android	A speech-to-text option that allows users to dictate text to their phone instead of typing it.	No
	Siri	iOS	A speech-to-text option that allows users to speak voice commands on the phone.	No
Font Settings	Device Settings	iOS, Android	Allows users to modify font size, font type and font boldness on built in system applications.	No
Contrast/ Brightness	Device Settings	iOS	Allows users to control display brightness and contrast.	No

Table 2: Tools used by participants on mobile devices.

devices, though three participants also used it on their computers. On touch devices, participants mainly used screen readers (VoiceOver or TalkBack), but struggled controlling them. The main problem with screen readers was that they were designed for eyes-free interaction, but our low vision participants wanted to use their vision to control them. For example, participants wanted to choose what would be read aloud, scroll through irrelevant text and read visually while listening to the speech by using Zoom or pinch-to-zoom. Another challenge was that interacting with screen readers required gestures that could not be combined with non-screen reader gestures. Thus, the screen reader gestures did not work well with other low vision enhancements gestures such as Zoom or pinch-to-zoom. In contrast to touch devices, on the computer, participants used text-to-speech, but none used screen readers, which made their interactions more efficient. Three participants used "Speak Selection" on Mac for reading long texts and Ethan used NVDA [14] on his PC, a program that allowed users to move the cursor to positions that would be read aloud.

4.1.4 Appropriating the Phone's Camera as a Magnifier

While the previous accessibility tools improved access to the device's interface, the phone's camera can improve access to the environment. Six participants appropriated the phone's camera as a digital magnifier to enlarge objects in the environment. Three participants compared the phone's camera to a portable CCTV. Participants complained about the camera's autofocus and the low resolution of the pictures. For example, Marie said she always used her magnifying lens first, because the camera goes "in and out of focus." Still, she said she liked the phone's camera because it allowed her to modify magnification while the magnification level of the magnifying glass is fixed. Ethan used a dedicated applications with OCR technology (see **Table 2**) to convert images to digital texts that can be read more easily (because fonts and colors can be adjusted) or used with text-to-speech.

4.2 Knowing What's Available

Participants' knowledge of accessibility tools varied. While some participants were proficient users of multiple accessibility tools (e.g., Ethan, Kate, Gordon), others did not know what was available or how to operate them (e.g., Marie, Oprah). Several times during the study the researcher asked about an accessibility tool, and participants wanted to be taught how to use it.

Ten participants used a smartphone daily (all participants except for Lora who owned a feature phone) , but none of our participants were trained to use their smartphones' accessibility tools. This lack of knowledge, led many to struggle using accessibility tools on their smartphone and to use their phones in general. For example, five participants did not know about the option to use a screen magnifier (e.g., Zoom). Moreover, all participants were confused at some point during the study regarding whether pinch-to-zoom can be used to magnify content (note that the screen magnifier can always be used). For example, Joanna explained she didn't use Zoom because its magnification level is limited, when in fact it's pinch-to-zoom level magnification that is limited. Yasmin, did not know about Zoom, and held an optical magnifier over her phone.

4.3 Discomfort Disclosing Oneself as LV

Participants discussed their discomfort with having people around them know they are visually impaired, since in most cases their disability was invisible. There was, however, one outlier, Adam, who was active in blind culture and occasionally used a cane, was very comfortable with his low vision identity. Except for Adam other participants' discomfort disclosing their disability affected their use of technology.

Participants felt uncomfortable modifying programs in ways that allowed them to see more easily, when it made their disability apparent in social settings. Gordon, a university student, avoided inverting colors on Microsoft Word despite the significant visual assistance it provided because he was worried it would attract attention. Instead, he would take notes in a coding editor, which is more commonly used with inverted colors, and thus did not attract attention. Moreover, Gordon also avoided increasing the font size on his computer's settings. He said, "I'm definitely a little self conscious about it, which might also be a subconscious reason I don't change as many things on my computer."

Similarly, other participants did not use certain technologies because strangers were in the vicinity. For instance, Richard did not use text-to-speech software, because he was worried what strangers would think about him, and Marie did not use her smartphone on the subway because she was worried that the magnified content would attract attention and put her at risk as a person with a disability. Participants who did use technology did so discreetly. For example, Joanna used the phone's camera to look at street signs and to recognize people approaching her, but was worried strangers would get upset if they thought she was photographing them. She used the camera covertly: "I pretend like I'm talking on the phone and not taking a picture."

4.4 Changes in Visual Experiences

One main challenge of low vision is that the visual experience of people with low vision varies across time (months or even during the day) and scenarios (e.g., lighting conditions). This challenge was amplified for our participants when using their devices, because the content on their devices changed constantly (e.g., between applications) and so their ability to comfortably see it.

Inconsistent experiences stemmed from different factors. Some were due to limited abilities of accessibility tools. For example, increasing the font in the settings of devices only affected built-in applications on the phone, and the pinch-zoom worked only on some websites. Another challenge was the variability of content itself—designs of websites can include multiple background colors, font styles and sizes. This created issues for participants, who had to adjust the zoom level and invert colors accordingly. For example, in Messages application on the iPhone the user's messages have a different background color than the messages sent by others. When inverted, the user's own messages have an orange background and black text, making it difficult to read. Gordon explained how he had to constantly switch colors to use the applications, "let's say someone sent me a text and I'm trying to read it, I'll read it, type it, invert, read it, type, invert back to normal."

4.5 Difficulty with Gestures

Participants struggled to use multiple gestures to adjust the content to see it comfortably. When using invert colors, participants often had to switch between turning it on and off, to allow them to read easily (see example in Section **4.4**). Similarly, using screen magnifiers required panning, which was especially demanding on touch devices, because it required scrolling with multiple fingers (see **Table 3**). Moreover, participants regularly switched between zoom levels according to the font size on the screen. In many cases the difficulty performing multiple gestures led participants to ignore certain content on the screen. For example, Adam did not look at photos of products because switching between the reverse colors modes to be able to read text versus seeing images was too much work, and Yasmin missed an error message because she did not pan the magnifier around the page.

Although performing gestures was difficult for participants, they wanted more options to control the interface. For example, participants who used VoiceOver wanted to be able to use their ability to see screen content to control VoiceOver and even combine it with using the Zoom simultaneously. Ethan was the only participant who used "Speak Selection" on his phone, which gave more control over what would be read out loud and was clearly an advantage, but even he still used VoiceOver occasionally. Participants also wanted to control font size and colors in menus of different applications.

4.6 Confusion and Loss of Control

Participants often felt a loss of control when they interacted with their devices. For example, when Adam used a Zoom gesture that also initiated a VoiceOver action, he said that he feels like he has a ghost in his phone. Marie, was panning on a shopping website and suddenly the product image appeared huge because her mouse cursor hovered over it. She felt disoriented: "Now I'm lost, and I don't even know how I got here."

Participants also frequently made mistakes that caused disorientation or annoyance. Adam said that needing to pan the magnifier as he read interrupted his flow. At some point when he was panning, he was confused because he accidentally clicked an ad. Similarly, Ethan clicked a popup ad by accident and then described how upsetting it can be to try and close it: "I would get so annoyed, because I would be trying to find the close button for that." These miss-clicks are noteworthy especially since both Ethan and Adam were tech savvy participants, Ethan was an IT contractor and Adam had built his own computer.

4.7 Inefficiency When Using Technology

Participants were inefficient when performing common tasks because they made errors, were slow, and did not see items on the screen. Even tech-savvy participants made mistakes by clicking on wrong items on the screen (see above, section **4.6**). Moreover, because low vision is associated with low visual acuity, it was hard for participants to see items on the screen. For example, when Lora was asked to choose an article from the finance section, she panned around the menus several times but missed the button. The difficulty seeing items made performing tasks time consuming. For example, when visiting new webpages with a screen magnifier, Lora described how she had to slowly pan around the page to learn its layout and menu locations, which made her anxious.

Software updates came up as an issue for two participants because they had to learn new interactions, but learning itself was difficult because the accessibility of the device had changed due to the update. For example, Gordon mentioned an update that changed menu items to a thin font, which he could barely see, and Kate said she prepared herself ahead of time to learn how to deal with software updates in the fall. Kate summarized the inefficiency of using low vision accessibility tools:

I can still somehow or another, with magnification, with taking a picture, with doing whatever, I can force myself to do most things. It's all about the time. It's not about whether or not there's a way to get it done, it's about how to get it all done in one day. (Kate)

5. DISCUSSION

Low vision has been described as an "invisible disability" [29] because it is not apparent to the surroundings, but it is also invisible in the sense that it lacks public awareness [19], especially in how it affects people's daily life.

Our results emphasize how different visual abilities lead to different interactions with technology. People with little to no vision use eyes-free interaction, and mostly gain information through screen readers. For example, a blind person may use Jaws [2] to interact with their PC and VoiceOver to interact with their iPhone. Although not all content will be accessible, this person would rely on a screen reader to receive auditory information and the quality of the auditory information would be similar (e.g., pitch or speed). In contrast, our participants juggled many accessibility tools that provided a variety of functionalities (see **Tables 2-3**). Although these tools helped our participants customize the visual content, participants still struggled seeing items on the screen and used multiple gestures to control their experience. Still, participants described they preferred accessing information visually than with screen readers. Our participants' challenges also emphasize the difference between people with low vision and sighted people. While people with low vision do have functional vision, it is not nearly as good as sighted people's vision (see **Table 1**). Although some of the problems our participants encountered are also common to sighted people (e.g., accidentally clicking an ad or the annoyance of software updates), the frequency and variety of the issues in conjunction with the many tools participants used illustrate the extra challenges low vision imposes on users. This made their interactions with technology inefficient and often led even tech savvy participants to feel frustrated.

Our study offers a new perspective into the use of technologies by people with low vision. Most previous research on low vision has examined low vision aids (e.g., [10, 16, 21, 23, 24, 32]), rather than low vision software accessibility tools. Only a few studies examined computer interactions, measuring the performance of only one task (e.g., icon identification [27, 28] or mouse movements [18]). One study, performed over a decade ago, examined the challenges and strategies of low vision people on a computer when browsing a government website [30]. They found that the limited field during magnification confused participants. Our study expands this result by finding additional challenges with screen magnifiers on the computer and by also examining the use of screen magnifiers on smartphones. We found that panning gestures were cumbersome and that navigation was difficult because magnification enhanced also pictures and spaces (see Section 4.1.1). Thus, our results highlight how little software accessibility for low vision has improved over the past decade, even given the advances in mobile and computer technologies.

5.1 The Need for Better Vision Enhancement

We found that although participants used many tools, existing tools did not provide adequate support for their needs. On the one hand, existing vision enhancement tools provided ineffective support. All our participants required some level of magnification on their devices, but they struggled using screen magnifiers. Participants found panning difficult and confusing, had to constantly change magnification levels and miss-clicked items. Similarly, color inversion, used by many, provided only limited support because it inverted all colors and thus distorted images and did not help when content was already inverted. On the other hand, screen readers were not a good solution for our participants. Screen readers rely on eyes-free interactions, but our participants stressed they wanted to control screen readers by using visual information. For example, they wanted to use their vision to choose what would be read aloud and to be able to listen to speech while reading visually. However, combining screen magnification gestures with VoiceOver gestures was confusing and hard to manipulate correctly. Furthermore, the majority of participants explained they relied on vision for comprehension, so text-to-speech options did not address all their needs.

These challenges illustrate the need to improve the usability of low vision tools. For example, participants desired smarter color inversion tools that would always provide dark background and light text. Participants also wanted more options to customize text on applications, such as the ability to choose color, background and font size. They also wanted to be able to modify settings across all applications, instead of only on system applications. Improving panning gestures is critical for users to adopt screen magnifiers, especially on touch devices. Participants did not like using multiple fingers for panning, and found the interaction with pinch-to-zoom much easier, probably because it only requires one finger to move the view. Website designers should consider allowing pinch-to-zoom to operate on mobile website versions or at least allow users to switch to desktop website versions so users can use pinch-to-zoom.

Another issue our participants faced was a constant need to adjust to different visual designs. Future research should examine the possibility of using machine learning to learn user's visual abilities and adapt content automatically. For example, systems can infer what font sizes users can see comfortably by capturing users' interactions, possibly in combination with eye tracking. Users may also have similar use patterns, and those could also be learned automatically. Automatic adjustment of content to abilities of users has been shown to be useful [11], and has the potential to benefit also low vision users.

5.2 Training and Discoverability

Prior research showed that training services improved the use of LVAs [32]. Our study further illustrates the importance of such training. For example, none of our participants were trained on using accessibility tools on their smartphones. As a consequence, participants did not know about screen magnifiers on the phone, confused screen magnifiers and pinch-to-zoom, and struggled controlling screen magnifiers. Because smartphones are widely used by low vision people [9] (as also evident in our study), it is important that vision services also teach how to use touch devices in addition to LVAs and computer programs. In addition, designers should also consider the discoverability and usability of accessibility tools.

6. LIMITATIONS

Our goal was to study software accessibility tools on mainstream devices using common tasks like reading email. However, there are additional scenarios that should be explored in future research, such as software tools used at the workplace. We asked participants to use their devices to add ecological validity to our study, but that also limits our results to devices participants owned. Future research should address the challenges of tools and devices that participants may not be familiar with.

7. CONCLUSIONS

In this paper, we presented findings from a study designed to understand the challenges people with low vision face when accessing interfaces on their computing devices. We found that participants faced challenges using accessibility tools, mainly because tools did not provide adequate support for their needs. While accessibility tools required many gestures, they did not provide enough control for participants to see content comfortably. Our study also illustrated how people with low vision rely on their vision to comprehend information, and their need for more sophisticated vision enhancement tools. Our work provides opportunities for future research for an important and ignored user group.

8. REFERENCES

[1]   Beyer, H. and Holtzblatt, K. 1997. *Contextual Design: Defining Customer-Centered Systems*. Elsevier.

[2]   Blindness Solutions: JAWS:
        *http://www.freedomscientific.com/Products/Blindness/JA
        WS.* Accessed: 2016-05-06.

[3]   Brody, B.L., Field, L.C., Roch-Levecq, A.C., Depp, C.,
        Edland, S.D., Minasyan, L. and Brown, S.I. 2012.
        Computer Use among Patients with Age-Related Macular
        Degeneration. *Ophthalmic Epidemiology.* 19, 4 (Aug.
        2012), 190–195.

[4]   Casten, R.J., Maloney, E.K. and Rovner, B.W. 2005.
        Knowledge and Use of Low Vision Services Among
        Persons with Age-related Macular Degeneration. *Journal
        of Visual Impairment and Blindness.* 99, 11 (2005), 720–
        724.

[5]   Chiang, M.F., Cole, R.G., Gupta, S., Kaiser, G.E. and
        Starren, J.B. 2005. Computer and World Wide Web
        accessibility by visually disabled patients: problems and
        solutions. *Survey of ophthalmology.* 50, 4 (Jan. 2005),
        394–405.

[6]   Common Types of Low Vision:
        *http://www.aoa.org/patients-and-public/caring-for-your-
        vision/low-vision/common-types-of-low-vision?sso=y.*
        Accessed: 2015-09-21.

[7]   Congdon, N., O'Colmain, B., Klaver, C.C.W., Klein, R.,
        Muñoz, B., Friedman, D.S., Kempen, J., Taylor, H.R.
        and Mitchell, P. 2004. Causes and prevalence of visual
        impairment among adults in the United States. *Archives
        of ophthalmology (Chicago, Ill. : 1960).* 122, 4 (Apr.
        2004), 477–85.

[8]   Crossland, M.D., Macedo, A.F. and Rubin, G.S. 2010.
        Electronic books as low vision aids. *British Journal of
        Ophthalmology.* 94, 8 (Aug. 2010), 1109–1109.

[9]   Crossland, M.D., S. Silva, R., Macedo, A.F., Silva, R.S.,
        Macedo, A.F., S. Silva, R. and Macedo, A.F. 2014.
        Smartphone, tablet computer and e-reader use by people
        with vision impairment. *Ophthalmic and Physiological
        Optics.* 34, 5 (Sep. 2014), 552–557.

[10]   Dougherty, B.E., Kehler, K.B., Jamara, R., Patterson, N.,
        Valenti, D. and Vera-Diaz, F. a. 2011. Abandonment of
        Low-Vision Devices in an Outpatient Population.
        Optometry and Vision Science. 88, 11 (Nov. 2011),
        1283–1287.

[11]   Gajos, K.Z., Wobbrock, J.O. and Weld, D.S. 2008.
        Improving the performance of motor-impaired users with
        automatically-generated, ability-based interfaces. *Proc.
        CHI '08,* ACM, New York, New York, USA, 1257-1266.

[12]   Gill, K., Mao, A., Powell, A.M. and Sheidow, T. 2013.
        Digital reader vs print media: the role of digital
        technology in reading accuracy in age-related macular
        degeneration. *Eye.* 27, 5 (May 2013), 639–643.

[13]   Gill, K., Mao, A., Powell, A.M. and Sheidow, T. 2013.
        Digital reader vs print media: the role of digital
        technology in reading accuracy in age-related macular
        degeneration. *Eye (London, England).* 27, 5 (May 2013),
        639–43.

[14]   Home of the free NVDA screen reader:
        http://www.nvaccess.org/. Accessed: 2016-05-06.

[15]   Horowitz, A., Reinhardt, J.P., Boerner, K. and Travis,
        L.A. 2003. The influence of health, social support quality
        and rehabilitation on depression among disabled elders.
        Aging Ment Health. 7, 5 (Sep. 2003), 342–350.

[16]   Humphry, R.C. and Thompson, G.M. 1986. Low vision
        aids--evaluation in a general eye department.
        *Transactions of the ophthalmological societies of the
        United Kingdom.* 105 (Pt 3, (Jan. 1986), 296–303.

[17]   Jacko, J. a and Sears, A. 1998. Designing interfaces for
        an overlooked user group: Considering the visual profiles
        of partially sighted users. *Annual ACM Conference on
        Assistive Technologies, Proceedings.* New York, NY,
        United States (1998), 75–77.

[18]   Jacko, J.A., Barreto, A.B., Marmet, G.J., Chu, J.Y.M.,
        Bautsch, H.S., Scott, I.U. and Rosa R.H., J. 2000. Low
        vision: The role of visual acuity in the efficiency of
        cursor movement. *Annual ACM Conference on Assistive
        Technologies, Proceedings.* (2000), 1–8.

[19]   Janiszewski, R., Heath-watson, S.L., Adrienne, Y.,
        Rosenthal, A.M. and Do, Q. 2006. The Low Visibility of
        Low Vision : Increasing Awareness through Public
        Health Education. *Journal of Visual Impairments and
        Blindness.* 100, Special Supplement (2006), 849–862.

[20]   Kane, S.K., Jayant, C., Wobbrock, J.O. and Ladner, R.E.
        2009. Freedom to Roam: A Study of Mobile Device
        Adoption and Accessibility for People with Visual and
        Motor Disabilities. *Proc. ASSETS '09,* ACM, Pittsburgh,
        Pennsylvania, USA. (2009), 115–122.

[21]   Margrain, T.H. 2000. Helping blind and partially sighted
        people to read: the effectiveness of low vision aids.
        British Journal of Ophthalmology. 84, 8 (Aug. 2000),
        919–921.

[22]   Massof, R.W. 2002. A model of the prevalence and
        incidence of low vision and blindness among adults in
        the U.S. *Optometry and vision science : official
        publication of the American Academy of Optometry.* 79,
        1 (Jan. 2002), 31–8.

[23]   McIlwaine, G.G., Bell, J.A. and Dutton, G.N. 1991. Low
        vision aids--is our service cost effective? *Eye (London,
        England).* 5 (Pt 5), 5 (Jan. 1991), 607–11.

[24]   Minto, H. and Butt, I.A. 2004. Low vision devices and
        training. *Community eye health / International Centre for
        Eye Health.* 17, 49 (Jan. 2004), 6–7.

[25]   Owsley, C., McGwin, G., Lee, P.P., Wasserman, N. and
        Searcey, K. 2009. Characteristics of low-vision
        rehabilitation services in the United States. *Archives of
        ophthalmology (Chicago, Ill. : 1960).* 127, 5 (May 2009),
        681–9.

[26]   Saldaña, J. 2013. *The Coding Manual for Qualitative
        Researchers.* (2nd ed.). Los Angeles, CA: Sage

[27]   Scott, I.U., Feuer, W.J. and Jacko, J.A. 2002. Impact of
        graphical user interface screen features on computer task
        accuracy and speed in a cohort of patients with age-
        related macular degeneration. *American Journal of
        Ophthalmology.* 134, 6 (Dec. 2002), 857–862.

[28]   Scott, I.U., Feuer, W.J. and Jacko, J.A. 2002. Impact of
        visual function on computer task accuracy and reaction
        time in a cohort of patients with age-related macular
        degeneration. *American Journal of Ophthalmology.* 133,
        3 (Mar. 2002), 350–357.

[29]   Shinohara, K. and Wobbrock, J.O. 2011. In the shadow

of misperception. *Proc. CHI '11*, ACM, New York, New York, USA, 705-714.

[30]   Theofanos, M.F. and Redish, J.G. 2005. Helping Low-vision and Other Users with Web Sites That Meet Their Needs: Is One Site for All Feasible? *Technical communication*. 52, 1 (2005), 9–20.

[31]   Virtanen, P. and Laatikainen, L. 1991. Primary success with low vision aids in age-related macular degeneration. *Acta ophthalmologica*. 69, 4 (May 1991), 484–90.

[32]   Watson, G.R., De l'Aune, W., Stelmack, J., Maino, J. and Long, S. 1997. National survey of the impact of low vision device use among veterans. *Optometry and vision science : official publication of the American Academy of*

Optometry. 74, 5 (May 1997), 249–59.

[33]   ZoomText Magnifier/Reader: *http://www.zoomtext.com/products/zoomtext-magnifierreader/*. Accessed: 2016-05-06.

[34]   CDC - About Vision Health - Common Eye Disorders - Vision Health Initiative (VHI).

[35]   Massof, R.W. and Lidoff, L. 2001. Issues in low vision rehabilitation: Service delivery, policy, and funding. *American Foundation for the Blind*. Vancouver

Real-Time Mobile Personalized Simulations of Impaired Colour Vision

Rhouri McAlpine
University of Dundee
Dundee, Scotland, UK
r.mcalpine@dundee.ac.uk

David R. Flatla
University of Dundee
Dundee, Scotland, UK
d.flatla@dundee.ac.uk

ABSTRACT

Colour forms an essential element of day-to-day life for most people, but at least 5% of the world have Impaired Colour Vision (ICV) – seeing fewer colours than everyone else. Those with typical colour vision find it difficult to understand how people with ICV perceive colour, leading to misunderstanding and challenges for people with ICV. To help improve understanding, personalized simulations of ICV have been developed, but are computationally demanding (so limited to static images), which limits the value of these simulations. To address this, we extended personalized ICV simulations to work in real time on a mobile device to allow people with typical colour vision greater freedom in exploring ICV. To validate our approach, we compared our real-time simulation technique to an existing adjustable simulation technique and found general agreement between the two. We then deployed three real-time personalized ICV simulations to nine people with typical colour vision, encouraging them to take photos of interesting colour situations. In just over one week, participants recorded over 450 real-world images of situations where their simulation presented a distinct challenge for their respective ICV participant. Through a questionnaire and discussion of photos with participants, we found that our solution provides a valuable mechanism for building understanding of ICV for people with typical colour vision.

Keywords

Impaired colour vision; colour vision deficiency; colourblindness; mobile personalized simulation

1. INTRODUCTION

In a recent topical thread on Reddit discussing poor treatment by employers,[1] a contributor relayed this experience:

> I'm colorblind. My boss assigned me a work task once that was color-coded in a way that I couldn't see. When I brought up my vision issues – not refusing to do the work, but asking for accommodation – I was written up for what they perceived as "insubordination".
>
> When I filed a complaint with HR asking for the write-up to be removed, the HR rep "graciously" gave me what she perceived as a solution: that I should go use the company's Tuition Reimbursement program to go take a remedial art class at my local community college. "So that you can finally learn your colors", she said.

Yes, it's Reddit, but the Internet abounds with similar stories of others' lack of awareness of what it is like living with Impaired Colour Vision (ICV – commonly called colourblindness).[2] Similar challenges have been documented in the academic literature [5, 27, 26, 15].

Accounts documenting the day-to-day challenges faced by people with ICV often reveal a *lack of awareness* among people with typical colour vision about what people with ICV actually perceive. Indeed, there seems to be a range of severities of this lack of awareness, from those who are entirely unaware that ICV exists, to those who have a general understanding of the colours that are indistinguishable for someone with ICV, but little comprehension of how the visual experience of people with ICV differs from their own.

A recent survey of 27 web designers found that 25/27 (93%) of respondents were aware of the existence of ICV, suggesting that the number of people who are entirely unaware of ICV is low. However, the same study found that substantially fewer (13/27 – 48%) respondents considered end users with ICV when working on a project, with 17/27 (63%) of respondents considering end users with ICV 'never' or 'rarely' [29]. Although many factors likely influence a designer's decision to consider end-user abilities (e.g., contract constraints), it is possible that these designers also lack understanding of how ICV influences colour perception, leading to a lack of accommodation in their designs.

In order to help improve awareness of how people with ICV perceive colours, simulations of ICV have been proposed [20, 17, 30, 4, 19] in which an image's colours are modified to illustrate how those same colours appear for someone with ICV. These simulation techniques provide an approximate representation of experiencing ICV, but lack the ability to precisely represent an individual's unique colour per-

---

[1] https://redd.it/4fzph7

ASSETS '16 October 23-26, 2016, Reno, NV, USA

© 2016 Copyright held by the owner/author(s).

ACM ISBN 978-1-4503-4124-0/16/10.

DOI: http://dx.doi.org/10.1145/2982142.2982170

---

[2] www.colourblindawareness.org gives one work-related account and provides others. https://redd.it/310n73 is a more general conversation about ICV challenges. www.colorblindness.com lists many challenges related to ICV.

ception abilities due to a lack of precise diagnosis of ICV or the presence of simultaneous or compound ICVs. To address these limitations, *personalized* simulations of ICV have been developed [11], but are computationally demanding and have only been applied to preselected images in a lab environment. As a result, personalized simulations are not available to our original Reddit contributor's co-workers (boss and HR rep) to help them understand exactly how their colleague sees the world.

To address this, we extended personalized simulations of ICV to operate in real time on mobile platforms. To do this, we build an Android app that: 1) measures an ICV individual's colour perception abilities to produce a personalized simulation, and 2) applies the personalized simulation to the live video feed from the device's camera and displays the ICV-simulated video feed on the device's screen. The result is a 'magic window' application that allows someone with typical colour vision to see real-world colours as someone with ICV by peering through the 'magic window'.

To accomplish this, the colour perception abilities of someone with ICV are captured via a calibration task [9]. The resulting values are used to execute the personalized simulation algorithm (described in [11]) on an image containing every RGB666 colour to generate a Look-Up Table (LUT) that maps original RGB values to personalized simulation RGB values. We use the LUT in OpenCV and RenderScript to modify each pixel of each frame from the video camera in parallel, then draw the simulated frame to the screen.

In addition to providing personalized simulations, we also corrected an error in the original algorithm (as identified in [11]), and added standard (i.e., non-personalized) simulations for common severe types of ICV to our application.

We evaluated our simulation application in two ways. First, we compared our corrected simulation algorithm to an existing adjustable ICV simulation technique (described in [19]) to understand if our personalized simulation technique agreed with other simulation techniques. We found some differences between the approaches, but overall our simulation technique generally agreed with the adjustable technique.

Second, we generated personalized ICV simulations for three people with ICV (one protan, one deutan, one near-monochromatic), and deployed our app with these simulations to nine people with typical colour vision. We added a 'capture image' feature to our simulation app that allowed participants to capture both the original and simulated current image at any given time. Participants had the simulation for 7-10 days, and gathered 461 images representing a diverse set of situations. Participants with typical colour vision reported increased understanding of the visual abilities of their particular ICV participant.

This paper makes three contributions. First we correct existing personalized ICV simulations, and describe the first ever real-time mobile personalized simulation of ICV. Second, we compare our personalized ICV simulation technique to an existing adjustable ICV simulation technique, identifying future extensions of our approach. Third, we present empirical data suggesting that real-time, mobile personalized simulations of ICV help improve ICV awareness for people with typical colour vision. In combination, our contributions provide a new opportunity to help improve general awareness of ICV.

2. BACKGROUND & RELATED WORK

2.1 Impaired Colour Vision

Commonly referred to as colourblindness or Colour Vision Deficiency (CVD), Impaired Colour Vision (ICV) affects anyone who has difficulty discriminating between colours that the majority of people can differentiate [8]. The terms 'colourblindness' and 'CVD' typically apply to only the inherited forms of ICV; but the term 'ICV' includes three broad classes of this impairment: inherited, acquired, and situationally induced [10].

Three types of retinal cone cells are responsible for typical human colour vision; long (l), medium (m), and short (s) wavelength sensitive cones respond to varying ranges of electromagnetic radiation between 700nm and 380nm [31]. Colour is perceived when light differentially stimulates the cone cells. Differential stimulation of the l and m cones allows discrimination between reds and greens; differential stimulation of a combined $l+m$ and the s cones allows discrimination between yellows and blues [28].

Inherited ICV affects the l and m cones in over 99% of cases, resulting in reduced discriminability between colours that differ in their respective amounts of red and/or green (e.g., green and orange, blue and purple) [2]. The taxonomy of inherited ICVs include *dichromacy* (one cone type absent; 1/4 of cases) – *protanopia* (missing l cones), *deuteranopia* (missing m cones), and *tritanopia* (missing s cones) and its less-severe but more common form *anomalous trichromacy* (3/4 of cases) – *protanomalous* (l-cone sensitivity shifted toward m-cone sensitivity), *deuteranomalous* (m-cone shifted toward l-cone), and *tritanomalous* (s-cone shifted toward m-cone). In more severe cases, two cones (*cone monochromacy*) or three cones (*rod monochromacy*) may be missing, leading to total absence of colour vision [3, 5]. Inherited ICV affects approximately 8% of males and 0.5% of females in Caucasians, with variable rates in other populations [3].

In addition to inheritance, ICV can also be acquired either permanently or temporarily. Permanent causes of acquired ICV are typically related to trauma either to the eye (e.g., diabetic retinopathy [12], glaucoma [21], exposure to solvents [7]) or to the brain (e.g., stroke or aneurysm leading to cerebral achromatopsia [23]). Acquired ICV can also be temporary in cases where it is induced by medication (e.g., Viagra [33], antidepressants [18]), or in cases of temporary inflammation in the visual system (e.g., optic neuritis [24]). In most cases of trauma to the eye, the individual's ability to discriminate between blues and yellows is reduced [12], but acquired ICV can lead to a mix of blue-yellow and red-green impairment [24], and even occassionally total loss of colour vision, as in cerebral achromatopsia [23]. ICV acquired as a person ages is typically less severe than other forms of acquired ICV [16], but is much more common – one study found that 64% of British over-65s and 32% of African over-40s [6] had some degree of acquired ICV.

Situationally-induced ICV occurs when any environmental factor inhibits a person's colour differentiation abilities. When using a screen, this can occur when environmental lighting is high or screen brightness is low [22].

2.2 Existing ICV Simulation Apps

Searching on the Google Play Store or Apple's iTunes Store for 'colorblind' turns up a number of mobile apps that provide real-time simulations of ICV (e.g., Color Blind Pal by Vincent Fiorentini on iOS and Android). However, every app we have found only provides simulations of dichromacy (one missing cone), so can not simulate the full range of types and severities of ICV that exist because they do not provide a personalized simulation.

2.3 ICV Simulation

Almost all attempts at simulating ICV have focused on dichromatic or anomalous trichromatic inherited ICV. The earliest simulation work [20, 17, 4]) defined the mechanism still in use today, described now.

The theoretical approach to simulate inherited dichromatic ICV is to represent each colour as a tristimulus value that represents the degree to which that colour stimulates the three types of cones (l, m, s) [20]. Once a colour is translated into this l-m-s colour space, the colour information encoded by the missing cone is removed or replaced with the information from another cone, thereby effectively reducing the dimensionality of the l-m-s representation of any colour from three to two dimensions [4].

In practical terms, this manifests as 'shifting' colour within a colour space such that a three-dimensional colour space is compressed into two dimensions. Using the CIE L*u*v* colour space, which has a luminance ($L*$) axis running from black to white, a $u*$ axis from greenish to reddish, and a $v*$ axis running from blue to yellow, simulating protan or deutan inherited ICV leads to a compression of the u* axis (red-green) toward the v* axis (yellow-blue) [4, 11].

When simulating anomalous trichromacy (or other partial ICVs), the degree of colour space compression is modulated by the severity of anomalous trichromacy – lower severity gives less compression, greater severity leads to more compression. Machado's adjustable ICV simulation technique [19] takes as input the degree of anomalous cone sensitivity shift, and compresses the colour space accordingly. Flatla and Gutwin's personalized ICV simulations [11] measure the colour differentiation abilities of the person whose vision is to be simulated, and uses these measurements to determine the magnitude of a fixed-distance shift within the CIE L*u*v* perceptually-uniform colour space. Our simulation technique is based on the personalized technique, so we next describe how we extended it to mobile.

3. MOBILE PERSONALIZED ICV SIMULATIONS

The personalized ICV simulation technique described in [11] performs the simulation colour shifting described above on a per-pixel (per-colour) basis. As mentioned earlier, this is computationally demanding, thereby preventing the simulation technique from running in real time.

3.1 Moving to Real Time

The computational overhead of the original personalized simulation technique is attributable to the algorithm employed. This algorithm uses a two-pass approach in which a 'primary ICV' is simulated first (either red-green or blue-yellow) and then a 'secondary ICV' (opposite of the primary ICV) is simulated using the output from the primary simulation. The primary and secondary ICVs are to accommodate people who have multiple or compound ICVs (e.g., inherited protanomalous with age-related ICV).

For given primary and secondary ICVs and their respective severities, plus an input colour (in RGB), the algorithm:

1. Converts the input RGB colour to CIE L*u*v*.

2. Determines the L*u*v* primary ICV dichromatic simulation colour for the input colour (using a pre-calculated look-up-table – LUT).

3. Creates a sphere around the input colour in L*u*v* space with radius equal to the input severity.

4. Casts a ray from the input colour to its dichromatic version in L*u*v*.

5. Solves the parametric equation for the intersection between the ray and the surface of the sphere.

6. Identifies the L*u*v* colour at the ray-sphere intersection point.

7. Repeats Steps 2-6 once more for the secondary ICV, but using the intersection L*u*v* colour as the input.

8. The intersection L*u*v* colour from the second pass is the final personalized ICV simulation colour.

Although no single step in the above algorithm is egregiously demanding in terms of processing power or memory, the combined effect of all of the steps results in a simulation technique that cannot operate in real-time. Processing a single 512x512 image requires approximately 1.3s on a 2.8GHz i7 mid-2015 MacBook Pro with 16 GB RAM – a relatively small image, but not nearly real-time performance.

Our solution to this is relatively simple – we extended the use of Look-Up-Tables (LUTs) from storing the pre-calculated dichromatic simulation colours for all possible input RGB colours to also storing the personalized simulation results for all possible input RGB colours. For a given participant's primary and secondary ICVs and respective severities, we calculate their personalized simulation colours for every RGB colour, and store the results in an image file that serves as our LUT. We use the RGB value for a given input pixel as the index into the LUT image's pixel array to access that pixel's pre-computed simulation colour. We are currently exploring shaders to further improve performance.

3.2 Correcting Previous Algorithm

As pointed out in the Discussion section of [11], the personalized ICV simulation algorithm presented there contains a bug that manifests when the severity of both the primary and secondary ICVs is high. The original algorithm utilized the standard dichromatic simulation during the second pass (secondary ICV). However, this sometimes results in the colour-space compression from the primary ICV becoming 'undone' by the secondary ICV compression on account of the radial direction of compression inherent in ICV simulations. As a result, the simulation for someone with monochromatic ICV incorrectly contains colours.

To address this, we incorporated an additional shifting mechanism in which the dichromatic version of the input colour for the second stage is shifted according to the primary ICV's type and severity. This results in truly monochromatic ICV simulation when the severities for the primary and secondary ICVs are both high.

3.3 Mobile Calibration

In order to provide personalized ICV simulations, the colour differentiation abilities of people with ICV need to be captured. To do this, we ported the calibration procedure used in the original personalized ICV simulation technique [11] (originally described in [9]) directly to mobile. A screenshot of the calibration on an Android device is shown in Figure 1.

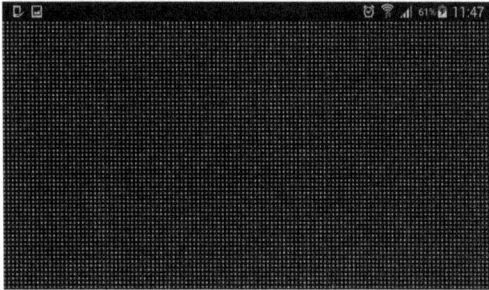

Figure 1: Screenshot of a single mobile calibration task on Android.

Once a person has completed the calibration, a personalized ICV simulation LUT is generated for them. The measurements from the calibration are also recorded in a unique user profile in case the LUT is accidentally deleted. The LUT and/or profile can be transferred to any other mobile running our simulation app to allow easy access to the personalized ICV simulations without requiring the person with ICV to recalibrate on each individual device.

3.4 Mobile Implementation

We developed an application for the Android 4.1 operating system on a Samsung Galaxy S5 development platform. We used OpenCV (opencv.org) to gain access to individual frames from the mobile's rear-facing camera, and RenderScript to parallelize access to the personalized ICV simulation LUT. During real-time simulation, write-access to the LUT is not needed; parallel read-only access allows RenderScript to look-up the personalized ICV simulation colour for multiple pixels simultaneously.

To help reduce LUT generation time and app memory footprint, we opted to use RGB666 (six bits each for red, green, and blue) instead of the standard RGB888 (eight bits each). No differences were visible when visually comparing RGB666 and RGB888 simulation results, so we opted for the lower-footprint version.

In addition to personalized ICV simulations, we also provided standard dichromatic simulations for protanopia, deuteranopia, and tritanopia, as well as monochromacy to allow someone to use the system immediately without having to obtain a personalized ICV colour vision profile. We did include personalized ICV simulation profiles directly in our evaluation deployment (see Section 5), so similar profiles could be included in any future commercial release.

4. COMPARATIVE EVALUATION

The personalized ICV simulation approach has previously been shown to be significantly more precise than standard dichromatic simulations [11] by comparing ICV participant colour vision test scores and non-ICV participant test scores when using ICV simulations. However this was shown for only the limited sets of colours used in colour vision tests.

To expand our understanding of the quality of our personalized simulation approach, we conducted a follow-on quantitative evaluation in which we measured the difference in simulation between our personalized approach and the state-of-the-art in adjustable ICV simulations (developed by Machado, Oliveira, and Fernandes [19]). Machado's adjustable simulation algorithm is described in an online tutorial[3] that outlines their simulation approach and provides a comprehensive set of RGB-to-RGB multiplication matrices that permit a straightforward implementation of their simulation technique.

Choosing the matrix for a given type (protan, deutan, tritan) and severity (0.0 for no ICV, up to 1.0 for dichromacy, in increments of 0.1) of ICV, allows simulation of that type and severity. The individual R,G, and B values for a given pixel are defined as a vector that is multiplied with the selected matrix (and clamped if necessary) to create a new vector containing the simulated R, G, and B values.

As the direct correlation between Machado's severity levels and the severity level measured by our calibration technique is unknown, we compared our simulation using a fixed severity of known type to all severity levels of the same type for Machado's simulation. Based on our previous experience with our calibration, we chose a mid-severity ICV value of 35.0 for each of protan and deutan ICVs, and compared each of these to all severities of Machado's adjustable simulation for the corresponding type of ICV. We calculated the Euclidean distance in CIE L*u*v* colour space (an approximation of perceptual difference [32]) between our simulation result and Machado's simulation result for every RGB666 colour for each level of severity and selected the severity that resulted in the lowest average Euclidean distance.

Machado's severity level that resulted in the minimum average Euclidean distance between our simulation technique and theirs was at severity 0.3 for both protan and deutan. At this severity, the minimum average distance was 12.46 CIE L*u*v* colour space units for protan and 13.12 CIE L*u*v* units for deutan. These values suggest that there is substantial agreement between the two simulation techniques; assuming that a distance of 2.3 represents the Just-Noticeable Difference (JND) point between any two colours ([14] citing [25]), the average disagreement between the two simulation techniques is approximately 5-6 JNDs. To put this in context, mapping the sRGB colour space into the CIE L*u*v* (using a D65 whitepoint) results in an L* range of 0-100 (43 JNDs), a u* range of -83 to 175 (112 JNDs), and a v* range of -134 to 107 (105 JNDs).

The distribution of distances for the protan and deutan personalized and adjustable simulations is shown in Figure 2. For each distribution, over 90% of the distances are less than 21 CIE L*u*v* units, but there is a long tail extending to 65 for protan and 63 for deutan.

So where do the differences lie between our personalized simulation technique and Machado's adjustable simulation technique? Upon further investigation, we discovered two situations that result in differences:

1. **Large Shift-Potential Colours:** The two techniques differ in the level of modification for colours that have the potential for substantial shifting during simulation. Our personalized technique tends to shift these colours towards their dichromatic counterpart less ag-

---

[3]www.inf.ufrgs.br/~oliveira/

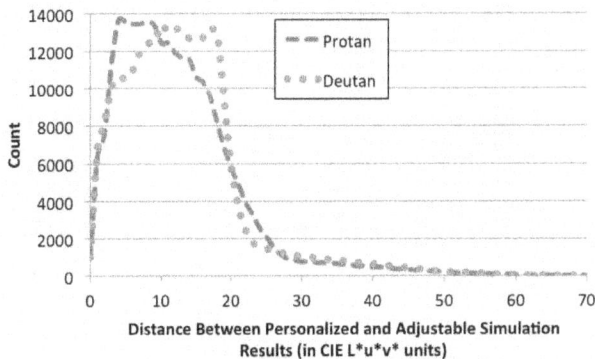

Figure 2: Histogram of differences between adjustable simulation and personalized simulation results for every RGB666 colour.

gressively than Machado's algorithm. This is illustrated on the right-hand side of Figure 3, which shows Machado's (blue lines) more aggressive shifting of reds and purples compared to our personalized simulation technique (yellow lines).

2. **Small Shift-Potential Colours:** The two techniques also differ for colours that are close to the yellows, greys, and blues that colours are shifted toward during simulation. These colours appear to be shifted more aggressively by our personalized simulation technique compared to Machado's adjustable simulation. This is illustrated on the left-hand side of Figure 3, which shows Machado's (blue lines) less aggressive shifting of blues and greens compared to our personalized simulation technique (yellow lines).

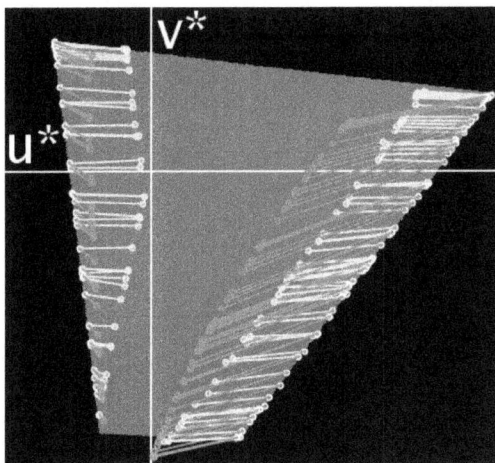

Figure 3: Illustration of shift amounts for our personalized simulation technique (protan, 35.0) and Machado's adjustable simulation technique (protan, 0.3). Original colours are white circles, personalized simulation results and shift lines in yellow, adjustable simulation results and shift lines in blue.

The difference between these two simulation techniques appears to be our reliance upon fixed shift distances in our simulation technique and the use of scalable shift distances

in Machado's technique. In recent discussions about this difference with colour scientists at the Norwegian Colour and Visual Computing Laboratory[4], we have identified strengths and weaknesses of each approach and concluded that more work is needed. In spite of these differences, the shift directions (towards blues, yellows, and greyscales) and shift magnitudes for each simulation technique largely agree, so we leave further examination and possible refinement of ICV simulation techniques as future work.

5. USER EVALUATION

In addition to the comparison evaluation described above, we also conducted a user evaluation in which we used our app to provide personalized simulations of three participants with ICV to nine participants with typical colour vision.

5.1 Participants

Twelve participants were recruited for the study. Three participants had some degree of ICV and nine participants had typical colour vision. The colour vision of all participants was assessed using the HRR Polychromatic Plates [13].

The participants with ICV were all male between the ages of 22 and 28, each with a different type of ICV: 1 mild protan, 1 mild deutan, and 1 near-monochromatic (degenerative incomplete achromatopsia) with self-reported perception of only extreme blues and yellows. The participants with typical colour vision consisted of two females (aged 22 and 25) and seven males (aged 18 to 29).

5.2 Experimental Design

This evaluation comprised an in-the-wild deployment of our app that allows people with typical colour vision to see the real-world colours as someone with ICV sees them.

To help capture what the participants with typical colour vision experienced during the deployment, we added a 'Capture Image' feature to our app. This feature allowed participants to record both the original and ICV-simulated versions of whatever was currently being displayed by our application. Each pair of images (original and simulated) were recorded to the device's local storage and retrieved later for analysis. We asked each participant to take pictures of anything they found of interest.

In conjunction with the image gathering step, we discussed the process with each typical-colour vision participant in an informal interview process. This interview was centered on discussing each participant's general impressions of experiencing a personalized simulation of ICV, as well as specific details about the circumstances and reasoning for each image they captured.

5.3 Procedure

Participants with ICV were recruited first. For each of these participants, we tested their colour vision using the HRR plates [13] and then had them run the calibration procedure twice on our development Samsung Galaxy S5 device. We generated simulations for each calibration for each participant and visually compared them (along with the ICV participant) to ensure the calibration accurately reflected the ICV participant's vision. The simulations appeared very similar for each ICV participant, so we arbitrarily chose one

---

[4]NTNU (Norwegian University of Science and Technology), Gjøvik, Norway

of each pair to serve as the simulation profile for each ICV participant. This profile was then incorporated into our app to be deployed to participants with typical colour vision.

Participants with typical colour vision were recruited next. Each of these participants was tested using the HRR plates (to verify they had no ICV). Then we installed our simulation app on their personal Android device, and loaded one of the ICV profiles gathered from the participants with ICV. One ICV profile was chosen for each non-ICV participant to give them a concentrated experience of a single person's ICV vision as this reflects the likely use case in real world deployment (e.g., a mother trying to understand the colour vision of her son with ICV).

With nine participants with typical colour vision and three participants with ICV, a 3:1 assignment ratio would have been natural. However, near-monochromatic vision is both much rarer than the protan and deutan vision of the other two ICV participants, and it is also very similar to seeing in greyscale. As many people will have had the opportunity to see greyscale versions of photographs and television, we opted to assign the near-monochromatic simulation to a single typical colour vision participant, and four of these participants to each of the deutan and protan simulations.

Participants with typical colour vision then used our simulation app in their day-to-day lives for between seven and ten days. Participants were encouraged to capture photos of anything interesting they experienced during this time. After this deployment period, we met with each participant individually to collect their images, and to speak with each participant about their experiences using the simulation.

Although we originally wanted to hold the data collection and discussion session collectively with all twelve participants (ICV and typical colour vision), timing and scheduling constraints of our participants made this impossible. We still believe that there would be great value in coordinating a joint discussion session with ICV and non-ICV participants (as done in the previous work on personalized simulations [11]), so plan to do this in the future.

5.4 Results

We met with each typical colour vision participant individually to transfer their photos, discuss the context around each photo they took, and to gather their thoughts via an open-ended questionnaire.

5.4.1 Photos Gathered

Overall, our nine participants recorded 461 unique images (with original and simulated versions of each) over the span of 7-10 days. The maximum captured by one participant was 125, the minimum was 16 (mean of 51).

After transferring the photos, we discussed each photo with the participants, using "What does this picture show?" and "Why did you take this picture?" as prompts to gather their reasoning behind each photo. Using this feedback, we classified the photos into categories, which represent many day-to-day challenges identified by previous work [27, 11]: 44% of photos were of products, 21% of photos were of challenges around the home, 17% of photos were within the context of work or education, 10% were outside, and 7% of photos were of leisure activities (e.g., watching sports).

The most informative photos taken by participants were ICV simulations of shopping for food and products. Participants identified the very visual nature of selecting food (e.g.,

ensuring something is fresh or ripe), and most participants noticed that fresh fruit and vegetables looked discoloured and not very fresh, as illustrated in Figure 4, bottom.

Figure 4: Original image (top), and deutan ICV simulated image (bottom) of a produce stand.

Another theme related to shopping was the reduced visual distinctiveness of product packaging. Product packaging colours are often chosen to be eye-catching or familiar to shoppers, but the yellow and green patterns on the dental dog biscuits shown in Figure 5 are much less apparent in the CVD simulation.

A final theme that emerged from the discussions with participants about their photos was how the use of colour to distinguish between products did not work well in their simulations. An example of this is shown in Figure 6, in which the lime (green) and lemon (yellow) versions of body wash are nearly indistinguishable in the CVD simulation image.

5.4.2 Questionnaire Reponses

As previously stated, the protan and deutan ICV simulations were given to four typical colour vision participants each, with the near-monochromatic ICV simulation given to a single typical colour vision participant. Because of the differences between the red-green and the monochromatic simulation, we treat feedback from these two sets of participants separately, first reporting the responses from those with the protan and deutan simulations. Our interview questionnaire contained four questions (discussed here) and one additional question (presented in Section 6). We list each question here and briefly summarize user responses.

What did you immediately notice about colours in the simulation you received? Participants with protan and deutan simulations all commented on the apparent 'dullness' or 'muted' nature of colours when viewed through the simulation. Participants with the protan simulation identified green as a particularly challenging colour as it typically appeared brown or yellow in the simulation, leading to confusion. Participants also perceived that the following sets of colours are often difficult to distinguish: reds, pinks,

Figure 5: Original (top) and protan ICV simulation (bottom) of dog dental biscuits packaging. Packaging colours are not very distinctive in the simulation.

Figure 6: Original (top), and protan ICV simulation (bottom) of green (lime) and yellow (lemon) body wash. The two body wash types are not visually distinct in the simulation.

and greys; blues and purples; and greens and yellows, which agrees with the experience reported by people with ICV [27].

Did you find any specific areas of interest? As reflected in the photo results listed above, participants identified food (e.g., produce) and packaging (of food and products) as interesting because of the stark differences between the simulation and their own experience. Two participants with the protan simulation identified the appearance of their own simulated skin colour as a surprise. The greyness of Caucasian skin tones, as well as the invisibility of rashes and burns have also been previously identified [11]. The simulations helped one deutan simulation participant realize that their workplace could present challenges, and another identified choosing and applying make-up as a difficulty.

Did anything surprise you? Participants with protan simulations highlighted the difficulty in telling the ripeness of bananas as well as repeated how food generally appeared to not be fresh and was quite 'off-putting'. Those with deutan simulations did not identify anything specific, but reiterated how the over-reliance on colour makes many general tasks more difficult for people with ICV.

Did the application improve your understanding of ICV? Every participant readily agreed that our app was an effective means of building understanding. One participant remarked that "it was pretty amazing".

It is difficult to identify whether these findings are attributable to seeing *personalized* ICV simulations rather than standard dichromatic ICV simulations, and did not design our study to test this. However, we hold that a more precise simulation will naturally afford greater empathy and understanding in people with typical vision; knowing that they see colours as another human being sees them must offer greater personal value than using an ill-fitting standard simulation.

5.4.3 Near-Monochromatic Results

The typical vision participant who received the near-monochromatic ICV simulation had an experience that was at once both similar and different from that of the participants who had the protan and deutan simulations.

There was an immediate shock value when looking at this simulation, as it was almost entirely devoid of colour save for anything that was intensely yellow or blue (to the non-ICV participant). This resulted in almost all of the photos gathered with this simulation profile being entirely greyscale – it was difficult for the typical colour vision participant to find situations in which any colour remained in the simulation (see Figure 7 for one example of successfully capturing some residual colour). The challenges (and shock) experienced by the participant using this simulation are evident in some of their responses to the questionnaire: *"There weren't any [colours]. At all. It was like the world was a black and white movie. I noticed there was some yellow and blue but there really wasn't much of it unless it was very bright. Most of the time it was just a total absence of all colours."*

In spite of the immediate shock and disbelief, this non-ICV participant did come to understand much more about ICV and the challenges that such an extreme form of ICV would give rise to: *"How could someone possibly have that as their vision? You would miss out on so many colours and so much detail on things. It must be horrible to have to deal with that all day every day!"* and *"It looks like everything is an issue with this type of ICV. It's pretty hard to tell things apart when they're just shades of grey."*

"When I thought of colourblindness [ICV], I never realised that it could be as bad as that...it was really just like taking pictures in black and white mode."

6. DISCUSSION

Our findings suggest that providing a real-time mobile personalized simulation technique to people with typical colour vision can indeed help them gain insights into the challenges that ICV presents. This applies to both more-common forms of ICV (inherited protan and deutan ICV) as well as

Figure 7: Original (top), and near-monochromatic simulation (bottom) of a blue sign and yellow street lines. Only the bright blue of the sign posts remain in the simulation.

less-common forms of ICV (as represented by our participant with degenerative incomplete achromatopsia).

The real-time nature of our app allowed participants to use ICV simulations in their day-to-day lives, and was less cumbersome than a simulation technique based on static photos (as used in previous studies). Similarly, the mobile nature of the app allowed participants to take the simulation with them anywhere, although some participants commented on the awkwardness of using a mobile app in this way in public – taking pictures of produce displays or road signs is not a 'normal' activity, and can easily lead to suspicion from others, and self-conscious feelings in the user.

That said, it is arguable that the 'personalized' feature of our tool was not adequately evaluated in our user study. We wanted to provide non-ICV participants with a rich and deep experience of a single individual's ICV, so participants did not get to experience a wide range of ICV types and severities. However, we did provide default dichromatic simulations to participants in addition to the personalized simulation, so participants may have experimented with the different simulations, although none explicitly commented on doing this. Our suspicion is that a personalized ICV simulation provided specific value to the non-ICV participants, in that they knew that their simulation was another human being's actual colour vision. Indeed, this was reflected in the near-monochromatic simulation participant's comments when they expressed disbelief that someone could actually have such severe colour vision loss.

Further to this, we also asked non-ICV participants if they identified anything that they anticipated would be a problem for people with ICV, but learned from using our app that it actually was not an issue. Participants with protan simulations identified that road signs were still quite vibrant (partly due to the 'mild' nature of their ICV simulations), and participants with deutan simulations identified traffic lights as not actually presenting a problem. Participants also

commented that distinguishing between money and football (soccer) uniforms was less challenging than they anticipated.

6.1 Extensions & Future Work

Using an in-situ real-time simulation in which people with typical colour vision were able to see the world through someone else's eyes proved to be a valuable and insightful mechanism for improving understanding of ICV. In the future, we would like to extend this work in four ways.

First, participants commented on the cumbersome nature of having to hold their mobile device to view the ICV simulations. To help address this, we are developing wearable ICV 'goggles' which provide a hands-free mechanism for 'seeing the world through someone else's eyes', similar to [1] but using personalized ICV simulations.

Second, the original personalized simulation paper explored how ICV simulation helped non-ICV participants understand the ICV of someone close to them (friend or family) [11]. In this paper, we explored enhancing the understanding of a general population that did not necessarily know the participants with ICV. We anticipate that there is great value in providing personalized ICV simulations to designers (to aid in the development of ICV-friendly designs) and teachers (who will have children with ICV in their classes), so are currently making plans to explore the value of ICV simulation with these specialist populations.

Third, our personalized ICV simulation technique and Machado's adjustable ICV simulation technique [19] both provide a mechanism for allowing people with typical colour vision to explore the range of severities of ICV. In recent demonstrations of these techniques to people with little previous understanding of ICV, we found that providing a simulation with a tuneable amount of severity (ranging from none to full dichromatism) was a valuable learning mechanism – seeing *how* colours shift as ICV severity increases helped people understand ICV more clearly. We are currently investigating this through continued public demonstrations, and plan to explore this empirically in the future.

Finally, we are looking to provide our system to the public, either by releasing our product commercially or by providing our codebase for free download. In the meantime, we invite interested parties to contact us directly so we can provide access to our software.

7. CONCLUSION

In this paper, we describe extending personalized simulations of ICV to real-time operation on mobiles by incorporating automatic LUT generation, and using these LUTs to increase the speed of the personalized simulation algorithm. We also present a comparison of our simulation to an existing adjustable ICV simulation technique – showing that they are similar, but also that more work is needed. Finally, we present findings from an in-the-wild user study in which participants with typical colour vision demonstrated their increased understanding through the collection of photos illustrating problematic uses of colour for people with ICV.

To further contribute to our goal of increasing awareness of ICV, we are now working on extending our simulation further by building and testing our hands-free ICV 'goggles', exploring how tuneable ICV simulations can contribute to learning, and working with specialist populations to help increase their understanding of ICV.

8. REFERENCES

[1] H. C. Ates, A. Fiannaca, and E. Folmer. Immersive simulation of visual impairments using a wearable see-through display. In *Proceedings of the Ninth International Conference on Tangible, Embedded, and Embodied Interaction*, pages 225–228. ACM, 2015.

[2] J. Birch. *Diagnosis of defective colour vision*. Elsevier Health Sciences, 2001.

[3] J. Birch. Worldwide prevalence of red-green color deficiency. *Journal of the Optical Society of America A*, 29(3):313–320, 2012.

[4] H. Brettel, F. Viénot, and J. D. Mollon. Computerized simulation of color appearance for dichromats. *Journal of the Optical Society of America A*, 14(10):2647–2655, October 1997.

[5] B. L. Cole. The handicap of abnormal colour vision. *Clinical & Expirimental Optometry*, 87(4-5):258–275, July 2004.

[6] I. R. Davies, G. Laws, G. G. Corbett, and D. J. Jerrett. Cross-cultural differences in colour vision: Acquired 'colour-blindness' in africa. *Personality and Individual Differences*, 25(6):1153–1162, 1998.

[7] F. Dick, S. Semple, R. Chen, and A. Seaton. Neurological deficits in solvent-exposed painters: a syndrome including impaired colour vision, cognitive defects, tremor and loss of vibration sensation. *QJM: An International Journal of Medicine*, 93(10):655–661, 2000.

[8] D. R. Flatla, A. R. Andrade, R. D. Teviotdale, D. L. Knowles, and C. Stewart. ColourID: Improving colour identification for people with impaired colour vision. In *Proceedings of the 33rd Annual ACM Conference on Human Factors in Computing Systems*, pages 3543–3552. ACM, 2015.

[9] D. R. Flatla and C. Gutwin. Improving calibration time and accuracy for situation-specific models of color differentiation. In *ASSETS '11: Proceedings of the 13th International ACM SIGACCESS Conference on Computers and Accessibility*, pages 195–202, 2011.

[10] D. R. Flatla and C. Gutwin. Situation specific models of color differentiation. *TACCESS: ACM Transactions on Accessible Computing*, 4(3):13:1–13:44, 2012.

[11] D. R. Flatla and C. Gutwin. "So that's what you see!" building understanding with personalized simulations of colour vision deficiency. In *ASSETS '12: Proceedings of the 14th International ACM SIGACCESS Conference on Computers and Accessibility*, pages 167–174, 2012.

[12] D. S. Fong, F. B. Barton, G. H. Bresnick, and E. T. D. R. S. R. Group. Impaired color vision associated with diabetic retinopathy: Early treatment diabetic retinopathy study report no. 15. *American Journal of Ophthalmology*, 128(5):612–617, 1999.

[13] L. H. Hardy, G. Rand, and M. C. Rittler. HRR polychromatic plates. *Journal of the Optical Society of America*, 44(7):509–521, 1954.

[14] J. Heer and M. Stone. Color naming models for color selection, image editing and palette design. In *Proceedings of the SIGCHI Conference on Human Factors in Computing Systems*, pages 1007–1016. ACM, 2012.

[15] C. Kaufman-Scarborough. Seeing through the eyes of the color-deficient shopper: Consumer issues for public policy. *Journal of Consumer Policy*, 23(4):461–492, December 2000.

[16] K. Knoblauch, F. Vital-Durand, and J. L. Barbur. Variation of chromatic sensitivity across the life span. *Vision Research*, 41(1):23–36, 2001.

[17] S. Kondo. A computer simulation of anomalous color vision. *Color Vision Deficiencies*, pages 145–159, 1990.

[18] O. Lagerlöf. Tricyclic psychopharmaca and colour vision. *Documenta Ophthalmologica Proceedings Series*, 1982.

[19] G. M. Machado, M. M. Oliveira, and L. A. F. Fernandes. A physiologically-based model for simulation of color vision deficiency. *IEEE Transactions on Visualization and Computer Graphics*, 15(6):1291–1298, 2009.

[20] G. W. Meyer and D. P. Greenberg. Color-defective vision and computer graphics displays. *IEEE Computer Graphics and Applications*, 8:28–40, September 1988.

[21] M. Pacheco-Cutillas, D. Edgar, and A. Sahraie. Acquired colour vision defects in glaucoma–their detection and clinical significance. *British Journal of Ophthalmology*, 83(12):1396–1402, 1999.

[22] K. Reinecke, D. R. Flatla, and C. Brooks. Enabling designers to foresee which colors users cannot see. In *Proceedings of the 34th Annual ACM Conference on Human Factors in Computing Systems*, pages 2693–2704. ACM, 2016.

[23] O. Sacks. *An anthropologist on Mars: Seven paradoxical tales*. Vintage, 2012.

[24] M. E. Schneck and G. Haegerstrom-Portnoy. Color vision defect type and spatial vision in the optic neuritis treatment trial. *Investigative ophthalmology & visual science*, 38(11):2278–2289, 1997.

[25] G. Sharma and R. Bala. *Digital color imaging handbook*. CRC press, 2002.

[26] J. A. B. Spalding. Confessions of a colour blind physician. *Clinical and Experimental Optometry*, 87(4-5):344–349, 2004.

[27] J. M. Steward and B. L. Cole. What do color vision defectives day about everyday tasks? *Optometry and Vision Science*, 66(5):288–295, May 1989.

[28] M. Stone. *A field guide to digital color*. CRC Press, 2013.

[29] G. W. Tigwell, D. R. Flatla, and N. D. Archibald. ACE: A usable tool for designing accessible colour palettes. *TACCESS: ACM Transactions on Accessible Computing*, 0(0):30 pages, In submission 2016.

[30] F. Viénot, H. Brettel, L. Ott, A. B. M'Barek, and J. D. Mollon. What do colour-blind people see? *Nature*, 376:127–128, July 13 1995.

[31] B. A. Wandell. *Foundations of vision*. Sinauer Associates, 1995.

[32] G. Wyszecki and W. S. Stiles. *Color Science: Concepts and Methods, Quantitative Data and Formulae*. Wiley New York, 2nd edition, 2000.

[33] C. D. Zippe, A. W. Kedia, K. Kedia, D. R. Nelson, and A. Agarwal. Treatment of erectile dysfunction after radical prostatectomy with sildenafil citrate (viagra). *Urology*, 52(6):963–966, 1998.

Should I Trust It When I Cannot See It?
Credibility Assessment for Blind Web Users

Ali Abdolrahmani and Ravi Kuber
UMBC
Baltimore, MD 21250
{ aliab1, rkuber } @umbc.edu

ABSTRACT

As users become increasingly more reliant on online resources to satisfy their information needs, care is needed to ensure that these resources are credible in nature, especially if a decision is to be taken based upon the information accessed. The credibility of a web site is known to be heavily influenced by its visual appearance. However, for individuals who are blind, challenges are often faced accessing these visual cues when using assistive technologies. In this paper, we describe an observational study to examine the strategies and workarounds developed by individuals who are blind to perform credibility assessments. These are compared with those used by sighted users. Findings from the study have highlighted the relationship between accessibility and credibility. The features used to form assessments non-visually have also been identified. Insights from the study can be used to support the design of highly credible interfaces for blind screen reader users.

CCS Concepts
• **Human Centered Computing→Accessibility**

Keywords
Accessibility; Blind; Visually-Impaired; Web Credibility

1. INTRODUCTION

Recent advances in technology have revolutionized the ways in which information can be accessed and shared with others. As the volume of information available online increases, researchers suggest that the content available may not be subject to filtering through professional gatekeepers. This therefore raises issues surrounding the credibility or quality of content [15]. As users become increasingly more reliant on online resources to satisfy their information needs, the presence and prominence of incorrect and misleading content can have serious consequences for users [19], particularly for those who make decisions based upon the information accessed. The burden is placed on the user to assess levels of credibility [14]; however, difficulties are often faced by users during this process [15].

According to Fogg et al. [7], the two key components of credibility include trustworthiness and expertise. The

ASSETS '16, October 23-26, 2016, Reno, NV, USA.
© 2016 ACM. ISBN 978-1-4503-4124-0/16/10...$15.00.
DOI: http://dx.doi.org/10.1145/2982142.2982173

trustworthiness dimension captures the perceived goodness or morality of the source, while the expertise dimension captures the perceived knowledge and skill of the source. When individuals explore online content, their assessment about the credibility of the information involves both objective judgments of information quality or accuracy, as well as subjective perceptions of the source's trustworthiness, expertise, and attractiveness [9,15]. Additionally, the visual appearance of a web page plays a significant role in attracting information seekers, as well as impacting their perception of its credibility [8].

For individuals who are blind, obtaining these visual cues using screen readers can prove to be challenging. Assistive technologies, such as screen readers, are able to translate textual content from a web page into auditory or tactile format, enabling users to gain an overview of content. However, graphical information and structural layout can be difficult to perceive non-visually. As information is outputted in a linear and time-consuming fashion through a screen reader, it can be a frustrating process when attempting to traverse through content-heavy sites. Furthermore, features such as banners or menus may not vary from page-to-page, and may consequently be presented multiple times when exploring the contents of a site, thereby "overloading" the user [1]. Further details relating to the limitations associated with screen reading technologies can be found in [1,3,16].

In this paper, we describe an observational study examining the strategies and workarounds used by individuals who are blind to perform credibility assessments when using a screen reader. Findings have been compared with those of sighted users. The definition of credibility used for this study refers to the believability of some information and/or its source [11,15]. We are particularly interested in examining: (1) the non-visual cues and credibility criteria used to make judgments (termed: features); and (2) the relationship between accessibility and credibility when making assessments.

2. RELATED WORK
2.1 Credibility assessment

The process of assessing credibility has been examined by a range of researchers. Hilligoss and Rieh [10] proposed a framework of credibility assessment in which credibility is characterized across a variety of media and resources with respect to diverse information seeking goals and tasks. The researchers conducted a diary study, where participants performed various information-seeking tasks. Through a grounded theory analysis, three distinct levels of credibility judgments emerged: construct (how a person constructs, conceptualizes, or defines credibility), heuristics (which involves general rules of thumb used to make judgments of credibility applicable to a variety of situations), and interaction (which refers to credibility judgments based on content, peripheral source cues, and peripheral information object cues). Wathen and Burkell [20] also proposed a model of credibility assessment. The researchers suggest that surface characteristics (e.g., appearance, interface design including download speed and interactivity, and organization of information) are rated once a web site is accessed. If this initial evaluation passes the user's criteria, then they will move to the next "level" of evaluation where the source and message are rated. Factors such as source expertise, competence, trustworthiness, accuracy, currency, and relevance would be taken into account. The third aspect of the process involves the interaction of presentation and content with the user's cognitive state. The researchers suggest that if these assessments meet the user's criteria for credibility, the user accepts the information as credible, and decides to evaluate the information content. If they do not, the user will likely leave the site.

Through a series of studies, Fogg et al. [5-8], have focused on determining the features of sites used for credibility assessment. In their 2003 paper [8], the researchers have described the Prominence-Interpretation Theory to model the ways in which credibility can be assessed. The theory posits that the impact an element has on perceived credibility is a product of its prominence (how likely it is to be noticed) and interpretation (what value or meaning people assign to that element) [19]. Fogg et al. [8] introduced 2684 participants to web sites, covering a range of topics including news, health, travel, e-commerce, and asked them to review and rank these in terms of credibility. Participants commented on the 'design look' of the site more often than any other feature (46.1%). Information visual design/structure (28%) and information focus (25%) were also identified more frequently by participants. Interestingly, functionality, clarity and readability were mentioned less often. In order to develop a highly credible web site, the researchers suggest investing in the visual aspects of a site. Designers should be aware that some highly prominent elements which may impact credibility, are sometimes outside of their control. Care should also be taken when making decisions about prominence, as "not everything can stand out at once". The perceived credibility of a web site is thought to hinge on these decisions [8].

Schwarz and Morris [19] examined page features which are currently difficult or impossible for end users to assess, yet provide valuable signals regarding credibility. These included examining: (1) on-page features (e.g., spelling errors, number of advertisements), (2) off-page features (e.g., awards won, sharing/hit rate of the page through social media), and (3) aggregate features (e.g., general popularity, geographical reach, expert popularity). The researchers proposed visualizations to augment search results and web pages using the most promising of these features. Findings revealed that augmented search results were found to be particularly effective at increasing the accuracy of users' credibility assessments.

The importance of using visual aesthetics to create favorable first impressions of a site has been described by Robins and Holmes [17]. The researchers presented the same content to participants in their study, using different levels of aesthetic treatment. The content with a higher aesthetic treatment was judged as having higher credibility. Kim and Moon [13] found that it is possible to manipulate the visual design factors of an interface in order to induce a target emotion, such as trustworthiness. They suggest that interfaces should be designed which create trustworthy feelings among users, which in turn will influence the decision to use the system. However, Blythe et al. [2] highlight that there may be instances where interfaces on the surface may appear trustworthy, but may need further checks to verify their intent. Difficulties were faced by participants in their study when attempting to detect 'phish' when visual cues, such as professional-looking logos, were present on an interface.

2.2 Information seeking by sighted and blind web users

Studies have been conducted examining the ways in which information seeking habits differ between individuals who are sighted and blind/visually impaired, and the features influencing impressions of the sites accessed. Examples include the study by Craven and Brophy [4], where the researchers presented four information seeking tasks using four different electronic resources. Results confirmed that it took visually impaired participants longer to complete searching and browsing tasks, with times varying considerably depending on the design of the site. Search time was impacted when encountering pages which contained more information, or ones that contained a number of hyperlinks. Ivory et al. [12] presented web-based search tasks to ten sighted and six blind participants. Findings from their study showed that participants initially used the page's summary, title, and URL to predict search result relevance. They then considered additional features (words, ads, and quality) to decide whether or not to explore the page, regardless of their relevance predictions. Similar to [4], blind participants were found to spend more time on tasks. They spent on average twice as long as sighted participants to explore search results and three times as long to explore web pages. Sahib et al. [18] found that the average number of results viewed by sighted participants was significantly higher than visually impaired participants. Sighted participants were also found to submit significantly more queries. However, observations showed that visually impaired searchers expressed their complete information needs in the form of long precise queries, and as a result, their queries were found to be more expressive. Sighted participants were found to place a strong emphasis on layout and aesthetics, while screen-reader users' impressions were thought to be largely dependent on content.

While prior work has offered an insight into the ways in which individuals who are blind explore and search for content, further work is needed to determine the ways in which credibility can be assessed. The study described in this paper, has aimed to identify the features on a web page used by individuals who are blind to assess credibility, and identify the browsing strategies/workarounds taken to make these assessments, compared with sighted peers. We have also aimed to examine the relationship between accessibility and credibility when exploring web content to make assessments. Insights from our study are thought to help to inform the design of highly credible interfaces for blind screen reader users.

3. OBSERVATIONAL STUDY

To investigate the ways in which credibility assessments are made, an observational study was undertaken. While the study primarily focused on the issues faced by individuals who are blind, sighted participants were also recruited in order to compare strategies/workarounds between groups.

3.1 Participants

Eleven legally-blind and eleven sighted volunteers were recruited for the study (aged 19 to 64: mean: 36). The snowball sampling technique was used, in order to identify blind participants with varying levels of experience using technology. All eleven legally-blind participants (B1-B11) had either limited or no residual vision, and relied upon screen readers to access content from the Web (9 PC users favoring JAWS, 2 Mac users favoring VoiceOver). Six of the participants described themselves as congenitally blind, with the remaining five stating that they became blind in later life. Three had some level of light perception. The sighted group followed a similar age and sex distribution to the blind group.

Each of the participants described their level of web expertise on a scale of 1 to 5, where '1' related to being a 'novice user', while '5' related to being an 'advanced user'. Blind participants rated themselves as 4 on average, while sighted participants rated themselves as 4.55. Examples of tasks that advanced users mentioned they could perform independently included regular online shopping, purchasing tickets online, searching for information needed for purposes of college/work, and using social media.

All eleven blind participants expressed confidence in using their screen reader commands for browsing purposes (e.g., quick key navigation to more efficiently jump between different HTML elements on the page such as headings, links, and landmarks). They mentioned that the browsing process could be hindered if pages were designed without consideration for accessibility. For example, difficulties could be faced gaining an overview of content if pages were not designed with the appropriate HTML tags, or if graphics were not labeled.

3.2 Task design
Two tasks were designed which were presented to all participants:

- Task 1: Browsing 5 pairs of web pages examining a topic related to a specific query and then rating the credibility of these pages. *Example: Exploring two web pages which appear in the search results associated with the search term: "How to Reduce Personal Debt."*

- Task 2: Browsing 5 sets of search results present on a search engine results page (SERP), generated using a specific query, and then selecting the most credible result (i.e., which result would be most likely selected for purposes of exploration to satisfy the query). *Example: Assessing the search results found when searching for the term: "Renewable Energy."*

Stimuli for our study were selected from the dataset[1] generated by Schwarz and Morris [19]. The dataset contains 1,000 URLs and their corresponding cached web pages (covering five topics, with five queries per topic, and 40 search results per query), along with subjective topic expert credibility ratings for each URL. For the study described in this paper, the web pages selected covered five topics (celebrity news, environment, health, personal finance, and politics). Pages selected for both tasks varied in terms of credibility ratings assigned by topic experts in the study by Schwarz and Morris [19]. A further check was then performed by both authors/investigators from our paper (one using a screen reader) to independently rate the pages, and check for potential issues which may arise. For Task 2, as search result snippets were not present in the dataset used in Schwarz and Morris' study [19], these snippets were generated using a popular search engine. These were then ordered in a similar way to the original searches conducted in [19].

3.3 Running the study
The study was conducted both in-person and remotely. While all sighted participants were able to attend the testing venue, due to difficulties recruiting blind participants from the local area, ten were asked to perform tasks remotely using video conferencing software.

---

[1] http://research.microsoft.com/credibility

Participants were provided with ten minutes of training, and then asked to perform both sets of tasks while thinking aloud. It was suggested that tasks should be completed as quickly as possible, without compromising quality. If the task could not be completed within a five minute period, participants were asked to move to the next task.

For Task 1, participants were asked to rate the credibility of each page examined and rate their confidence in assigning credibility ratings using Likert scales (1-5). Blind participants were also asked to rate the accessibility of each page. Participants were then asked to reflect upon their experience browsing each of these pages for Task 1, along with their experiences exploring the search results presented in Task 2. The post-task discussion helped us to clarify browsing strategies observed when performing the web-based tasks, as well as enabling participants to describe their reasoning behind their credibility assessment ratings.

Two investigators (one visually impaired, one sighted) were present for each session. Both took detailed notes. For purposes of analysis, both sets of notes were compared. Each session was audio recorded. The primary investigator (who identifies as visually impaired) listened to each recording, carefully examining the output from participants' screen readers when performing tasks. This step was taken to better understand the browsing strategies adopted, which might not have been explicitly verbalized during the sessions.

Table 1: Credibility ratings by user group, and the difference between these ratings with the corresponding values from the dataset used by Schwarz and Morris [19].

Web site	Credibility rating (mean)		Difference between ratings from our study compared with [19]	
	Sighted	Blind	Sighted	Blind
Michael Jackson-NYT	4.36	4.09	-0.64	-0.91
Michael Jackson- Flixster	3.09	2.55	0.09	-0.45
Organic-Heall	3.45	3.18	0.45	0.18
Organic-Grinning	2.73	4.00	-1.27	0.00
Autism-MedicineNet	4.27	4.27	-0.73	-0.73
Autism-AllExperts	2.73	2.70	-0.27	-0.30
Personal Debt-WiseGeek	2.27	3.09	0.27	1.09
Personal Debt-IdeaMarketers	2.36	2.89	0.36	0.89
Obama-CBS	4.36	4.18	-0.64	-0.82
Obama-FactCheck	4.09	3.55	-0.91	-1.45

4. RESULTS AND DISCUSSION

4.1 Quantitative findings
In order to analyze data from our study, the credibility ratings assigned to each web page selected for Task 1 were averaged for both blind and sighted groups. The difference between the average credibility rating for each page from our study and its corresponding rating from Schwarz and Morris' dataset [19], was then calculated. This step was taken to provide a point of comparison (Table 1). For sighted participants, the greatest difference (-1.27) was identified for the Grinning page which related to organic eating (average rating of 2.73 vs. dataset rating

of 4– Figure 1). For blind participants, the greatest difference (-1.45) was identified for the FactCheck page (average rating of 3.55 vs. dataset rating of 5 – Figure 2). The features used to assess the credibility of these pages are described in 4.2.

Figure 1: Grinning page   **Figure 2: Fact Check page**

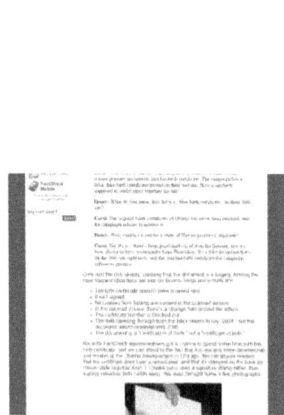

The sighted group were found to assign ratings which were closer in value to the ratings from Schwarz and Morris' dataset [19] (mean difference: 0.56/5), when compared with the blind group (mean difference: 0.68/5). Interestingly, the sighted group reported lower levels of confidence in assigning credibility ratings (4.28/5), compared with the blind group (4.36/5).

In order to examine the relationship between accessibility and credibility, a Spearman's rank-order correlation was run on the ratings provided by blind participants (110 ratings from a total of 11 blind participants). Findings showed a positive correlation between both types of assessment, which was statistically significant (r_s= .3352, n=110, p=.0003). The correlation indicates a weak relationship between the accessibility of a web page and its perceived credibility.

4.2 Perceptions of credibility

Features influencing credibility varied between groups. Sighted participants identified using visual aesthetics and structural layout in order to assess credibility, similar to the findings of Fogg et al. [8], while blind participants focused more on the textual content. For example, one of the pages related to organic eating (Grinning) (Figure 1) was rated 2.73/5 by sighted participants. When questioned about their reasons for the rating, participants suggested that the page was not considered to be visually appealing, appearing somewhat outdated due to an "old-fashioned appearing color scheme". The single column design was thought to be "fairly amateur-looking" in design. In contrast, the more "professional-looking" New York Times article (Michael Jackson-NYT) with a "clearer structure" and "more consistent formatting", was rated higher (4.36/5). The New York Times was thought to be a brand that was recognizable and known for high standards in reporting, which contributed to the rating.

The FactCheck page (Figure 2) received a rating of 3.55/5 from blind participants. When questioned about their reasoning behind the rating, participants highlighted that the page lacked headings, and its main content appeared image-heavy. Although images were labeled, these were not as meaningful to the user, leading to difficulties gaining an overview of content. In contrast, sighted participants rated the page as more credible (4.09). They could swiftly skim the textual content present on the page to gain an overview. The images were found to complement the text, aiding better comprehension of content.

4.3 Browsing Behavior

4.3.1 General browsing strategies

Browsing strategies were found to vary considerably between sighted and blind participants. Sighted participants were able to generally gain a near-instant overview of content and were able to traverse through longer pages with relative ease. Content could be skimmed fairly swiftly. The act of skimming enables users to glean more information about the 'look and feel' of a page (e.g., use of colors, typefaces and themes, visual structure of the page). Participants stated that features such as the presence and quality of images, and details relating to the author or reviewer of the content, would be helpful for making a more informed assessment of the page's credibility.

In contrast, blind participants were observed following a more structured set of steps to gain an overview of content, with the goal of assessing credibility. Upon opening a new web page, participants were observed attempting to locate the main textual content present, to gauge the intended purpose of the page. To do this, a range of techniques were used, described in more detail in 4.3.2.

After locating and reading the main content, some of the blind participants were observed attempting to browse other sections of the page, in order to locate other features (e.g., menus or links to external resources) which would help lead to a more informed assessment of credibility. This attempt could have either a negative or positive impact on their perception of the page's credibility, depending on how easily they could move around the page using their screen reader navigation shortcut keys (e.g., to navigate through headings, lists, etc.).

Blind participants stated that in order to browse pages containing considerable amounts of content (termed: 'busy' pages), reading speed and verbosity was adjusted to streamline the process of moving through information present. This would result in the participants expending considerable cognitive effort to listen attentively for certain terms or cues voiced by the screen reader, which would enable them to make a decision on how to proceed.

4.3.2 Non-visual browsing strategies

The following strategies were observed when blind participants were attempting to traverse content to make credibility assessments:

Avoiding extraneous content: Six blind participants were observed to use commands to skip over menu list items with the aim of moving straight to the main content present on the page. Participants who had accessed similarly structured pages in the past, described attempting to recall the steps previously taken to avoid extraneous information, including ads, list of links serving as menus, and social media links (e.g., Facebook, Twitter and Google Plus). On occasion, participants were noted to overshoot the main content. If this happened, participants would use commands such as the up arrow key to return back to the content that they had passed over.

Skipping graphics with inappropriate alternative descriptions: Images can be used for either decorative or informative purposes, when integrated with a web page. Six blind participants mentioned images without useful alternative descriptions would be bothersome and cognitively overloading when attempting to gain an overview of content, preventing them from focusing on making an informed credibility assessment. B6 stated, "when I hear the term 'graphic', meaningless long numbers or things like '% &? 1287958445643 @' outputted by my screen reader while browsing, I know that these images or frames are useless to spend time on, making me think that this content is not helping me in the least to determine the credibility of the page." Participants were largely aware that sighted users could glance over these images easily, without wasting any time. However, they were willing to put in the time to traverse content sequentially, in order to reduce the risk of assessing the credibility poorly, particularly if information from the page would be used to support a decision.

Browsing sequentially not to miss information: Seven of our participants were observed browsing content line-by-line, even though it was more time-consuming than using other techniques. Since many of the pages presented were unfamiliar to them, participants mentioned that line-by-line browsing would help to reduce the likelihood of missing important pieces of information. This led to the participants feeling more confident that they had made fair assessments of a page's credibility.

Using "HTML element" quick navigation: Participants were found to express greater levels of confidence when browsing familiar web pages, compared to ones that had not previously been accessed. Participants described developing mental structural representations of layout when exploring a page. While committing these representations to memory was found to be demanding, the technique could 'pay-off' if it helped to streamline the navigation process when visiting the site at a later time. Seven participants took advantage of their screen reader's navigation features when exploring familiar pages. Actions performed included jumping between headings, buttons, or links present on pages. These could be used to gain an overview of content, on which they could form their decision about the credibility of the page. If satisfied, they would then switch back to sequential reading as their typical behavior to pay close attention to the content. B9 stated, "If I know the layout of the page, I mostly find the heading first to save time, then just press 'say all' command ['Insert key plus Down arrow'] to read down."

Reading text character-by-character: Four of the participants used this technique to read certain sections of a page, even though the process was time consuming in nature. This strategy was used to read URLs to determine credibility. Domain name extensions such as '.org' were thought to include content that was more strongly vetted for presentation, compared with other extensions. Similar to Blythe et al. [2], participants described situations where they had selected URLs which were spelled or read by their screen readers in a similar way to commercial sites, but had inadvertently led them to unintended sites. Recovering from the error could be challenging, so it made sense to more cautious users to spend time going through the URL to avoid this from happening.

Searching for copyright and author information: In addition to checking URLs, four participants were observed checking for copyright symbols and digital certificates when exploring web pages. This technique has also been highlighted by Lazar et al. [14], as a method of assessing credibility. B1 was noted to spend time searching for the copyright symbol when exploring the Flixter page. After reading content present on the page, he was observed moving to the end of the page using the Ctrl and End keys. The up arrow key was then selected where he assumed using previous experience of accessing similar pages, that the copyright symbol would most likely be located. He stated "I know that jumping up back to where I was before [in the text] can be a hassle." He highlighted that it was worth making a trade-off, spending more time to locate features on a page which would inform a credibility assessment, rather than attempting to make a

decision based on content from a page which may not be trustworthy.

Participants were found to also search for information about the page author(s). The presence of names along with credentials (e.g., MD, Ph.D.) would signify whether content had been written by someone qualified for the role. This would in turn impact the assessment of the page's credibility.

4.4 Credibility assessment criteria

4.4.1 General characteristics of the page
Blind participants were observed focusing upon non-visual features present on web pages to support the assessment of credibility. These are described below.

Intention: Six blind participants attempted to identify the main message that each page was intending to convey (i.e., what was it selling, etc.) prior to providing a credibility assessment. They described searching for evidence in the textual content present on each page, to determine if the site appeared to be 'professional-looking' in nature, or whether it seemed more like a blog which may not have been vetted by a third party. The presence of ads, links to commercial products, and discussion related to the content, were criteria which used to determine the credibility of the page. As an example, while looking at the AllExperts web page which related to early signs of autism, B11 stated, "Oh, there are just questions and answers here. It seems that this page is nothing but just a blog post where advocates have posted responses." As a result, the participant felt inclined to close the page and move to the next link.

'Information Focus' *(term used by Fogg et al. [8])*: Two participants (B5 and B6) closely examined whether content present on a page differed from the intended purpose of the site. For example, if participants detected links or discussions about topics other than the main topic associated with the page, it would raise doubts about the quality and validity of the content. For example, when browsing the Flixter page relating to Michael Jackson (MJ), B5 pointed out, "it seems that it is just a kind of media page with videos and images of many people. So it is not a specific page dedicated to MJ, making me doubtful about its credibility, compared to what I read about him on the New York Times page." In contrast, sighted participants were not observed spending time attempting to differentiate between content on a site and its intended purpose.

4.4.2 Textual sensitivity
Textual content was found to be more heavily scrutinized by blind participants compared with the sighted group. The following highlights the textual characteristics which blind participants described they would use to help assess credibility.

Quality of the writing: Five participants stated that the quality of writing can provide a valuable insight into the accuracy of content. Depending on the context of the topic, this included how clearly the text was written, the sophistication of the writing (e.g., the use of technical terms), and how relevant the content was to the headings on the page. For example, looking at a blog-like web page with a casual style of writing, B11 pointed out, "The text does not appear to be expertly written when I skim it. It doesn't pass my trust test." Looking at the same page, B5 mentioned, "I cannot tolerate written text on a page that does not match its main purpose or topic."

'Tone of the writing' *(term described by Fogg et al. [8])*: Three participants were found to skim the text using the 'Say-all' command, to establish whether the content was well constructed, and to identify the 'tone' of the writing. They pointed out if they felt the text was written in a casual style, especially in pages with a scientific topic, they would not rate the information to be as highly credible. Looking at a page which related to the early signs of autism, B11 mentioned, "It looks that there is just a kind of casual conversation going on here between someone who has asked a question and the responder. I will never take contents like this seriously. I prefer reading pages [relating to medical conditions] which are more professionally written, with scientific information present."

Writing neutrality: Six blind participants stated when they skimmed through the main content of a web page, they would try to understand if the text was written as an opinion piece or a factual piece. If it was an opinion piece, participants described attempting to identify whether bias was present in the content. Although sighted participants mentioned this issue, they were found to mainly form their judgment based on whether or not the source appeared to be a neutral content provider (e.g., web sites with a reputation for presenting information with minimal bias), rather than spending time examining the content.

Writing mechanics: Grammatical errors and typos in the text negatively impacted the credibility ratings among four blind participants, while no sighted participants from our study explicitly referred to these. B5 pointed out, "...I can easily distinguish where there is a typo or grammatical error especially if I listen to the screen reader at a slower [reading] speed. You know it is quite clear through the change in tone of the spoken text. How can I trust the content and author when no-one has even proof read what they are presenting to me?"

4.4.3 Supporting Evidence as Criteria

The ability to locate supporting evidence in the main content of a page was found to impact credibility ratings among blind participants. Although sighted participants would take some of these factors into account, none of these were among the main criteria that they described as impacting their assessments.

Dates and **statistics**: When skimming text, three blind participants stated if they browsed a scientific or sensitive topic, they would pay close attention to statistical information present to support existing content, and any dates indicating when the page was developed, particularly when judging the credibility of time-sensitive topics (e.g., news articles, etc.). Participants were aware that older pages may contain information which may be out-of-date. Decisions based on out-of-date/inaccurate content were thought to lead to negative outcomes.

Presence of relevant links and citations: Seven blind participants stated that the presence of relevant links and citations would help to boost their perceptions of the page's credibility. If they were not familiar with the topic associated with the page, links would be useful to identify more information about that topic. For example, when looking at a medical web site relating to autism (Medicine.net), B11 stated, "The page appears to be credible as it has links to provide an explanation of the terms that may be unfamiliar to its readers. This site seems to be more credible, as it supports the needs of users with limited knowledge of medical terms." The page was noted not to contain links which were unrelated to the topic (autism).

Meaningfulness of the content and flow of the text: Four blind participants expected highly credible sites to be well structured, with text that flows well. Detailed relevant content on the page also led to perceptions of higher credibility. B6 highlighted that the lack of information present on a page explaining issues related to autism (AllExperts site) made it difficult to determine whether much time had been spent developing the site. As a result, it was not thought to be as credible as the autism article on the Medicine.net site.

4.4.4 Familiarity with topic or site

Both blind and sighted participants used criteria such as personal expertise/prior knowledge about the topic, to support their judgments of credibility. For instance, B10, who defined himself as being knowledgeable about organic eating practices, stated while referring to the Heall page, "I am well familiar with this subject. When I read this page, it is obvious that there is some bias in the language." This appeared to negatively impact his rating of credibility.

4.5 Impact of accessibility on perceptions of credibility

Blind participants emphatically stated that accessibility challenges when browsing web sites would not influence their perceptions of credibility. For example, B6 mentioned, "You know what? I know that people out there may not necessarily take accessibility into account when designing sites, but it does not mean what they present is not credible. I do my best to read the text and see what else I can find there to make an informed credibility assessment." However, in practice, observations revealed that when accessibility barriers were encountered, ratings often appeared to be impacted. Instances are described in 4.5.1-4.5.3.

4.5.1 Page layout and inappropriate usage of visual UI elements

Inappropriate design was one challenge described by participants that could impact the process of skimming the main content. Three blind participants were observed to struggle traversing through the tables (used for layout purposes) embedded within the Grinning page relating to organic eating. These were used to visually organize objects and text on the page. Ironically, the layout of content was not appreciated by sighted participants (4.2). When asked to describe his experience accessing the page using a screen reader, B1 stated, "It is taking too much time to explore. I usually don't care about pages that waste my time just to find content in them." Although he mentioned that this influenced his credibility rating, he highlighted that there were positives which could help to offset the rating (e.g. the clarity of textual content present on the page).

When describing general experiences browsing sites, B1 stated that tags are often misused by interface designers, which can impact the accessibility of content. For example, the tag <b> may be used by designers to embolden content when developing headings. However, heading tags (e.g., <h2>, <h3>), which make text appear visually similar to emboldened content, would be more useful, as screen readers are able to present lists of headings to the user to help gain an overview of content.

4.5.2 When content loaded slowly or was incomplete

The loading speed of the page content, though not directly an accessibility issue, was another factor that impacted credibility for four blind participants in our study. There were several instances when pages loaded more slowly than expected. Participants began to listen to the content present. However, only part of the information was present at this time as the page was still loading, which led to a negative perception of the site. Participants thought that either the page was not finished by the author, or that part of the content was inaccessible. This was not observed as a problem for sighted participants because they were able to visually recognize whether or not the pages were loaded completely.

4.5.3 Inaccessible media objects

The presence of inaccessible media objects including Flash content, unlabeled buttons, or images without appropriate alternative descriptions negatively impacted the credibility rating for some pages. The impact was most obvious when the page was unfamiliar to the user. For example, when browsing a web page relating to a celebrity, which contained multiple images of the star, B8 stated, "I am not sure if these are his photos as there is no description that I can trust. Should I trust it when I cannot see it? Sighted users can see them, so it must be simpler for them to identify if the page is credible." In contrast, on pages where graphical objects which were informative in nature, and associated with alternative descriptions (e.g., on the page related to organic eating), participants reacted to the page content with a more positive view relating to its credibility.

4.6 Exploring search results

Blind participants in our study were generally confident with the process of conducting online searches, and were able to move quickly through the search results present in Task 2. Findings from Task 2 highlighted certain parallels between both groups of users when attempting to gain an overview of content. For example, sighted participants were able to skim through the search result titles, which were larger in size and blue in color, and therefore more noticeable on the SERP. Blind participants tended to use shortcut keys to move through the search results, skimming titles in a similar fashion to sighted users. As the search result titles generated by the Google site, are tagged with "Heading 3" tags, selecting either "H" or "3" keys would help a screen reader user to jump quickly between search result titles in sequence. After skimming through titles, both groups could focus on the longer snippets, to identify the relevance and associated credibility of the page.

Both blind and sighted participants described using similar subjective criteria to evaluate search results. For example, familiarity with the topic, source of the search result, and purpose of the search were taken into account when making credibility assessments. Both groups were also noted to place a certain amount of trust in the algorithms used by Google, Bing, and other popular search engines, which enabled them to feel more confident that results on the first page of the SERP might be more relevant, and likely credible. Neither group favored spending time moving to a second page of results, should they be unable to locate appropriate results from the first page. They favored reformulating the query instead.

5. INSIGHTS FROM THE STUDY

Researchers suggest that web users are becoming more skeptical of the information they find online and may be wary of web-based experiences [7]. The onus is placed upon interface designers to enhance credibility. While design guidance has often focused upon improving the visual appearance of a site, findings from our study reveal that to better meet the needs of individuals who are blind, other considerations need to be made.

- **Designers should be aware that perceptions of credibility differ when exploring content visually and non-visually. Attempts should be made to bridge this gap**. Sites which are more visually-appealing were found to be associated with greater levels of credibility among sighted participants (e.g., Flixter page - Table 1). In contrast, sites with rich, well formulated textual content, and a strong structure, led to

more favorable credibility ratings by blind participants, even though some of these pages appeared less visually attractive and therefore less credible to sighted participants (e.g., Grinning page). Interface designers should consider ways to ensure that all users, irrespective of ability, are able to obtain the cues they need to make an informed decision as to the credibility of content.

- **Designers should be aware of features which are important to assess credibility non-visually, and note that relative importance of features may vary between user groups**. Findings from our study highlighted that pages found to be highly credible by blind participants, stayed on topic (information focus), and contained limited extraneous information (e.g., adverts, links to unrelated topics). Credibility was negatively impacted by inappropriate tagging, and poor layout of content, both of which would make the process of navigating with a screen reader more challenging. In terms of textual content, the quality and 'tone' of the writing were found to influence ratings. While some of these features influenced ratings by sighted participants, visual aesthetics and structural layout were found to be the most important for purposes of making an assessment.

- **Sites should be designed taking into account the browsing strategies that are used by blind users**. In order to explore unfamiliar pages, techniques such as moving from heading-to-heading or link-to-link were often used to gain a quicker overview of page content, with a view to making credibility assessments. If a page is inappropriately coded, these strategies would be difficult to perform. Furthermore, information which may be helpful to sighted users may be extraneous to blind users (e.g., listening to the alternative text associated with non-informative images), and therefore may be skipped over to save time in this process. Pages which were more familiar to blind users (e.g., search result pages presented by a search engine which is frequently visited) could be explored with greater levels of confidence, removing an additional hurdle to making a credibility assessment.

- **Cautious users should be supported when making credibility assessments**. Some of the blind participants in our study favored reading content line-by-line or character-by-character, depending on whether important decisions rested upon whether the content presented was credible or not. Similar to [2], the screen reader could be used as a 'security device', enabling users to examine URLs which may be similar sounding to a commercial site's URL, but may lead to a different, or possibly malicious site. Blind participants felt that a greater time investment at this stage would lead to a more informed decision relating to credibility.

- **Design for accessibility, which in turn may influence credibility**. Findings from our study confirmed the presence of a positive correlation between accessibility and credibility. While blind participants in our study were hesitant to describe a link between the two factors, their browsing behavior indicated otherwise (see Section 4.5). Thorough accessibility testing is needed with individuals who are blind and visually impaired to reduce the risk of issues that may be faced when using a screen reader to browse a page. Additionally, identifying credibility and confidence in the rating provided during the testing stage would also present considerable value.

6. CONCLUSION AND FUTURE WORK

The observational study described in this paper has examined the credibility assessment process undertaken by individuals who are blind and sighted. Two sets of web-based tasks were presented to participants. The features which are used to help inform credibility assessments have been identified. Furthermore, the relationship between accessibility and credibility has been described. Insights from the study can be used by interface designers when developing highly credible sites to cater to the needs of individuals who are blind and use screen readers to access the Web.

As the next logical step in the research, we aim to conduct a study where participants are presented with interfaces with varying levels of accessibility. Findings would offer a deeper insight into the ways in which inappropriate design can impact both accessibility and credibility assessments of a site. Further work may also be conducted to examine the ways in which assessments of credibility may vary when the situation, context, or environment differs (e.g., investigating search results while on-the-go using mobile devices). Findings would help to develop and strengthen guidance for interface designers aiming to support levels of credibility among users with diverse needs and abilities.

7. ACKNOWLEDGMENTS

We would like to thank Leila Heroabadi, Dhuel Fisher and William Easley, who helped prepare study materials and run study sessions; Josanne Revoir, Stacy Branham and Flynn Wolf, who helped proof-read the document; and Erick Ronquillo and Nasrin Attaran, who helped the visually impaired author format the manuscript. We also thank our participants for their valuable feedback.

8. REFERENCES

[1] Andronico, P., Buzzi, M., Castillo, C. and Leporini, B. 2006. Improving search engine interfaces for blind users: a case study. *Universal Access in the Information Society*. 5, 1 (2006), 23–40. DOI= http://dx.doi.org/10.1007/s10209-006-0022-3

[2] Blythe, M., Petrie, H. and Clark, J.A. 2011. F for fake: four studies on how we fall for phish. In *Proceedings of the SIGCHI Conference on Human Factors in Computing Systems*. CHI'11. ACM, New York, NY, 3469–3478. DOI= http://doi.acm.org/10.1145/1978942.1979459

[3] Borodin, Y., Bigham, J.P., Dausch, G. and Ramakrishnan, I.V. 2010. More than meets the eye: a survey of screen-reader browsing strategies. In *Proceedings of the International Cross Disciplinary Conference on Web Accessibility*. W4A'10. ACM, New York, NY, Article No. 13. DOI= http://doi.acm.org/10.1145/1805986.1806005

[4] Craven, J. and Brophy, P. 2003. *Non-Visual Access to the Digital Library (NoVA): the Use of the Digital Library Interfaces by Blind and Visually Impaired People*. Technical Report. Centre for Research in Library & Information Management, The Manchester Metropolitan University.

[5] Fogg, B., Marshall, J., Kameda, T., Solomon, J., Rangnekar, A., Boyd, J. and Brown, B. 2001. Web credibility research: a method for online experiments and early study results. *Extended Abstracts on Human Factors in Computing Systems*. CHI'01. ACM, New York, NY, 295–296. DOI= http://doi.acm.org/10.1145/634067.634242

[6] Fogg, B., Marshall, J., Osipovich, A., Varma, C., Laraki, O., Fang, N., Paul, J., Rangnekar, A., Shon, J., Swani, P. and Treinen, M. 2000. Elements that affect web credibility: early results from a self-report study. *Extended Abstracts on Human Factors in Computing Systems*. CHI'00. ACM, New York, NY, 287–288. DOI= http://doi.acm.org/10.1145/633292.633460

[7] Fogg, B.J., Marshall, J., Laraki, O., Osipovich, A., Varma, C., Fang, N., Paul, J., Rangnekar, A., Shon, J., Swani, P. and Treinen, M. 2001. What makes web sites credible?: a report on a large quantitative study. In *Proceedings of the SIGCHI Conference on Human Factors in Computing Systems*. CHI'01. ACM, New York, NY, 61–68. DOI= http://doi.acm.org/10.1145/365024.365037

[8] Fogg, B.J., Soohoo, C., Danielson, D.R., Marable, L., Stanford, J. and Tauber, E.R. 2003. How do users evaluate the credibility of web sites?: a study with over 2,500 participants. In *Proceedings of the Conference on Designing for User Experiences*. DUX'03. ACM, New York, NY, 1–15. DOI= http://doi.acm.org/10.1145/997078.997097

[9] Freeman, K.S. and Spyridakis, J.H. 2004. An examination of factors that affect the credibility of online health information. *Technical Communication*. 51, 2 (2004), 239–263.

[10] Hilligoss, B. and Rieh, S.Y. 2008. Developing a unifying framework of credibility assessment: construct, heuristics, and interaction in context. *Information Processing & Management*. 44, 4 (Jul. 2008), 1467–1484. DOI= http://dx.doi.org/10.1016/j.ipm.2007.10.001

[11] Hovland, C.I., Janis, I.L. and Kelley, H.H. 1953. Communication and persuasion; psychological studies of opinion change. Yale University Press, New Haven, CT.

[12] Ivory, M.Y., Yu, S. and Gronemyer, K. 2004. Search result exploration: a preliminary study of blind and sighted users' decision making and performance. *Extended Abstracts on Human Factors in Computing Systems*. CHI'04, ACM, New York, NY, 1453–1456. DOI= http://doi.acm.org/10.1145/985921.986088

[13] Kim, J. and Moon, J.Y. 1998. Designing towards emotional usability in customer interfaces—trustworthiness of cyber-banking system interfaces. *Interacting with Computers*. 10, 1 (Mar. 1998), 1–29. DOI= http://dx.doi.org/10.1016/S0953-5438(97)00037-4

[14] Lazar, J., Meiselwitz, G. and Feng, J. 2007. Understanding web credibility: a synthesis of the research literature. *Foundations and Trends® in Human-Computer Interaction*. 1, 2 (2007), 139–202. DOI= http://dx.doi.org/10.1561/1100000007

[15] Metzger, M.J. 2007. Making sense of credibility on the Web: models for evaluating online information and recommendations for future research. *Journal of the American Society for Information Science and Technology*. 58, 13 (Nov. 2007), 2078–2091. DOI= http://dx.doi.org/10.1002/asi.20672

[16] Murphy, E., Kuber, R., McAllister, G., Strain, P. and Yu, W. 2008. An empirical investigation into the difficulties experienced by visually impaired Internet users. *Universal Access in the Information Society*. 7, 1–2 (Apr. 2008), 79–91. DOI= http://dx.doi.org/10.1007/s10209-007-0098-4

[17] Robins, D. and Holmes, J. 2008. Aesthetics and credibility in web site design. *Information Processing & Management*. 44, 1 (Jan. 2008), 386–399. DOI= http://dx.doi.org/10.1016/j.ipm.2007.02.003

[18] Sahib, N.G., Tombros, A. and Stockman, T. 2012. A comparative analysis of the information-seeking behavior of visually impaired and sighted searchers. *Journal of the American Society for Information Science and Technology*. 63, 2 (Feb. 2012), 377–391. DOI= http://dx.doi.org/10.1002/asi.21696

[19] Schwarz, J. and Morris, M. 2011. Augmenting web pages and search results to support credibility assessment. In *Proceedings of the SIGCHI Conference on Human Factors in Computing Systems*. CHI'11. ACM, New York, NY, 1245–1254. DOI=http://doi.acm.org/10.1145/1978942.1979127

[20] Wathen, C.N. and Burkell, J. 2002. Believe it or not: factors influencing credibility on the web. *Journal of the American Society for Information Science and Technology*. 53, 2 (2002), 134–144. DOI= http://dx.doi.org/10.1002/asi.10016

Blind Photographers and VizSnap: A Long-Term Study

Dustin Adams, Sri Kurniawan, Cynthia Herrera, Veronica Kang, Natalie Friedman

University of California, Santa Cruz
1156 High St.
Santa Cruz, CA 95064
{duwadams,skurnia,cjherrer,vkang,nvfriedm}@ucsc.edu

ABSTRACT

This paper describes a long term user study in which 13 blind participants were asked to use a blind friendly iPhone app, VizSnap – an app designed to assist blind people in organizing and browsing a photo library without sight – for a total of two months. VizSnap records audio while the user is aiming the camera, and allows an optional voice memo to be recorded, to allow the user to give custom information to accompany the photo, as well as capturing time, date, and location the photo was taken. All this information is available to the user when browsing through VizSnap's photo library. The participants met with us every two weeks, in which we discuss general VizSnap usage, conduct a short user study with their photos, as well as upload all data that was gathered using VizSnap. The user study aims to determine whether accompanying audio, time, date, and location metadata assists in memory retrieval of photos by blind people. We found that in general, both ambient audio and voice memo are considered most helpful for memory retrieval.

Keywords

Blind Users; Photography; Mobile; Accessibility.

1. INTRODUCTION

Blind people often face challenges when accessing photographs that have already been taken and are stored in a photo library [1]. Since photography is inherently a visual undertaking, photographs often times only contain visual information. With the advent and recent ubiquity of smartphones, photographs can be complemented with other information (such as time, date, and location information).

Some researchers have made an application to make photographs more accessible to people who are blind by adding location (using reverse geo-coded GPS information) and general, nonspecific information about what is in a photograph (such as IQEngines) to help users browse and navigate a photo album without sight [6]. However, little research has been done to assess whether audio recorded while the photograph was taken, as well as a custom, spoken, voice memo to accompany the photograph could be used to help browse and navigate a photo album without sight.

This paper reports on a long-term user study that aims to investigate whether accompanying audio to a photograph enhances memory retrieval of an event for people who are blind, in addition to time, date, and location information, which are already available with the default photo album with iPhone. With

ASSETS '16, October 23 - 26, 2016, Reno, NV, USA
Copyright is held by the owner/author(s). Publication rights licensed to ACM.
ACM 978-1-4503-4124-0/16/10 $15.00
DOI: http://dx.doi.org/10.1145/2982142.2982169

the default iPhone photo album, time, date, and location are information given to the user through VoiceOver. Through VoiceOver, the iPhone user is also able to give a custom tag of the photo, once they have located it in the photo library (which is not available upon taking the photo – it must be done afterwards in the photo library), which may be a daunting task for someone who is unable to see the photograph. Giving a custom label in text is a multi-stage and sometimes time consuming process, meaning several gestures are required in order to open up the label creator, and typing with VoiceOver on requires three times as many gestures as it would without VoiceOver.

2. RELATED WORK

2.1 Social Networking among Blind People

Voykinska et al. conducted interviews with 11 blind people and conduct a survey among 60 blind people investigating blind people's interaction with photos on social media [11]. They found that most participants in their study use social networking services for the same reasons sighted people do, and 100% of their survey respondents use Facebook. While many of their totally blind participants face many accessibility challenges, there were plenty of participants who were engaged with visual content on Facebook, such as photos. However, the researchers reported that this often times required sighted help. They also reported only 23% of participants post photos on Facebook, mainly because of the difficulty associated with taking a "good" photo, and selecting the correct (or desired) photo from their photo album.

Wu et al. ran a study with 50,000 blind or visually impaired Facebook users to investigate general Facebook usage and problems faced by visually impaired users, compared with a random sample of 160,000 Facebook users [12]. The researchers discovered that comparing the "amount of photos that are produced and shared to Facebook" of the visually impaired group compared to the random sample, the difference is statistically significant for a Wilcoxon rank sum test on the difference in medians (p-value $< 1.2 \times 10^{-14}$). They do, however, report that users of the visually impaired sample do upload slightly fewer photos than the random sample, despite this statistical significance regarding "the amount of photos that are produced and shared to Facebook."

Qiu et al. conducted interviews and observations with six blind and visually impaired people to investigate their use of social media on mobile devices, in Hong Kong [9]. Some of their participants in the study have expressed desire for "real-time acoustic information of scenarios (record the synchronous sound when taking the photo), and acoustic description of photo contents (such as information of object, location, and color), " within the social media apps. One of VizSnap's purposes is to provide the user with both of these aforementioned features, through ambient audio and voice memo, respectively. However, the audio information is not currently targeted to be integrated with social media applications; they exist within VizSnap simply to enhance the user's memory of photographs.

Ahmed et al. conducted a user study with 14 visually impaired people to investigate the privacy concerns of visually impaired people, how visually impaired people manage their privacy, and which new technologies could offer enhanced privacy for visually impaired users [2]. They found that visually impaired users of social networking services are often concerned about the privacy of their personal content, including photos, on those social networking services. Participants also noted being concerned about strangers eavesdropping on audio played from a screen reader of the visually impaired person's mobile device. Many of their participants reported using headphones as a way to keep audio private.

2.2 Blind-Friendly Smartphone Apps

Many different blind-friendly photography apps have been developed targeted to allow app users to use their smartphone's camera to help assess the world around them – [4,6,7] – to name a few. Bigham et al.'s work on VizWiz shows that many blind people are willing to use their smartphone's camera to take photos and ask a question about the photo, using crowdsourcing as a way to get answers to their questions [4]. One example of a question asked about a photo is "Can you please tell me what this can is?" where the contents of the photo are a can of food with a label.

2.3 Blind Photography

As our own research as has shown [1], as well as Ahmed et al. [2], blind photographers are hesitant to share photos without knowing whether the photograph is "good," or acceptable to the photographer. This shows a necessity to help people who are blind with taking a good, or at least acceptable photo. Balata et al. describes a system that helps blind people aim a camera to achieve the Golden Ratio (which is a design principle roughly based on the ratio of 1 to 1.618) using vibration from a smartphone [3]. Vazquez et al. have also shown a system to help visually impaired people aim a camera giving feedback to the user indicating how they should move the camera [10]. The feedback is available in three different modes: speech, tone, and silent feedback.

3. METHOD

As the first step of understanding the problems that blind photographers face, we analyzed thousands of forum posts by tens of thousands of users with limited vision as well as photos posted by these users and concluded with the most common obstacles, techniques for taking photos, personal reflection, and common technological help sought out. These photographs came from a Flickr group called Blind Photographers, which restricts the uploaded photos to those taken by visually impaired photographers. Please note that the members are self-proclaimed to be visually impaired, and there is no test or verification done by the forum administration.

From the forum postings and the analysis of photos for quality problems, we found several problems (although we should note that over one third of the photos analyzed do not have any obvious problems we can pinpoint). The two biggest problems (combined made up almost half of the problems) are the photos being obviously cut off or out of focus. While better and better features are available in terms of helping a blind photographer focus their camera, few techniques are available to help avoid cut-off photos (e.g., a person with missing top part of the face/head). This suggests that there is a need to design a system that can inform the users about whether the object of interest is captured in its entirety.

The photo tag analysis revealed that the number one object taken was of people, in which there is good support already in terms of face detection (although not so much in making sure that the head is not cut off). The second most frequent tag, nature, is more difficult to support in terms of ensuring good quality photos, opening opportunities to think of an interactive system that can help in this kind of photographed object.

We should note that the analysis was done on a forum in which the photographers posted their photos, perhaps indicating that they have a certain level of confidence to show their photos to the general public (although the forum postings were also populated by those who are just beginning to take photos and are seeking help). By understanding the photography needs of blind photographers, we hope to come up with technologies and techniques to address those needs.

3.1 Research Questions

Based on our analysis, the primary research questions of the user study reported in this paper are:

1. What kind of photographs do blind photographers take?
2. Do blind photographers make use of sound recordings, time, date, and location information to help them recognize their photo?
3. What are some of the issues that blind photographers face when using VizSnap?

To answer question 1, all photos taken by participants during the user study were collected and combined to form a corpus of photos. The photos were analyzed by two researchers to categorize them into meaningful groups, which will be explained in depth in section 5.

To answer question 2, the participants were given the description of five photographs, and asked to retrieve the photo using only audio, time, date, and location metadata. After three minutes, if the user had not located the photo based on the description or has located a different photo, then retrieval of that photo is considered unsuccessful. It should be noted that no participants had to be cut off after the three-minute mark; this limit only existed to stop the participant from over-analyzing.

To answer question 3, participants were asked a short questionnaire during each two-week meeting about their general usage of VizSnap throughout the two-month period.

Approval from the Institutional Review Board (IRB) was obtained for this research before the study began.

3.2 Equipment

The main equipment for our study is an iPhone running an iPhone app we developed called VizSnap. VizSnap allows users to attach additional information to a photograph. VizSnap is available on the App Store for free. A precursor of VizSnap (called Phodio) has been documented and its user study had been published in [5]. VizSnap records ambient audio while the user is aiming the camera, then allows the user to take a picture using gestures provided by VoiceOver, and adds the option to record a VoiceMemo.

One gesture captures a photo, and one additional gesture records voice memo (fewer than the two gestures required by the built in iPhone camera app (using VoiceOver) to just take a photo). Once the user finished taking photos, they may exit the camera view (using one gesture), and are automatically taken to the photo album. In the photo album, the user uses one finger to swipe left and right to hear the voice memo, ambient audio, time, and date of earlier, and later photos, respectively. Upon hearing the desired photo, the user can use more gestures to replay the voice memo and ambient audio, and location information, as well as send the photo as an email attachment, post to Facebook, or delete the photo.

3.3 Participants

The users for this study are people who are totally blind or with light perception, and who need VoiceOver to use an iPhone. This user study targets both adventitiously blind and congenitally blind people. While it is intended that this app be implemented through Android at some point, right now, it is only available for iPhone, the most commonly used smartphone by blind persons [8]. For that reason, in addition to being blind, users must also have an iPhone.

The user study involved 13 participants, aged 18-65 years old, seven females and six males. There were users from USA (11), Canada (one), and New Zealand (one). There were seven adventitiously blind participants, and six who are congenitally blind. Nine participants were totally blind, and two still had some light perception.

The user study required that participants use VizSnap for two months, taking at least five photos every two days, and meeting with us (either in person or over the network) every two weeks. For each participant we also asked if biweekly was considered fine, and only two participants requested 3-week spacing for 1 session. The goal was to have the user take at least 30 photos in the two week period so that a legitimate assessment could be made as to whether the participant had used VizSnap sufficiently to form an opinion of the app, as well as for us to objectively assess the participant's usage of the app based on data recorded by the application. The participants were asked to upload their photos, along with all of the photos' audio, time, date, and location data to a server, to allow us to analyze the data, the day before the meeting. Please note that the VizSnap version in the app store does not require nor have the facility to upload to a server for privacy purposes.

From the data, five photos were chosen at random, and during the meeting with the participant, each photo was described to the participant, and the participant was asked to navigate through their photo album on VizSnap and locate the photo using only the audio, time, date, and location information of the photo. The participant was also asked a short questionnaire about their general usage of VizSnap during the previous two weeks.

3.4 Study Procedure

Since participants of this study are located throughout the US and outside the US, the users had to download the test VizSnap app with the capability to upload their data to a server for analysis. VizSnap was made available to participants using a service called TestFlight, provided to developers by Apple [13].

TestFlight involves registering the build of the App, as well as the email addresses of the participants. TestFlight then simply sends each participant an invitation to download the app, and the app is easily downloaded with the click of one link. The only caveat is that each build of TestFlight expires after 30 days, and since the user study lasted roughly two months, the participants had to

download updates, which retains all the users' previous data of VizSnap.

The user study was conducted over four sessions, and each session is described as follows:

3.4.1 First Session (Introductory Session)
The introductory session involved several steps. First, making sure VizSnap downloaded successfully on the participant's iPhone. All participants had successfully downloaded VizSnap.

Next, the participants were asked the following demographics questions:

1. How old are you?
2. Since when were you blind?
3. Preferred choice of camera device.
4. Since when did you use the camera device?
5. In a typical week, how often do you take photos?
6. How often do you browse through your photos?
7. What's your strategy for taking photos?
8. What's your strategy for browsing photos?
9. What's your strategy for sharing photos with others?

Next, the participants were instructed how to use VizSnap through a step-by-step demonstration of every feature and gesture. The participants were asked to repeat the use of each feature and gesture. All participants were successful in this step.

The next step involved the explanation of the user study, which highlights that the participants were required to take at least five photos every two days, such that at least 30 photos were present for the next meeting session (occurring every two weeks). The participants were given a $10 Amazon Gift Card for every session as long as they took at least five photos every two days prior to that session.

Finally, the consent form was read aloud to the participant, and the participant was asked if they consent to taking part in the user study and having their data used for analyses. The participants were given the consent form in advance (electronically with accessibility features) to read over if they so desired, in addition to having it read aloud do them during the meeting.

3.4.2 Second and Third Sessions
Sessions two and three were identical. The goal of these sessions was to assess the participants' long-term usage of VizSnap in their day-to-day life. The participants were interviewed following these guiding questions:

1. What do you think about this app VizSnap?
2. What problems have you experienced with VizSnap these last two weeks?
3. Out of the voice memo, ambient audio, time, date, and location information, which do you find the most useful in locating photos after you've taken the photo?
4. How often did you send your photos via email this last week? 0, 1-5, 6-10, more than 10?
5. How often did you post your photos on Facebook this last week? 0, 1-5, 6-10, more than 10?
6. What features do you think are missing from this app?

This was followed by a short exercise, in which we had chosen five photos, at random, prior to the meeting. We gave a short description to the participant of what was in the photograph, and asked them to locate the photo using only time, date, location, and the audio taken while the photo was captured. The participant provides the time and the date of the photo they think is correct, and we verified whether their photo matches the photo we asked them to find.

Here are some examples of the descriptions that were given to the participants:

- Photo on a sidewalk with a wooden garden in the frame.
- Photo inside a plane taking a picture out the window.
- Photo of a classic car parked in a driveway.

4. PILOT STUDY

Over the Summer of 2015, a pilot study was conducted with two blind participants to assess the viability of the long term user study. The two users were asked to use VizSnap in their day to day life, taking as many photos as possible, and were met with once every two weeks to assess their use of VizSnap through a short questionnaire, and to perform a short user study in which 3 photos were chosen at random, described to the participants, and the participants were asked to retrieve the photos using only the audio, time, date, and location information of the photograph.

The sessions in this stage of the user study took place in person; one participant lives in San Francisco, CA, the other participant lives in Hollister, CA. The first session began by asking the participant the same demographics questions listed in Section 3.4.1.

Next, the participants were shown all the features of VizSnap, including how to take a photo using gestures as well as taking photos using button mode, how to browse through their photo library, how to access the details of photos, send via email and Facebook, how to delete photos, and how to access the settings. The participants were then asked to repeat these steps to demonstrate that they understood how to use VizSnap in its entirety. Finally, the participants were taken on a small outing, in which the participant and us walked around outside of their home, taking pictures of various things in their surroundings, along with recording ambient audio and voice memos. Afterwards, we went back inside to review the photos.

The participants were encouraged to take photos in their day-to-day life, such that when the next meeting took place, they could answer a questionnaire of their general usage of VizSnap, followed by a user study. In the follow-up session, we asked the same set of guiding questions listed in Section 3.4.2.

Next, we chose three of their photos at random, described the photo to the participant, and asked the participant to browse through their photo album and find the photo we described, using only audio, time, date, and location information.

The participants were met with a total of three times, such that the above session described took place twice, while the initial session took place once.

Participant 1: 25 years old when the user study began. She has been blind since birth

Participant 2: 18 years old when the user study began. He has been blind since birth. He gave the following answers for the initial questionnaire:

The purpose of the pilot user study was to have a run-through with only a couple participants to make sure all the steps of the user study would be necessary, no steps would be extraneous, and that necessary steps would not be left out. The most important realizations from the pilot user study came as follows:

- The user study did not need to take place in-person, it could be performed remotely, through Skype, FaceTime, or Google Hangout meetings.
- There needs to be a system in place to encourage participants to take photos. Sometimes, the two participants took very few photos, which made the user studies of subsequent meetings unreliable. From this experience, we decided that for the real study, the participants would be paid a $10 Amazon gift card if and only if they took at least five photos every two days.
- Meetings should take place once every two weeks. Less often means the participants forgot some of their suggestions and experience, and more often was considered a burden.

5. RESULTS

The primary data we analyzed are the voice memos and ambient audio of the photos, time, date, and location photos were taken, participants' answers to the two different set of questions (see Sections 3.4.1. and 3.4.2), the accuracy of photo retrieval, participants' memory elicitation of the photo described to them, and a general analysis of the types of photos that were taken by participants as well as trends with the photos.

5.1 Session One

Session one analyzes which users took part based on age, location, blindness level, since when they were blind, and their photography preferences. Participants were asked the following questions with their respective answers given:

1. How old are you?

Ages given were {18, 18, 25, 28, 34, 37, 46, 50, 52, 54, 58, 61, 65}, showing a well-represented range of ages from 18 – 65.

2. Since when were you blind?

Seven participants were adventitiously blind, while six were congenitally blind.

3. Preferred choice of camera device.

Eleven out of the 13 participants stated the iPhone was their device of choice for taking photographs. While only iPhone users participated in this study, it was still enlightening that they use a smartphone as their main camera device.

4. Since when did you use the camera device?

Answers to this question varied from "I've rarely ever used this camera device" to the last six years. Eleven out of 13 participants stated they have been using their iPhone to take photos since at least the last two years. The other two participants stated some variation of they have rarely used the camera device.

5. In a typical week, how often do you take photos?

Seven participants stated that they take photos on a regular basis, meaning (for this user study) at least one per week.

6. How often do you browse through your photos?

Only three participants answered that they browse through their photos more than once a month. Most participants had some variation of the answer "I do not browse through my photos."

7. What's your strategy for taking photos?

Figure 1. Sample photos taken by various participants after two weeks of use.

Several participants stated multiple strategies for taking photos. Five participants stated using the "Point and shoot" method, such that photographers point in the general direction they know their subject is, and snap the photo. Four participants use the method of touching the subject, backing away, and then taking the photograph. Two participants stated using sighted help. Two stated utilizing face detection on the iPhone. Two stated knowing all you could about the lighting of the setting helps to take good photographs. And one participant uses the strategy of taking lots of photos, then weeding them out later.

8. What's your strategy for browsing photos?

Several participants stated multiple strategies here as well. Four participants stated uploading to a cloud sharing service (such as Dropbox) immediately to facilitate easier browsing later on. Three participants stated using the date and time information. Two

5.2.1 Session Two
Thirteen participants took part in session two.

There were two parts to session 2; during part I, participants were asked six questions regarding their use of VizSnap the previous two weeks, seen directly below. Part II entailed a short user study in which five of each participant's photos were chosen at random, described to the participant, and they were asked to locate the photo in their photo album using only voice memo, ambient audio, time, date, and location information.

5.2.1.1 Part 1
Open-coding by three researchers was performed on the open-ended responses to the questionnaire in order to extract themes which occurred for participants' responses. The open-ended questions were questions 1, 2, and 6. Questions 3, 4, and 5 were quantitative in nature. A summary of themes (along with the number of occurrences) observed for open-ended questions and analysis of quantitative questions are given below:

1. What do you think about this app VizSnap?

There were a variety responses to this question, such that the only theme that seemed to reoccur during this question was "Getting used to the app," which concretely occurred twice. Most users were pleased with the app, and only one participant expressed that using the app to be a negative experience, stating "I've got a couple things that I find, like, a little frustrating."

2. What problems have you experienced with VizSnap these last two weeks?

- Performing the right gestures (4)
- Knowing the photo quality (2)
- The volume is too low (2)

participants stated using location information. Two participants stated using labels in VoiceOver. One participant stated using sighted help, and one participant stated uploading the file the computer immediately and renaming the file.

9. What's your strategy for sharing photos with others?

Several participants stated multiple strategies here. Nine participants stated using Facebook, six through text message, three through email, two through Twitter, one through Shutterfly and one through Instagram.

5.2 Sessions Two and Three
Sessions two and three were identical in terms of what was required of the participants. Figure 1 shows sample photographs taken by four different participants after two weeks of use.

3. Out of the voice memo, ambient audio, time, date, and location information, which do you find the most useful in locating photos after you've taken the photo?

Some participants reported two different modes of information to be the most useful for locating photos after they are taken. Seven (54%) participants reported ambient audio to be the most useful information. Five (38%) participants reported the voice memo to be the most useful information to locate photos after they have been taken. Four (31%) participants reported the date to be most useful. Three (23%) reported the time to be most useful. One (8%) participant stated that they went back to look at photos after they had been taken for the first time in that session.

This data indicates that some form of audio (which is VizSnap's novelty) recording is most useful when locating a photo after it has been taken. The next two useful modes reported were the date and time. The only piece of information that was not reported as being the most useful was the location.

4. How often did you send your photos via email this last week? 0, 1-5, 6-10, more than 10?

Only three (23%) participants reported sending photos via email. Others remarked they only felt comfortable sending photos via email if they knew the quality of the photograph beforehand. One (8%) participant noted that sending photos via email was their way of verifying the quality of the photo.

5. How often did you post your photos on Facebook this last week? 0, 1-5, 6-10, more than 10?

Only one (8%) participant reported posting photos to Facebook using VizSnap. All other participants reported not having posted any photos to Facebook using VizSnap.

6. What features do you think are missing from this app VizSnap?

- Photo quality feedback (3)
- Access to camera flash (3)
- Volume should be louder (2)
- Accessing front facing camera (2)

5.2.1.2 Part II

As mentioned before, during part II, five photos from each participant was chosen at random, the contents of the photos were described to the participant, and the participant was asked to locate the photo – giving the time and date of the photo they chose in order to verify whether it was the correct photo.

To browse their photographs, a user begins by exiting the camera view using a single-finger left swipe gesture (a list of available gestures are read aloud to the user via VoiceOver). Swiping left and right give VoiceOver focus to newer and later photographs in a list view, respectively. As VoiceOver has focus on a photograph, the voice memo of the photo is first played, automatically followed by the ambient audio of the photo, and finally followed by the date and time the photograph was taken.

The following list shows the accuracy of retrieval for each participant:

- P1: 5 out of 5 – 100%
- P2: 3 out of 4 – 75% (technical difficulties led to not assessing the fifth photo)
- P3: 5 out of 5 – 100%
- P4: 4 out of 5 – 80%
- P5: Did not take enough photos to complete Part II.
- P6: 5 out of 5 – 100%
- P7: 5 out of 5 – 100%
- P8: 4 out of 5 – 80%
- P9: 5 out of 5 – 100%
- P10: 5 out of 5 – 100%
- P11: 3 out of 5 – 60%
- P12: 5 out of 5 – 100%
- P13: Did not take enough photos to complete Part II.

Out of the 11 participants that were able to complete Part II of Session II of the user study, 49 out of 54 photos (90.7%) were identified correctly. Three out of four participants who did not identify 100% of the photos correctly were congenitally blind.

5.2.2 Session Three

Eight participants participated in session three of the user study; five had dropped out since the first two meetings due to time commitment and phone issues (not related to VizSnap). Two had phone issues (one dropped the phone and the other one's phone just stopped working) and three had vacation/sickness issue that prevented them from participating in Session 3.

As mentioned before, the method for session three of the user study was identical to session two, consisting of a questionnaire followed by a short user study exercise (in which users retrieve the time and dates of photos described by the researcher).

5.2.2.1 Part 1

A summary of themes (along with the number of occurrences) observed for open-ended questions and analysis of quantitative questions are given below:

1. What do you think about this app VizSnap?

- Incredible/neat application (5)
- Well organized (4)
- Likes voice tagging/voice memos (2)

2. What problems have you experienced with VizSnap these last two weeks?

- The volume is too low (4)
- Knowing the photo quality (2)
- Issues with sound recordings (2)

3. Out of the voice memo, ambient audio, time, date, and location information, which do you find the most useful in locating photos after you've taken the photo?

Five (55%) participants reported the voice memo to be the most useful piece of information in locating photos after they are taken. Three (33%) participants reported the date to be the most useful. Two (22%) participants reported the ambient audio to be the most useful. It should be noted that one participant reported all five modes of information to be equally useful. It should also be noted that one participant who reported ambient audio to be most useful uses the ambient audio as a voice memo (sometimes with long stories accompanying photographs). This would make the number of participants who reported the voice memo as most useful actually 6 and not 5, but since the participant stated ambient audio was most useful, we interpreted her response literally.

4. How often did you send your photos via email this last week? 0, 1-5, 6-10, more than 10?

Three (33%) participants reported having used the email function to email photographs through VizSnap. This could indicate that the longer that people use VizSnap, the more comfortable they feel to sending photos through email. Many participants stated that during the previous session, they do not feel comfortable sending photos through email because of being unsure of the quality of the photo. Since participants are sending more photographs, this could indicate that participants feel more confident in the quality of the photographs they are taking, through using VizSnap regularly.

5. How often did you post your photos on Facebook this last week? 0, 1-5, 6-10, more than 10?

Four (44%) participants reported posting photos to Facebook. Last session, only 8% of participants reported posting photos to Facebook. This could be interpreted as people are becoming more confident in their photo taking ability (as participants noted that photo quality uncertainty was the main reason participants do not share photos) the more they use VizSnap.

6. What features do you think are missing from this app VizSnap?

- Volume should be louder (2)
- Access to the camera flash (2)

5.2.2.2 Part 2

All nine participants had sufficient photos to take part in Part II of Session 3 of the user study. The following list shows the accuracy of retrieval for each participant:

- P1: 5 out of 5 – 100%
- P3: 3 out of 5 – 60%
- P6: 5 out of 5 – 100%
- P7: 4 out of 5 – 80%
- P8: 3 out of 5 – 60%
- P9: 5 out of 5 – 100%
- P10: 4 out of 5 – 80%
- P11: 5 out of 5 – 100%

Total retrieval accuracy for all participants for this session was 34 out of 40, 85%. Overall retrieval accuracy was less compared to the last session. One reason this could be is that the participants have twice as many photos to choose from in their photo album (at least 70 per person) than last session, thus more photos to sift through. Out of the four participants who did not get perfect retrieval, two were adventitiously blind, and two were congenitally blind.

5.3 Analysis of the Photos

There were exactly 800 photographs collected from participants throughout the user study. For creating the categories for photos, two researchers made one pass each looking at all 800 photographs, then made another pass creating the categories. Another researcher compared the two categories and noted the categories that were semantically identical between the two researchers, and had a discussion with the 2 researchers on the categories that were not unanimous. At the end of the meeting, a set of categories were agreed on by all researchers. The same two researchers then categorized the photographs and the third

collected photos that were unanimously categorized. The photos that were not unanimously categorized were then discussed again until all researchers agreed on the categorization. The categories were the following, with the number of photos falling into each category listed alongside:

- Animal/Pet - 46
- Electronics - 40
- Food/Drink - 82
- Group - 46
- Household item - 54
- Individual person - 103
- Outdoor scenery - 225
- Plant - 59
- Toy/Craft - 69
- Vehicle - 73
- Whole room - 36

It should be noted that some photos fell into multiple categories.

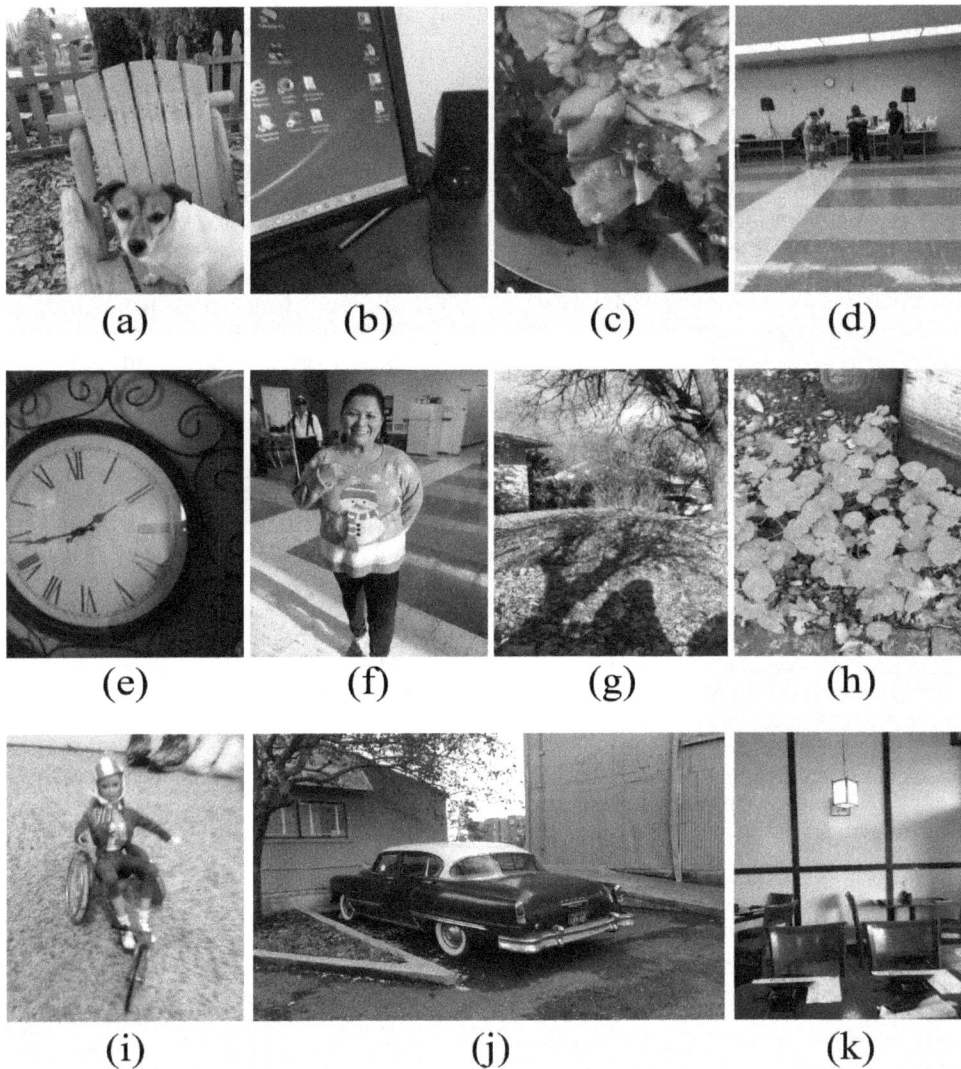

Figure 2. (a) Animal/Pet, (b) Electronics, (c) Food/Drink, (d) Group, (e) Household item, (f) Individual person, (g) Outdoor scenery, (h) Plant, (i) Toy/Craft, (j) Vehicle, (k) Whole room

Figure 2 shows a sample photograph from each category.

6. DISCUSSION

This user study set out to answer three research questions:

1. What kind of photographs do blind photographers take?
2. Do blind photographers make use of sound recordings, time, date, and location information to help them recognize their photo?
3. What are some of the issues that blind photographers face when using VizSnap?

In regards to research question 1, our analysis of the photo corpus indicated that outdoor scenery is by far the most common type of photographs blind persons take (double any other category). This is an interesting finding as there is much support for face detection that can help browsing without sight when the topic of the photograph is person(s) but not much support is available for outdoor scenery recognition.

In regards to research question 2, during session two, 54% of participants reported ambient audio to be the most useful mode of information for retrieving photos after they have been taken, while 38% of participants reported the voice memo to be the most useful. During session three, 55% of participants reported the voice memo to be the most mode of information for retrieving photos, followed by the date (33%), and finally the ambient audio (22%). We see a shift between sessions two and three from users finding the most useful mode of information when retrieving photos to go from ambient audio to voice memo. The growing number of photographs could account for this; users rely on more specific information, i.e. a voice memo, to retrieve photos rather than the audio that is being recorded while the user aims the camera. Participants' responses indicate they do indeed make use of audio recordings, time, date, and location information when retrieving photographs.

As noted in the Results section, participants achieved an accuracy of 90.7% when retrieving photos during session 2 and 85% accuracy when retrieving photos during session 3. While we would like to see these numbers closer to 100%, they nonetheless indicate that participants retrieve photos accurately an overwhelmingly majority of the time when presented with voice memo, ambient audio, time, date, and location information.

In regards to research question 3, out of the problems that participants experienced using VizSnap, knowing the photo quality and the volume being too low seemed to persist from session two to session three. Performing the correct gestures was a theme that was observed as a problem for participants during session two, however, this theme was not observed during session three. The reason this theme disappeared could be due to the repeated use of VizSnap, thus the participants were practicing and learning the gestures and no longer found them to be a problem.

During session two, the themes that occurred when participants were asked which features they felt were missing from VizSnap were Photo quality feedback, Access to camera flash, Volume should be louder, Accessing front facing camera. During session three, the themes that occurred when asked the same question were Volume should be louder, and Access to the camera flash. Participants no longer expressed desire for Photo quality feedback, or Accessing front facing camera. As mentioned before, more participants were sharing their photographs from session two to session three, possibly indicating they had more confidence in their photo taking ability. This could also account for the participants no longer desiring feedback of the photo's quality.

7. CONCLUSION

The overarching goal of this user study was to determine whether appending voice memo, ambient audio, time, date, and location information to a photograph assists blind smartphone-based in taking photos and maintaining a photo album. Observing the increased rate of sharing photos online, along with positive feedback from participants regarding their usage of VizSnap, and finally the observed lack of desire to continue having photo quality feedback from session two on to session three – signifying an increased confidence in photo quality – we believe that appending the aforementioned metadata to a photograph not only assists with organizing a photo album, but also increases confidence with taking, retrieving, and sharing photographs.

8. ACKNOWLEDGMENTS

Thanks to all participants who completed the user study.

9. REFERENCES

[1] Adams, D., Morales, L., & Kurniawan, S. A qualitative study to support a blind photography mobile application. In *Proc. of PETRAE '13* (2013), p. 25-33.

[2] Ahmed, T., Hoyle, R., Connelly, K., Crandall, D., & Kapadia, A. Privacy concerns and behaviors of people with visual impairments. In *Proc. of CHI '15* (2015), 3523-3532.

[3] Balata, J., Mikovec, Z., & Neoproud, L. (2015, June). BlindCamera: Central and Golden-ratio Composition for Blind Photographers. In *Proc. of MIDI '15* (2015), 8-16.

[4] Bigham, J. P., Jayant, C., Ji, H., Little, G., Miller, A., Miller, R. C., Miller, R., Tatarowicz, A., White, B., White, S., and Yeh, T. Vizwiz: Nearly real-time answers to visual questions. In *Proc. of UIST '10* (2010), 333-342.

[5] Harada, S., Sato, D., Adams, D. W., Kurniawan, S., Takagi, H., & Asakawa, C. Accessible photo album: enhancing the photo sharing experience for people with visual impairment. In *Proc. CHI '13* (2013), 2127-2136.

[6] Jayant, C., Ji, H., White, S., & Bigham, J. P. Supporting blind photography. In *Proc. of ASSETS '11* (2011), 203-210.

[7] Liu, X. A camera phone based currency reader for the visually impaired. In *Proc. of ASSETS '08* (2008), 305-306.

[8] Morris, J., & Mueller, J. Blind and deaf consumer preferences for android and iOS smartphones. In Inclusive Designing (2014), 69-79.

[9] Qiu, S., Hu, J., & Rauterberg, M. Mobile Social Media for the Blind: Preliminary Observations. In *Proc' of ICEAPVI '15* (2015), 152-156.

[10] Vázquez, M., & Steinfeld, A. Helping visually impaired users properly aim a camera. In *Proc. of ASSETS '12* (2012), 95-102.

[11] Voykinska, V., Azenkot, S., Wu, S., & Leshed, G. How Blind People Interact with Visual Content on Social Networking Services. In *Proc' of CSCW '16* (to appear) (2016).

[12] Wu, S., & Adamic, L. A. Visually impaired users on an online social network. In *Proc' of CHI '14* (2014), 3133-3142.

[13] TestFlight Beta Testing – App Store – Apple Developer. https://developer.apple.com/testflight/

Using Dynamic Audio Feedback to Support Peripersonal Reaching in Young Visually Impaired People

Graham Wilson & Stephen A. Brewster
Glasgow Interactive Systems Group
School of Computing Science, University of Glasgow, G12 8RZ UK
{first.last}@glasgow.ac.uk

ABSTRACT
Blind children engage with their immediate environment much less than sighted children, particularly through self-initiated movement or exploration. Research has suggested that providing dynamic feedback about the environment and the child's actions within/against it may help to encourage reaching activity and support spatial cognitive learning. This paper investigated whether the accuracy of peripersonal reaching (space within arm's reach) can be improved by the use of dynamic sound from both the objects to reach for and the reaching hand itself (via a worn speaker). We ran two studies that tested the efficacy of static and dynamic audio feedback designs with blind and visually impaired young people, to identify optimal feedback designs. Study 1 was with young adults aged 18 to 22 and Study 2 involved children aged 12 to 17. The results showed that dynamic audio feedback helps to build spatial connections between the objects and the reaching hand and participants were able to reach more accurately, compared to unchanging feedback.

Keywords
Sound perception; reaching; visual impairment.

1. INTRODUCTION
Children who are congenitally or early blind can be less engaged with objects in their immediate environment [4,22] due to a lack of location awareness and a slower cognitive development of object existence/permanence [27]. Sound and touch can be used to inform the child of the object's existence/location and encourage him or her to reach for it [14]. However, these activities typically require a parent or caregiver to facilitate the interaction, by moving the object, touching the child or making sounds. Providing a means with which children could, of their own accord, learn of the existence of objects, and their own position relative to them, might encourage more self-initiated movement [22,27]. Sounding objects have been used several times (e.g., [11,29,34]) but they require adult activation. A computer-based system that can control the playing of environmental sounds based on the child's activity could provide more complex and engaging feedback to encourage the child to be "more active against the world" [27]. As these children get older, even into adulthood, environmental sound may also be a way to support the development of accurate reaching within peripersonal space (i.e., space within arm's reach [19,23]).

ASSETS '16, October 23 - 26, 2016, Reno, NV, USA
Copyright is held by the owner/author(s). Publication rights licensed to ACM.
ACM 978-1-4503-4124-0/16/10...$15.00
DOI: http://dx.doi.org/10.1145/2982142.2982160

The ABBI project [12] is developing technologies and procedures to (re)habilitate spatial cognition in visually impaired children through natural audio-motor associations. The primary focus is developing the ABBI bracelet, which is placed on the wrists of children (and adults) with visual impairments: it detects movement (acceleration and orientation) and produces sound based on the nature of that movement. Thus it uses the auditory modality to convey spatial information about the movement of the person's own body within personal and peripersonal space, in a natural and direct manner similar to feedback provided by the visual modality in sighted people. These sound sources may then allow the visually impaired child to build a better representation of his/her movement in space and, ultimately, a representation of space itself.

The research in this paper investigated extending the audio-motor association beyond the limb to build associations with objects in the environment. Environmental sounds can encourage reaching [22,29,34] and wrist-based sound can improve spatial movements [8,12]. Therefore, this research looked at whether the combination of environmental sounds and wrist-based sound can guide and improve peripersonal reaching in blind and visually impaired people. The paper describes two studies that measured reaching accuracy and got subjective responses about the feedback design, including which was preferred and whether it established a connection between the hand and the reached-for object. The studies were similar other than the age of the participants taking part. Access to young (< 5) blind children is very limited, as is the amount of time that it is possible to engage them in experimental situations [2]. Older children and young adults can provide more detailed and reasoned feedback than young children to the the the design process. Therefore, as a first step, Study 1 was run with blind and visually impaired young adults (aged 18 to 22) to determine which of three audio designs best supports reaching. The results showed a benefit of dynamic audio feedback but no clear advantage for either sound design and so we continued to Study 2 involving blind and visually impaired children aged 12 to 17.

2. RELATED RESEARCH
2.1 Reaching in Peripersonal Space
In a series of experiments, Brungart and colleagues looked at the localisation of sound sources within 1 metre of the head [6,7]. Blindfolded sighted participants sat in an anechoic chamber and placed their chin on a rest to immobilise the head. The experimenter placed a sound source on the end of a curved tube and manually placed the source in positions around the participant's head from 0° to 180° azimuth, -90° to +90° elevation and distances of ~15cm to 1m, all relative to the chin. Participants closed their eyes and, after the sound played, they used the end of a 30cm wooden rod to point to the perceived sound location.

They first tested localisation of white noise (200Hz – 15kHz) pulses (5 x 150ms, separated by 30ms) with amplitude-based distance cues removed [6]. Azimuth error averaged at 12.6°, with error decreasing as distance increased. Azimuth error was higher for targets at lower elevations (below head-level) and more so for near distances. Average elevation error was 11.3°, with higher error in front of the participant, than at the sides. As distance cues were removed, distance error was unsurprisingly high (30-40%). A follow-up study, using the same experimental setup, tested the effects of different stimulus characteristics on localisation [7]. They used the same fixed amplitude to provide distance cues and compared the same previous white noise stimulus with two filtered versions (low and high pass) and a monaural stimulus, by blocking the sound in one ear. The smallest azimuth error (12.2°) and elevation error (10.5°) came from the fixed-amplitude original broadband noise stimulus, with the low pass filter resulting in the highest azimuth error (14.7°) and both filtered version having equal elevation error (~15.5°). Providing distance cues improved distance perception but azimuth error decreased as distance increased. These results impact the use of sound in peripersonal reaching, as 1) they show that the sound design will impact localisation and 2) objects are commonly nearby and below head-level, so their sound will be more difficult to localize than distant sources, or those nearer head-level.

Brungart *et al.* [6,7] gave participants a wooden rod with which to point to the perceived location, but we are interested in reaching with an open hand, as that is how children will reach for and interact with objects, and research suggests the method used to indicate perceived direction influences accuracy [16]. One of few studies to examine the accuracy of pointing with the finger in reaching space was conducted by Macé *et al.* [19]. Blind and blindfolded sighted participants sat in front of a semi-circular horizontal array of loudspeakers, arranged in 5 columns of 5 speakers placed at 30° intervals through 120°, starting straight in front. They studied the effect of varying the length and number of white noise (20Hz to 20kHz) bursts: single bursts of 10, 25, 50 or 200ms and multiple bursts of 2, 3 or 4 25ms bursts (separated by 30ms silence). Following stimulus presentation, the participant was to point to the perceived location and then return to facing straight ahead. They found that blind participants were significantly more accurate along the azimuth, although only by 0.5°, but were significantly *less* accurate in judging distance, but again only by ~10mm. Azimuth and distance errors decreased as the length of single bursts increased, but all multiple burst stimuli were more accurately localised than single burst stimuli, although only significantly so compared to the shortest single burst. Multi-burst error sat at around 10.5-11°. This suggests that multi-burst stimuli may better support reaching, over single sounds.

Parseihian *et al.* [23] extended the study by Macé *et al.* [19] looking at the effect of dominant vs. non-dominant hand and using physical touching (with tip of the fingers) instead of pointing to indicate the perceived location of the sound. This is important, as the physical contact is a more direct correlate of reaching for objects. They found no effect of reaching hand on azimuth or distance errors. They found that, potentially due to biomechanical limitations, placing the hand at nearby objects (33cm) was difficult and so led to significantly worse azimuth judgements, compared to distant objects. This may also be related to the poorer localisation of sounds nearer the head [6,7].

2.2 Sound Localisation
Reaching accuracy is inherently influenced by the perceived location of the sound source. We are primarily interested in the accuracy of the reaching movement itself (we do not measure localisation alone) and a full discussion of localisation research is outside the scope of this paper. Therefore, we present a discussion only of particularly relevant research, focusing on the effects of sound

parameters on localisation, as we are interested in identifying suitable audio designs to support reaching. Localisation accuracy is typically measured by the 'minimum audible angle' (MAA) [24] or 'localisation blur': the smallest perceivable change in location. Localisation in sighted people is more accurate straight ahead (and behind) compared to directly at the sides [3]. In a series of experiments, Hartmann & Rakerd looked at various stimulus (and room) effects on localisation of sound sources [17,25]. Removing attack transients (very slow onsets) led to only chance-level localisation accuracy for 200Hz and 500Hz sine tones, but broadband noise stimuli were better localised. In general, the greater the spectral complexity of a stimulus, the better localised it will be [17].

Having shown that slow onsets disrupt localisation, Rakerd & Hartmann [25] identified the threshold onset length for poor localisation as somewhere between 100ms and 500ms, depending on room acoustics. Accuracy improves as onset reduces to 0ms. They also found no effect of stimulus duration, and little effect of stimulus offset on localisation. Perrott [24] also found that the MAA increased as duration increased from 1ms to 500ms, but only for 2kHz stimuli, not low (500Hz) or high (5kHz) stimuli. However, research is currently split on whether blind and visually impaired people have better or worse auditory localisation than sighted people [15,19,26]. Macé *et al.* [19] found that longer stimulus durations led to better pointing accuracy, although they used white noise, rather than the sine tones used in these other studies. Overall, the research suggests that sounds we use should have fast onsets (<=100ms) and should avoid simple sine tones.

2.3 Environmental Engagement
Congenitally or early blind children develop motor skills more slowly than sighted peers and can be less engaged with objects in their immediate environment [4,22] due to a lack of awareness of their locations and a slower cognitive development of object existence or permanence [27]. Millar [22] provides recommendations on how to support a blind child's understanding of, and interaction with, the space around them. She stresses that simple audible 'lures' are an insufficient substitute for the visual feedback that attracts attention in sighted children. Instead, she suggests, "what is needed...is some means whereby sounds can be *systematically connected* with more than one other source of information" (Ch. 9, emphasis added). Hearing should be connected with reaching in the same way that vision is. The ABBI bracelet can provide information about the position and movement of the arm [12,13], but dynamic feedback coming from the arm and/or external objects will provide information about 1) arm location relative to the person, 2) object location and 3) the proximity of the hand to the object. This may add some redundancy of information, but this is recommended, particularly for young children [22]. Millar also suggests some ways to encourage reaching, including placing objects nearby that make noises when touched.

Ross & Tobin [27] also discuss the need for more complex sounds than simple 'lures'. They recommend that an infant be provided with access to changes in sound over time, sounds that inform the child about the object's existence or action. They use the word "Flux" to refer to these changes and that perceptual information comes from how objects change over time. In particular, to counter a blind child's lack of self-initiated action, they recommend the adoption of a rehabilitative program that forces the child to be "more active against the world". The earlier children are engaged in rehabilitation, the more benefit is gained from them [27].

The Royal National Institute of Blind People (RNIB) in the UK recommends the use of "sensory resource boxes" [28], wooden structures that hang objects with different sounds and textures for a child lying underneath to interact with (see Figure 1). The RNIB guide says these boxes "motivate children to notice the changes in their environment and then to begin to explore these changes". The boxes initially rely on the accidental contact of the child's limb with the objects, or the parent/carer moving the child's hand into contact with them. After this the child may remember the location to deliberately reach for the objects. The ABBI device can inform the child of the location of his/her arm, and a sensory resource box augmented with sounding objects could use the spatialised sound to inform the child of the location of objects they might enjoy interacting with. Tracking hand position relative to the objects could mean that the sounds could provide more information, support or encouragement for reaching.

Figure 1: Blind children reaching for hanging objects in a "sensory resource box" (L) and for sounding chains (R)

The research in this paper sought to design a system that *systematically connects* [22] a person's movement to objects nearby that, when applied to children, might encourage them to be "active against the world". It is "systematic" as the feedback was designed to vary in predictable and logical ways, and the feedback designs were tested with target user groups to ensure they were useful. The dynamic changes in feedback based on proximity are aimed to "connect" the hand and the object and encourage action.

3. EXPERIMENTAL APPARATUS

The apparatus consisted of 7 small speakers connected to a Windows 8.1 PC via USB soundcards and a Microsoft Kinect v2 depth camera, which tracked hand and speaker positions. Six of the speakers (KitSound [18] Mini Buddy "Magic 8 Ball") were used as the target objects and a variant of the same model was used for the wrist speaker ("Owl") (see Figure 2). The back surface houses the speaker (which always faced the participants) with the following characteristics: 100Hz to 20kHz frequency response, 36mm driver, S/N of 85dB and output of 2W RMS @ 4 ohms. Hand tracking was achieved using Kinect's in-built API with a One-Euro Filter [10] applied for smoothing.

Figure 2: Speakers used as targets ("8 Ball", left) and placed on the wrist ("Owl", right). Images from [18].

An ABBI device was not used at this time because the dynamic audio feedback required was not yet incorporated into the device. The KitSound speakers were chosen for several reasons. The ABBI device is deliberately designed to be small, light and cheap to produce, to maximise its validity and usefulness in clinical and home settings with children as young as several months. The use of large or high quality speakers would not reflect the capabilities

of the ABBI device, nor likely those of sounding toys, so the results may not be transferrable. These KitSound speakers are similar in size and weight to ABBI so can be held on the wrist with a strap, and they are representative of the intended final sound capabilities. They also allowed us to test more complex feedback in preparation for that functionality being added. While the speakers were connected to audio cables, the cable length and low speaker weight (50g) meant there was no movement restriction or encumbrance. As we are working with blind and visually impaired children, these speakers were also chosen because they include fun and colourful designs (for low-vision), and have different tactile qualities, which would provide a constant base across qualitative/quantitative research opportunities.

The "Magic 8 Ball" was chosen for its smooth and uniform shape, to provide no distractions, obstacles or haptic cues during reaching. The "Owl" was chosen as the protruding 'ears' provided purchase for the elastic bands holding the speaker to a rubber watchstrap and the 'feet' helped keep the otherwise spherical speaker from rotating during use, which would result in the speaker facing the wrong direction. The 6 target speakers were placed on top of 10cm high plastic beakers, to give them greater size and have them at a height suitable for reaching (see Figure 3).

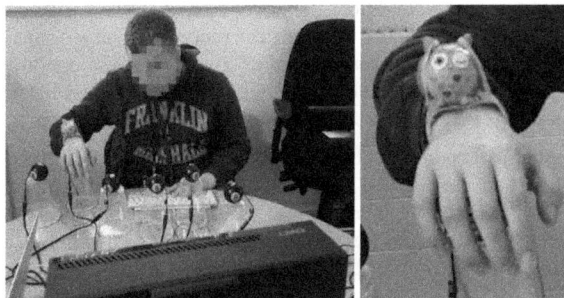

Figure 3: Experimental setup (left), speaker on wrist (right)

4. FEEDBACK DESIGNS

The purpose of the research was to determine which of several potential sound designs best supports accurate reaching and best conveys an *interconnection* between the hand and the object being reached for. While both are desirable, a design that only accomplishes one could still be of benefit in helping a child (or adult) relate his/her own movements to available objects nearby. The two studies presented below looked at both *dynamic* audio designs, which change based on the proximity of the hand to objects, but also constant, unchanging feedback. This was to establish if dynamic feedback, which would require more complex and expensive computing hardware in order to track the hands and object locations, provides any extra benefit in reaching accuracy over more basic feedback, which could be provided more simply and cheaply by a continually playing toy.

Three feedback designs were compared: 1) a dynamic Geiger counter, 2) a dynamic pitch and 3) a constant (unchanging) design that remained the same regardless of proximity. A Geiger counter is a common design that has been used successfully in navigation [21], and changes in pitch have strong effects on perceptual *streaming* [5]. Also, changes in frequency (pitch) and tempo (similar to Geiger counter) are commonly associated with changes in size [30] (in our case distance changes in size). We wanted to measure the effect of feedback emanating from the object alone, the wrist alone and the object and wrist combined, and so each feedback design had two aspects: an *Individual*, single speaker design and a two-speaker *Coalescent* design.

Both designs, but particularly the *Coalescent* design, were based on perceptual streaming [5], where sounds are perceived to be from one or multiple sources. Alternating notes that are close together in time or pitch are perceived as coming from the same source, while more distant notes are separated into multiple streams [5]. Therefore, the feedback designs changed in a way that, at a distance, the hand and object may be perceived as separate, but as proximity increases, they may be perceived as a single source, increasing the association of hand to object. The designs provided multiple interconnected pieces of information [22] and may provide "Flux" information [27].

For the interaction to be accepted by children, the sounds need to be enjoyable, or at least pleasant. A workshop with blind and visually impaired children revealed that synthetic sounds were as preferable as natural sounds, and were more easily tracked in 3D space [33]. To minimise experimental complexity as much as possible, all the sound designs were made using 0.2s synthetic "pluck" tones (similar to a guitar string) of different pitch generated from the free Audacity application [1]. They are composed of a single pitch (e.g., 523.25Hz) but with a non-sinusoidal waveform which, in combination with an onset of 0ms and rapid decay, should increase localisation accuracy over pure sine tones [25]. Regardless of the condition, the target speaker always played C^5 (523.25Hz) to provide a constant reference. The target speaker was always indicated by a burst of five C^5 tones, one every 200ms. A burst was used over single tones to increase localisation accuracy, as per Mace *et al.* [19].

It should be noted that ABBI habilitation activities are deliberately short and periodic, to help children develop their own skills, rather than replacing them or providing a crutch on which they depend. Therefore, the feedback designs were intended to be simple, minimalistic and so (potentially) easily understandable.

4.1 Geiger Counter
In this design, a pluck tone of pitch C^5 was played at an increasing rate/rapidity as the hand approached the object. For the *Individual* speaker design, the sound was produced by either the object or wrist, depending on the condition. Research has suggested that there is an inherent association between increasing the rapidity of sounds and decreasing proximity [32]. Therefore, the feedback began when the hand was 50cm from the target, with a tone playing every 900ms. As the hand approached the object, inter-tone delay decreased by 100ms for every 5cm advance, to a minimum delay of 100ms (10 per second) when the hand was within 7.5cm of the target centre (see Table 1). The two-speaker *Coalescent* design was similar, but the tones alternated between playing on the object and the wrist. The sound from the object and wrist speakers changed in rapidity (based on proximity) the same way as the *individual* design, but the tones were played in alternation, up to a maximum rapidity of 50ms (100ms alternated). To increase the perceptual distinction [35] between object and wrist, the object played C^5 and the wrist played G^4 (392Hz) and both tones played together when touching the target.

4.2 Increasing Pitch
Bregman [5] suggested that rapid notes close in pitch are grouped into a single stream, while notes distant in pitch are perceived as two separate streams. Therefore, the *Individual* design played the 8 tones in a C major scale that increased in pitch from C^4 (261.63Hz) up to C^5 as proximity increased (Table 1). A discrete mapping was chosen over a continuous function to provide perceptually clear changes but also to provide potentially more pleasant feedback, using harmonious musical steps and feedback that

was not constantly changing. The notes were played at a constant rate of 200ms. The mapping of *increasing* pitch (notes) to a decrease in distance is based on previous research that found it more in line with mental models of size compared to *decreasing* pitch for decreasing size (distance) [30]. For the *Coalescent* design, both the object and wrist speakers played tones at 100ms rapidity, but played alternately, resulting in an overall frequency of 50ms. In this case, the target always played the highest C^5 tone and the wrist tone increased based on proximity as in the *Individual* design, so that the tones matched when the target was touched.

Table 1: The mapping of Geiger inter-tone delay (ITD) and Pitch to the distance of the hand to the centre of the target

Distance (cm)	50	45	40	35	30	25	20	15	7.5
ITD (ms)	900	800	700	600	500	400	300	200	100
Pitch Note	C^4	C^4	D^4	E^4	F^4	G^4	A^4	B^4	C^5

4.3 Constant Design
The constant audio design was a continual repetition of the target object sound throughout the entire reaching action: a C^5 tone repeated constantly every 200ms. It either played from the target object, the wrist or both the object and the wrist. When both the object and wrist played, the tones were alternated at 100ms, like the Geiger counter and the wrist played G^4 (392Hz).

5. STUDY 1: REACHING IN ADULTS
As access to blind children is very limited we first used blind and visually impaired young adults, with the intention that the best sound design identified during the study would be used in future research with children. Six participants aged 18 to 22 (mean = 18.8) took part (1 female). All were legally blind: four totally blind, one had minimal light vision (Leber congenital amaurosis) and one had retinal dysfunction (the latter two wore a blindfold). Participants took part in all conditions and were paid £10.

The experiment had a 3 x 3 (*Feedback Design x Sound Source*) within-subjects design, giving 9 conditions, but a *Control* condition was added, where only the initial target sound was played (no other signals during the reaching action). Participants completed these 10 conditions over 60 minutes in a random order. Within each condition, each object speaker was the "target" to be reached for 3 times in a random order, following 6 practice trials. At the start of each trial the "target" object was indicated by five C^5 pluck tones played every 200ms. The participant was then free to start reaching for the target with the right hand. They were free to touch multiple objects in their hunt for the perceived target but were instructed to be as fast and accurate as possible. To "select" a speaker, the participant was instructed to place the palm of their right hand on top of it (see Figure 3) and press the space bar on a keyboard with the left hand.

5.1 Speaker Positions
Due to the number of conditions, two different speaker layouts were used to minimise the likelihood that participants would learn the positions, and so reach for a known location, rather than the location of the sound. The two layouts of the targets relative to the participant are shown in Figure 4. As it was not possible to fully counterbalance speaker position with the experimental conditions, speaker layouts were alternated between successive conditions.

Research has suggested that reaching accuracy is similar for the dominant and non-dominant hands [23] and so, to limit the length of the experiment, only the right hand was tested. The participant sat at the left-edge of a desk, facing forward. As distance and relative position can influence peripersonal pointing accuracy

[6,7,23] the speakers were placed so that they varied in both, while reachable with an out-stretched arm. In both layouts, two speakers were each placed on an arc 55cm, 61cm and 67cm from the participant. The azimuth angles for each speaker in each layout, relative to speaker 1 at 0° straight ahead, were 7°, 14°, 36°/31° (layout 1/layout 2), 44°/50° and 52° for speakers 2, 3, 4, 5 and 6 respectively. This had the effect of varying the azimuth angle between speakers, to determine if this had an effect. Distances of 50cm+ were chosen due to the difficulty in localising [23] and reaching for [6,7] nearer sounds.

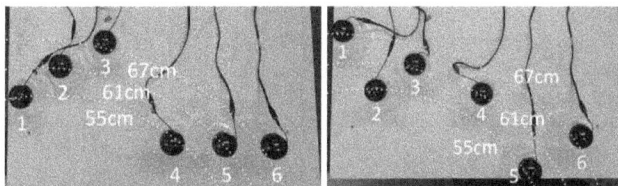

Figure 4: Target speaker layouts 1 (left) and 2 (right), including distance arcs. Participant sat facing speaker 1.

5.2 Variables & Measures

The Independent Variables were *Feedback Design* (Geiger, Pitch and Constant), *Sound Source* (Object, Wrist and Both), *Speaker Layout* (1 and 2) and *Speaker Position* (1 to 6). The Dependent Variables were: *Accuracy* (whether the correct speaker was chosen) and *Task Time* (time between the "target" sound finishing and participant selection, in milliseconds). We also recorded the participants' *Movement Trace* (all their hand movements during the trial in metres) to measure if different audio designs supported more direct and less exploratory reaching. This was done by summing the Euclidean distances between all Kinect hand positions. After each *Feedback Design* we asked three questions rated on 7-point Likert scales from "Strongly Disagree" (1) to "Strongly Agree" (7): *"The sounds created a connection between the hand and the object"*, *"The combination of the hand and object speakers was beneficial"*, *"The sound was pleasant"*. We also asked for *Feedback Design* preferences. While subjective views are important, Walker *et al.* suggest that experimentally derived mappings are better than only using "what sounds good" [30,31].

5.3 Results

5.3.1 Accuracy

No significant learning effect on accuracy was observed ($F_{(2, 538)}$ = 0.65, p > 0.05) and so the accuracy data were analysed using a 3 x 3 repeated-measures ANOVA and is summarised in Figure 5. There was a significant main effect of *Feedback Design* ($F_{(2, 214)}$ = 13.838, p < 0.001), Bonferroni pairwise comparisons showed that the *Constant* design had a significantly higher error rate (24.1%) than both the *Geiger* counter (12.0%) and *Pitch* (12.7%) designs. There was no significant main effect of the *Sound Source*: the *Wrist* speaker resulted in 18.5% error, *Both* speakers were 14.5%, and the *Object* speaker was 15.7%. There was no significant interaction effect between *Feedback Design* and *Sound Source*.

Each individual *Feedback x Sound Source* condition was compared to the *Control* condition, to look at the effect of adding feedback. A one-way repeated-measures ANOVA with the 10 conditions was run, followed by Bonferroni-corrected paired comparisons. There was a significant effect of Condition ($F_{(9, 963)}$ = 7.672, p < 0.001): the *Control* condition resulted in significantly more errors (36.1%) than all *Dynamic* feedback conditions except *Geiger + Wrist*. There were no differences between the *Control* condition and the *Constant* conditions. A 6 x 2 repeated-measures

ANOVA found no significant effect of either *Speaker Position* (6) or *Speaker Layout* (2) and no interaction effect. Based on the pattern of selection errors and the azimuth positions of the speakers, the average angular error was 11.4°, with means for the two layouts of 15.5% (layout 1) and 13.3% (layout 2).

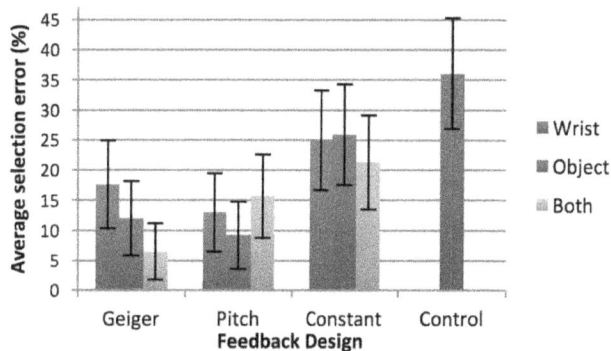

Figure 5: Mean Study 1 target selection error for all Feedback Designs and Speaker Locations. Error bars = 95% CI.

5.3.2 Selection Time

The selection time data violated the normality assumption, and so non-parametric analyses were carried out. Two separate Friedman tests were run to analyse *Feedback Design* and *Sound Source*. Following a significant effect, Bonferroni-corrected Wilcoxon pairwise comparisons were carried out (the necessary value for significance was p = 0.05/3 = 0.0167). A summary of the data can be seen in Figure 6. There was a significant effect of *Feedback Design* on reaching time (χ^2 (2)=13.16, p=0.001), with the *Pitch* design being significantly faster (mean = 3237ms), than both the *Constant* (3488ms) and *Geiger* (4103ms) designs.

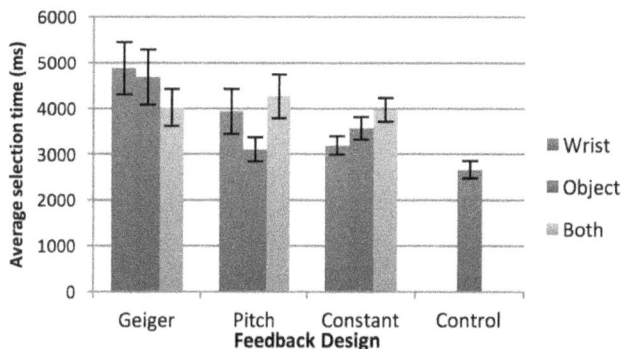

Figure 6: Mean Study 1 target selection times for all Feedback Designs and Speaker Locations. Error bars = 95% CI.

There was also a significant effect of *Sound Source* on reaching time (χ^2 (2)=22.80, p<0.001). Sound from the *Object* alone resulted in significantly faster times (mean = 3784ms) than sound from *Both* speakers (4079ms). The *Wrist* condition had a mean time of 4011ms, between the other two. Similar to the accuracy data, we compared movement time during the *Control* condition to the other conditions. The *Control* condition resulted in significantly faster selection times (χ^2 (9)=106.43, p<0.001; 2666ms) than all other conditions, except for *Pitch* with the *Wrist Speaker*.

A Friedman test found a significant effect of *Speaker Position* on Movement Time (χ^2 (5)=13.45, p<0.05), as Position 1 took significantly longer (mean = 4237ms) than Positions 4 (3705ms) and 5 (3697ms). A Wilcoxon comparison found no significant effect of *Speaker Layout*: mean Times were 3936ms for Layout 1 and 3619ms for Layout 2.

5.3.3 Movement Traces

We looked at the total distance the reaching hand travelled during each trial (in metres) to see if any feedback design led to more direct movement towards the target (a shorter distance would suggest less searching behaviour). As the data were not normally distributed, we used Friedman tests in the same way as for the time data. There was a significant main effect of *Feedback Design* on the total movement distance ($\chi^2(2)=15.63$, $p<0.001$). The Constant feedback resulted in significantly less movement (mean = 1.23m) than both the *Geiger* (1.62m) and *Pitch* (1.56m) designs. There was no main effect of *Sound Source*, with means of 1.52m, 1.45m and 1.67m for the *Wrist*, *Object* and *Both*, respectively.

5.3.4 Subjective Responses

In response to the statement *"The sounds created a connection between the hand and the object"*, the average response was 6 for Geiger and 6.3 for Pitch (between "Agree" and "Strongly Agree") but only 4.7 for the Constant design (between "Neutral" and "Slightly Agree"). Based on the average responses to *"The combination of the hand and object speakers was beneficial"*, providing sounds from both the Wrist and Object did not really provide any benefit over one speaker alone. All ratings were <4, between "Slightly Disagree" and "Neutral". Two participants said expressly that providing sounds from both was unnecessary, as sound from only one (particularly the Object) was sufficient. One participant also commented that having two different Pitches in the Coalescent design made it more difficult to process the feedback. However, two participants said having the two sounds meant that comparing the two could help to guide the hand. Two participants expressed that having sounds coming only from the wrist made reaching more difficult than having it from the Object, or having sounds from Both. All Feedback Designs were "pleasant" (> 4), with the Dynamic designs having slightly higher ratings.

When participants were asked which of the audio designs they preferred, one expressed no preference, one preferred the Geiger counter, three preferred the Pitch design and one expressed preference for different aspects of both the Geiger and Pitch designs. When asked why they chose these, the participant that preferred the Geiger counter, and the one who preferred aspects of both, said it was because they thought the changes in sound (based on proximity) were more "intuitive" or "instinctual" than the changes in pitch, as people who are not musical may struggle to make use of the pitch changes. In contrast, one of the participants who preferred the Pitch feedback believed *it* to be the more "intuitive" design, while the other two preferred it because the changes were more obvious and so easier to distinguish, making it more helpful.

The participant who preferred aspects of both designs said that he appreciated the immediate feedback in the Pitch design, as the Geiger counter inter-tone delay is long (900ms) when the hand is far away, so it requires more time to hear any feedback, compared to the Pitch design. This may be why Pitch was significantly faster than the Geiger design. He is the participant who stated that having two Coalescent Pitches made them more difficult to process, which may have been exacerbated by his difficulty in making use of Pitch changes in general. Finally, two participants said that dynamic changes were "necessary" in order to help reaching accuracy, as the constant feedback was not helpful.

5.4 Initial Discussion

Both Dynamic feedback designs led to greater accuracy and more positive subjective responses than the Constant design, and Pitch-based feedback was also significantly faster than the other designs. Constant feedback provided no benefit in accuracy over providing only a brief cue (Control), despite the Constant condition taking significantly longer than the Control. We interpret the shorter movement distance and faster movement time for the Constant/Control conditions as meaning that, in the absence of useful feedback, participants are left with only their initial location perception to rely on, and so make direct movements to the perceived (but more often incorrect) source.

Comparing the two Dynamic designs, the Pitch design had a significantly faster Movement Time than the Geiger counter, but there was no significant difference in accuracy, suggesting that participants were more hesitant in moving using the Geiger counter, potentially due to the long initial ITD in the Geiger, as the lack of a difference in reaching distance suggests they were not searching or investigating during this time. The subjective responses were more strongly in favour of the Dynamic designs, based on the higher average ratings of 6-6.3 compared to 4.7 for the Constant design, as well as individual comments from participants, such as the perceived *requirement* of dynamic changes to reach accurately. Therefore, the results from Study 1 suggested that dynamic audio feedback may be useful in helping blind and visually impaired children accurately reach for nearby objects. The reasons given for preferring either the Geiger or Pitch designs were similar: the changes were clearer, more "intuitive" and more helpful. There is a suggestion that pitch-based sonifications are more effective than tempo-based designs [31] (like the Geiger), although musical ability may play a part in how participants understand and make use of pitch sonifications [20].

The position of the Sound Source (Wrist, Object or Both) also had a moderate impact on objective and subjective results. There was no significant effect on accuracy, despite some moderate differences between the values. Providing sound through Both speakers provided little benefit over a single speaker alone. Using Both resulted in the lowest error value, but this was not significant, and using the Object alone was significantly faster than using Both, with the Wrist in between these values. Subjective participant responses generally did not agree that providing sound from both speakers provided a benefit (3.2-3.8 out of 7), perhaps because it did not provide additional information over one speaker.

There was no effect of target azimuth on reaching error, and only Speaker Position 1 vs. Positions 4 and 5 were different in reaching time (but only by ~540ms), suggesting that azimuth had little effect on reaching accuracy. Research that shows an effect of azimuth on auditory localisation tends to use short sound bursts presented to stationary ears [3], whereas the sounds here were more often continuous and the head was free to move. The average azimuth angular error of 11.37° is similar to the figure found by Macé *et al.* [19] (10.8°) using multi-burst sound in their peripersonal reaching study. The two Speaker Layouts equally affected performance and did not interact with Speaker Position.

Overall, the results showed a benefit of dynamic audio feedback but no clear advantage for either sound design or sound source and so we carried out Study 2 involving blind and visually impaired children to gain further insight.

6. STUDY 2: REACHING IN CHILDREN

Study 2 was largely the same as Study 1 but was conducted with blind and visually impaired children to establish if age has an influence in what sound designs are most useful. Eight children (3 female) aged 12 to 17 (mean = 14) were recruited from the visual impairment unit at a local school. The experiment took place in a school office and the distance to the speakers was reduced by approximately 20cm to accommodate the shorter arm reach of the children. The experimental setup and procedure were almost identical to Study 1, with the exception that the number of repetitions was reduced to minimise fatigue in the younger participants. Each child still completed all ten conditions, but only one trial for each speaker (instead of the three in Study 1). The order of *Feedback Designs* was counterbalanced and the order of the *Sound Source* conditions randomised. Due to the limited number of trials, only Speaker Layout 1 was used for all conditions. The same variables and measures as Study 1 were also used, except for Layout.

6.1 Results

6.1.1 Accuracy

The accuracy data were analysed using a 3 x 3 Repeated-measures ANOVA and are summarised in Figure 7. There was a significant effect of *Feedback Design* ($F_{(2, 94)}$ = 3.456, p < 0.05, η_p^2 = 0.07): Bonferroni pairwise comparisons showed that the *Pitch* design had a significantly higher error rate (36.1%) than the *Geiger* counter (24.3%). The *Constant* design was in between (30.6%). There was no significant main effect of the *Sound Source*: the *Wrist* speaker resulted in 38.9% error, *Object* was 27.1%, and *Both* speakers were 33.3%. There was no interaction effect.

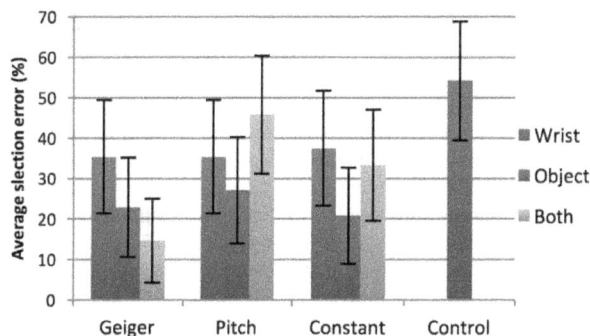

Figure 7: Mean Study 2 target selection error for all Feedback Designs and Speaker Locations. Error bars = 95% CI.

Each individual condition was compared to the *Control* condition. A one-way repeated-measures ANOVA with the 10 Conditions was run and found a significant effect of Condition ($F_{(9, 423)}$ = 3.803, p = 0.01, η_p^2 = 0.07): the *Control* condition resulted in significantly higher errors (54.2%) than the *Geiger + Both* speakers (14.6%) and *Constant + Object* speaker (20.8%). A one-way repeated-measures ANOVA found a significant effect of *Speaker Position* on accuracy ($F_{(5, 395)}$ = 9.259, p < 0.001, η_p^2 = 0.10), with mean error values of 15%, 27.5%, 50.0%, 33.8%, 41.3% and 28.8% for Positions 1 to 6, respectively. Position 3 had significantly higher error than Positions 1 and 2, and Position 1 also had significantly lower error than positions 4 and 5. Like the young adults, the majority of confusions were for speakers adjacent to the actual sound source (only 6.6% of responses perceived the sound as further away). The average angular error was 9.88°.

6.1.2 Selection Time

The selection time data again violated normality and so non-parametric analyses were used. There was a significant effect of *Feedback Design* on Selection Time (χ^2 (2)=22.545, p<0.001), with the *Constant* design being significantly faster (mean = 3665ms), than both the *Geiger* (4937ms) and *Pitch* (4830ms) designs. There was also a borderline significant effect of *Sound Source* (χ^2 (2)=5.972, p=0.05), with *Wrist* sounds resulting in significantly slower times (mean = 5076ms) than *Object* sounds (4211ms). *Both* sounds were in between (4428ms). As with the accuracy data, we compared Selection Time during the *Control*

condition and found a significant effect of Condition (χ^2 (9)=41.16, p<0.001), with the *Control* condition resulting in significantly faster selection times (3058ms) than all the Dynamic conditions except for *Geiger + Object* and *Pitch + Both*.

6.1.3 Movement Traces

There was no significant main effect of *Feedback Design* on the total movement distance, with mean movement distances of 1.83m, 1.73m and 1.84m for the *Geiger, Pitch* and *Constant* designs, respectively. There was also no main effect of *Sound Source* on movement with means of 2.0m, 1.62m and 1.74m for *Wrist, Object* and *Both*, respectively.

6.1.4 Subjective Responses

In response to the *"Connection"* statement the average response was 5.6 for Geiger, 5.7 for Pitch and 4.9 for the Constant design. The average responses to the *"benefit of combination"* statement were below 4 ("Slightly Disagree") for the Geiger and Constant designs but 4.5 for the Pitch ("Slightly Agree"). Most participants said that providing sounds from both locations made the task more difficult, as the extra sounds were distracting and confusing. All Feedback Designs were rated as similarly "pleasant" (> 4). 3 participants preferred the Geiger counter, 2 preferred the Pitch and 3 had no preference.

6.2 Initial Discussion

As there were a different number of data points for the two groups, we did not carry out a statistical comparison of the results. However, there are still some clear differences between the age groups. Accuracy levels were much worse in the children: the young adults had an overall mean error of 17.7% while the children's overall value was 30.3%. In particular, the young adults gained more benefit from the Dynamic feedback designs: error was significantly lower under the Dynamic designs compared to the Constant in young adults. In the children, there was no significant difference between the Dynamic and Constant designs, and the Pitch design was actually significantly worse than the Geiger. Also, while the Control condition led to the highest errors in both groups, it was only significantly worse than two other conditions in young children; it was worse than almost all conditions in young adults. However, comparing Figures 5 (Study 1) and 7 (Study 2) show very similar patterns of reaching error based on condition, even if the absolute values are much higher in children. Reaching times were just under 1 second longer on average in children, which constitutes approximately a 30-40% increase, but is not a high value in real terms, and reaching distance was also slightly higher, but only by around 20-30cm.

Azimuth position had different effects on the groups: there was no effect of Speaker Position on accuracy in young adults, but there was with younger children. Position 3 (Figure 4, left) had significantly higher error than Positions 1 and 2. Position 3 was the most physically distant along the median plane from the children, although the distance was set to be within arm's reach (37cm) and Position 6 had the same distance. Positions 1 and 6 had low error in both groups, as they only have one adjacent speaker, so it may be the combination of physical distance and close azimuthal proximity (to Positions 2 and 4) that made Position 3 hard to find. Despite the differences, the two groups had similar average azimuth errors (11.37° in Study 1 and 9.88° in Study 2) that were similar to Macé *et al.* [19] (10.8°), but lower than in other research [6,7]. It should be noted that, while we deliberately limited the number of trials to minimise fatigue, it is possible that performance could improve over time or more experimental sessions, despite the lack of a learning effect among the Study 1 data.

Subjective views were similar, with the Dynamic designs creating more of a connection between the hand and the object, and providing sound from both the Wrist and Object together was not seen as providing much benefit over just one speaker alone. The feedback preferences were slightly at odds with the objective measurements in Study 2. While the Pitch design resulted in significantly more errors than the Geiger, and also in the longest movement time, it had the highest ratings for all three subjective responses. However, only two participants preferred the Pitch design, with three preferring the Geiger counter (three had no preference). This contrasts with the young adults, three of whom preferred the Pitch design (only one preferred the Geiger). As mentioned earlier, musical ability can influence the usefulness of pitch-based sonifications [20] and so it may be that the two groups had different musical ability, but it could also be that the more developed older adults were better able to make sense and use of the changes in pitch. We will investigate this in the future. Either way, the results strongly suggest that personalisation is an important part of feedback design, and previous research on what kinds of sound blind and visually impaired children like/dislike showed a large degree of variety [33].

Young visually impaired children develop spatial and motor skills more slowly than sighted peers [4,22] and auditory spatial perception is worse at a young age [9]. These findings, along with our own (which show a similar trend), highlight the poorer spatial cognition in younger visually impaired children, bolstering the case for ABBI and using sound to support rehabilitation and improve spatial cognition in young children.

7. GENERAL DISCUSSION

Overall, the results from the two studies suggest that dynamic auditory feedback better supports reaching movements compared to constant (unchanging) feedback or only a brief initial cue (Control condition). Subjective comments from participants also showed a clear preference for dynamic changes, including the view that dynamic changes are "necessary" to guide movement. The results also suggest that sounds from nearby objects are more conducive to accurate reaching than sounds from the wrist, and providing feedback from both the wrist and the object does not appear to provide any benefit over sounds from a single speaker. There was only one significant difference between *Sound Sources:* the *Object*-only condition leading to faster Movement Times than when using *Both* speakers in Study 1.

However, there were some large differences in the results from children compared to young adults. The results from Study 1 (young adults) show a much clearer benefit of dynamic audio feedback over constant (unchanging) feedback, as dynamic feedback did not provide a strong benefit to younger children in Study 2. The control condition had the highest error in both studies, which suggests that these brief signals are not sufficient to inform children or young adults about the location of objects nearby.

7.1 Implications for ABBI & Rehabilitation

Our results have important ramifications for the use of spatialised and on-body sound in learning or habilitation activities. Providing hand guidance information through dynamic changes in sound is a potentially beneficial approach, which suggests that more complex engagement and play setups for children, such as 'sensory resource boxes' augmented with tracking and sounding objects, could be more beneficial than simple adult-activated 'lures' [22]. However, providing sounds from the wrist alone (as in ABBI), or both the wrist and the object, may only partially support accurate reaching, and less so than providing sound through only the object

to be reached for. Still, it should be noted that the results from Study 2 suggest that object (e.g., toy) positioning might also be important in encouraging accurate reaching: the high errors suggest objects should be placed more than 10° apart. Also Position 3 was more difficult to find so it may be best to position objects much closer than an arm's reach (even though near sounds are harder to localise in adults [6,7]).

In the case of our feedback designs, the *Coalescent* design does not appear to have added beneficial information over the *Individual* designs. While this is disappointing, we believe our findings can still be useful to other researchers, but there are a few points to consider. Firstly, there is the manner in which sound from the wrist was incorporated into the design. Previous focus group participants suggested that sound from the wrist, together with sound from the environment, would be appreciated in guiding the person to objects of interest in the room. However, it may be that continuous feedback from the wrist distracts attention from the location of the environmental source, and more sporadic or discrete feedback that compliments the environmental sound may be more suitable. Some participants commented that sound from the wrist, physically distant from the target, was distracting or confusing.

A second point is Millar's recommendation to provide redundancy and multiple pieces of systematically interconnected information in the sounds presented to young blind children [22]. We hypothesised that the *Coalescent* feedback may provide these, which may benefit children, but this does not seem to be the case. It may be that the two perceptual streams [5] utilised in the feedback presented additive, and so more perceptually saturating, information rather than repeating (redundant) information. While it is possible that younger children (0-12 years) may make different use of the *Coalescent* feedback, the drop in accuracy with age observed here suggests they may not find benefit in the specific design implemented here. Finally, it should be kept in mind that a key aim for the research, which the Dynamic feedback designs appear to have achieved, was to identify a design that creates a *connection* between the hand and the object: informing the child that there are objects nearby and that they are reachable. In future, we will test if this encourages children to self-initiate engagement with their environment more often. In this case, precise reaching is less important than the elicitation of the reaching itself.

8. CONCLUSIONS

This paper presents the results from two studies involving young visually impaired people aged 12-22 that looked at whether dynamic audio feedback from nearby objects and from a speaker on the wrist can improve peripersonal reaching, compared to unchanging feedback and no online feedback at all. The results showed that children (aged 12-17) were less accurate than young adults (18-22) but, overall, both studies showed a benefit of dynamic feedback on reaching accuracy and sounds from reachable objects are more likely to help reaching than sounds from the wrist or from both the object and wrist together. The dynamic sounds established a perceived connection between the hand and object, which may help young children create an internal connection between his/her movements and the environment, and so support self-initiated engagement.

9. REFERENCES

1. Audacity. Audacity: open source, cross-platform software for recording and editing sounds. Retrieved September 25, 2015 from http://audacityteam.org/
2. Ann E. Bigelow. 1986. The development of reaching in blind children. *British Journal of Developmental Psychology* 4, 4: 355–366.

http://doi.org/10.1111/j.2044-835X.1986.tb01031.x

3. Jens Blauert. 1999. *Spatial Hearing*. MIT Press, Massachusetts.

4. Michael Brambring. 2006. Divergent Development of Gross Motor Skills in Children Who Are Blind or Sighted. *Journal of Visual Impairment & Blindness* 101, 12: 620–634. http://www.afb.org/jvib/jvibabstractnew.asp?articleid=jvib001008

5. Albert S. Bregman. 1994. *Auditory Scene Analysis*. The MIT Press, Cambridge, MA.

6. Douglas S. Brungart, Nathanieal I. Durlach, and William M Rabinowitz. 1999. Auditory localization of nearby sources. II. Localization of a broadband source. *The Journal of the Acoustical Society of America* 106, 4: 1956–1968. http://doi.org/10.1121/1.428212

7. Douglas S. Brungart. 1999. Auditory localization of nearby sources. III. Stimulus effects. *The Journal of the Acoustical Society of America* 106, August 1999: 3589–3602. http://doi.org/10.1121/1.428212

8. Giulia Cappagli, Gabriel Baud-bovy, Elena Cocchi, and Monica Gori. 2014. Audio and proprioceptive space perception in sighted and visually impaired children. *Proceedings of International Multisensory Research Forum (IMRF '14)*.

9. Giulia Cappagli, Elena Cocchi, and Monica Gori. 2015. Auditory and proprioceptive spatial impairments in blind children and adults. *Developmental Science*: n/a–n/a. http://doi.org/10.1111/desc.12374

10. Géry Casiez, Nicolas Roussel, and Daniel Vogel. 2012. 1€ Filter: a Simple Speed-Based Low-Pass Filter for Noisy Input in Interactive Systems. *Proceedings of the SIGCHI Conference on Human Factors in Computing Systems (CHI '12)*, 2527–2530. http://doi.org/10.1145/2207676.2208639

11. Marsha G Clarkson, Rachel K Clifton, and Barbara A Morrongiello. 1985. The effects of sound duration on newborns' head orientation. *Journal of experimental child psychology* 39: 20–36. http://doi.org/10.1016/0022-0965(85)90027-X

12. Sara Finocchietti, Giulia Cappagli, Gabriel Baud-bovy, et al. 2015. ABBI, a new technology for sensory-motor rehabilitation of visual impaired people. *Proceedings of International Conference on Enabling Access for Persons with Visual Impairment (ICEAPVI '15)*, 1–5.

13. Sara Finocchietti, Giulia Cappagli, Lope Ben Porquis, Gabriel Baud-Bovy, Elena Cocchi, and Monica Gori. 2015. Evaluation of the Audio Bracelet for Blind Interaction for improving mobility and spatial cognition in early blind children - A pilot study. *Proceedings of the Annual International Conference of the IEEE Engineering in Medicine and Biology Society, EMBS* 2015-November: 7998–8001. http://doi.org/10.1109/EMBC.2015.7320248

14. Selma Fraiberg. 1977. *Insights from the blind: Comparative studies of blind and sighted infants*. Plenum Press, New York.

15. Monica Gori, Giulio Sandini, Cristina Martinoli, and David C Burr. 2014. Impairment of auditory spatial localization in congenitally blind human subjects. *Brain* 137, 1: 288–293. http://dx.doi.org/10.1093/brain/awt311

16. Lyn Haber, Ralph N. Haber, Suzanna Penningroth, Kevin Novak, and Hilary Radgowski. 1993. Comparison of nine methods of indicating the direction to objects: data from blind adults. *Perception* 22: 35–47. http://doi.org/10.1068/p220035

17. William M. Hartmann. 1983. Localization of Sound in Rooms. *Journal of the Acoustical Society of America* 74, 5: 1380–1391.

18. KitSound. KitSound. Retrieved January 28, 2015 from www.kitsound.co.uk

19. Marc J M Macé, Florian Dramas, and Christophe Jouffrais. 2012. Reaching to sound accuracy in the peri-personal space of blind and sighted humans. *Proceedings of International Conference on Computers Helping People with Special Needs (ICCHP '12)*, 636–

643. http://doi.org/10.1007/978-3-642-31534-3_93

20. Lisa M. Mauney and Bruce N. Walker. 2007. Individual Differences and The Field Of Auditory Display: Past Research, a Present Study, and an Agenda For The Future. *Proceedings of ICAD*, 386–390.

21. David McGookin, Stephen A Brewster, and Pablo Priego. 2009. Audio bubbles: Employing non-speech audio to support tourist wayfinding. *Proceedings of International Workshop on Haptic and Audio Interaction Design (HAID '09)*, 41–50. http://doi.org/10.1007/978-3-642-04076-4_5

22. Susanna Millar. 1994. *Understanding and Representing Space: Theory and Evidence from Studies with Blind and Sighted Children*. Oxford Press, Oxford. http://doi.org/10.1093/acprof

23. Gaetan Parseihian, Christophe Jouffrais, and Brian F. G. Katz. 2014. Reaching nearby sources: comparison between real and virtual sound and visual targets. *Frontiers in Neuroscience* 8, September: Article 269. http://doi.org/10.3389/fnins.2014.00269

24. David R Perrott. 1969. Role of signal onset in sound localization. *The Journal of the Acoustical Society of America* 45, 2: 436–445. http://doi.org/10.1121/1.1911392

25. Brad Rakerd and William M. Hartmann. 1986. Localization of Sound in Rooms, III: Onset and Duration Effects. *Journal of the Acoustical Society of America* 80, 6: 1695–1706.

26. Brigitte Röder, Wolfgang Teder-Sälejärvi, Anette Sterr, Frank Rösler, Steven A. Hillyard, and Helen J. Neville. 1999. Improved auditory spatial tuning in blind humans. *Nature* 400, July: 162–166. http://doi.org/10.1038/22106

27. Stuart Ross and Michael J Tobin. 1997. Object Permanence, Reaching, and Locomotion in Infants Who Are Blind. *Journal of Visual Impairment & Blindness* 91: 25–32. http://www.afb.org/jvib/jvibabstractNew.asp?articleid=jvib910105

28. Royal National Institute of Blind People. Sensory Development Resource Boxes. Retrieved March 18, 2015, rnib.org.uk/sites/default/files/sensory_development_resource_boxes[1].doc

29. Dale M Stack, Darwin W Muir, Frances Sherriff, and Jeanne Roman. 1989. Development of infant reaching in the dark to luminous objects and "invisible sounds." *Perception* 18: 69–82. http://doi.org/doi:10.1068/p180069

30. Bruce N. Walker, Gregory Kramer, and David M. Lane. 2000. Psychophysical scaling of sonification mappings. *Proceedings of ICAD 2000*, 99–104. http://dev.icad.org/Proceedings/2000/WalkerKramer2000.pdf

31. Bruce N. Walker and Gregory Kramer. 2005. Mappings and metaphors in auditory displays: an experimental assessment. *ACM Transactions on Applied Perception* 2, 4: 407–412. http://doi.org/10.1145/1101530.1101534

32. Bruce N. Walker and Lisa M. Mauney. 2004. Individual differences, cognitive abilities, and the interpretation of auditory graphs. *Proceedings of ICAD 2004*, 6–10. http://citeseerx.ist.psu.edu/viewdoc/download?doi=10.1.1.101.1938&rep=rep1&type=pdf

33. Graham Wilson, Stephen A. Brewster, Hector Caltenco, et al. 2015. Effects of Sound Type on Recreating the Trajectory of a Moving Source. *Proceedings of the SIGCHI Conference on Human Factors in Computing Systems (CHI '15) Extended Abstracts*, 1645–1650. http://doi.acm.org/10.1145/2702613.2732821

34. Jennifer G. Wishart, T. G R Bower, and Jane Dunkeld. 1978. Reaching in the dark. *Perception* 7: 507–512. http://doi.org/10.1097/00001756-199010000-00004

35. Eberhard Zwicker, G Flottorp, and Stanley S Stevens. 1957. Critical Band Width in Loudness Summation. *The Journal of the Acoustical Society of America* 29, 5: 548–557.

Nothing to Hide: Aesthetic Customization of Hearing Aids and Cochlear Implants in an Online Community

Halley P. Profita[1], Abigale Stangl[2], Laura Matuszewska[1], Sigrunn Sky[1], Shaun K. Kane[1,2]

[1]Department of Computer Science, [2]ATLAS Institute
University of Colorado Boulder
{halley.profita, abigale.stangl, laura.matuszewska, sigrunn.sky, shaun.kane}@colorado.edu

ABSTRACT

Hearing aids and cochlear implants can improve accessibility and quality of life for people with hearing impairments. However, use of these devices may cause concern amongst some users due to sociocultural issues such as unwanted attention and perceived stigma. While some individuals may respond to these concerns by attempting to conceal their devices, or even abandoning their devices, others have responded by making their devices more visible through aesthetic customization, and some have begun to share these customizations online. In this paper, we describe community interactions in an online forum dedicated to customized hearing aids and cochlear implants. We found that community members discussed customization tools and techniques, shared their customizations, and provided each other with encouragement and support. Community members customized their devices as a means of self-expression that demonstrated the wearer's fashion sense, revealed favorite sports teams and characters, and marked holidays and personal milestones. Our findings may inform the design of assistive technologies that better support personalization, customization, and self-expression.

CCS Concepts

• **Human-Centered Computing → Interaction Paradigms → Web-Based Interaction**

Keywords

DIY Assistive Technology; Online Communities; Hearing Aids; Cochlear Implants; Deafness; Social Acceptability

1. INTRODUCTION

Approximately 48 million people in the United States, representing 20% of the population, exhibit some degree of hearing loss [25]. People with hearing loss may use assistive technologies (AT) such as hearing aids (HAs) and cochlear implants (CIs) to compensate for their hearing loss. While HAs and CIs can restore some functional hearing to many users, use of HAs and CIs can present trade-offs such as poor functional performance, poor ergonomics, device invasiveness, and high cost [23]. Some potential users may be dissuaded from using HAs and CIs due to sociocultural concerns, such as worrying that using these devices will attract too much attention, or worrying that they will be treated differently [8, 26]. Sociocultural concerns about the use of AT may lead to social stigma and isolation, intermittent use of AT, or even abandonment of one's AT [8, 21, 22, 31]. Abandonment rates may be especially

Figure 1: An online community member shares an example of customized hearing aids decorated to celebrate the Christmas holiday. The hearing aids are decorated with glitter tape, tube wraps, and rhinestones.

high for hearing-related AT; it has been reported that abandonment rates for hearing aids may approach 75% [30].

Some individuals may respond to these concerns by avoiding use of HAs and CIs despite the potential functional benefits. Manufacturers of these technologies have responded to these concerns by producing smaller devices that are easier to conceal [15]. However, some have responded to this concealment by making their devices even more visible. There is a growing community of HA and CI users that decorate and customize their devices to increase the device's visibility, express their interests or personality, or demonstrate pride in their disability.

Because off-the-shelf HAs and CIs offer little variety in their design, people who wish to wear aesthetically pleasing devices may resort to do-it-yourself (DIY) modification of their AT, such as adding stickers or colorful tape to change the appearance of their devices. Recently, these DIY decorators have begun to share examples of their customizations online, and have formed communities to share design ideas, learn new techniques, and provide mutual support.

In this paper, we present an analysis of one such community that is dedicated to sharing custom decorations of HAs and CIs. This community, a Facebook group with over 4,800 members, represents what may be an early example of the growing phenomenon of DIY AT communities. We analyzed four months of activity within this community. Because a prominent theme of this community is to share one's own customized HAs and CIs, our analysis considers both users' preferences and practices around customizing their devices, as well as their interactions related to sharing and discussing their customizations online. Our findings illuminate why and how users customize their devices, which may inform the design of AT devices that better support customization and online communities that facilitate and support sharing of customized AT devices.

2. RELATED WORK

As the present work discusses aesthetic modifications to AT, we discuss related work in aesthetic beautification of AT, along with research into the developing DIY AT movement.

2.1 Aesthetic and Expressive AT

Early assistive technologies were designed to blend in with the wearer's body, to mimic the "missing" body part, or to present a neutral design [28]. However, some designers and users of assistive devices have responded by creating AT with a strong sense of aesthetic style, with the aim of instilling pride and empowerment in its users. For example, some companies have begun to design "expressive" prosthetics that offer alternative perspectives on the aesthetic design of a prosthetic limb [13]. Companies such as Unyq [36], Prosthetic Ink [27], and The Alternative Limb Project [34] create designs for prosthetic limbs such as patterned covers, tattoo-inspired body art, and designs that extend beyond biomimicry, respectively.

The notion of "expressiveness" in AT may extend beyond prosthetic limbs. Expressiveness appears in other forms of AT, including wheelchairs, crutches, insulin pumps, eye glasses [28], and hearing aids [10]. Companies such as Hayleigh's Cherished Charms [16], Hearrings [17], and Tubetastic Pimps [35] have begun to produce jewelry, clip-on accessories, and tube wraps that can be attached to HAs and CIs. Our present study documents use of some of these products by individuals with hearing loss, as well as DIY practices by individuals who desire further customization.

More broadly, these types of designs may represent movement away from a medical model of disability in which AT is used to restore missing functionality, to a model of disability that is socially constructed. As individuals choose clothing, jewelry, and other worn items to represent their identity [9], these expressive AT devices may empower the users to express themselves, their identity, and their disability [24].

2.2 Do-It-Yourself Assistive Technology

The burgeoning "maker movement" emphasizes a commitment to craft and Do-It-Yourself (DIY) solutions, while taking advantage of developments in fabrication tools such as consumer-grade 3D printers and laser cutters [12]. The DIY ethos has also been adopted by people with disabilities and their friends and families. Hurst and Tobias found that creating one's own AT can solve problems where solutions do not currently exist or are not affordable, give users a greater sense of ownership over their AT devices, and increase users' sense of personal agency and investment in the design process [20]. Perhaps the most well-known example of DIY AT practice is e-NABLE, an online community that facilitates the design, 3D printing, and distribution of customized prosthetic hands [11].

Several recent studies have explored practices of the Do-It-Yourself Assistive Technology (DIY AT) movement. Buehler et al. [3] explored a sub-community of Thingiverse, a large repository for 3D-printable models, dedicated to creating assistive technology, and found that devices were created and shared by a variety of stakeholders, including engineers and students, friends and family of a person with a disability, and the person with a disability themselves. Hook et al. [19] interviewed stakeholders related to DIY AT and found several barriers to producing DIY AT, including perceptions that DIY devices would have poor aesthetics. Bennett et al. [2] and Hofmann et al. [18] studied individuals who had used 3D-printed prosthetic hands, and found that these devices often encouraged their users to explore aesthetic and personally meaningful designs. Other studies have explored the use of DIY AT

practices and methods related to communication aids [14] and accessible learning materials [4, 32]. Our study presents an analysis of an active community engaging in DIY AT practices, and highlights specific challenges and opportunities related to the customization of hearing aids and cochlear implants.

3. STUDY

To explore how individuals with disabilities, as well their friends and family members, customize their AT to achieve aesthetic goals, we studied an online community dedicated to sharing aesthetic customizations of hearing aids and cochlear implants. People who are deaf and hard of hearing have been early and fervent adopters of online communities, which they use to build social connections and express themselves [1], and to practice communication strategies with people similar to themselves [5]. This study presents an analysis of an online community dedicated to addressing the emerging practice of customizing HAs and CIs.

3.1 The Online Community

We identified a Facebook group dedicated to posting and sharing customized HAs and CIs by searching through a variety of social networks, message boards, and mailing lists to identify communities engaging in DIY AT practices. Throughout the remainder of the paper we refer to the Facebook group as the "online community". Our analysis focused on members' interactions with the community, their modification practices, and the challenges and workarounds inherent in modifying the aesthetic qualities of these devices. As of July 2016, this group had over 4,800 members, and contained sub-groups for off-topic discussion and for suppliers of DIY resources. At the time of the study, the group could be found via Facebook search, but required permission from a moderator to join. As the community facilitates interactions between several different stakeholder groups (end users, parents and caretakers of end users, and community administrators), we may consider this community a boundary object [33] used by an emerging community of practice [37].

We established contact with the group after receiving permission from our IRB. We then contacted the moderators, identified ourselves as researchers, and explained the goals of our study. Our data collection methods were approved by the IRB and group moderators: we analyzed an anonymized subset of posts and present our aggregate analysis here. When sharing any individual's contributions, such as photographs or post text, we received explicit permission from the poster.

3.2 Data Collection

We collected a set of posts from the online community's main discussion page over a period of four months, from September 1, 2015 to December 31, 2015. Posts were captured using a Python script that downloaded the content of each post and replaced each poster's name with a unique, anonymized ID. We collected a total of 365 posts during this date range. We collected posts from the main discussion page only, and did not include the community's secondary pages (a social-oriented discussion page and a marketplace), as we were primarily interested in how individuals shared and discussed their customized devices. We also collected comments to posts, but do not analyze them here, as their content primarily contained brief reactions to the main posts.

3.3 Data Analysis

We analyzed the collected data using an open coding approach [7]. We conducted two stages of analysis. First, we analyzed the entire set of posts to identify the type of content included in posts, underlying themes of the posts, and the identity of the designer (i.e., whether they were designing for themselves or for someone else). Next, we analyzed each of the themes separately to identify common questions and comments, customization materials and methods, customization themes, and challenges related to customizing devices.

3.3.1 Post Types and Themes

Two co-authors reviewed 50 posts to independently develop codes, and reviewed and reconciled these codes together to create a coding manual. Analysis of the posts included both the post text and any associated media (e.g., images or video). These codes were discussed and refined with a third co-author in order to reconcile overlap and inconsistencies, and the raters coded an additional 50 posts to identify any issues or concerns with the codes.

The finalized coding manual contained 11 codes and definitions describing the types of posts made by community members, challenges and themes that appeared across posts, and the role of the poster (posting on their own behalf or on someone else's behalf). Some posts contained multiple codes.

Following two rounds of reconciliation, the two raters independently coded the remaining data. Disagreements were resolved by the two raters. We calculated inter-rater reliability for these themes using Cohen's kappa [6], which is reported in the following sections.

3.3.2 Community Interactions and Design Practices

Following this analysis, we separately analyzed posts within several categories to identify trends in the posted questions, advice, and shared customizations. We separately coded the types of questions asked by community members, the types of feedback and advice offered by posters, the materials used in posted customizations, and the design themes of posted customizations. These coding schemes were developed and iteratively discussed by the research team. Each category of posts was coded by one member of the research team, and the findings were shared and discussed within the research team.

4. FINDINGS

Our analysis addresses the following topics: who participated in the community, the types of posts made by community members, the methods used to customize HAs and CIs, the design themes of the customized HAs and CIs, and challenges experienced by community members when customizing their devices.

4.1 Community Members

Our set of 365 posts contained contributions from 191 different community members. The average number of posts made by each community member was 1.9 (SD=2.6). As with many online communities, participation in this community follows a long-tail distribution: 133 community members only posted once during the data collection period, 27 posted twice, and only 31 posted three or more times.

While our study was not focused on the demographics of our community members, we collected an anonymous count of posters by gender using a script that counted the gender of each poster who included their gender in their public Facebook profile. The gender distribution of community members is relevant to our research both because prior work has shown that online communities around design or fashion may skew female [29], and because aesthetic customization practices may differ based on gender. Of the 191 posters in our data set, 143 (74.9%) were female and 7 (3.7%) were male; 41 (21.5%) did not publicly disclose their gender.

In our preliminary review of the data, we noticed a number of posts from parents asking questions or demonstrating customizations related to their child. Therefore, we analyzed posts to determine whether the post referred to the end user of the HA or CI, or to another person. Of the 365 posts, 94 of the posts were made by someone clearly posting about their own needs (κ=.95), and 117 posts were made by someone clearly posting on behalf of another person (κ=.92).

Although we did not perform a thorough analysis of the third parties discussed in community postings, we observed that many posts related to children. A keyword search of 365 posts found that 22 posts included the term "son" and 45 included the term "daughter."

4.2 Types of Posts

We analyzed posts to identify their purpose, which included sharing customizations, asking questions, providing advice, sharing stories and life experiences, and community building.

4.2.1 Sharing Customizations

By far the most common type of post involved the poster sharing an example of a customization to their hearing aid or cochlear implant. This code applied to 330 of 365 posts (κ=.80). Most of these posts contained one or more photographs demonstrating the customization (see examples in Figure 2). Community members often described their customizations using colloquial terms such as "bling out" and "pimp" (inspired, perhaps, by the car-customization show *Pimp My Ride*). It is interesting to note that the community chose to provide alternative text descriptions for their shared photos to accommodate members with vision impairments. When a poster neglected to provide this alternative text, a moderator would typically add a comment requesting this information.

Because many of our research questions relate to how individuals customize their devices, we analyze the content of the customizations in detail in sections 4.3 and 4.4.

4.2.2 Asking Questions

The second most common type of post included questions, describing 102 of 365 posts (κ=.96). Table 1 summarizes the types of questions asked.

In some cases, community members asked for help solving a particular design problem, or requested help with finding the right design to suit their personality. For instance, one community member posted a request for "tomboyish" designs:

> I want to pimp my hearing aids, but i'm tomboy [sic]. And i'm not like a feminine. so, who can anyone help me how to make in accordance with my background tomboyish?

4.2.3 Sharing Advice, Resources, and Tips

Community members also shared advice, resources, and tutorials. These posts comprised 25 of 365 posts (κ=.86). Of these posts, 14 posts included information about where to find specific materials, six posts described sales on materials, one post included a tutorial for performing a specific kind of modification, and one post described a news media event about device customization. The remaining three posts provided reviews, feedback, or commentary related to use of specific materials or techniques.

4.2.4 Sharing Experiences

While much of the community's discussion focused on sharing of customizations and answering questions, participants also shared stories about their experiences wearing and using their customized devices. These posts comprised 25 of 365 posts (κ=.90).

Table 1. Questions asked by community members.

Question Type	#
Questions about obtaining supplies – where to obtain supplies, sales on supplies.	36
Questions about functional issues – how to avoid damaging HAs and CIs during customization, managing wear and tear, removing residue and artifacts between designs, customizability of specific HAs and CIs.	19
Questions about how to use supplies or techniques – how to apply materials such as Washi tape and nail stickers.	14
Requesting feedback – asking for feedback on a recently posted design, choosing between different designs or raw materials.	14
Requesting examples – asking for examples that use specific supplies, soliciting gender-specific design examples, or requesting examples from specific members.	11
Questions about general deafness-related issues – how adopting CIs will affect life, how to adapt to increased hearing loss, how to negotiate with clinicians or equipment suppliers.	6
Requesting help – requests for someone else to create a specific design for them.	2

Many of these stories described day-to-day living with customized HAs and CIs, described instances in which they wore their customized devices out, described their process of finding materials and customizing their devices, or shared anecdotes such as when a community member's hearing aids were chewed up by a pet.

Many of the stories demonstrated the positive feelings that community members experienced when wearing their customized devices in public:

> I wore Jamberry Jams today and my students loved the designs. I half joked "I'll bling your hearing aids and processors" and all six BOYS jumped at the idea.

Several stories from new members discussed challenges in using their HAs and CIs, and expressed optimism that customizing their devices could make them more desirable:

> I have had a hearing aid for almost a year now and am very conscious of it and hate having it on show. Now I have seen this page I can't wait to get pimping my aid and showing it off! Thank you!!

Another community member shared a similar comment about their son, who was unhappy about having to wear hearing aids:

> My son got aids today but is a bit upset at how dull they are so I showed him some pics I found online on pimped hearing aids he LOVES them …

Overall, the tone of these stories was quite positive, as community members expressed their excitement about being able to improve their devices by themselves, and about having customized devices.

---

[1] https://www.etsy.com/

4.2.5 Administration and Community Building

The online community is supported by the efforts of 10 volunteer moderators, who actively work to maintain the quality of the discussion. Posts related to administration and community building comprised 11 of 365 posts (κ=.97). These posts included reminders about community rules, links to tutorials, reminders to post alternative text descriptions for images, contest announcements (e.g., a contest for best Halloween-themed customization), encouraging comments, and community polls. The group maintains several how-to guides that document basic customization techniques and lists materials that are appropriate for use in customization, as well as those that may be problematic, such as materials with strong adhesives.

4.3 Customization Methods and Materials

Community members used a variety of techniques and materials to customize their HAs and CIs, including off-the-shelf products, purchased add-on accessories, and DIY materials. In this section we analyze the methods and materials used in community members' shared customizations.

4.3.1 Fashionable Off-the-Shelf Devices

Some community members shared their HAs and CIs without any DIY modification, but had selected attractive devices that represented their stylistic preferences. These devices often featured brightly colored cases or aesthetically pleasing materials, such as inner ear molds with sparkles embedded within the plastic.

4.3.2 Purchased Accessories

Community members often shared customized designs that featured off-the-shelf HAs and CIs decorated with commercially available accessories. These accessories included a variety of items that were specifically designed to enhance HAs and CIs, which can be purchased on company web sites or on marketplaces such as Etsy[1]. These accessories included colorful add-on device covers, stickers provided by the HA or CI manufacturer, device clips for attaching the HA or CI to clothing, and "tube riders" that enable the wearer to hang charms from their device's tubes or cables.

While these accessories were often chosen for their aesthetic properties, some accessories often have functional benefits as well. For example, covers can protect a device from damage, while device clips can keep the device from falling off during vigorous activity.

4.3.3 Do-It-Yourself Modifications

Many community members created their own aesthetic customizations, or combined off-the-shelf products with their own customizations. Customizations typically took one of several forms: applying foil, tape, or other materials to the surface of the device, decorating the device with stickers or stick-on gemstones, and hanging charms from the device tubes.

Community members used a variety of materials to decorate their HAs and CIs, including some materials originally designed for this purpose (such as tube riders), but also repurposed craft materials such as nail wraps, Washi tape (often used in scrapbooking), and stickers. These materials are often layered to produce more complex patterns. We analyzed the most commonly used materials based on manual inspection of photos and the alternative text provided by posters. Table 2 lists the most common materials found in our data set. Other, less commonly used materials included nail

Table 2. Materials used by community members to customize their hearing aids and cochlear implants.

Material	Description	#
Nail art	Nail foils, stickers, and wraps, especially those with mild adhesives.	61
Stickers	Generic stickers, not intended for HAs or CIs.	31
Gems	Gems and rhinestones with adhesive backings.	30
Duct tape	Easily removable tape that is often available in bright colors.	28
Tube riders	Commercial accessories and charms that hang from the HA tube.	27
Washi tape	Colorful tape often used in scrapbooking.	23
Glitter	Glitter, glitter tape, and glitter foil added to the HA or CI.	21
Charms	Charms representing characters, symbols, or shapes.	19

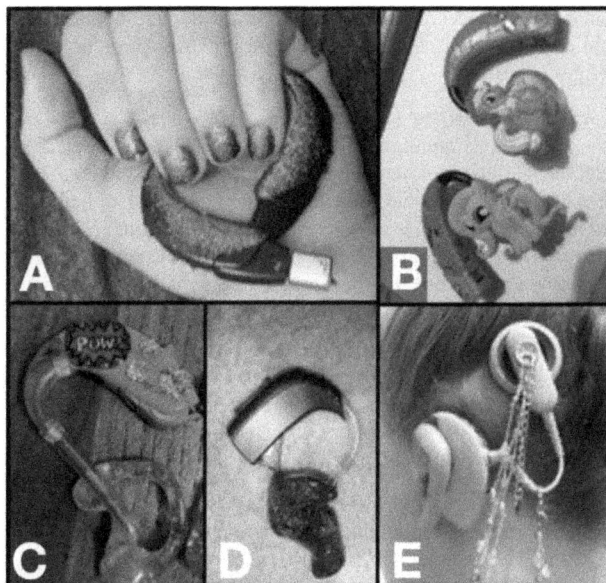

Figure 2. DIY customization of HA and CIs. A) Blue and silver glitter-decorated HAs with matching nails; B) HAs with My Little Pony character stickers and tube riders; C) HAs with silver dots, "POW" stickers, and a sparkly ear mold. D) HA with purple ear base and shimmering emerald ear mold; E) Cochlear Implant with ankle bracelet repurposed as a bangle.

polish, beads, pearls, googly eyes, elastic, felt, pipe cleaners, chain, fabric, hair clips, hair bands, foam, glue, thread, decals, buttons, generic tape, and string.

4.4 Customization Themes

Participants exercised their creativity to create a diverse range of customized devices. Customizations included changing colors and/or adding patterns and textures, celebrating holidays and seasons, an affinity for popular fictional characters, coordinating with clothing and worn accessories, celebrating life events, and showing affiliations for sports teams. Customization themes are discussed based on the frequency (most common to least common) with which they occurred.

4.4.1 Adding Colors, Patterns, and Textures

The most common customization strategy was to augment the HA or CI with colors, patterns, or textures, typically by adding tape, nail foils, or stickers (e.g., Figure 2A, 2C). Many of the DIY patterns shared with this online community included flowers, happy faces, sparkly materials, and geometric shapes.

Some community members created more elaborate patterns by layering tape, foil, gems, and other materials over the body of the device. Other community members added objects to their HA or CI to add color or texture or to change the shape, such as one community member who repurposed an ankle bracelet as a cochlear implant bangle (Figure 2E).

4.4.2 Celebrating Holidays and Seasons

Community members often decorated their HAs and CIs to celebrate a specific holiday or season. For example, one participant decorated their hearing aid with red and white rhinestones and green pine tree stickers to celebrate Christmas (Figure 1). Our data set contained 59 holiday-themed customizations: 41 for Christmas, 17 for Halloween, and one for Remembrance Day. Common holiday elements included spiders at Halloween, and stockings, reindeer, candy canes, trees, and Santa at Christmas. Some community members even decorated their devices to match their Halloween costumes.

Holiday-themed customization was encouraged by the community moderators, who organized Halloween- and Christmas-themed design contests. Moderators encouraged members of the community to mark their Christmas-themed customizations using

the hashtag #christmaspimps – this hashtag was used 26 times during the contest period.

4.4.3 Showing Favorite Characters

Community members used stickers and charms to decorate their devices with favorite characters from television and movies. Our data set contained 36 character-themed customizations. Popular characters included Buzz Lightyear and Lotso Bear (Toy Story), Cookie Monster and Elmo (Sesame Street), Darth Vader (Star Wars), Elsa and Olaf (Frozen), Stewie (Family Guy), Lightning McQueen (Disney's Cars), Minions, Peppa Pig, Minnie Mouse, Hello Kitty, Fluttershy and Applejack (My Little Pony, Figure 2B), Teenage Mutant Ninja Turtles, and Sonic the Hedgehog. One customization featured a Lego brick.

4.4.4 Matching Clothing, Nails, or Other Devices

Reinforcing the notion that a hearing aid is both an assistive technology and wearable technology, community members sometimes decorated their HAs and CIs to match other elements of their wardrobe. Our data set contained two instances of HAs or CIs decorated to match the wearer's clothing, one instance of matching a Halloween costume, and five instances of matching one's nails. Because nail art supplies such as nail foils were often used for decorating HAs and CIs, individuals could coordinate their devices with their wardrobe by using the same materials on both their nails and their devices (Figure 2A).

Community members sometimes decorated other devices to match their HAs or CIs: community members shared decorated crutches, a hand splint, earbuds, and a keychain battery holder. Community members also decorated other assistive listening devices, such as a ComPilot audio streaming device. Our data set contained seven instances of decorated assistive devices that were not HAs or CIs; three of these were shown paired with a matching HA or CI.

Additionally, many hearing aid and cochlear implant users wear more than one HA or CI at a time. When sharing images of two customized devices, members sometimes decorated both devices similarly (Figure 2A), and sometimes chose complementary designs (Figure 2B).

4.4.5 Celebrating Life Events
Just as some community members decorated their devices to celebrate holidays, other community members customized their devices to mark personal life events. Our data set contained eight instances of HAs or CIs customized to mark a personal life event: three for the first day of school or work, two for weddings, one for attending church, one for participating in a parade, and one to celebrate a charity event.

In some instances, the notion of decorating a hearing aid or cochlear implant became a broader part of the celebration itself. One community member shared an image of their child's birthday cake in which the cake was decorated with an image of the child's own customized cochlear implant.

4.4.6 Showing Team Affiliations
A small number of community members customized their HA or CI with logos or color schemes associated with sports teams. We identified three instances in which community members shared sports-themed customizations: the Green Bay Packers, Seattle Seahawks, and a South African rugby team. As with adding characters or references to life events, customizing a HA or CI with the wearer's favorite sports team provides the wearer with an opportunity for self-expression.

4.5 Challenges to Customization
Although many of the customizations shared by the community appear relatively simple, community members often encountered difficulties finding appropriate materials, matching their desired materials to the HA or CI, and assembling the customized device. Here we describe some of the common challenges expressed by community members.

4.5.1 Finding Appropriate Materials
Many of the customizations shared within the community involved working with found materials, such as repurposed craft materials. Community members often sought materials with specific characteristics such as texture, color, stiffness, or ease of use. Members of the community often discussed where to find specific materials and what materials might be used for a specific task. For example, one community member was looking for a colorful ear mold that would work with their hearing aids:

> I'm 22 and have these BTE aids... I want to jazz them up a bit.. I've seen kids with coloured plastic bits (not stickers) all pink/blue/orange etc... I'd really like them but I know I probably can't get them from my ENT and Audiology as an adult! Has anyone got suggestions of where I can get them or the coloured moulds from?

Some materials could cause problems if used to customize a hearing aid or cochlear implant. For example, some adhesives could damage the device. The community maintains several how-to documents which include a list of do's and don'ts related to customizing these devices.

4.5.2 Matching Customizations to the User's Device
Due to variations in the size, shape, and features of specific models of HAs and CIs, not all customization could be applied to every device. Some devices could not support a specific customization because the device was too small, had the wrong shape, or had a critical component in the area that the wearer wished to decorate, such as a volume switch, battery door, microphone, or FM connection ("boot"). Because customization options vary based on

the specific device model, community members often mentioned their specific HA or CI when sharing their customizations and when asking for advice. Of the 365 posts analyzed, 118 posts mentioned the specific brand or model of hearing aid or cochlear implant.

4.5.3 Challenging Assembly Processes
Even customizations that appear simple can involve multiple steps, including delicate operations such as cutting and gluing very small objects, and working with fragile materials. Many of the customizations shared involved only a few steps, although some did create more elaborate designs. Community members often asked for advice about how to perform customizations, especially when starting out. Some community members even practiced on other objects before performing the "real" customization, such as this parent who performed a practice customization on a stuffed animal:

> So I hope y'all don't think I am crazy, but my daughter was implanted this past Monday and I have been practicing pimping the CI that came along with our Cochlear koala! Glad I took some time to practice because I don't know that I have the fine motor skills for this and semi-botched it! I think I had better continue practicing before we get her real ones next week.

4.5.4 Limited Time and Resources
In some cases, community members were not able to acquire the desired materials needed for their planned customization. In those cases, they often substituted some other material to replace the missing resource. In other cases, community members had the available resources, but lacked the time to create a sophisticated design, especially those that involved intricate patterns or layering multiple materials. Community members occasionally expressed frustration when a customization did not turn out the way that they had planned, as they were hesitant to go through the complex series of steps all over again.

5. DISCUSSION
Our analysis of this community revealed a variety of motivations for customizing HAs and CIs, and multiple approaches to performing these modifications. The community itself, supported by moderators, encouraged sharing ideas and techniques and encouraged further customization. Here we consider more broadly the motivations for this type of customization; the connection between decoration, customization, and do-it-yourself AT; and opportunities to better support users in customizing their AT and sharing their AT customizations.

5.1 Why People Customize their Devices
Our analysis of HA and CI customization practice showed that community members put significant effort into customizing their devices. Why does this work happen? Is it simply that existing devices are unaesthetic, or are there other factors motivating this work? In examining the comments, questions, and customizations shared within this community, several motivations become clear.

First, many community members were motivated, and sometimes desperate, to find solutions that would motivate the individual to want to wear their HA or CI. This motivation was true both for those who were participating in the community to meet their own needs, as well as those who were seeking solutions for another person in their life. A substantial number of posts made by parents displayed a recurring theme of being unable to convince their children to wear their HAs or CIs. Community members, both adults and children, reported excitement after seeing others' customized devices, and expressed hope at the possibility of owning more attractive devices that they could wear with pride.

Second, community members used customization as a medium for self-expression. Descriptions of HAs and CIs included references to favorite colors, beloved characters, and important life events. This customization can enable the wearer to exert more control over how they present themselves to the outside world. When considering why people customize their HAs and CIs, it is natural to wonder whether this practice is motivated mainly by the poor aesthetic qualities of existing devices. If hearing aid manufacturers produced more aesthetically pleasing devices, would these customization practices end? Our data suggests that the answer to this question is a resounding no. Community members often created and shared multiple designs, and created temporary customizations to mark holidays and other events. This behavior strongly suggests that these customization practices are not entirely a response to ugly consumer devices, but rather that the act of customization itself provides the wearer with some intrinsic value.

Finally, it seems clear that the structure of the community itself facilitated participation and experimentation from members. Moderators engaged the community by posting encouragements, polls, and invitations to local events. Moderators further motivated the community through seasonal contests, and used social networking features such as hashtags to draw increased attention to these contests. In addition to the moderators, many members of the community were active in posting their customizations, offering tips, answering questions, and providing encouragement to others. Communities designed around shared self-expressions can strongly motivate participation, as has been shown in online communities surrounding fashion brands such as Warby Parker [29].

5.2 Customizing as DIY AT Practice

Much of the existing research on DIY AT practices focuses primarily on meeting functional needs: individuals create their own AT devices because the devices that they need do not exist, are not sufficiently customized, or are too expensive. Participants in this online community did utilize some functional customizations, such as adding clips to their device so that they could be attached to hair or clothing. However, the majority of customizations shared within this community focused on altering the appearance of the device.

While this paper explores a somewhat atypical DIY AT community, it is worth noting that this community is also quite successful in that it supports thousands of current members. While it is difficult to know why this particular group has been successful, there are several characteristics of the community that may help explain its popularity. First, this community addresses a problem that affects a rather large user group, and a problem with few existing solutions. Second, the barrier for entry into this type of DIY AT practice is low, as the tools and materials needed are inexpensive and readily available. Finally, because the customizations primarily affect the device's appearance, it is easy for community members to share their work by posting photos. It is possible that other DIY communities will appear around problems that have similar characteristics.

In considering this community as an example of a DIY AT community, we may also see areas in which this community differs from other communities of DIY AT practice. In particular, because this community is focused on aesthetic issues, members of the community may speak more directly about issues related to aesthetics and identity. Issues of aesthetics have appeared in other DIY AT communities: the e-NABLE community is known for producing desirable and exciting prosthetic limbs, such as hands inspired by superhero costumes [11], while Hook et al. found that the rough aesthetic qualities of DIY AT devices may dissuade potential users from adopting those devices [19]. However, in the community we studied in this paper, aesthetics and self-expression were central to most discussions.

In considering how members of this community expressed their preferences for aesthetically pleasing AT devices, we note two points that frequently reappeared during our analysis. First, community members were not simply interested in how the devices looked, but considered the process of customizing devices as part of a process of self-expression. Thus, it is important to consider not only the appearance of an AT device, but also its flexibility, including the ability to be decorated for special occasions and to be coordinated with other worn objects.

Second, it is clear that customization of AT, especially in the context of aesthetic customization, can be a gendered activity. Customized devices in our data set often reflected cultural gender norms, including gender-targeted colors, patterns, and characters. Many community posts contained questions about how to convince a child of a certain gender to adopt a hearing aid or cochlear implant. In some ways, it seems that even the concept of decoration may be gendered: decorating and embellishing worn objects may seem more culturally appropriate for girls and women, while making an AT device acceptable to boys and men may require another approach, such as incorporating a favorite character or sports team.

5.3 Supporting Device Customization

In many ways, we may consider this community a successful example of a community practicing DIY AT. While community members sometimes encountered challenges when customizing their devices, they were generally able to create and share their customizations. Thus, this community may offer insight on how to create other communities that support DIY AT practice, and may also offer insight on how to create more customizable AT devices.

As discussed previously, the structure of the community offered several features that supported members in creating and sharing customizations. First, community members were able to easily share their work by posting photos of their customizations, and some even posted tutorials to teach more complex techniques. Second, the community maintained a series of how-to documents to support new members of the community. Finally, moderators further encouraged continued engagement and participation through contests based around specific themes. These techniques may be useful in building other communities that support DIY AT practice.

These community features, while successful, may be improved in several ways. For example, as many members of the community asked questions about how to use specific materials or achieve specific looks, the site could offer a database of prior solutions by theme, materials, or device. The community might also support better documentation of customization techniques by making it easier to record videos or to author step-by-step guides.

Our analysis of community members' questions, comments, and challenges reveals several opportunities to improve customizability of the AT devices themselves. First, community members often decorated their devices multiple times, suggesting that AT devices should be easy to decorate and re-decorate. Manufacturers could support this feature by providing replaceable skins and covers. Second, community members sometimes experienced difficulties finding places to attach their decorations because the decorations would obstruct functional features of the device, such as the microphone or battery door. Manufacturers should aim to provide surfaces that can be decorated or ornamented whenever possible. Finally, community members often asked questions about what techniques and materials would be most compatible with their own device, suggesting that device manufacturers could provide clearer instructions about what modifications are possible. Manufacturers could also provide templates for device wraps, or offer 3D models of their devices to facilitate the creation of add-ons (some community members reported using manufacturer-provided stickers, but these reports were rare). Manufacturers could also connect device owners with one another through an online community to support exchanging of ideas and techniques.

6. LIMITATIONS AND FUTURE WORK

Our study presents an analysis of four months of communication in an active online community exploring DIY AT practice. Our findings illustrate community members' preferences and practices in customizing their AT devices. However, this study is limited in some ways that may be addressed in future work. First, our study addressed only one type of AT: hearing aids and cochlear implants. It is likely that communities that focused on other AT devices, such as prosthetic limbs, would present some differences. However, we believe that the broader findings related to community members' preferences for customized AT, their questions and concerns about customizing their devices, and their practices in creating and sharing customized AT, will apply to other such communities. In the future, we would like to compare this community to communities that create different forms of AT.

Second, our analysis included four months of posts only, and did not include analysis of post comments. We believe that focusing on this data set allowed us to identify broader themes that will carry over to future studies. As the majority of comments in our data set consisted of clarification questions and encouragement, analyzing these comments in the future set will allow us to better understand how community members work together and support each other in creating customized AT.

Finally, our data collection was limited to studying existing posts; we did not directly engage with the community or specific community members beyond requesting consent to use members' data. We made this choice both to maintain a manageable data set for our analysis, as well as to minimize our intrusion upon a growing online community. However, interacting directly with community members through interviews or focus groups would allow us to fill in some of the gaps regarding how members previously experienced their hearing loss, how they found and entered this online community, their personal motivations for customizing their HAs and CIs, and how use of customized HAs and CIs has affected their everyday lives. In the future, we plan to conduct interviews with community members to better understand these issues.

7. CONCLUSION

The practice of creating or customizing one's own assistive technology devices is becoming increasingly common, supported in part by online communities that enable AT users to share ideas, questions, and examples of these customized devices. For users of hearing aids and cochlear implants, decorating one's own device presents an opportunity to compensate for the limited aesthetic qualities of commercial devices, to express one's personal style and interests, and to counteract the perceived stigma and shame of wearing an assistive device. This study explored how users of HAs and CIs customized their devices and shared them in an online community. Our analysis of posts and shared customizations in this community improves our understanding of users' preferences for customizing their AT, their questions and concerns about performing these customizations, and the strategies used to create

DIY solutions to customizing AT. Understanding the customization practices that occur in this community also provides insight about how to design online communities to facilitate DIY AT practice, and how to design more customizable AT devices that will enable users to express themselves with pride.

8. ACKNOWLEDGEMENTS

We thank the administrators and members of the online community for their participation in this research.

9. REFERENCES

[1] Glívia A.R. Barbosa, Ismael S. Silva, Glauber Gonçalves, Raquel O. Prates, Fabrício Benevenuto, and Virgílio Almeida. 2011. Characterizing interactions among members of deaf communities in Orkut. In *Human-Computer Interaction–INTERACT*, 280-287. http://dx.doi.org/10.1007/978-3-642-23765-2_20

[2] Cynthia L. Bennett, Keting Cen, Katherine M. Steele, and Daniela K. Rosner. 2016. An intimate laboratory?: prostheses as a tool for experimenting with identity and normalcy. In *Proceedings of the CHI Conference on Human Factors in Computing Systems* (CHI '16), 1745-1756. http://dx.doi.org/10.1145/2858036.2858564

[3] Erin Buehler, Stacy Branham, Abdullah Ali, Jeremy J. Chang, Megan Kelly Hofmann, Amy Hurst, and Shaun K. Kane. 2015. Sharing is caring: assistive technology designs on Thingiverse. *In Proceedings of the ACM Conference on Human Factors in Computing Systems* (CHI '15), 525-534. http://dx.doi.org/10.1145/2702123.2702525

[4] Erin Buehler, Shaun K. Kane, and Amy Hurst. 2014. ABC and 3D: opportunities and obstacles to 3D printing in special education environments. In *Proceedings of the ACM SIGACCESS Conference on Computers and Accessibility* (ASSETS '14), 107-114. http://dx.doi.org/10.1145/2661334.2661365

[5] Anna C. Cavender, Daniel S. Otero, Jeffrey P. Bigham, and Richard E. Ladner. 2010. ASL-STEM Forum: enabling sign language to grow through online collaboration. In *Proceedings of the SIGCHI Conference on Human Factors in Computing Systems* (CHI '10), 2075-2078. http://dx.doi.org/10.1145/1753326.1753642

[6] Jacob Cohen. 1960. A coefficient of agreement for nominal scales. *Educational and Psychological Measurement* 20, 1, 37-46.

[7] Juliet Corbin and Anselm Strauss. 2014. *Basics of Qualitative Research: Techniques and Procedures for Developing Grounded Theory*. Sage Publications.

[8] Katherine Deibel. 2013. A convenient heuristic model for understanding assistive technology adoption. In *Proceedings of the ACM SIGACCESS Conference on Computers and Accessibility* (ASSETS '13), Article 32, 2 pages. http://dx.doi.org/10.1145/2513383.2513427

[9] Lucy E. Dunne, Halley Profita, Clint Zeagler, James Clawson, Scott Gilliland, Ellen Yi-Luen Do, and Jim Budd. 2014. The social comfort of wearable technology and gestural interaction. In *Proceedings of the International Conference of the IEEE on Engineering in Medicine and Biology Society* (EMBC '14), 4159-4162. http://dx.doi.org/10.1109/EMBC.2014.6944540

[10] Tameka Ellington and Stacey Lim. 2013. Adolescents' aesthetic and functional view of hearing aids or cochlear

implants and their relationship to self-esteem levels. *Fashion Practice* 5, 1, 59-80. http://dx.doi.org/10.2752/175693813X13559997788763

[11] Enabling The Future. Enabling The Future. Retrieved May 4, 2016 from http://enablingthefuture.org/

[12] Neil Gershenfeld. 2008. *Fab: The Coming Revolution on Your Desktop–From Personal Computers to Personal Fabrication.* Basic Books.

[13] Martha L. Hall and Belinda T. Orzada. 2013. Expressive prostheses: meaning and significance. *Fashion Practice* 5, 1, 9-32. http://dx.doi.org/10.2752/175693813X13559997788682

[14] Foad Hamidi, Melanie Baljko, Tony Kunic, and Ray Feraday. 2014. Do-It-Yourself (DIY) assistive technology: a communication board case study. In *Proceedings of the International Conference on Computers for Handicapped Persons* (ICCHP '14), 287-294.

[15] Jon Hamilton. Listen up to smarter, smaller hearing aids. NPR. Retrieved July 21, 2016 from http://www.npr.org/sections/health-shots/2013/04/08/176225511/listen-up-to-smarter-smaller-hearing-aids

[16] Hayleigh's Cherished Charms. Hayleigh's Cherished Charms. Retrieved May 4, 2016 from http://www.hayleighscherishedcharms.com/

[17] Hearrings. Turning hearing aids from a necessity to a must have accessory. Retrieved May 4, 2016 from http://www.hearrings.co.uk/

[18] Megan Hofmann, Jeffrey Harris, Scott E. Hudson, and Jennifer Mankoff. 2016. Helping hands: requirements for a prototyping methodology for upper-limb prosthetics users. In *Proceedings of the CHI Conference on Human Factors in Computing Systems* (CHI '16), 1769-1780. http://dx.doi.org/10.1145/2858036.2858340

[19] Jonathan Hook, Sanne Verbaan, Abigail Durrant, Patrick Olivier, and Peter Wright. 2014. A study of the challenges related to DIY assistive technology in the context of children with disabilities. In *Proceedings of the Conference on Designing Interactive Systems* (DIS '14), 597-606. http://dx.doi.org/10.1145/2598510.2598530

[20] Amy Hurst and Jasmine Tobias. 2011. Empowering individuals with do-it-yourself assistive technology. In *Proceedings of the ACM SIGACCESS Conference on Computers and Accessibility* (ASSETS '11), 11-18. http://dx.doi.org/10.1145/2049536.2049541

[21] Shaun K. Kane, Chandrika Jayant, Jacob O. Wobbrock, and Richard E. Ladner. 2009. Freedom to roam: a study of mobile device adoption and accessibility for people with visual and motor disabilities. In *Proceedings of the ACM SIGACCESS Conference on Computers and Accessibility* (ASSETS '09), 115-122. http://dx.doi.org/10.1145/1639642.1639663

[22] Anja Kintsch and Rogerio DePaula. 2002. A framework for the adoption of assistive technology. In *Proceedings of*

SWAAAC: Supporting Learning through Assistive Technology (SWAAC '02), 1-10.

[23] Sergei Kochkin. 2000. MarkeTrak V: "Why my hearing aids are in the drawer": the consumers' perspective. *The Hearing Journal* 53, 2, 34-36.

[24] Richard E. Ladner. 2015. Design for user empowerment. *interactions* 22, 2, 24-29. http://dx.doi.org/10.1145/2723869

[25] Frank R. Lin, John K. Niparko, and Luigi Ferrucci. 2011. Hearing loss prevalence in the United States. *Archives of Internal Medicine* 171, 20, 1851-1853.

[26] Phil Parette and Marcia Scherer. 2004. Assistive technology use and stigma. *Education and Training in Developmental Disabilities* 39, 3, 217-226. https://www.learntechlib.org/p/71944

[27] Prosthetic Ink. Prosthetic Ink–Helping you Stand Tall. Retrieved May 4, 2016 from https://prostheticink.com/

[28] Graham Pullin. 2009. *Design Meets Disability.* MIT Press.

[29] Karim Said, Michele A. Burton, Amy Hurst, and Shaun K. Kane. 2014. Framing the conversation: the role of Facebook conversations in shopping for eyeglasses. In *Proceedings of the ACM Conference on Computer Supported Cooperative Work & Social Computing* (CSCW '14), 652-661. http://dx.doi.org/10.1145/2531602.2531683

[30] Marcia J. Scherer, 1996. *Living in the State of Stuck: How Technology Impacts the Lives of Persons with Disabilities.* Brookline Books.

[31] Kristen Shinohara and Jacob O. Wobbrock. 2011. In the shadow of misperception: assistive technology use and social interactions. In *Proceedings of the SIGCHI Conference on Human Factors in Computing Systems* (CHI '11), 705-714. http://doi.acm.org/10.1145/1978942.1979044

[32] Abigale Stangl, Jeeeun Kim, and Tom Yeh. 2014. 3D printed tactile picture books for children with visual impairments: a design probe. In *Proceedings of the Conference on Interaction Design and Children* (IDC '14), 321-324. http://dx.doi.org/10.1145/2593968.2610482

[33] Susan Leigh Star and James R. Griesemer. Institutional ecology, 'translations' and boundary objects: amateurs and professionals in Berkeley's Museum of Vertebrate Zoology, 1907-39. 1989. *Social Studies of Science* 19, 3, 387-420.

[34] The Alternative Limb Project. The Alternative Limb Project–imaginative and bespoke prosthetics. Retrieved May 4, 2016 from http://www.thealternativelimbproject.com/

[35] Tubetastic Pimps. Tubetastic Pimps Shop. Retrieved May 4, 2016 from http://www.tubetasticpimps.co.uk/

[36] Unyq. UNYQ: Personalized Prosthetics & Orthotics. Retrieved May 4, 2016 from http://unyq.com/

[37] Etienne Wenger. 1999. *Communities of Practice: Learning, Meaning, and Identity.* Cambridge University Press.

How Designing for People With and Without Disabilities Shapes Student Design Thinking

Kristen Shinohara*, Cynthia L. Bennett†, Jacob O. Wobbrock*

Information School*, Human Centered Design and Engineering†

DUB Group | University of Washington

{kshino, bennec3, wobbrock}@uw.edu

ABSTRACT

Despite practices addressing disability in design and advocating user-centered design (UCD) approaches, popular mainstream technologies remain largely inaccessible for people with disabilities. We conducted a design course study investigating how student designers regard disability and explored how designing for both disabled and non-disabled users encouraged students to think about accessibility throughout the design process. Students focused on a design project while learning UCD concepts and techniques, working with people with and without disabilities throughout the project. We found that designing for both disabled and non-disabled users surfaced challenges and tensions in finding solutions to satisfy both groups, influencing students' attitudes toward accessible design. In addressing these tensions, non-functional aspects of accessible design emerged as important complements to functional aspects for users with and without disabilities.

CCS Concepts

• **Human-centered computing~Accessibility theory, concepts and paradigms** • **Human-centered computing~Accessibility design and evaluation methods** • **Social and professional topics~People with disabilities**

Keywords

Accessibility; Assistive Technology; Design; Design Thinking.

1. INTRODUCTION

User-Centered Design (UCD) approaches emphasize the user experience in the design of technologies such as laptops, mobile phones and wearables [16]. In UCD, including people with disabilities is considered part of addressing the user experience, where stakeholders are involved in the design process [29]. Some variations of UCD specifically advocate that people with disabilities should be included in the design process to create technologies that are accessible [18,24,35]. Nevertheless, current mainstream personal technologies are often inaccessible; people who create mainstream technologies do not regularly incorporate accessible design except perhaps to satisfy legal requirements [8]. Thus, despite research espousing the benefits of working with people with disabilities in the design process [18,24,29,35], the lack of accessible mainstream technologies indicates that few designers effectively do so. Promoting inclusion in the design process has not been enough to motivate a sweeping change in making technologies accessible. Instead, accessibility is often approached as "someone else's job," and the responsibility of accessible design is relegated to a niche group of designers [6,7].

ASSETS '16, October 23-26, 2016, Reno, NV, USA
© 2016 ACM. ISBN 978-1-4503-4124-0/16/10...$15.00
DOI:http://dx.doi.org/10.1145/2982142.2982158

Figure 1. A student designer works through a design sketch with a blind "expert user."

Although prior work has demonstrated that designing directly with people with disabilities can improve accessible technology outcomes [1,20,33], we focused our research on which elements of inclusive design influenced student designers to incorporate accessibility in their design process and thinking, not just as a "special topic," or an afterthought of heuristics or guidelines for legal requirements. We conducted a design course study focused on how working with disabled *and* non-disabled users influenced student designers' perspectives on accessibility and design (Figure 1). Although it is well known and accepted that people benefit in awareness and empathy from exposure to people not like themselves [20,33], a specific account of how novice student designers come to think about accessibility (and people with disabilities) during the formative stages of their design thinking has not, to date, been provided. Our account here adds insight into the evolving thinking of students as they address users with and without disabilities and become aware of the need for accessibility in their design thinking. Our study demonstrates how expanding accessible design to include a broader, diverse view of users can positively influence the design process.

We found that designing for both disabled and non-disabled users surfaced unique tensions between non-functional and functional needs across both user groups. We use the term "non-functional" to refer to aspects of the design that are not related to how the technology works, *per se*, but other factors influencing the use and perception of the technology, like social appropriateness, professional presentation, adherence to decorum (is it loud during a work meeting when people should be quiet?), and so on. Addressing functional/non-functional tensions challenged students to re-assess their view of disability and accessibility, and stretched their capacity as designers of accessible solutions. Overall, engaging tensions that emerged from designing for two user populations challenged students to balance requirements from both sides, encouraging them to shift from ableist perspectives of disability toward a more inclusive approach to design overall. This work offers implications for accessible design based on improving ways users with disabilities can be included in the design process and the likely beneficial effects that has on how designers think.

2. BACKGROUND AND RELATED WORK

People choose from a variety of technologies to help them do more. However, most mainstream technologies are not accessible, and people with disabilities instead use assistive technologies. Inaccessible technologies are indicative of a shortcoming in most current approaches to technology design. We therefore see an opportunity to encourage technology designers to incorporate accessibility into their design thinking and work [10]. We separate related work into two categories, disability-specific design approaches and accessibility as taught in design courses.

2.1 Disability-Specific Design

User-Centered Design (UCD) emphasizes inclusion by focusing on users and the user experience in the design process [29]. UCD relies on inclusion—inviting others to participate in the process— also to address issues of disability. In theory, emphasizing the user at the center of the design process *should* provide opportunities for designers to seek out users with disabilities and become familiar with accessibility issues [29]. But in practice, the dearth of mainstream technologies that are accessible out-of-the-box without added accommodation suggests that most designers tend to assume an audience without disabilities.

Research has shown that rather than expecting disability to fall under the umbrella of "user experience," specifically encouraging accessibility and working with users with disabilities can help designers create more accessible technologies [1,20,24,33]. In contrast with design approaches like UCD, where designers tend to assume a non-disabled target user population, disability-specific approaches explicitly emphasize that to make design accessible, designers should include people with disabilities in the design process itself. Popular approaches include: *Universal Design (UD)* [1,21], which focuses on principles like equitable use, flexibility in use, and simple and intuitive use; *User-Sensitive Inclusive Design (USID)* [24], which emphasizes getting to know disabled users and focusing on specific needs; *Design for User Empowerment (DUE)* [18], which includes people with disabilities as the designers and engineers creating accessible technologies; and *Ability-Based Design (ABD)* [35], which emphasizes ability, and tries to design systems aware of and responsive to those abilities. Such disability-centric focus is a lingering aspect of assistive technology's relationship with rehabilitation engineering [6,17], the result of which is a "special" category of technologies specific to people with disabilities [4,19,27].

Assistive technologies may bridge the need that people with disabilities have for technical access. But it is increasingly common for assistive technologies, created exclusively for disabled users, to have mainstream counterparts with the same capabilities. An example is a refreshable Braille note taker, which has similar functionality as a laptop. Disability-specific design approaches help create technologies that people with disabilities can use, but the specificity of the approach often results in technologies *only* disabled people can use. In comparison, mainstream technologies are typically only usable by *non-disabled* people. Unfortunately, disability-only devices perpetuate an ableist view; mainstream devices remain inaccessible because "special" accommodations are available for those who cannot use them [19]. Ableism is a tendency to consider non-disabled people as superior to disabled people; the consequences of ableism have far-reaching historical and socially detrimental effects [4,9,19]. These topics are outside the scope of this study, but we highlight ableism to raise awareness of implications of design that assumes non-disabled users [34].

Including people with disabilities in the design process has been studied as a way to help designers create accessible technologies, but focusing solely on disability results in a schism: separate technologies for people with disabilities and for people without disabilities, regardless of whether the capability exists to make a holistic solution accessible to all. Despite positive outcomes when designers work with disabled users, more must be done to raise awareness of who benefits from accessibility and how. One way to address gaps in research and practice has been to focus on what designers do and why [15,26,36], and how to effect change. We studied novice designers to understand specific characteristics of inclusion that shaped their design thinking when required to create solutions for both disabled and non-disabled users.

2.2 Accessibility in Design Courses

Previous research in post-secondary design courses examined how college students address disability in requirements gathering, brainstorming, and prototyping solutions [1,20,33]. These courses introduced engineering and computer science students to accessibility, highlighting the benefits of working with users with disabilities. Ludi and Waller et al. [20,33] focused primarily on requirements gathering and the engineering process. Bigelow [1] incorporated UD principles in engineering courses to get students into a more human-centered mindset in design. In these studies, students worked directly with people with disabilities in at least one instance throughout the design process. In our study, we expanded opportunities for students and users with disabilities to interact by facilitating multiple feedback sessions throughout the course. Further research in UD in education facilitates ways to increase awareness of accessibility in teaching and learning [2]. Such research confirms that prioritizing accessibility and including people with disabilities improves understanding about disabled technology users' needs. Yet, while UD in education promises to increase student exposure to diverse abilities, strategies for inclusive design tend to remain disability-specific. Training engineering and computer science students to include disability in design may result only in functional disability-specific solutions, it may not translate into accessible *mainstream* technologies. To avoid creating this bias, we expanded our course project to challenge students to design for both disabled and non-disabled users in an effort to promote the view that disability is just one part of diversity among technology users. We purposefully structured the course to engage disability not as separate from design, but as part of a greater socio-technical community of users.

3. METHOD

To investigate how inclusion increases designer awareness of accessible design, we built on disability-specific design approaches with some modifications. We conducted a design course study with student designers as they learned UCD, focusing our investigation on how students engaged users with disabilities, and on student reactions and reflections throughout the design process. We built on inclusive design approaches by staying close to the UCD process, which also minimized cost and resource requirements. We modified inclusive design approaches by having student designers work with *both* disabled and non-disabled users to facilitate awareness from different perspectives. We prompted students to reflect on their experiences, specifically how they viewed and interacted with disability and design.

The curriculum of our undergraduate-level course on design thinking—a course utilizing Norman's and Buxton's popular texts

[3,25]—focused primarily on needs assessment, ideation, low- and high-fidelity prototyping, and user-testing. Students conducted interviews, created personas and scenarios, generated conceptual models, sketched and ideated, created paper-based and interactive prototypes, applied usability heuristics, and tested their designs with users. We set an expectation that accessible design was part of design overall and a requirement to design both for users with and without disabilities. The rationale for tasking students to design for both user groups was that rather than designing a "specialized" technology specifically for people with disabilities, students were to design an accessible technology usable and appealing to anyone. Students worked in groups and each group was paired with a person with a disability. They were largely left on their own to find non-disabled users, although we facilitated in-class paired feedback sessions, heuristic evaluations, and usability testing to assess non-disabled user interactions. Each week, students were introduced to a new concept and participated in activities to gain experience working with different techniques around that concept. Students applied this new knowledge in a term-long project to develop a usable prototype by the end of the course.

Table 1. "Project A" groups and expert users.

Project A: Real-Time Augmented Reality Navigation		
Grp.	Student Designers	Expert User
G1	S12 (M), S22 (M), S41 (M), S31 (F)	E1 (M), Blind
G2	S1 (F), S26 (M), S28 (F), S36 (M)	E2 (M), Blind
G3	S19 (M), S21 (M), S33 (M), S35 (F)	E3 (F), Low Vision
G4	S6 (F), S8 (M), S23 (M), S34 (M)	E4 (F) Low Vision
G5	S2 (F), S9 (M), S15 (F)	E5 (F), Blind
G6	S11 (M), S13 (M), S25 (F), S42 (M)	E6 (F), Blind

Table 2. "Project B" groups and expert users.

Project B: Real-Time Live Captioning		
Grp.	Student Designers	Expert User
G7	S14 (M), S30 (M), S38 (M), S39 (M)	E7 (F), Deaf
G8	S3 (M), S5 (F), S20 (M), S32 (M)	E8 (F) Hard of Hearing
G9	S10 (F), S16 (F), S29 (M), S37 (M)	E9 (M), Deaf
G10	S4 (M), S7 (M), S27 (M)	E10 (F) Hard of Hearing
G11	S17 (M), S18 (M), S24 (F), S40 (M)	E11 (M), Deaf

3.1 Participants

Forty-two undergraduate students (12 female) participated in the study. No students had any known disabilities, few students had design experience, and only a handful of students had interacted with people with disabilities prior to the course. Students worked with 11 (seven female) users with disabilities. We referred to users with disabilities as "expert users" to reinforce their expertise as users of accessible technology. Expert users were recruited through local disability groups and assistive technology listservs: Department of Services for the Blind, National Federation of the Blind, Hearing Loss Association, and the university disability club. The study was restricted to people with sensory disabilities.

3.2 Design Projects

Students' groups were randomly assigned design projects: "Project A" groups worked with blind or low vision expert users and were tasked to design an application providing real-time augmented reality (walking) navigation; "Project B" groups worked with deaf or hard of hearing expert users and were tasked to design an application providing real-time captioning of nearby speakers.

Groups met with expert users four times throughout the 10-week term: interviewing, iterating on brainstormed ideas, eliciting feedback on sketches, and then on paper prototypes, and conducting usability tests on interactive high-fidelity prototypes. Each session with expert users lasted approximately one hour, during which time student groups shared design artifacts for feedback. Expert users evaluated the final designs.

At the beginning of the term, a question and answer forum with a blind guest speaker familiarized students with appropriate etiquette for interacting with people with disabilities. The course also included relevant readings and introductory lectures to orient students to existing approaches to design for diverse populations: User-Sensitive Inclusive Design [24], Ability-Based Design [35], Universal Design [21], Participatory Design [28], Design for Social Acceptance [30], and Value Sensitive Design [13]. We consider it compulsory to include design approaches specific to disability and related issues due to course expectations to create accessible designs. Tables 1 and 2 describe groups, expert users, and projects.

3.3 Data and Analysis

Our data comprise student assignments including weekly reflective journals, interview protocols and summaries, observations, brainstorms, sketches, design rationales, user testing results and heuristic evaluations, final design specifications, design process books, and expert user evaluations of student designs. Expert users evaluated student work mid-term and at the end of the course.

Data were analyzed deductively and inductively following systematic qualitative data analysis methods [23,32]. Deductive codes were generated from related work to accentuate known issues about assistive technology use [27,30,31]. Two coders openly and separately coded two groups' data to generate an inductive code list, and discussed and refined code definitions. (See Table 3 for a summary of codes.) Similar concepts that arose were discussed and combined where relevant, and connections were drawn across categories. Then, the two coders independently coded 10% of the student journal entries. A Cohen's Kappa calculated on the coders' results yielded $\kappa = 0.79$, indicating strong agreement between the coders. A single researcher coded the remaining data. All researchers discussed and confirmed the final categories and themes. Analysis focused on how students considered disability as they developed an understanding of design.

4. FINDINGS

All groups successfully created high-fidelity prototypes that they could test with expert users at the end of the 10-week term (Figure 2). Expert users judged that the final designs met their expectations. Thus, our findings confirm that inclusion of diverse users can indeed influence designers toward accessible solutions. We also found new evidence that working with *both* disabled and non-disabled users surfaced different tensions and challenges that encouraged designers to consider accessibility as a key component of all design, not just a specialty, guideline fulfillment, or after-thought. We focus on how tensions across non-functional and functional issues for both groups of users manifested.

4.1 Perceptions of Accessibility

Tensions that emerged from designing for both disabled and non-disabled users were different from challenges typically faced when designing for only one group or the other. These tensions influenced student perceptions of the difficulty or feasibility of accessible design. Learning about expert users' experiences as disabled people encouraged students to re-assess the need for accessible design, while including non-disabled users prioritized non-functional needs. For example, working with expert user E2 emphasized the disparate state of technologies:

We have also paid more attention to refining our choices regarding the placement, sizing, and labeling of inputs and information, all areas in which small changes can modify the effectiveness and physical usability of the application. These changes reflect, for me, a broader change in my understanding of design and accessibility. E2's encouragement to investigate the existing marketplace showed me just how separate the industrial fields of design and design for those with disabilities have become. Seeing him use his devices firsthand has demonstrated why that practice is flawed, ignorant, and impractical. The structure of this course has also been encouraging for me in thinking about the inclusion of users in the design process. (S26, Journal 9)

Table 3. A summary of deductive and inductive codes.

Deductive codes from prior work
Ability and equal access: just like everyone else
Aesthetics and form factor, user appearance
Avoidance
Safety and help
Attitude
Ignorance
Contextual influence
Employment
Technology type: mainstream or proprietary
Breakdowns: functional and social
Social expectations, transitional encounters
User confidence, showing technical savviness, educating/sharing
User self-consciousness
Mis/perceptions: social, technical, contextual, neutral
Inductive codes
Perceptions, expectations: learning and design
Attitude, reflection, learning: disability, accessibility, design thinking
Tensions, challenges: design for disability, cost, complexity
Techniques and tools
Design decisions: accessibility, usability, prioritizing, assumptions
Working with users with disabilities, in groups: prior experiences

Indeed, the challenges we put before students stretched their experience with design and disability; addressing both target user populations was daunting, particularly if student designers had little or no experience with design or disability. As S26 discussed, student perceptions of accessibility changed as they continued to work with expert users. Initially, students had altruistic reactions to the design project. However, despite feel-good attitudes and a desire to "be helpful" to people with disabilities, altruism stemmed from a sympathy toward disability. Sympathetic attitudes are not necessarily a bad thing—sympathy exposes misperceptions and assumptions—but sympathy can manifest as ableist and create barriers to understanding and creating accessible design. Only six students had substantial interactions with people with disabilities before the course, such as having a close friend who is blind. Fifteen students reported limited interactions, from meeting blind massage therapists to grandparents with hearing loss. Of those, four had working interactions, such as briefly tutoring a deaf student. Thus, few of the 42 students interacted with people with disabilities before the course, and almost all students expressed discomfort and self-consciousness prior to meeting expert users, despite the guest lecture about appropriate etiquette. S30 related common concerns:

The nervousness comes from the fact that I'm not quite sure how to act around [disabled people] and I really don't want to say the wrong thing and upset my client. The last thing I want to do is offend them in any way since I have a lot of respect for them. I can't

really imagine what it would be like to live without either sight or hearing or even both. I thought about what it would be like before and every time I come to the conclusion that there is no way that I could even come close to imagining it. (S30, Journal 2)

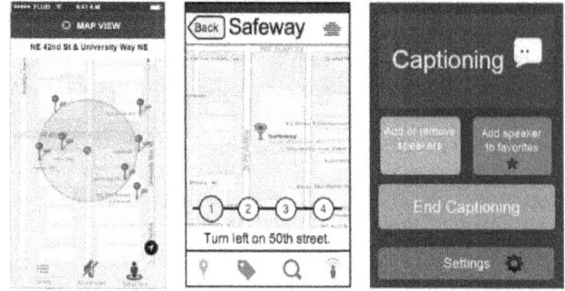

Figure 2. Student designs (from left): G1's and G5's way-finding map interfaces. G11's captioning-in-progress.

Like S30, student designers were self-conscious about their own ignorance of disability. S1 worried she might offend others:

I felt sad and was worried that I could unintentionally hurt [people with disabilities] through my ignorance. The worst fear was sparked by blind people and there were a couple of reasons. First of all, I consider myself a visual thinker, so the loss of vision seems one of the most terrifying complications to me. Therefore, I am worried that I can unintentionally hurt a blind person—I feel so sorry for blind people, but they want to be treated like everyone else. (S1, Journal 2)

Ignorance and discomfort were grounded in inexperience with disability—students were self-conscious about being offensive because they did not know what was acceptable or unacceptable behavior around people with disabilities—the knowledge void was filled by ableist perspectives. The view that, "loss of vision seems one of the most terrifying complications," highlight that students focused on the disability ahead of the person. Understandably, students were unaware of the ableist tendency in this thinking, and they were not expected to know or think otherwise. But what are the implications of such thinking? Do designers with an ableist view create inaccessible technologies? Our findings indicate that students initially assumed it unnecessary to include accessibility:

Working with a person with a disability will affect the considerations I put into the project. If I were making a device for someone without disabilities, I sadly would not have considered factoring in people with disabilities. (S16, Journal 2)

Because he was not disabled, S28 did not think about accessibility:

[E2] had me thinking about things that I don't really pay much attention to, because I have normal vision. (S28, Journal 3)

S28 considered an experience vastly different than his own:

Talking to our expert user made me think about things that I don't really usually think about. That is why our expert user's input is valuable. I could see that being even more evident once we get feedback after presenting our ideas to him. (S28, Journal 4)

Working with expert users, students became aware of the implications of inaccessibility. S36 disregarded what he was taught about accessibility, until he noticed how it affected his expert user:

To be honest, I never find the value of labeling my button when I design a website or other product, because when the professor said we need to focus on the accessibility of our design, I often just let it slip away. However, I realized the importance of labeling when I heard my interviewee saying unlabeled buttons are the most frustrating factor when using applications. (S36, Journal 3)

Because we cannot know exactly what students thought, it would be hard to say whether working with disabled users eliminated ableist tendencies in students or not. But S28 and S36's comments were representative of what students reported as the weeks went on, and here the data confirms findings in prior work [20,33]: Interacting with expert users opened students' minds to a diverse view on accessibility. More time with expert users was beneficial—misconceptions faded as students and expert users developed friendly working relationships. As students adjusted to using appropriate disability etiquette (i.e., asking if a person needs help instead of assuming their impairment means they need help) and overcame communication barriers, the unknowns that made design for disability seem impossible became more passé. As S17 noted:

I have also found more confidence working with deaf people through our interactions with E11. Trying to tiptoe around the fact that he is deaf wastes valuable time we could use discussing button layout and font sizes. (S17, Journal 8)

Multiple sessions helped students learn about their expert user as a person, not a disability, and helped students to learn from their mistakes; one awkward meeting would make the next more productive as students learned better ways to ask questions. Students found that incorporating accessibility did not detrimentally affect the rest of their design; instead it could help the design become more usable overall:

Working with accessibility as one of your central focuses when designing a product does seem to improve the quality and usability of the final design overall. What I was surprised about is that I don't feel this is just because an accessibility focus forces the design to be "easier to use," but because the focus of people with accessibility issues is to be able to behave just like everyone else. Thus, working with people with hearing loss, sight loss, movement problems, etc., helps you focus with laser-precision on the most important and basic human needs. (S40, Journal 8)

As S40 mentioned, students learned that accessibility did not have to be an excessive burden on design, but could be another way to improve design overall. Key to this understanding was for students to be able to see: (1) the multiple issues at play for the various users, and (2) that the students, as designers themselves, could meet the challenges emerging from the tensions between the different issues. We next discuss how a focus on disabled and non-disabled users gave rise to both functional and non-functional issues.

4.2 Functional and Non-Functional Factors

Students struggled to bridge functional and non-functional needs of users with and without disabilities. Students were overwhelmed by what they needed to learn about how disabled people used technologies. Ableist attitudes at first narrowed their perspective: students considered the disability before the person, sometimes myopically focused on functional issues, despite the emphasis in UCD on holistic user *experience*. To address disabled user needs, students began by asking, "what functionality will address impairments?" rather than other concerns, like what a user might find socially acceptable or aesthetically pleasing. Indeed, S2 considered "intuitive aesthetics" unnecessary for blind users:

Though our product will still have to be usable for able-bodied people, it will be interesting to design something that has to have a very intuitive layout rather than intuitive aesthetics. For a blind person, it doesn't necessarily have to look pretty, but the way things are laid out has to provide smooth navigation. I think that might be one of the biggest challenges we'll face; how to organize the features we want to include. (S2, Journal 2)

There exist functional differences between disabled and non-disabled users, but the language S2 used reflected an assumption that disabled users may not care about "aesthetics" as much as non-disabled users. The benefit of working directly with expert users was that students learned about the non-functional needs they otherwise might have overlooked. Expert user E7 emphasized that accessibility was more than just about functionality, it included her busy schedule, safety, and financial security:

Learning about how E7's iPhone was her go-to device was really valuable, because we were then able to identify that we should be designing for an iPhone. We knew it needed to be cheap and simple, because E7's a busy woman, and she's a college student with a light budget. These kinds of facts about our expert user that we learned through the interview helped create more physical and practical constraints on our design. (S14, Journal 8)

S14 highlighted real experiences he was privy to and could draw on as he worked with E7. S21's expert user also prioritized non-functional issues, like safety and customizability:

Our client emphasized that her priorities are customizable fonts, portability, and the fact that she is a single woman with a vision impairment. What she meant with that last bit is that she tries hard not to look lost and vulnerable when she's alone and using her mobile devices. (S21, Journal 4)

The non-functional needs enumerated by expert users contrasted with the function-only view that students initially held. Students benefited from working with expert users who gave feedback highlighting non-functional needs. Students benefited from also designing for non-disabled users because it challenged students to strategize ways to address tensions exposed by non-functional needs. Specifically, students did not try to "imagine what it would be like" to be a user with a disability as a strategy (which tends to be an ableist exercise); they learned that expert users prioritized non-functional characteristics important to any user. Understanding that characteristics like safety and social appeal were important to expert users and non-disabled users alike made students aware of what they had (or did not have) in common with expert users. S16's group referenced its understanding of social decorum and cell phone use supported by feedback from E9:

…we examined the social implications of always having a phone out and reading off a phone while talking with someone. Since so many people find that to be rude, we began to explore ways of allowing our users to read the text while staying engaged in the conversation. E9 was a great help with this by pointing out how important eye contact and facial expressions are to him. (S16, Journal 4)

Another non-functional concern unique to expert users was the aspect of disability itself. Managing an image-as-disabled was an experience of disability that students may not have anticipated.

One of her biggest concerns was the aesthetic of the device and how it should be discreet enough so as to not give away her disabilities. This point has had a conscious impact on my mentality when going about doing the sketches. (S3, Journal 4)

Specifically, some non-functional issues were unique to the experience of disability, and it made sense that as time went on, these issues organically arose:

Perhaps the most important discovery was that two particular factors were most important to our target user: accuracy and unobtrusiveness… She also said that she wanted the application not to call unnecessary attention to her hearing loss; she did not want it [to] be stigmatizing. (S7, Journal 3)

S7's expert user prioritized accurate functional accuracy and unobtrusiveness. Although these two issues are not always opposing, for a person with a disability, they could be. We discuss how students addressed some of these tensions in the next section.

4.3 Tensions and Opportunities

Students applied different strategies to challenges highlighted by tensions between functional and non-functional issues. Our findings indicate that having a requirement to also design for non-disabled users gave students another tool with which to strategize. Like S7's group above, S24's group learned the severity of the non-functional issue of drawing "unnecessary attention" because E11 was less likely to use technology that was not discreet.

We were also able to learn what is important to them when it comes to assistive hearing technology; for example, E11 made it very clear that inconspicuousness is important to them in a product–if something isn't discreet or just about invisible, they are much less likely to use it. (S24, Journal 3)

For E11, functional success alone did not necessarily translate into access. Students took this feedback to heart. E11's group reflected:

Glasses were chosen because, as a group, we figured that holding a device up while talking, or listening to someone would be distracting for all parties involved. We wanted to reduce this social awkwardness as much as possible. (E11's group design rationale, see Figure 3)

Figure 3. A sketch of E11's group's glasses design, described as: "designed to have a profile of modern 'hip' glasses."

With a clearer awareness of what they, as non-disabled users, had in common with expert users, students sometimes referred to a non-disabled understanding of non-functional issues to find solutions. S10's group referenced its understanding of social cues when deciding on form factor:

In my experience, most people find it rude when people look down at their phone while in a conversation and avoid eye contact. This is why our group decided to avoid a mobile device or other device where a user would have to look away from the person they are speaking with to comprehend the conversation. (S10, Journal 5)

Indeed, students focused on what users have in common:

When looking to create a product for those with and without a visual impairment, it is a great start to focus on what they can do in common... (S23, Journal 3)

Another strategy was to start from expert user's requirements and find ways it might also appeal to non-disabled users:

He constantly suggests things that would make using applications easier for him, and we've figured out ways to turn the interactions that facilitate his accessibility into cool design features that people without disabilities will find useful and interesting. (S31, Journal 6)

S23's group circled between the requirements of both user groups:

We need to constantly be looking back at the problems that we set out to solve with our design. Is this helping people navigate even

with visual impairment? Will this let people explore what is around them? By continually referring to these questions and considering if we are still answering a definitive yes then I have confidence our design will stay on track. (S23, Journal 4)

Finally, some challenges that students encountered were due to inaccessible aspects of tools and techniques used and these challenges highlighted the shortcomings of UCD for accessible design. For example, most prototyping techniques assumed that users can see representations, and students found it difficult to work around the inaccessibility of paper prototyping for visually impaired users. The interchangeable parts on S6's perceived flexible prototype fell apart during testing:

For paper prototyping, we tried just having buttons placed on top of the paper. When we did that, it would be lifted and the pieces would fall off. Eventually we got tape to help stick the pieces on, which did help, but the delay made it not as helpful as it could have been. (S6, Journal 8)

In the event that a technique was inaccessible, we encouraged students to seek creative solutions on their own and they were mildly successful at devising accessible workarounds. In one example, S13's team worked around paper prototyping by "having [E6] test the application on her own phone... and a team member voiced the computer and spoke appropriate feedback." Although interacting with the sleek, glass touch screen of a smartphone might feel like a high-fidelity experience, the fidelity of the interaction was considerably lower due to the draft script.

Not all groups were successful at workarounds. E9's group tried to facilitate a realistic user experience by creating a high-fidelity prototype with glasses that captioned in real-time. The group tried to Wizard-of-Oz the interaction with a "captioner" who live-typed conversations that appeared on a tablet in front of the user (Figure 4). The transition from typist to screen was slower than speech-to-text engines and did not create the desired experience. E9 inadvertently relied on lip-reading and an ASL interpreter rather than the prototype, missing much of what appeared on the screen:

Although the captions weren't showing, we felt like we were very close because there were times during the testing where the captioning was on time and E9 used our prototype. We also knew we were close to captioning fast enough because we noticed that the second after E9 would look up to read lips, the captions would almost always appear at the same time. As far as improvements go, we feel the only improvement we can make would be to type faster or to find a way to have speech to text technology be implemented, but the latter would be going towards the actual product rather than a prototype and we don't have the resources for that technology. (S29, Journal 9)

Figure 4. E9 tests a high-fidelity prototype, simulating glasses (he is wearing) displaying captions in real time (on the tablet).

Many user-centered techniques and tools make assumptions about ability. Paper prototyping assumes vision, few prototyping tools support speech-to-text functionality, and students struggled at times to work around these issues. Students persevered with few resources, but it is unclear how much more successful they could have been if tools supported their accessibility needs.

Ideally non-functional issues were brainstormed and prototyped with regard to user-experience, but unique disability-related issues distracted students from these considerations. The design prompt for disabled and non-disabled users challenged students not to disregard one for the other.

4.4 Changing Attitudes Toward Design

Weekly journals served the purpose of tracking issues, difficulties with subject matter, or problems within groups. Journals provided rich data on student effort throughout the term, including how accessibility requirements challenged and changed student perspectives on design for disability. S36 expressed a common concern students had early on about their ability to create a design that would adequately address tradeoffs for both user groups.

I think one aspect that might detract me from my design is the over emphasis on accessibility and make [sic] the product significantly more difficult to use by people without disabilities, and often impossible to use by people with a different type of disability. One thing that I've [sic] keep reminding myself in the process of design is how to balance my design between normal people and people with disability. (S36, Journal 3)

Fortunately, attitudes about possible negative impacts of accessible design and the needs of "normal people" gave way, in the end, to a more enlightened understanding. The impact of expert users was evident, as S37 wrote:

I think I've learned a lot about disabilities by working with E9. Lip reading, accessibility devices, and the challenges of being deaf have all been illuminated to me. A lot of my preconceived notions about people with disabilities have proven to be false, and I feel much more comfortable interacting with someone who may have a disability. I have learned that design can be made universal for people, regardless of the level of their abilities. (S37, Journal 8)

The reflective journals provided a way to track student perceptions and ideas. S25 reflected on how she felt she had changed:

Personally, I believe my perspective on designing for accessibility has done a complete '180', so to speak. Towards the beginning of the class, I was afraid I would have limited knowledge to contribute to my team, because it was a realm I knew very little about. Truthfully, when I had wireframed or designed web pages in the past, it never occurred to me that it is so crucial to design for accessibility. I had always thought, "what is some cool iconography I could use to make this look modern and minimalistic?" Now I just kind of think back on that, and laugh at myself. Design is much more multidimensional, and I not only feel like I've grown with my team, but also as an individual designer with more empathy for all users. (S25, Journal 9)

Similarly, S28 shared how her expert user had influenced her:

I think that having these meetings with our expert user has made me think more actively about accessibility for all. I honestly now find myself always thinking about how disabled people might use an object or interact with a system. I have also experienced having to weigh decisions regarding aesthetics and "innovation" based on their usability. Although I can't say I know for sure what I would do whenever decisions regarding these things are to be made, I now give it a little more thought. (S28, Journal 8)

Toward the end of the course, S13 wrote:

I also used to think that accessibility design is a separate branch of design, but that is not at all design. We can design for accessibility by considering the same parameters you would consider for a regular design and just thinking of different use cases. (S13, Journal 9)

Corroborating S25's, S28's, and S13's sentiment, most students confessed they expected design for users with disabilities to be more difficult than for non-disabled users. But, at the course conclusion, 21 out of 36 students admitted that designing for disability was not as hard as they thought it would be. Ten reported no change, and only 2 felt it was harder. Interactions with expert users helped students gain an appreciation for accessibility.

5. DISCUSSION

Despite emphasis on the user in UCD, current mainstream personal technology design is predominately inaccessible, disregarding disabled users as part of that user-base. To understand how design thinking changed when disability was emphasized, we investigated how designing for disabled and non-disabled users in the UCD process influenced student perspectives. Our findings about student attitudes and perspectives on accessibility corroborated related work indicating that separating disability and mainstream design approaches reinforces the notion that accessibility is someone else's job [2,20,33]. We add to the existing body of research in UD in education [2] an empirical study of students tasked with inclusively designing for people with disabilities in a classroom setting. Our findings expand on strategies bolstering awareness of the importance of accessibility. We found evidence of ableist attitudes implicit in students' initial approaches to accessibility, confirming and extending work by Ludi [20] and Waller [33], that interacting with people with disabilities can help students develop a better understanding of disability and design. In distilling implications for accessible design, we identify key characteristics that facilitated awareness of the disabled experience as it might contribute to a designer's conception of design overall.

5.1 Agency in Accessible Design

The assumptions about design and disability that student designers initially had led us to understand that most first-time designers do not typically come to technology design with an appreciation of the needs of disabled users. Social psychology literature informs us that student designers' expectations around disability are almost certainly shaped by previous experience [5,22]. Students' prior experiences led them to feel uncomfortable with the idea of working with people with disabilities, and some students exhibited ableist views. If students did not regularly engage with disabled people before the course (and most did not), they were unfamiliar with how to approach and interact with people with disabilities.

Students situated their perceptions toward disabled users as a stigmatized "other" [11,12,14]. S1's confession that, "I... was worried I could unintentionally hurt them through my ignorance... I feel so sorry for blind people," revealed bias: as a sighted person, she could not imagine the loss of vision and concluded blind people have it impossibly harder, in a way she could only pity. Sidelining the disabled experience, or like S1, pitying disability, led students to feel self-conscious about offending expert users. Indeed, present-day society socializes disability-sympathetic, if not patronizing and ableist, behaviors [4,10]. Students came to the course influenced by social and cultural stereotypes, and their reactions to disability were likely biased by assumptions of ability. It was not that students felt they should not design for disabled users, but they believed non-disabled users were the presumptive *de facto* target audience.

Simply put, in their role as designers, students did not think it was their job to design for disability.

One way ableism manifested as a barrier to accessible design was that students considered themselves "normal" and addressed accessible needs as separate from needs of non-disabled users. Disability-specific approaches can feed ableist attitudes perpetuating a divide between users with and without disabilities. A divide does not mean one user group is superior to another, but there was evidence that students already had these tendencies likely indicating ableist attitudes toward design for disability. Opening up the concept of the "user" to include disabled and non-disabled people gives more stakeholders an equal chance to influence design. With this requirement, students were prevented from separating "normal" from accessible.

The guest speaker was helpful in setting expectations and clarifying etiquette, the single question and answer forum did not sufficiently provide the perspectives needed to persuade students to weigh accessibility seriously. Instead, perceptions about accessibility and disability changed with increased time spent working with expert users. Addressing challenges in design for disabled and non-disabled users helped students cultivate open-minded views of accessibility, bolstered by their growing ability and confidence as designers to make design accessible. What does this mean for the broader view of design overall? Including people with disabilities involves more than just face time [20,33], it involves enmeshing disabled *and* non-disabled viewpoints throughout the design process. Our findings translate into a need for designers to consider disabled users as part of the whole user base, not as a separate group or set of requirements. When student designers regarded accessibility as part of their larger aims they: (1) gave agency to the disabled user as a *person* (not a disability) with an equal stake in design outcomes like any non-disabled user, and (2) they saw *themselves* as having agency and skill as designers to create technology that fulfilled needs for both groups.

5.2 Implications for Accessible Design

We compile our findings into implications for incorporating accessibility in design. Designers should include disabled and non-disabled users because challenges arise that are unique to the intersection of both groups. Our study suggests extended exposure to expert users helped students understand how the disabled experience amounts to more than functional limitations. Students learned about non-functional issues expert users experienced, such as social use, safety, and discretion, and saw how important such issues were. Although these issues are important for non-disabled users, too often functional needs in disability-centric design overshadow or complicate non-functional issues for disabled users. For example, text-to-speech was a popular design component in projects for blind and low-vision users, but some expert users were sensitive to talking devices attracting attention, for social or safety reasons. Finally, requiring two user groups was one way to challenge ableism by creating a socio-technical space where disabled and non-disabled users were equal contributors.

Tensions between functional and non-functional issues led to the second implication: designers should consider functional *and* non-functional features in their design. In finding ways to bridge different requirements for the two user groups, student designers needed to find solutions that would work across the tensions that emerged. In addition, it was through the process of addressing these tensions between seemingly disparate groups (users with and without disabilities) that students could see that they were capable of creating *accessible*, rather than just *assistive*, technologies.

Our data suggest that the tensions students faced while designing for disabled and non-disabled users and the ways they addressed those challenges allowed students to see the power of their own agency. We recall this sentiment by S25: "Design is much more multidimensional, and I not only feel like I've grown with my team, but also as an individual designer with more empathy for all users."

6. LIMITATIONS AND FUTURE WORK

Our study is limited by students' novice design experience. We captured students' perspectives, but we do not know how professional designers would handle similar challenges, and we cannot be sure how *learning* design may impact perspectives. We did not evaluate how specific tools and techniques contributed to design thinking, despite some of the accessibility challenges uncovered in UCD methods. Although we recruited disabled expert users, we did not recruit non-disabled users, and students' success reaching non-disabled users on their own was varied. Future work will involve explicit recruitment from both populations. In addition, teaching multiple design approaches facilitated an opportunity to compare across them, but our study was not designed to facilitate controlled comparisons. Including approaches in a curriculum that otherwise does not train students to design for disability strongly restricts any pedagogical conclusions and we refrain from making any. Despite this, student experiences and design artifacts speak to the veracity of our findings. Future work will focus on nuanced differences and involve professional designers.

7. CONCLUSION

We studied how student designers cultivate their design thinking when tasked with designing for users with and without disabilities. Addressing tensions between functional and non-functional factors revealed challenges at the intersection of designing for both user groups simultaneously. When students engaged requirements to design for users with and without disabilities, they broadened their conception of accessible design. We distilled our findings into implications for accessible design: (1) target users should include those with and without disabilities (not just one or the other); and (2) designers should consider functional and non-functional elements across both user groups. In tackling these issues, students not only changed their perception that accessible design is possible and feasible, but also that they had the ability and responsibility to achieve accessible design.

Working with users in the design process leads to useful designs [16], and working with disabled users is likely to produce more accessible designs [1,18,20,24,33]. Yet, the dearth of accessible mainstream technologies reveals an opportunity to understand how designers are (or are not) addressing design for disability. Although inclusion of disabled users is effective, more needs to be done to effect change in the way designers approach their own practice of design. Increasing the number of technologies usable by people with disabilities, whether assistive or mainstream, is a positive shift because it improves the ability for a diverse population of users to participate in society. But having similar functionality in different devices is not the same as making all technologies accessible. Thus, we see an opportunity to change how designers engage disability and incorporate accessibility in their overall understanding of technology design.

8. ACKNOWLEDGMENTS

This work was supported in part by the National Science Foundation under grants IIS-1217627, IIS-1230435, and IIS-0952786. Any opinions, findings, conclusions or recommendations expressed in this work are those of the authors and do not necessarily reflect those of any supporter listed above.

9. REFERENCES

[1] Bigelow, K.E. 2012. Designing for Success: Developing Engineers Who Consider Universal Design Principles. 25, 3 (2012), 211–225.

[2] Burgstahler, S. 2015. *Universal design in higher education : from principles to practice*. Cambridge, Massachusetts : Harvard Education Press.

[3] Buxton, W. 2007. *Sketching user experiences : getting the design right and the right design*. Elsevier/Morgan Kaufmann.

[4] Charlton, J.I. 1998. *Nothing about us without us: disability oppression and empowerment*. Univ. of California Press.

[5] Christiansen, C.H. 1999. Defining Lives: Occupation as Identity: An Essay on Competence, Coherence, and the Creation of Meaning. *The American Journal of Occupational Therapy*. 53, 6 (Nov. 1999), 547–558.

[6] Cook, A.M. and Hussey, S.M. 2002. *Assistive technologies : principles and practice*. St. Louis : Mosby.

[7] Cook, A.M., Polgar, J.M. and Livingston, N.J. 2010. Need- and Task-Based Design and Evaluation. *Design and Use of Assistive Technology: Social, Technical, Ethical, and Economic Challenges*. M.M.K. Oishi, I.M. Mitchell, and H. f. M.V. der Loos, eds. Springer. 41–48.

[8] Crutchfield, B. 2016. ADA and the Internet: ADA Settlements-Fitting Accessibility Compliance into Your Product Lifecycle. *SSB Bart Group*.

[9] Davis, F.D. 1989. Perceived Usefulness, Perceived Ease of Use, and User Acceptance of Information Technology. *MIS Quarterly*. 13, 3 (1989), 319–340.

[10] DePoy, E. and Gilson, S. 2014. *Branding and designing disability : reconceptualising disability studies*. Abingdon, Oxon : Routledge.

[11] Elliott, G.C., Ziegler, H.L., Altman, B.M. and Scott, D.R. 1982. Understanding stigma. *Deviant Behavior*. 3, 3 (1982), 275–300.

[12] Fine, M. and Asch, A. 1988. Disability Beyond Stigma: Social Interaction, Discrimination, and Activism. *Journal of Social Issues*. 44, 1 (1988), 3–21.

[13] Friedman, B., Kahn, P. and Borning, A. 2006. *Value Sensitive Design and Information Systems*. M.E. Sharpe.

[14] Goffman, E. 1963. *Stigma; notes on the management of spoiled identity*. Prentice-Hall.

[15] Goodman, E., Stolterman, E. and Wakkary, R. 2011. Understanding interaction design practices. *Proc CHI '11* (Vancouver, BC, Canada, 2011), 1061–1070.

[16] Gould, J.D. and Lewis, C. 1985. Designing for usability: Key principles and what designers think. *CACM*. 28, 3 (1985), 300–311.

[17] Kondraske, G.V. 1988. Rehabilitation engineering: Towards a systematic process. *IEEE Engineering in Medicine and Biology Magazine*. 7, 3 (1988), 11–15.

[18] Ladner, R.E. 2015. Design for user empowerment. *interactions*. 22, 2 (2015), 24–29.

[19] Linton, S. 1998. *Claiming Disability: Knowledge and Identity*. New York University Press.

[20] Ludi, S. 2007. Introducing Accessibility Requirements through External Stakeholder Utilization in an Undergraduate Requirements Engineering Course. *Proc. Soft. Eng. '07* (2007), 736–743.

[21] Mace, R.L., Hardie, G.J. and Plaice, J.P. 1991. Accessible environments: Toward universal design. *Design Intervention: Toward a More Human Architecture*. W. Preiser, J. Vischer, and E. White, eds. Reinhold. 155–176.

[22] Mead, G.H. 1962. *Mind, self, and society from the standpoint of a social behaviorist*. Univ. of Chicago Press.

[23] Miles, M.B. and Huberman, A.M. 1994. *Qualitative data analysis: an expanded sourcebook*. Sage Publications.

[24] Newell, A., Gregor, P., Morgan, M., Pullin, G. and Macaulay, C. 2011. User-Sensitive Inclusive Design. *Universal Access in the Information Society*. 10, 3 (Aug. 2011), 235–243.

[25] Norman, D. 1988. *The Design of Everyday Things*. Basic Book.

[26] Roedl, D.J. and Stolterman, E. 2013. Design research at CHI and its applicability to design practice. *Proceedings of the SIGCHI Conference on Human Factors in Computing Systems* (Paris, France, 2013), 1951–1954.

[27] Scherer, M.J. 1993. *Living in the state of stuck: how technologies affect the lives of people with disabilities*. Brookline Books.

[28] Schuler, D. and Namioka, A. 1993. *Participatory Design: Principles and Practice*. Erlbaum Assoc.

[29] Sharp, H., Rogers, Y. and Preece, J. 2007. *Interaction design: beyond human-computer interaction*. Wiley.

[30] Shinohara, K. and Wobbrock, J.O. 2011. In the shadow of misperception: Assistive technology use and social interactions. *Proc. CHI '11* (Vancouver, BC, 2011), 705–714.

[31] Shinohara, K. and Wobbrock, J.O. 2016. Self-Conscious or Self-Confident? A Diary Study Conceptualizing the Social Accessibility of Assistive Technology. *ACM Transactions on Accessible Computing (TACCESS)*. 8, 2 (2016), 1–31.

[32] Strauss, A.L. and Corbin, J.M. 1998. *Basics of qualitative research*. Sage Publications.

[33] Waller, A., Hanson, V.L. and Sloan, D. 2009. Including accessibility within and beyond undergraduate computing courses. *Proc. ASSETS '09* (Pittsburgh, PA, USA, 2009), 155–162.

[34] Winner, L. 1980. Do Artifacts Have Politics? *Daedalus*. 109, 1 (1980), 121–136.

[35] Wobbrock, J.O., Kane, S.K., Gajos, K.Z., Harada, S. and Froehlich, J. 2011. Ability-based design: Concept, principles, and examples. *ACM TACCESS*. 3, 3 (2011), 1–27.

[36] Zhang, X. and Wakkary, R. 2014. Understanding the role of designers' personal experiences in interaction design practice. *Proceedings of the 2014 conference on Designing interactive systems* (Vancouver, BC, Canada, 2014), 895–904.

Breaking Barriers to Digital Literacy: An Intergenerational Social-Cognitive Approach

Keith Atkinson
Michigan Technological
University
1400 Townsend Drive
Houghton MI 49931 USA
kwatkins@mtu.edu

Jaclyn Barnes
Michigan Technological
University
1400 Townsend Drive
Houghton MI 49931 USA
jaclynb@mtu.edu

Judith Albee
judyalbee708@gmail.com

Peter Anttila
bustera@att.net

Judith Haataja
jhaataja@yahoo.com

Kanak Nanavati
kbnanavati@gmail.com

ABSTRACT

In entering the digital realm, older adults face obstacles beyond the more clearly understood physical and cognitive barriers traditionally associated with accessibility. This experience report is a collection of narratives from learners and student tutors who participate in our digital literacy sessions for seniors. We point out ways in which attitudes and motivations, framed by social and cultural factors, can either hinder or assist with adoption of commodity digital technology among older newcomers. We also show how a social-cognitive approach can help learners overcome barriers to digital literacy.

CCS Concepts

•Social and professional topics → Seniors; •Applied computing → Collaborative learning; *Personal computers and PC applications;* •Human-centered computing → *Empirical studies in accessibility;*

Keywords

Digital literacy; Senior citizens; Collaborative learning; Accessibility

1. INTRODUCTION

From the confluence of two social phenomena—an aging population and an increased dependence on digital technology—a critical need has emerged for older citizens to develop digital literacy. The barriers to access are substantial, spanning from traditionally accepted factors like physical, motor, and perceptual impairments [9] to less measurable factors such as motivation, awareness, and perceived benefit [6, 3, 7]. Ironically, the task of exploring and mastering digital technology is often left to the adopters themselves, with an implicit requirement of the very skills that they lack: "If digital literacy is necessary, how can a person become digitally literate if the means to become so are inaccessible or unusable?" [5]

Listening to older adults and addressing their learning needs as we develop the technologies of tomorrow is a moral imperative. Since 2011, the Breaking Digital Barriers group at Michigan Tech has run a program called BASIC (Building Adult Skills in Computing) that pairs our students with community members, most of them 60 years of age or older, who are seeking help with computing technology. In this experience report, participants in our program relate their challenges and the role of the BASIC program in their trajectory toward digital literacy.

2. BARRIERS TO DIGITAL LITERACY

We find recurring themes in our interactions [4]:

Anxiety stifles exploration. The experience of using a computing device is known to cause anxiety in older people, and our experiences bear this out. A common concern for participants in our group is that something they do will "break" their investment. Even routine activities cause anxiety as users fear accidentally going "off script".

Danger online. Many learners are fearful of going online because of stories of fraud and identity theft they have heard in the media. Without a basis of understanding for how malware and other threats work, they have no model for how to minimize their threat level.

Context sensitivity and non-obvious affordances. A shift toward mobile devices with small displays and a shift toward "clean" design have led to a decrease in affordances and other cues in user interfaces. To use these interfaces effectively, the user must be willing to explore the space and uncover the functionality. A change triggered by an inadvertent action makes older users feel anxious and out of control.

Details obscure abstraction. Not so long ago, users typically accomplished activities like email and word processing through dedicated applications specific to a particular personal computer. The movement toward mobile computing devices and cloud-based storage and applications has abstracted those activities into general "services". For many of our learners, conceiving of computing in this abstract way runs contrary to their script-based style of learning about computers.

ASSETS '16, October 23-26, 2016, Reno, NV, USA

© 2016 ACM. ISBN 978-1-4503-4124-0/16/10. . . $15.00

DOI: http://dx.doi.org/10.1145/2982142.2982183

Functionality across devices. Most older adults do not use the same services across different devices; rather, they use different devices for different tasks. For example, seniors might not use a tablet to check the weather if they associate that ability with a PC. Also, many older users do not realize that content on the Internet, especially "cloud" services, is accessible and consistent across devices.

Issues like these cannot be explained satisfactorily through traditional factors like age-related cognitive, perceptual, or motor changes. Usability tests focused purely on external behavior, like eye tracking or measuring response time, are insufficient. In general, a focus purely on end goals ("completing the task") without taking the method of learning into account will hide important cognitive and social barriers to digital adoption.

3. OUR SOCIAL-COGNITIVE APPROACH

Bandura's Social Cognitive Theory (SCT) informs our approach to digital literacy [1, 2]. According to this theory, an individual's functioning is the product of an interaction between cognitive, behavioral, and contextual factors. It emphasizes the social context of learning and the importance of observation. In opposition to a behaviorist approach, learning and the demonstration of what has been learned are separate, so learning involves not just the acquisition of new behaviors, but also acquisition of knowledge, cognitive skills, concepts, rules, values, and other cognitive constructs.

SCT provides a foundation for interventions designed to improve people's learning. Below we review several key SCT principles and describe how our instructional practices are connected to each [8].

Observational Learning/Modeling. SCT's most basic instructional implication is that learners require access to models of the knowledge, skills, and behaviors they are expected to learn. Multiple types of models (e.g., instructors, peers) and various forms of modeling (e.g., cognitive, verbal, mastery, coping) should be used. Instruction must support learners' engagement in observational learning.

Our BASIC program pairs each learner with a tutor who models behaviors and strategies that we hope to reinforce in the learner. The simplest form of modeling is when our tutors demonstrate how to conduct an action. To make their actions and intentions more obvious, they typically vocalize what they are doing while they are doing it.

Tutors model not only behavior but also problem solving and exploration. We believe it is important for our learners to see that learning the skills to find the answer is often more important than knowing the answer. Tutors also model their emotional reactions to not knowing the solution. It is critical for tutors to demonstrate to learners that, while it is reasonable to feel annoyed when something is not easy to figure out, there is no need to feel anxious; there are ways to find a solution and recover from mistakes.

Outcome Expectations. Instruction should help people see that situated learning and the demonstration of that learning lead to personally valued or important outcomes. Lessons should emphasize real-world applications and the relevance of material to the learners' lives.

Rather than delivering predefined training sessions, we invite learners to come to us with their specific needs. We then tailor our one-on-one tutoring sessions accordingly. Addressing the learner's specific problem often affords opportunities to address specific digital literacy competencies along the

way. In this way, the skills we teach are tied to problems of personal value to our learners. We also invite our learners to bring their own devices to our tutoring sessions. This ensures that learners are developing skills on the devices they will be using in their day-to-day lives. To support an understanding of functionality across devices, we often encourage learners to use multiple devices in the same session. For example, when a learner is interested in learning about the cloud, we may work with him or her to synchronize files across devices and access information from the cloud from a variety of platforms and devices.

Goal Setting. Instruction needs to help students set effective goals—goals that are attainable, clear, specific, and moderately challenging. To facilitate progress and self-efficacy, learning goals should be attainable with moderate levels of effort. Goals that learners set or endorse themselves have a bigger effect on their behaviors than assigned goals.

As mentioned above, our tutoring sessions are driven by the requests and goals of our learners. Even in the cases in which learners specify a general goal of "learning about computers", our tutors spend time talking to them about their lives to identify potential computing needs and to choose learning goals that may be most relevant to each learner.

Perceived Self-Efficacy. People will be more active, effortful, and effective learners when they are confident in their ability to complete tasks successfully. Instruction should be designed to help learners develop and sustain self-efficacy: the belief in one's capabilities to organize and execute the courses of action required to manage prospective situations.

Our learning sessions are hands on, and whenever possible, we ask the learner to "drive". Although we may model behavior by demonstrating a sequence of steps, our tutors ask the learners to repeat the steps themselves to help ensure they will be able to address the problem on their own at home. As noted above, our tutors do not always know the answers to a learner's problems and may need to seek assistance online or from another tutor. In doing this, we hope to reinforce that even "experts" need help finding the answer and that having questions about how to do things on a computer or handheld device is normal and not something to feel ashamed about.

Self-Regulation. All students should be supported in their efforts to be self-regulated learners. Three processes involved here are self-observation (monitoring one's own behaviors and outcomes), self-judgment (evaluating whether one's actions are effective), and self-reaction (responding to the self-evaluations by changing, rewarding, or discontinuing the behavior). Instructors can promote self-observation by helping people learn how to monitor different aspects of their learning behavior through aids such as checklists.

Our program currently offers only limited support for self-regulation. Tutors provide models of self-observation, self-judgment, and self-reaction, and they can encourage similar behavior in learners, but the limited contact time makes it difficult to practice these behaviors. Future work may include self-guided learning tasks done outside of the group sessions. Also our planned tool support for wayfinding (discussed in the next section) offers an opportunity to record learning progress and present it to the learner.

4. PARTICIPANT ACCOUNTS

In this section, we relate the experiences of several participants in the BASIC program. Keith and Jaclyn are student tutors in the program, and Judy, Peter, Judy, and Kanak are regular attendees and learners.

4.1 Keith

I am a third-year computer science undergraduate student at Michigan Technological University. I originally joined BASIC after watching a documentary on the challenges elderly people face with technology, and I have been an active volunteer for about a year. As a tutor for BASIC I gained a great deal of personal insight into how newcomers use and learn about new technologies, such as tablets, computers, smartphones and everything in between.

Conceptual challenges. A major issue for someone entering a new technology is that as it has advanced, it has built off of previous advancements, whether it be physical or software. A good example is the iCloud, having photos be stored in something called a gallery and divided into albums is generally intuitive for someone accustomed to interacting with it, and the addition of cloud storage isn't a big leap. If a person doesn't understand the idea of a digital photo album, then they now struggle with trying to grasp the idea of digital photo storage and what a cloud storage is, something that can be complicated even for a veteran of the system.

The upgrade train — when to get on, when to get off. Patrons can sometimes display a dislike to new things, and that can sometimes be difficult to overcome. A very common situation is when being forced to go from a completely standard cellphone to a smartphone. Patrons typically feel overwhelmed by the new features they don't intend to use, coupled with the immediate frustration of not having had a choice can sometimes be a recipe for disaster, especially if their cellphone is their primary phone.

When helping a person who has been unwillingly "upgraded" the best practice has been to walk them through the necessities such as making phone calls and then moving into what the person seems interested in using. Camera functions are the best place to start because it becomes apparent that it is useful to have such a small camera on you, and then moving onto other things they might be interested in such as facetime, email, and favourite sites.

Left in the cold. When first using a device such as a tablet, there may be a very short instruction on how to use some features, but normally there is nothing beyond telling the user to open an apps menu. This is a greatly overlooked issue, especially because people tend to exhibit a fear of breaking the device, they do not "play around", so without any instruction it is frustrating to the user. Even with the addition of simple tutorials or guide a language barrier can develop very quickly. The difference between the Facebook app and website, for example, if you don't have any concept of an "app" or concept of what a website actually is, trying to use them interchangeably can be extremely difficult because the app and website offer different layouts and features as well as being device specific.

Making it your own. Many patrons after a few sessions tend to become familiar enough to start taking full advantage of their devices. Patrons also tend to have more advanced questions their familiarity increases, such as in depth questions about the differences between Android and Apple devices. After a few sessions many begin customizing their devices or asking how to; this is a highlight for me because the device becomes theirs, with custom pictures, third party apps, and creating albums or libraries.

It is a truly fulfilling experience working with patrons to get over tech related hurdles. I gain a lot of education personally from volunteering as well. Almost all of my peers and the people I work with day to day are very comfortable using all kinds of new technology. After working in the BASIC program, I can bring different approaches to software design by recognizing design choices that tend to ostracize technological newcomers, and that is an experience and an understanding that is not taught in class.

4.2 Jaclyn

I am a second-year PhD student in the Computer Science program at Michigan Technological University. I grew up watching my grandfather struggle with technology as it became more important in daily life. I started working with the BASIC program as soon as I came to grad school to get a better perspective on difficulties seniors had with tech.

My primary research has turned out to deal with children rather than the elderly, but I continue to tutor when time permits. I find it rewarding and refreshing to interact with seniors who attend in particular because their perspectives are so far from my own and serve as a reminder of both the broader goals of studying HCI — making actual users' interactions with technology, and perhaps even their lives in some small way, better — and the world outside academia since grad school can be a bit all consuming. The format makes it easy even for a deeply introverted person like me to engage with strangers because it is not the undirected small talk of mingling, but rather a purposeful encounter that sometimes includes small talk and the conversation can naturally be redirected to the task at hand when it becomes uncomfortable. We also get a lot of repeat patrons, so many do not stay strangers for long.

Tutoring was very uncomfortable at first. We get a lot of questions about laptops, smartphones, tablets, and popular applications. I knew I did not (and do not) have an encyclopedic knowledge of PCs or Macs. I did not even own a smartphone or tablet when I started. When you sit down to help someone else, it feels like you are expected to be a tech whiz who knows all the answers. It took a while to get comfortable saying "I don't know. Let's find out." to the patrons and within the hearing of my peers and professors. However, I have never had a bad reaction to saying that. On the contrary, many of the seniors are cheered to find that someone they view as knowledgeable is also at a loss. Not to mention the occasions they know something I do not or are better at something. Instead of being upset, most enjoy the role reversal.

A lot seems to be made of being a digital native or not. I am not sure that is a helpful metaphor. For one thing, it implies that people cannot attain proficiency if they were not exposed to technology as children. For another, often times, if not most of the time, neither the digital native tutors nor the seniors we're working with have enough "native" fluency in a particular app or device to immediately know exactly how to accomplish a task. Knowing the jargon and some common conventions most certainly helps as we figure it out, but being a digital native does not mean you can understand an app with the same degree of confidence a native speaker understands a sentence. It seems that the more significant differentiator is that the tutors are more comfortable exploring the device and trying things to see if they work. Many of the seniors are concerned that they will break their devices, but tutors know that there are not very many settings you can fiddle with that will irrevocably destroy a device and those are usually protected.

Where the digital native distinction might apply is with mental models for computer systems. Many seniors just do not seem to have them or have something inaccurate. This can be especially difficult when you need to explain a high-level concept that relies on lower-level concepts that are equally unfamiliar. The cloud is an example. Most people who come in do not understand the cloud, but may very well use it on their Apple device, eReader, or Android. What I want to tell them is that using the cloud is a way to have your files on a company's computer somewhere else where you can get to them. That is understandable as far as it goes, but it usually takes either a specific example or analogy to explain why before it seems to make sense. Using the cloud for backup can be explained by saying that backing up their phone to the cloud means that if their phone breaks they can connect a new phone to their account and download the things they've previously entered. Alternatively, an analogy like a safety deposit box can serve similar purposes. I often combine both approaches. When you start getting follow-up questions that show understanding, like asking about Google's cloud compared to Apple's cloud, you know you are on the right track or ready to move on.

One good rule of thumb is to always ask why a patron is trying to learn or do something. Like during requirements gathering, people often ask for what they think they want instead of what they actually want. "I want to get to the library site from my Kindle." is very different from "I want to download library books to read offline while I'm on vacation." Asking why and what they want to accomplish not only helps identify these confusions, but it also gives you an idea of what the person already knows.

It helps to make the conversation as much of a dialogue as possible. Ask a lot of questions and work in small chunks to identify miscommunications quickly. I keep the conversation polite, but friendly and informal. Not only is it appropriate for the culture of the region, but it helps diminish the awkwardness of an elder being taught by a young person.

Patrons usually want to learn how to do things step-by-step. It Is not uncommon to have people try to write down exactly what they need to do to reference when they are at home. Unfortunately, step-by-step processes are very brittle. People can miss a step in their list or not understand something they wrote and be completely lost. Even more troublesome, when an interface changes, those steps may be wrong. This seems to cause a fear of computer and applications updates for some, which can result in important security updates not being applied for fear they will change a familiar process. There is comfort in having the notes for later reference and writing does help people learn, so I do not try to stop notetakers. However, I do try to get people to teach why things are done rather than just how.

There is a tricky balance to deciding when to do something yourself and when to have the patron do it. That is partially personal style. I tend to do more myself than most other tutors seem to. If I need to figure out something new and I expect there to be a lot of backtracking and redoing as I learn, I'll do that myself rather than try to walk the senior through physically doing the exploration. First, it is more efficient. Second, it is less confusing for the patron. A good argument could be made that it is better to teach

that process of figuring things out and let the patron do it themselves, but I have not figured out how to do that well. What I usually try to do instead is narrate what I am doing and explain that they do not have to remember the steps as we will do it from the beginning once I have learned how.

Most of the sessions are conducted in close proximity, so everyone can hear everyone else. That can be both embarrassing and helpful. On the one hand, both the tutors and the patrons are forced to admit their ignorance semi-publicly. For instance, I had one woman who could not reboot her new phone. Several people were watching the interaction when the phone booted for me in a couple seconds. The problem was not the phone as I initially assumed; the problem was the woman had been pressing the home button instead of the power button. It would have been less embarrassing had it not been witnessed by the woman's watching friends. However, it can also be helpful because hearing what everyone is working on and how they are doing it can give new tutors models to follow and allow us to learn the specialties of each person. Finally, on occasions we need to work with more than one person, it is much easier to go back and forth when they are close together.

It is fairly common, particularly around holidays and exams, for there to be more patrons than tutors. There have been occasions I've worked with three people at the same time. It Is usually possible to balance the timing so that you are leaving each person while they are writing something down, practicing a procedure, or waiting for a process to complete. Interleaving the sessions this way makes it a bit more efficient, but overall you do get less accomplished in the hour per person. The only practical way I can see to avoid this would be to turn away latecomers, but I would rather help a few people partially than help one person fully and the rest none at all.

4.3 Judy Albee

Although I have been retired for 15 years, I was employed as an elementary classroom teacher, full or part time, for over 35 years. I strongly believe in "hands-on" learning for young children, which did not entail being attached to an "electronic tether". I did use a personal computer during the last few years of my career. It was basically to generate banners for my classroom, communicate with parents and organize my lessons.

I took computer classes to help me with the technology, but the BASIC sessions are much better. After reading an article in our newspaper and the recommendation of a colleague, I decided to check out the program. I continue to return to the library program for a couple of reasons. First of all I know I will receive the specific help I need, and secondly I return when I have exhausted the personal resources I have to meet current needs.

I still struggle with the excess of options, continual updating and the transition from our Microsoft laptop to our Apple ipad. Setting up laptops and tablets is like learning a foreign language. I have tried the *Computers for Dummies* books, but they are continually obsolete. I look for help through Google search, but my sons say I am not wording things the right way. From my perspective, that is not my fault; I speak and write clearly, and if the computer cannot understand English, that is its problem, not mine.

I am still afraid of pop ups, and the constant updates. Computers have so many bells and whistles; I just want a generic version, and I do not need updates to complicate my life. The dead ends that I encounter make me feel that it is all done by the drug companies, to raise your frustration level. One thing that drives me to distraction is the clutter; there are so many visual items to confuse me. I thought that a smaller device (iPad mini) would help with this problem, but it did not.

I do not have time to play with silly machines; if it is a helpful aid, like when I check the weather while traveling, that is fine, but I do not really embrace it as a tool, especially if I have to expend so much time and energy on it. That said, I have made some things using the computer: for instance, a 50th wedding anniversary book, and a video for our granddaughter. Those are things that I would not have been able to do earlier.

Learning or gradually internalizing the basic terms, icons and sequencing of steps to complete a task are some of the most important things I've learned from the library program. The students in the library program know this is a limited commitment, have the ability to give advice from different perspectives, and can assist me in my fear of "breaking something" or losing material in the "black hole" — unlike our children, who often do not have patience and do not explain. The tutors do a good job of breaking things down into bite-sized pieces. Still, there is so much sequencing, and often that extra step that the students help you make — I can get up to four or five steps, but beyond that I need an extra push. I take notes of what we do and use that as a memory aid. You have to do something numerous times to internalize it.

4.4 Peter

I have had some experience with computers over the years; they interest me sometimes, but other times I feel like driving over them. Several years ago, I ran a business doing welding, building, and contracting; I had a bookkeeper who used QuickBooks, and I knew enough to get by. When I started working for the University, I had to take a technology class. Thank goodness for the other students in the class who helped me; they had less experience than I did but still learned more. I feel like I get a brick wall in front of me sometimes when I am learning this technology.

Lately I was asked by the insurance company handling my disability to learn more about computing. I do not see myself making a living with computers; everything I have done has been hands on. The company calls periodically to ask if I have updated my resume, but it is not easy for me.

I am pretty good at surfing the Web; I have done research on fishing and cooking, and it is my main source for news. Listing a truck on Craig's List was a monumental task, but I was able to do it, with the help of a friend. The problem with searching for answers online is that often you do not even know what the options are, so how do you know what to search for? Also, I am not fluent enough with the language to know where to look. Organizing files and icons is a challenge. I struggle because I do not use the computer all the time, while students even in elementary school around here go home with tablets.

The BASIC program is the best thing ever: one on one help, for as long as needed; we keep going until the problem is solved. It is better than a class because it is productive 100% of the time; there is no down time. My son helps sometimes, but it is different; he gets frustrated with me and

tells me, "just do this!" It is exciting being with the students because they are patient, and I can see myself learning; I look forward to going back and learning more.

4.5 Judy Haataja

I am a native of the Houghton area, a college graduate in my 70's. I love flowers, and I like to read and be outdoors. I was working in the school superintendent's office when computers were just being introduced to our local school system. I got frustrated early on when you were expected to do basic actions like initializing disks and I could not find the directions to do that. In the evening, I took computer classes, mainly on how to use Microsoft Office. I do not feel computer literate, though I know that everyone will be in twenty years or so. I am not happy with the "phone culture" of today, where everyone is looking at their devices.

The BASIC program caught my attention because I wanted answers to questions that kept popping up — questions that I can't get answers to by Googling. I have never managed to get help from the online help; it just makes me more confused. My ego is such that I do not want to appear "dumb", so I look for help in books, like the *Windows 10 for Dummies* book that I checked out of the library. I do not like the title "dummies", but that is what I need. I read the book but still did not understand. I need someone to be patient and help me through what the book is saying.

It is frustrating to know that you can do something but just not know *how* to do it. I know that there are programs available out there that can enhance my life, but I do not know how to find them. A big problem for me is keywords. For instance, I was looking online for ways to give away books; I searched on Google for a while without success, but my friend got the answer right away with the right keywords. Also, the special vocabulary of computers is difficult. I feel that I do not make myself clear and that I do not explain things well. For instance, I tried Amazon's interactive help service, to help with my Kindle, but they did not understand what I was asking and went and did something I did not understand. I did not learn how to do it myself.

The BASIC program was very good at giving me advice on purchasing a smartphone versus a tablet. There are nice people at the program who are willing to help and take you seriously. It is good to have interaction too. For instance, I was having trouble copying and pasting between documents. The problem was that I thought the actual dimensions of what you are copying and where you are pasting it had to be identical; instead, the copy and paste is just about text. I had written down instructions on how to do it, but it did not transfer. By doing it with a tutor, I discovered the problem.

The personal contact is important; I know that when I visit nursing homes as a volunteer, everyone says thank you for coming, and I feel the same way about BASIC. My son also helps me when he comes to visit, and he helps remotely through screen sharing. He organizes things, putting files in the right places, but he does not have a lot of time to explain. It is harder when family members are helping you; there is a tradeoff between helping with computers and spending time in other ways. With BASIC, everyone is there and dedicated to helping with computers.

I find surprising things like pop ups confusing. You are asked: do you want to do this or do that? What are the options, and will I get in trouble with one or the other? It feels like I am expected to give an answer right away, but

I do not have one. I really do not want to get myself into trouble with computers and the Internet. Some of the advice that I get comes up out of the blue. For instance, one tutor was helping me download a book, and we came across a dangerous website; she told me "don't ever go here". That kind of advice to be safe, to keep me from going off where I shouldn't go, is very valuable, and I would not even know to ask for it.

4.6 Kanak

I am 69 years old, originally from India but settled in Copper Country since fall of 1973. After losing my husband in 1986, I got busy raising 4 kids single-handedly but continued painting to develop my hobby by attending art workshops, taking part in juried shows and solo exhibits, and also teaching art. I continue my passion for art and exhibitions, plus I sell my work at local galleries. One big reason for using computers for me is to store images of my paintings as well as photographs of the area.

My experience with computers prior to coming to the BASIC program was minimal, but not nil: I knew how to do email and how to store photos. My first experience with computers was scary. My son bought me a laptop and filled in everything for me. I started with a laptop, then an iPad and an iPhone. Currently I use email, Picasa for photos, and Skype, with help from my nephew.

My knowledge of computers is expanding over time. I started with a Hotmail email account, then learned about Gmail from my daughter. It was news to me that that you don't have to have just one account. Moving from a digital camera to an iPhone, I am now taking many more photos than before. More recently, I have learned that you *need* to know about computers nowadays: to pay bills, look at bank statements; even depositing a check by taking a photo of it.

Some of the upgrades I have experienced have been difficult. For instance, when my computer kept telling me about Windows 10, I was surprised: I did not need a big change and did not want an upgrade. I knew that I should OK it, but I what would the consequences be, and would I have to pay? Virus protection messages confuse me too. My iPhone has complications: at first I did not understand about photos in iCloud, but I learned at the help sessions. Still, it is confusing when iCloud gets full. I do feel that it would be better to go back to a simpler time with my old camera.

In the BASIC program, I have learned not to be afraid to ask; earlier, I did not know who to approach with questions or how to put them. The BASIC program keeps me wanting to come back and learn more. I am always curious to see if I can adapt. For instance, I heard about GPS: can I learn to use it on my phone? I learn about things I was not even aware of from the student tutors — like calling internationally through the Internet. Sometimes I realize that certain things are possible but too much trouble; for instance, once Keith showed me how to transfer music from tapes to CD, but I realized that it would take too much time.

The sessions are 100% enjoyable: they are one to one and face to face, so the tutors can see the problem. They also make me feel good about asking questions. The tutors don't know everything, but they say, "let's figure out how to do that". That gives me confidence that I can do it too — I am no longer afraid to ask. My kids help me too, but they like to fix things themselves — for instance, my daughter had me send her my phone so she could fix it, rather than tell

me how to do it. I also learn from other people who have come for help. For instance, one woman had learned about the difference between updates and upgrades, and what you could safely skip; she gave me advice about that. Another woman showed me a template for quilting that she had found online. The sessions make me feel like I am keeping pace with technology; that makes me feel good.

5. CONCLUSION

These narratives, from a range of learner backgrounds, reveals common themes that can inform more accessibility-aware design in commodity hardware and software: the confusing and changing vocabulary; the question of where to turn for information on "unknown unknowns"; the feelings of anxiety and lack of control precipitated by constantly updated/upgraded technology. The interactive nature of our help sessions, with tutors modeling the kind of critical inquiry that we wish to infuse in our learners, is an effective way to mitigate demotivating feelings of anxiety and confusion. Moreover, our student tutors constitute a learning community of their own, familiarizing themselves with the perspectives of technology users who are different — yet not too different — from themselves.

6. ADDITIONAL AUTHORS

Kelly Steelman, Michigan Technological University (email: `steelman@mtu.edu`), Charles Wallace, Michigan Technological University (email: `wallace@mtu.edu`).

7. REFERENCES

[1] A. Bandura. *Social Learning Theory.* Prentice-Hall, 1977.

[2] A. Bandura. Organisational applications of social cognitive theory. *Australian Journal of Management,* 13(2):275–302, 1988.

[3] S. Czaja, J. Guerrier, S. Nair, and T. Landauer. Computer communication as an aid to independence for older adults. *Behavior and Information Technology,* 12:197–207, 1993.

[4] S. Kumar, L. C. Ureel, H. King, and C. Wallace. Lessons from our elders: Identifying obstacles to digital literacy through direct engagement. In *Proceedings of Pervasive Technologies Related to Assistive Environments (PETRAE),* 2013.

[5] D. Leahy and D. Dolan. Digital literacy — is it necessary for einclusion? In *HCI and Usability for e-Inclusion,* pages 149–158. Springer LNCS 5889, 1991.

[6] R. Mackie and C. Wylie. Factors influencing acceptance of computer-based innovations. In M. Helander, editor, *Handbook of Human-Computer Interaction,* pages 1081–1106. Elsevier, 1988.

[7] A. Melenhorst, W. Rogers, and D. Bouwhuis. Older adults' motivated choice for technological innovation: Evidence for benefit-driven selectivity. *Psychology and Aging,* 21(1):190, 2006.

[8] K. S. Steelman, K. L. Tislar, L. C. Ureel, and C. Wallace. Breaking digital barriers: A social-cognitive approach to improving digital literacy in older adults. In *Proceedings of HCI International,* 2016.

[9] N. Wagner, K. Hassanein, and M. Head. Computer use by older adults: A multi-disciplinary review. *Computers in Human Behavior,* 26(5):870–882, 2010.

Remote Access Programs to Better Integrate Individuals with Disabilities

Thomas Hahn
Dept. of Info. Sciences
Univ. of AR at Little Rock
Little Rock, AR, USA
+ 1 (501) 301 4890
Thomas.F.Hahn3@gmail.com

Hidayat Ur Rahman
Lahore Leads University
Lahore, Pakistan
+92-3329702722
Hidayat.Rhman@gmail.com

Richard Segall
Dept. of Comp. & IT
Arkansas State University
Jonesboro, AR, USA
+ 1 (870) 972-3989
rsegall@astate.edu

**Christoph Heim &
Raphaela Brunson**
Business – Consulting - Services-
Schwerin, Germany
+49 (385) 550 83 78
info@bestercomputerservice.com

Ankush Sharma
Inst. of Clinical Physiology,
National Research Council,
Siena-, Italy
-+393318316370
ankush.sak@gmail.com

Maryam Aslam
Quaid-i-Azam University
Islamabad, Pakistan
+92-3323177741
Maryamch67@gmail.com

Ana Lara-Rodriguez
Dept. de Ciencias Biologicas
Universidad de los Andes
Bogota, Colombia
+57 321 3723159
ac.lara422@uniandes.edu.co

Md. Sahidul Islam
Dept of Statistics
University of Rajshahi,
Rajshah, Bangladesh
+0088 01737 272633
ripon.ru.statistics@gmail.com

Neha Gupta
Dept. of Comp. Science
Lamar University
Beaumont, TX, USA
+ 1 (409) 223 4571
nneha2ggupta@gmail.com

Charles S. Embry
Dept. of Info. Sciences
Univ. of AR at Little Rock
Little Rock, AR, USA
+ 1(501) 541-9073
csembry@ualr.edu

Patrick Grossmann
Dept. of Biostatistics
Harvard University
Cambridge, MA, USA
+ 1 (781) 859 7190
patrick@jimmy.harvard.edu

Shahrukh Babar
Silverback Pvt. Ltd. & RMS Inc.
Islamabad, Pakistan
+92 3347090717
Shahrukh.swam@gmail.com

Gregory A. Skibinski
Dept. of Biol. Sciences
Univ. of AL in Huntsville
Huntsville, AL, USA
+ 1 (205) 936-4040
greg.skibinski@gmail.com

Fusheng Tang
Dept. of App. Sciences
Univ. of AR at Little Rock
Little Rock, AR, USA
+1 (501) 569-3507
FXTang@UALR.edu

ABSTRACT

Sensory impaired individuals are at a disadvantage in accessing and processing electronic information. The first author (i.e. Thomas Hahn) is legally blind due to Albinism. In this experience report we describe challenges faced by the visually impaired and explain how remote access programs in combination with voice communication programs can be used to—at least partially—compensate for those disadvantages because they don't transmit magnification. This property is especially important to effectively train visually impaired individuals on new applications and interfaces remotely because it allows them to view exactly the same information simultaneously with their sighted trainers.

Since the technical prerequisites for this information exchange, skill transfer, and knowledge acquisition approach have already been freely available for at least 7 years, but are still not widely used, this approach needs to be impressively demonstrated at conferences like this one to increase the odds that its participants will share this approach with those who could potentially benefit from it. This approach could make computer labs with expensive software not only accessible to the disabled, but instead, to everyone around the clock while saving money, which is still being spent to pay lab

supervisors to keep the labs open for a few hours without losing—but instead—gaining functionality. Offering virtual remote office hours would benefit disabled and non-handicapped students and faculty alike.

Providing remote access to lectures can make them available to a wider audience and thus could decrease costs for tuition. Obvious benefits of this approach for the mobility impaired and soon to be expected benefits for the hearing impaired are mentioned. Allowing faculty to remotely participate in oral exams increases choices for possible specializations. Making information more accessible to the disabled has obvious synergistic benefits for non-handicapped people alike as reflected by the importance of the concept of workforce diversification for overcoming unexpected future challenges and potential stumbling blocks. This approach makes it possible to magnify lecture presentations directly onto the screen of visually impaired students and could improve real-time interactions in the classroom. Remote access for everyone could reduce the perception of disabilities. Handicapped people could be considered early adopters because they are more in need of improvements since the present circumstances and limitations are much less acceptable to them. This article concludes by describing current bottlenecks to accessibility and information transfer, and ends with an overall optimistic outlook to the future.

CCS Concepts: Human-centered Computing →
Accessibility • Social and professional topics → People with
disabilities • *Applied computing ~ Education*

Keywords: Visual impairment; magnification; remote control; knowledge-, skills-, and information transfer; inclusive design; e-learning; virtual classroom; education; collaboration, tutoring

ASSETS '16, October 23-26, 2016, Reno, NV, USA.
© 2016 ACM. ISBN 978-1-4503-4124-0/16/10...$15.00.
DOI: http://dx.doi.org/10.1145/2982142.2982182

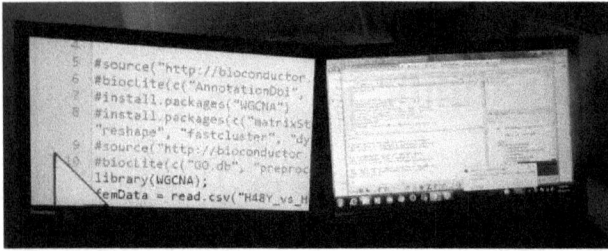

Figure 1: On the right laptop screen, the normal view of the programming interface of R Studio (see https://www.r-project.org/) is shown. The left laptop screen shows the alterations that are necessary for me to access and process electronic information. The setting displayed here closely simulates situations when sighted people train me to learn new interfaces or to follow instructions on how to use them.

1. CHALLENGES

The ability to quickly access and process electronic information has become a major key qualification. This, unfortunately, puts people with sensory impairments at a severe disadvantage. Generally, information accessing and processing skills can be acquired relatively easily as long as there is no big variation in the perceived sensory input information at the computer-human interface. But what if the input information must be altered before it can be processed?

Severely visually impaired people often struggle when trying to accomplish the two mutually exclusive goals, which are having high enough magnification for reading while simultaneously trying to maintain their remaining visual field as large as they possibly can to keep their orientation on the screen. But the lower the remaining vision the more magnification is needed and consequently the smaller the remaining visual field. This causes severe limitations because only a very small portion of the visual information can be accessed at any particular time. This makes it very challenging to learn new programming and web application interfaces. Moreover, it limits collaborations because visually impaired and normal sighted people encounter severe problems when trying to work together using the same computer screen, e.g., during peer programming sessions or hackathons, because normal sighted people feel limited by the small remaining visual field needed by the visually impaired to accommodate their need for high magnification. Figure 1 shows how the input information must be altered before I (legally blind first author) can access it.

For example, it is challenging for visually impaired and normal sighted people to troubleshoot the R program shown in Figure 1 together by trying to look at it simultaneously. Moreover, it is much harder to keep track of many variables if one can only see such a small portion of the screen. Furthermore, important communication across the human-computer interface could easily be lost, e.g., when the user needs to confirm an action by clicking OK, if the OK-button is not displayed within the small vision field of ZoomText. ZoomText is a screen reader and screen magnification software especially developed to meet the special needs of visually impaired computer users (see http://www.aisquared.com/products/). Because I am a bioinformatics student I need to use programs that only run on Linux. But there is no good screen reader and screen magnification program like ZoomText available for Linux since many fewer visually impaired people use it.

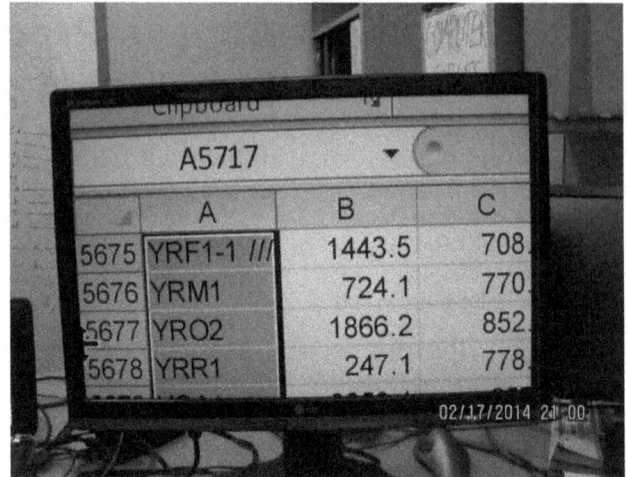

Figure 2: Shows how little I can see of an Excel file containing normalized intensity values computed from our in-house yeast microarray data (project focused on studying biological networks with Dr. Ankush Sharma)—even on my large, external 27-inch monitor.

I found a way to magnify Linux with my ZoomText by installing Virtual Box (see https://www.virtualbox.org/) on my Windows 7 laptop, but unfortunately, ZoomText cannot track the cursor and the appearance of other computer-human interface communication windows because—although it recognizes the Virtual Box as a separate application running under Windows 7—it cannot distinguish between applications running within the Virtual Box. Therefore, if for example, applications running in the Virtual Box appear not to respond anymore, the visually impaired user needs to scroll the entire screen with the small remaining vision field hoping to place the magnification window exactly above a newly popped up communication window.

When using ZoomText its user must remember the exact locations of the buttons for the functions of an application, such as safe, send, upload, compute, etc., to know in which direction on the screen to scroll to access them. This takes away the intuition for using new applications, programs and interfaces. In Excel, for example, relationships between multiple columns may not be observed simply because they cannot be fitted within the small remaining visual field of ZoomText. See Figure 2. When extending columns to their entire width, sometimes not even a single column can fit within the zoomed in window. This makes it then harder to jump to the next column, especially when the font has to be enlarged so much that not even a single column can fit on the screen even without using ZoomText. Hence, one needs to know the columns very well to work with such kinds of multi-dimensional data.

When searching for resources on the web, such as conferences that offer travel grants for students, it is challenging to find all critical information because if one cannot find the travel grant information for a particular conference although "travel grant" was entered as one of the search criteria, one never knows whether this information is not available or whether one only failed to find it when trying to scroll across an unfamiliar website with only a very small visual field inevitably caused when needing high magnification. Being dependent on a small visual field or even on screen readers makes it difficult to search for new information because visually skimming for keywords or phrases is impossible. Hence, one can spend lots of time searching for information that is not available or one may miss out on opportunities when giving up the search too quickly.

2. REMOTE ACCESS

Programs for remotely accessing other computers through the internet are available free of charge for non-commercial use for many years already. They were initially developed to allow system administrators to maintain the computers of their clients remotely. However, most information needed for programming and data intensive tasks can be shared via remote access. Two such remote access programs, with which I had positive experiences, are TeamViewer (see https://www.teamviewer.com/en/ and AnyDesk (see http://anydesk.com/remote-desktop). Although they were not initially developed for teaching and sharing information, skills, techniques, and knowledge, they have proven to be extremely suitable for those purposes. For conveying audio information, programs such as Skype (see https://www.skype.com/en/), Google Hangout (see https://hangouts.google.com/) or Yahoo Messenger (see https://messenger.yahoo.com/) or many others can be used.

The main advantage is that these remote access programs don't transmit the magnification and thus it's inevitably connected small visual field to the screen of the computer, which has taken remote control. Thus, visually impaired people can use magnification viewing the same information on their computer as sighted people without limiting their visual field. This property is very important because it allows sighted people to train me remotely on new interfaces and applications.

Remote access allows me to keep working in an already configured interface, where font sizes and colors are already optimized to meet my specific low vision needs instead of requiring me to adapt to a different interface configuration on, for example, lab computers.

3. TUTORING/TRAINING

The perspectives of the sighted trainer and the visually impaired trainee are shown in Figure 3. This setup allows me to contribute much more to my hackathon team while, for example, troubleshooting problems.

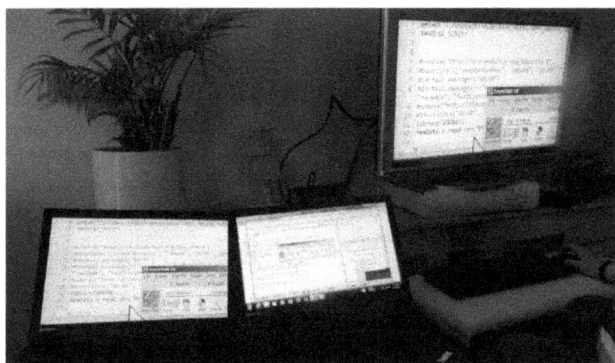

Figure 3: Showing the perspective of the sighted tutor and his/her visually impaired student. On the left, the student's laptop with 2.5 times ZoomText magnification is shown. In the middle, the perspective of the tutor, who is not affected by the screen magnifier, is shown. The tutor is not getting distracted by the limited vision field of his visually impaired student using ZoomText. Moreover, as shown on the right, the laptop of the visually impaired student can be connected to an even larger external monitor, thus maximizing the remaining visual field by minimizing the needed level of magnification even further.

Being a bioinformatics student requires me to quickly learn how to use many new interfaces and applications. Unfortunately, the locations of their functions on the screen often vary to such an extent that they are unpredictable when depending on a small visual field thus making it difficult to find them. In such cases it has been very helpful when a sighted person already familiar with a particular application or interface has trained me remotely by taking over my mouse to show me where, for example, the upload, calculate, or submit button is located. When learning complex applications with many options, such as Cytoscape (see http://www.cytoscape.org/), my sighted trainer could follow me remotely while I was navigating through a new application to verify that all my steps were correct and could intervene at any time when I needed additional help. On the other hand, these remote access programs allow me to take over the computer of my tutor/trainer thus enable me to introduce my approaches for solving a particular problem. Such experiences have given me the confidence that I can become an excellent instructor despite my visual impairment. By the time I need to apply for jobs I hope that using remote access to convey information and knowledge has become more widely accepted because not only does it allow for me to receive training but also vice versa, it enables me to train others by logging into their computers and magnifying their screen with my ZoomText.

4. THE NEED FOR DEMONSTRATIONS

Before such remote control programs were available my assistants/ tutors/trainers always had to be at the same location as me to train me. As I advanced through my education my tasks eventually became so complex and specialized that I no longer could find anybody who could assist me, at the same location. Due to this limitation I was unable to continue my education in Dallas in 2010 despite the availability of these remote access programs because nobody had made me aware of their potential benefits in overcoming accessibility barriers to the visually impaired. Most people who taught me new applications, I have never met in person, but I could not have learned the new application or interface they taught me without their assistance, unless I'd have spent much more time learning them on my own by going through many more frustrating and exhaustive trial-and-error experiences.

Therefore, I feel very strongly that it is very important to be given the opportunity to demonstrate the benefits of using these remote access software for the visually impaired firsthand and to give good examples showing how this approach has helped me. I'd like to present this to as many people as possible by impressively demonstrating at conferences, such as this one, to increase the odds that they'll remember so that they are more likely to share this information with others, who could potentially benefit tremendously.

That is why I feel that it is very important to be given the opportunity to demonstrate this approach at this conference because people tend to remember much better when seeing something working well firsthand instead of only reading about it. People are often overwhelmed with consciously selecting their reading material on the web because too much information is competing for their attention. However, while attending a demonstration much less information is competing for their attention and hence they are much more likely to remember it for much longer. I found sharing screens to be especially helpful for brainstorming and collaborating in searching for new information together in real time because it allows for understanding and adopting new search strategies and for adjusting them based on obtained results. Moreover, it allows for quickly finding suitable materials to convey new concepts. It also allows for developing and verifying applied procedures to ensure that the same kind of data is processed in the same way by different people. I found that I am much more alert, concentrated, motivated and attentive when working with somebody in real time than when working alone.

5. MAKING COMPUTER LABS ACCESSIBLE

Due to my visual impairment, I could not work fast enough to complete the computer lab work for my ecology and biometry class during the times at which the computer lab was open. Fortunately, my instructor agreed to set up TeamViewer for unattended access on one of the lab computers, thus providing me with unlimited access to expensive software packages, such as SPSS (see http://www.jmp.com/en_us/home.html), using my ZoomText, and thus enabling me to complete my assignments despite me needing many more hours than my sighted peers to complete them. After I turned in all my assignments I suddenly realized that universities could save much more money if they'd make their computer labs remotely accessible to all students instead of needing to pay a computer lab supervisor to keep the lab open for only a few hours per day. This is again a synergistic effect where those remote access programs can benefit visually impaired and non-handicapped people alike.

Fortunately, my instructor let me have remote access to his lab computers to help me compensate for my vision loss, but this solution, which we found by necessity to compensate for my visual disability, could benefit so many more people and save lots of money, if more people would be aware of its benefits. Hence, it is not only important for a solution to become available, but it is at least equally important that people, who could potentially benefit from it, are made aware of it. In this respect, I feel that this conference would have a strong information multiplication and dissemination effect.

6. REMOTE OFFICE HOURS

I have struggled hard to get access to information for many computer science classes. To receive help I often visited my instructors during their office hours. I remember spending lots of time troubleshooting problems, whose solutions seemed to depend on the computer used, with my instructors trying to understand why I kept getting wrong results despite me following each and every step as instructed. In such situations it was helpful to give my instructors remote access to my computer because this was the only way we could follow my steps together. But not all instructors were open to this approach thus creating a situation where either the instructor or I—but not both of us together—could observe what happened. That is why I feel that especially computer science instructors should be encouraged to offer remote office hours using remote access programs, such as TeamViewer or AnyDesk, in combination with voice transmitting programs, such as Skype, Google Hangout or Yahoo messenger, because not only would this allow visually impaired students to simultaneously look at the same problem with their instructors using their large external monitor, but it would also benefit non-handicapped students to communicate much more effectively with their instructors about anything that can be shown on computer. Offering remote office hours could save driving time and increase the flexibility of the busy schedules of students and instructors alike to unexpected short notice changes. Remote office hours would also allow students to consult with their instructors much more spontaneously and informally when stuck on a problem and only needing a little bit of help to proceed.

7. REACHING A WIDER AUDIENCE

Offering lectures remotely would also allow many more students to enroll in a particular class virtually, thus causing tuition to decline. Since the proportion of information that is communicated through computers is steadily rising, this approach can become beneficial for a rising number of situations, subjects, and topics. During traditional classroom lectures information must pass the computer-human interface twice, i.e., firstly, from the PowerPoint presentation into the classroom; and then, secondly, again from the perception of the students back into their computers. Passing through the computer-human and human-computer interface twice is causing more loss of information than when conveying it from the computer of the instructor directly into the computer of the student. Moreover, students could record any sessions for later review using free programs, such as Krut Computer Recorder (see http://sourceforge.net/projects/krut/) and many others for later review. Furthermore, lectures could be archived by the university thus making them available to a wider audience.

8. BENEFITS FOR THE MOBILITY AND HEARING IMPAIRED

The described benefits not only apply to the visually impaired but even more so to the mobility impaired because they'd be no longer required to attend any session in person since they can join remotely using TeamViewer or AnyDesk, especially when most of the visual information is conveyed by PowerPoint presentations, while the audio information can easily be conveyed using programs such as Skype, Google Hangout or Yahoo Messenger. Hence, constraints regarding physical locations are no longer limiting factors.

Furthermore, the development of speech recognition software and new hardware for accommodating its demand for more memory, processing power, and storage space is advancing very rapidly hence soon allowing for synchronous computer-based closed captioning of everything spoken during lecture and archiving it for later use. Actually, when testing the speech recognition software named "Dragon Dictate" in 2010, I was impressed by its ability to make my computer write what I said. Hence, I believe that by now we should already have the needed hardware and software, but we must become much keener in utilizing them for these purposes. As we have seen with the very slow adoption of this approach despite its very obvious benefits for the visually and mobility impaired, the eagerness to practically implement such new technical options is at least as important as making them available in the first place.

9. INCREASING FACULTY CHOICES

Sharing remote computer access using a combination of voice communication and remote access programs allowed my external adviser to fully participate in the oral defense of my master's thesis because he could take control over my laptop and point to any item I discussed. This gave me much more flexibility in finding committee members who'd be willing to work with me despite some things taking me still longer due to my visual impairment. It saved one of my committee members from driving more than 6 hours because he no longer needed to attend my master's defense in person. Hence, if one cannot find a supportive person locally one can search globally to increase the odds of succeeding. I often feel that somewhere in the world there must exists at least one person who could help me in solving a particular problem, but the hard part is finding this person.

10. WORKFORCE DIVERSIFICATION: BENEFITS FOR THE NON-HANDICAPPED

Using ZoomText's screen reader function resulted in unexpected benefits when, for example, editing documents or PowerPoint presentations in a team also using TeamViewer and Skype. We all could listen to the voice through Skype, which helped us to much better identify errors and contribute to their corrections from many perspectives. This is another synergistic effect, where accommodations to compensate for shortcomings caused by disabilities have beneficial effects even for non-handicapped people. This is another reason for integrating more disabled people into the workforce.

The concept of workforce diversification is very empowering. It is important to not view disabilities as necessarily always negative but rather to focus on aspects under which adaptations for compensating for shortcomings caused by disabilities could become beneficial to everyone. In situations when methods used by non-handicapped people fail, adaptations to compensate for the unavailability of those methods may still work. For example, I have met several people, who'd love to have the screen reader voice of my ZoomText for better learning how to properly pronounce English words and for subconsciously remembering new information without having to actively read them. Furthermore, I only recently learned that one of my tutors got a new idea from working with me resulting in a great publication.

Moreover, forming virtual teams via TeamViewer and Skype made it possible for me to form a new startup company with people I never met before, where we are using machine learning to improve breast cancer diagnostics. Sometimes I feel that I can form much stronger bonds of friendship with people I only met remotely than with people I met in person because we have a much greater overlap of common interests.

11. MAGNIFYING LECTURES

Visually impaired students face the dilemma of needing sufficient magnification for reading while at the same time maintaining a large enough visual field to keep their orientation on the computer screen. Also, when using low vision aids when trying to follow PowerPoint presentations during lectures—although the slides can be magnified using telescope glasses—the remaining visual field is often too small for following the small laser pointer, hence making it very challenging to grasp complex relationships shown in those figures. Fortunately, those remote control programs can be used to display PowerPoint presentations directly onto the large screen of a visually impaired student by remotely logging into the presentation computer and magnify them with ZoomText, as shown in Figure 4.

The main advantage of this approach is that visually impaired students are no longer limited by the much smaller visual field of their telescopes because now their visual field is as large as their monitor.

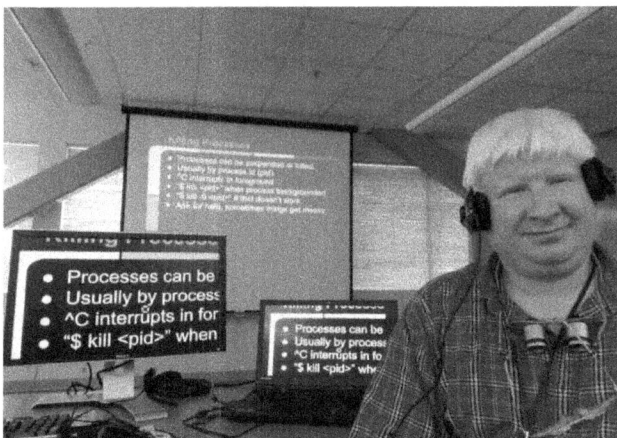

Figure 4: Showing Thomas Hahn (legally blind main author) using TeamViewer in combination with ZoomText to magnify the lecture content during a bioinformatics internship at the National Center for Genomic Resources in Santa Fe, NM (http://www.ncgr.org/) in June 2015.

Furthermore, it is now possible to adjust the magnification to accommodate different font sizes, which is not possible with telescope glasses because their level of magnification is fixed. Visually impaired people constantly struggle in striking the best balance between the contradictory objectives of having high enough magnification for reading and viewing graphical details in figures, while—at the same time—having still a large enough remaining visual field for maintaining their visual orientation in order to follow presentations. If their visual field becomes too small, relationships between items shown on a slide can no longer be seen. Many computer science classrooms are already equipped with computers at the seats of each student. Hence, installing these programs on classroom computers used by visually impaired students would greatly improve their ability to follow lectures more efficiently due to a larger visual field and adjustable levels of magnification. Furthermore, it would allow visually impaired students to demonstrate their work or questions to the entire classroom using ZoomText but without limiting the visual field of their sighted peers. Moreover, the telescope glasses hanging around my neck as shown in Figure 5 are very heavy and cause headaches. Hence, they cannot be worn for extended times because using them is much more exhausting and tiresome than looking at a large computer screen.

Installing such kinds of remote access programs on the classroom computer of each student would allow them to point with their mouse to any item or text on their instructor's computer about which they might have questions. Moreover, the instructor could look at the code of each student from his/her computer. Furthermore, the instructor could monitor the steps students take to navigate new interfaces. Hence, using these remote computer access programs would benefit visually impaired and non-handicapped students alike.

12. VIRTUAL ACCESS REDUCES PERCEPTION OF DISABILITIES

Providing virtual access to everyone would also break down communication barriers between visually impaired and sighted students because they could look at the same problem simultaneously. Thus visually impaired students would no longer be separated from their sighted peers. From the virtual perspective provided by these remote computer access programs it is much less possible to tell whether somebody depends on screen reader and screen magnification programs to compensate for the shortcomings caused by disabilities, thus making it possible to perceive oneself as being closer to normal. The reduced perception of disability and the reduction of the feeling that something is wrong with being disabled can contribute to an even better integration; and feeling of an improved ability to function more similar to the mainstream, which boosts one's confidence.

13. DISABLED PEOPLE ARE OFTEN SIMPLY EARLY ADOPTERS OF BETTER WAYS TO DO THINGS

Adding this virtual interaction component could aid information exchange and discussion in the classroom. As we have seen, adding virtual components, such as remote access, to traditional classroom education can benefit disabled and non-handicapped people alike. It would also make it easier for disabled instructors to give high-quality lectures. There are many ways in which the additional benefits of the added virtual components could be evaluated and quantified, thus allowing better determination of the optimal combination and usage of virtual components to maximize educational success for everyone. And here we see again that—

although disabled people require adding more virtual components sooner to better accommodate their disabilities—non-handicapped people would benefit from that as well. The only difference in my eyes is that the threshold for requiring and demanding changes and improvements, such as more virtual components, is lower for disabled people—but eventually everyone will benefit. For example, since I am visually impaired I was the first in my family to use CD-ROMs to look up phone numbers, whereas everyone else still used the traditional, thick, old, yellow phone book. But eventually everyone started to use CD-ROMs. The only difference was that—since it was more difficult for me to use a phone book because of my visual impairment—the threshold for switching to better methods, such as CD-ROMs, was much lower for me because the traditional way to look up phone numbers did not work for me. But eventually, everyone figured out the additional benefits and today we all use the Internet. Hence, one can conclude from this observation that disabled people are more on the lookout for better ways to compensate for the shortcomings caused by their impairments, but often, if they find better ways, they often benefit everyone eventually. Disabled people are just more likely to adopt them sooner because the status quo is less acceptable to them.

14. CURRENT BOTTLENECKS

Current limitations for this approach to be more widely used in research are caused by the difficulties to quickly convey characters that are not on our keyboard. However, tablet computers are already available for about $1,000, which allow for well legible handwriting. As soon as they become more widely used, even that kind of information can be exchanged remotely much faster in real time. Currently, this is still a bottleneck preventing me from advancing in higher mathematics when the equations become too long for me to fit on even large paper.

The counteracting objectives to have at least enough magnification to read while keeping the remaining visual field large enough to keep ones orientation on the screen inevitably requires compromise either on the magnification or the size of the visual field. The 27-inch external monitors I am currently using were all purchased in 2008 (see Figure 2). Back in 2008, these were the biggest available monitors that could be bought for an at least somewhat reasonable price. Hence, the 27-inch display diagonal has been the limiting factor for the maximally available visual field. Fortunately, display technology has advanced rapidly since 2008, thus bringing down the prices for high resolution 4K external monitors with display diagonals of up to 65 inches to less than $2,000. I was extremely delighted when my rehab counselor indicated recently that it might be possible for him to justify purchasing such a large 65-inch high resolution 4K external monitor to enable me to see two application windows simultaneously. It is my hope that this will allow me to finally view a programming or application interface simultaneously with the instructions on how to use them. Until now, I have only been able to view one or the other, but never both at the same time. If I could view a particular interface simultaneously with the instructions explaining its usage, it would be a quantum leap forward in my ability to access and process electronic information. This would increase the benefits of using computer access and voice communication programs even more because if I had access to such a large external monitor I could work much more similar to sighted people and hence could learn much faster from them remotely. Maybe that would also allow me to view large figures and their corresponding captions simultaneously since this has been a huge bottleneck in my ability to understand visually intensive scientific

publications. And here we see again that a larger screen will generally be demanded sooner by the visually impaired but non-handicapped people benefit from this improvement as well.

15. FUTURE OUTLOOK

If this remote access approach is eventually used much more widely as more appropriate hardware and software become available, it will become easier for visually impaired people like me to better integrate into an increasingly competitive and specialized workforce. Our ability to exchange information remotely in real time will be further improved, and the more this approach is used, the fewer people will be aware of my visual handicap since one cannot even tell from such remote communication whether somebody like me depends on screen reader and screen magnification programs to compensate for the shortcomings caused by disabilities. Thus, at least some disabled people would feel less singled out because fewer people would realize that they must work in different ways to overcome limitations caused by disabilities. As we improve our abilities to better generate living and working environments, in which the adverse effects caused by disabilities can be increasingly minimized, most disabled people will experience a huge improvement in their quality of life. They will start feeling that there is a place for them in our society when their disability is much less of a limiting factor to their opportunities and development of other potentials and interests. It feels very good if one can gain increasing control over one's life by learning to compensate for the adverse effects caused by disabilities, eventually well enough that they no longer constitute the limiting factor. However, this requires much timelier implementation of new technological advances in overcoming limitations caused by disabilities. What really worries me is—that despite their relatively easy implementation, their enormous benefits, their availability free of charge—I only know of very few handicapped people who actually benefit from combining remote access with screen magnification and voice communication.

Therefore, I very strongly feel that conferences, such as this one, are extremely essential for connecting disabled people with the approaches that best meet their needs, and that allow them to maximize their potentials despite being disabled. That is why I very strongly feel that it is very essential that I be given the opportunity to present in person all the beneficial effects I have described in this experience report. As cognitive performance declines with age, training older people remotely to better adapt to changes in their virtual environments could enormously contribute toward maintaining their virtual independence for much longer. I noticed that—at least the quality of my life—depends much more on virtual than on real relationships because virtual interactions much better allow me to reach my potentials despite being disabled, for all the reasons I have described in this experience report. I must admit that I generally feel much more accepted by my virtual partners than by many people I interact with on a personal level. I feel that this experience is indicative of how much more exciting one's life could potentially become if one can improve on a virtual level.

16. FUNDING ACKNOWLEDGMENT

This project was supported by the Arkansas INBRE program, with grants from the National Center for Research Resources (NCRR, P20RR016460) and the National Institute of General Medical Sciences (NIGMS, P20GM103429) at the National Institute of Health (NIH).

Clinical and Maker Perspectives on the Design of Assistive Technology with Rapid Prototyping Technologies

Megan Hofmann*, Julie Burke$^{\Omega\dagger}$, Jon Pearlman$^{\Omega}$, Goeran Fiedler$^{\Omega}$, Andrea Hess$^{\beta}$, Jon Schull$^{\pi\dagger}$, Scott Hudson*, Jennifer Mankoff*†

{meganh@cs.cmu.edu; {julieburke, jpearlman, gfiedler}@pitt.edu; andrea.hess@ottobock.com; jschull@gmail.com; {scott.hudson, jmankoff}@cs.cmu.edu;

| *HCI Institute | $^{\Omega}$School of Health and Rehab. | $^{\beta}$Independent | $^{\pi}$MAGIC ACT Rochester | † e-NABLE |
| Carnegie Mellon | Sciences, University of Pittsburgh | Prosthetist | Institute of Technology | |

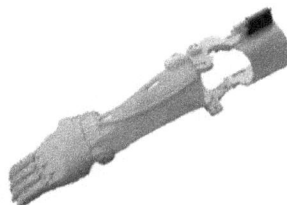

A: The RIT E-NABLE Lab is representative of many maker spaces, including tools like consumer 3D printers. The designs that come from e-NABLE are characterized by bright colors and mechanical simplicity similar to toys and puppet hands, such as this Raptor Reloaded hand.

B: University of Pittsburgh Prosthetists use this state of the art lamination room to build professional prosthetic sockets. The shown prosthetic is the Michelangelo Arm, an advanced myoelectric arm by Ottobock, a prior employer of an attending prosthetist.

Figure 1. We compare the experiences of clinicians and researchers (A) to those of the e-NABLE community (B). One clear contrast is the level of fabrication technology used by both communities, and this impacts the complexity of the produced devices. This is shown by contrasting the products of attending institutions, a Raptor Reloaded Arm from e-NABLE and a Michelangelo Arm from the prosthetic company Ottobock.

ABSTRACT

In this experience report, we describe the experiences of volunteer assistive device designers, clinicians, and human computer interaction and fabrication researchers who met at a summit on Do-It-Yourself Assistive Technology. From the perspectives of these stakeholders, we elucidate significant challenges of introducing rapid prototyping to the design of professional assistive technology, and opportunities for advancing assistive technology. We describe these challenges and opportunities in the context of an emerging gap between clinical and volunteer assistive device design. Whereas clinical process is fully led by the question, "will this do harm", while volunteers chaotically pursue the lofty goal of providing assistive technology to all. While all stakeholders hold the same core goals, there are many practical limitations to collaboration and development.

Keywords

Assistive technology, clinical practice, clinician, design, do no harm, experience report, prosthetic, prosthetist, prototyping, rapid fabrication, regulation, safety, 3D printing, 3D scanning

ASSETS '16, October 23 - 26, 2016, Reno, NV, USA
Copyright is held by the owner/author(s). Publication rights licensed to ACM.
ACM 978-1-4503-4124-0/16/10...$15.00
DOI: http://dx.doi.org/10.1145/2982142.2982181

1. INTRODUCTION

3D printed and non-professional assistive technology design has stimulated new questions about the future while presenting unique challenges for collaboration among volunteers and clinicians. What technologies and practices will be appropriate for creating effective and safe assistive devices as rapid prototyping technology becomes ubiquitous? What role should clinicians have when non-professionals can create assistive technology in the home? What assurances can we make that Do-It-Yourself assistive technology (DIY-AT) is safe, and works properly? We address these questions from the perspectives of several stakeholders in the design of rapidly fabricated prosthetic devices (volunteers, clinicians, and technologists).

In this experience report, we document challenges and opportunities with introducing rapid prototyping technologies into the field of assistive technology. These findings are the result of a summit on DIY-AT, focusing on the future of 3D printed prosthetics, such as devices created by the e-NABLE Community of volunteers. The summit brought together: Enable Community Foundation leaders and volunteers (e-NABLErs); human computer interaction/fabrication researchers; rehabilitation scientists and engineers; and clinicians (occupational therapists, orthotists, and prosthetists) (Figure 1). We describe their shared experiences of using rapid prototyping technology such as 3D printers and 3D scanners in the design and life cycle of assistive technology, primarily focusing on upper limb prosthetics.

During the summit, we identified two main perspectives on the introduction of rapid prototyping to assistive technology design. First is the perspective of the clinicians, which revealed an unmet role in the research, development, and release of open-source and 3D printed devices. Second is the perspective of makers and their role: to create DIY designs that provide a wider population of users access to assistive technology.

Clinicians' concerns centered on their obligation to "do no harm" and whether volunteers can design and support safe devices without the expertise and experience of clinicians. Clinicians also wondered how to safely contribute to DIY devices within the current structure of volunteer organizations. The attending clinicians identified many aspects of their research process that was missing from e-NABLE's practices, and argued that pre-patient device testing and more validation measures would produce improved designs. Clinicians acknowledged the important role of rapid prototyping in their practice: as a tool to create highly customized devices and to advance clinical research.

E-NABLErs, in turn, noted that many of their developments could improve professional practice. For example, DIY-AT can help to provide highly customized and easy to produce terminal devices for standard prosthetics, and has brought inexpensive upper limb prosthetics to children and other underserved populations for whom traditional medical prosthetics are less practical or accessible. These developments, they argue, are the result of a rapid and somewhat chaotic "maker" approach to design. They pointed to successes in creating a wide variety of customized terminal devices and an international impact by supporting people without access to professional prosthetics. They see their role as filling in the gaps where clinicians cannot support all users, all the time.

While this summit brought together a large group of diverse perspectives and stakeholders in the design of assistive technology, we limit the scope of this report to perspectives of professionals and experienced volunteers who primarily create prosthetic devices. The focus of many of the summit attendees is in the design of upper limb prosthetic devices, or other assistive technology for people with limb differences, such as gripping aids or orthotics. Further, we note that none of the authors of this paper use prosthetic devices. We limit the scope of this report to our multi-stakeholder perspective on the experience of designing assistive technology and the rapid prototyping technologies that support and disrupt the design process. We do not focus on the utility of prosthetics or any other assistive technology.

2. BACKGROUND
The first amateur-buildable 3D printed prosthetic-like device was created in 2011, and since then the e-NABLE network of volunteers has grown into an international movement creating and distributing 3D printed prosthetic-like devices [22]. The story has gained massive popularity as it introduced a new aspect of 3D printing and assistive technology to the public at large [12, 13, 27]. E-NABLE has the potential to make inexpensive prosthetic-like devices available to underserved populations, such as: children who outgrow traditional prosthetics [9], or people in countries with developing health care systems where access to prosthetics and the clinicians who create them may be limited [18].

2.1 A CLINICAL PERSPECTIVE
Since the 1990s, 3D printing has been a topic of interest in the professional prosthetics world [25]. From the use of 3D printing as a rapid prototyping method, to studies investigating its viability and usage in socket fabrication, and the release of cosmetic prosthetic attachments, 3D printing has made its mark on the professional field and will continue to do so [14, 19].

One possible value of rapid prototyping is in follow up. It is difficult to study assistive technology in the wild and most literature documenting abandonment rates use surveys [3, 23]—improved sensor integration could change this, as it has with wheelchairs [26] (which provide an easy platform for sensor deployment).

Among clinicians, there appear to be conflicting opinions and ambivalence. Clinicians may embrace 3D printing technology or becoming defensive or resistant against it [30]. Perceived job insecurity may also make clinicians hesitant to encourage or participate in research and development of 3D printing technologies for use in the professional world [20].

2.2 A MAKER'S PERSPECTIVE
DIY-AT and 3D printing have been studied in many assistive technology domains [4, 7, 8, 15]. DIY-AT can improve user relationships with devices [2, 17], by allowing for cost effective customization of devices [7, 8, 9] which may reduce abandonment rates [16, 23, 24]. Further, digital fabrication technologies supports sharing these designs online, providing opportunities for collaboration which produces improved designs [29]. However, with respect to sharing assistive technology online, few designers report having a disability or designing for themselves, and few designers have clinical expertise [5]. 3D modeling tools are also being created to support different aspects of device design [10, 21] for assistive technology in particular [1, 4, 7, 11, 28].

3. DIY-AT SUMMIT
It is difficult to bridge the gap between clinical and non-professional assistive technology designers. Clinicians have safety regulations that limit what they create to assure patient safety. Non-professionals may circumvent many of these regulations and constraints. For example, e-NABLE can circumvent medical device requirements by referring to their prosthetic-like devices as toys. This allows them to produce a wide variety of designs rapidly. However, the e-NABLE community has few formal mechanisms for assuring safety and quality. These regulatory factors and cultural differences impede collaboration between clinical and non-professional assistive technology designers.

This report is the result of a two-day summit of e-NABLE volunteers, Enable Community Foundation representatives, clinicians (prosthetists, orthotists, and occupational therapists), and human computer interaction and fabrication researchers. The goal of this summit was to discuss the value of 3D printing and rapid prototyping technology, and identify the challenges to introducing the technology to clinical and volunteer practices. Many stakeholders in the domain of prosthetic design attended, in hopes of sharing their experiences and learning from designers on either side of the clinical / non-professional gap.

Table 1. Presenters, affiliation, and presentation titles for the presentations that set discussion topics for the DIY-AT Summit

Presenter	Affiliation	Presentation title
Jon Schull	MAGIC ACT, Rochester Institute of Technology; Enable Community Foundation	The status of e-NABLE: volunteers printing prosthetic-like devices
Andrea Hess	Independent Prosthetist	Clinical research goals regarding rapid prototyping
Ben Salatin	Clinical Rehabilitation Engineer for the Albuquerque Veterans Medical Center	Clinical concerns regarding 3D printed prosthetic-like devices
Scott Hudson	Human Computer Interaction Institute of Carnegie Mellon University	A technical perspective of rapid prototyping assistive technology
Jeffery Bigham	Human Computer Interaction Institute of Carnegie Mellon University	A technical perspective of behavioral science and assistive technology
Skip Meetze	e-NABLE Volunteer	Recent technical advances for 3D printed prosthetic-like devices

This summit began with six presentations of differing perspectives on rapid prototyping and its role in the creation and design of prosthetic devices. These presentations titles, presenters, and affiliations are in Table 1.

Following these presentations, attendees broke out into groups to discuss current research and experiences regarding different topics. These topics were broken into three categories, which bridged different stakeholder's expertise, including augmenting clinical expertise among makers; improving tools for clinicians and makers; and advancing 3D printed prosthetics. Finally, the groups reconvened to discuss the greater challenges to introducing rapid prototyping technology into the design and creation of prosthetics. These discussions elucidate various challenges to introducing rapid prototyping technology into the practices of different stakeholders. This introduces opportunities for new research, invention, and innovation.

4. BRING "DO NO HARM" TO DIY-AT

The core concern of clinicians, when presented with DIY-AT, was how to enforce a clinician's' Hippocratic Oath to "Do No Harm"[1]. From one perspective, clinicians can support the design of better open source assistive technology by applying the validation methods used in their practice, and supporting patient follow-up on devices already in use. From another perspective, a clinician's involvement in the design of open source assistive technology gives them liability if the designs fail, both legally and morally. Finally, clinicians were concerned by the response of regulators and insurance companies, and how this may limit users' access to professional devices.

4.1 The Design Phase

Clinicians train to identify safety and biomechanical flaws at each stage of the design process. For example, prosthetists are the product of rigorous education in clinical decision-making, techniques for assessing the appropriate application of assistive technology, and the design of safe devices. Attending clinicians described their research as a highly structured process that ensures they fully validate devices before a patient ever tests one. They worried that communities of volunteers lack the training and insight needed to validate open source designs.

The US Food and Drug Administration (FDA) classifies prosthetics as low risk devices. Because prosthetists are the only licensed professionals who can provide a medically certified prosthetic, the FDA enables them to produce prosthetics with

little interference on a case-by-case basis. More regulation is required for the manufacturers of prosthetic parts; the FDA ultimately holds these manufacturers responsible for any malfunction and injury resulting from a flawed design. However, makers act as both manufacturer and prosthetists. An attending e-NABLEr described the lack of regulation as one of the factors that contributes to their diversity of devices; however, he thought that the regulatory environment might change as the community develops advanced devices (*e.g.*, myoelectric prosthetics).

The attending e-NABLErs characterize their "maker" perspective as a drive to invent new, creative solutions with "down and dirty" iteration cycles and rapid prototyping. Maker culture has no barrier to entry. Makers are self-trained and unregulated. They build on the diversity of experiences provided by novice and expert creators. The e-NABLErs described their methodology as trial-and-error based, with little structure, follow-up, or feedback methods; they argue this allows them to conduct collaborative, large-scale, open-sourced research and development. The attending e-NABLErs preached caution, however: There are no formal mechanisms for enforcement of best practices, or suspension of dangerous activities.

Whereas traditional clinical research methodologies intend to reduce risk to patients, attendees from both groups were concerned about the research methodology of makers. Both groups acknowledged that unregulated processes pose potential risk to users, as failures found in testing often happen during use. The clinicians believe that, by bringing a clinical perspective, they could obtain evidence as to whether or not a method, fabrication technique, or device is truly beneficial to the user. The e-NABLErs recognized the importance of clinicians, and often encourage recipients to seek professional support. However, in general e-NABLE cannot and will not require access to clinicians. In fact, much of the population they support cannot access clinicians due to location or cost. Further, clinicians, when approached by patients who are seeking support with an e-NABLE device, may fall into the "do no harm" conflict: Supporting an unknown device could put the patient at risk, but turning them away could result in no treatment or unregulated treatment by volunteers.

4.2 Follow Up

One clinician noted that the most important role she provides to patients is to follow up on a device after she releases it. This reflects her clinical knowledge regarding the importance of education in patient care and the long-term effects of devices. The clinician cited how she adjusts devices to fit a growing patient, and how she recognizes that a device is injuring the

---

[1] "Do No Harm" refers to the Hippocratic Oath taken by many clinicians in western cultures. The concept refers to a clinician's job: first, do no harm to a patient, and then help the patient.

patient through use. It may be damaging the skin or requiring an awkward, straining motion. She specifically commented on the awkward grasping motion in e-NABLE devices. To close the fingers, a user must bend his wrist, which she says would cause strain and could eventually cause a repetitive strain injury. The clinicians thought that their understanding of biomechanics might have prevented this design flaw.

Clinical practice provides a system to support follow up in the form of regular medical appointments. The e-NABLErs recognized the value of this, as there is no current formal expectation for recipients to follow up with their assigned volunteer. However, e-NABLErs rebutted that the prohibitive financial and time costs of meeting clinicians were as disruptive as seeking out their volunteer. Both groups wished to find a balance between the expertise of clinicians and the access to the crowd of supportive and invested volunteers e-NABLE can provide.

4.3 Device Access

There is another challenge regarding open source designs: how do these designs affect an individual's access to assistive technology? From the e-NABLE perspective, designers without clinical training or engineering experience may be able to collect assistive technology designs from the Internet. Shared designs remove the need for design expertise with rapid prototyping technology. However, there was a prevailing concern among the attending clinicians that these freely available designs could do harm to the populations they support because people may lose access to professional devices.

One presenter remarked that a colleague of hers was in court because a medical insurance company no longer considered his devices medically necessary. The company argued that 3D printed trans-radial prosthetics became exceedingly popular because the media misreported and presented them out of context. This caused the company to recognize the devices as a widely appropriate assistive technology, so they are denying claims on more expensive, but medically valuable, advanced devices. For the populations that e-NABLE supports, this is less of an issue, because many cannot currently access advanced devices through a medical practitioner. From e-NABLErs perspective, any hand is better than no hand. This was a main point of contention at the summit.

5. MOVING BEYOND MAKING HANDS

In general, the clinicians encouraged the advancement of 3D printed prosthetics and pushed the attending e-NABLErs to iterate on terminal devices rather than the gauntlets and hands they currently release. This meets the clinical need for safety regulations at the level of the prosthetic socket, and still leverages the value of 3D printed devices. With current modeling practices, it is much easier to create a custom terminal device than a form fitting socket [15]. From the perspective of e-NABLErs, this may be a more exciting task as it allows for the creation of a plethora of task-specific devices. It builds on the strengths of maker communities to create unique designs and to iterate and customize these designs for individuals.

Clinicians felt that there are not enough professionals able to create and support the current populations of prosthetic users who require task-specific terminal devices. Communities like e-NABLE may be able to fill this void. However, clinicians raised specific concerns regarding potentially dangerous activities—*i.e.*

steering wheel and bike attachments that a user cannot quickly detach in an emergency, or swimming equipment that could increase drowning risk. One prosthetist described her experience building a terminal device for a surfer; she was extremely worried that if the design failed to float or broke, it could lead to the death of her patient. She wondered if communities like e-NABLE could limit themselves to safer activities.

Concerning how devices connect to users, clinicians believed that research of rapid fabrication technology and socket fitting should remain a topic for professional practice. The prosthetists argued that this was the most complex part of their craft, and that it posed the greatest risk to patients. As they see it, if digital rapid prototyping technology could support the ambiguity and freedom of their craft, it would be a valuable asset because it enables the reproduction of a crafted design. However, current systems are limited. One prosthetist referred to 3D scanning technology's ability to produce a rigid representation of an amputated limb; however, this did not reflect the malleability of flesh. The more standard practice of constructing casts of a limb includes a prosthetist fitting around unseen structures in the limb, such as malleable muscle groups and non-standard bone structures. He worried that 3D scanning and printing cannot express the complex relationship between a socket and a patient's physiology.

Rapid fabrication tools may support customizing devices to fit to a user in another way. It may be possible that 3D scanning could support reproducing previously fitted designs. One attendee was an engineer for the US Department of Veterans Affairs (VA) who prototypes 3D printed assistive technology for occupational therapists (OTs) in the VA's hospital system. The attendee had been working with thermo-forming and scanning techniques for creating reproducible arm splints. In his case, he took the common orthotist practice of creating a thermoformed orthotic and 3D scanning it. The e-NABLErs drew comparisons to their practice of creating thermoformed gauntlets with 3D printed PLA sheets. Both groups remarked that these techniques could allow clinicians and users to reproduce devices by sharing 3D model files. In the VA, OTs could reproduce the scanned version and mail it to patients if the original were broken. For e-NABLE device users, they can reprint a gauntlet and reform it in the home with some support from a volunteer or friend.

6. "ENABLING THE FUTURE" OF AT WITH RAPID PROTOTYPING

Rapid prototyping technology is valuable because it supports design innovation. This leads to many new directions for clinicians to explore when supporting a patient with unique needs. An attendee representing the VA had expertise in rapid fabrication as well as clinical design. This afforded him unique opportunities to negotiate the high standards of clinical practice while introducing the customization and innovation benefits of rapid prototyping. However, he can only support a small number of OTs, and most clinicians do not have the expertise needed to include rapid prototyping in their practice. He believes this is because of lack of training or access to the technology. Without a full understanding of the potential of the technology, the extra time required to learn 3D modeling or to scan a device before sending it out seems prohibitive to many of his OT collaborators.

Some clinicians raised another concern for integrating rapid prototyping into their practice; under current systems: it may be difficult to compensate clinicians for the time-spent prototyping. For example, an OT's primarily income is for time spent with patients. If clinicians must prototype outside of a care session, it is not clear that medical insurance companies will compensate them for their time. In the case of prosthetists, their income is from the sale of devices. The amount of money reimbursed by insurance companies to a prosthetist is dependent on the original cost of the materials, the estimate on time and labor required for the job, and the time the prosthetist will spend seeing the patient for evaluation, delivery, and subsequent maintenance and follow up visits. Due to this billing structure, prosthetists may not be as interested in creating rapid prototype items: The time they spend designing, modeling, and printing may not be covered for insurance reimbursement. In addition, medical insurance companies are likely to tie reimbursement to FDA approval of the devices a clinician produces and getting approval for every custom device is not feasible.

Cost was less of a concern for e-NABLErs, as the volunteer community had not needed to work with medical insurance companies or the FDA. Rather, rapid prototyping excited them because it could remove some of the costs of creating devices, and some of the barriers to accessing clinicians for devices and maintenance. From their perspective, the cost or location of a practitioner can inhibit many people from accessing professional assistive devices. For instance, it may be difficult for children to get prosthetics covered by insurance because they outgrow them. Further, they argue, it can be difficult to get professional care for a device at a moment's notice. Since the e-NABLE devices are "do-it-yourself" and made by non-professionals, it should be easier to fix a device when it breaks, or adjust it to the user's particular needs. However, many of the clinicians were skeptical of this benefit in e-NABLE's current practice. One prosthetist argued that someone without a hand could not construct the devices, and that scheduling time with a volunteer is less reliable than scheduling time with clinicians.

Many clinicians saw the role of rapid prototyping as furthering research in the prosthetics field. One clear example was how rapid prototyping technology could support embedding custom data collection sensors into prosthetics. They described the value of these sensors for studying device use in the wild. This may support research on usage and abandonment. One clinician compared this to tracking location data on wheelchairs; this data supports research into wheelchair accessibility and usage. It is currently difficult to collect sensor data on prosthetic devices, because of prohibitive cost and difficulty integrating new sensors into standard prosthetics. The clinicians believed that rapid fabrication could make it easier to use sensors by embedding them in devices. This requires further research into rapid manufacturing techniques that support sensor integration. The data collected from these devices could benefit many fields of research. It could support the testing of new devices, or lead to discoveries on the causes of device abandonment.

7. DISCUSSION

Both the attending clinicians and e-NABLErs recognized a common goal: for people with limb differences to access devices that improve their quality of life. However, the backgrounds each group led to a constant tension between the clinicians' cautious optimism and the unqualified exuberance of volunteers.

Out of this tension, we elucidate many potential avenues of research that could bridge the gap between these communities as well as advance each individually.

"Do no harm" is central to clinical practice, and is relevant to every portion of the life cycle of DIY-AT. This poses major challenges to volunteer groups and is a unique area of interest for researchers investigating multiple stakeholder collaboration. How can we regulate large groups of people, without tying their hands to legal and bureaucratic systems that delay design iteration? The systems used by professionals assure that devices are safe and properly maintained, however the lack of oversight on groups like e-NABLE allows for rapid and unhindered growth, in both positive and negative directions.

One method for supporting collaboration may be to separate the domains of each group. There seemed to be consensus that each group could support research on different portions of the prosthetic: the sockets that connect the prosthetic-like device to a user, and the terminal devices that allow users to interact with the environment. Clinicians considered the design of sockets to be one of the most difficult and technically challenging portions of their craft; they encouraged the e-NABLE community to avoid this area of design. However, terminal devices may cover a larger variety of tasks, many of which are relatively safe. Focusing design efforts on these devices may allow e-NABLE's resource of thousands of designers to create a huge repository of customizable designs. Advances in rapid prototyping technology and 3D modeling technology support both these goals. 3D modeling software should better support clinical practice by integrating into the crafting style of socket design, while software for volunteers should support the design of validatable devices with minimal expertise.

Finally, clinicians perceive the current state of rapid prototyping technology as prohibitive to them and their patients, making it difficult to access many of the benefits reaped by e-NABLE. It is important that users can easily alter their assistive devices or have an accessible support system for maintaining them. Researchers should explore how volunteers, clinicians, and patients can collaborate over the life cycle of a design. This includes validation of designs, tools for adjusting designs during use, and techniques for conducting research that leverages the capabilities of rapidly prototyped devices.

8. CONCLUSION

Currently, there is a large divide between clinical practice and the work of volunteer assistive device designers. Both groups provide value: clinicians produce safe and robust devices, while e-NABLE produces a large quantity of unique and customized designs. There seems to be a consensus that rapid prototyping technology can play a significant role in the future of assistive technology. However, if we do not overcome the challenges of these conflicting methodologies the gap may persist and worsen in the years to come. Clinicians may continue to have difficulty leveraging rapid prototyping in their practice, while e-NABLE will produce more devices that they cannot validate and fully support. To bridge this gap, there must be new ways for clinicians to share their expertise with volunteer communities, and volunteers must support a collaborative design process that provides clinicians and assistive technology users access to a wide variety of validatable designs.

9. ACKNOWLEDGEMENTS

We would like to thank the attendees of the DIY-AT summit as well as the sponsoring institutions, Carnegie Mellon University, The University of Pittsburgh, and the Enable Community Foundation.

10. REFERENCES

[1] Bastian, A. 2016. *LimbForge Wiki*.

[2] Bennett, C.L., Cen, K., Steele, K.M. and Rosner, D.K. 2016. An Intimate Laboratory?: Prostheses As a Tool for Experimenting with Identity and Normalcy. *Proceedings of the 2016 CHI Conference on Human Factors in Computing Systems* (New York, NY, USA, 2016), 1745–1756.

[3] Biddiss, E. and Chau, T. 2007. Upper-limb prosthetics: critical factors in device abandonment. *American Journal of Physical Medicine & Rehabilitation*. 86, 12 (2007), 977–987.

[4] Brown, C. and Hurst, A. 2012. VizTouch. *Sixth International Conference on Tangible, Embedded and Embodied Interaction* (Feb. 2012), 131–138.

[5] Buehler, E., Branham, S., Ali, A., Chang, J.J., Hofmann, M.K., Hurst, A. and Kane, S.K. 2015. Sharing is Caring: Assistive Technology Designs on Thingiverse. *Proceedings of the 33rd Annual ACM Conference on Human Factors in Computing Systems* (New York, NY, USA, 2015), 525–534.

[6] Buehler, E., Comrie, N., Hofmann, M., McDonald, S. and Hurst, A. 2016. Investigating the Implications of 3D Printing in Special Education. *ACM Trans. Access. Comput.* 8, 3 (Mar. 2016), 11:1–11:28.

[7] Buehler, E., Hurst, A. and Hofmann, M. 2014. Coming to Grips: 3D Printing for Accessibility. *Proceedings of the 16th International ACM SIGACCESS Conference on Computers & Accessibility* (New York, NY, USA, 2014), 291–292.

[8] Buehler, E., Kane, S.K. and Hurst, A. 2014. ABC and 3D: Opportunities and Obstacles to 3D Printing in Special Education Environments. *Proceedings of the 16th International ACM SIGACCESS Conference on Computers & Accessibility* (New York, NY, USA, 2014), 107–114.

[9] Burn, M.B., Ta, A. and Gogola, G.R. 2016. Three-Dimensional Printing of Prosthetic Hands for Children. *The Journal of hand surgery*. 41, 5 (2016), e103–e109.

[10] Chen, X. "Anthony," Coros, S., Mankoff, J. and Hudson, S.E. 2015. Encore: 3D Printed Augmentation of Everyday Objects with Printed-over, Affixed and Interlocked Attachments. *ACM SIGGRAPH 2015 Posters* (New York, NY, USA, 2015), 3:1–3:1.

[11] Creuzer, M., Jones, A., Ortiz, R. and Popkin, L. 2015. *Hand-O-Matic*.

[12] Dickeson, T. 2015. Pontypool girl's prosthetic hand made with 3D printer. *BBC News*.

[13] Domanico, A. 2015. Cheaper prosthetic arms let kids become a Jedi Knight, Iron Man or Elsa - CNET. *CNET*.

[14] Herbert, N., Simpson, D., Spence, W.D. and Ion, W. 2005. A preliminary investigation into the development of 3-D printing of prosthetic sockets. *Journal of Rehabilitation Research and Development*. 42, 2 (Mar. 2005), 141–6.

[15] Hofmann, M., Harris, J., Hudson, S.E. and Mankoff, J. 2016. Helping Hands: Requirements for a Prototyping Methodology for Upper-limb Prosthetics Users. *Proceedings of the 2016 CHI Conference on Human Factors in Computing Systems* (New York, NY, USA, 2016), 1769–1780.

[16] Hook, J., Verbaan, S., Wright, P. and Olivier, P. 2013. Exploring the Design of technologies and services that support do-it-yourself assistive technology practice. *Proceedings of DE*. 2013, (2013).

[17] Hurst, A. and Tobias, J. 2011. Empowering Individuals with Do-it-yourself Assistive Technology. *The Proceedings of the 13th International ACM SIGACCESS Conference on Computers and Accessibility* (New York, NY, USA, 2011), 11–18.

[18] Ishengoma, F.R. and Mtaho, A.B. 2014. 3D printing: developing countries perspectives. *arXiv preprint arXiv:1410.5349*. (2014).

[19] Judith Otto 2014. 3D Printing: Opportunity for Technicians? | July 2014 | The O&P EDGE | oandp.com. *oandp.com*.

[20] Kesselring, J.A., Fiedler, G. and Pearlman, J. 2016. Prosthetist's Assessment of Additive Manufacturing as an Alternative to conventional manufacturing techniques in P&O. *Proceedings of the 42nd Annual AAOP Meeting and Scientific Symposium* (Orlando, FL, 2016).

[21] Koyama, Y., Sueda, S., Steinhardt, E., Igarashi, T., Shamir, A. and Matusik, W. 2015. AutoConnect: Computational Design of 3D-printable Connectors. *ACM Trans. Graph*. 34, 6 (Oct. 2015), 231:1–231:11.

[22] Owen, J. 2014. ABOUT US. *Enabling The Future*.

[23] Phillips, B. and Zhao, H. 1993. Predictors of assistive technology abandonment. *Assistive Technology*. 5, 1 (1993), 36–45.

[24] Riemer-Reiss, M.L. and Wacker, R.R. 2000. Factors associated with assistive technology discontinuance among individuals with disabilities. *Journal of Rehabilitation*. 66, 3 (2000), 44.

[25] Rogers, W., Crawford, R., Beaman, J. and Walsh, N. 1991. Fabrication of prosthetic sockets by selective laser sintering. *1991 Solid Freeform Fabrication Symposium Proceedings, Marcus, HL, Beaman, JJ, Barlow, JW, Bourell, DL, and Crawford, RH, eds., Austin, TX* (1991), 158–163.

[26] Sonenblum, S.E., Sprigle, S., Harris, F.H. and Maurer, C.L. 2008. Characterization of power wheelchair use in the home and community. *Archives of physical medicine and rehabilitation*. 89, 3 (2008), 486–491.

[27] Spencer, S. 2015. Watch what happens when boy puts on prosthetic hand. *USA TODAY*.

[28] Taking Measurements in Tracker - Cyborg Beast: 2014. *http://www.cyborgbeast.org/taking-measurements-tracker/*. Accessed: 2015-09-13.

[29] Torrey, C., McDonald, D.W., Schilit, B.N. and Bly, S. 2007. How-To pages: Informal systems of expertise sharing. *ECSCW 2007*. Springer. 391–410.

[30] Travis M. Andrews 2013. Can We Really 3-D Print Limbs for Amputees? - The Atlantic. *The Atlantic*.

OnScreenDualScribe with Point-and-Click Interface: A viable computer interaction alternative based on a virtual modified numerical keypad*

Kavita Krishnawamy[†]
University of Maryland
Baltimore County
1000 Hilltop Circle
Baltimore, MD 21250
kavi1@umbc.edu

Patricia Ordóñez
University of Puerto Río
Piedras
P.O. Box 70377
San Juan, PR 00936-8377
patricia.ordonez@upr.edu

Phillip Beckerle
Technical University of
Darmstadt
Karolinenpl. 5
64289 Darmstadt, Germany
beckerle@ims.tu-
darmstadt.de

Stephan Rinderknecht
Technical University of
Darmstadt
Karolinenpl. 5
64289 Darmstadt, Germany
rinderknecht@ims.tu-
darmstadt.de

Torsten Felzer[‡]
Technical University of
Darmstadt
Karolinenpl. 5
64289 Darmstadt, Germany
felzer@ims.tu-
darmstadt.de

ABSTRACT

This paper describes the experience of the first author with the *Point-and-Click Interface* of the *OnScreenDualScribe*, created by the last author. The new interface is an innovative extension to the previous interface which required the use of the *DualPad*. The main differences between the two interfaces are highlighted. The user took several writing tests with the *Point-and Click Interface* and compares her results with two of interfaces she uses the most for writing, *Dragon NaturallySpeaking* and *SofType*. Finally, the first author recommends several improvements to the interface which would make the software a better alternative for her.

CCS Concepts

•Human-centered computing → Keyboards; Accessibility design and evaluation methods; Accessibility technologies;

---

*An Extension of the *OnScreenDualScribe with DualPad*
[†]The experienced report primary user.

[‡]The designer and creator of the *OnScreenDualScribe* and the *Point-and-Click Interface*

ASSETS '16, October 23-26, 2016, Reno, NV, USA

© 2016 ACM. ISBN 978-1-4503-4124-0/16/10... $15.00

DOI: http://dx.doi.org/10.1145/2982142.2982184

Keywords

Virtual Keyboard; Assistive Technology; Text Entry

1. INTRODUCTION

The *OnSreenDualScribe* with the *Point-and-Click Interface* is a tool to aid users who are unable to use the standard keyboard or mouse. It replaces the large keyboard and mouse with a virtual on-screen keyboard that is aimed at reducing the number of keystrokes that are required to type a word by incorporating features such as word prediction. It is capable of empowering a person with limited mobility in their hands to type by only moving the mouse over the virtual keyboard.

The first author of this report has Spinal Muscular Atrophy. She requires assistance for all activities of daily living. Her movement is limited and she is only able to interact via a few fingers in one hand. She prefers using a track ball on a mouse for pointing as she requires assistance for from her caregiver to place her hand on the device and to reposition her hand when it slips. After about 1-2 hours of using a virtual keyboard, she fatigues and begins to feel "stiffness in her hands." This requires that she ask her caregiver to submerge her hand in water and massage her fingers for relief of the symptoms. Her two favorite interfaces for text entry are Dragon NaturallySpeaking, the current voice recognition gold standard for dictation and SofType for its word prediction capabilities. Word prediction tools are known to aid users when entering text on both desktop and mobile interfaces.

SofType[TM] by Origin Instruments is a Windows software that provides an alternative to a standard keyboard's functionality with a virtually accessible on–screen keyboard [16]. A user's mouse or preferred pointing device may be used to select a character on the computer screen that will generate

257

the corresponding keystroke on the active application. Additionally, a list of words are presented in the typing process with word prediction to reduce the number of keystrokes because the word can be selected from the prediction list and a space is automatically added at the end of the selected word. Different layouts of the keyboard can be changed based on the preferences and needs of the user. Other features include the AutoClick and Dragger with the common clicking functions of Double Click, Left Drag, Right Click and Right Drag for mouse usage. as an alternative to a standard keyboard's functionality with a virtually accessible on–screen keyboard [16]. A user's mouse or preferred pointing device may be used to select a character on the computer screen that will generate the corresponding keystroke on the active application. Additionally, a list of words are presented in the typing process with word prediction to reduce the number of keystrokes because the word can be selected from the prediction list and a space is automatically added at the end of the selected word. Different layouts of the keyboard can be changed based on the preferences and needs of the user. Other features include the AutoClick and Dragger with the common clicking functions of Double Click, Left Drag, Right Click and Right Drag for mouse usage.

Dragon NaturallySpeaking is a popular speech recognition system developed by Nuance [15]. A user creates a voice profile a completes the training process by pronouncing a list of words. The software learns overtime and transcribes spoken words accurately.

2. RELATED WORK

With improving computer technology, advanced methods to support individuals with disabilities in text entry evolve. Early alternatives rely on conventional keyboards and facilitate input by word prediction [9]. However, the analysis of spoken words and even video recordings in real-time is feasible nowadays. Hence, speech recognition [24, 7] and eye tracking [10, 1, 25, 19] are applied to control a personal computer. Regarding text entry, eye tracking serves as a mouse pointer allowing to operate an on-screen keyboard.

Contemporary, input devices with alternative hardware compared to the standard keyboard that do not require extensive computational power are available. Examples for such systems are EdgeWrite [23, 22] and Dasher [21]. While EdgeWrite uses two dimensional traces to represent individual characters, Dasher uses a pointing device for text entry. Various other systems rely on small keyboards: MessageEase [14] is an ambiguous keyboard with 12 keys similar to a phone keypad. Further approaches replace the standard keyboard by switch-activated scanning systems, e.g., Sibylle [20] and HandiGlyph [2]. Beyond those, OneKey and Qanti combine scanning with ambiguous keyboards [13].

Yet, these approaches might either demand too much or too little from a user with certain disabilities, e.g., Spinal Muscular Atrophy. The combination of small keypads and word prediction can reduce the typing effort and fatigue [18]: although some subjects might perform well with speech recognition, they might benefit from a physical entry device that is meeting their ergonomical needs. The user tester of this study can easily perform lateral movements on the screen using pointing devices but experiences distinct limitations in moving up and down. Thus she can make only limited use of approaches such as Dasher but can exploit systems that are more complex than single-switch input devices

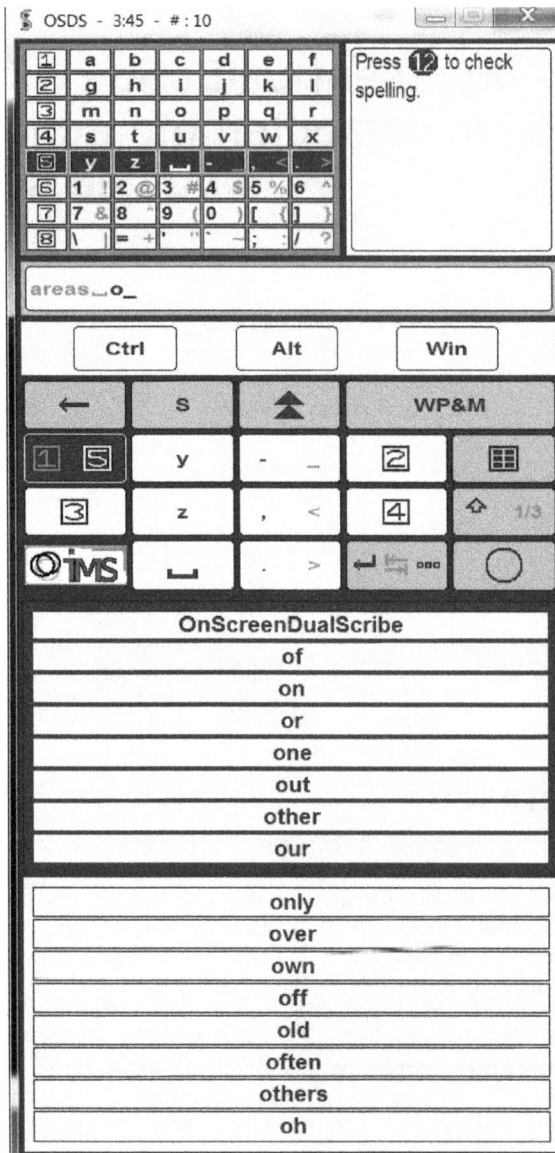

Figure 1: The OSDS interface.

such as MessageEase. Due to her limitations in motion capabilities and fingers that can be used during typing, special keyboards combined with word prediction seem appropriate to meet her needs [18]. According to [4], such keyboards can further be beneficial in pointing compared to standard keyboards [17], head tracking systems [6, 11, 8], or speech recognition [12].

3. THE POINT-AND-CLICK INTERFACE

Previously. the *OSDS* required the use of the *DualPad*, which in its latest form, is an off-the-shelf numeric keypad. It's smaller in size and the fewer keys made it possible for people with limited mobility in their hands to hold the keyboard and type with their two thumbs as did the last author of this paper. He was able to double his words per minute rate with the DualPad [5].

OnScreenDualScribe is a very powerful device with over 12 modes, but for the purpose of this report we will focus solely on the default mode - the Dual Mode. This mode emulates the hardware in software; however, it does not require installing any software. You simply copy all the files to your machine and click on the executable [3]. The software captures all the interaction between the keyboard and the graphical user interface that has the focus. The Point-and-Click Interface was added for people who are not able to physically press down on the keys or hold the keypad in their hands as is the first author of this paper, but may have the similar challenges he had such as of not being able to use voice recognition. Video demos are online 1) https://www.youtube.com/watch?v=9N3bqeyyNjg and 2) https://www.youtube.com/watch?v=ZKku59T-gYo. Please visit url: http://www.felzer.de/data/osds_v309_build1003.zip to download the *OnSreenDualScribe* for free.

When participating in a study which examined the usability of OSDS, the first author was unable to exert sufficient pressure on the keypad buttons. The first author relies instead on the Wheel Mouse. As long as someone can place her hand on the mouse, she can use her index finger to move the mouse. Lateral motion is easier than vertical movement of the pointer for her using the Wheel Mouse. The Point-and-Click Interface is a viable option for her.

OSDS Dual Mode interface can be seen in Figure 1. The interface consists of four square parts. The top square basically presents the use with a new keyboard. The second square down contains the avatar which is where the user can interact with the interface. The third and fourth squares represent the powerful word prediction mechanism of the interface that contains over 100,000 words. The paper will briefly describe the features of the interface that were examined in the writing studies.

3.1 Clicking on Candidates

The Point-and-Click Interface allows for using the mouse button on the avatar to select potential candidate letters and to select words from the lower word prediction squares. So for example, if the user wanted to type the word *often* , the user would:

1.) roll mouse wheel over the [3] button and hover or press,
2.) roll over the [1][5] button and hover or press and finally
3.) select the word from the list of auto-completion options in the bottom dialog box, as seen in Figure 1.

3.2 Dwell Time Clicking

Taking into consideration users that might not be able to click on the interface using the mouse, the interface automatically issues a click if the user points at a clickable area for longer than a certain time period. That period of time is configurable and is called the *dwell time*.

For more information on the interface, reference the file in info directory of the software [3].

4. METHODS

The last author created a writing test suite of 5 random sentences that he asked the evaluator to enter using the OSDS and their favorite text input method. The entering of every sentence was timed and recorded automatically and statistics such as the number of edit operations, correct sentences and characters entered versus total characters was recorded. Thus, for every test in Table 1, five random sentences were typed to determine the Words Per Minute (WPM) and Errors. The test was taken over 7 days with complete rest breaks on Day 4 and Day 6.

5. RESULTS

On examining Figure Table 1 and Figure 2, it is evident that the first author's most efficient method for text input was Dragon NaturallySpeaking. However, it merits saying that in one week of using the interface, her words per minute doubled with the application. As the last author and creator of the interface recognized, the OSDS software requires period of adaption as most users are accustomed to using a qwerty keyboard.

The following are a list of comments from the first author on using the Point-and-Click interface of the OnScreenDualScribe software.

1. Volume is automatically adjusted when the application starts. In fact, even when the system is on mute on the volume control before opening the program, the application automatically turns the volume back on.

2. There is a sound effect after each keystroke that is distracting.

3. A tooltip on menu buttons could be helpful as clear instructions are provided only through the manuals. Since the keyboard is so novel, incorporating help into the interface could improve adaptation.

4. A space should be automatically added after each word completion.

5. When a word is typed with an alternative input (i.e. SofType keyboard) and then edited in OnScreenDualScribe, the word is not recognized with a multimodal interaction use.

6. Dragon NaturallySpeaking says "The correction hot key has been disabled because the same hot key is in use by another application. You may use the Options dialog to select a different hotkey" with a multimodal use.

7. Greek symbols and mathematical symbols can be inserted by OnScreenDualScribe.

8. The alphanumeric layout is difficult to adapt from the traditional qwerty layout. Users should be able to customize their preferred layout.

9. There are several bugs in the program because after maximizing the window, the application automatically closes down after pressing the apostrophe key twice.

10. Once the dwell feature is turned on, there is no way to turn it off unless the application is closed and re-opened.

11. Once the application is maximized to the large size, there is no way to bring it back to the default size unless you reopen the application.

12. All of the application components are at the top right/left hand of the screen and that may be difficult for many users. It occupies a vertical screen space that is too narrow and difficult to navigate the mouse. Even if a word appeared into the prediction list, the first author

Table 1: Summary of Results for Each Method over 7 days

Day	Type	WPM	Errors	WPM Avg	Error Avg
5	Dragon	29.544	0.4		
5	Dragon	30.186	0.2	31.3	0.3
5	Dragon	34.23	0.2		
1	SofType	8.494	1.8		
3	SofType	9.516	2	9.4	1.5
5	SofType	10.3	0.8		
1	OSDS	2.69	2.2		
2	OSDS	2.282	7.2		
2	OSDS	2.864	0.8		
3	OSDS	2.832	1.6		
3	OSDS	3.376	0.2	2.0	3.7
5	OSDS	4.532	0.4		
5	OSDS	4.284	0.6		
7	OSDS	5.688	2		
7	OSDS	4.97	3		

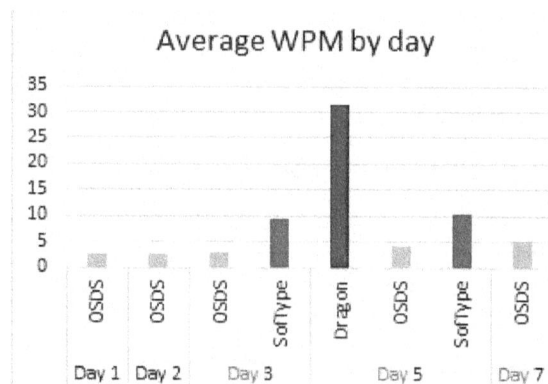

Figure 2: Comparison of OSDS Point-and-Click Beta Interface to SofType version 4.2 and Dragon NaturallySpeaking version 12.5

kept typing the word out letter by letter to avoid moving a mouse to the location because of the difficulty.

13. The word predictions are helpful and the prefix of a word allows easy word changes. For example, to type the word "Anything", type 'A' then select "An" from word prediction list then "Anything" from word prediction list.

14. Font size cannot be changed.

15. Words with apostrophe do not show in prediction.

16. Only rows 1-5 are displayed even though there are 8 rows. Selecting rows 6-8 is little confusing because you have to remember how to alternate between rows 1-5.

17. After awhile the user becomes accustomed to remembering the letter of each row.

18. The test caused fatigue at times. Punctuation is the greatest challenge.

19. Different colors of the interface would be nice.

20. Selecting the rows is an efficient concept.

6. CONCLUSIONS

Whereas the interface of the virtual keyboard is very novel, it is complex and there is a steep learning curve. However, in one week of working with the interface, the first author was able to double her WPM with the *OSDS*. It is quite an achievement seeing as in the first week, the author can see the potential in interface and has suggested several improvements to the system.

In summary, the user's comments referring to the interface can be placed in six categories.

6.1 Customization

Research software may lack the extensive customization abilities of a more mature commercial tools which can cause barriers for new users, or test users. So there is little control over the volume and sound effects, the ability to customize the keyboard layout, or the ability to adjust the font size and the layout of the controls.

6.2 Usability

Most research software is not very customizable beyond the practical functionality such as the ability to minimize the window or to turn off dwell time. This first author has a preference for horizontal over vertical movement because of the fact that she can only use her index finger. She is not able to adapt the software to her needs. She also reported that she found the sound a little bothersome and would like to have the ability to turn the sound off.

6.3 Learning Curve

The interface was developed by an expert user who understood the complexity of the application. New users require time to learn the interface, although tutorial videos were provided. However, the more the experience report user began to use the interface, the more she was able to see the potential of the word prediction in the interface. For a new user, the interface may not be intuitive and there is a steep learning curve.

6.4 Multimodal Interaction

OSDS allows for the use with other methods like speech input and SofType. the benefit is that for some tasks such as dictation for a user who is able to speak using an alternate voice recognition method would be more efficient for using OSDS. However, for something like Latex or programming the OSDS, interface would be better. Having the ability to combine two or more techniques makes the interface more efficient and useful. However, there seem to be bugs with the multimodal interaction.

6.5 Efficient Row Selection

Efficient row selection combined with auto-completion allows for the pressing of as many or fewer characters than those in most words. So for example pressing the button [1][5] followed by [3] will populate the word completion with the all the words that begin with the letters in row [1] and are followed by the letters in row three. If the word is not listed but the combination is, the user can select the combination and pick another row, for example [4], where now the word completion is filled with all the words in its dictionary that begin with the first two letters and are followed by one of the letters in row [4].

6.6 Benefits

Finally, there are some benefits of OSDS over other systems such as the ability to type Greek Symbols and mathematical symbols. That makes it a much easier interface for programming. The efficient row selection in conjunction with the word prediction are novel and speed up the process of typing a word by a factor of 2 in most cases. Giving users the ability to have the best of both (many) worlds when the software can be combined with other assistive and allow the user to switch between the methods to use the most efficient or preferred method for the task.

7. ACKNOWLEDGMENTS

The authors would like to acknowledge Dr. Torsten Felzer for his tireless work in developing assistive technology not only for himself, but also for others. He developed this interface after realizing that his original solution was not accessible for the first author. He listened to her suggestions and implemented them and then developed a test suite for them. He was a model of academic excellence and an inspiration for assistive technology research. Dr. Torsten Felzer will always be remembered in the field of accessible computing.

8. REFERENCES

[1] B. Ashtiani and I. S. MacKenzie. Blinkwrite2: an improved text entry method using eye blinks. In *Proceedings of the 2010 Symposium on Eye-Tracking Research & Applications*, pages 339–345. ACM, 2010.

[2] M. Belatar and F. Poirier. Text entry for mobile devices and users with severe motor impairments: handiglyph, a primitive shapes based onscreen keyboard. In *Proceedings of the 10th international ACM SIGACCESS conference on Computers and accessibility*, pages 209–216. ACM, 2008.

[3] T. Felzer. Onscreendualscribe software. http://www.felzer.de/data/osds_v309_build1003.zip, 2016.

[4] T. Felzer, I. S. MacKenzie, and S. Rinderknecht. Efficient computer operation for users with a neuromuscular disease with onscreendualscribe. *Journal of Interaction Science*, 2(1):1–10, 2014.

[5] T. Felzer and S. Rinderknecht. It's a curse... and a gift: Developing the own input alternative for computer interaction. In P.Langdon, J. Lazar, A. Heylighen, and H. Dong, editors, *Designing around People CWUAAT 2016*, chapter 18, pages 177–186. Springer, 2016.

[6] J. Gips, M. Betke, and P. Fleming. The camera mouse: Preliminary investigation of automated visual tracking for computer access. In *In Proc. Conf. on Rehabilitation Engineering and Assistive Technology Society of North America*, pages 98–100, 2000.

[7] T. Hirsimäki and M. Kurimo. Analysing recognition errors in unlimited-vocabulary speech recognition. In *Proceedings of Human Language Technologies: The 2009 Annual Conference of the North American Chapter of the Association for Computational Linguistics, Companion Volume: Short Papers*, pages 193–196. Association for Computational Linguistics, 2009.

[8] R. Javanovic and I. S. MacKenzie. Markermouse: mouse cursor control using a head-mounted marker. In *International Conference on Computers for Handicapped Persons*, pages 49–56. Springer, 2010.

[9] H. H. Koester and S. P. Levine. Modeling the speed of text entry with a word prediction interface. *IEEE transactions on rehabilitation engineering*, 2(3):177–187, 1994.

[10] P. O. Kristensson and K. Vertanen. The potential of dwell-free eye-typing for fast assistive gaze communication. In *Proceedings of the symposium on eye tracking research and applications*, pages 241–244. ACM, 2012.

[11] M. Kumar, A. Paepcke, and T. Winograd. Eyepoint: practical pointing and selection using gaze and keyboard. In *Proceedings of the SIGCHI conference on Human factors in computing systems*, pages 421–430. ACM, 2007.

[12] F. Loewenich and F. Maire. Hands-free mouse-pointer manipulation using motion-tracking and speech recognition. In *Proceedings of the 19th Australasian conference on Computer-Human Interaction: Entertaining User Interfaces*, pages 295–302. ACM, 2007.

[13] I. S. Mackenzie and T. Felzer. Sak: Scanning ambiguous keyboard for efficient one-key text entry. *ACM Transactions on Computer-Human Interaction (TOCHI)*, 17(3):11, 2010.

[14] S. B. Nesbat. A system for fast, full-text entry for small electronic devices. In *Proceedings of the 5th international conference on Multimodal interfaces*, pages 4–11. ACM, 2003.

[15] Nuance. Dragon naturallyspeaking online exclusive. http://shop.nuance.com/store/nuanceus/Custom/pbpage.resp-dragon-naturallyspeaking-premium-13. Accessed: 2016-06-26.

[16] Origin Instruments. Softype^{TM} 5 on-screen keyboard for windows. http://www.orin.com/access/softype/. Accessed: 2016-06-26.

[17] RH Designs. Mouse emulator. http://rhdesigns.browseto.org/mouseemulator.html. Accessed: 2016-06-27.

[18] S. Saulynas, L. Albar, R. Kuber, and T. Felzer. Using onscreendualscribe to support text entry and targeting among individuals with physical disabilities. In *Proceedings of the 17th International ACM SIGACCESS Conference on Computers & Accessibility*, ASSETS '15, pages 303–304, New York, NY, USA, 2015. ACM.

[19] O. Špakov and D. Miniotas. On-line adjustment of dwell time for target selection by gaze. In *Proceedings of the third Nordic conference on Human-computer interaction*, pages 203–206. ACM, 2004.

[20] T. Wandmacher, J.-Y. Antoine, F. Poirier, and J.-P. Départe. Sibylle, an assistive communication system adapting to the context and its user. *ACM Transactions on Accessible Computing (TACCESS)*, 1(1):6, 2008.

[21] D. J. Ward, A. F. Blackwell, and D. J. MacKay. DasherâĂŤa data entry interface using continuous gestures and language models. In *Proceedings of the 13th annual ACM symposium on User interface software and technology*, pages 129–137. ACM, 2000.

[22] J. O. Wobbrock, B. A. Myers, H. H. Aung, and E. F.

LoPresti. Text entry from power wheelchairs: Edgewrite for joysticks and touchpads. In *ACM SIGACCESS Accessibility and Computing*, number 77-78, pages 110–117. ACM, 2004.

[23] J. O. Wobbrock, B. A. Myers, and J. A. Kembel. Edgewrite: a stylus-based text entry method designed for high accuracy and stability of motion. In *Proceedings of the 16th annual ACM symposium on User interface software and technology*, pages 61–70. ACM, 2003.

[24] W. Zhang, V. G. Duffy, R. Linn, and A. Luximon. Voice recognition based human-computer interface design. *Computers & industrial engineering*, 37(1):305–308, 1999.

[25] X. A. Zhao, E. D. Guestrin, D. Sayenko, T. Simpson, M. Gauthier, and M. R. Popovic. Typing with eye-gaze and tooth-clicks. In *Proceedings of the Symposium on Eye Tracking Research and Applications*, pages 341–344. ACM, 2012.

Exploring the Use of a Drone to Guide Blind Runners

Majed Al-Zayer
malzayer@cse.unr.edu

Sam Tregillus Jiwan Bhandari
tregillus@cse.unr.edu bhandari@nevada.unr.edu

Dave Feil-Seifer
dave@cse.unr.edu

Eelke Folmer
efolmer@cse.unr.edu

Human+ Lab - Computer Science - University of Nevada

ABSTRACT

People with visual impairments have a hard time getting consistent physical exercise, as they can not do some exercises, such as running outside, without a sighted guide. People with visual impairments have been shown to have higher spatial localization skills than sighted people, which lead us to believe that they could follow a drone on a running-track environment. This paper presents a feasibility study where we investigate the ability to localize and follow a low-cost flying drone in people with visual impairments. A Wizard of Oz style study was conducted with 2 blind participants. Our results indicate that blind individuals can accurately localize the drone and follow it. Qualitative results also indicate that the participants were comfortable with following the drone and had high efficacy when it came to following and localizing the drone. The study supports future development of a fully functioning prototype.

Keywords

Exercise; Obesity; Health disparities; Drones; Running;

1. INTRODUCTION

Obesity has become one of the biggest drivers of preventable chronic diseases and health care costs in the United States. The problem is of a higher significance on people with visual impairments due to their fewer opportunities to be physically active. Even with the few options available to the visually impaired, they require a sighted guide for such options to be accessible [5]. Our project aims to explore the usage of low-cost unmanned aerial vehicles (drones) as autonomous guides for individuals with visual impairments. Drones can maintain a speed that is fast enough to keep up with a runner, and can ignore uneven ground surfaces. This paper describes a pilot study where we evaluate the feasibility of using a consumer-level drone as a guide in a track-like situation. In our design, the drone flies ahead of the blind individual, who follows it using the sound of the rotors. We test how accurately blind individuals can localize the drone, try to determine the optimal distance to keep the drone for the most accurate localization, and see how accurately blind individuals can follow the drone.

ASSETS '16 October 23-26, 2016, Reno, NV, USA

© 2016 Copyright held by the owner/author(s).

ACM ISBN 978-1-4503-4124-0/16/10.

DOI: http://dx.doi.org/10.1145/2982142.2982204

Figure 1: Our project explores the use of a low cost quadrotor drone as a substitute for a sighted guide.

2. RELATED WORK

Past research has explored the assistive capabilities of robots for the visually impaired. Most of this research has involved slow, grounded robots that are attached to the user with a leash. Mori and Kotani [6] created a robotic travel aid that was mounted onto a wheelchair using a camera and sonar for collision detection and a GPS for localization. Kulyukin [4] created a guide robot for indoor environments that used radio frequency identifier (RFID) tags to localize the robot. Some non-robotic research into helping blind athletes has also been done. Several studies have explored electromagnetic walls where two transmitting units are positioned to create 2 walls of detectable radiation patterns on either side of the user, forming a corridor between the walls [7, 2].

Utilizing drones as running companions have been demonstrated via Joggobot [3], but it was meant for sighted runners. For blind users, Avila et. al conducted a few small experiments where a blind participant followed a drone piloted by the experimenters [1].

3. EXPERIMENT

Our primary goals for this experiment were to determine whether further development on a guide drone for blind athletes was worthwhile by evaluating three main questions. First, can people with visual impairments accurately localize and orient towards a drone using only the sound of its rotors? Second, can people with visual impairments accurately follow a drone and stay within a running-track width lane? Third, will people with visual impairments trust the drone and feel that they are accurately tracking and following the drone?

We recruited 2 blind participants (males, 35 and 36 years old), one of whom was legally blind. Each subject participated in two tasks: a localization task and a navigation task. The goal of the localization task was to test the participants ability to accurately locate a drone using the sound of its rotors. Participants were asked to estimate the location of the drone after it was flown to 10 predefined locations organized in 2 semicircles of radii 3 and 4 meters, respectively. Participants wore a video recording helmet from which their estimation accuracy was determined. The goal of the navigation task was to test the participants ability to walk in a straight line by following the sound of the drone's rotors. Participants were asked to walk in a straight line within a track of 12.6 meters long and 1.22 meters wide in two conditions: one without drone guidance and another with drone guidance. In the latter, the drone was distanced at 3 meters from the participant. Participants were asked to walk at any speed that they felt comfortable with, and they were told that the track was simply a straight line with no obstacles. All participants were asked to perform the task without their cane. Participants continued to wear the video recording helmet for their safety and to video record the trials for our reference. Two experimenters, one on each side, walked next to the participant to ensure his safety. Each participant performed a total of 10 trials, 5 for each condition. A stopwatch was used to record the overall trial time and the amount of time the participant spends outside the walking lane. The order of two the conditions was counterbalanced among participants with the first participant assigned to the With-Drone condition. The Bebop drone [1] and the Contour Roam 3 [2] camcorder were used in this experiment. When both tasks were completed, participants were asked to fill a post-experiment questionnaire to provide demographic information in addition to their qualitative feedback.

4. RESULTS

For the localization task, results show that the drone was never far from the center of the camera frame for any of the trials, indicating that blind individuals can accurately localize the drone from the sound of its rotors. We found no difference between the data for locations at 3 meters and 4 meters. For the navigation task, we divided the error time by the total time for each participant for both conditions and Table 1 shows the results. For the post-experiment questionnaire, both participants had relatively similar responses. Both felt extremely confident that they were able to accurately localize the drone, that the sound of the drone was sufficient for localization, and that they were able to accurately follow the drone. They both felt relatively comfortable following the drone and were mostly confident that they were walking in a straight line with assistance from the drone. However, they were uncertain about their ability to follow the drone while running, and uncertain about the role that drones might play in assisting them with their own physical activity.

Condition	Participant 1	Participant 2
With Drone	10%	0%
Without Drone	28.51%	2.86%

Table 1: Average percentage of time that participants 1 and 2 were out of the lane for the conditions with drone and without drone

5. CONCLUSION AND FUTURE WORK

We acknowledge that this experiment had several limitations that we plan to overcome in future studies. We mention the major ones here for brevity. The study was performed in an indoor space that had no windows opened, resulting in a high level of echo that amplified the drone's sound cues. We ran our experiments in a walking track of 12.6 meters long which we believe was too short to reliably measure blind people's ability to maintain walking in a straight

line. While performing the navigation experiment with the second participant in the condition without the drone, we noticed that the participant was able to maintain walking in a straight line almost perfectly and were able to predict the end of the track. Because the experimenters were walking next to the participant on both sides, we suspect that the participant could have used their walking steps as sound cues to help him stay on track. Our experiments were conducted with only 2 participants which is not sufficient to perform effective statistical analysis and arrive at reliable conclusions. Each participant covered a total distance of 126 meters at the navigation task, which we believe is too short compared to the relatively few participants that we were able to recruit. Both experiments tasks were carried out in a Wizard-of-Oz style where one of the experimenters controlled the drone manually, which may have introduced some inaccuracies to the experimentation procedure.

Future work will involve a working prototype with a low-cost drone, such as the Parrot AR.Drone 2.0[3]. The AR drone has built-in tag detection that can determine the distance from it to a specific tag that could be worn on a participant's shirt. It also has a downward facing camera, which with computer vision techniques could be used to automatically orient and move along the lines of a normal running track. Ideally, this would be done with an Android application that could be run on the user's phone, and physical feedback via vibration on the phone could be explored as an additional channel of feedback. We also will do user studies to determine how blind users feel about following the drone at a running pace.

6. ACKNOWLEDGMENTS

This work was made possible by the support of the National Science Foundation under Grants No. IIS-1445380 and IIS-1528137.

7. REFERENCES

[1] Avila, M., Funk, M., and Henze, N. Dronenavigator: Using drones for navigating visually impaired persons. In *Proceedings of the 17th International ACM SIGACCESS Conference on Computers & Accessibility*, ACM (2015), 327–328.

[2] Cerri, G., De Leo, A., Di Mattia, V., Manfredi, G., Primiani, V. M., Petrini, V., Pieralisi, M., Russo, P., and Scalise, L. The electromagnetic technology for safe mobility of visually impaired people. In *Control and Automation (MED), 2014 22nd Mediterranean Conference of*, IEEE (2014), 164–168.

[3] Graether, E., and Mueller, F. Joggobot: a flying robot as jogging companion. In *CHI'12 Extended Abstracts on Human Factors in Computing Systems*, ACM (2012), 1063–1066.

[4] Kulyukin, V., Gharpure, C., Nicholson, J., and Osborne, G. Robot-assisted wayfinding for the visually impaired in structured indoor environments. *Autonomous Robots 21*, 1 (2006), 29–41.

[5] Lieberman, L. J., Robinson, B. L., and Rollheiser, H. Youth with visual impairments: Experiences in general physical education. *RE: view 38*, 1 (2006), 35.

[6] Mori, H., and Kotani, S. Robotic travel aid for the blind: Harunobu-6. In *European Conference on Disability, Virtual Reality, and Assistive Technology* (1998).

[7] Pieralisi, M., Petrini, V., Di Mattia, V., Manfredi, G., De Leo, A., Scalise, L., Russo, P., and Cerri, G. Design and realization of an electromagnetic guiding system for blind running athletes. *Sensors 15*, 7 (2015), 16466–16483.

---

[1] http://www.parrot.com/products/bebopdrone/
[2] http://contour.com/cameras/roam3

---

[3] http://www.parrot.com/usa/products/ardrone-2/

Impact of Word Presentation for Dyslexia

Damien Appert
University Toulouse & CNRS / IRIT
Toulouse, France
Damien.Appert@irit.fr

Philippe Truillet
University Toulouse & CNRS / IRIT
Toulouse, France
Philippe.Truillet@irit.fr

ABSTRACT

In this paper, we present an experiment that uses eye-tracking system to measure the effect of word presentation on reading performance and fixation duration. Twelve subjects without dyslexia and eight with dyslexia read thirty-six words and non-words with three kind of presentation. We show that one type of presentation leads to significant better results for people with dyslexia.

Keywords
Design; experimentation; dyslexia.

1. INTRODUCTION

Dyslexics are around 10% of the population worldwide. Scientific studies [5] have reported difficulties for them with phonological processing, rapid naming, deficits of vision, working memory, processing speed, etc. Regardless, reading problems and spelling difficulties continue to cause concerns, especially in the school system where dyslexic children experience every day the lack of consensual educational instructions regarding their learning problems. The work presented in this paper is related to text presentation. The main contribution is that some visual clues have a significant impact on reading performance for people with dyslexia.

2. RELATED WORK

Whereas the phonological deficits seem to be established, the presence and nature of visual impairments is still quite debated. Some authors have shown that dyslexics' eye movements are quite different from those of normal readers: each letter tends to be fixed and there are frequent movements backwards to scan the same letters several times. Many works test the impact of visual perception with eye-tracker systems [7, 8].

Recent findings argue that letter size and crowding do not affect dyslexics and normal readers differently [3, 7]. Typographic characteristics such as font, type size, spacing between words and letters contrast are all thought to influence legibility in a fashion well known to font designers. Hughes reports an influence of text size on both speed and error [4]. Moreover, having tested subjects on their susceptibility to visual stress, the authors found that children who were susceptible to visual stress performed significantly more poorly when asked to read the smaller texts. Accordingly, the dyslexic community and the websites addressing it recommend a pared down presentation of the information and adapting the reading material. Hence, special fonts for dyslexic

have been designed (for example, see Boer, Lexia Readable Gill Dyslexic or Gonzalez works). Rello measured the impact of font type on reading performance [8]. They showed that some font types improved significantly the reading performance. Moreover, we can note that most of the interfaces developed for dyslexics allow a display adaptability.

Gattegno proposed several decades ago a method named "*Words in Color*" which addressed the problem of learning to read and write [2]. Briefly, it consists of a series of word charts using a color code in which each color represents a phoneme of the language. The charts are used to provoke the phonological awareness in students of the sounds they are making. This work is the basis of the study we conducted with an eye tracker. This served us of playback control tool.

3. EXPERIMENTAL DESIGN

The primary purpose of our study is to test the impact of three different word presentation on eye movements for subjects with dyslexia. Can reading process be improved with a color code or semantic code? Are there any interesting visual cues? We defined three types of presentation (see Figure 1): the reference presentation, a "syllabic presentation" where each syllable is separated by a vertical bar -This bar is used as a visual clue- and a "differentiation highlights presentation" where the "d" (colored in cyan) and "t" (colored in orange) letters are colored relatively to "*Words in color*" method [2]. These phonemes are close and cause frequent errors in decoding for people with dyslexia.

Figure 1. Illustration of three presentations: standard, syllabic and differentiation highlights for the word "document".

We used the Sassoon Sans Bold font in this experiment. This font (see http://www.sassoonfont.co.uk) is a typeface designed with and for children and know to be easily readable.

4. METHODOLOGY
4.1 Design

The type of presentation and the type of subject (Dyslexics and Non Dyslexics) are our independent variables and we used two dependent variables: The numbers of fixations and the number of read errors. We used the number of fixations as an objective clue of readability. According to Hyönä and al., fixations patterns reflect difficulties in successfully identifying words [5]. We can correlate this variable with reading errors because participants read the texts aloud so we were able to relate oral reading to eye behavior.

The experimental platform is designed from an eye tracker (SMI Eyelink II), PTZ cameras and a microphone to collect the activity of the subjects. We used a 21-inch TFT monitor with a resolution of 1024x768 pixels. The time measurements of the eye-tracker have a precision of 0.004 second. The subjects were placed at 570 mm from the screen so that any movement of 1° angle corresponds to exactly 10 mm (e.g. 26 pixels) on the screen.

4.2 Experimental task

After reading instructions and calibration phase, subjects began the testing phase This phase consisted of three pre-determined sets of different presentations. Each series consisted of twelve words, chosen pseudo-randomly from the set of thirty-six words in order to balance the non-words and words 3 and 4 syllables. To control the impact of visual cues on word reading strategies, words are placed at the same height, but still shifted (between 1 to 4 cm, randomly) to the right of the screen centre. This configuration requires to perform at least one jerk to be able to read the word. At the end, all subjects read all thirty-six words through three different sets of presentations. The order of presentation was counterbalanced between subjects. Users should read aloud the presented word and repeat it.

4.3 Results

The study was conducted with 12 non-dyslexic subjects and 8 dyslexic subjects (8 women and 12 men). The ages ranged from 19-50 years with an average of 27.3 years. Nobody had mental disabilities and all participants had a good view (no glasses). The subjects first had to pass a preliminary test ("L'Alouette" [6]) to determine their reading level. Note that all dyslexic subjects were recognized as disabled by the MDPH[1].

We compute the number of visual fixations for the three of presentations and for dyslexic and non-dyslexic users.

There are more fixations when the user is dyslexic. For dyslexic users, we found a significant effect between types of presentation (Kruskall-Wallis χ^2=12.90, df=2, p<0.01). Moreover, the differentiation highlights and standard presentations are significantly different (Wilcoxon rank sum Pairwise post-hoc p<0.02). Compared to the standard form of presentation, our results show an average reduction of 10.8% of fixings with differentiation highlights form. By cons, we did not find any significant effects between differentiation highlights and standard presentations for non-dyslexic subjects (Kruskall-Wallis χ^2=14.1, df=2, p=n.s.).

This is why we focused thereafter only with results from standard and differentiation highlights layout. The next question was whether this result could be correlated with improved playback performance aloud. As we recorded the words read, we could compare with them with presentation type.

For the standard presentation, there is a significant effect of the number of visual fixations between dyslexic and non-dyslexic subjects (Kruskall-Wallis χ^2=59.95, df=1, p<0.001 the number of words read correctly (Kruskall-Wallis χ^2=5.29, df=1, p<0.03).

Regarding the differentiation highlights presentation, we also found a significant effect on the number of visual fixations between dyslexic and non-dyslexic subjects (Kruskall-Wallis χ^2=33.69, df=1, p<0.001). However, there is no significant effect on the words read correctly (Kruskall-Wallis χ^2=1.13, df=1, p=n.s.). Actually, it seems that the differentiation highlights presentation reduces reading errors. The performance of dyslexic subjects approaches the performance of normal-readers. Finally, it should be noted that this presentation does not affect the performance of normal-readers.

5. DISCUSSION

Actually, it seems that the differentiation highlights presentation can greatly reduce reading errors. Moreover, the performance of dyslexic users approaches the performance of non-dyslexic users.

It may be argued that our results obtained using a reading aloud task would not necessarily generalize to silent reading. However, we can argue (as for [5]) that in oral reading, eye movements are closely linked with word recognition processes.

Our results on reading and spelling performances provide evidence that word presentation have an impact for dyslexic readers. These results are consistent with many researches on text design recommendations for people with dyslexia [1, 8, 9]. Nevertheless, these studies focus mainly on fonts or document structure, but few on word or text salience. This could be interesting to link this result to neuroscience studies. Does the salience layout allow to "see" in a better way and understand what is written? Is it more effective than cutting words into syllables for example?

6. CONCLUSION AND FUTURE WORK

The main conclusion of this preliminary work is that the "differentiation highlights" presentation has an impact both on number of fixations for dyslexic users and on readability. These findings can guide some analysis, design and evaluation of reading interfaces for Dyslexics. We currently integrate this work on an interface in order to evaluated this work with more complex texts in a natural interaction.

7. REFERENCES

[1] French M., Blood A., Bright N. D., Futak D.; Grohmann M. J., Hasthorpe A., Heritage J., Poland R., Reece S., Tabor J. Changing Font in Education: How the benefits vary with ability and dyslexia , The Journal of Educational Research, 106:301-304, 2013

[2] Gattegno C., Teaching Reading with Words in Color: A Scientific Study of the Problems of Reading, Educational Solutions, 1967-2011

[3] Gregor P., Newell A., An empirical investigation of ways in which some of the problems encountered by some dyslexics may be alleviated using computer techniques, ASSETS'00, pp. 85-91

[4] Hughes, L.E. & Wilkins, A.J. 2000, Typography in children's reading schemes may be suboptimal: Evidence from measures of reading rate. Journal of Research in Reading, 23(3), pp. 314-324.

[5] Hyönä J., Olson R. K., Eye Fixation Patterns Among Dyslexic and Normal Readers: Effects of Word Length and Word Frequency, Journal of Experimental Psychology, Learning, Memory and Cognition, 1995, vol.21 n°6, pp. 1430-1440

[6] Lefavrais P., Description, définition et mesure de la dyslexie, Utilsiation du test « L'Alouette ». Revue de Psychologie Appliquée, 15 (1), pp. 33-44, 1965

[7] MacKeben M, Trauzettel-Klosinski S, Reinhard J, Dürrwächter U, Adler M, Klosinski G., Eye movement control during single-word reading in dyslexics, Journal of Vision, 2004 May 14;4(5): pp. 388-402.

[8] Rello L, Baeza-Yates R., Good Fonts for Dyslexia, ASSETS'13, October 21-23 2013, pp. 14-22

[9] Rello L., Baeza-Yates R., How to Present more Readable Text for People with Dyslexia, Univ Access Inf Soc (2015). doi:10.1007/s10209-015-0438-8

---

[1] Departmental House of Disabled Persons in France

A Tool for Capturing Essential Preferences

Dana Ayotte[1], Michelle Brennan[2], Nancy Frishberg[3], Cynthia Jimes[2], Lisa Petrides[2],
Whitney Quesenbery[3], Madeleine Rothberg[4], Rich Schwerdtfeger[5], Jim Tobias[6],
Jutta Treviranus[1], Shari Trewin[5], Gregg C. Vanderheiden[7]

[1]Inclusive Design Research Center,
OCAD University, Toronto, Canada
dana.ayotte@gmail.com,
jtreviranus@ocadu.ca

[2]Institute for the Study of Knowledge
Management in Education, CA, USA
{michelle,lisa,cynthia}@iskme.org

[3]Center for Civic Design, MD, USA
{whitneyq,nancyf}@civicdesign.org

[4] National Center for Accessible
Media, WGBH, Boston, USA
madeleine_rothberg@wgbh.org

[5] IBM/IBM Research, Texas/NY, USA
{schwer,trewin}@us.ibm.com

[6]Inclusive Technologies, NJ, USA
tobias@inclusive.com

[7]Trace R&D Center Madison WI &
Raising the Floor – International,
Geneva, Switzerland
gregg@raisingthefloor.org

ABSTRACT

For some people, interaction preference settings like large fonts or speech output are essential for technology access. We demonstrate a 'First Discovery Tool' intended as an easy and accessible way for people to discover and set preferences to address major access barriers. The tool is designed to support people who have limited technology experience or confidence. Testing in educational and senior settings found that most participants were able to understand the preferences offered, and some discovered helpful options they were previously not aware of.

Keywords: Preferences; older adults; education; independence.

1. INTRODUCTION

Users of information technologies often have preferred ways of interacting. Sometimes their preferences are essential for access, but discovering and activating these settings is difficult to do independently on an unadapted device. Even among technology users, there is a lack of awareness of preference options, and limited customization of those options (Spool, 2011; Anthony, 2013). Our tool supports would-be technology users in getting their most important preferences in place, with minimal assumptions about their background and abilities.

2. BACKGROUND

The Global Public Inclusive Infrastructure (GPII) is an initiative to improve access to Internet-based resources to everyone who faces barriers due to disability, literacy, digital literacy, or aging (gpii.net). It is building an infrastructure that provides automatic adaptation of any device based on user preferences. Techniques for gathering user preferences include online self-assessment methods such as Mada (http://mada.org.qa/assessments/en/Q1.htm), and operating system wizards (e.g. Microsoft Windows accessibility wizard) that help users navigate through the many options. IBM's WebAdapt2Me (Hanson et al., 2006) is an early example of an end-user preference gathering system, aimed initially at seniors. With one-click access to a preference toolbar in their browser, users could adjust preferences

ASSETS'16, October 23–26, 2016, Reno, NV, USA.
ACM ISBN 978-1-4503-4124-0/16/10.
DOI: http://dx.doi.org/10.1145/982142.2982155

and immediately see the impact on their current web page. Their preferences were applied to every page they visited.

3. TOOL REQUIREMENTS

The First Discovery Tool is designed to provide enough customization to overcome major barriers and get a person started online. It will be part of a series of preference tools designed to adapt systems and content to a best fit for each user. Education and senior settings are the primary use cases for the tool. Other scenarios include voting or public kiosks. For example:

Bob is a 16-year-old student who injured his right arm. Bob opens his school's Learning Management System from home, and on his dashboard is a link from his teacher, to access the First Discovery Tool. Bob uses the tool to set up preferences that will allow him to complete his schoolwork one-handed, with minimal use of the keyboard and mouse.

Maude is an 86-year-old retired teacher whose daughter bought her a laptop. She is having difficulty seeing the icons and using the keyboard. Her daughter helps her access the First Discovery Tool so that she can set preferences that make icons bigger and the keyboard easier to use.

The tool can make few assumptions about a new user. They may not be able to see, or to hear. Their primary language and literacy level are unknown. They may never have used a mouse before, or a touch screen. The scope of the tool covers any preference that can be enacted purely in software. Individuals who need specialized devices like eye-tracking systems would normally have a professional assessment, and training.

4. FIRST DISCOVERY TOOL

The First Discovery Tool prototype is a multimodal web-based application designed for both tablet and desktop presentation. The visual interface presents two panels – one for adjusting a preference, and the other providing a preview of the effect of the preference (Figure 1). In earlier testing of a prototype without a preview, users found it hard to know what effect their settings would have on the kinds of information they wanted to access. Previews allow users to try out a preference before selecting it, and to see the effect in the context of use. The

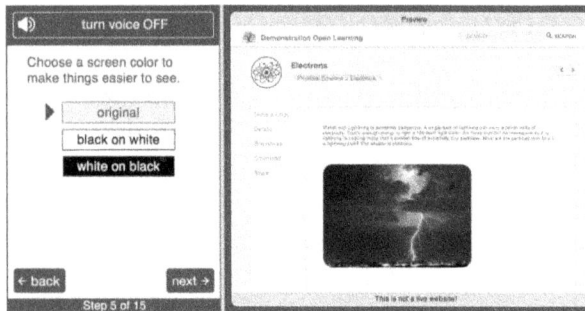

Figure 1. The text contrast preference screen with preview.

preview content can be customized to suit a particular deployment setting, as can the set of preferences included.

The interaction takes 15 steps, and covers 11 preferences: language, speech output, speech rate, screen color, text size, line spacing, letter spacing, captions, screen flash, on-screen keyboard, and sticky keys (one-finger typing). These settings have been identified as important for seniors and cover both audio-only and visual-only access.

The steps are ordered so as to establish communication as early as possible. First the user selects a language, then they receive instructions. These early steps are presented with built-in speech turned on and a fairly slow speech rate (too-fast speech is an access barrier while too-slow speech is an annoyance). Users then have the option to deselect the speech, or select a speech rate. Visual presentation options follow, then visual replacements for audio, followed by the dexterity options. Finally, a summary of selected settings is presented, users have the option to finish and save their settings, or to go back and repeat some steps. These settings would then be saved so they can be applied easily to any device that supports the same or similar settings and has GPII installed. Users would be able to access these settings through many methods, such as logging in with a username and password, or simply swiping a card near the computer's card reader.

5. USER TESTING

User testing was conducted at four sites: two U.S. nonprofit organizations that provide technology training for adults aged 50 or over; and a high school and a university that make strong use of online digital resources.

5.1 Participants

A total of 27 adults (6-8 from each site, 14 male, aged between 18 and 94) representing a diversity of accessibility needs and preferences, participated. Six (all seniors) had no previous experience of computers or tablets, and 12 did not know in advance what accommodations they would need or want. All of the students used computer technology for school work.

Two participants were Braille readers. Two were experienced screen reader users, two were considering or transitioning to a screen reader, and one used a large monitor and magnifiers at home. Approximately 10% used hearing aids, one person had a developmental disability, and some used adaptations for learning differences. No participant was Deaf or had a dexterity impairment. All were comfortable reading English.

5.2 Procedure

In facilitated individual think-aloud testing sessions of up to one hour, each participant worked through the steps of the tool, as independently as possible at first, followed by a more detailed pass-through with discussion. Our goal was to learn whether these specific preferences were well-described, and whether the preview helped participants understand the effect of the setting.

5.3 Findings

All but one participant successfully completed the steps, although the participants who were new to computers struggled to use the mouse effectively. However, several participants were confused by preferences they did not understand, that they felt were not appropriate for them, or that were not responsive in the prototype. In one example, a blind participant was annoyed at having to work through text display preferences. However, other participants found that going through all the steps introduced them to helpful options they were previously unaware of. For example, many participants were unfamiliar with and pleasantly surprised by different screen contrast settings. The preview panel was helpful but also introduced new problems: participants were unsure which panel to pay attention to, navigating between panels made the interaction more complex, especially in audio presentation, and the effect of some of the settings (eg speech rate, Sticky Keys) was not reflected in the preview panel.

The different contexts of use impacted how participants approached the tool. Students assumed they would use it independently, just as their study is self-directed. The seniors were at a center where they came to be taught to use technology, and were more likely to turn to the moderator as a resource.

In general the idea of being able to personalize settings and have those settings persist across equipment was positively received. For example, a husband and wife indicated that they share their home machine and want different settings, or a user wants the same settings on a library machine as his/her home machine.

6. CONCLUSIONS

Our prototype tool for gathering essential preferences was tested by seniors and students, who found it usable with assistance even without computer experience. A preview pane helped participants to evaluate some visual preferences, but did not help for other preferences, and makes the interaction more complex. Next steps include testing with other user groups, and evaluating whether the selected preferences do enable a basic level of access.

7. ACKNOWLEDGMENTS

We thank the staff and participants at our four testing centers. This material is based upon work supported by U.S Department of Health and Human Services (HHS), Administration for Community Living (ACL), and National Institute on Disability, Independent Living, and Rehabilitation Research (NIDILRR) under contract No. ED-OSE-12-D-003. Any opinions, findings, conclusions, or recommendations expressed in this material are those of the authors and do not necessarily reflect the views of U.S. government agencies listed above.

8. REFERENCES

[1] Anthony, L., Kim, Y. and Findlater, L. (2013). Analyzing user-generated YouTube videos to understand touchscreen use by people with motor impairments. *CHI 2013*.

[2] Hanson, V., Snow-Weaver, A., and Trewin, S. (2006). Software personalization to meet the needs of older adults. *Gerontechnology* 5(3), pp. 160-169.

[3] Spool, J. (2011). Do users change their settings? Retrieved June 2016 from http://www.uie.com/brainsparks/2011/09/14/do-users-change-their-settings/

Designing a Kinect2Scratch Game to Help Teachers Train Children with Intellectual Disabilities for Pedestrian Safety

Yao-Jen Chang[1], Ya-Shu Kang[2], Yao-Sheng Chang[3], Hung-Huan Liu[1],
Yu-Ling Chiu[2], Chia Chun Kao[1]

[1]Department of Electronic Engineering, Chung Yuan Christian University, Taiwan

[2]Department of Special Education, Chung Yuan Christian University, Taiwan

[3]Department of Tourism and Leisure Management, Chung Chou University of Science and Technology, Taiwan

{yjchang, yashu, hhliu}@cycu.edu.tw; yschang@dragon.ccut.edu.tw

Abstract

Children with intellectual disabilities (ID) may need to undergo long-term cognitive training to enhance the possibility of social inclusion. Pedestrian safety is a critical issue when it comes to participating in community activities for children with ID. Currently, no commercial pedestrian safety training products are available for public special education schools. Consequently, teachers normally gave lectures with the support of slides and pictures to enhance children's ability of getting around in the community. This study employs the Microsoft Kinect technology and image recognition technology to create a pedestrian safety training system which may be applicable for people with ID. To motivate people with ID to engage in the training, we gamified the training of pedestrian safety for children with ID in special education school settings. By leveraging the Scratch language and Kinect2Scratch tool, the teacher who will use the system may be able to do the customization without technical support. Preliminary results of 15 children with ID, aged 9-10, testing the game are presented.

Keywords

serious games; gamification; Kinect; Scratch; Kinect2Scratch; pedestrian safety.

Introduction

With sufficient and appropriate support, many people with cognitive impairments are capable of participating in the world of work, which provides both financial support and the opportunity for social integration (community-based living, recreation and leisure pursuits, use of community services, and use of public transportation). However, with increased

ASSETS'16, October 23–26, 2016, Reno, NV, USA
ACM 978-1-4503-4124-0/16/10
http://dx.doi.org/10.1145/2982142.2982185

independence and integration comes greater risk. To decrease risk for individuals with disabilities as they increase community participation and seek social inclusion, recent strategies focus on increased autonomous functioning [1]. Because individuals with intellectual disabilities (ID) are frequently dependent on others for support across environments, these strategies and skills must directly help access such support. Staff supervision can increase commuter safety; however, it is time-consuming and expensive. Furthermore, protracted or indefinite staff supervision emphasizes the dependence of persons with ID, minimizing the value of responses. The pedestrian safety problems that children with ID typically have include insufficient sense of danger, not knowing the meaning of traffic lights, not being able to pay attention to cars or traffic lights, and lack of practice.

In [2, 3] a Kinect-based system was used to assist young adults with motor impairments in rehabilitation. In this study, we designed a Kinect-based training game to be used by teachers for pedestrian safety lessons. Pedestrian safety lessons are difficult to implement because teachers normally do not train students in the street for the reasons of safety. On the other hand, lectures in the classroom do not help much. Therefore, it is much desired to design a game that can simulate street and traffic scenarios in the special education school setting. Unfortunately, there was no such facility to the best of our knowledge. The teacher that we worked with decided to take the initiative to design such games for the students.

Game Design

This study primarily employed the Microsoft Kinect sensory device to measure the distance of the user by leveraging its depth imaging. The design was inspired by a special education teacher who collaborated with the research team during implementation. This system enables teachers to develop a series of street and traffic scenarios based on the level of ID for each child. Moreover, this Kinect-based system calculates the performance for the mentioned scenarios to determine whether the outcome of each student corresponded to teacher's expectations.

In specific, Kinect and its SDK automatically detect the student's depth in front of the Kinect device, and use the depth data to determine whether the students' distance. The system also includes an interactive interface with audio and video feedback to enhance students' motivation, interest, and perseverance to engage in training sessions.

Based on student ability and Individualized Education Program (IEP), a teacher in a special-education school developed various training scenarios. To motivate the students to engage in such exercises, a game approach was adopted. The game was called Cat Walk which is implemented using the Kinect2Scratch tool, Kinect API for the Scratch programming language. Using Scratch means that the teacher can easily customizes the games we developed with less technical support after delivery. The screenshots of Cat Walk are shown in Figure 1.

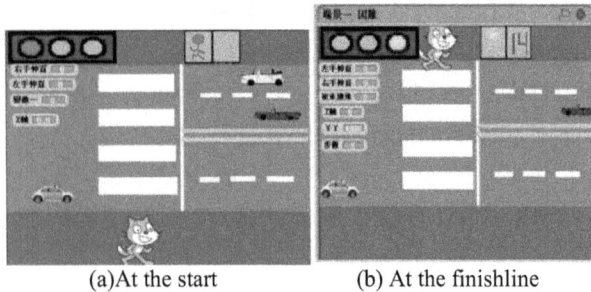

(a)At the start   (b) At the finishline
Figure 1: Game screenshots

To play the game, a child with ID stood at the start and was told to walk to the Kinect sensor when the traffic light on computer screen turned green. The child had to walk 3 meters that simulated using a crosswalk on the screen. Three levels were designed so far: entry, medium, and advanced. For the entry level, no traffic conditions were designed and what the child needed to watch was the traffic light. The child learned to walk on green and stopped on red. For the medium level, there was traffic in both directions on the street in addition to traffic lights. However, the cars always followed rules of the road. At this level, no cars ran through a red light and none violated speed limits. At the advanced level, more cars were added and occasionally some cars violated the road rules.

Experiments and Results

In our experiment, 15 primary school students with an IQ of less than 70 were invited to test the games. Seven students were 9 years old and eight were 10 years old. The teacher instructed the students to play the games three times per week for 18 times in total. Each game play took 2 min. The players were requested to rest for 5 min before proceeding with the next gameplay.

Two scenarios were created: one is with traffic lights (TL) and the other is without traffic lights (WTL). For both scenarios, no cars showed up at the entry level, an average of three cars per min showed up in the line of sight at the medium level, and an average of ten cars came into the scene at the advanced level. At the advanced level of the TL scenario, some cars ran though the red light on purpose.

For the TL mode, a trial was considered a success if the player stopped on red, walked on green, and was not hit by any car while crossing the street. For the WTL mode, a trial was considered a success if the player was not hit by any car while crossing the street. For the TL mode as shown in Figure 2, 75% of trials were successful at the entry level. This indicated that most students could tell red lights from green ones. For the WTL mode (Figure 3), 100% of trials were successful at the entry level because no traffic lights existed. Furthermore the TL performance differed from the WTL performance at both the medium and advanced levels. The results showed it was more difficult for students to walk across the road without traffic lights.

Every child was interviewed after the experiment was finished. Most children enjoyed the Cat Walk game. Only two of them did not like it because they thought the screen was too small. The teacher that used the game in the IEPs considered the game useful and interesting. She was willing to recommend the game to her colleagues. She also suggested the game be adopted in the kindergarten for typically developing children in addition to special education schools.

The preliminary results show the Kinect2Scratch games have the potential to motivate pedestrian safety training for children with ID. The teacher was happy with the feasibility study and prepared to introduce the game to the prospective students by including the game-based training in the IEP. Special education teachers in the same school district also showed interest in Cat Walk and considered the use of the game in their curriculum.

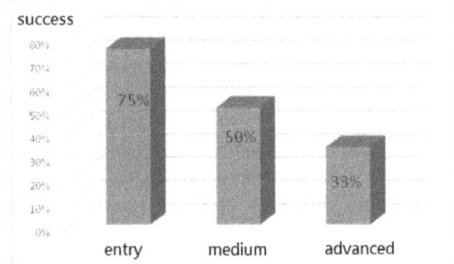

Figure 2: Scenarios with Traffic lights

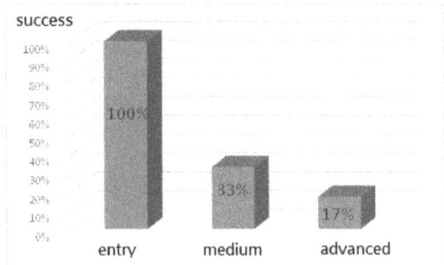

Figure 3: Scenarios No traffic lights

References

[1] Yao-Jen Chang, Tsen-Yung Wang, Shu-Fang Chen, Tien-Shyan Ma, Anomaly Detection to Increase Commuter Safety for Individuals with Cognitive Impairments, *Journal of Developmental and Physical Disabilities*, Volume 24, Issue 1 (2012), Page 9-17

[2] Chang Y. J., Chen, S. F., Huang, J. D. A Kinect-based system for physical rehabilitation: A pilot study for young adults with motor disabilities, *Research in Developmental Disabilities*, 2011(32):6, 2566–2570

[3] Yao-Jen Chang, Ya-Shu Kang, Yao-Sheng Chang, Hung-Huan Liu, Cheng-Chieh Wang, Chia Chun Kao, Designing Kinect2Scratch Games to Help Therapists Train Young Adults with Cerebral Palsy in Special Education School Settings, Proceedings of ACM Computers and Accessibility, Lisbon, 2015 Oct. 26~28.

Deaf and Hard of Hearing Individuals' Perceptions of Communication with Hearing Colleagues in Small Groups

Lisa Elliot, Michael Stinson,
James Mallory, Donna Easton
National Technical Institute for the Deaf
Rochester Institute of Technology
Rochester, NY 14623
{lbenrd, msserd, jrmnet, dlencr}@rit.edu

Matt Huenerfauth
Golisano College of Computing
and Information Sciences
Rochester Institute of Technology
Rochester, NY 14623
matt.huenerfauth@rit.edu

ABSTRACT

This survey-based study investigated the the perception of deaf and hard of hearing (DHH) individuals' perceived need for technologies that may facilitate communication when meeting in small groups with hearing colleagues. Participants were 108 DHH postsecondary students who participated in co-op (internship) and capstone experiences at workplaces with hearing employees within the past two years. Participants' responses to a survey indicated that they were generally not satisfied with their current strategies and technologies for communicating with hearing persons in small groups.

CCS Concepts

• **Human-centered computing → Accessibility → Empirical studies in accessibility • Human-centered computing → Collaborative and social computing → Empirical studies in collaborative and social computing**

Keywords

Deaf; hard-of-hearing; small groups; communication; survey

1. INTRODUCTION

A variety of methods are available to provide accessible information during meetings, classes, and live events for people who are deaf or hard-of-hearing (DHH); this includes sign-language interpreting and as well as live-captioning services, in which a trained provider uses a computerized system to transcribe the spoken information, with the words displayed on a screen for those in attendance. Having reliable access to a signed or text version of the spoken information aids DHH individuals' understanding and effective participation in educational or employment settings.

Automatic Speech Recognition (ASR), software that converts audio input of human speech into text displayed on the screen, holds exciting promise for making spoken content accessible for people who are DHH – especially when access services such as captioning/transcription performed by a human are currently not provided or are prohibitively expensive.

Prior studies have investigated DHH individuals' acceptance of

ASSETS '16, October 23-26, 2016, Reno, NV, USA
ACM 978-1-4503-4124-0/16/10.
http://dx.doi.org/10.1145/2982142.2982198

ASR technologies [4], fully automatic captioning of classroom lectures using ASR [6], professional re-speaking of classroom content to semi-automate caption production [3], or the use of human workers to repair ASR errors [1]. While state-of-the-art ASR is still imperfect, especially in the noisy and complex audio environment of multi-party meetings, in this work, we focus on supporting communication in one-on-one meetings or small groups. In contrast to a lecture context, in small group meetings, the potential that communication partners may adapt their speaking behavior could increase the likelihood of ASR success.

This study investigated DHH individuals' perception of the need for technologies and strategies that will facilitate communication between deaf and hearing colleagues in small groups. Prior to conducting technological research and development on using ASR in small teams with DHH and hearing colleagues, it was important to first determine the DHH individuals' attitudes about the need for improving communication with hearing teammates. If DHH individuals were to report that they experience significant difficulties communicating with hearing teammates, even with the use of current technologies and strategies, this finding may justify exploration of use of ASR, and possibly other technologies, as technological solutions to facilitate communication.

The study addressed two questions: (a) To what extent were the current strategies that DHH individuals used satisfactory for communication in teams? (b) What were the relative preferences among various technologies and strategies used for communication?

2. METHOD

The participant pool for this study consisted of postsecondary students (n=379) who are deaf or hard of hearing and who participated in co-op (internship) and capstone experiences at workplaces with hearing individuals within the past two years. The invitation to participate was transmitted by email and included a link to the survey. Respondents who offered contact information received a $20 gift card for their participation.

The survey consisted of 16 questions, including multiple-choice, Likert-scale type, and open-ended short-answer questions. The survey was created using the Survey Monkey survey tool. Following the methodology of prior studies published at ASSETS [2, 5], our online survey of DHH participants was presented bilingually with questions provided in the form of ASL videos and redundantly as onscreen English text. The videos were prepared by students whose first language is ASL, and the quality of the ASL videos was analyzed by a professor of ASL-English Interpretation who is a native ASL signer.

2. RESULTS

2.1 Participants.

For this study, survey responses were analyzed using descriptive statistics. The survey was completed by 108 respondents for a response rate of 28%. Respondents were: enrolled in college full-time (n=69); working (n=28); or graduated and unemployed (n=5). 73% of respondents preferred to use American Sign (ASL) either alone or in combination with voice. In contrast, on average, 66% of respondents regularly interacted with individuals who did not know American Sign Language.

2.2 Communication Strategies

For both one-to-one and small group meetings, respondents were asked whether they had tried technology-based and non-technology-based communication strategies and to rate their satisfaction with each (1=not at all satisfied, 4=very satisfied). Table 1 displays the strategies and complete results. In one-to-one meetings the top 3 technology-based strategies used were: email before or after meetings (94%; average satisfaction 3.06/4.0); writing on paper (84%, average satisfaction, 2.44/4.0); and texting (82%, average satisfaction, 2.59/4.0). In small group meetings, the top 3 technology-based strategies were email before or after meetings (88%, average satisfaction, 2.67/4.0); writing on paper (79%, average satisfaction 1.99/4.0); and using a computer word document (72%, average satisfaction 2.04/4.0).

Table 1: Technology-based and Non-Technology-based Communication Strategies Reported by Participants

Strategy	One-to-One Meeting % used strategy; (number of responses) avg. satisfaction with strategy (std. dev)	Small Group Meeting % used strategy, (number of responses) avg. satisfaction with strategy (std. dev)
Technology-based Strategies		
Write on paper	84 (104) 2.44 (1.41)	79 (103) 2.16 (1.38)
E-mail before/after meeting	94 (103) 3.06 (1.09)	88 (103); 2.67 (1.27)
Computer word document	75 (104) 2.29 (1.54)	72 (103) 2.04 (1.51)
Notes phone app with typing	65 (104) 1.93 (1.60)	56 (103) 1.55 (1.57)
Notes phone app with voice recognition	51 (104) 1.32 (1.53)	49 (103) 1.25 (1.51)
Texting	82 (104) 2.59 (1.45)	67 (103) 1.89 (1.58)
Chat programs on computer/phone	70 (104) 2.13 (1.60)	64 (103) 1.75 (1.51)
Share pictures	55 (103) 1.60 (1.64)	54 (103) 1.42 (1.53)
Non-Technology based Strategies		
Voice	73 (103) 2.14 (1.43)	75 (102) 1.81 (1.34)
Speech-reading	88 (101) 2.30 (1.28)	83 (103) 1.82 (1.22)
Gestures	86 (103) 2.29 (1.21)	85 (101) 1.99 (1.15)

3. CONCLUSION

The results of this survey indicate that while students relied on ASL as a primary form of communication, they were frequently in work situations where the majority of their interactions were with individuals who did not know ASL. Respondents reported that they relied on a variety of strategies to communicate in the workplace. The most frequently used technology-based strategy, email before or after meetings, did not afford individuals who are DHH with a real-time means of participation in work meetings. Other strategies relied on potentially cumbersome approaches such as writing on paper, texting, or using a word-processing program. Results of this survey suggest the need for new strategies or technologies for real-time communication for individuals who are DHH in the workplace. In future work, we will investigate the use of ASR-based technologies in this context.

3. ACKNOWLEDGMENTS

This material is based on work supported by the National Technical Institute for the Deaf.

4. REFERENCES

[1] Yashesh Gaur, Florian Metze, Yajie Miao, and Jeffrey P. Bigham. 2015. Using Keyword Spotting to Help Humans Correct Captioning Faster. In Sixteenth Annual Conference of the International Speech Communication Association.

[2] Hernisa Kacorri, Matt Huenerfauth, Sarah Ebling, Kasmira Patel, and Mackenzie Willard. 2015. Demographic and Experiential Factors Influencing Acceptance of Sign Language Animation by Deaf Users. In Proceedings of the 17th International ACM SIGACCESS Conference on Computers & Accessibility (ASSETS '15). ACM, New York, NY, USA, 147-154. DOI=http://dx.doi.org/10.1145/2700648.2809860

[3] Marc Marschark, Greg Leigh, Patricia Sapere, Denis Burnham, Carol Convertino, Michael Stinson, Harry Knoors, Mathijs PJ Vervloed, and William Noble. 2006. Benefits of sign language interpreting and text alternatives for deaf students' classroom learning. Journal of deaf studies and deaf education 11, 4 (2006), 421–437.

[4] Soraia Silva Prietch, Napoliana Silva de Souza, and Lucia Villela Leite Filgueiras. 2014. A Speech-To-Text System's Acceptance Evaluation: Would Deaf Individuals Adopt This Technology in Their Lives? Universal Access in Human-Computer Interaction. Design and Development Methods for Universal Access (2014), 440–449.

[5] Jessica J. Tran, Eve A. Riskin, Richard E. Ladner, and Jacob O. Wobbrock. 2015. Evaluating Intelligibility and Battery Drain of Mobile Sign Language Video Transmitted at Low Frame Rates and Bit Rates. ACM Trans. Access. Comput. 7, 3, Article 11 (November 2015), 26 pages. DOI=http://dx.doi.org/10.1145/27971

[6] Mike Wald. 2005. Using automatic speech recognition to enhance education for all students: Turning a vision into reality. In Frontiers in Education, IEEE FIE'05. Proceedings 35th Annual Conference. DOI: http://dx.doi.org/10.1109/FIE.2005.1612286

VizMap: Accessible Visual Information Through Crowdsourced Map Reconstruction

Cole Gleason, Anhong Guo, Gierad Laput, Kris Kitani, Jeffrey P. Bigham

School of Computer Science, Carnegie Mellon University, Pittsburgh, PA, USA

{ cgleason, anhongg, gierad.laput, kkitani, jbigham }@cs.cmu.edu

ABSTRACT

When navigating indoors, blind people are often unaware of key visual information, such as posters, signs, and exit doors. Our *VizMap* system uses computer vision and crowdsourcing to collect this information and make it available non-visually. VizMap starts with videos taken by on-site sighted volunteers and uses these to create a 3D spatial model. These video frames are semantically labeled by remote crowd workers with key visual information. These semantic labels are located within and embedded into the reconstructed 3D model, forming a query-able spatial representation of the environment. VizMap can then localize the user with a photo from their smartphone, and enable them to explore the visual elements that are nearby. We explore a range of example applications enabled by our reconstructed spatial representation. With VizMap, we move towards integrating the strengths of the end user, on-site crowd, online crowd, and computer vision to solve a long-standing challenge in indoor blind exploration.

Categories and Subject Descriptors

H.5.2 [**Information interfaces and presentation**]: User Interfaces - *Input devices and strategies*; K.4.2 [**Computers and Society**]: Social Issues - *Assistive technologies*

Keywords

Blind users; accessibility; crowdsourcing; indoor navigation.

1. INTRODUCTION

Exploring unfamiliar indoor environments can be difficult for blind people. Many use obstacle-avoidance measures, such as navigating with a cane or guide dogs, to make their way through indoor spaces, but these aids do not provide access to critical navigation cues such as signs or the location of doors. Likewise, relevant points of interest (POIs) pertinent to a location (*e.g.*, bathroom signs, trash cans, posters) are equally inaccessible. Sighted users take these visual cues for granted, but most objects lack salient non-visual hints to their presence, making even everyday environments difficult for blind users to access effectively.

ASSETS '16, October 24–26, 2016, Reno, Nevada, USA.

© 2016 Copyright held by the owner/author(s).

ACM ISBN 978-1-4503-4124-0/16/10..

DOI: http://dx.doi.org/10.1145/2982142.2982200

In outdoor environments, GPS applications for smartphones have made blind navigation and exploration much easier, as the application can detect the user's location within a few meters and provide information about nearby landmarks. For instance, the popular BlindSquare[1] application describes outdoor points of interest (*e.g.*, businesses and streets) to blind users based on their current location. Indoor localization systems have not yet achieved that level of utility for blind users due to limited maps of points of interest. Indoor environments also suffer from poor GPS signal reception, so researchers have tried many other approaches to find a blind user's position inside a building. Becaon-based approaches use the signals of devices placed throughout the environment, but require instrumenting the building and maintaining the system. Google's Project Tango[2] enables indoor navigation with depth sensors in smartphones, but RGB-D cameras are not yet in widespread use. Impressive projects like Navatar solve this problem by reducing localization drift in dead-reckoning by having the user periodically confirm their location based on nearby landmarks [2].

Computer vision approaches such as Structure from Motion can be used to create models of environments and localize users in them [3], but often have no semantic understanding of the visual information. Prior research has also explored the utility of providing point of interest awareness [4], but annotating all indoor points may be time consuming. Projects like VizWiz proved that crowd workers can provide good semantic labels and human understanding for blind users [1] via a smartphone application. Our system fuses these two approaches to embed the crowd's labels of visual information into a model of the environment. We also explore how this information might be accessed using a smartphone.

2. VIZMAP

We introduce VizMap, a system that captures indoor visual points of interest and makes them available to blind people. VizMap uses OpenMVG's Structure from Motion pipeline[3] to automatically construct a model of an indoor environment, and embeds crowdsourced semantic annotations of visual points of interest. In general, on-site sighted volunteers with smartphones (or wearable cameras) act as distributed physical crawlers to collect video footage of a building's interior. These videos are used to build a 3D point cloud representation of the environment for localization and navigation. Once representative video frames are collected, an online annotation interface allows remote crowd workers to generate semantic labels for important visual cues in key video frames. These labels are then embedded in the underlying 3D point-cloud representation, which

---

[1] http://blindsquare.com/

[2] https://get.google.com/tango/

[3] https://github.com/openMVG/

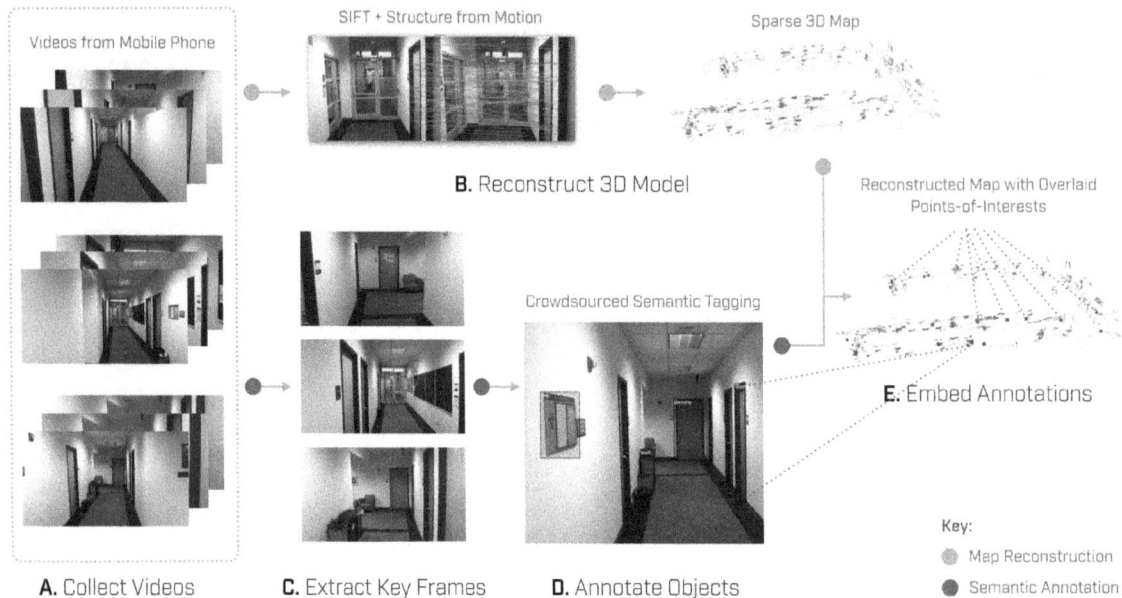

Figure 1: VizMap system infrastructure. VizMap collects videos from sighted volunteers (A) and constructs a sparse 3D model of the environment (B). At the same time, clear key frames are extracted (C) for the crowd to annotate points of interest (D). Finally, the crowd labels are embedded into the generated points cloud (E), shown here as blue squares.

a blind user with a smartphone can interact with by simply taking a photo. Using SIFT features from the captured photo, VizMap determines the user's indoor location and heading to sub-meter accuracy. With that information, it is simple to retrieve all labels in the user's vicinity (*e.g.*, 3 meters) and display them relative to their current direction.

VizMap leverages the strengths of the on-site crowd to provide access to the environment; the online crowd to offer always available sight and general intelligence; computer vision to deliver automation, speed, and scalability; and the end user to build a mental model of the environment based on the embedded points of interest. Our approach also takes advantage of the ubiquitously available smartphones instead of instrumenting the environment.

3. EXAMPLE APPLICATIONS

VizMap produces a point-cloud representation of an indoor environment with embedded semantic labels. To explore interaction techniques with this model, we designed and built three prototype applications using the VizMap infrastructure on an iPhone, taking advantage of the built-in accessibility and screen reader features (*e.g.*, VoiceOver). Whenever the blind user takes a photo in the mapped environment, the image is sent to a server which performs real-time localization and finds the user's orientation.

- **Nearby POIs:** The server finds all POIs within a predefined radius of the user. The orientations for the retrieved POIs are then computed relative to the user and read aloud in a clockwise fashion via VoiceOver (*e.g.*, "3 o'clock: door").

- **Fine-grained interrogation:** VizMap determines all POIs directly within the user's field of view and allows the user to interact with these POIs by tapping buttons on screen, using an interface similar to RegionSpeak [5].

- **Dynamic messages:** In a third prototype, a sighted or blind user can take a photo and embed a message into the environment in order to mark dynamic information like ongoing construction or social events.

A blind user evaluated these three applications (the second in a Wizard of Oz fashion) in a campus corridor, but she had difficulty taking a good photo, as many of the bare walls lacked enough feature points to localize. Future work will allow the user to continuously pan the camera until localization succeeds, removing the need to aim. Dead-reckoning and other approaches will provide smooth localizations between those successful frames. Alternatively, the annotated 3D map could use different indoor localization methods, such as beacons, in supported buildings.

4. REFERENCES

[1] J. P. Bigham, C. Jayant, H. Ji, G. Little, A. Miller, R. C. Miller, R. Miller, A. Tatarowicz, B. White, S. White, et al. Vizwiz: nearly real-time answers to visual questions. In *Proceedings of the 23nd annual ACM symposium on User interface software and technology*. ACM, 2010.

[2] N. Fallah, I. Apostolopoulos, K. Bekris, and E. Folmer. The user as a sensor: navigating users with visual impairments in indoor spaces using tactile landmarks. In *Proceedings of the SIGCHI Conference on Human Factors in Computing Systems*. ACM, 2012.

[3] A. Irschara, C. Zach, J.-M. Frahm, and H. Bischof. From structure-from-motion point clouds to fast location recognition. In *IEEE Comference on Computer Vision and Pattern Recognition*. IEEE, 2009.

[4] R. Yang, S. Park, S. R. Mishra, Z. Hong, C. Newsom, H. Joo, E. Hofer, and M. W. Newman. Supporting spatial awareness and independent wayfinding for pedestrians with visual impairments. In *The proceedings of the 13th international ACM SIGACCESS conference on Computers and accessibility*. ACM, 2011.

[5] Y. Zhong, W. S. Lasecki, E. Brady, and J. P. Bigham. Regionspeak: Quick comprehensive spatial descriptions of complex images for blind users. In *Proceedings of the 33rd Annual ACM Conference on Human Factors in Computing Systems*. ACM, 2015.

Promoting Strategic Research on Inclusive Access to Rich Online Content and Services

Clayton Lewis and Shaun K. Kane
Department of Computer Science
University of Colorado
Boulder CO USA
clayton.lewis@colorado.edu,
shaun.kane@colorado.edu

Richard Ladner
Department of Computer Science
University of Washington
Seattle WA USA
ladner@cs.washington.edu

ABSTRACT

How can the broader field of computer science research be harnessed to address challenges and opportunities in accessibility? This poster summarizes the findings of a workshop, sponsored by the Computing Community Consortium (USA), that brought together computer scientists, representatives of disability advocacy organizations, people from industry, and government employees to develop an agenda for strategic research. Members of the ASSETS community may find the reports useful in organizing collaborative projects with others in the computer science community.

CCS Concepts

• **Human-centered computing**☐**Accessibility technologies** • *Human-centered computing*☐*Interaction design* • *Human-centered computing*☐*Accessibility systems and tools* • *Social and professional topics*☐*Government technology policy*

Keywords

Strategic research; collaborative research

1. INTRODUCTION

Solving the difficult problems in accessible computing requires both computing innovation and user-centered design. While much research in accessible computing is conducted by researchers who themselves are accessibility experts, there is value in bringing in researchers who do not typically conduct accessibility research. This paper summarizes findings from a workshop held in September 2015, organized by the Computing Community Consortium, to frame an agenda for strategic research on promoting inclusion of people with disabilities online. A report of the findings is available online [1]. This poster summarizes the findings, so that members of the ASSETS community can help draw attention to and create support for the agenda. The report identifies opportunities

for collaborative research by researchers in technology and disability, working with researchers in other areas of computer science.

2. NEED, OPPORTUNITY, AND IMPACT

The report contains references to many indicators of the importance of inclusion online. It cites relevant policy commitments in the USA, and at the international level. It provides illustrations of the impact on the lives of citizens that can be realized by well directed research, such as a job seeker finding job opportunities and completing job applications online, regardless of disability, or a blind student choosing from a wide array of advanced technical courses, available online, knowing that all the information presented via diagrams and interactive simulations will be accessible.

The report argues that the time is ripe for increased research, for three reasons. First, the aging population means that the impact of inclusion will increase. Second, there are barriers to inclusion that are increasing, rather than decreasing, and we need to act now to reverse this trend. Finally, recent advances in technology are creating opportunities to reduce existing barriers.

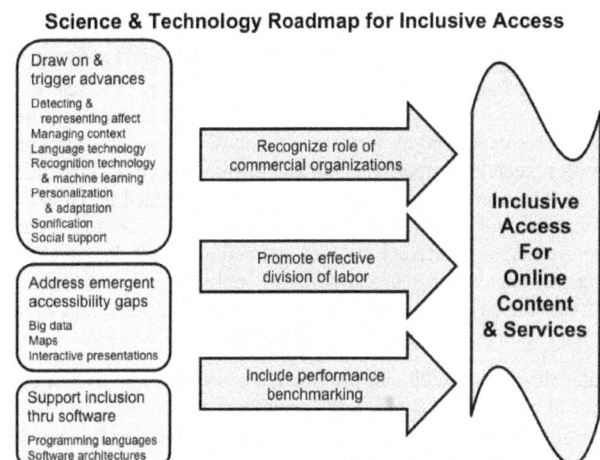

Figure 1. Roadmap for research in inclusive access.

3. ROADMAP FOR RESEARCH

Figure 1 summarizes the findings from the workshop, highlighting the logic for addressing the needs and opportunities. The left side of the figure shows the areas of research with most promise, both as sources of new solutions for people with disabilities, and as opportunities for progress from focusing on the needs of inclusion.

The middle of the figure shows the key actions needed to reach the key goal of inclusive access.

Participants identified two broad classes of research opportunities. First, there are new developments in science and technology that can help address existing barriers. Major advances in inclusion are possible if researchers and developers working on accessibility can work cooperatively with researchers who are developing new technologies for other purposes, as well as with scientists seeking fundamental understanding of relevant problems. We can not only exploit progress being made in other areas, but also trigger new advances, by contributing our understanding of important problems. Second, some opportunities arise because new technologies for delivering content and services create new barriers. For example, the increasing use of games and simulations, for education as well as for entertainment, creates a need for research on how to support the use of these media by people with disabilities.

3.1 Drawing On Advances in Other Fields
Participants identified the following topics as especially promising. Rationale and detail are included in the report.

- Detecting and representing affect
- Managing attention in multi-stream communication
- Managing context in interpreting communication
- Automated natural language processing
- Accessibility of machine learning
- Personalization and adaptation in user interfaces
- Sonification
- Tactile displays
- Social support for technology use and development

3.2 Addressing Emergent Accessibility Gaps
Participants identified the following research needs, associated with new, or newly important, technologies:

- Exploring and understanding large quantitative datasets
- Maps and navigation
- Inclusive design of interactive presentations

3.3 Supporting Inclusion through Software
A broader need that emerged in this survey of research opportunities is for software structures that make accessibility enhancements easier to implement. Today, adding accessibility features, such as support for a tactile display, requires substantial implementation effort. Software structures are needed that make it easier to substitute different representations for the same information, and different ways of interacting with it. Research on programming languages and software architectures that aims to address this challenge includes the KORZ, NewSpeak, and Fluid projects. Enhanced support for this line of work is needed.

This software research can provide a crucial added benefit: it can make it easier for people with disabilities themselves, and their caregivers, to create useful technology that meets individual needs. Making software development tools themselves more accessible, and easier to use by people with less technical skill, is an important research challenge. Research in end user programming, including programming by demonstration and by example, has much to contribute here.

4. RESEARCH GOALS
For research to meet the goals of inclusion online, the contributions of individuals with different skills, and organizations with different roles and capabilities, need to be coordinated. Participants recommended the following approaches.

4.1 Include Commercial Organizations
Results of value for consumers will happen much more quickly if the companies that create those products and services participate in the research.

A public-private partnership may be a way to create the needed collaboration. Government agencies could broker funding for cooperating teams of researchers and developers in academe and industry.

4.2 Promote Effective Division of Labor
Many of the technical and scientific advances that have promise for enhancing inclusion online are being made by people with little or no understanding of the opportunities to serve the needs of people with disabilities. At the same time, people well informed about these needs, and these behavioral science methods, may have little understanding of the scientific and technical developments to be exploited. Research sponsors should be proactive in assembling the teams needed to carry on this work.

4.3 Include Performance Benchmarking
Relatedly, research sponsors should develop benchmarks that will allow the field to determine when progress is being made in meeting inclusion goals. Recruitment of test participants, and the conduct of the assessments, would be provided for any participating, funded project. Thus technology researchers can propose promising work without undertaking the assessment work themselves.

5. CONCLUSION
As information increasingly moves online, we must support full participation from people with disabilities. New forms of interaction bring with them the need to make them help include, rather than exclude, people with disabilities. At the same time, the opportunities to build on research progress in other computing fields are increasing. The time is right for researchers, and those who support research, to step up our efforts to address these needs by grasping these opportunities.

6. ACKNOWLEDGMENTS
We are grateful to all of the workshop participants, who are listed in the Workshop Report [1]; to Ben Shneiderman for suggestions about the presentation; and to the Computing Community Consortium, the National Science Foundation, and the National Institute for Disability, Independent Living, and Rehabilitation Research, for supporting the workshop.

7. REFERENCE
[1] Kane, S., Ladner, R., and Lewis, C. (2016) Promoting Strategic Research on Inclusive Access to Rich Online Content and Services. Computing Community Consortium. Online at http://cra.org/ccc/wp-content/uploads/sites/2/2016/04/Inclusive-Access-Report.pdf.

#accessibilityFail: Categorizing Shared Photographs of Physical Accessibility Problems

ABSTRACT

Social media platforms are existing online spaces where users share their daily encounters, providing a large dataset of photographs of inaccessible environments. We analyzed 100 posts from Twitter and Instagram that describe accessibility problems. Our findings suggest these posts are helpful to locate, identify and communicate accessibility problems, and provide design ideas for potential assistive technologies. We suggest design implications using social media posts to improve physical accessibility.

Keywords

Physical accessibility; photography; social media.

1. INTRODUCTION

Inaccessible environments are often obvious to people with disabilities and disability advocates, but may not be as obvious to the general public who do not typically encounter them when navigating physical spaces.

Photographs are useful for learning about accessibility problems. Applications like VizWiz [3] and RemoteLogCam [5] ask users to take accessibility-specific photographs *in situ*, and use those photographs to provide accessible information. Other projects leverage existing datasets of photographs that were not collected for accessibility purposes, like street-level images in Google Street View which were used to evaluate accessibility in the environment [6]. Both sources of photographs offer valuable information about accessibility problems but have limitations. Projects that solicit accessibility-specific photographs often have limited samples, and projects that use general datasets may lack the context needed to identify accessibility problems.

Many social media platforms like Instagram are built specifically around sharing, which allows users an opportunity to document daily experiences and provides a rich source of user-generated data. YouTube videos uploaded by users with motor impairments using touchscreens have given researchers valuable insights into technology design [1]. By examining accessibility-related social media posts, we can learn about everyday accessibility problems.

In this paper we identify three themes in social media posts about accessibility "fails", problems with accessibility infrastructure. This analysis can be used to inform future projects that leverage social media posts about accessibility.

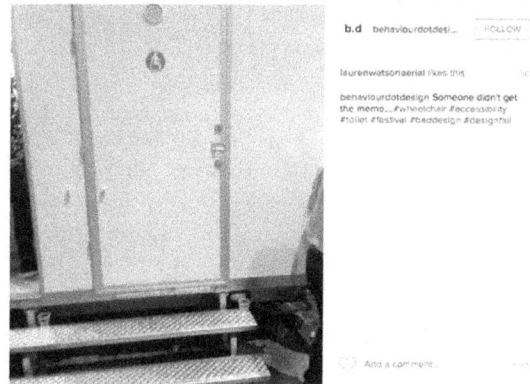

Figure 1: An accessibility problem on Instagram. While the festival had a portable restroom that was marked as "wheelchair accessible", it was only reachable via a flight of inaccessible stairs.
This photograph was taken by Linda van de Sande of behavior.design, and is used with her permission. [instagram.com/p/BES1nLRsrex/]

2. ACCESSIBILITY FAIL POSTS

We selected a sample of posts from Twitter and Instagram from September 2012 to February 2016 containing photographs and the hashtag *#accessibilityFail*, a commonly-used term to describe accessibility problems. We used two platforms' native search function to extract 100 post and image pairs. The posts were then manually screened by two researchers for relevance to our study resulting in 93 posts which were analyzed. A diversity of disabilities was mentioned in the sample, including deafness, visual impairment, and mobility impairment, but the majority of sampled posts (73%) dealt with wheelchair use.

Two researchers performed open coding on the posts during which unclear codes were discussed to reach a consensus. The open coding process resulted in 23 codes. Those codes were then iteratively refined through affinity diagramming [2] into three higher-level themes that describe how people use photographs to document and communicate accessibility issues.

2.1 Details of Accessibility Problems

41 of the 93 posts analyzed **gave details about the accessibility problem pictured** in some way. This theme took multiple forms across the posts: describing the issue seen in the photograph (17 posts); talking about what type of person it impacts (12); including the location of the problem (21); and naming or at-mentioning the person responsible for the problem or facility (15).

Individual posts could have multiple descriptive features. One Instagram user posted a picture of two clothing racks positioned close together, with the accompanying text:

> *Irritated with this stupid mall... Can't fit in between the effing racks... They are supposed to leave enough room for wheelchairs and don't! Ugh! #accessibilityfail #Deb*

These descriptive details could be useful both to broad audiences as an introduction into this type of accessibility problem and its' consequences, and to other local wheelchair users who may want to avoid Deb (a junior's clothing shop) until it is made accessible.

2.2 Sharing Experiences and Reactions

29 of the 93 posts analyzed **shared experiences and reactions** around the accessibility problems encountered. Posts categorized within this theme were either user's personal experiences with a problem (11 posts), or emotional reactions to a problem that may have been encountered by themselves or others (26 posts).

Some posts that shared personal experiences. Users self-identified a problem and sometimes used the text to convey strong emotions, such as outrage about accessibility inequality or sadness over the consequences of accessibility problems:

> To wheelchair and scooter users, be advised that the @etsyvancouver event on today is not accessible. ... The volunteers were sincerely apologetic, **but I am still very disappointed having just wasted my morning trekking downtown for this**... [emphasis added]

Other users employed humor, snark, or sarcasm in describing accessibility problems. One Instagram user posted a photograph of an unfinished ramp up a flight of stairs with the sarcastic text:

> You can manage those last three steps with your wheelchair, right? ...

2.3 Prompting Corrective Action

33 of the 91 posts analyzed **prompted corrective actions or education about accessibility**. Within this theme, we identified three sub-themes that used distinct but complementary approaches to try to persuade others to improve accessibility: requests to report problems, general advocacy, and criticizing or shaming.

Directives for others to *report problems* were the least-common, but most informative posts within this theme. These users utilized their social network not as a passive audience but as active voices who could put pressure on others to resolve problems. This type of 'slacktivism' is a common way people leverage their existing social networks to impact political processes or support pro-social causes [4]. These posts included calls to action – a photograph of a broken cobblestone sidewalk on Instagram included the post:

> Taxachusetts.   #harvardsquare   #accessibilityfail @cambridgepolice Intersection of Bow and DeWolfe on odd side, v. unsafe for persons with mobility and balance issues, in wheelchairs, after dark, strollers, etc. **Please advise DPW** [Department of Public Works, emphasis added]

The detailed location information in this post could be used to identify street-level accessibility problems, similar to approaches in [6]; the use of an at-message to the local police's Instagram account *("@cambridgepolice")* helps route the request to an appropriate authority who might be able to resolve the problem.

Other posts shared general *accessibility advocacy*. These posts included information about common accessibility problems and solutions, promoted specific causes, or linked to more information outside the photo-sharing platform. Many of these posts used rhetorical tactics in engaging readers to identifying accessibility problems by posting a photograph of an accessibility problem and asking users to comment with the problem's description (e.g., *"Can you figure out what's wrong with this picture?"*).

Posts in the final sub-theme, *criticizing or shaming*, used their photographs to directly critique places where accessibility was not considered, or was implemented poorly.

> This is a perfect example of how meeting minimum building requirements does not make a space #accessible or #inclusive. And in a brand new build from a chain that claims to be socially responsible? ...

Some of these posts also identified the correct way to make things more accessible in their accompanying text.

3. FUTURE WORK

The wide range of accessibility issues and environments highlighted in the images, combined with the descriptive text posted by the users and conversations that they engage in, create a rich dataset of annotated accessibility problems and solutions. Many of these metadata provide information that could be useful for locating problems, or collecting a repository of proposed solutions from people with disabilities or involved in advocacy for broader accessibility. Below we discuss future work we are undertaking to make this dataset more useful.

The intermixing of humor or sarcasm in some of the posts might make automated approaches difficult. Crowdsourced or human-powered accessibility tools might be the most appropriate method for comprehending the information available from each post, and we plan to analyze how crowdsourced annotations compare to the original metadata available with the posts.

The tenor of conversations on Twitter and Instagram were significantly different. In one example in our dataset, a user had posted an image about an accessibility problem at an event on both Twitter and Instagram. On Twitter she received an apology from the organizers with a promise to make things accessible the next year. On Instagram she received support from her friends, as well as a place to complain further about her frustrations. Understanding how users choose what platform to post to and how this might impact the data generated on those platforms is crucial to using this data for accessibility. Further analysis of the conversations that took place in the comments of these posts and platform differences will broaden our understanding of how posts are used to influence accessibility. This data will seed our examination of the feasibility of crowdsourcing to identify and propose solutions to accessibility problems remotely.

4. REFERENCES

[1] Anthony, L. et al. 2013. Analyzing user-generated youtube videos to understand touchscreen use by people with motor impairments. *Proceedings of the SIGCHI Conference on Human Factors in Computing Systems* (2013), 1223–1232.

[2] Beyer, H. and Holtzblatt, K. 1997. *Contextual design: defining customer-centered systems.* Elsevier.

[3] Brady, E. et al. 2013. Visual challenges in the everyday lives of blind people. *Proceedings of the SIGCHI Conference on Human Factors in Computing Systems* (2013), 2117–2126.

[4] Christensen, H.S. 2011. Political activities on the Internet: Slacktivism or political participation by other means? *First Monday.* 16, 2 (2011).

[5] Güldenpfennig, F. and Fitzpatrick, G. 2013. A monitoring device as assistive lifestyle technology: combining functional needs with pleasure. *Proceedings of the 4th augmented human international conference*, 190–193.

[6] Hara, K. et al. 2015. Improving Public Transit Accessibility for Blind Riders by Crowdsourcing Bus Stop Landmark Locations with Google Street View: An Extended Analysis. *ACM Transactions on Accessible Computing (TACCESS).* 6, 2 (2015), 5.

Exploration of the Use of Auditory Cues in Code Comprehension and Navigation for Individuals with Visual Impairments in a Visual Programming Environment

Stephanie Ludi
Department of Computer Science and Engineering
University of North Texas
Denton, USA
Stephanie.ludi@unt.edu

Jamie Simpson
Department of Computer Science and Engineering
University of North Texas
Denton, USA

Wil Merchant
Department of Physics
Coastal Carolina University
Conway, USA

ABSTRACT
Visual programming languages are commonplace in engaging novice programmers. Accessibility challenges persist in these systems. This study investigates whether auditory cues improves a visually impaired programmer's ability to navigate and understand source code in a block-based language. The type of auditory cue that best serves this purpose is also investigated. The participants' comprehension of source code using three trials with two tests each is presented, with each trial corresponding to a different form of audio cue. Participants are graded on how accurate their written source code is in comparison to the actual source code.

Keywords
Audio cues; accessibility; block-based programming; program understanding; visually impaired

1. INTRODUCTION
People with visual impairments face challenges in programming. Traditionally source code is text-based. While there are many visual cues used to improve the clarity of source code in a text based programming environment (whitespace, indentation, highlighted text, etc.), these cues are inaccessible to individuals with visual impairments. Being unable to use these visual cues, programmers with visual impairments must struggle to contend with the complexities of writing source code such as resolving syntax errors and determining nesting levels. With improved accessibility to source code, not only would more people with visual impairments be able to participate in programming.

Visual Programming Languages (VPLs) such as Scratch could be useful in resolving several issues involved with writing source code by allowing users to construct programs using coding blocks that represent functions and commands. These blocks can be constructed and attached to each other in a way that allows users to construct a full program with little text input. VPLs also have the advantage of limiting syntax errors during source code generation by disallowing users to attach ineligible blocks together.

ASSETS '16, October 23-26, 2016, Reno, NV, USA
ACM 978-1-4503-4124-0/16/10.
http://dx.doi.org/10.1145/2982142.2982206

While the simplicity of visual programming languages allows for an introduction to programming for novice users, there is a possibility that the structure of VPLs could serve as a tool to aid users with visual impairments in programming. Before this can be a possibility, there are some improvements that must be made to the design of VPLs before programmers with visual impairments can use them reliably.

One method that could be implemented to improve the accessibility of visual programming environments is using auditory cues to signify the various components of source code. Audio cues are auditory mechanisms used to enhance text-to-speech representations of data [4]. The usage of audio cues in aiding people with visual impairments has been researched extensively in other fields such as mathematics and literature. While there are many visual cues in programming that make writing and navigating programs easier, audio cues are an innovation that have rarely been implemented in visually programming. Our research questions include:

- Are auditory cues used in a visual programming environment effective in aiding users in navigating and understanding source code?

- Which form of auditory cue is the most effective?

This study explores the above questions by conducting an evaluation a prototype user interface with 7 programmers with visual impairments. A modified version of the visual programming editor Blockly was chosen for its simple user interface, customizability, and the navigability tools that the application provides through the use of keyboard shortcuts. Along with Blockly, this study employs the use of auditory cues, specifically earcons and spearcons. Earcons are abstract sounds, usually musical, that are used to represent objects or ideas [3]. Spearcons, on the other hand, are sounds generated from sped up speech [2].

2. RELATED WORK
Stefik's study [5] focused heavily on the comprehension of source code in aural form using musical elements and prosodic elements to represent different aspects of source code. In the first experiment, a group of 64 sighted users were tasked with listening to auditory representations of 10 different programs. The participants would then write their interpretations of the source code structure for each program. The results showed that the group that received scoping had improved comprehension of the source code compared to the other group. The results of this experiment found that sighted users performed best in visual

environment, and an auditory environment that provides semantic cues about the source code of a program.

Baker et al's work [1] discusses the development and evaluation of a plug-in for the Eclipse IDE called StructJumper. This plug-in was used to assist blind programmers in navigating through Java source code via a hierarchical tree of the nesting structure of a program's source code. The results of the study showed that participants were able to complete tasks quicker and understand the source code more than those that did not use the tool.

3. EVALUATION

Seven programmers with varying visual impairments participated in this study. The average age of the participants was 24.1 years (SD = 5.30) with an average of 3.25 years of programming experience. While VPL's are associated with novice programmers, participants with some experience were used so as to minimize issues with controlling for concept understanding. Skype was used to contact the participants since Skype allowed the authors to monitor the participants' tasks. The Evaer Skype call recorder was used for video recording of the experiments.

Before participating in the study, users were required to complete a short preliminary survey that asked participants to provide demographic information, programming experience information, and information about the accessibility tools commonly used by the participant. Experimental sessions consisted of three trials with each trial differing in the auditory cue used. Training was conducted.

The study consists of three trials using a different type of auditory cue for each trial. Participants used their typical screen readers for all tasks. For the first test, participants were provided with a pre-generated block of source code and were then tasked with finding a specific block in the code using the auditory cues available. Participants were timed on how long it took them to find the designated code block. For the second test, participants were asked to listen to a short audio description of a set of source code. Participants then wrote down their interpretation of the source code's structure. Their results were graded using a technique known as artifact encoding that analyzed the accuracy of their interpretation - derived from [3]. In artifact encoding, the user's responses and the correct answers are coded into strings and compared to each other. After comparing the two encoded strings, the users were given a score based on how well the two strings match up. The survey at the end of each trial then asks the user questions about their overall experience with auditory cues.

4. RESULTS

For the first part of each trial, we recorded the amount of time it took each participant to find a certain block in a set of pre generated source code. After the times were recorded they were grouped by auditory environment (speech, earcons, spearcons) and averaged. Of all the auditory environments, participants completed the navigation task the fastest in the spearcon auditory environment (39.51 s, SD = 16.93). The second fastest of the three environments was speech (40.25 s, SD = 23.06), followed by earcons (45.27 s, SD = 22.62).

The second task of the each trial trial focused on comprehension, and the data recorded from that task was participants' scores after being calculated using artifact encoding. Similarly to the data from task 1, the scores were grouped based on auditory environment and averaged. Of all the auditory environments,

participants had the best comprehension scores in the speech auditory environment (0.94, SD = 0.13), followed by spearcons (0.92, SD = 0.08), and the worst performance being in earcons (0.80, SD = 0.14).

At the end of each trial in an experimental session, the users were given a short survey asking questions about their experience with the auditory environment presented to them. In this survey, participants were asked to rate the usefulness of the auditory cues in terms of navigation and comprehension of the source code on a scale of 1 (not useful at all) to 5 (very useful). For these Likert scale questions, the participants' responses were grouped by auditory environment, and averaged. When asked how useful they felt that the auditory cues were for navigation, participants gave speech a rating of 4.83 (SD = 0.41), earcons a rating of 3.67 (SD = 1.75), and spearcons a rating of 4.33 (SD = 1.63). When asked how useful they felt that the auditory cues were for comprehension, participants gave speech a rating of 4.67 (SD = 0.52), earcons a rating of 3.17 (SD = 1.47), and spearcons a rating of 4 (SD = 1.64). The postsurvey data shows the participant's overall thoughts on the Blockly program. Earcons were rated to be the worse auditory cue chosen for the experiment while spearcons were shown to roughly match regular speech when conveying the nesting level. The advantage of spearcons over speech lies in the amount of time needed to convey meaning.

While Blockly still has many accessibility limitations, it would be interesting to have a study done to investigate whether or not auditory cues can help a programmer with visual impairments program source code in this type of environment. It would also be interesting to see how these auditory cues would work for larger segments for code.

5. ACKNOWLEDGMENTS

Thank you to the participants and to the IECS team overall. This work was supported by the National Science Foundation (Award # 1240809, 1460894).

6. REFERENCES

[1] C. M. Baker, L. R. Milne, R. Ladner. "StructJumper: A tool to Help Blind Programmers Navigate and Understand the Structure of Code." n Proceedings of the 33rd Annual ACM Conference on Human Factors in Computing Systems, ACM New York, pp.3043-3052. April 2015.

[2] S. A. Brewster. "Using Earcons to Improve the Usability of a Graphics Package." In HCI '98, Hilary Johnson, Laurence Nigay, and Chris Roast (Eds.). Springer-Verlag, London, UK, 287-302. 1998.

[3] E. Gellenbeck, and A. Stefik. "Evaluating Prosodic Cues as a Means to Disambiguate Algebraic Expressions: An Empirical Study." Proceedings of the Eleventh International ACM SIGACCESS Conference on Computers and Accessibility (ASSETS 2009), Pittsburgh, pp. 139-146. October 2009.

[4] MIT Media Lab. "Kids coding in the cloud." MIT News. Retrieved: July 28, 2015, From: http://newsoffice.mit.edu/2013/scratch-two-released-0514.

[5] A. Stefik, C. Hundhausen, R. Patterson. "An Empirical Investigation into the Design of Auditory Cues to Enhance Computer Program Comprehension." The International Journal of Human-Computer Studies, vol. 69, pp. 820-838, 2011.

Tag Thunder: Towards Non-Visual Web Page Skimming

Elena Manishina, Jean-Marc Lecarpentier, Fabrice Maurel
Stéphane Ferrari, Maxence Busson
Normandie Univ, UNICAEN, ENSICAEN, CNRS, GREYC, 14000 Caen, France
{firtsname.lastname}@unicaen.fr

ABSTRACT

Tag thunder is an audio version of a visual tag cloud content representation. Tag thunders aim to bring quick reading strategies, such as skimming, to blind people. Tag thunders vocalize the key terms of a page using concurrent speech paradigm coupled with additional audio effects, similar to visual effects in a tag cloud. In this paper we present our implementation of the tag thunder concept. Our system comprises three modules: page segmentation, key term extraction and tag thunder vocalization. The evaluation results show the viability of the tag thunder concept.

CCS Concepts

•Human-centered computing → Accessibility; Accessibility technologies; Accessibility systems and tools; Accessibility theory, concepts and paradigms;

Keywords

Web content accessibility, Speech Synthesis, Content Segmentation, Keyword Extraction

1. INTRODUCTION

When accessing web pages, readers get a first glance of the page content (skimming), followed by a scanning phase in order to find information. Page layout and typographic effects play an important role in facilitating this process. However, these visual clues are not available in non-visual web browsing environments [5]. A number of reading strategies have been developed to facilitate the process of web page skimming and scanning [1], such as using screen readers with faster speech rate depending on block size, shortcuts to jump from heading to heading, reading the beginning and the end of a paragraph, etc. However, these solutions are far less efficient than skimming and scanning strategies used in visual environments [3]. This work is based on two main techniques: content summarization and concurrent speech synthesis. Tag thunders combine these techniques to provide a

ASSETS '16 Reno, Nevada USA

© 2016 Copyright held by the owner/author(s).

ACM ISBN 978-1-4503-4124-0/16/10.

DOI: http://dx.doi.org/10.1145/2982142.2982152

Figure 1: Segmentation and key terms extraction

quick overview of the page content in an audio format.

In this paper, we propose a system which allows blind users to get a first glance of web page content. We introduce and implement the concept of tag thunder. Tag thunder is an audio version of a visual tag cloud. Tag thunders use a concurrent speech strategy in order to represent the dense visual stimulus embodied by tag cloud. It is based on the *Cocktail Party Effect* [4]: a user may identify key terms pronounced simultaneously and focus his attention on key terms that interest him amongst all the others.

Our implementation comprises three main steps, as illustrated in Figure 1. First, we segment a web page into a given number of zones. Then we select key terms for each zone using extraction techniques and key terms visual properties. Finally, the vocalized key terms are simultaneously placed on an audio track in order to reflect the position and visual properties of its zone. Our implementation is available online at https://tagthunder.greyc.fr/demo/.

In the following Section, we describe the architecture of our tag thunder implementation.

2. ARCHITECTURE

2.1 Page segmentation

To segment a web page, we use the K-means++ clustering algorithm [2]. It groups visible HTML elements into a given number of zones based on their Euclidian distance. To optimize convergence and efficiency, each HTML element is enhanced with its computed styles based on CSS and Javascript. Elements that are not part of the visual layout are ignored.

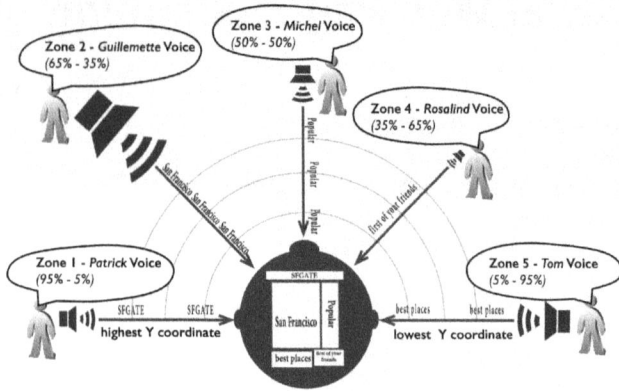

Figure 2: Stereo perception of a 5-zone tag thunder

2.2 Key terms extraction and weighting

For each zone, we extract a given number of key terms. In this implementation, the key terms are n-grams of different lengths. For each n-gram we compute tf-idf, where tf is the frequency of a term within its zone and idf is the number of documents containing this term in a corpus of 953K entries. We couple the tf-idf score with several additional parameters which reflect the visual properties of the zone and the key term itself, such as font color, font size, background color, etc. We compute the final key term score using the Formula (1).

$$Score = tf(term, zone) \cdot idf(term, C) \cdot \sum_{i=1}^{n} \sigma(c_i) \qquad (1)$$

where $tf(term, zone)$ is the frequency of the term within its zone, $idf(term, C)$ is the number of occurrences of the term in our corpus C. σ is the weight for additional parameters c_i. Weight ranges from 0.5 to 5 depending on the parameter's perceived importance.

2.3 Vocalization

Finally we generate the audio signal for each key term. Our vocalization module uses the Kali TT Synthetizer [8], developed at the University of Caen Normandie. Voices are equally distributed in the 2D stereo space depending on the zone's centroid coordinates, with a total number of sound sources equal to the number of zones. For each key term, the silence between repetitions is proportional to the relative size of its zone. Volume is set within a given interval, using the average of normalized color contrast and key term frequency of its zone. The resulting key term vocalizations are placed on an audio track which is played in a loop. This helps the user to detect the sound of potential interest, determine its source and navigate to a desired zone or term. Figure 2 illustrates tag thunders in action.

3. CONCLUSION

According to the evaluation results [6], our system produces audio representations that provide sufficient information about web page content and layout: the participants were able to measure the correspondence between a tag thunder and a web page.

Our future work focuses on improving the performance of each module. The segmentation module may combine visual (image based) and logical (DOM based) page segmentation methods. Key term extraction module may be enhanced with new solutions such as 'wikify!' [7]. Also, we need to find the best associations between the visual page properties and acoustic and prosodic characteristics of the tag thunders. In addition, binaural audio techniques would provide more options for the spatialization of key terms. Finally, an important direction of our future work is to find a compromise between the number of zones and key terms and the perceptive capacity of users.

4. ACKNOWLEGMENTS

This research work was funded by the 'Region Normandie' with the CPER NUMNIE project.

5. REFERENCES

[1] F. Ahmed, Y. Borodin, A. Soviak, M. Islam, I. Ramakrishnan, and T. Hedgpeth. Accessible skimming: Faster screen reading of web pages. In *25th Annual ACM Symposium on User Interface Software and Technology (UIST)*, pages 367–378, 2012.

[2] D. Arthur and S. Vassilvitskii. k-means++: The advantages of careful seeding. In *Proceedings of the eighteenth annual ACM-SIAM symposium on Discrete algorithms*, pages 1027–1035. Society for Industrial and Applied Mathematics, 2007.

[3] J. P. Bigham, A. C. Cavender, J. T. Brudvik, J. O. Wobbrock, and R. E. Lander. Webinsitu: A comparative analysis of blind and sighted browsing behavior. In *9th International ACM SIGACCESS Conference on Computers and Accessibility (ASSETS)*, pages 51–58, 2007.

[4] E. C. Cherry. Some experiments on the recognition of speech, with one and with two ears. *Journal of the acoustical society of America, 25(5)*, pages 975–979, 1953.

[5] G. Dias and B. Conde. Accessing the web on handheld devices for visually impaired people. In K. Wegrzyn-Wolska and P. Szczepaniak, editors, *Advances in Intelligent Web Mastering*, volume 43 of *Advances in Soft Computing*, pages 80–86. 2007.

[6] J.-M. Lecarpentier, E. Manishina, F. Maurel, S. Ferrari, E. Giguet, G. Dias, and M. Busson. Tag thunder: Web page skimming in non visual environment using concurrent speech. In *7th Workshop on Speech and Language Processing for Assistive Technologies (SLPAT)*, 2016.

[7] R. Mihalcea and A. Csomai. Wikify!: linking documents to encyclopedic knowledge. In *Proceedings of the sixteenth ACM conference on Conference on information and knowledge management*, pages 233–242. ACM, 2007.

[8] M. Morel and A. Lacheret-Dujour. Kali, synthèse vocale à partir du texte : de la conception à la mise en oeuvre. *Traitement Automatique des Langues 42*, pages 193–221, 2001.

A Platform Agnostic Remote Desktop System for Screen Reading

Syed Masum Billah   Vikas Ashok   Donald E. Porter   IV Ramakrishnan

Stony Brook University

{sbillah, vganjiguntea, porter, ram}@cs.stonybrook.edu

ABSTRACT

Remote desktop technology, the enabler of access to applications hosted on remote hosts, relies primarily on scraping the pixels on the remote screen and redrawing them as a simple bitmap on the client's local screen. Such a technology will simply not work with screen readers since the latter are innately tied to reading text. Since screen readers are locked-in to a specific OS platform, extant solutions that enable remote access with screen readers such as NVDARemote and JAWS Tandem require homogeneity of OS platforms at both the client and remote sites. This demo will present Sinter, a system that eliminates this requirement. With Sinter, a blind Mac user, for example, can now access a remote Windows application with VoiceOver, a scenario heretofore not possible.

1. INTRODUCTION

Remote desktop technology is primarily used to access applications that are hosted on remote machines, such as a physician accessing a medical records application running on an office server from her home. The graphical display of the remote system is virtualized and shipped across the network to the client. Virtualization emulates the graphics card frame buffer in which the pixel values are scraped from the screen of the remote system, and redrawn as a simple bitmap on the client's local screen. This approach yields seamless access to remote applications, as if they were running on the local desktop. Remote desktop access is indispensable to users engaged in activities such as telecommuting, distance learning, remote troubleshooting and maintenance.

Unfortunately, remote desktop technology in its current incarnation, namely via emulation of the graphics frame buffer, simply will not work for blind users. These users rely on screen readers to interact with digital content. Screen readers require semantic information, such as text and hierarchical relationships to narrate screen contents—all of this information is lost by the time the screen is rendered as a bitmap.

ASSETS '16 October 23-26, 2016, Reno, NV, USA

© 2016 Copyright held by the owner/author(s).

ACM ISBN 978-1-4503-4124-0/16/10.

DOI: http://dx.doi.org/10.1145/2982142.2982151

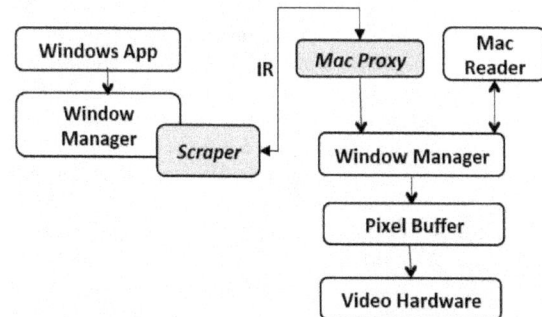

Figure 1: A schematic of remote access in Sinter.

One obvious solution is to run a screen reader on the remote host and relay the synthesized audio to the client. But network delays, especially over WANs, can introduce unacceptable latencies to relaying audio, a fact validated by our experiments [1]. A second approach, exemplified by commercial systems such as NVDARemote [3] and JAWS-Tandem [2], is to intercept text from the remote screen reader just before audio synthesis, relay this text to the local client and synthesize audio locally. Getting this to work requires identical screen readers, one running remotely and the other locally. The serious problem with such a solution is that screen readers are locked into a single operating system platform; the differences in the underlying accessibility APIs (e.g., Microsoft's MSAA and UI Automation, Apple's Accessibility, and GNOME's ATK & AT-SPI) has been a strong barrier to portability. Consequently, NVDARemote-like solutions require both the remote and local platforms to be similar. Platform-specific remote access solutions are clearly inadequate in the modern computing era where computer users increasingly use applications designed for different OSes, spanning desktops, laptops, tablets, mobile devices, cloud and other platforms. For instance, a Mac user may access a cloud-based Windows remote desktop to run an application required for her job. Similarly, a Windows desktop user may use VMware workstation to develop and test a Linux server application. Such scenarios are the norm these days and, thus, calls for platform-independent remote access solutions for screen reader users. Our Sinter system [1] provides such a solution.

2. *SINTER* SYSTEM OVERVIEW

Sinter is predicated on the observation that applications on every OS consist of similar User Interface (UI) widgets such as buttons, drop-down menus, text fields, etc. The key idea then is to create a UI model of the application's GUI from the existing, platform-specific accessibility APIs, analogous to an HTML document object model (DOM) tree, convert the model into a generic intermediate representation (IR), and finally render the IR encoding of the application GUI on a different platform, using native UI widgets. A screen reader on the client system can then read the native rendering of the IR. Fig. 1 is a high level schematic of this idea. The figure corresponds to a scenario where a user wants to run VoiceOver, the Mac screen reader, to read a Windows application on a remote system. In Sinter, a scraper on Windows mines the Windows-specific UI model of the application, and converts it into Sinter's IR which is shipped to a client system–Mac in this example, where a proxy converts the IR back to a native representation of these elements that VoiceOver understands. The Sinter proxy relays keystrokes and other user inputs back to the scraper, and the scraper relays incremental changes in the UI back to the proxy. In Sinter, the IR is a generic XML which we found to be sufficiently expressive for encoding a majority of standard UI element types on Windows and Mac. Having an IR opens up powerful opportunities for personalizing or making application specific modifications of the UI itself. For example, we made a mega-ribbon for Word in Fig. 2, which avoids cumbersome ribbon navigation for frequently-used buttons.

3. CURRENT STATUS

The Sinter idea and the engineering that went into building the system was presented in the 2016 European Systems Conference [1]. Since then, we have completed the implementation of a fully functional Sinter system. Furthermore, following IRB approval we also conducted a preliminary user study with 21 blind subjects at Lighthouse Guild. Currently, Sinter enables to screen-read the remote Windows application locally on a Mac with VoiceOver, and conversely, remote Mac application locally on Windows with JAWS and NVDA. Windows applications that can be accessed remotely from Mac clients include Microsoft Word, Windows Calculator, Windows Explorer, the Windows registry editor, and the DOS command line (command.exe) while remote Mac applications accessed from Windows clients include Apple Mail, HandBrake (a media ripping and transcoding utility), Messages, Calculator, and Contacts. Fig. 2 presents snapshots of Windows applications accessed remotely on an Mac client with Sinter.

A Sinter demo, which will be the first of its kind to the accessibility community, will exercise the functionalities of Sinter with these applications in place.

4. PRELIMINARY USER STUDY

21 blind subjects participated in a preliminary study primarily primed to get an initial assessment of Sinter, and gather additional requirements from users. Towards that they were given tasks to calculate with a remote calculator, and edit documents using Notepad running remotely. A System Usability Scale (SUS) questionnaire was administered at the end of the study relating to usability, ease of use, learning curve, etc. Sinter averaged a SUS score of around 78 which is considered good from a usability perspective. More importantly, a noteworthy highlight that emerged from the

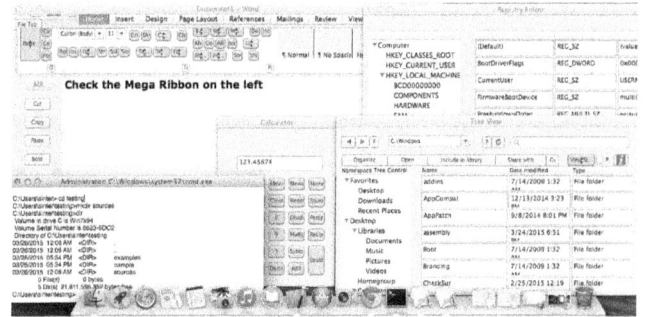

Figure 2: Clockwise from the top left: Microsoft Word, the Windows registry editor (regedit) Windows Explorer, Windows Calculator, and the Windows command line (cmd.exe). Word also displays the mega ribbon on the left hand side, automatically saving the most frequently used buttons.

study was that users very much liked the fact that they can access remote applications using their preferred screen reader with customized settings. This eliminates the need to learn new screen readers or platforms, and thus allows them to stay in their own comfort zone. They also felt Sinter had the potential to be a game changer since it does not need a screen reader to be installed on a remote host which is often the situation they encounter in practice.

5. DISCUSSION

Sinter requires only two simple conversions for each OS: one from the native accessibility API to the IR, and one from the IR back to the native accessibility API. Our experience with Sinter has been that, if one can reuse native libraries, this translation can be done in a few thousand lines of code in each direction. As a point of comparison, the NVDA Windows screen reader is over 50,000 lines of code. We found that IR transformation is a potent meta-programming tool for making accessibility enhancements that are desirable but missing in the original application. Their full potential remains to be explored. Finally, an extensive user study examining important aspects of Sinter such as impact of platform independence, and accessibility enhancing IR transformations is a task that we will undertake in the near future.

Acknowledgments: This research was supported in part by NSF grants IIS-1218570, IIS-1447549, CNS-1149229, CNS-1161541, CNS-1228839, CNS-1405641, CNS-1408695, CNS-1526707, and VMware.

6. REFERENCES

[1] S. M. Billah, D. E. Porter, and I. V. Ramakrishnan. Sinter: Low-bandwidth remote access for the visually-impaired. In *Proceedings of the Eleventh European Conference on Computer Systems*, pages 27:1–27:16, New York, NY, USA, 2016. ACM.

[2] Freedom Scientific. Jaws tandem quick start guide. http://www.freedomscientific.com/JAWSHq/JAWSTandemQuickStart. [Online; accessed 11-Jun-2016].

[3] NVDA. NVDA Remote brings free remote access to the blind. http://nvdaremote.com/.

Ad-Hoc Access to Musical Sound for Deaf Individuals

Benjamin Petry[1]
bpetry@acm.org

Thavishi Illandara[2]
thavishi@ahlab.org

Juan Pablo Forero[1]
juan@ahlab.org

Suranga Nanayakkara[1]
suranga@sutd.edu.sg

[1] Singapore University of Technology and Design, Singapore
[2] University of Moratuwa, Sri Lanka

Figure 1. Development of MuSS-Bits: (a) prototype iteration 1, (b) prototype iteration 2, (c) latest prototype

ABSTRACT

Learning a musical instrument can be a challenging task for a deaf person due to limited access to sound. Prior work has developed visual and vibrotactile approaches to provide music-to-sound feedback to deaf people. However, these systems are not designed for ad-hoc access to sound, which enables a deaf person to explore sound from various audio sources and receive real-time feedback. In this paper we present the development of a music sensory substitution system that enables ad-hoc access to musical sounds. It provides the technical basis to study deeper research questions about understanding and creating sound.

Categories and Subject Descriptors

K.4.2 [**Computers and Society**]: Social Issues – *Assistive technologies for persons with disabilities*

Keywords

Music; Sensory Substitution; Assistive Technologies; Deaf

1. INTRODUCTION

Music is an important part of our daily life. We listen to the radio, enjoy concerts or make music. This excessive exposure of music makes even children experts in music-listening [6]. In music-making activities, this expertise enables humans to compare the created with the intended sound and completes the feedback-loop for music-making (play, listen, evaluate, adjust). However, this is a challenging task for a deaf (deaf, deafened or hard of hearing) individual interested in learning to play an instrument.

Exploration is an important part of learning [3]. Learning about sound and its relationships through exploration requires the ability to sense sound from different *sound sources* at different *places* and perceive *feedback in real-time*. Prior work has developed visual and vibrotactile sensory substitution systems that enable access to musical sounds for deaf people [2,4,7]. While those systems are well studied and deliver accurate musical information in real-time, often the input possibilities (sound sources) and

ASSETS '16, October 23-26, 2016, Reno, NV, USA
ACM 978-1-4503-4124-0/16/10.
http://dx.doi.org/10.1145/2982142.2982213

portability are limited or pre-defined. Wearable electronics, such as smartwatches, mobile phones and MUVIB [5] could provide pervasive access to sound through vibrations. However, they use pancake motors with a slow response (lag time: ca. 40ms; rise time: ca. 100ms). These are not able to provide real-time feedback with the accuracy needed for musical sounds. The Basslet Kickstarter project[1] (a technology still being built) seems to be promising, enabling high temporal resolution in a wearable product, and able to be connected with different audio capturing mechanisms. This paper addresses the research question:

How can we provide a deaf person with an easy ad-hoc access to sound and music in particular?

In this work, we present the design process of Music Sensory Substitution (MuSS) Bits (see Figure 1). MuSS-Bits consist of wearable sensor-display pairs that were to allow ad-hoc access to sound. Best to our knowledge, we did not find a technology, that provides real-time feedback from different audio sources, such as instruments, digital devices or environmental sounds, and is made portable to cater for ad-hoc sound access. The focus of this paper is the detailed description of the challenges, problems and design decision for MuSS-Bits.

2. Development of MuSS-Bits
2.1 Initial Goals

Our main goals were to provide (1) real-time feedback, (2) input from different audio sources and ensure (3) wearability to allow ad-hoc sound access. Further initial goals were:

- **Support for Rhythm**: Designing a mapping for a sensory substitution system (e.g. audio-to-vibrotactile) is a challenging task, but crucial for the system's success. In the terms of music, our goal was to use a mapping that at least provides access to rhythm information, since steady-beat and rhythm are commonly introduced first in deaf music lessons [1].
- **Audio Source Selection:** We aimed to make it easy for the users to select a specific audio source, such as an instrument.
- **Simple to Operate:** We assume that this technology will be used by non-experts, and therefore we aimed to keep the interaction with MuSS-Bits simple and intuitive. At the same time, the use of MuSS-Bits should be un-obstructive to ease exploration and music performances.

---

[1] https://www.kickstarter.com/projects/basslet/the-basslet-a-wearable-subwoofer-for-your-body

2.2 Iteration 1

Our first prototype (see Figure 1a) used vibrotactile feedback, which has been successfully applied in previous music sensory substitution systems for deaf people [4,7]. Different actuators can be used to implement vibrotactile feedback (see Table 1). We used ERM motors (model 307-103 from precisionmicrodrives[2]) in our prototype, since these are light weighted, responsive (important for real-time feedback) and have a high amplitude.

Table 1. Overview of vibrotactile actuators we considered

	Frequency Span	Lag Time*	Weight	Power
Voice Coil	20Hz – 20kHz	Instant	++	++
LRA Motor	20Hz	ca. 40ms	--	--
ERM Motor	0 – 250Hz	ca. 8ms	-	+

* time until the motor reaches 0.08G

As a starting point we used a simple mapping inspired by MUVIB [5]. Auditory loudness was mapped to the motor's intensity. This was sufficient to convey rhythmical information and therefore fulfills our goal for rhythm support.

We gave this first prototype to 2 deaf musicians and interviewed them in separate sessions. We explained our intention to develop a technology for music teaching sessions and access to sound. The prototype was wired to a computer. We played music videos and used the computer's microphone to demonstrate the prototypes functionality. The musicians held the prototype in their hands.

Both musicians liked the vibrotactile feedback, but they stressed that we should add visual effects, since deaf people appreciate those a lot. Furthermore, they confirmed that in their teaching sessions they introduce rhythm first (as Fawkes [1]) before they go on to tuned instruments, such as a guitar. During these sessions we also observed that the wires became obstructive thereby drawing our attention towards a wireless approach.

2.3 Iteration 2

We decided to split the sensing from the feedback part (Sensor-Bit and Display-Bit) for the second prototype (see Figure 1b). This enables intuitive audio source selection by attaching a Sensor-Bit to the audio source and also provides feedback on the user's body.

Input and Output: The Sensor-Bit embodied one omni-directional in-air microphone and an audio jack to provide ad-hoc access to air-conducted sound and to digital devices and instruments. The Display-Bit contained one ERM motor and a single pixel display (RGB LED) to provide visual feedback. The LED's brightness (we used white as color) changed according to the loudness, complementing our existing mapping.

Communication: We decided to implement a wireless approach for the second prototype to avoid obstruction through entangled cables. We used WiFi (ESP8266-12F) to establish a wireless connection that allows us to transmit real-time audio. We used a one-to-one relationship between Sensor- and Display-Bit. To identify a pair we color coded the casings.

Form Factor: We used a rectangular shape to fit the electronics inside it, minimizing the size (LWH: 5cm x 5cm x 3cm; weight:

---

2 https://www.precisionmicrodrives.com/product/307-103-9mm-vibration-motor-25mm-type

---

65 – 70g). Furthermore, we implemented various attachment mechanisms to simplify the deployment of MuSS-Bits: (1) sticky tape, (2) slots for velcro band, (3) magnets, and (4) sewing holes.

User Feedback: We gave this prototype to 4 deaf children (12-17 years) at a residential deaf school (group 1) and to 7 deaf young adults (17 – 25 years) of a local music group (group 2). They explored MuSS-Bits with instruments and music teaching videos.

We received positive and constructive feedback. Group 2 said that MuSS-Bits could help new group members to follow the rhythm. However, they stressed that there is no difference in the feedback between voice and instruments. Furthermore, they raised aesthetic concerns and suggested to reduce the prototype's size and make it look like a garment. In group 1 the participants mixed up Sensor- and Display-Bits due to their similar shape.

2.4 Iteration 3

The latest prototype (see Figure 1c) was reduced in size (LWH: 4.4 cm x 3.5 cm x 1.5 cm) and looks closer to a smartwatch. The Display- and Sensor-Bit can be easier differentiated by the shape. The single LED was replaced with four Nano Pixel LEDs to improve the visual effect's visibility. WiFi was replaced by Bluetooth module to reduce power consumption and allow to connect e.g. a mobile phone. Further, we integrated a contact microphone, to provide a better audio signal from instruments through directly sensing the instrument's sound from its surface.

3. Limitations and Future Work

In this work, we presented MuSS-Bits that aim to enable intuitive audio source selection and provide real-time rhythm information to a deaf user. MuSS-Bits enables to study further questions, such as: *Does MuSS-Bits help a deaf person to build a conceptual model of sound? Does MuSS-Bits support music-learning for a deaf person? Does MuSS-Bits support collaborative music play among deaf musicians?* We plan to investigate these questions in the future with MuSS-Bits.

4. ACKNOWLEDGMENTS

The authors gratefully acknowledge the support of Dr. Reijntjes School for the Deaf, Sri Lanka and ExtraOrdinary Horizons, Singapore. This work is partially funded by the SUTD President's Graduate Fellowship.

5. REFERENCES

[1] Fawkes, W.G. *The Teaching of Music to Hearing Impaired Children and Teenagers*. 2006.

[2] Fourney, D.W. and Fels, D.I. Creating access to music through visualization. *Science and Technology for Humanity (TIC-STH)*. 2009, 939–944.

[3] Jr, T.G.R. Active Exploration. In S. Goldstein and J.A. Naglieri, eds., *Encyclopedia of Child Behavior and Development*. 2011, 26–27.

[4] Karam, M., Branje, C., Nespoli, G., Thompson, N., Russo, F.A., and Fels, D.I. The Emoti-chair: An Interactive Tactile Music Exhibit. In *CHI EA '10*. 2010, 3069–3074.

[5] La Versa, B., Peruzzi, I., Diamanti, L., and Zemolin, M. MUVIB: Music and Vibration. In *Proc. ISWC'14 Adjunct*. 2014, 65–70.

[6] Levitin, D.J. *This is your brain on music: Understanding a human obsession*. Atlantic Books Ltd, 2011.

[7] Nanayakkara, S., Taylor, E., Wyse, L., and Ong, S.H. An Enhanced Musical Experience for the Deaf: Design and Evaluation of a Music Display and a Haptic Chair. In *Proc. CHI'09*. 2009, 337–346.

Towards a Sign-Based Indoor Navigation System for People with Visual Impairments

Alejandro Rituerto, Giovanni Fusco and James M.Coughlan

The Smith-Kettlewell Eye Research Institute

2318 Fillmore Street San Francisco, California 94115

{arituerto, giofusco, coughlan}@ski.org

ABSTRACT

Navigation is a challenging task for many travelers with visual impairments. While a variety of GPS-enabled tools can provide wayfinding assistance in outdoor settings, GPS provides no useful localization information indoors. A variety of indoor navigation tools are being developed, but most of them require potentially costly physical infrastructure to be installed and maintained, or else the creation of detailed visual models of the environment. We report development of a new smartphone-based navigation aid, which combines inertial sensing, computer vision and floor plan information to estimate the user's location with no additional physical infrastructure and requiring only the locations of signs relative to the floor plan. A formative study was conducted with three blind volunteer participants demonstrating the feasibility of the approach and highlighting the areas needing improvement.

Keywords

Navigation, wayfinding, blindness, low vision.

1. INTRODUCTION

Blind or visually impaired people face severe difficulties navigating indoors and in other GPS-denied environments, which creates barriers to independent travel needed for a variety of daily activities related to work, health care, leisure and education. Different approaches and sensors have been proposed to assist a visually impaired person to navigate in an unknown environment [1]. Headlock [2] uses Google Glass to help users with visual impairment to navigate in large open spaces. The user can lock onto a salient landmark in the space and the system will provide audio feedback to guide him/her towards the target. On the other hand [6] presents the Digital Sign System, a computer vision approach that uses infrared retroreflective markers and a hand-held camera with an infrared light that enhances the markers' detectability and can be used for both indoor exploration and navigation.

A key part of any navigation aid system is the estimation of the localization of the user. Smartphones provide a powerful sensor platform to perform such localization. Pedestrian Dead Reckoning approaches (PDR) [5, 9] use inertial sensors to estimate how the user moves. Other approaches make use of computer vision techniques to process the images acquired with a phone to estimate the position [8]. Bluetooth beacons are becoming very popular, but by themselves they don't provide directional information and have batteries that must be replaced periodically,

ASSETS '16, October 23-26, 2016, Reno, NV, USA
ACM 978-1-4503-4124-0/16/10.
http://dx.doi.org/10.1145/2982142.2982202

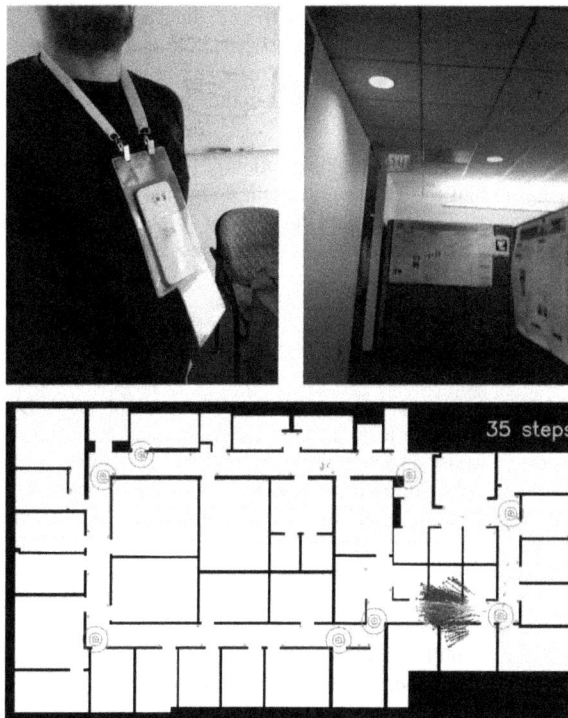

Figure 1 (a) User wearing the lanyard with the smartphone. (b) Camera image showing an Exit sign detection (blue rectangle). (c) Floor plan of the environment (39x21 m) with particles (short line segments) shown around the estimated user location. Red particles correspond to impossible positions while blue particles correspond to plausible position hypotheses (brighter blue means better particles). Exit signs are shown as green points inside two concentric red circles.

which can represent a burden when including all the beacons in an entire building.

In this work (see Fig. 1) we estimate the user's location in an indoor environment using a minimum of infrastructure, namely a map annotated with a few features that can be detected and recognized using computer vision techniques. We restrict these features to be existing Exit signs and printed barcodes (ArUco markers [4]) that we post near existing signs. In the future we will rely solely on existing signage. We also rely on inertial odometry to estimate the user's movements.

2. APPROACH

Our approach is based on Particle Filtering, a method widely used for robot localization. This method allows different sources of information to be combined to estimate the user's position in the environment. In this work, we combine information from three

287

different sources: a map of the environment, an inertial odometry system and a computer vision algorithm for object detection.

We incorporate information about the environment in the form of a digitized floor map in which walls, corridors and rooms are labeled and the positions of some important signs (such as Exit signs and fiducial markers) are annotated. The inertial odometry system, based on the work described in [7], enables us to track the user's footsteps and their heading, while the computer vision module processes the acquired images (at a framerate of 2 FPS) and detects the annotated signage using the method in [3].

We use an off-the-shelf Android smartphone and we access its IMU (Inertial Measurement Unit) and the RGB camera. The current prototype transmits the sensor readings and camera images in real time from the phone (using a Wi-Fi connection) to a laptop, where the data is processed; in the future, the entire system will run on the smartphone alone.

Our system is able to track the position of the user while he/she is moving around the environment and communicates, via text-to-speech, a list of nearby rooms or marked points of interest when the user stands in one location for longer than 5 seconds.

3. FORMATIVE STUDY

We began a formative study of our prototype with three blind participants with no usable vision. Two participants were familiar with the environment, while the third had little prior knowledge of it. The users wore a lanyard that held the smartphone (without covering the camera lens) on their chest, leaving both hands free for other purposes, such as holding a white cane, while holding the camera stable in order to acquire good-quality images. Users were instructed to walk as usual through their environment, without aiming the camera in any particular fashion; however, they were told that additional visual information could be obtained whenever needed by standing still while slowly rotating their torso to pan the camera left and right. Note that the use of a white cane didn't cause any significant occlusions in the video captured by the camera, and we expect the same to be the case for guide dog use.

Currently, the weakest part of the system is the step detection algorithm which estimates when each step is taken by analyzing the accelerometer readings over time. This estimation process is noisy because: (a) each individual has a different style of walking; (b) gait characteristics change under different conditions, e.g., walking straight along a corridor vs. turning at a corridor junction; and (c) increased uncertainty about the path immediately ahead, causes the person to slow down his/her steps, which may lead to the steps being missed by the step counter (since the acceleration amplitude is attenuated under these conditions).

The detection of map features in the camera images improved the estimation of the user position. Even the detection of just standard Exit signs (when the detection of the markers was switched off) was enough to correctly track the user motion on the map. The ability to recognize more visual features in the future will lead to greater robustness of the localization algorithm.

The annotated floor map helped to remove invalid position estimations (to rule out hypothetical paths hitting or entering walls), allowed the system to calculate the visibility of features in the map from the current estimated position and to look for map features nearby when the user stopped.

4. CONCLUSION

This formative study has shown the feasibility of our approach and helped us to assess its weaknesses and to plan the next steps

towards our objective. In the future we will study the inclusion of more sources of information such as beacons and more computer vision signage detection algorithms, eliminating the use of markers. An important goal is to transform the current prototype into a true navigation aid that provides turn-by-turn directions to a desired destination (instead of the current functionality which is limited to providing information about the user's current location). We also plan to test our system in different environments of bigger size and to assess the precision of the localization in a quantitative way. We will involve more potential end users to test navigation and localization performances and to determine the type of interface that will most benefit the users.

5. ACKNOWLEDGMENTS

Rituerto was supported by a Rachael C. Atkinson Fellowship; Fusco and Coughlan acknowledge support from the National Institute on Disability, Independent Living and Rehabilitation Research, grant 90RE5008-01-00.

6. REFERENCES

[1] Dakopoulos, D., & Bourbakis, N. G. (2010). Wearable obstacle avoidance electronic travel aids for blind: a survey. IEEE Trans. on Systems, Man, and Cybernetics, Part C (Applications and Reviews), 40(1), 25-35.

[2] Fiannaca, A., Apostolopoulous, I., & Folmer, E. (2014, October). "Headlock: A wearable navigation aid that helps blind cane users traverse large open spaces", In Proc. of the 16th intl. ACM SIGACCESS conference on Computers & accessibility (pp. 19-26). ACM.

[3] Fusco, G., Tekin, E. & Coughlan, J. M. (2016). "Sign Finder Application Technical Report." Retrieved from http://www.ski.org/project/sign-finder

[4] Garrido-Jurado, S., Muñoz-Salinas, R., Madrid-Cuevas, F. J., & Marín-Jiménez, M. J. (2014). "Automatic generation and detection of highly reliable fiducial markers under occlusion." Pattern Recognition, 47(6), 2280-2292.

[5] Harle, R. (2013). A survey of indoor inertial positioning systems for pedestrians. IEEE Communications Surveys & Tutorials, 15(3), 1281-1293.

[6] Legge, G. E., Beckmann, P. J., Tjan, B. S., Havey, G., Kramer, K., Rolkosky, D., & Rangarajan, A. (2013). Indoor navigation by people with visual impairment using a digital sign system. PloS one, 8(10), e76783.

[7] Li, F., Zhao, C., Ding, G., Gong, J., Liu, C., & Zhao, F. (2012, September). "A reliable and accurate indoor localization method using phone inertial sensors." In Proc. of the 2012 ACM Conf. on Ubiquitous Computing (pp. 421-430). ACM.

[8] Murillo, A. C., Gutiérrez-Gómez, D., Rituerto, A., Puig, L., & Guerrero, J. J. (2012, June). Wearable omnidirectional vision system for personal localization and guidance. In 2012 IEEE Computer Society Conference on Computer Vision and Pattern Recognition Workshops (pp. 8-14). IEEE.

[9] Yang, Z., Wu, C., Zhou, Z., Zhang, X., Wang, X., & Liu, Y. (2015). Mobility increases localizability: A survey on wireless indoor localization using inertial sensors. ACM Computing Surveys (CSUR), 47(3), 54.

"Holy Starches Batman!! We are Getting Walloped!": Crowdsourcing Comic Book Transcriptions

Christine Samson[1], Casey Fiesler[2], and Shaun K. Kane[1]

Department of Computer Science
University of Colorado Boulder
Boulder, CO 80309 USA
{christine.samson, shaun.kane}@colorado.edu

Department of Information Science
University of Colorado Boulder
Boulder, CO 80309 USA
casey.fiesler@colorado.edu

ABSTRACT

Comic books are among the most popular forms of popular media, but most comics are not provided in an accessible format. Creating an accessible transcript of a comic book may be more challenging than simply describing the images, as comics involve complex interplay between words and images, and often feature long-running and complex storylines. In this poster we describe a pilot study exploring the feasibility of crowdsourcing transcriptions of comic book pages. We recruited 60 crowd workers and asked them to transcribe a page of a comic book; half were told that the description was for a blind person, and half were not. We found that people who knew that they were transcribing for a blind person produced longer, more detailed descriptions. Our results also suggest that comic book knowledge may have at least some small impact on description detail.

Keywords

comics; crowdsourcing; fandom; visual impairment

1. INTRODUCTION

Comics are a unique source of literature and entertainment that combine text and graphics to tell a story. However, the foundation of comics—combining graphics and text—poses a problem to blind readers. Most mainstream comics are not produced in an accessible format. Furthermore, translating comic pages to an accessible representation can be challenging, as comic storytelling often involves a complex interplay between words and images [4].

In this exploratory study, we consider how we might use crowdsourcing to generate descriptions of graphics for blind comics readers when official transcripts are not available. We engaged 60 crowd workers to describe two pages from a comic book [7]. We examine how two variables might impact these descriptions: (1) how much of a comic fan the worker is; and (2) whether the worker knows the purpose of the task (i.e., that the description is for a blind reader).

The results of this study suggest important directions for future work, including how to leverage fan communities rather than paid workers for crowdsourcing. This study presents a first step towards the design of a system to support transcriptions of media from fan communities.

ASSETS '16, October 23-26, 2016, Reno, NV, USA
ACM 978-1-4503-4124-0/16/10.
http://dx.doi.org/10.1145/2982142.2982211

2. RELATED WORK

Making visual content accessible to people with vision impairments typically involves translating the visual content to audio (e.g., speech or sonification) or tactile (e.g., Braille and tactile graphics) formats [3]. Each solution has its limitations: translating to audio provides broad accessibility, but removes the spatial and visual elements that are essential to comic storytelling [5]. Translating visual art into tactile format typically requires an expert to perform the translation, and works best with simple images [4]. Our preliminary experiments in creating tactile comics have shown that the amount of text in a typical comics page prevents the text from being overlaid as Braille without significantly increasing page size. In this work, we focus on creating text transcriptions of the content, which could later be presented in the user's preferred modality.

A significant challenge in this work is translating images into text. While solutions exist for automatically captioning images (e.g., [1]), these systems require significant training data sets, and no such training set currently exists for comic images. Another approach is to recruit crowd workers to transcribe images, which can be effective for simple images such as charts and graphs, especially when workers are given clear instructions [6]. This work contributes an exploration of crowdsourced image transcription for comic book pages, which may present challenges beyond translating charts, such as identifying characters or interpreting the story.

3. METHODS

For this study, we deployed a survey on Mechanical Turk (MTurk). Crowd workers (Turkers) were shown a two-page spread from a Batman comic book (Figure 1), and were given the instruction: "Your task is to write a text description of the actions that occur in this comic page." We specified to Turkers that they did *not* need to transcribe any text, but rather only describe the action taking place.

We also asked Turkers to identify the characters that appear in the comic (by both their hero/villain identity and secret identity, if known—e.g., Batman/Bruce Wayne), and to report their familiarity with Batman comics (whether they had read Batman comics or seen Batman films). Finally, there were two conditions for the survey: *blind*, in which we instructed the Turker that their description was for a blind comics fan, and *non-blind*, in which we included no such instruction. We recruited a total of 60 Turkers who were paid $1 each. Turkers were randomly assigned into the blind or non-blind conditions upon accessing the survey, resulting in 27 Turkers in the blind condition and 33 in the non-blind condition.

Figure 1. Comics panel that we showed to crowd workers [7]. Image (c) DC Comics.

One challenge of our data analysis is that we do not currently have a metric for what is a "good" or "bad" transcription, or what constitutes an appropriate level of detail for a transcribed comic. For this preliminary study, we used word count as a metric for level of detail for descriptions, as descriptions with more words suggest that the transcriber put more effort into the task and included more detail in their transcription.

Our questionnaire included two questions to approximate Turkers' level of fandom and familiarity with the characters: (1) whether or not they reported having read a Batman comic book or had only seen a Batman movie or TV show; and (2) whether they were able to correctly identify the names and secret identities of the characters in the comic.

Using word count as a dependent variable, we performed one-way ANOVAs to determine whether these factors (blind versus non-blind survey condition, reading or not reading comics, and ability to recognize characters) had a significant impact on word count.

4. FINDINGS

Descriptions varied greatly in length and level of detail: word count ranged from 30 to 885 (mean 274, median 238). Brief descriptions included single sentences such as "batman get shot to an aircraft" or "Holy Starches Batman!! We are getting walloped!" Longer descriptions described the sequence of actions in the comic, and sometimes described each panel separately.

In analyzing this preliminary survey data, we focused on level of detail of the descriptions, approximated by word count. We hypothesized that: (1) Turkers who were told that they were describing for a blind person would provide longer descriptions; and (2) Turkers with more comics knowledge would provide longer descriptions.

Our first hypothesis was (marginally) accepted with a significance of p = 0.05. The mean word count of descriptions provided by participants in the *blind* condition was 323, and for those in the *non-blind* condition, 235. In other words, Turkers who were told that they were writing for blind readers produced longer descriptions than those who were not told this.

Our second hypothesis was that comics "fans" would produce more detailed descriptions. We operationalized this in two ways, by whether they reported reading comics, and whether they could correctly identify characters. For both of these metrics, our data

shows a trend in the direction we expected, though does not rise to the level of significance. Those who reported that they read comics provided descriptions with a mean word count of 304, and those who do not, 226 (p=0.09); those who can identify all characters correctly provided descriptions with a mean word count of 350, and those who could not, 261 (p=0.16).

5. DISCUSSION & CONCLUSION

These preliminary findings provide us with several potential avenues for future work.

First, it is important to note that using word count to determine what might be a "good" or "bad" description is obviously inadequate (since *amount* of detail may not be the most important or useful feature of a transcription for a blind comics reader). One next step is to use the descriptions generated by this survey to determine what kinds of descriptions are useful to blind comics fans, so that in future iterations of this work we can better determine "good" versus "bad" descriptions.

Second, though our findings regarding the effect of "fandom" level on transcription detail were not significant in this small sample, the directionality of our results are encouraging for continuing this line of inquiry moving forward. An obvious next direction is to look *outside* of MTurk for fans. Prior work shows that fan communities tend to be particularly oriented towards social justice, and in particular are concerned about issues of accessibility [2]. One motivation of this work is the intuition that not only might transcribers recruited from fandom communities provide *better* transcriptions than crowd workers, but that they might perform transcription and other accessibility-related tasks for altruistic reasons, rather than for pay.

Finally, this work begins what we hope to be a new research exploration in converting comic book stories into a more accessible format. We intend to develop a system that will allow a user to request crowd transcriptions for their comics, and perhaps even to specify the level of detail that they wish to include, so that dedicated fans could explicitly request more detailed descriptions. We may also extend this approach to transcribing other forms of media, such as movies and TV episodes. We hope that this work will contribute to making popular media more accessible to everyone.

6. REFERENCES

[1] Deng, J., Dong, W., Socher, R., Li, L. J., Li, K., & Fei-Fei, L. (2009). Imagenet: A large-scale hierarchical image database. *Proc. CVPR '09*, 248-255.

[2] Fiesler, C., Morrison, S., & Bruckman, A.S. (2016). An archive of their own: a case study of feminist HCI and values in design. *Proc. CHI '16*, 2574-2585.

[3] Jacko, J. A., Vitense, H. S., & Scott, I. U. 2002. Perceptual impairments and computing technologies. In *The Human-Computer Interaction Handbook*. L. Erlbaum Associates Inc.

[4] Jayant, C., Renzelmann, M., Wen, D., Krisnandi, S., Ladner, R., & Comden, D. (2007). Automated tactile graphics translation: in the field. *Proc. ASSETS '07,* 75-82.

[5] McCloud, S. (1993). Understanding Comics: The Invisible Art. New York: William Morrow Paperbacks.

[6] Morash, V. S., Siu, Y. T., Miele, J. A., Hasty, L., & Landau, S. (2015). Guiding novice web workers in making image descriptions using templates. *ACM TACCESS*, 7(4), 12.

[7] Parker, J., & Case, J. (2013). Batman '66, # 1. DC Comics.

Kirana: A Gesture-based Market App for Life Skills Learning for Individuals with Developmental Disabilities

Sumita Sharma[1], Saurabh Srivastava[2], Krishnaveni Achary[3], Blessin Varkey[3],
Tomi Heimonen[4], Jaakko Hakulinen[1], Markku Turunen[1], and Nitendra Rajput[5]

[1]University of Tampere, Tampere, Finland
[2]Xerox Research Centre India, Bangalore, India
[3]Autism Research Center, Tamana School of Hope, New Delhi, India
[4]University of Wisconsin-Stevens Point, Stevens Point, WI, USA
[5]IBM Research, New Delhi, India

{firstname.lastname, sumita.s.sharma}@sis.uta.fi, saurabh.srivastava@xerox.com, {krishnaveni.achary, blessinvarkey}@gmail.com, theimone@uwsp.edu, rnitendra@in.ibm.com

ABSTRACT

Kirana is a gesture-based application that simulates purchasing experience at a local Indian grocery store. It provides individuals with developmental difficulties a safe and controlled environment to explore the processes of purchasing an item: namely, deciding items to buy (decision making), calculating costs and balance (mathematical skills), and interactions via pointing (social interaction). Previous research has established that gesture-based interaction has the potential to enhance social, motor and cognitive skills for individuals with developmental disabilities. Currently, translating learnings from gesture-based virtual applications to real world scenarios is underexplored. Kirana is an approach to simulating practical real interactions, by breaking down complex tasks that require social, mathematical and decision-making skills, and encouraging self-efficacy. Skills learnt by purchasing items with *Kirana*, are potentially transferable to a real world store.

Keywords

Gesture-based interaction; Developing countries; Individuals with developmental disabilities

1. INTRODUCTION

Individuals with developmental disabilities face several challenges in learning skills that promote self-efficacy. There is a threat of being mistreated and misunderstood outside of their home or school and difficulties in arranging multiple self-paced practice sessions in the real environment. When attempting to perform daily living tasks such as purchasing items at a store, individuals with developmental disabilities can be overwhelmed by the number of smaller subtasks involved – of deciding which items to buy, of calculating costs and balances, and interacting socially with the shopkeeper. Therefore, it is important to provide a safe, controlled and self-paced learning environment to practice buying of items before exposing the individual to the real world environment.

Working with special educators, parents and teachers from the Nai Disha Tamana School in New Delhi, we designed and evaluated an interactive gesture-based application, called *Kirana*. The

application aims to teach the real life skill of purchasing items from local stores ("kirana") in India. These local stores usually consist of shelves full of items along the walls and a large rectangular table at the store entrance. On top of the table is a cash register, among other items. These stores are usually quite small where customers stand outside the store and point to the items they want. The application interface and interaction simulated the real world scenario of buying items from an actual store, and they are described in the next section.

2. KIRANA APPLICATION

The application's interaction and interface was designed to break down the task of buying groceries into smaller achievable tasks. Moreover, by designing within the Indian context and with Indian users, we aimed to promote socially acceptable gestures and behaviors. This helps ensure any insights gained from the application are culturally appropriate when translated to a real world setting [3]. With Kirana, a teacher or care giver can assign a customized task, for example, buying items from a given list, or buying items for breakfast (with a given budget). The task is then completed by buying the items using the application. The application also provides easy to configure task elements - *types of items, price of items and total available money* - to allow for individualized learning goals. Moreover, tasks can be made increasingly complex to encourage users to sharpen their skills. *Kirana* was evaluated with participants from Nai Disha Tamana School in New Delhi which is described in detail in [3]. We next describe the interface and interaction of the application with respect to the real world scenario of purchasing an item from such a store.

2.1 Interface

The interface of the application is shown in Figure 1. It contains two shelves with various items on each. The number of items are limited to four per shelf to reduce the complexity of the overall learning task. In the actual store, there would be several shelves alongside the walls with enough items on each shelf to hide the wall behind it. The application also has a large rectangular wooden table in front of it which also resembles the tables or counter in actual stores. This table usually has a cash register on it, and that is why the items being bought and money being paid are also kept on the table. The right side of the interface shows a user's wallet with the amount of money and the left side shows the current bill as one would expect from an actual store. We intentionally do not have an avatar for the shopkeeper for two reasons: to allow the mediator to incorporate personalized social interactions for each individual users, and to eliminate the complexity in attempting to simulate complex social interactions.

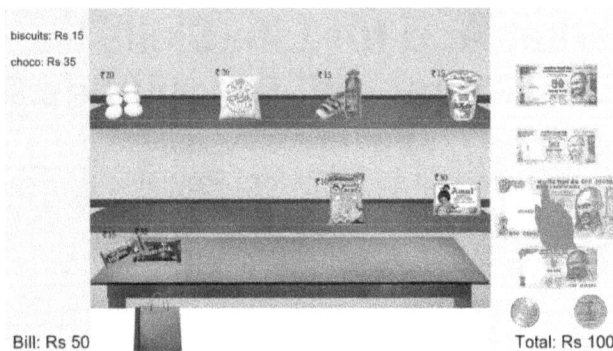

Figure 1: The *Kirana* application interface

2.2 Interaction

The interaction with the application is kept as close to the real world scenario as possible. To select an item on a shelf, users have to point at it for 1.5 seconds using their left hand. Likewise, money is selected by pointing at it for 1.5 seconds with the right hand. This two-handed selection mechanism isolated the item selection from the money selection and increased bodily movements (moving both arms instead of one), which was deemed desirable by the teachers. Once an item or money is selected, it animatedly flies onto the table. We intentionally animated item movements to eliminate the drag and drop gestures from the application because it was found to be confusing and difficult for the target users [3]. In the real world scenario, the shopkeeper would usually move the items from the shelf to the table.

2.3 System Description

The system consists of a laptop running the application software and connected to an HD display and a Microsoft Kinect 360 sensor[1]. The application was built using an in-house application framework (described in more detail in [2] and [3]), consisting of three main processes: a Kinect service, graphics engine, and application core logic. The Kinect service is a thin client over the Microsoft Kinect SDK that connects to the core logic over a TCP socket. Microsoft Kinect is used to track a user's hand with respect to their body within a 3D pointing area, called the physical interaction zone (PhIZ) [1]. The zone is relative to the user's body, and not the display. All audio and graphical content is rendered using the Panda 3D[2] graphics engine. The core logic is a Python based application that consists of an input/output management module, handling all the inter-process communication and acting as an interface between the core logic, the Kinect, and the graphics engine (ibid).

2.4 Transaction Flow

A typical session with the application consists of the following:

- **Start**: A user stands in front of the system. Upon detection by the Kinect, the initial black screen fades out to the application screen shown in Figure 1. A female voice (pre-recorded) greets the user by saying 'welcome to the virtual market', which is also shown textually on the screen. To remove learnability of item placements, the items are randomly arranged each time.
- **Select items:** The user can now select items by pointing at them for 1.5 seconds using their left hand. Once an

item is selected, it animatedly flies to top-left of the table, and the bill is updated with the item name and its cost. When browsing over items for selection, the item name is spoken out by the female voice.

The user can continue to select several items from the shelves until available funds are exhausted. That is, if the bill total will exceed the total money available, that item will not be selected and a female voice will remind the user that there is 'not enough money left', which is also displayed textually at the center of the screen. Thus, in this way, the application provides feedback for incorrect actions. However, the application intentionally does not provide additional prompts or hints to the user to allow them to spend as much time as they require on the task.

- **Paying for the items**: the user can select money by pointing at it for 1.5 seconds using their right hand. Money selected also animatedly flies but to the center of the table. Similar to the item announcement during selection, money denominations are also spoken by the female voice when browsing over them for selection. Money that is paid (selected) is reduced from the total bill amount to indicate the remaining cost. Once the cost is paid, the items fly into the blue shopping bag and any remaining monetary balance is returned to the table from where it animatedly flies back to the right side of the interface, and is added to the available money.
- **End**: A session ends when there is not enough money left to buy any more items or when the user walks away from the system (outside the tracking area of the Kinect sensor). This would typically take place after completing the desired transactions but can also be the result of the user accidentally leaving the area.

At the end of each session there is a loud applause and the female voice says 'well done' to all users.

3. ACKNOWLEDGMENTS

We thank all the Nai Disha Tamana School students for their time and efforts towards designing and evaluating *Kirana*. We are also grateful to Sanna Grönlund for designing the application interface.

4. References

[1] Microsoft Corporation. (2013). Kinect for Windows Human Interface Guidelines v1.8.0.

[2] Sharma, S., Srivastava, S., Achary, K., Varkey, B., Heimonen, T., Hakulinen, J. S., ... & Rajput, N. (2016, February). Promoting Joint Attention with Computer Supported Collaboration in Children with Autism. In *Proceedings of the 19th ACM Conference on Computer-Supported Cooperative Work & Social Computing* (pp. 1560-1571). ACM.

[3] Sharma, S., Srivastava, S., Achary, K., Varkey, B., Heimonen, T., Hakulinen, J. S., ... & Rajput, N. (2016, October). Gesture-based Interaction for Individuals with Developmental Disabilities in India. In *Proceedings of the 18th International ACM SIGACCESS Conference on Computers and Accessibility*. ACM

---

[1] developer.microsoft.com/en-us/windows/kinect

[2] www.panda3d.org

Autonomous Training Assistant: A System and Framework for Guided At-Home Motor Learning

Ramin Tadayon
Center for Cognitive Ubiquitous
Computing
Arizona State University
Tempe, AZ, USA
Ramin.Tadayon@asu.edu

Troy McDaniel
Center for Cognitive Ubiquitous
Computing
Arizona State University
Tempe, AZ, USA
Troy.McDaniel@asu.edu

Sethuraman Panchanathan
Center for Cognitive Ubiquitous
Computing
Arizona State University
Tempe, AZ, USA
panch@asu.edu

ABSTRACT

We present a novel framework and system for at-home rehabilitative exercise in the absence of a physical therapist. The framework includes metrics for assessing motor performance on a wide variety of exercises. We present our system, the Autonomous Training Assistant, which utilizes this framework and a low-cost accessible exercise device called the Intelligent Stick to deliver feedback as a user trains at home. We evaluated the system's multimodal feedback mechanism in a case study whose results indicate that individual preference may have a significant effect on modality assignment for optimal learning. We conclude with ideas for future work.

CCS Concepts

• Human-centered computing→Human computer interaction (HCI)→Interaction techniques.

Keywords

Rehabilitation; Human-Computer Interaction; At-Home Training; Motor Learning

1. INTRODUCTION

One of the many focuses in rehabilitative research is at-home exercise. This research aims to address the drop-off in compliance over time in at-home rehabilitation that results from a lack of therapist presence. In this work, we address guidance environments for home exercise in upper-extremity rehabilitation with a focus on unsupervised motor learning, or the improvement of motor function in the absence of a real therapist. The challenge is to develop a system which can assess performance, provide feedback, and guide the user through an exercise routine in the same manner as a physical therapist, while proving a meaningful abstraction of the exercises themselves to engage the user over a long period. To achieve this, we developed a framework for motor guidance and a system for at-home rehabilitation with a focus on three elements: assessment, feedback, and serious game design.

ASSETS '16, October 23-26, 2016, Reno, NV, USA
ACM 978-1-4503-4124-0/16/10.
DOI: http://dx.doi.org/10.1145/12345.67890

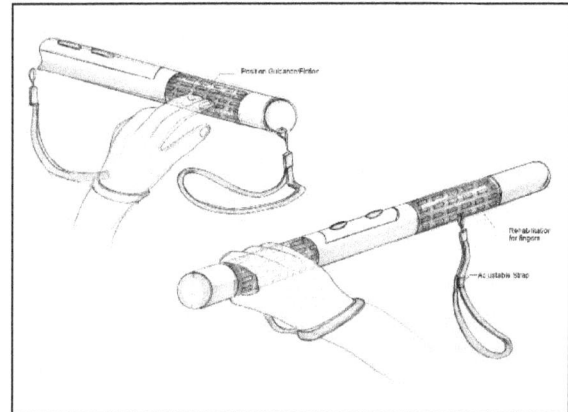

Figure 1. Intelligent Stick Design Sketch

2. RELATED WORK

As the volume of work related to at-home rehabilitation is extensive, we review some of the common approaches applied in recent work. Approaches toward rehabilitation systems range from virtual reality [2] to serious games developed using commercial hardware [3]. Several studies have yielded a series of common requirements for games developed in this space: they should be adaptable to a wide variety of individuals, easy to use/minimally intrusive, offer frequent and explicit feedback on performance, and adapt well to more complex motor tasks [1]. While many of these systems have offered encouraging results when used by subjects in rehabilitation, often the choice of feedback mechanisms and game archetypes in these systems is arbitrary, and as a result they are more effective for some users than others. To address this challenge, we first define a framework that links assessment and feedback in motor learning. We then present a system which implements this framework in practice, and discuss how game design can make use of this framework to optimize both learning and engagement.

3. MOTOR GUIDANCE FRAMEWORK

In previous work, we developed a framework which formalizes the process of motor assessment and motor feedback for use by an autonomous system [6]. To achieve this, we observed physical training sessions between trainer and trainee and derived three categories for motor assessment which describe any motor action: "posture" and "progression" in the spatial domain, and "pacing" in the temporal domain. We also described how these elements can be quantified and evaluated against a dynamic goal template managed by a trainer for each individual, such that our framework is person-centered. For simple single degree-of-freedom motions, these can

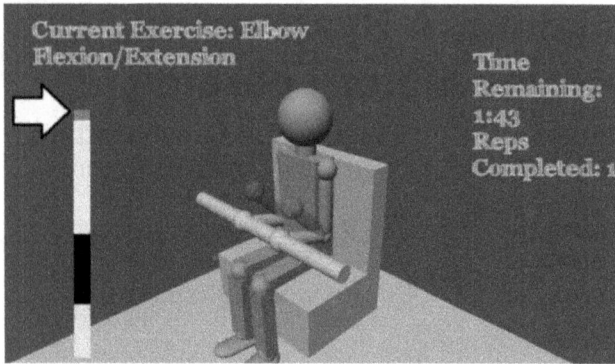

Figure 2. ATA Training Interface.

be measured using the rotational range of the primary limb or limbs involved in the motion, as well as the time required to complete a single iteration of the motion.

We then determined how to deliver feedback on motor performance. We had three channels through which feedback can be delivered during exercise: audio, visual, and haptic (vibrational). The goal of this phase was to determine how to map these channels of feedback to the categories of assessment listed above in a way that optimizes motor learning. As an initial point of guidance, we referred to a review by Sigrist et al. [4] on motor feedback which indicates how modalities can be assigned such that the system scales well with increasing motor task complexity.

4. AUTONOMOUS TRAINING ASSISTANT

With this framework in mind, we propose a system for at-home unsupervised motor learning entitled the "Autonomous Training Assistant" (ATA). This system consists of training software for at-home exercise including a virtual avatar for visual feedback, a Kinect camera for monitoring an individual's body posture, and a rod-shaped training device called the "Intelligent Stick" which includes an accelerometer for motion capture and vibrational motors for haptic feedback. The stick includes a modular design with flexible grip size which allows users with a wide variety of grip strengths to adapt the design to their needs. The design sketch for the Intelligent Stick prototype is shown in Fig. 1.

The software utilizes our motor guidance framework to interpret data from the Intelligent Stick and Kinect camera during exercise. For each motor exercise, a set of major joints is monitored by the system through the Kinect's joint tracking data for postural information, while accelerometer data from the Intelligent Stick is used to determine a user's motion range (progression) and speed (pacing). Trainers can input new motion exercises into the software using authoring software, which we described in previous work [5]. For each individual user, a profile containing the goals for that user in each category is provided and maintained remotely by the trainer over cloud storage. The ATA uses this information on each session to evaluate and provide feedback to the user. A virtual avatar acts as the visual representation of the trainer by demonstrating exercises on-screen and mirroring the user's motion to provide a visual point-of-reference. This interface is depicted in Fig. 2.

5. CASE STUDY: MULTIMODAL FEEDBACK

To determine how an individual's learning may be impacted by the modality assignments in our framework, we evaluated the system in a case study with an individual with hemiparesis resulting in impaired function in one arm. The subject used the ATA interface to perform a series of three exercises assigned by the subject's physical trainer: umbrella, witik and twirl. For each exercise, we generated a random selection of modality assignments. After a 1-minute calibration period, the user then repeatedly performed the motor task over a period of 2 minutes. Pre- and post-performance scores were determined in each category to provide a basis for improvement in each modality assignment. These results were compared to a control condition in which the user completed the exercise with no feedback from the system, and a condition in which the user chose the modality assignments by preference. In the preference condition, the user's performance significantly outweighed performance in the other conditions. This suggests that individual preference can have a significant impact on the optimal assignment of modalities in at-home training, although further evaluation is necessary to provide conclusive evidence.

6. CONCLUSION AND FUTURE WORK

Through a case study, we indicated in previous work that the system is capable of capturing and remotely managing a trainer's feedback and assessment protocol as well as a training regimen with a variety of upper-extremity motor exercises [6]. We also indicated that it may be important to consider an individual's preference for certain modalities when delivering feedback on motor performance, though future evaluations with multiple users will serve to validate this claim. We are currently in the process of designing games for rehabilitation using a spectrum of motor tasks of increasing complexity and an assignment of game archetypes to those tasks. This will add a layer of interactivity to make motor tasks more meaningful and interactive and is the subject of future work.

7. ACKNOWLEDGEMENTS

The authors would like to thank the National Science Foundation and Arizona State University for their funding support. This material is partially based upon work supported by the National Science Foundation under Grant No. 1069125.

8. REFERENCES

[1] Alankus, G. et al. 2010. Towards customizable games for stroke rehabilitation. Proceedings of the SIGCHI Conference on Human Factors in Computing Systems (New York, NY, USA, 2010), 2113–2122.

[2] Deutsch, J. 2009. Virtual reality and gaming for rehabilitation. Physical Therapy Reviews. 14, 5 (2009), 297–298.

[3] Deutsch, J.E. et al. 2008. Use of a low-cost, commercially available gaming console (Wii) for rehabilitation of an adolescent with cerebral palsy. Physical therapy. 88, 10 (2008), 1196–1207.

[4] Sigrist, R. et al. 2012. Augmented visual, auditory, haptic, and multimodal feedback in motor learning: A review. Psychonomic Bulletin & Review. 20, 1 (Nov. 2012), 21–53.

[5] Tadayon, R. et al. 2014. A Toolkit for Motion Authoring and Motor Skill Learning in Serious Games. 2014 IEEE International Symposium on Haptic Audio Visual Environments and Games (HAVE) (Oct. 2014).

[6] Tadayon, R. et al. 2015. Interactive Motor Learning with the Autonomous Training Assistant: A Case Study. Human-Computer Interaction: Interaction Technologies. M. Kurosu, ed. Springer International Publishing. 495–506.

"Turn Left After the Heater": Landmark Navigation for Visually Impaired Users

Robert Tscharn, Tom Außenhofer, Dimitri Reisler, Jörn Hurtienne
Julius-Maximilians-Universität
97074 Würzburg, Germany
{robert.tscharn, joern.hurtienne}@uni-wuerzburg.de
{tom.aussenhofer, dimitri.reisler}@stud-mail.uni-wuerzburg.de

ABSTRACT

Indoor navigation is a challenging task for visually impaired people. Existing technologies promise to provide support for autonomous way finding; however, the accuracy of low-budget approaches is low and can lead to frustration amongst users. The presented ongoing work is based on suggestions in the literature that contextual information such as sudden changes in the surface structure or landmarks could supplement distance estimations to improve the user experience during navigation tasks. Following a user-centered design approach, a real-time interactive prototype with localization was implemented and evaluated. First results from a pilot study confirmed the hypothesis that user experience is improved by contextual information and showed that contextual information are accepted and appreciated by users.

CCS Concepts

K.4.2. Computers and society: Social issues –assistive technologies for persons with disabilities.

Keywords

Indoor navigation; visually impaired people; iBeacons.

1. INTRODUCTION

Navigation in unfamiliar environments is a difficult task for visually impaired people [7]. Current technologies such as Global Positioning System (GPS) provide real-time localization for navigation solutions and enable autonomous way finding for this user group. But GPS is limited to outdoor navigation. For indoor localization, different approaches use signals such as WiFi, Radio Frequency Identification (RFID) or Bluetooth Low Energy (BLE) to estimate the user's current location within the building [6,9]. Several studies investigated the technical feasibility and optimization of these approaches to indoor navigation, an already proposed, but understudied approach [1]. However, these systems, are often either expensive, complex, or too inaccurate and not very reliable, which could lead to mistrust and poor user experience.

In this paper we present the human-centered development and evaluation of an indoor navigation application for visually impaired people based on iBeacons and built-in smartphone sensors. To counteract the limited accuracy in localization, we added contextual information along the navigation path [2]. We

ASSETS '16, October 23-26, 2016, Reno, NV, USA
ACM 978-1-4503-4124-0/16/10.
DOI: http://dx.doi.org/10.1145/2982142.2982195

expected that the additional context information would improve the user experience during indoor navigation.

2. DEVELOPMENT PROCESS

The prototype was developed following a user centered design process (ISO 9241-210). To understand the context of use and derive user requirements, semi-structured interviews with five visually impaired people were conducted (20 to 35 years, all male, remaining visual acuity: 2-20%, one had dyschromatopsia, one was a mobility trainer at an education center for visually impaired people). When participants already used or had used a navigation application, they demonstrated it in a short navigation task. Only observations or remarks that were stable over at least two participants were used as key requirements. For example, one re-occurring observation of normal navigation behavior was relying on familiar objects along the path. One key user requirement was therefore that navigation commands should include multimodally perceivable environment elements (e.g., landmarks such as heaters/radiators or changing surface structures; in line with e.g. [5, 8]). Also, all navigation steps should be presented in a preview mode (in line with [7]) and users should be able to individually customize the interaction with the application (e.g., distance in meters versus distance in steps). Based on the list of user requirements, we developed and evaluated a first digital Axure®-based prototype. Localization was provided through a Wizard-of-Oz setup and three students with simulated visual impairments (Cambridge Simulation glasses [3]) tested this first version.

Using insights from this first iteration, the final prototype was implemented for the Android platform (version 5.0) and used real-time iBeacon-trilateration with a localization accuracy of approximately 3m (95% of all estimations were within a 3m range of the true value). All UI-elements were labeled according to accessibility guidelines to guarantee compatibility with built-in Android accessibility features. The application allows users to turn contextual information "on" and "off". Based on the interviews, relevant contextual elements were included (e.g., surface changes: from soft carpet to stone; smell: coffee machines; temperature: sunlight or heaters/radiators).

3. PILOT STUDY

3.1 Method

Eleven participants (age: 21-48 years; 2 female; visual acuity < 0.2) were recruited from a local education center for visually impaired people, where the experiment took place. We used a within-subject design with three conditions in randomized order. In condition "only cane", all instructions were given before the participants started walking in form of a common description ("turn to the right in 10m"). In the condition "app without context", our smartphone application tracked the location on the navigation path and gave auditory navigation commands (e.g., "turn to the right in 10m") at certain waypoints. In the condition "app with context", navigation commands were enhanced by additionally providing information on the environment and its relevant elements (e.g., "Turn to the right in 10m after the heater"). The entire path was covered with signals from eleven iBeacon emitters (8 Onyx™-beacons, 3 iPods™). After each condition, participants completed an AttrakDiff-questionnaire [4], a subjective measurement for pragmatic quality (e.g., efficiency, effectiveness) and hedonic quality (the product's ability to satisfy the users' need for stimulation and identity). The attractiveness dimension of the AttrakDiff measures the perceived global value of the product. To keep the task comparable and due to location constraints, the route was not changed between conditions.

3.2 Results

As expected, the condition "only cane" was rated highest regarding the dimension of pragmatic quality (table 1), followed by "app with context" and "app without context". For hedonic quality, "app with context" was rated highest, followed by "only cane", and "app without context" was rated lowest.

Table 1. Mean and [Standard Deviation] of the AttrakDiff questionnaire. PQ: pragmatic quality, HQ: hedonic quality, GA: global attractiveness (scales range from -3 to +3).

Condition	PQ	HQ	GA
Only Cane	1.30 [0.94]	0.35 [0.40]	1.08 [0.97]
App without context	0.10 [1.33]	0.23 [1.44]	0.25 [1.75]
App with context	0.73 [0.94]	0.81 [0.83]	0.75 [1.00]

Statistical analysis was conducted using a repeated-measures ANOVA with planned Helmert contrasts (level 1: "only cane", level 2: "app without context", level 3: "app with context") for the dimensions pragmatic quality and hedonic quality, and a Difference contrast for the dimension global attractiveness. Regarding the pragmatic quality, the condition "only cane" was rated significantly higher compared to both versions of the application, $F(1, 10) = 5.45$, $p = .042$, but no significant difference could be found between both applications. On the dimension of hedonic quality, "only cane" did not differ significantly from both applications, but "app with context" was rated significantly higher than "app without context", $F(1, 10) = 5.15$, $p = .047$. None of the planned contrasts for global attractiveness was significant.

Since the main purpose of this pilot study was to test the new application, interviews focused on its functionality, accuracy, usability, and accessibility. 10 out of 11 participants stated that they were satisfied with the functionality of both versions (with and without context information) and would trust the navigation commands. The accuracy was described by half of the participants as accurate enough that it could be helpful in daily use. Participants did not encounter major problems while interacting with the application. Seven of the 11 participants report that they would prefer the version with context information, the remaining 4 would switch it permanently off. Participants stated that they worried about an overstimulation with contextual information in complex environments. It is therefore important to be able to customize the application regarding the quantity and quality of the information given.

4. DISCUSSION

Following a human-centered design process, we developed and tested an interactive prototype making use of contextual information for indoor navigation. First results indicate that adding contextual information to the navigation commands could lead to a better user experience compared to a version without landmarks. Still, both versions are rated lower in terms of pragmatic qualities compared to a condition, where participants used only their cane. One interesting implication of this finding is that the negative effect of an inaccurate localization on the user experience could at least partially be reverted by adding context information to navigation commands. Several methodological drawbacks narrow the generalizability of these findings. The rather simple navigation task, the small sample size, the within-participant design of the study, and a lack of performance data are certainly limitations. Despite these limitations, we gained first promising insights into context-supported, low-budget indoor navigation. The next iteration will include further improvements of the usability of the application and the main evaluation will overcome the aforementioned limitations.

5. ACKNOWLEDGMENTS

We thank the BFW Würzburg for the support and all the participants for their valuable feedback.

6. REFERENCES

[1] Corna, A., Fontana, L., Nacci, A.A., and Sciuto, D. 2015. Occupancy detection via iBeacon on Android devices for smart building management. In *DATE '15*. EDA Consortium, San Jose, CA, USA, 629-632.

[2] El-Shimy, D., Grond, F., Olmos, A., and Cooperstock, J.R. 2012. Eyes-free environmental awareness for navigation. *Journal on Multimodal User Interfaces*, 5(3-4), 131-141.

[3] Engineering Design Centre: Inclusive Design Tools. In: Inclusive Design Toolkit, Retrieved January 11, 2016 from http://www.inclusivedesigntoolkit.com/betterdesign2/inclusivetools/inclusivedesigntools.html

[4] Hassenzahl, M., Burmester, M., and Koller, F. 2003. AttrakDiff: A questionnaire to measure perceived hedonic and pragmatic quality. In *Mensch & Computer 2003*. Vieweg+ Teubner Verlag, 187-196.

[5] Chen, H.-E., Lin, Y.-Y., Chen, C.-H., and Wang, I.-F. 2015. BlindNavi: A Navigation App for the Visually Impaired Smartphone User. In *CHI '15 Extended Abstracts*. ACM, New York, NY, USA, 19-24.

[6] Fallah, N., Apostolopoulos, I., Bekris, K., and Folmer, E. (2013). Indoor human navigation systems: A survey. *Interacting with Computers, 25*(1), 21-33.

[7] Miao, M., Spindler, M., and Weber, G. 2011. Requirements of indoor navigation system from blind users. In *Proceedings of the 7th Conference of the Workgroup HCI and Usability Engineering of the Austrian Computer Society 2011*. Springer, Berlin Heidelberg, Germany, 673-679.

[8] Quinones, P.-A., Greene, Tammy, Yang, R., and Newman, M. 2011. Supporting visually impaired navigation: a needs-finding study. In *CHI '11 Extended Abstracts*. ACM, New York, NY, USA, 1645-1650.

[9] Ruffa, J.A. 2015. *Assessing iBeacons as an Assistive Tool for Blind People in Denmark*. Doctoral Thesis. Worcester Polytechnic Institute, Worcester.

Eye-Gaze With Predictive Link Following Improves Accessibility as a Mouse Pointing Interface

Jason Vazquez-Li, Lyle Pierson Stachecki, John Magee
Department of Mathematics and Computer Science
Clark University, Worcester, MA, USA
{jvazquezli, lpiersonstachecki, jmagee}@clarku.edu

ABSTRACT

We propose a target-aware pointing approach to address one predominant problem in using eye-controlled mouse replacement software: the lack of high-precision movement. Our approach is based on Predictive Link Following [4], which alleviates the difficulties with link selection when using mouse replacement interfaces by predicting which link should be clicked based on the proximity of the cursor to the link. For cursor control via eye movement, an eye tracking algorithm was implemented using the Tobii EyeX device to detect and translate gaze location to screen coordinates. We conducted an experement comparing eye-gaze controlled mouse pointing with and without the Predictive Link following approach. Our results demonstrate increased accuracy of our system compared to just using eye-controlled mouse pointing.

Keywords

Accessibilty, Mouse Replacement Interfaces, Eye-gaze Interfaces, Target-Aware Pointing

1. INTRODUCTION

Eye-gaze controlled software is a common interface modality for people with severe motion disabilities. However, tasks such as mouse control are difficult due to the natural jittery movements of the eyes, which prevents fine-tuned movement of the mouse from being made [2]. As most software is not designed for eye-gaze input, having small interactive elements,users are limited in what interactions they can reasonably do, which can cause frustration.

Most eye-gaze systems do not provide for high-precision movements to control a mouse. We base our system on an approach originally designed for the Camera Mouse. The Camera Mouse allows users to control the mouse using certain body parts (e.g. tip of nose), but it does not allow eye movement as a user input option [1]. This is a problem for people who cannot move their heads. Given that, our

ASSETS '16 October 23-26, 2016, Reno, NV, USA

© 2016 Copyright held by the owner/author(s).

ACM ISBN 978-1-4503-4124-0/16/10.

DOI: http://dx.doi.org/10.1145/2982142.2982208

system makes progress towards addressing the lack of high-precision movement when using eye-controlled mouse replacement software. We also base our approach on HMAGIC [3], a system that combines eye-gaze with the Camera Mouse. Other approaches include force fields, speed reduction, and warping [5]. Our approach here accumulates a score based on pointing *near a target* to assist in selecting the target even when the user is unable to actually click on it.

2. SYSTEM OVERVIEW

The Tobii EyeX eye tracking hardware was used for eye-gaze input. Traditional infrared eye tracking hardware has been cost-prohibitive, but the EyeX is a consumer-grade device, costing less than $200. Our system is arranged as follows:

2.1 Controlling Cursor Movement

The X and Y coordinates of the user's eye relative to the monitor are brought into our system and used to calculate the screen coordinate of where the mouse should be positioned. As a pre-processing step, in order to reduce the amount of mouse jitter, we set the mouse position to the average position of the last 20 gaze points. A gaze point is registered about every 15 milliseconds.

2.2 Clicking

Clicks are triggered by blinking of the eyes; a blink lasting approximately 275 milliseconds will trigger a click. This works because the EyeX device stops detecting gaze movement if the user closes their eyes. Thus, our system checks for interruption in gaze movement for a specific span of time to perform the clicks. To actually click, a "leftClick" method implements the system functions that simulate pressing and releasing the left mouse button.

2.3 Modification of Predictive Link

We modified the the Predictive Link function to better work for eye-gaze input. The original algorithm [4] had a discontinuity as the distance from the pointer to a target approached zero:

$$\text{pointer}(a) = \begin{cases} \frac{1}{\text{dist}(a, clickpoint)^\beta} * \gamma & \text{if clicked on page} \\ hoverScore & \text{otherwise,} \end{cases}$$

where hoverScore is the value assigned when the pointer is over a link.

In our system, a slight modification provides a function that approaches a constant as the pointer gets close to a link:

$$\text{pointer}(a) = \frac{1}{(\text{dist}(a, mousepoint) + 1)^{\beta}} * \gamma$$

The function is used to accumulate a score for how likely a user is trying to click on a particular link a based on the distance from the pointer to the link. β and γ are configurable parameters.

3. EXPERIMENTAL EVALUATION

A preliminary experiment was conducted to evaluate our software.

3.1 Apparatus, Procedure, and Users

Two versions of a website containing various-sized hyperlinks were used to test our system. The first version of the website (condition A) included the necessary JavaScript files for the Predictive Link technology software; the second version (condition B) did not. This was done to compare the effectiveness of the two different methods. Another script file running in the background for both website versions randomly selects and highlights a hyperlink on the website for the user to click on. The target link will remain highlighted for 5000 milliseconds before the script selects another hyperlink, with a pause time of 1500 milliseconds between trials.

For the website with the Predictive Link function, the user does not have to click directly on the link to register it as a successful click, rather, the output of the prediction algorithm is used to determine if the link was clicked. In contrast, the user must directly click on the hyperlink if using the website without the Predictive Link function. For each trial, the evaluation software stores either a successful click or a failed click (not clicking on the assigned hyperlink within the time limit, or clicking on another link). Each participant conducted 50 trials for each condition. At the end of the test session, the result is reported as a percentage.

Seven people without motion disabilities participated in our test. Each participant was given the same instructions and assigned a random order of conditions. That is, those that started with condition B had the first test as the webpage without the Predictive Link function, and then completed condition A, with the second webpage with the Predictive Link function. Six of the participants had minimal experience with eye gaze input. User 7 had been using eye gaze input for several weeks. In total, there were 700 trials conducted (7 participants, 2 conditions, 50 trials each).

3.2 Results and Discussion

Table 1 summarizes our results. Excluding User 7 (because that participant had significantly more experience with eye gaze) the means, standard deviations, and 90% confidence interval for a means difference test are as follows.
Condition A (with Predictive Link) mean: 35.7%
Condition B (without Predictive Link) mean: 21.7%
Condition A standard deviation: 13.8
Condition B standard deviation: 10.6

The 90% confidence interval of the means, calculated using the Student's t-distribution is [1.1, 26.9].

Table 1: Results

User	With Predictive Links	Without Predictive Links	First Condition
1	46% Correct	26% Correct	A
2	58% Correct	40% Correct	A
3	26% Correct	10% Correct	B
4	34% Correct	22% Correct	B
5	22% Correct	14% Correct	A
6	28% Correct	18% Correct	B
7	94% Correct	56% Correct	A

Subjects three and five had problems with the calibration of the Tobii EyeX.

Based on the results, using Predictive Link technology increased performance by 14%. However, even though using Predictive Link boosted performance significantly, the mean success rate of 35.7% for Condition A is still not high enough for a reliable interaction system. A contributing factor may be lack of experience using Tobii EyeX. We can see this in User 7, who scored 94% on the Condition A test (with Predictive Link). This participant was one of the developers of this software and thus used the device extensively; further testing will evaluate whether there is a learning effect on performance.

4. CONCLUSION

Pairing eye-controlled mouse replacement software with Predictive Link technology increased accuracy for tasks demanding high-precision cursor movement. Although the performance of inexperienced users in our initial test was not high, it seems likely that accuracy increases for users who have been using the system for longer periods. Future studies with more participants will examine this as well as provide data for further analysis of statistical significance.

5. ACKNOWLEDGMENTS

The authors would like to thank Jiri Roznovjak for his asstance in modifying the predictive link algorithm.

6. REFERENCES

[1] M. Betke, J. Gips, and P. Fleming. The camera mouse: Visual tracking of body features to provide computer access for people with severe disabilities. IEEE Trans. Neural Systems and Rehabilitation Engineering, 10:1-10, 2002

[2] R. J. K. Jacob. The use of eye movements in human-computer interaction techniques: What you look at is what you get. ACM Trans. Inf. Sys., 9(2):152-169. Apr. 1991

[3] A. Kurauchi, W. Feng, C. Morimoto, and Margrit Betke. HMAGIC: head movement and gaze input cascaded pointing. PETRA '15, 4 pages. 2015.

[4] J. Roznovjak, and J. Magee. Predictive Link Following for Accessible Web Browsing. ASSETS'15, pp 403-404. Oct. 2015.

[5] X. Zhang, X. Ren, and H. Zha. Improving eye cursor's stability for eye pointing tasks. CHI '08, pp 525-534. 2008.

Social Dimensions of Technology-Mediated Sight

Annuska Zolyomi, Anushree Shukla, and Jaime Snyder

Information School
University of Washington
Seattle, WA 98195 USA
{annuska, anushreeshuk, jas1208}@uw.edu

ABSTRACT

Users of wearable vision technology, such as eSight assistive eyewear, have a distinct relationship with sight influenced by personal, social, and cultural perceptions and practices. In order to better understand the ways in which vision is socially constructed through technology-mediated sight, we conducted qualitative, semi-structured interviews with 13 users of eSight glasses. Our interviews focused on eliciting narratives about eSight use from initial introduction of the technology to current daily practices. Emerging findings describe ways in which technology-mediated vision is experienced in relation to (1) adaptive practices, (2) social participation, (3) experiences of space, and (4) opportunities for choice and self-determination.

CCS Concepts

• **Human-centered computing → Accessibility → Empirical studies in accessibility.**

Keywords

Assistive technology; vision; qualitative research; interviews.

1. INTRODUCTION

Assistive technologies (ATs) for those with impaired vision improve the visual acuity of users through mechanical or digital adjustments to magnification and luminance. The most recent generation of these technologies use digital displays, sophisticated optics and radically smaller computer hardware to offer users extremely portable assistive devices that provide high resolution visual output calibrated to an individual's personal physiology. While early adopters of these technologies have contributed greatly to the refinement and continued development of assistive hardware and software technologies, these individuals are also valuable partners in understanding the sociotechnical implications of technology mediated vision. We interviewed 13 users of eSight wearable vision technology in order to identify personal, social, and cultural factors these individuals associate with the introduction of this AT into their lives.

2. BACKGROUND

2.1 eSight Assistive Eyewear

At first glance, eSight eyewear [12] looks like a pair of virtual reality goggles. The eyewear system is comprised of a molded plastic frame that encases a pair of LCD screens positioned in front

ASSETS'16, October 23-26, 2016, Reno, NV, USA
ACM 978-1-4503-4124-0/16/10
http://dx.doi.org/10.1145/2982142.2982190

of each eye. The plastic frame accommodates corrective lenses, positioned between the eye and the LCD screens. The glasses are wired to a hard drive and book-sized battery pack. The eSight device relies on a user having at least some functioning photoreceptors. Globally, 246 million people have moderate to severe visual impairments due to conditions such as Macular Degeneration, Stargardt Disease, and Ocular Albinism [10]. Currently, hundreds of people have eSight devices, which cost $15,000 US [12].

2.2 Related Work

People with low vision employ a range of adaptive strategies in order to work around inaccessible situations, including modifying their actions and environments [1,3,4]. There are also multiple vision ATs, including hand held and desktop devices that help to bridge gaps with the sighted world [3]. Less mainstream, but promising, are wearable vision devices currently in research and development [11], which are designed to provide assistive, augmented, and virtual alternatives. AT users grapple with their personal expectations of technology as well as the expectations of others, who can express limiting views about potential effectiveness of these devices [6]. AT users can be concerned about social acceptability [3,11]; they can also face social stigma, which is a key deterrent for AT adoption and use [7,8,9].

We situate our research as an extension of this body of work, with a focus on the in situ lived experiences of users of a commercially-available AT. Our research examines the social dynamics of low vision, sight, and accessible technology use within the context of family, work, and community. We build on a visual cultural studies perspective that vision is a social construct, comprised of a set of "practices related to vision, emphasizing ways in which power structures, visual orders…and various gazes direct our attention" [5:2]. When a person has a visual impairment, or "sees with special requirements" [5:2], vision practices exist within a different set of perceptions, frictions, and relationships. Our research illuminates the dynamic, personal vision practices of eSight users, probing into the social dimensions of sight.

3. METHOD

We conducted 13 semi-structured phone interviews with eSight users, each lasting for about one hour. Our goal with the interviews was to maintain a technology-agnostic perspective, focusing on participants' narrative accounts of personal experiences with the eSight eyewear. We asked our participants to first share details regarding their visual conditions. We then asked them to walk through the story of how they first heard about the eSight eyewear; their initial reaction to using the device; and how they came to make the decision to purchase the system. Next we asked them to tell us about the ways in which the eyewear played a role in their daily lives. We concluded by asking them to reflect on the ways the technology influences how they think about vision. Throughout the interview process, we employed a qualitative, grounded approach [2]. We compiled and discussed research notes; audio recordings were transcribed and verified. Our preliminary analysis of emergent themes is reported here.

4. EMERGENT THEMES

The following themes reflect the ways our participants described vision as being socially constructed through technologies.

4.1 Vision as Adaptation

Our participants talked about the many small and large ways they adjust their routines, habits, and actions to a highly visual world. Most users explicitly stated that the eSight device was not a replacement for being typically sighted, describing the many ways they still had to adjust their behaviors. While use of the eSight eyewear mitigated some adaptations (such as asking a waiter for recommendations rather than struggling to read a menu), the device introduced the need for others, such as awareness of battery life and ambient light levels. Participants described adaptations in terms of the technology, their naturally fluctuating visual abilities and contextual conditions, revealing a complex and dynamic ecosystem of sight.

4.2 Vision as Participation

Not surprisingly, individuals described the many ways that their vision influenced their degree of participation in daily activities. While many described very active and social lives, many also qualified these narratives by highlighting perceived limitations to their abilities to fully engage in activities such as shopping, travel, work, and transportation. When wearing eSight, many became aware of new visual details in their environment that provided the basis for additional, less direct interactions with others, as described by P1: *"Everywhere you go it's all about reading. You have to read signs; people hand you pamphlets; you have to fill out forms. Written information is a huge component of communication and there's something about it that just feels really good to take in."*

4.3 Vision as Space

Many of the participants talked about relationships between physical space, sight and social interaction. Without ATs, many described the social challenges of having limited depth of vision: facial expressions are often unclear and non-verbal communication can be missed. With more traditional ATs, smooth transitions from viewing something near to seeing something far away are often not possible. eSight enables users to control their visual reach (i.e., their access and proximity to visual information). For example, participants described feeling more comfortable participating in and even leading group discussions because they can relatively seamlessly transition from focusing on an individual to panning across a classroom or audience. P6 described the ways in which his relationship with space was enhanced by eSight while watching his grandson play hockey: *"My grandson was sitting in the penalty box and my son said, "I'd like to know what he's doing right now." I just beamed up [with the eSight] and I told him what he's doing right now."*

4.4 Vision as Choice

Wearable ATs face the challenge of balancing sometimes bulky physical hardware with comfort and socially acceptable form factors. Based on previous research [9], we anticipated that participants would be concerned about stigma; however, although some described being moderately self-conscious, their use and non-use of eSight were motivated by a range of factors including degree of familiarity with the setting, a desire to not become too dependent on the device, and physical comfort. Users make conscious tradeoffs between factors when deciding when and where to use their eSight. For example, while some chose to travel with their eSight in order to see new sights first hand, others opted to leave the device at home in order to minimize distractions, potential discomfort, and risk of theft.

5. CONCLUSION AND FUTURE WORK

In our qualitative interviews with early adopters of eSight glasses, interviewees shared their personal stories, including motivations, concerns, expectations and realities associated with their eSight experiences. Our initial inductive, thematic analysis captured their experiences of vision in terms of adaptation, participation, space, and choice. As we complete our analysis, we will refine our themes through focused coding [2] and reflect upon socio-technology systems of visual practices and issues of visual equity.

6. ACKNOWLEDGMENTS

We thank eSight and the interview participants.

7. REFERENCES

[1] Branham, S.M. and Kane, S.K. 2015. Collaborative Accessibility: How Blind and Sighted Companions Co-Create Accessible Home Spaces. In *Proc. CHI '15*, ACM, New York, NY, 2373–2382.

[2] Charmaz, K. Shifting the Grounds: Constructivist Grounded Theory Methods. 2009. In J.M. Morse, P.N. Stern, J. Corbon, B. Bowers, K. Charmaz and A.E. Clarke (Eds.), *Developing Grounded Theory: The Second Generation*. Left Coast Press, Inc., Walnut Creek, CA, 127–154.

[3] Kane, S.K., Jayant, C., Wobbrock, J.O., and Ladner, R.E. 2009. Freedom to Roam: A Study of Mobile Device Adoption and Accessibility for People with Visual and Motor Disabilities. In *Proc. SIGACCESS '09*, ACM, New York, NY, 115–122.

[4] Lazar, J., Feng, J., and Allen, A. 2006. Determining the Impact of Computer Frustration on the Mood of Blind Users Browsing the Web. In *Proc. SIGACCESS '06*, ACM, New York, NY, 149–156.

[5] Lehmuskallio, A. 2015. Seeing with special requirements: visual frictions during the everyday. *Journal of AESTHETICS & CULTURE 7*.

[6] Pal, J. and Lakshmanan, M. 2012. Assistive technology and the employment of people with vision impairments in India. In *Proc. Conf. on ICT4D*, ACM, New York, NY, 307–317.

[7] Pape, T.L.-B., Kim, J., and Weiner, B. 2002. The shaping of individual meanings assigned to assistive technology: a review of personal factors. *Disability and Rehabilitation 24*, 1-3, 5–20.

[8] Parette, P. and Scherer, M. 2004. Assistive technology use and stigma. *Education and Training in Developmental Disabilities 39*, 3, 217–226.

[9] Shinohara, K. and Wobbrock, J.O. 2011. In the Shadow of Misperception: Assistive Technology Use and Social Interactions. In *Proc. SIGCHI '11*, ACM, New York, NY, 705–714.

[10] World Health Organization. 2014. Visual impairment and blindness Fact Sheet N°282. Retrieved June 20, 2016 from http://www.who.int/mediacentre/factsheets/fs282.

[11] Zhao, Y., Szpiro, S., and Azenkot, S. 2015. ForeSee: A Customizable Head-Mounted Vision Enhancement System for People with Low Vision. In *Proc. SIGACCESS '15*, ACM, New York, NY, 239–249.

[12] eSight. http://www.esighteyewear.com

Not All Errors are Created Equal: Factors that Impact Acceptance of an Indoor Navigation Aid for the Blind

Ali Abdolrahmani[1], William Easley[1], Michele A. Williams[1], Erick Ronquillo[1]
Stacy Branham[1], Tiffany Chen[2], Amy Hurst[1]

[1]University of Maryland Baltimore County (UMBC)
{aliab1, easley1, mawilliams, erick4, sbranham, amyhurst} @umbc.edu
[2]Toyota Engineering and Manufacturing North America
tiffany.chen@tema.toyota.com

ABSTRACT

Large indoor spaces continue to pose challenges to independent navigation for people who are blind. Unfortunately, assistive technologies designed to support indoor navigation frequently make errors that are technically difficult or impossible to eliminate. We conducted a study to explore whether there are strategic ways designers can minimize the impact of inevitable errors on user experience. This paper summarizes an online survey of 41 blind individuals regarding their projected acceptance to three types of errors expected of these devices. We found that some errors were more acceptable than others. Factors that impacted results included the error type and the social/environmental setting.

General Terms

Design; Human Factors

Keywords

Navigation; assistive technology; blindness; errors; acceptance

1. INTRODUCTION AND BACKGROUND

Navigation technologies have greatly impacted the lives of blind individuals by providing complementary functions to traditional Orientation and Mobility (O&M) skills and mobility aids (white cane or guide dog). Standalone GPS devices (e.g., Humanware's Trekker Breeze), familiar smartphone apps (e.g., Google Maps), and smartphone apps for the blind (e.g., Ariadne, BlindSquare) have become ubiquitous tools for independent navigation. However, many of these technologies are designed for outdoor navigation and require map data and a GPS signal to work.

While several technologies exist which support indoor navigation, myriad logistical barriers make implementation a challenge. For example, to create virtual or tactile maps, technology designers must first have access to building blueprints. Additionally, the use of QR codes, NFC sensors, or RFID tags for feature identification and map building would require altering the building infrastructure [3,4,5]. Due to these barriers, computer vision presents itself as an alternative technology that is capable of identifying indoor building features without the need for building-specific background information or changes to the environment [8]. Drawbacks of a computer vision approach include

ASSETS '16, October 23-26, 2016, Reno, NV, USA
ACM 978-1-4503-4124-0/16/10.
http://dx.doi.org/10.1145/2982142.2982210

introduction of errors due to, for example, insufficient training data or changes in lighting or viewing angle.

Previous research has explored factors that lead to assistive technology (AT) adoption [6] and abandonment [7]. Factors include a lack of consideration for user opinion, ease of device procurement, poor device performance, and change in needs or priorities. Our goal is to better understand what constitutes poor device performance for indoor navigation AT.

We deployed a survey to 41 blind participants to evaluate their reactions to errors made by an imagined indoor navigation device in different scenarios of use. We found that error type, building feature for which the error is made, and social/environmental setting variously impact users' acceptance of the device.

2. SURVEY DESIGN AND ANALYSIS

Indoor navigation aids that rely on computer vision can make three kinds of errors: object misidentification, false negative (FN: failure to identify a trained object that is actually in view) and false positive (FP: identifying an object that is not in view). To explore how these errors impact device acceptance, we designed a survey that presented an imagined indoor navigation device and error scenarios to potential users.

The imagined device was described as a wearable technology with computer vision capable of recognizing building features in the 9-to-3-o'clock range. Features included detection of restroom signs, stairs and escalators, doors, and popular storefront logos (e.g., Starbucks). Five contextual factors, each with two extremes, were presented evenly in ten scenarios: crowd density (wide open or dense), familiarity of environment (unfamiliar or familiar), crowd attendees (stranger or family), environment setting (professional or leisure), and who notices the error (just you or others). Device features were also evenly distributed amongst the 10 scenarios. Each scenario presented one type of error in the given context. Following each scenario, participants provided free responses about how they would react to the error and steps they would take to work through the situation. They also indicated on a 7-point Likert scale how likely they were to continue using the device.

We chose this thought experiment technique instead of deploying an actual prototype for two reasons. First, it allowed users to consider a wide variety of familiar contexts without requiring travel to multiple locations. Second, it emphasized the general capabilities and errors made as opposed to specific interaction features of the navigation device.

We recruited 41 participants (31 female, ages 18-57) from existing contacts and snowball sampling. 34 participants used a white cane as their primary mobility aid, and two used guide dogs. Three participants used both white cane and guide dog, and one used white cane and wheelchair. One participant used no mobility aid. 410 responses (41 participants times 10 scenarios) were reviewed. Two researchers independently open-coded this data to find themes and then collectively reconciled to agree on a final list of codes and categories.

3. FINDINGS AND DISCUSSION
Our analysis revealed that 34% of responses indicated acceptance of the error, 18% were neutral, 27% indicated not accepting, and the rest considered the error irrelevant in the scenario. Type of the error the device made, building feature for which the device made the mistake, and social/environmental context were three factors that impacted whether or not the user would accept the error.

3.1 When Errors Were Forgiven
In 34% of total responses, participants indicated that they would accept the device error. Error acceptance is illustrated by P40 in this response: "I'm a bit more forgiving of when the device failed to notify me that I reached the intended target. Technology isn't always perfect and I believe there is a big difference between recognizing the wrong thing in failing to recognize something because it may look different from most things." Approximately 50% of error acceptance involved false negatives. In other words, false negatives were nearly twice as acceptable as false positive and gender misidentification errors. In 22 total responses, participants expressed an understanding of imperfections in AT. Nearly 73% (16 responses) of these happened in scenarios where the device made errors in identifying doors and stairs/escalators. Participants were also forgiving of imperfections in dense and unfamiliar environments (73% and 64%, respectively).

3.2 When Errors Were Not Forgiven
In 27% of total responses, participants' reactions indicated that they would not accept the device error. Consider P21's reaction to a restroom misidentification error: "I honestly admit I would be a bit exasperated. From what I know, restroom signs would be distinctive enough that I feel the machine should recognize where they are." In 70% (79 responses) of non-acceptance cases, participants expressed negative emotional reactions (e.g., feelings of anger, frustration, and embarrassment). Negative emotional reactions were predominantly associated with device errors involving restroom sign misidentification (35 responses) and scenarios that took place in professional settings (50 responses).

3.3 Implications
Our findings indicate that technical accuracy in computer-vision-based navigation aids is not the only important consideration towards adoption. There are at least three additional considerations that should be made. First, which indoor features are recognized by the device? Misidentification of doors and stairs/escalators was much more forgivable than misidentification of restroom gender, for example. Second, which types of errors should the device favor? False negatives were generally more acceptable than either false positives or feature misidentification. Third, designers should ask which social/environmental settings are most critical? We found that errors in densely populated settings are more forgivable than errors in professional settings.

These contextual factors are important, particularly for navigation tasks, because users may transition in and out of various settings throughout a typical day. Designers need to consider how setting transitions should alter the system's inclination toward different types of errors. Prior research has similarly found that attitudes toward AT change between the home and professional settings [1,2]. Our study supports this finding with a much larger

participant pool and adds important details about how users might react differently to device failures in these different settings.

4. CONCLUSION
This paper presents findings from an online survey about how blind individuals would react to errors while using an imagined indoor navigation aid. Five distinct social/environmental parameters as well as FN, FP, and misidentification errors were presented in ten scenarios of use. Participants' responses revealed that type of the error, building feature for which the error is made and social/environmental context in which the error happened impacted users' acceptance of the device errors. While device accuracy is an important design concern, more nuanced, naturalistic studies of user's varying tolerance of errors will lead to increased acceptance of not only indoor navigation aids for people who are blind, but any assistive technology device.

5. ACKNOWLEDGMENTS
We thank our participants for their valuable time and insights. This work was supported by Toyota Motor Engineering & Manufacturing North America.

6. REFERENCES
[1] Branham, S.M. and Kane, S.K. 2015. Collaborative Accessibility: How blind and sighted companions co-create accessible home spaces. Proceedings of the 33rd Annual ACM Conference on Human Factors in Computing Systems (2015), 2373–2382.

[2] Branham, S.M. and Kane, S.K. 2015. The Invisible Work of Accessibility: How Blind Employees Manage Accessibility in Mixed-Ability Workplaces. Proceedings of the 17th International ACM SIGACCESS Conference on Computers & Accessibility (2015), 163–171.

[3] Chumkamon, S. and Tuvaphanthaphiphat, P. et al. A blind navigation system using RFID for indoor environments. Proc. Electrical Engineering/Electronics, Computer, Telecommunications and Information Technology, 2008, 765-768.

[4] Idrees, A. and Iqbal, Z. et al. An efficient indoor navigation technique to find optimal route for blinds using QR codes. Proc. Industrial Electronics and Applications (ICIEA), 2015, 690-695.

[5] Ivanov, R. 2010. Indoor navigation system for visually impaired. Proceedings of the 11th International Conference on Computer Systems and Technologies and Workshop for

[6] Kane, S.K., Jayant, C., Wobbrock, J.O. and Ladner, R.E. 2009. Freedom to roam: A Study of Mobile Device Adoption and Accessibility for People with Visual and Motor Disabilities. Proceeding of the 11th international ACM SIGACCESS conference on Computers and accessibility - ASSETS '09 (New York, New York, USA, Oct. 2009), 115–122.

[7] Phillips, B. and Zhao, H. 1993. Predictors of assistive technology abandonment. Assistive Technology. 5, 1 (1993), 36–45.

[8] Tian, L. and Tian, Y. et al. Detecting good quality frames in videos captured by a wearable camera for blind navigation. Proc. Bioinformatics and Biomedicine (BIBM), 2013, 334-337

Using a Design Workshop to Explore Accessible Ideation

Cynthia L. Bennett[1], Kristen Shinohara[2], Brianna Blaser[3], Andrew Davidson[1], Kat M. Steele[4]
[1]Human Centered Design and Engineering, [2]iSchool, [3]DO-IT, [4]Mechanical Engineering
University of Washington, Box 352315
Seattle, WA 98195
{bennec3, kshino, adavid7, blaser, kmsteele}@uw.edu

ABSTRACT

Although a critical step in the technology design process, ideation is often not accessible for people with disabilities. We present findings from a design workshop facilitated to brainstorm accessible ideation methods. Groups, mostly engineers, ideated on a design challenge and documented access barriers encountered by participants with disabilities. They then ideated and prototyped potential solutions for decreasing access barriers. We offer suggestions for more accessible communication and ideation on a design team and insights from using a workshop as a site for rethinking ideation.

Keywords

Accessibility; Brainstorming; Design; Ideation; Disability

1. INTRODUCTION

Ideation, also known as brainstorming, is a crucial phase of the technology design process used to inspire and to refine designs. However, few projects have explored how to make ideation itself more accessible for people with disabilities. For example, many students are taught to ideate by sketching, but this method may be difficult for people with vision or mobility impairments. As efforts to increase the number of people with disabilities in computing and accessible products continue, it is imperative to explore how ideation can both be made more accessible for all designers and co-design participants.

We explored this question during a short design workshop, by prompting engineers, and participants with disabilities, some being engineers, to identify access barriers during an initial design challenge and to then prototype potential methods for making ideation more accessible. We offer two contributions: (1) We present accessible communication and ideation considerations prototyped during the design activity, and (2) We offer a design activity as a generative site for documenting and improving upon design-related access barriers. We hope designers can use these preliminary findings to ideate more accessibly and to motivate research on increasing the accessibility of the design process.

2. RELATED WORK

Researchers have introduced strategies for designing for people with disabilities such as Ability-Based Design [10], Design for Social Accessibility [6], and User Sensitive Inclusive Design [5]. One popular framework, Universal Design [8], advocates designing for the most people to have access, including those with disabilities. However, these strategies lack specific methods for accessibly navigating various phases of the design process.

ASSETS '16, October 23-26, 2016, Reno, NV, USA
ACM 978-1-4503-4124-0/16/10.
http://dx.doi.org/10.1145/2982142.2982209

Notably, Larsen *et al* [4] recommend ideation strategies for co-designing with children who do not speak, and Bueler *et al [2]* offer recommendations for teaching a 3D-printing course with students with and without intellectual disabilities. Design workshops are also a popular tool for introducing people to the design process. For example, IDEO offers a free toolkit [3] to K-12 educators on incorporating design thinking into curricula. The Hasso Plattner Institute of Design at Stanford introduces students to each phase of the design process [7] in a short workshop. Our approach was similar, as groups briefly ideated on a design challenge. However, we narrowed the challenge to focus on ideation to gather more targeted accessibility suggestions.

3. METHODS

Procedure. The 90-minute design workshop was conducted during a Capacity Building Institute sponsored by AccessEngineering [1] that gathered engineering educators, engineers, and disability service professionals, some of whom had disabilities. Everyone was introduced to the phases of the design process, with extra background on ideation methods. Each group was given a bag of supplies including sticky notes, pens, felt, pipe cleaners, popsicle sticks, Play-Doh, and other craft supplies. Groups of participants were asked to ideate solutions for making smart classrooms more accessible by first brainstorming several solutions and then choosing one for ideating refinements. Participants then reflected by identifying access barriers they encountered in this process, what went well, and what was challenging. Each group then chose one access barrier they encountered and ideated and prototyped potential solutions. Participants engaged in another reflection and presented their findings to the group. Data include a CART (communication access real-time translation) transcript of the activity, reflection sheets from each group, and field notes from two researchers. All data were thematically analyzed, and we present these findings along with solutions prototyped during the workshop.

Participants. We had about 40 participants divided into seven groups, with at least one member with a disability in each. Four workshop attendees offered to serve as the person with a disability for their group, and the remaining three were volunteers from the community. Three participants had vision impairments, one had a hearing impairment, one identified as neurodiverse, one had a learning disability, and one had physical disabilities and attended via a Beam remote presence robot [9].

4. FINDINGS

Communication. An emergent theme across groups was access barriers impacting communication during the workshop. Ideation is rooted in individuals sharing and building upon others' ideas; however, traditional ideation methods created persistent challenges. For example, conversation was difficult for deaf or hard of hearing participants to follow and contribute to the group. These participants expressed frustration lip reading or watching an interpreter during a fast paced conversation while also examining sketches or other artifacts. One group passed around a talking stick to discourage interrupting and to offer each member a chance to share. A participant from a different group realized that "each individual member of the group has a particular strength or weakness." They categorized preferences such as writer, speaker, and tactile in a matrix and asked each member to fill out their strengths, which were then used to allocate roles during the workshop. Groups realized that different communication styles and access needs prevented everyone from maintaining awareness and contributing. As demonstrated in the above examples, they found systematic and multimodal methods of communication helpful to ensuring that everyone could share their ideas.

Ideation. Beyond communication, the groups identified additional solutions for more accessible ideation. One group with a neurodiverse participant noted difficulty following the progression of ideas as they were tossed into a pile in the middle of the table. They designed a pattern and participants took turns placing ideas so it was easier to track the trajectory of the ideation session. Vision-impaired participants were unaware of sketched ideas and handwritten sticky notes as they piled on tables. In response, one group mocked up a Play-Doh design for a system to synchronize handwritten and typed ideas for participants to read visually or with audio. The group also noted the potential for such systems to better include remote collaborators such as people attending via a Beam. One group tried to make 2D ideas more accessible non-visually by adding textures to sketches, and cutting sticky notes into different shapes to categorize ideas tactually.

Workshop. To gather formative insights, we positioned a design workshop as a site for documenting access barriers and thinking of design solutions. Not only did groups think of creative ways to be more inclusive while ideating, the workshop itself prompted participants to rethink design. One participant concluded his group's presentation with, "Even in the [design] process, you have to consider accessibility. That was my aha moment." Positioning participants as co-designers in a workshop setting raised awareness about access barriers for some and helped them to think of quick solutions to try in their own design environments. However, the workshop itself contained access barriers. For example, hearing-impaired participants were unable to focus on interruptions by the facilitator and their groupmates at the same time. These access barriers raised an interesting tension around purposefully not making the workshop as accessible as it could have been to inspire ideas, though we did not do anything explicitly to make the workshop less accessible. While experiencing access barriers allowed them to be identified and used for ideating more accessible methods, we should consider how to most thoughtfully do this so not to position participants to have a negative experience. A potential solution is to incorporate accessibility considerations often not implemented during similar design workshops, such as visual and audio cues to, allow people to finish their thoughts before a facilitator speaks. Participants could reflect on how accessibility considerations impacted collaboration, which could then be used to begin refining existing solutions or generating new ones.

5. CONCLUSION

We presented findings from a workshop aimed at designing ways to ideate more accessibly. During the activity, participants found several access barriers to communication and ideation which prevented participants with disabilities from contributing equally. In response, they used common craft supplies, often employed during prototyping phases of the design process, to ideate more accessibly. The variety of supplies and multimodal communication methods seemed to provide more opportunities for greater participation by everyone. Though more work should be done to insure the workshops themselves are accessible, the setting built on [2] and [4] and allowed participants to immediately try solutions positioning it as a promising method for further improving design process accessibility.

6. ACKNOWLEDGMENTS

Thanks to our participants and AccessEngineering (NSF grant number EEC-1444961).

7. REFERENCES

[1] AccessEngineering. Overview. http://uw.edu/doit/programs/accessengineering/overview Retrieved 6/23/2016.

[2] E. Buehler, W. Easley, S. McDonald, N. Comrie, and A. Hurst. 2015. Inclusion and Education: 3D Printing for Integrated Classrooms. In Proceedings of the 17th International ACM SIGACCESS Conference on Computers & Accessibility (ASSETS '15). ACM, New York, NY, USA, 281-290. DOI=http://dx.doi.org/10.1145/2700648.2809844

[3] IDEO. Design Thinking Toolkit for Educators. https://www.ideo.com/work/toolkit-for-educators Retrieved 6/22/2016.

[4] H. S. Larsen and P. L. Hedval. 2012. Ideation and ability: when actions speak louder than words. In *Proc. PDC '12*, Vol. 2. ACM, New York, NY, USA, 37-40. DOI=http://dx.doi.org/10.1145/2348144.2348157

[5] A. Newell, P. Gregor, M. Morgan, G. Pullin, and C. Macaulay. 2011. User-Sensitive Inclusive Design. *Universal Access in the Information Society*. 10, 3, 235–243.

[6] K. Shinohara and J. O. Wobbrock. 2011. In the shadow of misperception: Assistive technology use and social interactions. In *Proc. CHI '11* (Vancouver, BC), 705–714. http://doi.acm.org/10.1145/1978942.1979044

[7] Stanford University Institute of Design. Design Project Zero: A 90 Minute Activity. http://dschool.stanford.edu/use-our-methods/design-project-zero-a-90-minute-experience/ Retrieved 6/22/2016

[8] C. Stephanidis, D. Akoumianakis, M. Sfyrakis, and A. Paramythis. 1998. Universal accessibility in HCI: Process-oriented guidelines and tool requirements. In *Proc. User Interfaces for All '98*.

[9] Suitable Technologies Beam Presence Smart System. https://suitabletech.com/beampro/ Retrieved 6/22/2016.

[10] J. O. Wobbrock, S. K. Kane, K. Z. Gajos, S. Harada, and J. Froehlich. 2011. Ability-based design: Concept, principles, and examples. *ACM TACCESS*. 3, 3, 1–27. http://doi.acm.org/10.1145/1952383.195238

Study of a Smart Cup for Home Monitoring of the Arm and Hand of Stroke Patients.

Maxence Bobin
LIMSI-CNRS
Rue John Von Neumann,
91405, Orsay
Building 508, France
maxence.bobin@limsi.fr

Mehdi Boukallel
CEA-LIST
Route de Gif, 91191,
Gif-sur-Yvette
Building 565, France
mehdi.boukallel@cea.fr

Margarita Anastassova
CEA-LIST
Route de Gif, 91191,
Gif-sur-Yvette
Building 565, France
margarita.anastassova@cea.fr

Mehdi Ammi
LIMSI-CNRS
Rue John Von Neumann,
91405, Orsay
Building 508, France
mehdi.ammi@limsi.fr

ABSTRACT

In this work, we present a platform for continuously monitor and guide stroke patient at home during Activities of the Daily Living. The platform consists of a smart cup which embeds sensors that monitor the patient's hand and arm motor activity at different times of the day. The cup detects its orientation, the liquid level, its position on a specific target, as well as tremors. Moreover, displays are provided to guide the patient's movement. Finally, the planned studies with both the therapists and patients are presented.

Keywords

Stroke; Monitoring; Home; Cup; Internet of Things

1. INTRODUCTION

15 million people are affected by stroke every year. Stroke patients encounter varied cognitive and motor impairments [3]. Stroke rehabilitation is very expensive in terms of infrastructures and medical staff. Moreover, patients are left alone at home without monitoring to assess their recovery. Usually, recovery progress are evaluated before each rehabilitation session by the therapist with empirical measures based on visual estimations [4]. Yet, many Activities of the Daily Living (ADLs) can provide relevant data about the patients' recovery [2]. The emergence of Internet of Things let us imagine to perform continuous monitoring of stroke patients at home. The collected data would allow the therapist to adapt the rehabilitation program according to the patients' progress. This paper presents the design and implementation of a smart cup, called SyMPATHy, based on a

common ADL: filling a cup and drinking. It aims to monitor the arm and hand activity of stroke patients and to provide a gestural guidance during recovery exercises.

2. CONCEPT

The design process of SyMPATHy includes five main steps and is based on the following methodology:

1 Identification

- Task to perform (see Section 2.1)
- Information to monitor (see Section 2.2)
- Sensory feedback to provide to the patient (see Section 2.2)

2 Implementation of the platform (see Section 2.3)

3 Data acquisition and processing (see Section 2.3)

4 Technical study of the platform (see Section 2.3)

5 Planned studies (see Section 3)

2.1 Task to perform

According to interviews with two qualified health professionals working at a stroke rehabilitation center, the work focused on the task of reaching, filling and transporting a cup. This task is based on different motor sub-tasks (arm movement, hand grasping, etc.) with the upper limb which is involved in other usual ADLs (cleaning, take a shower, etc.). Moreover, it simultaneously involves vision, tactile, proprioception and audio sensory feedback.

2.2 Features and feedback design

Drinking and filling task is composed of different steps which required monitoring: (1) Filling the cup, (2) Grasping the cup, (3) Holding and moving the cup and (4) Releasing the cup on the table. In addition to the monitoring, providing feedback is essential especially for patients with motor and sensory impairments. Alert and guidance during filling and drinking steps enhance the performances and motivations of the patients [5]. The visual feedback was preferred for step 1 (filling the cup). Informal study led us to use the visual channel by displaying colors vertically along the cup. Liquid level information is simplified by discrete colors chosen according to the European culture (red, orange, yellow and green). The selected feedback for the third step (hold and move the cup) is a visual feedback around the top of the cup. The LEDs display colors according to the inclination of the cup (green 0-20°, yellow 20-35°, orange 35-50° and red > 50°). Furthermore, the audio channel is used to alert the patient when he reaches a spatial target on the table. This allows to unload the visual channel. No sensory feedback was provided for the grasping and tremors data.

2.3 Implementation

SyMPATHy embeds a Raspberry Pi Zero and sensors which retrieve and process data in order to provide the correct feedback to the patient. Orientation detection is supported by the 9-DoF Inertial Movement Unit (IMU) MPU-9150. Industrial liquid level sensors having constraints (size, low-reactivity), a custom liquid level sensor based on liquid conductivity and tension divider bridges was added to the cup. For each level, an electrode is wired to a tension divider bridge. Measuring a tension allow to detect the presence or absence of liquid. The relative position to a given spatial target is assessed by a Near-Field Communication (NFC) Reader. Finally, Force Sensing Resistors (FSR) have been added to the grooves on the hand print in order to monitor the force applied on the cup while grasping.

A technological study have shown that the gyroscopic tremor detection is reliable with a error range of 3.6% and match the data-sheet of the IMU sensor which forecast an error range of 3%.

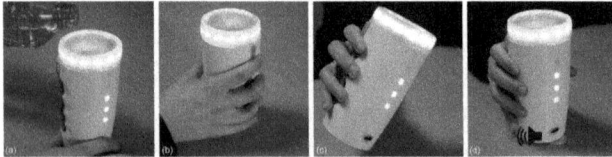

Figure 1: SyMPATHy cup used during steps: (a) filling, (b) grasping, (c) moving and (d) releasing.

3. PLANNED STUDIES

Based in this first SyMPATHy prototype, two series of studies are planned with both therapists and patients. The first goal is to retrieve feedback in order to improve the design and the technical features of the cup. The usability and acceptability of the platform will be also investigated. Finally, the impact of the device on the patients' health state should be assessed. The first study will be conducted with therapists in order to improve the cup. Then, a second study will be carried out with real patients to assess acceptability.

3.1 Study with therapists

The SyMPATHy cup provides a large number of relevant data on patient's activity (temporal records, mean values, 3D gestures, etc.). The collected data has to be displayed in order to provide usable information to therapists. A study with therapists working in a rehabilitation center will be carried out to provide understandable information and usable visualization tools. This study should highlight the most relevant information to display as well as the way to display it. The resulting recommendations should help us to upgrade the visualization interface on the basis of therapists needs. More fundamentally, the study will address the usefulness of the data of such type of platform to monitor the daily living activity of patient.

3.2 Study with patients

Another study with real patients in a rehabilitation center must be carried out. The aim of this study is to assess the acceptability of the cup in the rehabilitation process. The evaluation will be gradual. First, the smart cup (features, recorded data and displays) will be presented to the patients. Then, patients will be asked to use the cup without providing feedback. Afterwards, the sensory feedback will be enabled. During each step, the acceptability and the usability of the device will be investigated with both the patient and the therapist. The results of this study should highlight the features to improve and allow us to identify the weaknesses which could lead to the rejection of this technological concept [1].

4. CONCLUSIONS

SyMPATHy smart cup prototype have been developed for monitoring and guiding stroke patients during ADLs. Data collected provide relevant information about the patient recovery state and the therapist can adapt the rehabilitation program. Two studies are planned to improve the features of the cup as well as create a usable visualization tool for the therapist and investigate the usability of the cup both for patients and therapists.

5. REFERENCES

[1] M. Anastassova, C. Mégard, and J.-M. Burkhardt. Prototype evaluation and user-needs analysis in the early design of emerging technologies. In *Human-computer interaction. Interaction design and usability*, pages 383–392. Springer, 2007.

[2] B. Gialanella, R. Santoro, and C. Ferlucci. Predicting outcome after stroke: the role of basic activities of daily living predicting outcome after stroke. *European journal of physical and rehabilitation medicine*, 49(5):629–637, 2013.

[3] J. S. Kim. Delayed onset hand tremor caused by cerebral infarction. *Stroke*, 23(2):292–294, 1992.

[4] S. Pandian and K. N. Arya. Stroke-related motor outcome measures: Do they quantify the neurophysiological aspects of upper extremity recovery? *Journal of bodywork and movement therapies*, 18(3):412–423, 2014.

[5] R. Stanton, L. Ada, C. M. Dean, and E. Preston. Feedback received while practicing everyday activities during rehabilitation after stroke: An observational study. *Physiotherapy Research International*, 2014.

An Approach to Audio-Only Editing for Visually Impaired Seniors

Robin N. Brewer[1], Mark Cartwright[2], Aaron Karp[2], Bryan Pardo[2], Anne Marie Piper[1]
[1]Inclusive Technology Lab, Northwestern University, 2240 Campus Drive, Evanston, IL 60208
[2]Interactive Audio Lab, Northwestern University, 2133 Sheridan Road, Evanston, IL 60208
{rnbrewer, mcartwright, aaronkarp2017}@u.northwestern.edu
{pardo, ampiper} @northwestern.edu

ABSTRACT

Older adults and people with vision impairments are increasingly using phones to receive audio-based information and want to publish content online but must use complex audio recording/editing tools that often rely on inaccessible graphical interfaces. This poster describes the design of an accessible audio-based interface for post-processing audio content created by visually impaired seniors. We conducted a diary study with five older adults with vision impairments to understand how to design a system that would allow them to edit content they record using an audio-only interface. Our findings can help inform the development of accessible audio-editing interfaces for people with vision impairments more broadly.

CCS Concepts

• **Human-centered computing** → **Accessibility systems and tools;**

Keywords

Older adults; vision impairments; audio interface; editing

1. INTRODUCTION AND RELATED WORK

Seniors (60+) are increasingly relying on phones and audio content to access information (e.g. receiving weather updates by phone) and want to publish their own content [1]. We are interested in helping seniors with vision impairments create and edit audio content to be shared with others, (e.g. for podcasts). Despite being a task that is not inherently visual, existing audio editing software such as Avid's Pro Tools relies heavily on graphical interfaces. Yet, such interfaces present many challenges for with vision impairments. Screen readers are a common assistive technology that help visually impaired people use graphical interfaces, yet are difficult to learn and maintain (e.g. install software updates) [2]. It also can be difficult to access screen readers and to navigate them, due to complex navigational structures that are difficult to learn and to use [3]. Another approach is to use audio-only interfaces. However, graphical tools have not been developed or deployed for audio-only editing. Prior work has shown how traditional phone interfaces on landline and non-smart cell phones can be used to access online content for seniors and suggests this modality can be useful for visually impaired seniors [1]. However, it is not obvious how best to translate audio-only interfaces for editing voice content due to the lack of visual input and feedback.

Here, we present an in-depth diary study with seniors with vision impairments to learn about their post-processing needs for audio content. We use this diary study to design a system that would allow visually impaired seniors to edit content they record using an audio-only interface (e.g. phone). Our findings can help inform developers on how to create simple, accessible audio-editing interfaces for people with vision impairments. Our findings may also extend to other populations without easy access to mainstream graphical interfaces such as people in developing countries who may rely on phones and IVR systems.

2. METHOD

We conducted a two-week diary study with older adults (over the age of 60) with vision impairments to understand how they would create and potentially want to edit audio stories. We conducted pre-interviews to learn about their current technology use and provided them with an accessible audio recorder (Wilson Digital Voice Recorder, v5) to record their stories. Participants were instructed to record on any topic as often as they wanted for two weeks. In the post-interviews, we asked participants if and how they would want to edit their stories.

Participants were recruited through audio and printed flyers at a local residential community for people with vision impairments and at organizations that have support groups for visually impaired seniors. Five people participated in the diary study (average age=72.2 years old, min=60, max=96, male=3). Two participants are blind and three reported having low vision.

3. FINDINGS AND RECOMMENDATIONS

We learned that participants employed different preferred recording strategies. P2 wanted to record his diary entry in its entirety without stopping, but noted that he would repeat a phrase until he was satisfied before moving on. The "flow" of the recording was very important to P4 and P5. P4 preferred not to edit his recording at all and would rather rerecord his whole diary entry. P5 also recorded his entry in full to maintain the flow of the story, but he would go back to edit individual phrases, rather than rerecord a whole entry.

ASSETS '16, October 23-26, 2016, Reno, NV, USA
ACM 978-1-4503-4124-0/16/10.
http://dx.doi.org/10.1145/2982142.2982196

Also, participants wanted the quality of their recordings to resemble that of audio content with which they were familiar, where quality was both a reflection the quality of the audio production and performance. For example, P5 said, *"Make me sound like a professional"*. This participant was a musician. He enjoyed uploading music online and listening to music recorded by other artists on sites such as SoundCloud. Therefore, he wanted his recordings to mimic a similar level of audio-production quality. Also, P1 described how she wanted her recordings to be similar to the quality of the audio books she listens to weekly. Participants explained that removing filler words like "ahs", "ums", long pauses, or repeated words would increase the quality of performance and production. However, P5 noted that the occasional "um" is okay, a reflection of his desire to maintain a natural flow to his recordings. P2 and P4 said they would want their recordings to have limited background noise or to be able to remove any background noises such as thumps or deep breaths. P4 tried to achieve this same goal by creating a relaxing and quiet environment for recording.

After understanding what types of edits they would make, we asked participants how would they make such edits by voice. They described two primary models of navigation which we call \ *standard* and *bookmarking*. P1, P2, and P3 said they wanted to use physical buttons for standard audio navigation similar to how one may navigate an audio cassette---*stop*, *play*, *rewind*, and *fast forward*. However, in contrast to a cassette player in which playback speed and pitch are dependent on each other, participants noted they preferred "fast playback" (e.g. 1.5x, 2x, 4x speed), in which just the playback speed (and not the pitch) is affected---this is similar to the fast playback functionality found in text-to-speech screen readers and audio books which the participants are used to. P4 elaborated further and explained that he would want to perform such navigation using a combination of keypad and voice input. For example, he may use buttons to fast-forward to the approximate subsection of the recording and dictate by voice to delete *"a sentence before that."* P5 noted that this relative navigation could work well with absolute navigation where users can also say *"fast forward to one minute"* to find the appropriate place to edit, especially for longer recordings. These known editing locations are similar to what P1, P4, and P5 describe as navigation using bookmarks. People would be able to set bookmarks either while recording or during playback to quickly navigate recordings.

Therefore, we recommend that an accessible audio editing system provide multiple methods for navigation: *Standard*--- *stop*, *play*, *increase speed*; *Bookmarks*---jump to points in time saved previously the user (e.g. by user-provided or default labels) or defined by the system (e.g. filler words identified by the system); *Variable time interval*---jump forward/backward in time by "audio chunks", which are segmented by significant regions of silence; and *Fixed time interval*---jump forward/backward in time specified by minutes/seconds. To perform local edits, users would specify the boundaries of regions to be altered either by predefined locations *current location*, beginning, and *end*, or by bookmark locations.

4. PROTOTYPE DESIGN

Based on our findings above, we developed an initial voice interface with fixed and variable navigation functionality, the ability to delete and play segments, and a global and local silence reducer. To segment the audio and split it into sensible chunks for editing, we calculated the average power over a given frame length of the audio signal using the root-mean-square of the amplitude (RMS) for every frame of the given signal. Using these values, we determined a cutoff point to differentiate between periods of relative silence and periods of relative sonic activity. This resulted in "audio chunks" that primarily consisted of individual words or short phrases spoken in an elided manner. This "separation by silence" technique allows for variable time interval navigation. Navigation was implemented through two commands---next chunk, and previous chunk. Users can delete segments of audio by navigating to the chunk and pressing the corresponding "delete" button. The prototype's chunking system gives users the ability to remove individual words or phrases that are unnecessary. Given the importance placed on the awkward feeling of extended pauses in the post-interviews, the system also allows users to reduce the length of silences both locally and globally. Locally, this technique reduces the currently selected silence's length by a given scaling factor. Globally, all silence segments above a certain length are reduced by a given scaling factor, which is useful for longer recordings, as navigating linearly through the recording to find silences would be time-consuming for the user. We chose to focus on segmenting the audio because this is crucial for the functionality of the fixed and variable time navigation mentioned above and automatically creates bookmarks for users to more easily traverse through their recordings.

5. CONCLUSIONS AND FUTURE WORK

In this paper we investigated how older adults with vision impairments would edit voice input to explore how they could edit audio off of a computer. Our findings show how navigation and strategic audio deletion are preferred to produce high quality recordings. In the future we will further develop navigation functionality and test the prototype with older adults. This research contributes to designing voice interfaces that are accessible, flexible, and easy-to-use.

6. REFERENCES

1. Robin N. Brewer and Anne Marie Piper. 2016. "Tell It Like It Really Is": A Case of Online Content Creation and Sharing Among Older Adult Bloggers. *Proceedings of CHI 16.* http://doi.org/10.1145/2858036.2858379

2. Shaun K Kane, Chandrika Jayant, Jacob O Wobbrock, and Richard E. Ladner. 2009. Freedom to roam: a study of mobile device adoption and accessibility for people with visual and motor disabilities. *Proceedings of the 11th international ACM SIGACCESS conference on Computers and accessibility*, ACM, 115–122. Retrieved March 12, 2012 from http://dl.acm.org/citation.cfm?id=1639663

3. Anne Marie Piper, Robin N. Brewer, and Raymundo Cornejo. 2016. Technology learning and use among older adults with late-life vision impairments. *Universal Access in the Information Society.*

Accessible Online Indoor Maps for Blind and Visually Impaired Users

Tania Calle-Jimenez
Escuela Politécnica Nacional
Quito-Ecuador
tania.calle@epn.edu.ec

Sergio Luján-Mora
University of Alicante
Alicante-Spain
sergio.lujan@ua.es

ABSTRACT
This paper proposes alternatives for the development and improvement of maps to aid accessibility. Based on our analysis, we present an accessible online indoor map prototype that complies with WCAG 2.0. For the case study, the prototype displays an indoor map that is designed using Scalable Vector Graphics (SVG) format. This format can include information that helps the screen reader to interpret the visual graph information. In addition, the prototype can simulate the route that the users select so they can get an idea of the environment where they will mobilize. We tested the prototype in different browsers with the help of blind people.

CCS Concepts

• **Human-centred computing**→ Accessibility→ Accessibility design and evaluation methods • **Interaction design**→ Interaction design process and methods→ User interface design • **Visualization**→ Visualization application domains → Geographic visualization.

Keywords
Web Accessibility; Online Maps; Indoor Maps; SVG; Accessibility Guidelines; WCAG 2.0; Blind People; Visually Impaired People.

1. INTRODUCTION
Increasingly, the Web uses graphic content that is accessed by many users. Anyone with an electronic device can explore the Internet and access graphic content including geographic material. As many people require access to online maps, the study of web accessibility in maps is one of our interests. As maps are visual by nature, a blind person that interacts with a computer via a screen reader and keyboard cannot fully benefit, since the graphic part of the information is not visible to them. According to the World Health Organization, 39 million people are blind, which represents 0.7% of the world population [1]. These people have difficulty accessing the Web, in particular geographic content. Web accessibility means that people with disabilities will be able to make better use of it. Web accessibility is not concerned with the specific conditions of people who use the Web, but with the impact, their conditions have on their ability to use it [2]. To solve the problems of web accessibility, the WCAG 2.0 demands web developers to provide equivalent alternatives for non-text content [3].

ASSETS '16, October 23-26, 2016, Reno, NV, USA
ACM 978-1-4503-4124-0/16/10.
http://dx.doi.org/10.1145/2982142.2982201

This paper presents a prototype of an accessible online indoor map that solves the main access barriers for blind users. Users can use the prototype to help with mobility and learn about the environment using a keyboard. This prototype helps mitigate the visual barriers with the use of WCAG 2.0 and SVG.

2. PROPOSING ANSWERS TO ACCESSIBILITY BARRIERS
2.1 Maps as an Accessible Image
To overcome this barrier, we review principle one Perceivable of WCAG 2.0 that states that developers should provide text alternatives for any non-text content so that it can be changed into other forms that people need, such as large print, braille, speech, symbols or simpler language [3]. Fortunately, there are some formats such as SVG that developers can use to design maps as images; SVG includes some characteristics that allows the screen reader to interpret the map.

2.2 Maps Operable using a Keyboard
To ensure that maps are operable with a keyboard, we apply guideline 2.1 of the principle two Operable of WCAG 2.0 that states that all functionality should be available using a keyboard. We implement the SVG code and the use of arrow and tab keys that help users to navigate the map, and hear and understand it.

2.3 Maps with Readable Text
To resolve this problem, we apply the guideline 1.4.5 through of readable fonts inside of map. Besides, we provide that information of each component of indoor map, this information is to read by a screen reader.

2.4 Colour Maps
We propose the application of guideline 1.4 regarding distinguish ability, which makes it easier for users to see and hear content including separating the foreground from background. We apply the guideline 1.4.1 that says colour should not be used as the only visual means of conveying information and we propose applying guideline 1.4.3 regarding contrast, which says the visual presentation of text and images of the text should have a contrast proportion of at least 4.5:1 for normal size text and 3:1 for large-scale text [3].

3. PRACTICAL EXAMPLE
The interface of the prototype is displayed in a browser that includes a help menu, two accessible toolbar, and a general structure with three panels. The left panel represents the navigation in the text content, the centre panel shows the indoor map and the right panel displays information about the selected area.

3.1 Main Content
Figure 1 illustrates the general structure that consists of: view of indoor map, navigation and visual and auditory instructions. From the left panel, users can navigate through using the tab and arrow

keys. Users can use the keyboard shortcuts to exit, help, the principal menu and map. The left panel contains a search menu in alphabetical order and the search has been divided to facilitate navigation into four ranges (A-C) (D-L) (M-P) (Q-Z). This menu represents the names of teachers sorted alphabetically.

The central panel contains the SVG map, this map has elements of a floor, i.e. offices, meeting rooms, bathrooms, among others. Each element of the map contains information that is displayed when selected using the mouse or keyboard. After selection, the screen reader describes the information presented in the right panel to the user. The right panel shows a description of the item of the map selected. It contains three buttons: a "back to map" button that returns the user to the last selected item on the map, a "back to the main menu" button that returns the user to the search menu and a "start" button that returns the user to the top of the page.

Figure 1. Prototype interface

Similarly, Figure 1 illustrates the directions and the visual and auditory instructions for user mobility that is the route simulated when the users select an element. When the users select an item from the list of routes, the prototype draws the route in the map and the audio file indicates what the better route should be.

3.2 Accessibility Toolbars

The accessibility toolbars consist of two toolbars named "accessibility" and "advanced". Figure 2 shows "advanced" toolbar that users can select to change patterns. The prototype changes the "pattern" in the indoor map, in base to the algorithms proposed in [24], and in this study concluded that patterns improve users understanding. The "accessibility" toolbar allows the configuration of other properties of the webpage. The "saturation" "brightness", "hue", "grayscale", "sepia", "invert", "opacity" and "contrast" controls help users to obtain better tonality for improved readability and understanding.

Figure 2. Advanced toolbar

Additionally, the prototype changes the colours of the map in base to the algorithms proposed in [4][5]. These studies show what algorithm is used for users with problem of vision. Figure 3 shows an example. The "patterns" control changes the colour of the indoor map to help to users understand it better without the need of colours.

Figure 3. Pattern map

4. USER TESTING

Blind users used the prototype with Google CromeVox for the first time, this involved a difficulty when manipulating the application. This meaning that requires more number of visits to navigate more easily and quickly. Users mentioned that the prototype would be very useful for their everyday life: users prefer to know beforehand the environment that they will be mobilized. Besides, they explained that the simulation route is very important to the mobility in unknown premises.

5. CONCLUSION AND FUTURE WORK

The prototype was tested in three browsers: Google Chrome, Mozilla Firefox and Microsoft Edge. Google Chrome supports SVG and is compatible with web styles and colours, while, Mozilla Firefox and Microsoft Edge support HTML and SVG, but these browsers are not compatible with the tabindex property. Moreover, we evaluated the prototype with TAW and eXaminator that measure the compliance of the WCAG 2.0.

For future work we intend to apply tools with voice commands, that is to say, we should use tools that simulate and transform the voice to text, so that users can speak the name of the place where they want to go to and the prototype will relay information about that place.

6. ACKNOWLEDGMENTS

Our thanks to Cristina Rivera for allowing us to show some interfaces of her prototype that was developed for her studies of the systems engineer of Escuela Politécnica Nacional.

7. REFERENCES

[1] United Nations. 2008. Convention on the Rights of Persons with Disabilities and Optional Protocol.16-18.

[2] W3C. 2012. Introduction to Web Accessibility. Available Online: http://www.w3.org/WAI/intro/accessibility.php.

[3] W3C. 2008. "Web Content Accessibility Guidelines 2.0". Available Online: http://www.w3.org/TR/WCAG20.

[4] Zhou L., Bensal V., Zhang D. 2014. Color Adaptation for Improving Mobile Web Accessibility. In Computer and Information Science (ICIS). 291 – 296.

[5] Navadal B., Santhosh K, Prajwal S, Harikishan B. 2014. An Image Processing Technique for Color Detection and Distinguish Patterns with Similar Color: An aid for Color Blind People. In Circuits, Communication, Control and Computing (I4C). 333 – 336

FOQUS: A Smartwatch Application for Individuals with ADHD and Mental Health Challenges

Victor Dibia
IBM T.J. Watson Research Center,
Yorktown, USA
dibiavc@us.ibm.com

ABSTRACT

This paper reports on the design of *foqus*, an app running on a smartwatch to aid adults with mental health conditions like ADHD and mild forms of attention deficiency through two main routes – tools to foster extended focus and tools to reduce anxiety/stress. Using a user-centric design approach, three important features are identified, implemented and evaluated which aim to leverage the benefits of wearable devices: a flexible implementation of the Pomodoro time management technique, a tool for guided meditation, and positive message priming. Initial user test results suggest smartwatch-based interventions as a viable, ubiquitous tool for addressing mental health and stress related conditions.

Keywords

Wearables, Smartwatches, ADHD, Attention Deficiency, Mental Health.

1. INTRODUCTION

In the emerging era of wearables and the quantified self, new opportunities arise for the application of computing technology in the area of health and wellness. Whilst much work has been done regarding physical fitness tracking, a less addressed area of inquiry is the application of wearables to mental health and wellness issues. Mental health issues such as ADHD, which materialize in the form of obstacles to sustained task focus and constantly elevated levels of anxiety, can be a debilitating challenge to adults as well as children [2]. Unfortunately, the impact of such mental health issues on the quality of life, are less likely to be observed by the general public, and not given appropriate attention. In addition, for adults with mild forms of ADHD and stress, few tools exist that can help them adopt behavioral change approaches to improving their condition. To address this, the current study presents a working prototype (*foqus*) of a wearable application with feature that assist a user in improving task focus and reducing stress.

1.1 ADHD and Work

Traditionally, ADHD has been viewed as a childhood disorder which youngsters outgrow as they get older. However, recent studies have highlighted ADHD diagnosis within adolescents and older demographics [2]. Attention deficit problems in the workplace can cause an individual to exhibit symptoms such as anxiety, depression and low self-esteem. They appear to be flighty, edgy, late, disorganized, constantly unable to meet deadlines,

ASSETS '16, October 23-26, 2016, Reno, NV, USA
ACM 978-1-4503-4124-0/16/10.
http://dx.doi.org/10.1145/2982142.2982207

Figure 1. Interface screenshot for *foqus*.

prioritize appropriately, fidget and daydream. The work of de Graaf et al [2] shows that 3.5% of all working adults (age 18 – 44years, n = 7075) across 10 countries met the standard (DSM IV) diagnosis criteria for ADHD. This suggests that a significant percentage of ADHD cases persist into adulthood, and only a small amount receive appropriate treatment. Their findings also highlight the impact of ADHD on job role performance for workers (employed and self-employed). Specifically, workers with ADHD had an excess of 8.4 more sickness absence days per year and greater annualized average excess number of workdays associated with diminished work quantity (21.7 days) and quality (13.6 days). Taken together, it is projected that various forms of ADHD are associated with 143.8 million lost days of productivity each year [2]. For such adults, there is value in assistive tools that help manage their conditions.

2. DESIGNING A SOLUTION

Given the neurobehavioral nature of ADHD, this work explores the design of technology tools that implement behavioral management techniques (BMT) approaches to ADHD treatment. BMT covers a range of cognitive behavioral approaches such as cognitive training, and social skills training which have been identified to be particularly helpful when patients are unresponsive to medication, intolerant to medication, when symptoms are mild or where there are strong ethical or moral objections to medication [5]. Related work includes interventions where a video game gets harder when a player's brainwaves indicate waning attention[6], and a tool that utilizes skin conductance sensors to estimate stress and offer positive priming messages [7]. Other recent work in this area explore the use of smartphones, EEG and heart rate monitors to track ADHD behavior in children [6]. A drawback of these approaches is a lack of ubiquity and complexity of their setup that may limit their effectiveness especially within the workplace. These drawbacks can be addressed through the use of smartwatches (as highly ubiquitous and personal devices) while leveraging their multiple sensors such as heart rate, ambient conditions (light, pressure, UV) and proximity sensors [1]. To build the proposed solution, a user-centric design approach was adopted which began with a user survey (n=27, age 16-40), followed by artifact prototyping and usability tests (n = 10). Results from the survey showed that most of the individuals were highly interested in wearable devices and felt wearable apps were *more likely* to help them realize their mental health goals compared to smartphone or desktop apps. Participants also described their attention deficit issues mainly as an *inability to complete* extended tasks and *high levels of stress/anxiety.*

3. RESULTS

3.1 System Design
Based on the initial survey, the following app features were implemented.

Pomodoro: This feature implements the Pomodoro time management technique (see http://pomodorotechnique.com) which suggests tasks be broken down into 25 minutes of uninterrupted work sessions followed by 5 minute breaks. This technique has been acknowledged to help reduce procrastination, avoid distraction as well as engender flow and focus. In our implementation we abide by the tenets of the Pomodoro technique but allow for a flexible control of work and rest durations to accommodate users with diverse time schedule granularity. Haptic feedback (vibration cues) are also used to notify users of focus milestones and end of sessions.

Mindful Meditation: This feature provides timed visual and haptic cues which guide users on regulating their breathing pattern as a meditation session progresses. Users can adjust the inhale/exhale cycle duration for deeper meditation and vice versa as well as modify the length of the entire session. Users are then presented with their average heart rate before and after the session as an objective measure of its effectiveness. This instant feedback on the benefit/quality of the completed meditation session, coupled with a visualization of progress is designed to improve the user's motivation and effort.

Message Based Priming: Priming is implemented in two ways throughout *Foqus*. First, positive messages (e.g. Awesome job!) are displayed on successful completion of a Pomodoro or meditation session. Secondly, there is a dedicated Health Tips screen that provides mental health tips (adapted from the mental health foundation).

3.2 Usability Study Results

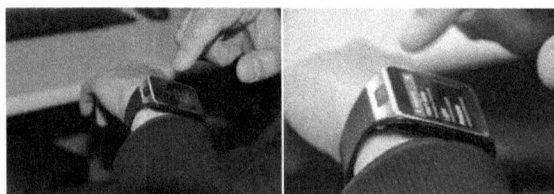

Figure 2: User test of *foqus* hi-fi prototype

To evaluate the usability of *Foqus*, a working prototype (see Figure 1) was developed and deployed on the Samsung Gear 2 smartwatch. A cognitive walkthrough was performed to ascertain functional completeness, followed by usability tests (n=10, age=21-30) with participants who indicated they struggled with attention deficiency in their daily work. Each was asked to perform at least one focus and one mindful meditation task over a 7-day period. The focus task involved the use of the Pomodoro feature in completing 2 hours of focused work while the meditation task involved completing at least 3 meditation sessions. They were then asked questions about the value of the app, its usability and to review the session results. Findings are summarized as follows:

i.) Users made less interaction mistakes on the interfaces where functions were disaggregated into multiple screens. E.g. rather than adding 4 buttons on the screen, a horizontal scroll menu with 4 distinct screens produced better results.

ii.) Context was an important factor for users in constructing the value of app functions. For example, a user mentioned "*This app would be most valuable to me ... especially during my yoga or meditation class*".

iii.) While there were concerns regarding the accuracy of the smart watch heart rate readings, users were excited about the *instant feedback* on the effect of their meditation session. A reduction in measured heartrate made users feel more satisfied with a session.

iv.) 8 users (80%) reported reduced levels of stress/anxiety after each meditation session.

v.) Inhale/exhale vibration cues helped users remain mindful during meditation session and was particularly amenable for sessions at their work desks.

4. CONCLUSION
In this work, a smartwatch app designed to help users improve their ability to focus on tasks (via a flexible implementation of the Pomodoro time management technique), reduce their anxiety via mindful meditation and improve their overall mental health via positive message priming was designed and implemented. The intervention provided in this study is put forward as a first step in designing assistive tools for adults with attention deficiency and stress challenges in the workplace. In conclusion, the choice of the wearable platform in this study is timely, given recent investments in smartwatch development from large technology companies like Google, Microsoft, Samsung, Asus, Apple as well as fashion and consumer electronics companies like Withings and Montblanc. As these firms push the envelope regarding the array and quality of sensors embedded within smartwatches, design direction from this work will likely become even more pertinent. Future work will entail a larger field study and in depth analysis of the efficacy of *Foqus*.

5. REFERENCES

[1] Dibia, V. An Affective, Normative and Functional Approach to Designing User Experiences for Wearables. *International Conference on Information Systems SIGHCI 2014 Proceedings*, (2014).

[2] de Graaf, R., Kessler, R.C., Fayyad, J., et al. The prevalence and effects of adult attention-deficit/hyperactivity disorder (ADHD) on the performance of workers: results from the WHO World Mental Health Survey Initiative. *Occupational and environmental medicine 65*, 12 (2008), 835–42.

[3] Pina, L., Rowan, K., Roseway, A., Johns, P., Hayes, G.R., and Czerwinsk, M. In Situ Cues for ADHD Parenting Strategies Using Mobile Technology. *International Conference on Pervasive Computing Technologies for Healthcare*, (2014).

[4] Pope, A.T. and Bogart, E.H. Extended Attention Span Training System: Video Game Neurotherapy for Attention Deficit Disorder. *Child Study Journal 26*, 1 (1995), 39–50.

[5] Safren, S.A., Otto, M.W., Sprich, S., Winett, C.L., Wilens, T.E., and Biederman, J. Cognitive-behavioral therapy for ADHD in medication-treated adults with continued symptoms. *Behaviour research and therapy 43*, 7 (2005), 831–42.

[6] Sonne, T., Obel, C., and Grønbæk, K. Designing Real Time Assistive Technologies. *Proceedings of the Annual Meeting of the Australian Special Interest Group for Computer Human Interaction on - OzCHI '15*, ACM Press (2015), 34–38.

Tactile Interface for Electric Wheelchair

Youssef Guedira[(1)], Liam Jordan[(2)], Clément Favey[(2)], René Farcy[(2)], Yacine Bellik[(1)]

LIMSI, CNRS
Univ. Paris-Sud,
Université Paris-Saclay
Orsay, France
<first name.last name>@limsi.fr

LAC
Univ. Paris-Sud,
Université Paris-Saclay
Orsay, France
<first name.last name>@u-psud.fr

ABSTRACT

In the framework of an augmented multimodal electric wheelchair for people with multiple disabilities, we propose a new user interface based on an Android application on a tablet to steer the wheelchair. The proposed system aims at overcoming some of the problems encountered with the traditional joystick interface like the involuntary arm extensions due to spasticity conditions. These often lead to unwanted movement of the chair and, in many cases, to accidents. The application uses different output modalities to allow the user keep his/her attention on the navigation task without having to visually focus on the tablet screen. We conducted some preliminary tests with some people with disabilities to engage them in the design process and get their feedback on the first prototype. The general impression was positive with insight on future improvements to the system.

Keywords

electric wheelchair; tactile interface; interaction modalities; design.

1. INTRODUCTION

Over the past few decades, joysticks have been widely used to steer electric wheelchairs. However, during our visits to care centers, some issues with the joystick interface have been reported to us by the occupational therapists. In the case of cerebral palsy, especially for kids, strong emotions may generate a sudden extension of the arms (spasticity). Thus, the user can accidentally push the joystick which moves the wheelchair and ends up hitting an obstacle causing injuries. Some users suffering from dystonia also find it difficult to grab the joystick. Therapeutic assistants often modify manually the shape of the joystick in order to fit the hand configuration of the person.

Different systems have been used to replace joysticks, some of them already commercialized. Some rely on occipital movement using either proximity sensors near the head or position an accelerometer on a headwear [1], others use a capacitive neckband to get the head movement [2]. However, such input modalities suffer from the interference of involuntary movements not meant for driving the wheelchair. Some researchers propose to double the movement if meant for driving but this becomes too tiring for the user and even dangerous when he/she needs an emergency stop. Brain-Computer Interfaces (BCI) have also been investigated for the control of the wheelchair. In [3], the authors use the EEG evoked potential to issue movement commands. However, this interaction technique is too slow and too intrusive to be practically used in daily life. Other BCI systems rely on

motor imagery [4] which is relatively fast but needs up to several months of user training. Some tactile interfaces have been proposed [5] but they only provide a visual feedback which requires one to constantly look at the touchpad.

The interface we propose comes in the framework of a multimodal, augmented wheelchair project for people with multiple disabilities [6]. At this stage, the interface allows the user to control the wheelchair through an Android application on a smartphone/tablet using input touch modality. It also provides multiple output modalities in order to help the user navigate without having to look directly at the interface. In later phases, we plan to integrate more input modalities and make the system adaptive to the user's handicap and environment conditions.

2. SYSTEM ARCHITECTURE

To control the wheelchair, we use an R-net Input/Output Module (IOM) that bypasses the control of the joystick. This allows us to control the wheelchair without interfering with its internal driving system[1]. To the input socket of the module, we connect a microcontroller. The exchange of data between the tablet and the microcontroller is achieved via a Bluetooth connection. Figure 1 gives an overview of this architecture.

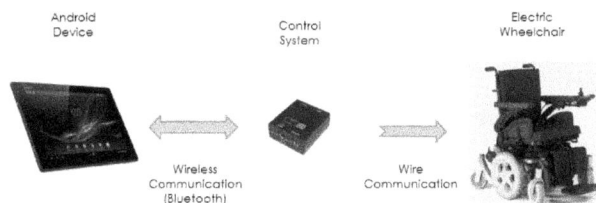

Figure 1. General architecture of the system

We implemented a bilateral communication between the Android device and the control system. This allows us to not only control the wheelchair but also to detect and handle communication errors like a sudden disconnection. In such cases, the wheelchair stops and waits for further action from the user. Using Bluetooth has many advantages since it is a lightweight solution and the user can even park the wheelchair in his/her room while lying in bed (at a reasonable distance). However, we can other communication channels straight wired communication if they are more efficient and more secure for a steering task.

The IOM offers different control modes. We started by implementing the control for the "switch mode". This mode allows to control eight directions for the movement: forward, backward, left, right as well as the diagonals. However, it does not allow a progressive control of the speed neither for the precise

ASSETS '16, October 23-26, 2016, Reno, NV, USA
ACM   978-1-4503-4124-
0/16/10.http://dx.doi.org/10.1145/2982142.2982189

---

[1] Furthermore, this lets us keep the wheelchair warranty that allows it to be driven by a person with disabilities.

direction angle. These features are only available in the "analog mode" that we are currently working on.

3. SYSTEM DESIGN

3.1 Input/Output Modalities

The Android application gives the user an interface to control the wheelchair offering the same functionalities as the joystick interface. We designed 4 different configurations, depending on 2 parameters: geometrical shape and number of directions. The geometrical shape of the interface can be circular or rectangular, while the number of directions can be 4 or 8. Figure 2 shows these different design choices.

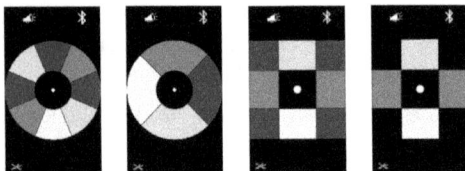

Figure 2. Different interface design choices

A tablet is intrinsically a visual device. However, we needed to add some feedback mechanisms that let the user position his/her fingers on the interface and control the wheelchair without looking directly at the tablet to keep the his/her visual focus on the environment. Hence, we added a 3D printed cover to the tablet to provide a haptic feedback. This cover delimits the areas of the different directions along with a bump on the central neutral zone. The latter is a little bit more elevated than the rest of the cover so it can be sensed by the user without touching the screen. Figure 3 shows the cover 3D model and the tablet wearing it.

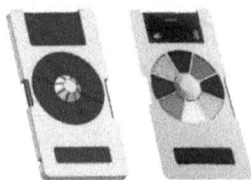

Figure 3. Tablet with cover for haptic feedback

We also added vibrations and beeps when the user touches a movement command. In addition, we wanted to use a visual feedback by displaying, on the upper black background, white blinking arrows that indicate the current movement direction. While the user can focus his/her central visual field on the road, the lateral vison can still pick up this piece of information since it is sensitive to luminosity and to movement [7].

3.2 Preliminary Evaluation

We organized few sessions where we gave the first prototype to 5 persons who use electric wheelchairs on a daily basis, and they used the tablet to control the wheelchair we are working on. The goal was to see how users interact with the system, how they learn to use it and how they perceive the different output modalities. After they got familiar with the interface, we gave them a System Usability Scale [8] to fill. We calculated a score of 85.5% which indicates a promising acceptance by our users. Also, these sessions gave us insight on different points. First, the "switch mode" was too abrupt for most users. It made them a little bit hesitant in the driving task. Thus, implementing the "analog mode" is our current priority. Second, not all users wanted full control over the 8 directions. Some users preferred having only

the 4 primary ones. Finally, the tactile interface can present a risk of accidental activation. Although this has not come up in our experiments (our users had full control over their hand movements, the experimentation time was limited...), we are aware of this issue and we are still working to address it.

4. CONCLUSION AND PERSPECTIVES

In this project, we introduce a system to control electric wheelchairs using an Android application. The application sends controlling commands to a microcontroller via Bluetooth. Then, using an IOM system, these commands get transferred to the internal driving system of the wheelchair. We have designed and implemented different touch interfaces that resolved classical joystick problems caused by spasticity and dystonia. We have conducted some preliminary tests with real users that provide encouraging results. At the same time, we are working on getting full control over the wheelchair movement to give a natural driving to the user. In later phases of the project, we plan to integrate other interaction modalities and make the system more adaptive to the specifics of the user's handicap. We also envision the tablet being not only a means of control of the wheelchair but also a means of accessing information and/or controlling other objects (light, TV ...) especially in a connected environment.

5. ACKNOWLEDGMENTS

We thank Tarbaya Video association and Ellen Poidatz foundation for facilitating the contact with real users/assistants to test our system and give us constructive feedback.

6. REFERENCES

[1] Pajkanović, A. and Dokić, B. 2013. Wheelchair Control by Head motion. *Serbian Journal of Electrical Engineering*, *10*, (1), 135-151.

[2] Hirch, M., Cheng, J., Reiss, A., Sundholm, M., Lukowicz, P. and Amft, O. Hands-free gesture control with a capacitive textile neckband. *Proc. of the 2014 ACM International Symposium on Wearable Computers*, (Seattle, WA,USA 2014), ACM New York, NY, USA, 55-58.

[3] Chen, T. L., Zeng, Q., and Ang Jr., M. H. Controlling a Wheelchair Indoors Using Thought. *IEEE Intelligent Systems, 22* (2), 18-24.

[4] Carlson, T. and del R. Millan, J. Brain–Controlled Wheelchairs: A Robotic Architecture. *IEEE Robotics and Automation Magazine*, *20*, (1), 65 – 73.

[5] Chen, T. S., Kuo, Y. C., Syu, Y. S. and Kuo, C. H. A Touch-Based Wheelchair Control Interface: Concept and Implementation. *Applied Mechanics and Materials*, *300-301*(1), 1471-1474.

[6] Favey, C., Villanueva, J., Zogaghi, A., Jordan, L., Guedira, Y., Bellik, Y. and Farcy, R. Guidage de Fauteuils Roulants pour Polyhandicapés par Profilométrie Optique Active. in *Handicap '16*, (Paris, France, 2016), IFRATH, 113-118.

[7] Legge, G. E. and Kersten, D. Contrast discrimination in peripheral vision. *Journal of the Optical Society of America A, 4* (8), 1594-1598.

[8] Brooke, J. SUS: a 'quick and dirty' usability scale. *Usability Evaluation in Industry, Chapter 21*, ed: P. W. Jordan, Taylor and Francis. Abingdon. UK,1996.

Facade: Auto-generating Tactile Interfaces to Appliances

Anhong Guo[1], Jeeeun Kim[2], Xiang 'Anthony' Chen[1], Tom Yeh[2], Scott E. Hudson[1],
Jennifer Mankoff[1], Jeffrey P. Bigham[1]

[1] Human-Computer Interaction Institute, Carnegie Mellon University, Pittsburgh, PA, USA
[2] Department of Computer Science, University of Colorado Boulder, Boulder, CO, USA

{anhongg, xiangche, scott.hudson, jmankoff, jbigham}@cs.cmu.edu,
{jeeeun.kim, tom.yeh}@colorado.edu

ABSTRACT

Digital keypads have proliferated on common appliances, from microwaves and refrigerators to printers and remote controls. For blind people, such interfaces are inaccessible. We conducted a formative study with 6 blind people which demonstrated a need for custom designs for tactile labels without dependence on sighted assistance. To address this need, we introduce *Facade*—a crowdsourced fabrication pipeline to make physical interfaces accessible by adding a 3D printed augmentation of tactile buttons overlaying the original panel. Blind users capture a photo of an inaccessible interface with a standard marker for absolute measurements using perspective transformation. Then this image is sent to multiple crowd workers, who work in parallel to quickly label and describe elements of the interface. These labels are then used to generate 3D models for a layer of tactile and pressable buttons that fits over the original controls. Users can customize the shape and labels of the buttons using a web interface. Finally, a consumer-grade 3D printer fabricates the layer, which is then attached to the interface using adhesives. Such fabricated overlay is an inexpensive ($10) and more general solution to making physical interfaces accessible.

Categories and Subject Descriptors

H.5.2 [**Information interfaces and presentation**]: User Interfaces - *Input devices and strategies*; K.4.2 [**Computers and Society**]: Social Issues - *Assistive technologies*

Keywords

Blind users; accessibility; crowdsourcing; personal fabrication.

1. INTRODUCTION

If a blind person could independently and inexpensively create a tactile interface to any appliance that they use regularly, touchpads on appliances from microwaves and refrigerators to printers to remote controls could be made accessible. A tool like this is needed because appliances with inaccessible interfaces are proliferating. The task of creating an appropriate tactile overlay currently requires sighted help and labeling device that can print embossed labels. However sighted assistance is not always available; and labels must be small enough to fit on or near the button. A more complete solution such as a tactile overlay would require detailed knowledge about the size and location of buttons in addition to labels. Our work addresses this by providing an end-to-end automated solution that can be done completely independently, and costs less than $10 per appliance.

Several projects have focused on augmenting existing interfaces for Internet of Things or accessibility for blind people, such as [3]. These systems require specific information of the interface to generate augmentation of the interface, and require the end user to design and instrument. Recent advances in consumer-grade 3D printers and do-it-yourself movement have changed the audience of 3D printing. It has already been established as a tool that addresses wide differences of needs for assistive technology [2]. Transcribing visual information into touchable tactile artifacts with 3D printer for non-visual access has been proposed in various domains. However, most approaches still require much initial transcription work from sighted assistants. Crowdsourcing is good at providing knowledge to arbitrary interfaces to be identified and augmented by tactile interface. A number of crowd-powered systems have been developed to make visual information accessible to blind people [1]. In these approaches, blind users send photos and audio questions to receive assistance from crowd workers.

To identify the existing challenges of using inaccessible interfaces of home and work appliances, we conducted a formative study with six blind participants. We first went to the home of a blind person, and observed how she cooked a meal and used home appliances. We then invited her and five other participants to the lab, and asked them to describe their home appliance usage, whether these appliances were accessible, and the strategies they employed to use these appliances without assistance. We identified four unique design requirements for a system to augment physical interfaces for non-visual access: *(i)* tactile labels must enable blind users to operate appliances without sighted assistance, *(ii)* blind users should not need to identify the original interface and design the augmentation themselves, *(iii)* the augmented labels should be customizable to address individual needs, and *(iv)* the system must support diverse appliances with a lot variations and distinctive features.

2. FACADE

We introduce *Facade*, a crowdsourced fabrication pipeline to make physical interfaces accessible by adding a 3D printed layer of tactile buttons overlaying the original panel (Figure 1). When a blind person encounters an inaccessible interface for the first time, he captures a photo of an inaccessible interface with a standard marker for absolute measurements using perspective transformation (Figure 1AB). Within a few minutes, crowd workers mark the

ASSETS '16, October 23-26, 2016, Reno, NV, USA
ACM 978-1-4503-4124-0/16/10.
http://dx.doi.org/10.1145/2982142.2982187

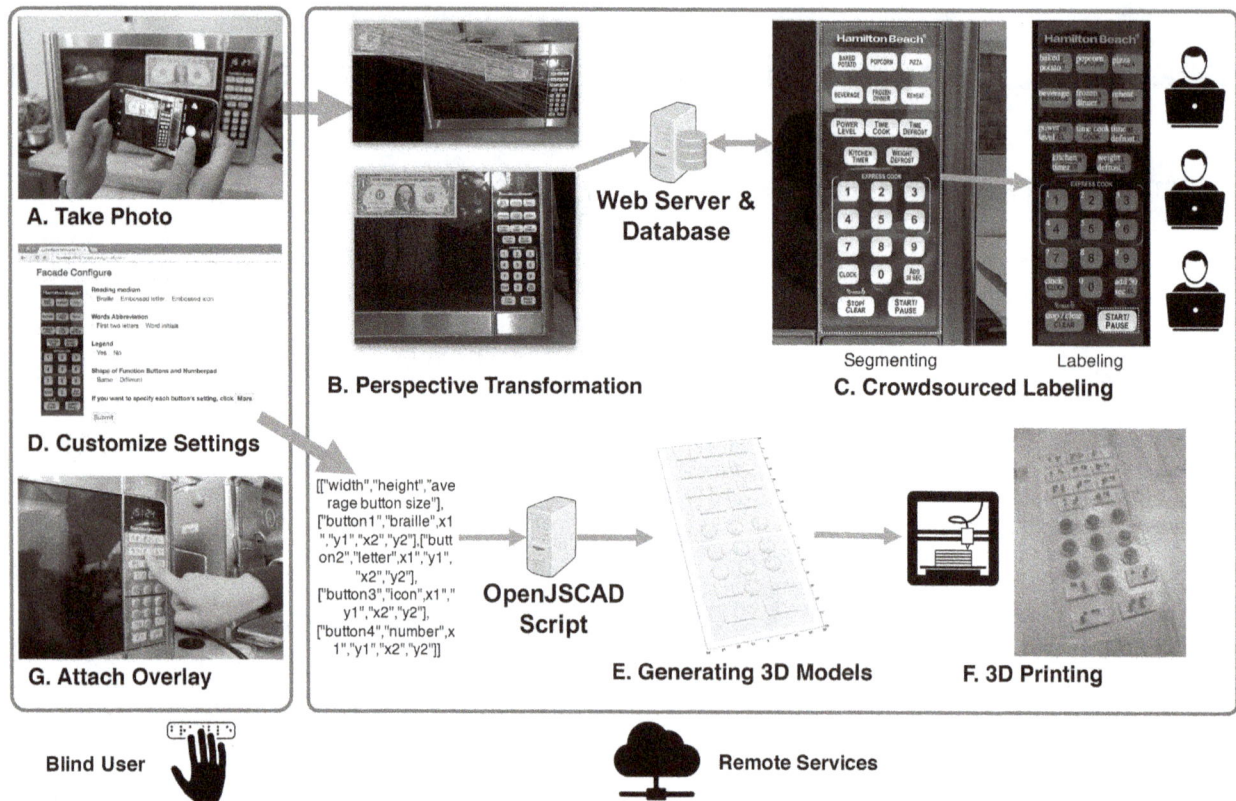

Figure 1: Facade takes user's photo to capture physical appliance's interface, acquires labels from crowd workers, and produces 3D printed tactile buttons overlaying the original panel.

Figure 2: Facade is a crowdsourced fabrication pipeline that enables blind people to make flat physical interfaces accessible by independently producing a 3D-printed overlay of tactile buttons. We demonstrate example applications including microwaves, refrigerators, and printers.

layout of the interface, annotate its elements (*e.g.*, buttons or other controls), and describe each element (Figure 1C). These labels are then used to generate the 3D models of a layer of tactile and pressable buttons matching the original controls (Figure 1E), which the blind users can customize the shape and labels of the buttons using a web interface (Figure 1D). Finally, an off-the-shelf 3D printer can be used to fabricate the layer (Figure 1F). The printed button facade is designed to be easily attached to its appliance using adhesives (Figure 1G). Although consumer-grade 3D printers might not be readily available to blind people at home, many print services are available from which a print can be mail-ordered. In addition, we can expect that consumer-grade printers will continue to improve in robustness. Even with the addition of mail-order costs, our approach is a cheap ($10 from a service such as 3D Hubs) and more accessible alternative to current solutions. As shown in Figure 2, Facade supports a wide range of interfaces, including microwaves, refrigerators, and printers. We fabricated tactile layers using different material settings and user customization settings.

3. REFERENCES

[1] J. P. Bigham, C. Jayant, H. Ji, G. Little, A. Miller, R. C. Miller, R. Miller, A. Tatarowicz, B. White, S. White, et al. Vizwiz: nearly real-time answers to visual questions. In *Proceedings of the 23nd annual ACM symposium on User interface software and technology*, pages 333–342. ACM, 2010.

[2] E. Buehler, S. Branham, A. Ali, J. J. Chang, M. K. Hofmann, A. Hurst, and S. K. Kane. Sharing is caring: Assistive technology designs on thingiverse. In *Proceedings of the 33rd Annual ACM Conference on Human Factors in Computing Systems*, pages 525–534. ACM, 2015.

[3] R. Ramakers, F. Anderson, T. Grossman, and G. Fitzmaurice. Retrofab: A design tool for retrofitting physical interfaces using actuators, sensors and 3d printing. In *Proceedings of the 34rd Annual ACM Conference on Human Factors in Computing Systems*. ACM, 2016.

An Accessible Blocks Language: Work in Progress

Varsha Koushik and Clayton Lewis
Department of Computer Science
University of Colorado, Boulder Colorado USA
vasr6678@colorado.edu, clayton.lewis@colorado.edu

ABSTRACT

Block languages are extensively used to introduce programming to children. They replace the complex and error prone syntax of textual languages with simple shape cues that show how program elements can be combined. In their present form, blind learners cannot use them, because they rely on graphical presentation of code, and mouse interactions. We are working on a nonvisual blocks language called Pseudospatial Blocks (PB), that supports program creation using keyboard commands with synthetic speech output. It replaces visual shape cues for language syntax, the key feature of block languages, with filtering of program elements by syntactic category.

CCS Concepts

• **Human-centered computing~Accessibility systems and tools**   • Human-centered computing~Auditory feedback   • **Software and its engineering~Visual languages**

Keywords

Accessible Interfaces; Barriers to programming; Learning to program

1. VISUAL PROGRAMMING ENVIROMENTS ARE INACCCESSIBLE TO BLIND USERS

Block languages like Scratch, Snap, MIT App Inventor, Microsoft Block Editor for BBC, and many more are among the most popular platforms for introducing children to the world of programming. Program elements are presented as blocks, which have tabs and sockets that show how they can be fit together, so that learners don't have to master the complex syntax of textual languages. However, non-sighted users cannot see these shape cues (nor can they perform the drag and drop mouse interactions used to assemble the blocks.)

A number of researchers have responded to the need to offer the potential conceptual benefits of block languages in a form accessible to blind learners. A team at Google is creating Accessible Blockly, (https://blockly-demo.appspot.com/static/demos/accessible /index.html), a system that presents blocks and blocks programs as HTML structures that can be read by a screen reader, a tool with which many blind users are already familiar. Stephanie Ludi [4] has proposed a related

ASSETS '16, October 23-26, 2016, Reno, NV, USA
ACM 978-1-4503-4124-0/16/10.
http://dx.doi.org/10.1145/2982142.2982150

approach, also based on Blockly, which will also support visual access, an advantage in many learning situations where blind and sighted learners work together. The Bootstrap system (http://www.bootstrapworld.org/) is being extended to support a blocks language made accessible by a screen reader (Emmanuel Schanzer, personal communication, July 15, 2016). Richard Ladner (personal communication, June 1, 2016) has proposed using a touchscreen to permit learners to explore and operate on blocks by touch. Like Ludi's work, these approaches may allow the same system to be used by blind and sighted learners. There are also projects aimed at coding with tangible, physical blocks; see e.g. http://cubescoding.com/, https://www.primotoys.com/, and https://projectbloks.withgoogle.com.

2. PSEUDOSPATIALITY – BEYOND THE SCREEN READER

Our approach to creating an accessible blocks language is based on the ideas of T.V. Raman, who suggests that many visual tasks can be replaced by nonvisual ones ([6], [7]; see also [2].) In Raman's thinking, one should create nonvisual presentations of content that work well in themselves, rather than seeking to make visual representations accessible, as a screen reader does.

Screen reader navigation is serial and hierarchical. Commands are provided to read all material, or to read only elements at a given level, or to skip to elements of a specified type, which provides some flexibility, but the underlying structure is still constrained. Some designers of applications for blind users have moved outside this structure to support navigation in a virtual two dimensional space, with operations provided that move right to left or up and down (for example, the TWBlue Twitter client, http://twblue.es/).

A navigation scheme can be *pseudospatial*, rather than simply spatial, if the geometry of movement is distorted. We describe here Pseudospatial Blocks (PB), a blocks language presentation based on arrow key navigation. In PB a toolbox of blocks is to the "left" of a workspace. The blocks in both areas, and parts within blocks, are arranged "vertically". The arrangement is pseudospatial in that a step "left" from a block in the workspace will reach the same location in the toolbox, regardless of the "vertical" position of the block in the workspace, and there are other distortions of actual space. Lewis [3] presented work on a nonvisual dataflow language with a similar liberal use of two-dimensional space.

Schiff and colleagues (see e.g. [9]) have shown that people navigating virtual environments have no greater difficulty learning environments that are distorted or impossible geometrically or even topologically than realistic ones (in a topologically impossible environment one can move from the outside to the inside of a closed contour without crossing the contour, for example.) We conjecture that distortions in the geometry of PB will not be an issue.

3. SHAPE CONSTRAINTS IN PB

As mentioned earlier, the distinctive feature of blocks languages is the use of block shape to indicate how blocks can legally be assembled. For example, a block representing a statement has a different shape from a block representing an expression. Statement blocks can fit together to make sequences of statements, but expression blocks cannot; similarly, expression blocks can fit into holes representing the inputs to operations, while statement blocks cannot fit there. How can these constraints on block placement be handled in a system with no visual presentation?

In PB, one constructs a program by selecting an insertion point, where a new block is to be placed. The system then prompts the user to select the desired block from a list of candidates, in the toolbox of available blocks. But the list of candidates is filtered, so that only legal candidates can be selected. For example, in the situations just compared above, if one selects an insertion point in a sequence of statements, only statement blocks are presented as candidates, while selecting an insertion point where an expression is legal gives only expression blocks as candidates.

Arguably, this selection scheme has advantages over shape-based constraints, in two ways. First, shapes have difficulty indicating when two or more different kinds of blocks can be used. For example, in Scratch, blocks that represent numeric quantities are shown as rounded shapes, and character strings are rectangles. But a rounded shape can legally be placed in a rectangular hole, even though it does not "fit". The numeric quantity is converted to a string, in such a situation, but there is no visual cue that this will happen until it is tried. Using filtered selection, this is no problem: all legal blocks are offered as candidates.

A second issue with shapes is that each kind of block that has distinctive fit constraints has to have a distinctive shape. But it seems that only so many shapes are workable, so some distinctions among blocks may go unmarked. For example, in the demo language at https://blockly-demo.appspot.com/static/demos/code/index.html, list blocks and number blocks have the same shape, but some list operations cannot be applied to numbers, and so number blocks will not always fit where their shape suggests. Distinctive colors are used for list and number blocks, which helps, but only for sighted users.

This situation is unproblematic for filtered selection. For example, PB has blocks representing sounds and numbers; in many situations only one or the other can be inserted, and the filtered selection process offers only legal candidates.

4. IMPLEMENTATION AND STATUS

The implementation of PB is based on the Blockly library (https://developers.google.com/blockly/; [1]), an extremely flexible and widely used platform for creating blocks languages. Blockly supports an XML representation of blocks programs, and can generate code for these in a number of languages. This support makes it easy to create new interfaces like Accessible Blockly or PB. PB is implemented as a Web application that builds a JSON (JavaScript Object Notation) representation of programs, converts this to XML, and then uses Blockly to generate JavaScript code. PB communicates with users via synthetic speech; it will also be possible support screen reader users by using an ARIA active region to generate responses via the screen reader.

4.1 Status of PB

PB supports a small number of statement types, for arithmetic, control structure, and sound. Sounds and operations on them are supported by two kinds of blocks. First there are sound statement blocks that simply play fixed, associated sounds. As statements, these blocks can be formed into sequences to play desired melodies. Second, there are sound expression blocks, that represent sounds (as lists of samples) but do not play them; they are played by providing them as input to a "play sound" statement block. Sound expression blocks support generating musical notes, attenuating or amplifying a sound (by multiplying the samples by a given number), concatenating two sounds, or mixing them, that is, playing the sounds simultaneously. As discussed earlier, the filtered selection mechanism enforces that (for example) only sounds and not numbers can be mixed. We believe PB is nearing readiness for user testing, which is obviously crucial. We expect many changes to be driven by user input.

5. ACKNOWLEDGMENTS

We thank Sina Bahram for telling us about TWBlue, and for suggestions for structuring pseudospatial interfaces; Richard Ladner for sharing his proposal for tactile support for blocks languages; Neil Fraser and Madeeha Ghori of Google for their help in our use of Blockly, and for sharing their work on Accessible Blockly; Ben Shapiro and Annie Kelly for advice on platforms; and Andy Stefik and Brian Harvey for convening a workshop on accessibility of block languages at MIT in April, 2015, that provided the inspiration for our work.

6. REFERENCES

[1] Fraser, N. (2015). Ten things we've learnt from Blockly. *In Blocks and Beyond Workshop (Blocks and Beyond)*, 2015 IEEE (pp. 49-50). IEEE.

[2] Lewis, C. (2013). Pushing the Raman Principle. *In Proceedings of the 10th International Cross-Disciplinary Conference on Web Accessibility* (W4A'13). ACM, New York, NY, USA, Article 18, 4 pages.

[3] Lewis, C. (2014). Work in Progress Report: Nonvisual Visual Programing. In B. duBoulay and J.Good (Eds) Proc. *PPIG 2014 Psychology of Programming Annual Conference*, 25th Anniversary Event. Brighton, England, 25th-27th June 2014.

[4] Ludi, S. (2015). Position paper: Towards making block-based programming accessible to blind users. *Blocks and Beyond Workshop (Blocks and Beyond)*, 2015 IEEE, Atlanta, GA, pp 67-69

[5] Maloney, J., Resnick, M., Rusk, N., Silverman, B., & Eastmond, E. (2010). *The scratch programming language and environment. ACM Transactions on Computing Education (TOCE)*, 10(4), 16.

[6] Raman, T.V. (1996) Emacsspeak—A speech interface. *In Proceedings of the SIGCHI Conference on Human Factors in Computing Systems* (CHI'96), Michael J. Tauber (Ed.). ACM, New York, NY, USA, 66-71.

[7] Raman, T.V. and Gries, D. (1997.) Documents mean more than just paper! *Mathematical and Computer Modelling*, Volume 26, Issue 1, July, 45-53.

[8] Zetzsche, C., Wolter, J., Galbraith, C., & Schill, K. (2009). Representation of space: image-like or sensorimotor?. *Spatial Vision*, 22(5), 409-424.

Demonstration: Screen Reader Support for a Complex Interactive Science Simulation

Taliesin L. Smith
Faculty of Design, Inclusive Design
MDes. Program, OCAD University
Toronto, Ontario, Canada
talilief@gmail.com

Clayton Lewis
Department of Computer Science
University of Colorado Boulder
Boulder, Colorado, USA
Clayton.Lewis@colorado.edu

Emily B. Moore
Department of Physics
University of Colorado Boulder
Boulder, Colorado, USA
Emily.Moore@colorado.edu

ABSTRACT

Interactive simulations are increasingly important in science education, yet most are inaccessible to blind learners. We demonstrate an accessible version of a simulation, *Balloons and Static Electricity*, that illustrates responses to key challenges in providing screen reader support: the need to describe unpredictable sequences of events, the manipulation of objects that act as both controls and displays, and the management of descriptions of changes in the state of the simulation as well as of the state of the interactive object, itself. Meeting these challenges requires extending current practices for verbal description of visual interactive content.

Keywords

Description; Accessibility; Visual Impairment; Usability Study; STEM Education; Interactive Science Simulation; PhET Simulation

1. INTRODUCTION

The availability of cheap, fast computers, with excellent graphics capability, and appropriate software tools, has led to the creation of large numbers of interactive simulations ("sims"), aimed at helping students understand concepts in many fields. Many are widely used; for example, the sims by the PhET Interactive Simulations project (http://phet.colorado.edu/) are run over 75 millions of times a year. But these sims use dynamic visual representations of science concepts, and mouse- and touch-driven interaction, that present barriers for learners who cannot see.

Figure 1 shows two screen shots from the *Balloons and Static Electricity* sim that we demonstrate. It allows a learner to rub a balloon on a sweater, and observe the rearrangement of electrostatic charges that result, as well as the consequences (for example, the balloon being attracted to the sweater or to the wall).

A number of approaches to making sims like this accessible can and should be explored. It may be possible to use dynamic tactile displays (though the small-scale electrostatic charges would be a challenge). There may be other nonvisual and engaging ways to convey the underlying content of the sim, such as the text-based command-response interactions seen in text adventure games.

The approach we demonstrate meets two constraints arising from the pedagogical use of the PhET sims. First, it must not require

ASSETS'16, October 23–26, 2016, Reno, NV, USA
ACM 978-1-4503-4124-0/16/10.
DOI: http://dx.doi.org/10.1145/2982142.2982154

hardware not widely available in classrooms today. Second, the accessibility features must be incorporated in the same sim used by sighted learners.

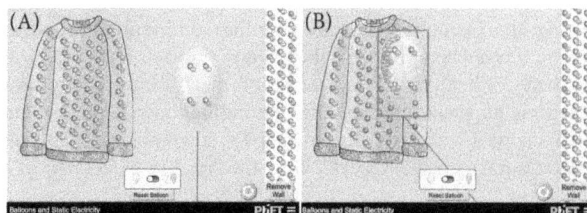

Figure 1. PhET Sim, *Balloons and Static Electricity*. (A) Sim on page load. (B) Negatively charged Balloon sticking to positively charged Sweater with keyboard focus (pink outline).

2. APPROACH

To meet these constraints, we designed and implemented 1) infrastructure, the *Parallel Document Object Model (PDOM)*, to support communication between the sim, a web browser, and a screen reader 2) keyboard navigation and interactions, and 3) descriptions to be read by the screen reader.

The PDOM is a data structure (built in Hypertext Markup Language, HTML) that represents the objects in the sim, such as the balloon, in a form that can be accessed by a screen reader program. This had to be added because, like most such programs, the preexisting sim on which we are building used graphical representations that cannot be accessed by a screen reader.

With the PDOM as an invisible layer on top of the visual sim, a blind learner can navigate much of the sim using familiar keyboard interactions and screen reader commands. However, some interactions required a customized approach. We designed custom hot keys to move the balloon quickly to important areas within the sim and to drag and rub it against other sim objects.

3. DESCRIPTIONS

The remaining design and implementation work focused on the descriptions to be read by the screen reader while the simulation is in use. An active range of work [1,2,3,6,7] on making diverse types of static and interactive science content accessible through the use of natural language is ongoing. In the iterative design and evaluation of our sim, we found that we needed to go beyond the recent guidance available for simple interactive scientific graphics [4]. We describe here the new challenges we encountered, and our approaches to them.

3.1 Unpredictable event sequences.

When describing a video, the describer knows the sequence of events, and can devise a description that works well for that fixed sequence. In an interactive sim, one knows the events that may occur, but not the sequence in which they will occur. This requires that descriptions be written modularly, so that event descriptions are intelligible when reordered and recombined.

The descriptions we demonstrate are adequate in this respect. But we believe more sophisticated methods should be developed, in which redundancy is reduced by making descriptions history dependent: the description of a second occurrence of an event should be shorter than the description of the first.

3.2 Objects as controls and displays.

Existing guidance on interactive diagrams [4] supports situations in which a learner controls the visual by setting parameters, e.g., by using a slider. While many interactive sims include this kind of control, other kinds of interaction are common. In our case, the balloon poses special challenges. It behaves somewhat like a control, in that moving it changes the state of the sim. But its role cannot be reduced to controlling a simple parameter, because rubbing the balloon on the sweater has different effects from rubbing it elsewhere. Further, the balloon also acts as a display, in two ways. First, visual indicators of electrostatic charges are shown on its surface. Second, if the balloon is released, it may move on its own, as it is attracted to other objects. Thus the balloon is not a control separate from the sim, but in fact part of it.

These complications required us to provide three distinct forms of description for the balloon. First, as a learner explores the simulation by navigating the PDOM, they will encounter the balloon as an object in the sim, and need a description of it. This includes the amount of charge on the balloon, its position, and its effect on nearby objects. Second, when the learner wants to interact with the balloon, they need a description of how to use it. Since the balloon is not a standard HTML control, users would not be familiar with the drag and release interaction from prior experience. Third, when the learner acts on the balloon they receive a description of the effects of the action, discussed next.

3.3 Describing states and state changes.

The action of rubbing the balloon on the sweater has two effects. First, it produces a *new state of the sim*: the distribution of charges after the motion is different from what it was before. Second, it *makes something happen*: negative charges move from the sweater to the balloon. These two aspects are integrated for sighted learners: they immediately see the new distribution of the negative charges as they disappear from sweater and instantly appear on the balloon. Blind learners see neither of these things.

We demonstrate descriptions that distinguish these aspects of the sim, using descriptions provided in two ways. The current state of any object, for example the charge on the balloon or the sweater, is given by a description as part of the element representing the object in the PDOM. The learner can access the current state information by navigating the PDOM. In addition, when the learner takes an action that makes something happen, they receive a description of the effect of the action, immediately. Changes to both types of descriptions are announced to the learner via ARIA Live Regions, a technical means of directing a screen reader to read out a change in the sim that is outside the student's current reading location (i.e., cursor focus). Thus both types of descriptions, the *new states* of the objects affected by the action, and the description of the change (i.e., *what happened*), are provided. The newly announced state information is the changed description available in an element in the PDOM. It is announced to connect the learner's actions with the changes. This state information can be reviewed or listened to again by navigating the PDOM. The description of the change; however, only makes

sense at the time of interaction. Thus, it is stored as hidden content in the PDOM to prevent hearing it out of context.

4. DISCUSSION

Existing research and resources provide very useful strategies for describing static content and simple interactive graphics, and are applicable to many aspects of more complex scenarios. But we found challenges unique to complex interactive simulations.

Our response to these challenges, as demonstrated was to:

- Create modular descriptions that can be reordered to accommodate unpredictable event sequences.

- Provide differentiated descriptions for objects that serve both as controls and as displays in the simulation.

- Recognize the need to provide separately (a) access to the current state of the objects, (b) access to new state information when actions are taken, and (c) descriptions of changes caused by actions.

We have explored in a limited way how point (c) might be supported by sonification [5], using sound together with language to convey information about dynamic processes like movement. This is one example of further work we and the research community can pursue, to increase accessibility of this important class of educational tool.

5. ACKNOWLEDGMENTS

Funding for this work provided by the National Science Foundation (DRL #1503439), the University of Colorado Boulder, and the William and Flora Hewlett Foundation.

6. REFERENCES

[1] Demir, S. 2008. TAIG: Textually Accessible Information Graphics. In *Proceedings of the 10th International ACM SIGACCESS Conference on Computers and Accessibility* (Halifax, Canada, October 2008) 313–314. DOI: 10.1145/1414471.1414555

[2] Diagram Center. 2015. Image Description Guidelines, *DIAGRAM Center*, 2015. [Online]. Retrieved February 9, 2016 from http://diagramcenter.org/table-of-contents-2.html

[3] Gerino, A. et al. 2014. MathMelodies: Inclusive Design of a Didactic Game to Practice Mathematics. In *Proceedings of the 14th Computers Helping People with Special Needs International Conference* (Paris, France, July 2014) 564–571. DOI: 10.1007/978-3-319-08596-8_88

[4] Keane, K. & Laverent, C. 2014. Interactive Scientific Graphics Recommended Practices for Verbal Description. Technical Report. Wolfram Research, Inc., Champaign, IL.

[5] Kramer, G. et al. 2010. Sonification Report: Status of the Field and Research Agenda.

[6] Smith, T. L., Lewis, C., & Moore, E. B. 2016. A Balloon, a Sweater, and a Wall: Developing Design Strategies for Accessible User Experiences with a Science Simulation. In *Proceedings of the 10th International Conference on Universal Access in Human-Computer Interaction* (Toronto, Canada, July 2016) 147–158. DOI: 10.1007/978-3-319-40238-3_15

[7] Sorge, V., Lee, M. & Wilkinson, S. 2015. End-to-end Solution for Accessible Chemical Diagrams. In *Proceedings of the 12th Web for All Conference* (Florence, Italy, May 2015) 1–10. DOI: 10.1145/2745555.2746667

TranslatAble: Giving Individuals with Complex Communication Needs a Voice through Speech and Gesture Recognition

Meredith Moore
Center for Cognitive Ubiquitous Computing
Arizona State University
Tempe, AZ, USA
Mkmoore7@asu.edu

Sethuraman Panchanathan
Center for Cognitive Ubiquitous Computing
Arizona State University
Tempe, AZ, USA
panch@asu.edu

ABSTRACT
This paper presents the design of TranslatAble, a new Augmentative and Alternative Communication system. Taking advantage of the convenience and mobility of modern smartphones, TranslatAble allows individuals with complex communication needs—specifically individuals with severe dysarthria or individuals who primarily use non-sign language gestures—to build their own system of communication through speech or gesture input. This system uses a machine learning model—specifically dynamic time warping—to match the user's input to their unique dictionary to help them be understood by their communication partner. TranslatAble is highly flexible and person-centered, which allows it to adapt to fit the unique needs of each user's unique communication needs. We expect this novel device to enable individuals with complex communication needs to interact with a larger social circle. This may help decrease feelings of loneliness and increase self-confidence, self-esteem, and independence, as well as help maintain strong relationships outside of the user's support network.

Keywords
Augmentative and Alternative Communication; AAC Device; Gesture Recognition; Speech Recognition; Complex Communication Needs

1. INTRODUCTION
Augmentative and Alternative Communication (AAC) professionals generally define communication as the ability for a person to establish meaning with another person or group[1]. This joint establishment of meaning is fundamental to most aspects of life. Individuals who have complex communication requirements may not have the communication skills necessary to meet all of their needs. Namely, an individual's ability to communicate effectively affects their ability to build and maintain relationships, make choices, and participate in everyday life. These components are all incredibly important for quality of life.

There are two main use cases that we will focus on for the purposes of this paper. In the first use case, the user is an individual who does not have speech, and communicates primarily through gestures. There have been a number of studies

that attempt to solve the problem described in case 1, but this body of work is generally focused solely on sign language translation. These solutions are divided by the type of data they use to classify the signs, but some of the common methods are to use sensor gloves or computer vision to classify hand gestures[2,4,5]. While data gloves have been used to achieve promising gesture recognition results, they have also shown to be too invasive and expensive for the everyday user. The main drawback of computer vision methods is that they prevent the user from being mobile. While both computer vision and sensor gloves may eventually work well to translate sign language, there also exists a group of people who may not have the cognitive ability to learn sign language. However, this group still uses concise and repeatable gestures to communicate. The only translation option available to these individuals currently is to draw a line down the middle of a notebook and describe the gesture on one side, and the translation on the other. While this rudimentary solution has helped many people communicate, the technology exists today to create a system that will recognize these gestures in real time to translate these individual's unique communication systems to their interaction partners.

In the second use case, the user is an individual who has speech, but their speech may be difficult for communication partners to understand. This area is a very underdeveloped field of research, but there is one app, Talkitt, that has yet to be released, which has a similar goal of giving individuals with speech difficulties a voice of their own by translating their speech to a more easily understood computer generated voice.

2. PROPOSED SOLUTION
To fill this gap in user needs and provide a pervasive and ubiquitous computing experience for individuals with complex communication needs, we developed a novel smartphone-based AAC device that translates both gestures and speech in real time.

2.1 Goals
We have three goals for the design of the application:

Pervasive/Non-Invasive Interface: The solution should not interfere with the user's daily activities.

Real-Time Accurate Translation: Communication is a real-time activity which necessitates fast response times. A timing delay of 0.1 s is considered 'instantaneous,' while a delay of 0.2 s is noticeable by the user, but still acceptable. Any response time greater than 1 s needs to be acknowledged as processing[3].

Facilitate Communication: The device should enable the user to easily facilitate communications with people around them.

ASSETS'16, October 24–26, 2016, Reno, NV, United States.
Copyright 2010 ACM 1-58113-000-0/00/0010 …$15.00.
DOI: http://dx.doi.org/10.1145/12345.67890

2.2 System Architecture

Input for TranslatAble comes from two main sources: the built in iPhone sensors and the Myo Armband (Fig 1C). Audio input is recorded from the built in microphone in the iPhone (Fig 1D), while both inertial data (acceleration and rotational data) and electromyography (EMG) data come from the commercial grade Myo Armband. Myo Armband has 8 EMG pods that record at a rate of 200 Hz, as well as an accelerometer and gyroscope that record at 50 Hz.

The Myo Armband is connected to the iPhone via a Bluetooth LE connection and is worn on the forearm. These features keep it from interfering with the user's daily activities.

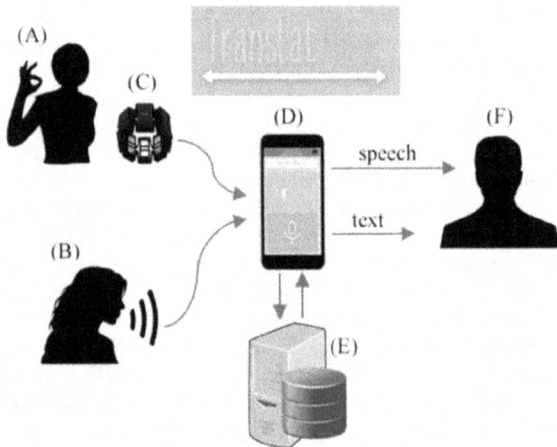

Figure 1: Overview of the TranslatAble System

2.3 Usage

There are two main ways to use TranslatAble, through gesture (Fig 1A) and through speech (Fig 1B). For both methods of communication, the process is very similar. For gestural communication systems, the user begins by building their unique library of gestures. The user individually adds the gestures into their library by performing the gesture 3-4 times. This repetition allows the system to obtain a template of the gesture. They then enter into translation mode, and perform the gesture. The data is sent to the phone (Fig 1D), which then processes the data and returns the recognized output to the user's screen. The user has the option to configure the output as either text or speech. For speech based communication systems, the process is very similar, but instead of performing gestures, the user speaks into the device for both the training portion and the translation portion.

2.4 Data Processing

The primary task of the system is to match gestures or audio input to the user-created templates. Once the input is collected, the data is sent to a remote database to be processed and matched against the other gestures or audio clips that are part of the user's profile. The input data is preprocessed, and the task is to recognize the gesture or audio based on the nearest matches between the input samples (received during translation mode), and stored samples (collected during training to build a user's library). To find these nearest matches, we are using Dynamic Time Warping (DTW), a well-established method for finding the optimal alignment between two given time-dependent sequences. DTW is performed on each modality of the input and a list of potential matches is created. From this list, the nearest match is chosen.

2.5 Output

There are two main output modalities that are being considered at this time: text and speech. The output modality will be an option that the user can control. Myo is also equipped with a vibration motor, and haptic feedback will be available to cue the user when Myo is ready to translate, as well as provide feedback when the recognition is successful.

3. FUTURE STUDIES

Thus far, we have built a prototype of the user interface, and have received some informal feedback on the usability of the interface. We are in the process of implementing the gesture and speech recognition functionalities of the application using Dynamic Time Warping. We are also in the process of creating a large dataset of gestures using the Myo armband in order to test more robust machine learning algorithms such as deep learning. While the prototype is being developed, we are setting up focus groups with speech and hearing clinicians, as well as individuals with complex communication needs and their support networks. The feedback we receive from these focus groups will further shape the design and functionality of the application. We are also planning user studies that will focus on discovering how well TranslatAble facilitates communication for individuals with complex communication needs.

4. ACKNOWLEDGMENTS

The authors would like to thank the National Science Foundation and Arizona State University for their funding support. This material is partially based upon work supported by the National Science Foundation under Grant No. 1069125.

5. REFERENCES

[1] Blackstone, S.W., Williams, M.B., and Wilkins, D.P. Key principles underlying research and practice in AAC. *Augmentative and Alternative Communication* 23, 3, (2007) 191-203.

[2] Kim, K.W., Lee, M.S., Soon, B.R., Ryu, M.H., and Kim, J.N., Recognition of sign language with an inertial sensor-based data glove. *Technology and Health Care* 24, s1 (2015), S223-S230.

[3] Miller, R.B. Response Time in Man-computer Conversational Transactions. *Proceedings of the December 9-11, 1968, Fall Joint computer conference, Part I* ACM (1968), 267-277.

[4] Praveen, N., Karanth, N., and Megha, M.X. Sign language interpreter using a smart glove. *2014 International Conference on Advances in Electronics, Computers and Communications (ICAECC)*, (2014), 1-5.

[5] Wu, Y. and Huang, T.S. Vision-Based Gesture Recognition: A Review. *Gesture-Based Communication in Human-Computer Interaction.* Springer Berlin Heidelberg, 1999, 103-115

Supporting Visual Impaired Learners in Editing Mathematics

Volker Sorge
Progressive Accessibility
Solutions, Ltd.
University of Birmingham, UK
V.Sorge@progressiveaccess.com

ABSTRACT

We present an extension to the Emacspeak audio desktop that provides support for editing mathematics in LaTeX. It integrates MathJax and the Speech Rule Engine to support users in reading LaTeX sources, manipulating mathematical formulas and verifying correctness of the rendered output.

Keywords

STEM Accessibility, Mathematics, MathJax

1. INTRODUCTION

Mathematics is still the single most significant hurdle for inclusive education for visually impaired students in the STEM subjects. In particular, in secondary education the increasing complexity of mathematical formulas makes it harder to communicate content equally effectively to both sighted and blind students. While mathematical formulas can be expressed in dedicated Braille formats, these become quickly unwieldy for more advanced mathematics and moreover it becomes impossible for students to communicate them to their peers or professors. Consequently they need to start using a linear format that is commonly understood. And indeed on transitioning from high school to University students often have to learn LaTeX to have a means to read and communicate advanced material.

While there are some specialist editors that support editing mathematics for the blind (e.g. [2]) there is very little support for reading or authoring LaTeX documents directly (cf. [3]). In particular, it is difficult for students to write mathematical content in LaTeX while checking that the rendered output indeed corresponds to the mathematical formula they intended to write. We aim to support this task by extending the Emacspeak audio desktop [4] with a mathematics option. It exploits the power of MathJax [1] to translate LaTeX expressions into MathML markup and the Speech Rule Engine (SRE) [5] to translate MathML into speech strings that can be passed to a TTS.

ASSETS '16 October 23-26, 2016, Reno, NV, USA

© 2016 Copyright held by the owner/author(s).

ACM ISBN 978-1-4503-4124-0/16/10.

DOI: http://dx.doi.org/10.1145/2982142.2982212

Our work focuses on supporting students in the aspects of learning, writing and working with LaTeX. In particular, to allow them to take source material, read it, browse it and manipulate it. We support learning LaTeX by offering ways to write and rearrange expressions and hear the effect, by using MathJax's error reporting mechanism to indicate incorrect expressions and by enabling interactive exploration of rendered expressions on the fly, while editing. As editing mathematics is already a time consuming task we aim to minimise the impact of having to listen to lengthy expressions multiple times by exploiting Emacspeak's prosody feature and SRE's ability to summarise sub-expressions meaningfully for concise aural rendering of expressions.

2. TECHNICAL REALISATION

Technically we realise our aims by combining Emacspeak with MathJax and the Speech Rule Engine.

Emacspeak is a speech interface that allows visually impaired users to employ the Emacs editor as the main tool for desktop activities. It supports tasks from implementing in different programming languages, writing documents in markup formats like markdown or LaTeX, to browsing the file system and the WWW. Emacspeak uses audio formatting via W3C's Aural CSS (ACSS) to produce rich aural presentations of electronic information with the aim of shifting some of the burden of listening from the cognitive to the perceptual domain. For instance, syntax highlighting is aurally rendered by changes in voice characteristic and inflection. Combined with appropriate use of non-speech auditory icons this creates the equivalent of spatial layout, fonts, and graphical icons important in a visual interface.

Speech Rule Engine (SRE) is a Javascript library that translates XML expressions into speech strings according to rules that can be specified in an extended Xpath syntax. It was originally designed for translation of MathML and MathJax DOM elements for Google's ChromeVox screen reader [6]. It has since been turned into a stand-alone application that can be installed server side as a NodeJS application as well as used in client side web applications. Besides the rules originally designed for the use in ChromeVox, it also has an implemententation of the full set of Mathspeak rules. In addition it contains a library for semantic interpretation and enrichment of MathML expressions, rules for intelligent summarisation of sub-expressions, facilities for the interactive exploration of mathematical expressions, highlighting of DOM nodes, etc. SRE runs both in browsers as well as in NodeJS. It can be installed via Node's package manager npm and offers a command line interface for batch translation of XML expressions.

MathJax is a JavaScript library for visual rendering of formulas across all platforms and browsers. It was originally built as a polyfill solution for rendering mathematics in browsers until the MathML standard would be sufficiently supported. But since most browsers still do not support MathML natively, MathJax has become the quasi standard for displaying Mathematics on the web. MathJax can render the most common mathematical authoring formats — LaTeX, ASCIIMath, and MathML — into high quality output represented either as HTML or as SVG. Although MathJax is built as a client side solution, to be included into webpages, there is a special NodeJS package release, which allows server side rendering of mathematical expressions from one of the three input formats into SVG. In addition, it offers a way to convert LaTeX into standardised MathML. MathJax can also use SRE as a dependency to produce speech strings for mathematical expression for inclusion into the rendered output.

NodeJS Bridge: The three systems are combined with a simple NodeJS bridge, whereby MathJax and SRE run within an inferior JavaScript process in Emacs. Emacspeak communicates with both systems by message passing between the different Emacs processes. Using an inferior process over a simple batch process integration does not only decrease potential lag due to delay in system startup but also has the advantage that both integrated systems can keep an independent internal state Emacspeak can refer to.

3. READING LaTeX IN EMACSPEAK

LaTeX formulas are spoken in Emacspeak in two different ways: Either integrated into the continuous flow when the entire document is read or speaking can be triggered interactively for a single formula. In either case Emacspeak detects the math delimiters and sends the expression to the node process. MathJax then translates it into MathML and passes it to SRE, which in turn performs a semantic analysis of the expression and then translates the expression into a speech string using a chosen set of speech rules.

One of Emacspeak's features is that it enables audio formatting, by employing changes in prosody (e.g., changes in pitch or stress), to indicate syntax highlighting, special text elements like links etc. Similarly, SRE supports prosody markup by allowing speech rules to define changes in pitch, rate, volume and by adding pauses. We combine this by translating mathematical expressions in SRE using a speech rule set that indicates two dimensional layout, such as sub and superscripts or positions in fractions with changes in pitch and rate, rather then employing more verbose indicator words like StartFraction or EndFraction. SRE then returns translated formulas as sexpressions that contain speech strings together with Aural CSS markup that Emacspeak can exploit for audio formatting.

Since mathematical formulas are often of a complex nature and just listening to an expression once is generally not enough for a user to fully take in its meaning, it is particularly important to be able to engage with them interactively by offering a means of traversing sub-expressions. SRE provides a number o different navigation options for mathematical expressions, which we exploit from Emacspeak. Thereby SRE keeps an internal state on the latest mathematical formula that it has rendered. Emacspeak then allows users to walk this formula using simple cursor key navigation, while SRE produces speech strings for the corresponding sub-expressions, potentially together with positional information, such as denominator, numerator etc.

4. LEARNING SUPPORT

One major difficulty presented to students new to LaTeX is learning the intricacy of its syntax and in particular to correctly implement complex, nested mathematical expressions. We provide a number of features that are aimed in particular at helping students understand expressions and write correct ones themselves. For this we exploit as much as possible the abilities of the systems we integrate:

Error Handling Since MathJax implements a version of the TeX typesetting system it can return fairly detailed error reports. We expose these directly to the reader together with an error earcon to allow users to quickly understand and rectify problems in their input expressions.

Syntax Highlighting Since LaTeX documents are implemented rather than composed in a WYSYG style, editors help authors to distinguish content from markup using syntax highlighting. Emacspeak can exploit its audio formatting to achieve a similar effect, making it possible to separate content from markup and giving the reader an indication of what layout elements markup would produce, such as bold type face, section headings etc. For math expressions audio formatting is used to indicate nesting depth of braces, giving a user an indication of the position within an expression they edit thus highlighting potential problems or errors.

Minimise Aural Rendering Since editing LaTeX can be a time consuming task, which is only compounded by the need to listen to lengthy audio output of mathematics, one of our main goals is to decrease the burden of listening. One way is by prefering rich audio formatting to more verbose traditional reading styles of mathematics (cf. MathSpeak for example). A second way is by exploiting the summarisation features SRE provides. For example, instead of reading a complete expression, SRE can use its semantic interpretation to produce summaries such as "sum with 5 summands", which are only expanded when explicitly prompted by a user, thus shortening aural output while editing.

Acknowledgements

The author is grateful for TV Raman's technical work on the Emacspeak integration.

5. REFERENCES

[1] MathJax Consortium. MathJax v2.6, 2015. http://www.mathjax.org.

[2] S. Dooley, D. Brown, E. Lozano, S. Park, and S. Osterhaus. Online nemeth braille input/output using content mathml. In *Proc of W4A*. ACM, 2016.

[3] NCBYS. Blindmath gems LaTeX. http://www.blindscience.org/blindmath-gems-latex.

[4] TV Raman. Emacspeak. http://emacspeak.sourceforge.net.

[5] V. Sorge. Speech Rule Engine. https://github.com/zorkow/speech-rule-engine.

[6] V. Sorge, C. Chen, TV Raman, and D. Tseng. Towards making mathematics a first class citizen in general screen readers. In *Proc of W4A*. ACM, 2014.

Motivating Individuals with Spastic Cerebral Palsy to Speak Using Mobile Speech Recognition

Zak Rubin, Sri Kurniawan, Taylor Gotfrid, Annie Pugliese
Dept. of Computer Engineering, Jack Baskin School of Engineering
University of California Santa Cruz, 1156 High St, Santa Cruz, CA 95060, USA
Ph: +1-831-459-1037
Email: {zarubin, skurnia, tgotfrid, abpugliese}@ucsc.edu

ABSTRACT

Individuals with cerebral palsy (CP) struggle with conditions such as dysarthria, dysphagia, and dyspraxia as they speak. While speech therapy is successful in practice, outside practice requires increased commitment and effort from caregivers. Researchers developed a speech recognition game designed to encourage out-of-office exercises and motivate users to practice. Next they recruited a participant with cerebral palsy to investigate the performance of the system in a live environment. The participant joined the game after demonstration from the caregiver and temporarily increased speech loudness and clarity during play. The participant found sound effects more rewarding than animations. The total number of sentences spoken during the session was found to be less than half that of a speaker without any impairment. Researchers also observed two instances of cheating. This work provides insight into the automated motivation of motivating speech production with individuals with cerebral palsy.

CCS Concepts

• **Human-centered computing~Usability testing abase management system engines**

Keywords

Cerebral Palsy; Speech Recognition Interface; Speech Therapy; User Study

1. INTRODUCTION

More than half of all individuals with cerebral palsy deal with some form of speech disorder [1]. These speech problems result in reduced ability to function in social situations leading to social isolation and depression. Cerebral palsy speech is considered dysarthric and is characterized by a variety of speech issues including slurring, chopping, speed issues, mouth movement issues, and voice quality issues [2].

Treatment of dysarthria presently involves direct intervention by a speech-language pathologist. Two-thirds of those who attempt speech therapy improve their intelligibility and communication

ASSETS '16, October 23-26, 2016, Reno, NV, USA
ACM 978-1-4503-4124-0/16/10.
http://dx.doi.org/10.1145/2982142.2982203

functioning. They also became intelligible to all listeners following intervention. The speech language pathologist determines if assistive technology would benefit the individual [3].

Despite assistive technology's potential benefit to this realm research conducted in 2013 found that speech language pathologists were unaware of any available assistive technology for those with speech impairments. An investigation of existing technologies found no technology developed to interact with speech impairments. Interviews with the primary stakeholders in speech therapy determined that a tool that motivated individuals in therapy and provided speech therapists with feedback about their practice and performance outside of the office would provide the most impact in the lives of those with speech impairments [4].

2. RELATED WORK

Researchers at the University of California, Berkeley investigated computerized speech recognition of individuals with dysarthria caused by cerebral palsy. Nine athetoid cerebral palsy speakers and one spastic speaker took part in a test investigating the performance of the Shadow/VET voice entry system. Researchers found that dysarthric speakers had a similar pattern of correct recognition to non-disabled speakers but the correct recognitions of dysarthric speakers was less than half that of non-disabled speakers. The researchers noted that the low recognition accuracy remains a serious problem [5].

Speech Adventure is a speech therapy tool suite intended for use by children enrolled in speech therapy. Speech Adventure utilizes a speech recognition engine capable of detecting coarse mispronunciations characteristic of speech impairments related to cleft lip and palate [6]. Researchers adapted the engine used in Speech Adventure to ignore mispronunciations and developed games focused on sound effects and animations.

3. SPEECH GAME

A graduate and undergraduate student developed a total of two levels. Five levels intended for plosive speech practice had their dictionaries replaced with command and control dictionaries containing fewer than ten words. Words were translated into their Arpabet equivalent via the lmtool provided by Carnegie-Mellon University [7].

These dictionaries were put into a rotating system of a total of seven mini-games. The game engine cycles through the games randomly, making sure each game is played at least once before repeating. Each level's time was set to 20 seconds, if the user does not finish the level in the allotted time the game moves to the next level. The system provides a timer for each level as well as on-screen prompts to guide the user what to say. As the user speaks the on-screen phrase highlights as the user speaks. If the user speaks the word or phrase correctly, an action occurs such as a sound effect or an animation.

Table 1. Sample In-Game Dictionary

Word	Arpabet Translation
BLAST	B L AE S T
BOOM	B UW M
BURST	B ER S T

Researchers evaluated the system on four native English speakers with no speech disorders. Three females and one male aged 21-27 took part in a playtesting session lasting a half hour. The mean speech rate in game was 17.2 words (SD = 1.92) per minute of playtime.

4. USER STUDY

Undergraduate students from the University of California, Santa Cruz recruited a 34-year-old female participant with spastic cerebral palsy as part of a course introducing beneficial technology to disabled groups. The participant had previous experience playing a variety of games on her own tablet. Testing took place in a quiet indoor location on campus. The participant's home support was present in place of the primary caregiver.

Figure 1 Fireworks Level. Players touch a rocket and then say the word in the text box to launch the rocket.

Initially the participant was reluctant to participate. The home support motivated the participant by playing tutorial levels. On the second in-game sentence the participant attempted to play, but let the home support finish the sentence. The participant began playing the game on her own on the second level of the tutorial and played along with the home support for the remainder of the levels as they played the main game together. The participant reacted positively to all in-game sound effects. During play of the main game (levels 3-10), the home support and observers noted a significant increase in the participant's pronunciation and volume.

Researchers witnessed the participant cheating in the game on two separate occasions. Cheating in this context was defined as any attempt to gain points or progress in the game without saying the on-screen sentence. In the first instance the participant exploited the caregiver's verbal motivation for all of game level seven. The participant would attempt to have the caregiver say the word loud enough so that the recognition engine would respond to the caregiver. In the second instance the participant could sometimes

trigger events in the game through any vocalization. This began on level eleven and continued until the game concluded.

The game reported that the participant played for 4 minutes. During that time they played 12 levels and spoke 34 valid sentences, for a speech rate of 8.5 sentences per minute. Of those 8 were utterances from the participant; the remainder came from the home support. Nine of the twelve levels played were unique and three were repeats. The participant expressed disinterest in the game at level ten, and was unable to complete any level before time ran out. The home support reported that the participant enjoyed the game overall, but grew bored primarily due to the repetition of the games.

5. DISCUSSION

We have described a speech recognition tool suite designed to motivate individuals with speech disorders to practice their voice in an engaging virtual environment. Testing on an adult participant with spastic cerebral palsy resulted in a temporary increase in both speech loudness and pronunciation. The system's initial results are promising in improving speech characteristics of those with speech impairments as well as the development of speech recognition systems designed for disabled users.

The adult participant required significant motivation from home support. The system also did not maintain the individual's interest beyond the first cycle of mini-games. Finally, the participant resumed normal speech patterns shortly after use so more application is necessary to realize the benefits. It is difficult to determine the degree of reluctance of the participant to join initially as the study was conducted in an unfamiliar environment. This work would most benefit from an expansion into home environments for long-term investigations to determine if the improvements transfer over to real-life conversational scenarios.

6. REFERENCES

[1] Nordberg, A., Miniscalco, C., Lohmander, A. and Himmelmann, K., 2013. *Speech problems affect more than one in two children with cerebral palsy: Swedish population-based study.* Acta paediatrica, *102*(2), pp.161-166.

[2] *Dysarthria.* ASHA http://www.asha.org/public/speech/disorders/dysarthria/ Retrieved 6/19/2016.

[3] Yorkston, K. *Treatment Efficacy Summary: Dysarthria (Neurlogical Motor Speech Impairment).* ASHA, 2003.

[4] Rubin, Z., Kurniawan S. *Speech Adventure: Speech Recognition for Cleft Speech Therapy.* Proceedings of 6th International Conference on Pervasive Technologies Related to Assistive Environments. PETRA 2013.

[5] Coleman, C., Meyers, L. *Computer Recognition of the Speech of Adults with Cerebral Palsy and Dysarthria.* Augmentative and Alternative Communication, 7:1, 34-42. 1991. DOI: 10.1080/07434619112331275663

[6] Rubin, Z., Tollefson, T., Kurniawan S. 2014. *Results from Using Automatic Speech Recognition in Cleft Speech Therapy with Children.* Computers Helping People with Special Needs, 283-286.

[7] Lenzo, K. *The CMU Pronunciation Dictionary.* http://www.speech.cs.cmu.edu/cgi-bin/cmudict. Retrieved 6/19/2016.

A Virtual Self-care Coach for Individuals with Spinal Cord Injury

Ameneh Shamekhi, Ha Trinh,
Timothy W. Bickmore
Northeastern University
Boston, MA, USA
{ameneh, hatrinh, bickmore}@ccs.neu.edu

Tamara R. DeAngelis, Theresa Ellis,
Bethlyn V. Houlihan, Nancy K. Latham
Boston University
Boston, MA, USA
{trork, tellis, bvergo, nlatham}@bu.edu

ABSTRACT

Most persons with spinal cord injury (SCI) require training and support for self-care management to help prevent the development of serious secondary conditions after hospital discharge. We have designed a virtual coach system, in which an animated character engages users in simulated face-to-face conversation to provide health education and motivate healthy behavior. We conducted an exploratory study with nine participants who have SCI to examine the acceptance and attitudes towards our system. Results of the study show that participants are highly receptive of the virtual coach technology and recognize it as an effective medium to promote self-care.

Keywords

Spinal cord injury; embodied conversational agent; healthcare.

1. INTRODUCTION

Spinal cord injury (SCI) is damage to the spinal cord that often results in partial or complete loss of motor and sensory functions. People with SCI are at risk of developing various secondary conditions, such as pressure ulcers, cardiovascular disease, and depression. Training and support for self-care management is essential to help people with SCI manage their own care and prevent the development of these secondary conditions after hospital discharge. To address this issue, a number of automated telehealth interventions have been developed to support the prevention and management of different secondary complications of SCI, such as pressure ulcers and depression [4].

Embodied Conversational Agents (ECAs) are animated characters that use verbal and nonverbal behavior to engage users in simulated face-to-face conversations (see Fig. 1). ECAs have been used in a number of interventions to facilitate learning of health concepts and self-care skills, and to motivate health behavior change [5]. Compared to existing telephonic interventions (such as [4]), ECAs enable the delivery of both auditory and visual content, and thus offer a richer and more flexible communication medium. ECAs have been found to be effective and highly accessible to various user populations, including older adults and those with little or no computer experience [5]. However, most studies on the efficacy of ECAs have primarily focused on non-disabled adults. An exception is Ellis et al.'s study, which demonstrated the feasibility of a coach ECA to promote exercise

ASSETS '16, October 23-26, 2016, Reno, NV, USA
ACM 978-1-4503-4124-0/16/10.
http://dx.doi.org/10.1145/2982142.2982199

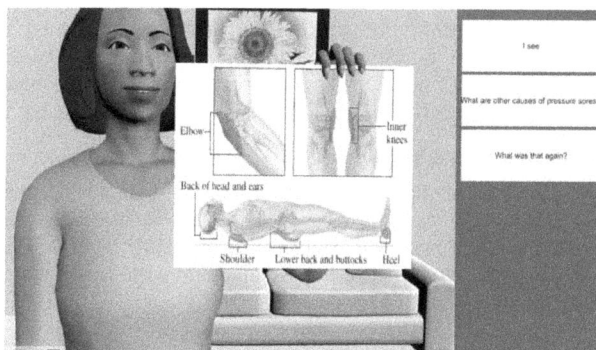

Figure 1. Embodied conversational agent as virtual coach.

among people with Parkinson's Disease [3]. However, there have been no studies to date that investigate how ECAs could be adapted for people with SCI.

Our research aims to explore the potential of ECAs to promote self-care management for people with SCI. We have designed a prototype ECA system, in which the agent plays the role of a virtual coach to support the prevention and management of pressure ulcers, a common secondary condition affecting 33% of people with SCI. Using the prototype as a technology probe, we conducted an exploratory study with nine participants who have SCI to understand their acceptance and attitudes towards the virtual coach technology.

2. VIRTUAL COACH DESIGN

Our current virtual coach prototype runs on a 21.5" touchscreen desktop computer. Users without upper limb function can use adapted devices to interact with the touchscreen. In future iterations, we aim to integrate other alternative access methods, such as speech recognition and gaze tracking.

Our virtual coach, named Tanya, is 3D character animated in the Unity game engine (Fig. 1). Tanya communicates with the user using synthetic speech. She is capable of displaying a variety of nonverbal conversational behavior, including facial display of affect, eyebrow movements, directional gazes, head nods, posture shifts, and hand gestures (e.g. deictic gestures for pointing to visual content). Most of her nonverbal behavior is automatically generated using the BEAT text-to-embodied speech system [2].

Human-agent dialogues are scripted using a custom scripting language based on hierarchical transition networks. User input to the conversation is obtained via multiple-choice selection of utterance options, updated at each turn of the conversation.

Each conversation begins with a brief introduction and greeting, followed by a short social chat that serves to build rapport with the user. The user is then offered a menu of three topics related to skin care management to discuss: skin inspection, bed pressure relief, and chair pressure relief.

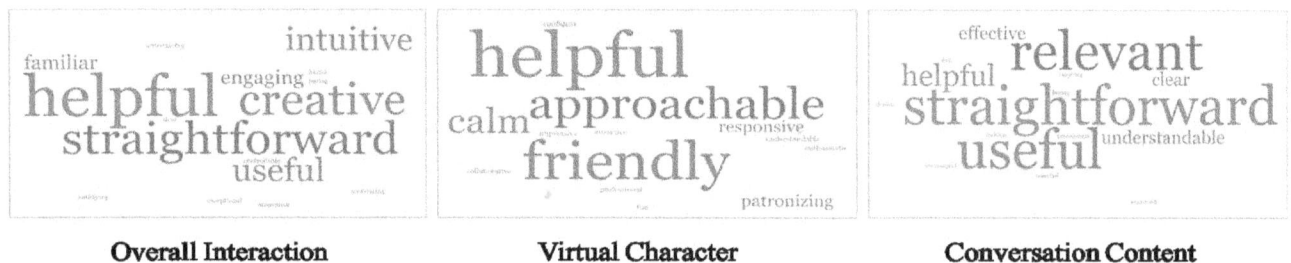

| Overall Interaction | Virtual Character | Conversation Content |

Figure 2. Word clouds generated from the Reaction Cards selection that describe the participants' impressions of the technology.

During the discussion, Tanya incorporates images and video to demonstrate skincare-related concepts, problems and processes. In addition, the user is also offered the option to listen to audio recordings of real people with SCI who share their personal knowledge and experiences.

3. EXPLORATORY STUDY

We conducted a single-session, qualitative study with people who have SCI to examine their experiences of the virtual coach. We recruited 9 participants with SCI (8 male, 1 female, ages 26-62, mean 38), who were 2.5-9 years post injury. Of these participants, 7 have tetraplegia and 2 have paraplegia.

3.1 Procedure

Each study session lasted between 90 and 120 minutes and consisted of a pre-interview, a Think Aloud session during which the participants interacted with the virtual coach, and a post-interview. The interviews were audiotaped and transcribed, while the Think Aloud session was videotaped for analysis.

During the pre-interview, we asked each participant about their experience with self-care management and technology. We then asked them to interact with Tanya while thinking aloud. Participants were encouraged to use the system in any way they wanted, and for as long as they wished. For participants who were unable to use the touchscreen, we asked them to speak aloud their conversational responses, and a research assistant selected the corresponding option from the touch screen. Following the Think Aloud session, we conducted a post-interview, asking questions in three main categories: (1) impressions of the overall interaction with the ECA; (2) impressions of the virtual character; and (3) impressions of the conversation content. For each category, we also asked the participants to select 3-5 word cards from a set of 25 cards that best described their impressions. These cards were taken from the Microsoft Product Reaction Cards [1], which has been used in desirability testing to gather participants' emotional responses to technology.

3.2 Results and Discussion

Figure 2 shows results of the participants' Reaction Cards selection. Most participants appreciated the flexibility and interactive nature of the conversation format, and felt that it could be a useful and accessible medium to learn health information: *"This is a good way to get the information across, especially to ask questions so you can kind of narrow it down, if there is something specific that you are looking for"* [P3]. Many participants envisioned that the technology could be particularly useful as a self-paced learning tool for newly injured patients, who might feel overwhelmed by other forms of media.

Participants commented positively on the virtual character's mannerism that helped keep them engaged in the conversation:

"The character is enthusiastic and promotes wanting to keep going... She is smiling and on a first name basis" [P3]. Talking with the agent provided the participants with a sense of collaboration, because: *"you're obviously working with her. You are answering her questions"* [P1]. Four participants expressed preferences for the agent to be on a wheelchair to represent a person with SCI: *"I think it would be good to have a peer that you are looking at and talking to"* [P9]. Two participants, however, felt that the virtual agent could *"end up being patronizing"* [P6], due to her *"cartoon"* style: *"The fact that it is a cartoon immediately makes you feel more childish about it"* [P6].

All participants appreciated the inclusion of images and audio recordings to facilitate learning. All of them particularly enjoyed listening to personal experiences shared by real people with SCI, because: *"when you hear information from them, their personal story, the information is more powerful"* [P4]. Participants suggested that the system could be a useful platform to provide health information on sensitive topics, such as bowel and bladder care or sexual relationships.

4. CONCLUSION

We present the design and formative study of a virtual coach system that aims to provide training and support for self-care management for people with SCI. Overall, participants were highly receptive of the virtual coach technology and considered it as a useful platform to promote self-care, especially for newly injured individuals. Future work will focus on expanding the system and evaluating it in a randomized controlled trial.

5. REFERENCES

[1] Benedek, J. and Miner, T. 2002. Measuring desirability: new methods for evaluating desirability in a usability lab setting. In *Proceedings of Usability Professionals Association, 2003*, 8-12.

[2] Cassell, J., Vilhjálmsson, H. H. and Bickmore, T. 2001. BEAT: The Behavior Expression Animation Toolkit. In *Proceedings of SIGGRAPH '01*, 477-486.

[3] Ellis T., Latham N. K., DeAngelis T. R. et al. 2013. Feasibility of a virtual exercise coach to promote walking in community-dwelling persons with Parkinson disease. *Am. J. Phys. Med. Rehabil. Assoc. Acad. Physiatr.* 92(6), 472–485.

[4] Houlihan B. V., Jette A., Paasche-Orlow M. et al. 2011. A telerehabilitation intervention for persons with spinal cord dysfunction. *Am. J. Phys. Med. Rehabil. Assoc. Acad. Physiatr.* 90(9), 756–764.

[5] King, A. C., Bickmore, T. W., Campero, M. I., Pruitt, L. A. and Yin, J. L. 2013. Employing virtual advisors in preventive care for underserved communities: results from the COMPASS study. *J. Health Commun.* 18(12)

Magic Touch: Interacting with 3D Printed Graphics

Lei Shi   Ross McLachlan   Yuhang Zhao   Shiri Azenkot

Jacobs Technion-Cornell Institute
Cornell Tech
New York, NY
(ls776, rdm257, yz769, shiri.azenkot)@cornell.edu

ABSTRACT

Graphics like maps and models are important learning materials. With recently developed projects [2,3,5], we can use 3D printers to make tactile graphics that are more accessible to blind people. However, current 3D printed graphics can only convey limited information through their shapes and textures. We present *Magic Touch*, a computer vision-based system that augments printed graphics with audio files associated with specific locations, or *hotspots*, on the model. A user can access an audio file associated with a hotspot by touching it with a pointing gesture. The system detects the user's gesture and determines the hotspot location with computer vision algorithms by comparing a video feed of the user's interaction with the digital representation of the model and its hotspots. To enable MT, a model designer must add a single tracker with fiducial tags to a model. After the tracker is added, MT only requires an RGB camera, so it can be easily deployed on many devices such as mobile phones, laptops and smart glasses.

CCS Concepts

• **Human-centered computing~Accessibility systems and tools**   • *Human-centered computing~Interactive systems and tools*

Keywords

Computer vision; 3D printing; visual impairments

1. INTRODUCTION

Graphics are important tools in our daily life. With 3D printing, we can use different shapes and textures to make visual information accessible to blind people. Researchers have proposed several ways to enable blind people to make and use tactile graphics with 3D printing. Brown *et al.* [2] developed 3D printing software that could automatically generate tactile line graphs. Kane *et al.* [3] used 3D printing technology to help blind students understand their Twitter visualizations. McDonald *et al.* [5] used a laser cutter and 3D printer to teach graphic design theory to visually impaired students.

While 3D printing is a powerful accessibility tool, 3D printed graphics can only convey limited information through their shapes and textures. Text, like annotations and legends, is hard to represent on these graphics due to limited printing and perceptual resolution and the complex topography of many graphics. For example, when designing an accessible world map using a 3D printer, model designers have to cut down some text to leave

ASSETS '16, October 23-26, 2016, Reno, NV, USA
ACM 978-1-4503-4124-0/16/10.
http://dx.doi.org/10.1145/2982142.2982153

Figure 1. We made three interactive graphics with our trackers: (a) a globe, (b) a cell model and (c) a tactile map.

space for the graphic information. Blind people, especially those who don't know Braille, will still rely on sighted people to understand these 3D printed graphics. The accessibility community has explored several accessible labeling methods for 3D printed graphics. Shi *et al.* [7,8] used acoustic sensing technologies to add accessible labels on 3D printed models. CamIO used bullseye fiducials to track hotspots of annotations on fixed models [6]. However, these systems required a relatively quiet environment or specific settings like mounting a depth camera in a room.

We present Magic Touch (MT), a system that can significantly enhance 3D printed graphics by providing an additional interaction modality, audition. Besides the tactile information from printed graphics, users can access audio information about pre-defined hotspots when they explore the graphics with our system. For example, when a user points to a continent (*i.e.*, one hotspot) on a globe using her index finger, MT will speak relevant information about that continent. MT only requires an attached 3D tracker to track a printed graphic. The system tracks the printed graphics and identifies gestures using the tracker and computer vision algorithms. It takes a video feed as input and outputs audio, so it can be deployed on a variety of devices including smart glasses, mobile phones, and personal laptops.

In this demonstration, we describe the design and implementation of MT. We made three interactive graphics with our trackers (as shown in Figure 1), and implemented our current system on a laptop. Our current system will speak out information corresponding to the hotspot a finger points to. In the future, MT will provide varied output information when users interact printed graphics with different gestures.

2. SYSTEM DESIGN

MT tracks hotspots on a printed graphic with the help of a 3D tracker. The tracker is a cube covered with fiducial tags, which provides spatial coordinates to our system. Hotspots are locations on a graphic that are associated with audio information. MT will record the coordinates of hotspots in a relative Cartesian coordinate system, whose origin is at a corner of the tracker. To make a printed graphic work with MT, a model designer needs to add one 3D tracker and hotspots onto the graphic. To add a hotspot, the designer needs to provide the Cartesian coordinate of the hotspot to our system, as well as the audio information of the

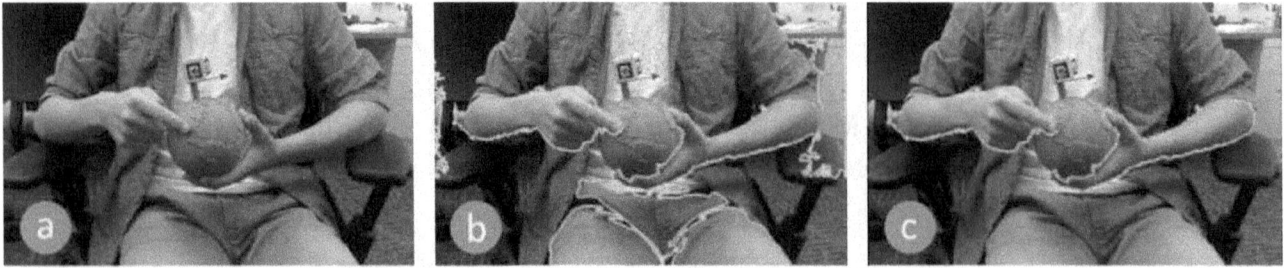

Figure 2. (a) First, our system finds the position of the model based on the tracker. Then, (b) it applies a detector to find all contours that contain skin color. (c) The system identifies gestures in contours that's close to the model, and speaks out information related to a nearby hotspot (marked in red dot).

hotspot. Blind users can run our system using cameras from laptops or smart glasses. When users perform gestures over a hotspot, our system speaks the associated audio information.

2.1 The Tracker

We designed a 3D tracker (as shown in Figure 1) with five fiducial tags, which can be tracked by RGB cameras. The tracker is a $2 \times 2 \times 2$ cm^3 cube. We used tags from Chilitags [1], and added one tag on each face of the tracker except its bottom face. With this tracker, a camera will be able to capture at least one tag when users hold models in different directions. The tracker and tags can be printed together in dual-extruder printers. Users can also easily glue paper tags to a tracker whenever dual-extruder printers are not available. The current tracker can be bulky when used with certain models, and we plan to explore less obtrusive tracker designs in our future work.

2.2 The Algorithms of MT

MT has three main functions: it (1) determines the orientation and location of a model in video stream, (2) identifies gestures on the model based on the locations of fingertips, and (3) plays audio files based on the position of the gestures and the hotspot locations.

The system calculates the position of a model by tracking the coordinates of the tags on the tracker. We used the Chillitags C++ library to compute the coordinates of the tags. Based on these coordinates, the system builds a relative Cartesian coordinate system with an origin at a corner of the tracker, and maps the 3D coordinates of hotspots into the current 2D video stream.

Our system uses a color-based skin detector [4] to identify hands. The algorithm finds all contours that contain skin color in the frame and then disregards contours that has no overlap with the model, as shown in Figure 2. For the remaining contours, the system identifies fingertips using a convex-hull algorithm, and recognizes hand gestures based on the locations of identified fingertips.

MT provides audio information about hotspots based on recognized hand gestures. Our current prototype only supports pointing gestures using one finger. The system finds the closest hotspot to the fingertip of the finger, and speaks out information corresponding to that hotspot.

3. PROTOTYPE AND SAMPLE MODELS

We implemented our current prototype in Python, and used the webcam of a Macbook. In the future, we plan to implement our prototype on other devices like tablets and smart glasses, which will provide different user experiences.

We printed three models using a Makerbot 5th generation printer and modified them by adding a bar that can host a tracker to each of the models, as shown in Figure 1. We printed the trackers separately and stuck paper tags on them. A researcher hardcoded the position and audio information of hotspots in Python scripts. We printed the following three models:

1. A globe model: we added a hotspot for each continent.
2. A cell model: we added a hotspot for each major component.
3. A tactile map: we added a hotspot for each building.

4. FUTURE WORK

In the future, we will design more gestures and make tactile graphics more powerful. Currently, MT allows blind users to inquire about specific elements on a graphic (*e.g.*, the name of each building in a tactile map). We plan on combining multiple gestures and non-speech audio to help users explore such information. For example, a user can perform a zoom-in gesture to browse the names of companies in a building, or uses a series of swipe gestures to select a certain store and read its description. With these new interaction techniques, for example, blind people can use our system to navigate with talking tactile maps when on the go. We will also develop tools to assist designers to add hotspots on 3D models.

5. REFERENCES

[1] Bonnard, Q. *et al.* Chilitags: Robust Fiducial Markers for Augmented Reality. http://chili.epfl.ch/software.

[2] Brown, C. *et al.* VizTouch: automatically generated tactile visualizations of coordinate spaces. TEI '12. http://doi.acm.org/10.1145/2148131.2148160

[3] Kane S. K. *et al.* Tracking @stemxcomet: teaching programming to blind students via 3D printing, crisis management, and twitter. SIGCSE '14. http://doi.acm.org/10.1145/2538862.2538975

[4] Mahmoud, T.M. A new fast skin color detection technique. WEAST 43, (2008).

[5] McDonald, S. *et al.* Tactile aids for visually impaired graphical design education. ASSETS '14, 275- http://doi.acm.org/10.1145/2661334.2661392

[6] Shen, H. *et al.* CamIO: a 3D computer vision system enabling audio/haptic interaction with physical objects by blind users. ASSETS '13, 41. http://doi.acm.org/10.1145/2513383.2513423

[7] Shi, L. Talkabel: A Labeling Method for 3D Printed Models. ASSETS '15. http://doi.acm.org/10.1145/2700648.2811327

[8] Shi, L. *et al.* Tickers and Talker: An Accessible Labeling Toolkit for 3D Printed Models. CHI '16. http://doi.acm.org/10.1145/2858036.2858507

Evaluation of Automatic Caption Segmentation

James M. Waller
University of Chicago
5801 S Ellis Ave
Chicago, IL 60637
jmwaller@uchicago.edu

Raja S. Kushalnagar
Gallaudet University
800 Florida Ave NE
Washington, DC 20002
raja.kushalnagar@gallaudet.com

ABSTRACT

Captions are typically segmented in a way that respects grammatical boundaries and makes them more readable. However, the growth of online video content with captions generated from transcripts means that this segmentation process is often ignored. This study evaluates the effects of text segmentation on caption readability, and proposes a program to automatically segment captions using a parser. The parser-segmented captions readability is also evaluated and compared to human-segmented captions and arbitrarily-segmented captions. Results indicate segmentation influences sentence recall, though other wise little difference is found between the different kinds of captioning.

CCS Concepts

•Human-centered computing → Accessibility design and evaluation methods;

Keywords

Caption Segmentation

1. INTRODUCTION

Closed Captioning is used to represent spoken and audio information as written language in real-time. Primarily used by Deaf and hard-of-hearing people, closed captions are beneficial for a number of people in many situations. The current study focuses on how to automatically divide up lines on captions to maximize readability and comprehension. Current guidelines for captions specify a number of rules explaining where lines breaks should and should not occur âĂŞ at the end of a sentence, never in the middle of a name or compound sentence, etc. [1] The goal is to keep words in the same grammatical phrase together as much as possible. While this is useful, currently captionists must do this work manually, and on some websites these conventions are ignored entirely. This study develops a prototype based on text parsing information to segment captions at the optimal line breaks, and evaluate the usefulness of the program.

2. RELATED WORK

2.1 Impact of Segmentation on Readability

Research suggests caption segmentation can have a positive impact, but is not conclusive. Rajendran et al. [6] found participants were able to focus more on the video itself when captions appeared one phrase or sentence at a time, rather than by one word. On the other hand Perego et al. [5] found that segmenting subtitles in inappropriate places had no impact on sentence recall or eye movement. One explanation for he difference is that Rajendran et al. looked at breakpoints between sequential captions segments, when one appeared after the other, while Perego et al.'s "ill-formed" segmentations mostly occur between two simultaneous lines that appear together. This suggests that good breakpoints are more important when one segment appears after the other. The current study involves breakpoints at between both simultaneous and sequential lines.

2.2 Automatic Segmentation of Captions

Only two studies to date have tested programs that automatically segment captions. Murata et al. [4] developed a program for segmenting Japanese captions, while another study by Álvarez et al. [2] developed a general program, which they applied to Basque subtitles. Both used machine learning to teach their programs to identify correct segmentation points. Both programs had about 70-75% agreement with human captionists, and were judged as more readable than a baseline. Álvarez et al. did not involve grammatical analysis, and noted it was limited by the lack of parsers available for Basque. For English, many parsers are openly available, such as the Stanford parser used in this study. The Stanford parser can parse a transcript and produce a hierarchical phrase structure for each sentence [3], making it easy to identify optimal breakpoints.

3. PROGRAM AND EXPERIMENT

3.1 Program Development

The ACS (Automatic Caption Segmentation) program developed for this experiment first applies the Stanford Parser to produce syntax trees for the sentences in the transcript. The sentence is broken into phrases all the way down to the level of words. The program uses this information to identify optimal point breaks. All potential breakpoints between

ASSETS '16 October 23-26, 2016, Reno, NV, USA

© 2016 Copyright held by the owner/author(s).

ACM ISBN 978-1-4503-4124-0/16/10. . . $15.00

DOI: http://dx.doi.org/10.1145/2982142.2982205

words are assigned indexes depending on how many parent nodes the words share. Since a separate syntax tree is created for each sentence, sentence boundaries have the lowest index and are the best candidates for breakpoints. If no sentence boundary is available, then the program searches within the program to the breakpoint with the next lowest index. If two adjacent words are deeply embedded together in a sentence, they will have a higher index, and will not be chosen, preventing phrases from being broken up.

The parser also puts additional emphasis on punctuation. Captioning guidelines also emphasize the importance of breakpoints at punctuation and "natural pauses" [1]. The program is modified to reflect this, by automatically reducing the index of punctuated breakpoints, thereby increasing the possibility they are selected as breakpoints.

3.2 Experimental Methodology

3.2.1 Participants 18 Deaf/hh participants were recruited for the first experiment, ranging from 20 to 28 years in age. All participants regularly use captions when watching online videos, TV, and other audio-video content. The entire experiment takes approximately 30-45 minutes and the participants are compensated for their time.

3.2.2 Procedure Each participant first watches two different 4-minute videos, each with a one of the following caption conditions:

- A: Segmented by a human captionist
- B: Segmented by the ACS program
- C: Segmented only by line-length (no parsing)

Thus each participant saw two of these three styles - condition A Human-generated captions follow standard conventions for breaking caption lines in suitable ways, while condition C captions simply obey a character-per-line limit and ignore phrase structure. There are eight comprehension questions given to the participant after the video, as well as two to three pre-test comprehension questions to check previous knowledge of the subject. The comprehension section consists of two kinds of multiple-choice questions: four general comprehension questions that asked about information presented in the text (i.e. What is the purpose of the video?) and four recall questions that asked gave the beginning of a sentence from the caption transcript and asked the participant to select the correct ending of the sentence from memory. Two subjective Likert-scale questions ask the participant to rate the readability of the captions and their satisfaction with the captions. There is also an open-ended question asking about general feedback on the questions, and if they noticed a difference between the two styles presented.

3.3 Results

No significant differences were found in subjective preference from the Likert question data, either in terms of satisfaction or readability across the three conditions, using Mann-Whitney tests. Parametric t-tests were used for data from the test questions. For comprehension question data (shown in Figure 1), there was no differences in general comprehension for the three conditions, but for sentence recall, participants performed significantly better for condition B (M = 2.08 out of 4 correct) than for C (M = 1.00, t(22) = 2.17, p < 0.05). There was no significant difference in recall between conditions A (M = 1.58) and either B or C.

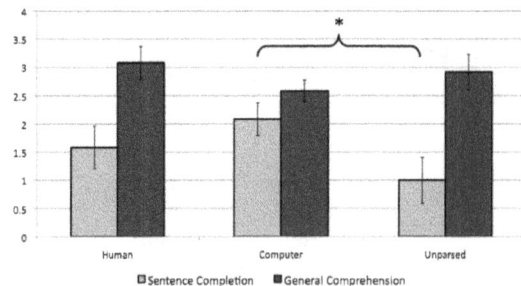

Figure 1: Average Number of Correct Questions

4. CONCLUSION

The general lack of differences between human-segmented (A) and arbitrarily segmented captions (C) may support Perego et al.'s conclusion [5] - that segmentation in captioning has little or no impact on readability. This study supports the notion that automatic segmentation could replace manual segmentation, since the two types performed very similarly.

Also, the difference between conditions B and C for sentence recall suggests that segmentation may indeed have an impact on our memory of the text. This result points to future ways to measure caption readability. Performance on content comprehension questions can involve many variables unrelated to the captions including background knowledge and inference from video graphics. Sentence recall questions more directly measure whether or not the participants recall the actual caption text itself. Future research could explore the viability of this kind of measurement, and improve it.

Any future work on caption segmentation must involve Deaf/hh people from a wider range of educational backgrounds, ages, and English reading skill to see if all benefit equally from caption segmentation.

5. REFERENCES

[1] Captioning key - text. https://www.dcmp.org/captioningkey/text.html. Accessed: 2015-06-08.

[2] Aitor Álvarez, Haritz Arzelus, and Thierry Etchegoyhen. Towards customized automatic segmentation of subtitles. In *Advances in Speech and Language Technologies for Iberian Languages*, pages 229–238. Springer, 2014.

[3] Danqi Chen and Christopher D Manning. A fast and accurate dependency parser using neural networks. In *EMNLP*, pages 740–750, 2014.

[4] Masaki Murata, Tomohiro Ohno, and Shigeki Matsubara. Automatic linefeed insertion for improving readability of lecture transcript. In *New Directions in Intelligent Interactive Multimedia Systems and Services-2*, pages 499–509. Springer, 2009.

[5] Elisa Perego, Fabio Del Missier, Marco Porta, and Mauro Mosconi. The cognitive effectiveness of subtitle processing. *Media Psychology*, 13(3):243–272, 2010.

[6] Dhevi J Rajendran, Andrew T Duchowski, Pilar Orero, Juan Martínez, and Pablo Romero-Fresco. Effects of text chunking on subtitling: A quantitative and qualitative examination. *Perspectives*, 21(1):5–21, 2013.

Utilizing Neural Networks to Predict Freezing of Gait in Parkinson's Patients

Jonathan Zia
Emory University School
of Medicine
Emory University
Atlanta, GA, USA
jzia@emory.edu

Arash Tadayon
Center for Cognitive
Ubiquitous Computing
Arizona State University
Tempe, AZ, USA
atadayon@asu.edu

Troy McDaniel
Center for Cognitive
Ubiquitous Computing
Arizona State University
Tempe, AZ, USA
troy.mcdaniel@asu.edu

Sethuraman
Panchanathan
Center for Cognitive
Ubiquitous Computing
Arizona State University
Tempe, AZ, USA
panch@asu.edu

ABSTRACT

With the appropriate mathematical models, data from wearable devices can be used to help Parkinson's patients live safer and more independent lives. Inspired by this idea, the purpose of this study was to determine the viability of neural networks in predicting Freezing of Gait (FoG), a symptom of Parkinson's disease in which the patient's legs are suddenly rendered unable to move. A class of neural networks known as layered recurrent networks (LRNs) was applied to an open-source FoG experimental dataset donated to the Machine Learning Repository of the University of California at Irvine. The independent variables in this experiment – the subject being tested, neural network architecture, and down sampling of the majority classes – were each varied and compared against the performance of the neural network in predicting impending FoG events. It was determined that single-layered recurrent networks are a viable method of predicting FoG events given the volume of the training data available, though results varied between patients.

Keywords

Parkinson's Disease; Freezing of Gait; Machine Learning; Wearable Devices.

1. INTRODUCTION

One common result of Parkinsonian Gait is "Freezing of Gait" (FoG), which refers to the patient having difficulty initiating movement or continuing it once it has begun. Though there are several methods of mitigating the severity of a FoG episode once it has begun, the lack of a viable method of prediction means that patients and caregivers may not have adequate time to prepare for the onset of such an episode [4]. To overcome this challenge, this study proposes using layered recurrent networks (LRNs) as a method of predicting FoG before its onset to improve the effectiveness of such therapeutic techniques. The LRN was chosen because of its noise-tolerance and ability to recognize patterns over time in large datasets. The LRN model used is shown in Figure 1.

In this study, LRNs of varying configurations were applied to three subjects chosen from the Machine Learning Repository [4] to obtain a preliminary indication of whether LRNs are a viable method of predicting FoG events.

ASSETS '16, October 23-26, 2016, Reno, NV, USA
ACM 978-1-4503-4124-0/16/10.
http://dx.doi.org/10.1145/2982142.2982194

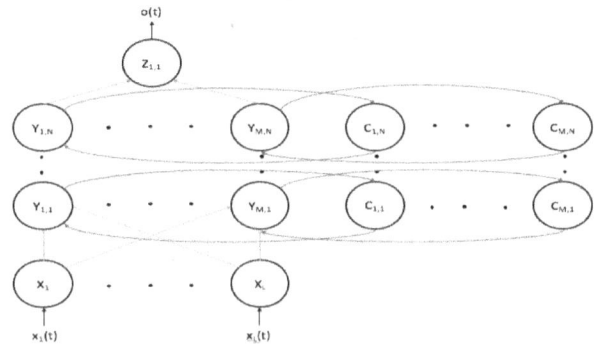

Figure 1. Layered Recurrent Network (LRN) Model

2. RELATED WORK

The effectiveness of neural networks in predicting the onset of Parkinsonian symptoms has not been extensively explored; however, previous publications have proposed other methods of predicting FoG. Such studies include analyzing skin conductance [6], motion data [7], and EEG data [1] using a variety of methods. Though previous studies have attained reasonable success in this area, neural networks provide the benefit of adaptability to each patient's unique symptom presentation while other methods require varying degrees of tailoring to account for human factors.

3. METHODS

In the dataset used for this study, motion data was captured from each subject using three accelerometers with different placement (shank, thigh, and torso). Any FoG events that occurred were then manually time-stamped into the dataset by an independent observer.

In this study, three subjects were chosen at random and only the data from the three-axis shank accelerometer was used. For each subject, neural networks were trained using the first half of their dataset. In this training period, each time-stamp where FoG occurred was shifted 1,000 samples (approx. 5 seconds) toward $t = 0$ such that the networks were trained to recognize the precursor symptoms of each FoG event. Once these networks were trained, they were tested using the second half of the dataset to yield the results shown in the following section. For each subject, several different neural networks were tested. The parameters that were varied include (1) N - number of hidden layers, (2) M - number of hidden units per layer, (3) f_0 - number of samples included in backpropagation through time (BPTT) algorithm, and (4) D - down sampling factor[1] [5]. This resulted in 48 different trials summarized in Table 1.

Table 1. Experimental Parameters

N	M	f_0	D
1	3	100	1
3	5	1000	3

4. RESULTS

After these trials were performed, the precision and recall for each network configuration were calculated. The precision is the percentage of FoG warnings by the trained network that correctly predicted a FoG event while the recall is the percentage of FoG events that were predicted by the trained network. Only the configurations which yielded statistically-significant precision and recall values are shown in the Table 2. Table 3 indicates the number of FoG events present in each dataset used for training and testing.

Table 2. Precision and Recall Values

				Subject 1		Subject 2		Subject 3	
f_0	D	N	M	P%	R%	P%	R%	P%	R%
100	1	1	3	-	-	100	11	-	-
100	1	1	5	-	-	100	4	-	-
100	3	1	3	-	-	89	30	57	27
100	3	1	5	-	-	96	16	62	25
1000	1	1	3	-	-	100	5	-	-
1000	3	1	3	42	47	100	2	-	-
1000	3	1	5	-	-	100	10	-	-

Table 3. Number of FoG Events per Dataset

	Subject 1	Subject 2	Subject 3
Training	18	9	39
Testing	5	15	26

Higher precision indicates that the network better identified FoG-specific patterns while higher recall indicates that it identified a wider range of FoG events. The values for precision and recall depend on how the network output is interpreted. In this study, the decision rule used to interpret the output was optimized using the receiver operating characteristic (ROC) of each network, thus maximizing precision and recall together. In certain applications, however, it may be more beneficial to bias the output toward one or the other. In the case of FoG, failing to predict an event may have more severe consequences than a false alarm.

5. CONCLUSION

5.1 Discussion

These results suggest that LRNs may be a viable method of predicting FoG events. The data shows that FoG events were predicted up to 47% of the time for Subject 1, 30% for Subject 2, and 27% for Subject 3 while the corresponding network precision was 42%, 89%, and 57% respectively. As listed in Table 2, the most effective networks (highlighted) were those that were both small

and utilized down sampled data. This may indicate that larger networks – which detect more nuanced patterns – require either more computation time or more extensive datasets to provide comparable predictive power. Based on the results, LRNs may be used in the future to assist Parkinson's patients in their daily lives.

5.2 Future Work

Future work should integrate other data modalities such as skin conductance, medication cycles [2], and physical location [3] as well as incorporate a greater number of subjects. The effect of processing the raw data before training should also be examined along with the effect of training the networks over several different subjects rather than training each network independently. Furthermore, the implication of using a fixed time-shift when training the networks was that they could not learn longer-term predictive patterns; these should be addressed in future work. Finally, exploring different types of neural networks and methods of counteracting class imbalance may also improve these results.

6. ACKNOWLEDGMENTS

We thank Dr. Charles Adler for his insight into the clinical aspects of Parkinson's and his valuable feedback in conducting this study.

7. REFERENCES

[1] A. Handojoseno, J. Shine, T. Nguyen, Y. Tran, S. Lewis and H. Nguyen, "Analysis and Prediction of the Freezing of Gait Using EEG Brain Dynamics", IEEE Trans. Neural Syst. Rehabil. Eng., vol. 23, no. 5, pp. 887-896, 2015.

[2] J. D. Schaafsma, Y. Balash, T. Gurevich, A. L. Bartels, J. M. Hausdorff, and N. Giladi, "Characterization of freezing of gait subtypes and the response of each to levodopa in Parkinson's disease," Eur J Neurol European Journal of Neurology, vol. 10, no. 4, pp. 391–398, 2003.

[3] J. Nonnekes, A. H. Snijders, J. G. Nutt, G. Deuschl, N. Giladi, and B. R. Bloem, "Freezing of gait: a practical approach to management," The Lancet Neurology, vol. 14, no. 7, pp. 768–778, 2015.

[4] M. Bachlin, M. Plotnik, D. Roggen, I. Maidan, J. Hausdorff, N. Giladi, and G. Troster, "Wearable Assistant for Parkinson's Disease Patients With the Freezing of Gait Symptom," IEEE Transactions on Information Technology in Biomedicine IEEE Trans. Inform. Technol. Biomed., vol. 14, no. 2, pp. 436–446, 2010.

[5] N. Chawla, K. Bowyer, L. Hall and P. Kegelmeyer, "SMOTE: Synthetic Minority Over-sampling Technique", Journal of Artificial Intelligence Research, vol. 16, pp. 321-357, 2002.

[6] S. Mazilu, A. Calatroni, E. Gazit, A. Mirelman, J. M. Hausdorff, and G. Troster, "Prediction of Freezing of Gait in Parkinson's From Physiological Wearables: An Exploratory Study," IEEE Journal of Biomedical and Health Informatics IEEE J. Biomed. Health Inform., vol. 19, no. 6, pp. 1843–1854, 2015.

[7] S. Mazilu, E. Gazit, D. Roggen, J. Hausdorff, and G. Tröster, "Feature Learning for Detection and Prediction of Freezing of Gait in Parkinson's Disease," in Machine Learning and Data Mining in Pattern Recognition, vol. 7988, a calatroni, Ed. New York, NY, 2013, pp. 144–158.

---

[1] A down sampling factor of 3 indicates that one out of every 3 data points in the raw data were used in neural network training.